STATIC AND EVOLUT
INTERPRETAT

How should international treaties be interpreted over time? This book offers fresh insights on this age-old question. The Vienna Convention on the Law of Treaties (VCLT) sets out the rules for interpretation, stipulating that treaties should be interpreted *inter alia* according to the 'ordinary meaning' of the text. Evolutive interpretation has been considered since the times of Gentili and Grotius, but this is the first book to address systematically what evolutive interpretation looks like in reality. It sets out to address how and under what circumstances it can be said that the interpretation of a treaty evolves, and under what circumstances it remains static. With the VCLT as its point of departure, this study develops a functional reconstruction of the rules of treaty interpretation, and explores and analyses how the International Court of Justice and the European Court of Human Rights have approached the issue.

CHRISTIAN DJEFFAL received his PhD from the Humboldt University of Berlin where he worked as a research assistant. He is currently a law clerk at the Higher Regional Court of Frankfurt. He has been visiting scholar at the Amsterdam Center for International Law at the University of Amsterdam, at the Lauterpacht Centre at the University of Cambridge and at the Max-Planck-Institute for Comparative Public and International Law.

CAMBRIDGE STUDIES IN INTERNATIONAL AND COMPARATIVE LAW

Established in 1946, this series produces high quality scholarship in the fields of public and private international law and comparative law. Although these are distinct legal sub-disciplines, developments since 1946 confirm their interrelations.

Comparative law is increasingly used as a tool in the making of law at national, regional and international levels. Private international law is now often affected by international conventions, and the issues faced by classical conflicts rules are frequently dealt with by substantive harmonisation of law under international auspices. Mixed international arbitrations, especially those involving state economic activity, raise mixed questions of public and private international law, while in many fields (such as the protection of human rights and democratic standards, investment guarantees and international criminal law) international and national systems interact. National constitutional arrangements relating to 'foreign affairs', and to the implementation of international norms, are a focus of attention.

The series welcomes works of a theoretical or interdisciplinary character, and those focusing on the new approaches to international or comparative law or conflicts of law. Studies of particular institutions or problems are equally welcome, as are translations of the best work published in other languages.

General editors
James Crawford SC FBA
Whewell Professor of International Law, Faculty of Law,
University of Cambridge
John S. Bell FBA
Professor of Law, Faculty of Law, University of Cambridge
A list of books in the series can be found at the end of this volume.

STATIC AND EVOLUTIVE TREATY INTERPRETATION

A Functional Reconstruction

CHRISTIAN DJEFFAL

CAMBRIDGE
UNIVERSITY PRESS

University Printing House, Cambridge CB2 8BS, United Kingdom

One Liberty Plaza, 20th Floor, New York, NY 10006, USA

477 Williamstown Road, Port Melbourne, VIC 3207, Australia

314-321, 3rd Floor, Plot 3, Splendor Forum, Jasola District Centre, New Delhi - 110025, India

79 Anson Road, #06-04/06, Singapore 079906

Cambridge University Press is part of the University of Cambridge.

It furthers the University's mission by disseminating knowledge in the pursuit of education, learning and research at the highest international levels of excellence.

www.cambridge.org
Information on this title: www.cambridge.org/9781107543645

© Christian Djeffal 2016

This publication is in copyright. Subject to statutory exception and to the provisions of relevant collective licensing agreements, no reproduction of any part may take place without the written permission of Cambridge University Press.

First published 2016
First paperback edition 2018

A catalogue record for this publication is available from the British Library

Library of Congress Cataloging in Publication data
Djeffal, Christian, author.
Static and evolutive treaty interpretation : a functional reconstruction / by Christian Djeffal.
pages cm – (Cambridge studies in international and comparative law)
ISBN 978-1-107-11831-7 (Hardback)
1. Treaties–Interpretation and construction. I. Title.
KZ1304.D54 2015
341'.026–dc23   2015020012

ISBN 978-1-107-11831-7 Hardback
ISBN 978-1-107-54364-5 Paperback

Cambridge University Press has no responsibility for the persistence or accuracy of URLs for external or third-party internet websites referred to in this publication, and does not guarantee that any content on such websites is, or will remain, accurate or appropriate.

CONTENTS

List of figures viii
List of tables ix
Preface xi
List of abbreviations xix
Table of cases xx

PART I **Definitions, assumptions and method** 1

1 **Two paths to interpretative method** 3
   1.1 What we are talking about: interpretative method and methodology 3
   1.2 Who we are talking about: international courts 5
   1.3 Interpretation 8
   1.4 Evolutive interpretation 18

2 **Suggested solutions** 28
   2.1 Suggested solutions after the coming into force of the VCLT 28
   2.2 Discussion within the ILC and at the Vienna Conference 37
   2.3 Suggested solutions prior to drafting the VCLT 48
   2.4 Transferring solutions from other jurisdictions 54

3 **Mode of inquiry: functional reconstruction** 67
   3.1 The problem of circularity 67
   3.2 Functional reconstruction 71
   3.3 Functional reconstruction in practice 76

PART II **The rule of interpretation in the VCLT: method and methodology** 81

4 **Historical account of the means of interpretation** 83
   4.1 Functional reconstruction in historical perspective 83
   4.2 The mechanical phase 85
   4.3 The flexible phase 91

4.4 The phase of codification   97
4.5 Summary and explanation   106

5 **Cardinal cores of the rule: features of the process**   109
   5.1 The nature of the rule core: legality   109
   5.2 The means core: techniques   114
   5.3 The activity core: balancing and weighing   126
   5.4 The core of argumentative weight and hierarchy: 2.5 steps   129
   5.5 The core of openness: broad and treaty related   134
   5.6 Synthesis: art not science   138
   5.7 Finale: the function as the core of the cores   140

6 **Interpretative knots: the system of the VCLT revisited**   147
   6.1 The goal knot   147
   6.2 Interpretation in good faith   150
   6.3 Ordinary and special meaning of the terms of the treaty   153
   6.4 Context   157
   6.5 Object and purpose   158
   6.6 Subsequent agreements and practice   162
   6.7 Relevant rules of international law   167
   6.8 *Travaux préparatoires*   170
   6.9 Circumstances of the conclusion of the treaty   171
   6.10 Other supplementary means of interpretation: facing the intertemporal knot   172
   6.11 Executive summary   181

7 **Shout of encore: evolutive interpretation in the context of the VCLT**   183
   7.1 Express regulation   184
   7.2 Reservations   189
   7.3 Temporal applicability   192
   7.4 Internal law   193
   7.5 Amendment   193
   7.6 Norm conflict   194
   7.7 Invalidity, termination and suspension   195
   7.8 Conclusions and reflection on intertemporal openness   201

PART III **Court practice**   203

8 **Profiling courts: a framework of analysis**   205
   8.1 Power: the actor dimension   208
   8.2 Perception: the material dimension   210
   8.3 Pace: the temporal dimension   211

9 The International Court of Justice: peacemakers and disputants   214
  9.1 Institutional aspects   214
  9.2 Stocktaking   216
  9.3 General approaches   234
  9.4 Justificatory patterns   251
  9.5 Summary   269

10 The European Court of Human Rights: an aging activist   272
  10.1 Institutional aspects   273
  10.2 Stocktaking: intertemporal instances   278
  10.3 General approach   301
  10.4 Justificatory patterns   314
  10.5 Summary and outlook   338

PART IV Summary and conclusions   345

11 Summary and conclusions   347
  11.1 Part I: definition of the problem, suggested solutions, mode of inquiry   347
  11.2 Part II: the rule of interpretation   350
  11.3 Part III: court practice   354
  11.4 Intertemporal openness as the solution and not the problem   357

Appendix 1 Schemes of interpretation   359
Appendix 2 Sample reservation clauses   367
Appendix 3 Sample conditional interpretative declaration clauses   368
Bibliography   369
Index   401

FIGURES

1 Method in context   5
2 Semiotic triangle modified   12
3 Distinction between means and results of interpretation   23
4 Discursive map: Suggested solutions to the intertemporal question   36
5 Techniques as filters   128
6 Weighing and balancing   128
7 Mixing console: Ways of limiting and enhancing static or evolutive interpretations   339

TABLES

1 Discourse on originalism   60
2 *Méthode scientifique et méthode évolutive*   65
3 Possible modes of inquiry   78
4 Frequency of intertemporal instances at the ICJ   230
5 Frequency of interpretative intertemporal instances at the ECtHR   300
6 Frequency of intertemporal instances of balancing at the ECtHR   300
7 Frequency and success rates of interpretative techniques   325

PREFACE

This is an inquiry into the question of how issues of static and evolutive treaty interpretation ought to be resolved in international law. It covers materials available until 31 December 2014.

Analytical division: Problems

A research question is a question, but also a choice. It is like turning the head to look in a certain direction, it is like looking at an object from a certain angle, it is like choosing the key before composing. The question does not necessarily entail the answer, but it narrows the scope of answers down substantially. The question this book is dealing with reads: How can and how do international courts and tribunals deal with questions of stasis and evolution. This question is basically a legal question, and it is far from being asked for the first time.

But the fact that there is a continuing and maybe even rising interest in that topic should make us attentive: Why is legal scholarship looking for answers to this question over and over again? Why are so few of the inquiries actively engaging with other solutions? Lawyers and, to a certain extent, also legal scholars are trained to find answers to questions. If no satisfactory solution is found, more answers are produced. This is what has happened to the question of static and evolutive interpretation. The underlying *problématique* is described in very abstract terms, opposing the state of the law as it is and the notion of legal security with possible changes and the need to adapt to new political, social or economic conditions. Departing from this very general view of the problem, scholars try to find a generally satisfactory legal solution. It is very tempting for a scholar to follow this example and to produce an at least partly new solution to this problem.

I have taken another road: I was more focused on problems underlying the question as opposed to possible answers. For more than 400 years, international legal scholars have grappled with questions of evolution and change. Courts and tribunals took different stances on the question, and, even within the institutions, views changed over time. As the reader will discover, I have arrived at the conclusion that these problems can be answered only to a limited extent and that this is not a flaw but actually a good thing. The research I have conducted was a process of discovery. I have not tried to prove something but to understand international interpretative method. The first part of my preface is, therefore, an introduction to the problems.

The first part of the book deals, on the one hand, with problems of definition and problems of the modus operandi of the inquiry. Questions of definitions are often conceived as rather insipid and lacklustre exercises. This does not, however, apply to the field of interpretation. Those call for precise definitions about the subject of research. For otherwise all is lost before it starts.

It is, therefore, of the utmost necessity to have a close look at the concepts used, such as interpretative method, methodology and interpretative practice (Part I). It is also required to render a precise definition of what interpretation ought to mean and in which circumstances one could speak of a static or evolutive interpretation (Chapter 1).

The second step is to look into scholarly attempts to deal with those questions. If there is no agreed solution, it might be helpful to go back in time and look at the preparatory works leading to the conclusion of the VCLT or even further back in time. If there is no solution within international legal discourse, one might also have a look at comparable situations in national law (Chapter 2).

Even though there is currently no agreed solution, we can say that Arts. 31 and 32 VCLT provide for an agreed interpretative method in international law. Since the intertemporal question of interpretation[1] is not expressly dealt with in the Convention, we need to find out whether and how the Convention can handle those issues. One could also say that we need to interpret the rule of interpretation. Is that possible, and, if so, how? This is one of the major problems to be dealt with in the present inquiry. It has previously been determined that the self-application of the rule of interpretation might result in an endless interpretative circle. Omitting to interpret rules of interpretation would lead to arbitrary interpretations of interpretative method (Chapter 3). The problem of interpreting the rule of interpretation is very serious, for it forces us to

---

[1] I.e. the question whether and under what circumstances the interpretation of treaties can change over time.

employ a workable method that is different from interpretative legal method. Part I ends with a theoretical outline of how the rule of interpretation can be reconstructed functionally. This could be shortly circumscribed as rephrasing the rule of interpretation in a way to bring out its defining features (cardinal cores) more precisely while also identifying open questions of interpretative method (interpretative knots).

Part II puts this functional reconstruction into practice. Yet, such a reconstruction can only be successful when one can identify the questions that need to be addressed when looking at a certain interpretative method. One way to find out what the questions are, is engaging into a historical inquiry and to see how international interpretative methodology has developed over time (Chapter 4).

The look into legal history enables us to bring out the defining features more clearly (Chapter 5). Knowing more about the process of interpretation could also help to determine the function of interpretation. To extrapolate the function can be useful if one deals with issues concerning the rule of interpretation that cannot easily be determined.

Those issues will be inquired into in turn (Chapter 6). The Convention has to be analysed to see in which relations there cannot be a determinative answer to questions. The assessment of the defining and the open features will show how the Convention works and to what extent the intertemporal question is determined.

While Part II deals with problems of methodology, Part III is focused on interpretative practice. It first focuses on how to collect all relevant data from certain courts on static and evolutive interpretation (Chapter 8). It will then inquire in an in-depth manner into the jurisprudence of the ICJ (Chapter 9) and the ECtHR (Chapter 10).

Contextual division: Comparisons

Set in stone like the Decalogue or engraved in a living tree like a constitution? Ossified or breathing? The nature of treaties in international law is one of the broader themes on which the limited question of this study is dependent. Can an interpreter change the meaning of an international treaty through interpretation and, if so, how? These two questions took me on an unexpected voyage starting with basic insights about interpretation, deep into the general rule of interpretation in the VCLT and from there to the practice of two international courts. On this road, narratives and metaphors often have to make way for precision and detail that are essential in an analytical inquiry. Therefore, I seek to appease the reader by borrowing from the beauty of other writers who in their fields expressed deep truths that are in harmony with the tunes of international legal interpretation. Publius Ovidus Naso introduces his metamorphosis with the following prooemium:

> In noua fert animus mutatas dicere formas
> corpora; di, coeptis (nam uos mutastis et illae)
> adspirate meis primaque ab origine mundi
> ad mea perpetuum deducite tempora carmen (1.1–4).

> My mind moves me to tell of shapes changed into new
> bodies; gods, inspire my beginnings (for you have changed even those)
> and spin a fine thread of continuous song
> from the first origin of the world to my own times.[2]

Magical tales follow these verses with which Ovid explains the coming into existence of the most ordinary and the most special things in the world: He tells us how the strong King Atlas turned into a mountain after refusing to receive Perseus as a guest but also how the beautiful Narcissus fell in love with himself and turned into a flower. Why is there an echo if we shout next to a wood? Because the nymph Echo was cursed by Juno to repeat everything that was said to her. Upon being rejected by Narcissus, she fled to the woods and the only thing that remained was her answering voice.

Classicists have quarrelled over whether the masterwork could be considered as an epos. To the many interpretations of the work, we could add that Ovid could be considered a scientist: He explained the world in his terms. For him, the essence of all phenomena lay in change: When things happened to special people, they changed into new bodies. Ovid explains the world we live in. There is even a method he pursues and a form to his inquiry. But his stories never have the same structure. Looking at changes, he looks at the time and his account goes back to the very beginnings of humanity which he sees as golden ages. The temporal dimension is important in each story, but also for the work in its totality. The changes he perceives are explained by divine power. And as was custom amongst the authors of that time, he thanked the gods in his first lines. Amongst PhD students, it is a longstanding custom to thank their supervisors. In line with this convention but also independent from it, I would like to express my sincere gratitude to my supervisor Professor Georg Nolte. When I came to Berlin to take up a

---

[2] Keith, 'Metamorphosis' 236.

position as an assistant to him, I was the same age as Werner Heisenberg, when he took up his first professorship in Leipzig in 1927. In the very same year, he published an article that changed physics and natural sciences substantially and profoundly. One important aspect of his findings can be expressed by a simple sentence:

> [T]he more precisely the position (momentum) of a particle is given, the less precisely can one say what its momentum (position) is.[3]

This was later denoted as Heisenberg's Uncertainty Principle. Heisenberg discovered that one could either know the movement or the position of particles in physics, but the simultaneous knowledge of both was impossible. This insight framed and influenced quantum experiments for the time to come. Many lessons can be derived from it and it might also be an apt metaphor for legal scholarship: Sometimes, I felt that it is either possible to state what the law is or where the law is heading. Yet, doing both things at the same time proved to be impossible since such a fundamental change of perspective would necessarily blur the other aspect. Writing this thesis was at times more a lesson of my limits. Many things I assumed and sensed I could not prove. Yet, this also made me think about what I can find out and know. There is an intricate relationship between cognition and ignorance that was famously expressed early on by Socrates. Looking back, I feel that the growing awareness of the limits and the insufficiency of my knowledge and method increased the precision and exactness of what I could express. What helped me was to meet so many interesting people during those four years. This applies to my colleagues as well as to my fellow doctoral students at the chair of Professor Nolte, where I regularly presented my research. I am indebted to Professor Christian Tomuschat for his opinion on my draft. For the very interesting conversations I would like to thank Ana Kolarov, Ariane Grieser, Ariane Richter, Birgit Heppt, Cindy Daase, Friederike Engler, Michael Fischer, Yoan Villain and Wulf Loh. Fiona Nelson diligently improved language and style.

The project was a journey in the literal sense since I had the opportunity to visit interesting and prestigious research institutions, where

---

[3] Heisenberg's conclusion reads: 'je genauer der Ort bestimmt ist, desto ungenauer ist der Impuls bekannt und umgekehrt'. Heisenberg, 'Über den anschaulichen Inhalt der quantentheoretischen Kinematik und Mechanik' 175. Translation by Hilgevoord and Uffink, 'The Uncertainty Principle'.

I gathered a lot of helpful insights: I visited chairs and institutes at the University of Amsterdam, in Berlin, in Cambridge at the Lauterpacht Centre, in The Hague, in Heidelberg at the Max-Planck-Institute, in Munich at the Ludwig-Maximilians-Universität and at the University of the Federal Armed Forces and in Paris. To present my research at the Research Forum of the American Society of International Law was a particular honour. For their kind hospitality and their views and critique I would like to thank Alexandra Kemmerer, Judge Bruno Simma, Judge James Crawford, Judge Leonid Skotnikov, Professor André Nollkaemper, Professor Armin von Bogdandy, Professor Bardo Fassbender, Professor Gerd Seidel, Professor Christian Walter, Professor Christoph Möllers, Professor Daniel Khan, Professor Gerhard Dannemann, Professor Giorgio Gaja, Professor Ingolf Pernice, Professor Jonathan Nash, Professor Marc Weller, Professor Philip Allot, Professor Stefan Vogenauer and Professor Rüdiger Wolfrum.

During the three months in Cambridge I had a very special encounter which contributed much more to the spirit than to the letter of what is to follow: the acquaintance of Sir Elihu Lauterpacht. Whenever I had the honour and privilege to meet with him, things turned out very differently than I expected: When I met him in his study for the first time, being ready to present and talk about my research, I discovered that he is a man of many interests and a *connoisseur* of classical music. When I met him at a pub to later attend a concert in an old church nearby Cambridge, I learned that he is a family man and that he is currently working on a photo-biography. On the third occasion in his beautiful garden in Cambridge, I had the opportunity to take a glance at some of the pictures. I saw the evidence of some of the occurrences that shaped international law that I knew and some I had not heard of. Yet, on this afternoon in the summer sun, lines I had read some years before filled with life. They were penned by Henry Cartier-Bresson:

> In photography there is a new kind of plasticity, product of the instantaneous lines made by movements of the subject. We work in unison with movement as though it were a presentiment of the way in which life itself unfolds. But inside movement there is one moment at which the elements in motion are in balance. Photography must seize upon this moment and hold immobile the equilibrium of it.[4]

---

[4] Cartier-Bresson, 'The Decisive Moment 1952' 385.

On the one hand, photography is an endeavour that has to grapple with similar hardships as legal scholarship: It follows movement but it can capture only the moment. Cartier-Bresson comments that if the photographer is prepared and perseveres, it might be possible to capture the decisive moment. In this moment, a simple photograph can achieve the impossible: It can transcend time: It displays the past, it points to the future. What is striking about Cartier-Bresson is the simplicity of the context in which he captures those moments: It happens on the streets in small towns, in flats of middle or working class people, in schools and hospitals. Instead of producing imaginary oil paintings of historic events, he was looking for real life and by close observation and attention anticipated those magic instances. Writing about the evolution of the law is in many ways also a quest for the decisive moment: like Ovid, one has to consider not only the present but also the past in many respects. One has to be mindful like Heisenberg that there are many uncertainties and impossibilities in the process of researching. But by sticking to one's method, it might be possible to be there at the decisive moment, in theoretical heights as well as on the ground of legal practice, where interpretation actually happens. Cartier-Bresson's simplicity is the simplicity of the appearance of the object, but it is also the simplicity of the means of photography: Followers would reject more refined technology in favour of their original cameras. Is an old camera not like a plain and simple style of writing? Everybody wants to have a new camera, to exhibit erudition and literacy even when it does not improve the quality of the pictures or texts. The present study has consciously opted for a plain, simple and analytical style. I do not know which sources fed into that decision: Possibly the limits of my ability, possibly also the convictions of the plain English movement that simple style furthers thinking and understanding of the reader and the author. And it might possibly have been influenced by *Erich Auerbach's* concept of *sermo humilis* and his belief that simplicity in the humanities was also necessary for democratic reasons. In the end, an important factor is my deep conviction that changes in information technology will soon necessitate more reform in academic communication: Not only knowledge production but knowledge organisation and quality management will be the quests of tomorrow's scholars. Not only originality but also embeddedness in the discourse will become increasingly relevant. With rising specialisation, researchers will need to think more complexly but also to express themselves more comprehensibly. This might in many instances require choosing the simple over the complex form. Simple is the expression of gratitude towards the people who have always been there for me in the decisive moments. All books in the world could not have expressed what I owe to my family, Carmen, Mostefa and Ramona Djeffal.

ABBREVIATIONS

AJIL	American Journal of International Law
ASIL	American Society of International Law
BYIL	British Yearbook of International Law
ECHR	European Convention on Human Rights
ECtHR	European Court of Human Rights
EJIL	European Journal of International Law
GC	Grand Chamber
ICJ	International Court of Justice
ICJ Rep	ICJ Reports
ILC	International Law Commission
ILC Ybk	Yearbook of the International Law Commission
ILO	International Labour Organization
PCIJ	Permanent Court of International Justice
RdC	Recueil des Cours de l'Académie de Droit International
RGDIP	Revue Générale de Droit International Public
RIAA	Reports of International Arbitral Awards
UN	United Nations
UNCITRAL	United Nations Commission on Trade Law
UNGA	UN General Assembly
UNTS	United Nations Treaty Series
VCLT	Vienna Convention on the Law of Treaties
WTO	World Trade Organisation

TABLE OF CASES

European Court of Human Rights and European Commission of Human Rights

A v. Croatia (First Section) App. no. 55164/08   340
A, B and C v. Ireland (GC) ECHR 2010 App. no. 25579/05   289, 307, 318, 337
Acmanne and others v. Belgium DR 1984 App. no. 10435/83   288, 331
Airey v. Ireland (Chamber) Series A no. 41 App. no. 6289/73   304, 305
Al Skeini and others v. the United Kingdom ECHR 2011 App. no. 55721/07   297
Al-Saadoon and Mufdhi v. the United Kingdom (Fourth Section) ECHR 2010 App. no. 61498/08   280, 310, 330, 332
Annoni di Gussola and others v. France (Third Section) ECHR 2000-XI App. nos. 31819/96, 33293/96   286, 308
Anthony M. Tyrer against the United Kingdom Report (1976) App. no. 5856/72 Report of the Commission   303
Aoulmi v. France (Fourth Section) ECHR 2006-I App. no. 50278/99   306
Austin and others v. the United Kingdom (GC) ECHR 2012 App. nos. 39692/09, 40713/09, 41008/09   285, 308, 313–14, 331
B v. France (Plenary) (1992) Series A no. 232-C App. no. 13343/87   288, 324, 337
Banković v. Belgium, the Czech Republic, Denmark, France, Germany, Greece, Hungary, Iceland, Italy, Luxembourg, the Netherlands, Norway, Poland, Portugal, Spain, Turkey and the United Kingdom (GC) (Decision) ECHR 2001-XII App. no. 52207/99   296–7, 307–8, 337
Bayatyan v. Armenia (GC) ECHR 2011 App. no. 23459/03   289, 304, 308, 326–8, 330–1, 333–4, 338, 342
Bayatyan v. Armenia (Third Section) App. no. 23459/03 (ECtHR, 27 October 2009)   285
Beganović v. Croatia (First Section) App. no. 46423/06 (ECtHR, 25 June 2009)   310
Brauer v. Germany (Fifth Section) App. no. 3545/04 (ECtHR, 28 May 2009)   293, 315
Catan and others v. Moldova and Russia (GC) ECHR 2012 App. nos. 43370/04, 8252/05, 18454/06   324
Centre for Legal Resources on behalf of Valentin Câmpeanu (GC) App. no. 47848/08 (17 July 2014)   257, 341
Chapman v. the United Kingdom (GC) ECHR 2001-I App. no. 27238/95   288, 319

Christine Goodwin v. the United Kingdom (GC) ECHR 2002-VI App. no. 28957/95   7, 279, 288, 292, 304, 314–17, 320–2, 324, 327, 333, 337–8, 341–3
Cossey v. the United Kingdom (Plenary) 1990 Series A no. 184 App. no. 10843/84   287, 291, 315, 322, 334, 338, 341–2
Cruz Varas and others v. Sweden (Plenary) Series A no. 201 App. no. 15576/89   298, 307, 323, 328–9, 331, 333
Demades v. Turkey (Third Section) App. no. 16219/90 (ECtHR, 31 July 2003)   305
Demir and Baykara v. Turkey (GC) ECHR 2008 App. no. 34503/97   275, 291, 330–4, 340
Deumland v. Germany (Plenary) Series A No. 100 App. no. 9384/81   308
Dikme v. Turkey (First Section) ECHR 2000-VIII App. no. 20869/92   282–3
Dudgeon v. the United Kingdom (Plenary) (1981) Series A no. 4 App. no. 7525/76   316, 322
Emonet and others v. Switzerland (First Section) App. no. 39051/03 (ECtHR, 13 December 2007)   288–9, 319, 321
Engel and others v. Sweden (Decision) (1994) App. no. 15533/89   305
F v. Switzerland (Plenary) (1987) Series A no. 128 App. no. 11329/85   292, 321
Ferrazzini v. Italy (GC) ECHR 2001-VII App. no. 44759/98   285, 324
Fretté v. France (Third Section) ECHR 2002-I App. no. 36515/97   293
Genovese v. Malta (Fourth Section) App. no. 53124/09 (ECtHR, 27 October 2011)   293, 319
Giusto and others v. Italy (Second Section) (Decision) App. no. 28972/06   310
Golder v. the United Kingdom (1973) Series A no. 18 App. no. 4451/70   275, 334
Gorou v. Greece (No. 2) (GC) App. no. 12686/03 (ECtHR, 20 March 2009)   310, 313
Grant v. the United Kingdom (Fourth Section) ECHR 2006-VII App. no. 32570/03   288
Haas v. Switzerland (First Section) ECHR 2011 App. no. 31322/07   288
Harroudj v. France (Fifth Section) App. no. 43631/09 (ECtHR, 4 October 2012)   287, 315, 318
Hassan v. the United Kingdom (GC) App. no. 29750/09 (ECtHR, 16 September 2014)   312, 331
Hatton and others v. the United Kingdom (GC) ECHR 2003-VIII App. no. 36022/97   312, 322
Hénaf v. France (First Section) ECHR 2003-XI App. no. 65436/01   282, 310
Herrmann v. Germany (GC) (2012) App. no. 9300/07 (ECtHR, 26 June 2012)   311
Hirsi Jamaa and others v. Italy (GC) ECHR 2012 App. no. 27765/09   275, 296, 323, 326–7, 337
Hirst v. the United Kingdom (No. 2) (GC) ECHR 2005-IX App. no. 74025/01   305
I v. the United Kingdom (GC) App. no. 25680/94 (ECtHR, 11 July 2002)   288
Inze v. Austria (Chamber) (1987) Series A no. 126 App. no. 869579   293, 319
Ireland v. the United Kingdom (Plenary) Series A no. 25 App. no. 5310/71   274
James and others v. the United Kingdom (Plenary) (1986) Series A no. 98 App. no. 8793/79   295, 334

Janowiec and others v. Russia (GC) App. nos. 55508/07 and 29520/09 (ECtHR, 21 October 2013)   306
Johnston and others v. Ireland (Plenary) (Judgment) (1986) App. no. 9697/82   275, 333
Kharin v. Russia (First Section) App. no. 37345/03 (ECtHR, 3 February 2011)   310
Klass and others v. Germany (1978) Series A no. 28 App. no. 5029/71   312
Konstantin Markin v. Russia (First Section) App. no. 30078/06 (ECtHR, 7 October 2010)   293
Konstantin Markin v. Russia (GC) ECHR 2012 App. no. 30078/06   293, 302, 308, 318–19, 321
Kress v. France (GC) ECHR 2001-VI App. no. 39594/98   305
Kroon and others v. the Netherlands, Series A no. 297-C App. no. 18535/91   321
KU v. Finland (Fourth Section) ECHR 2008 App. no. 2872/02   288, 321
L v. Lithuania (Second Section) ECHR 2007-IV App. no. 27527/03   288
Lebedev v. Russia (First Section) App. no. 4493/04 (ECtHR, 25 October 2007)   285
Leyla Şhahın (GC) ECHR 2005-XI App. no. 44774/98   296, 302, 311
Loizidou v. Turkey (Preliminary Objections) (Chamber) (1995) Series A no. 310 App. no. 15318/89   275, 297, 302, 306–7, 323, 327–8, 331–3
Lucky Dev v. Sweden (Fifth Section) App. no. 7356/10 (ECtHR, 27 November 2014)   306
Mamatkulov and Askarov v. Turkey (GC) ECHR 2005-I App. nos. 46827/99, 46951/99   298, 326, 329, 332, 334
Mangouras v. Spain (GC) App. no. 12050/04 (ECtHR, 28 September 2010)   284–5, 311
Marckx v. Belgium (Plenary) (1979) Series A no. 31 App. no. 6833/74   279, 292–3, 302, 305, 319
Matthews v. the United Kingdom (GC) ECHR 1999-I App. no. 24833/94   295, 302, 326–7
Mazurek v. France (Third Section) App. no. 34406/97 (ECtHR, 1 February 2000)   293, 319–20, 337
MC v. Bulgaria (First Section) ECHR 2003-XII App. no. 39272/98   282, 316–18, 321–2, 331
McVeigh and others v. the United Kingdom (Decision) (1981) App. nos. 8022/77, 8025/77, 8027/77   284, 312, 356
Mizzi v. Malta (First Section) ECHR 2006-I App. no. 26111/02   338
Moretti and Benedetti v. Italy (Second Section) App. no. 16318/07 (ECtHR, 27 April 2010)   305, 315
Mouvement Raëlien Suisse v. Switzerland (GC) ECHR 2012 App. no. 16354/06   290
Mubilanzila Mayeka and Kaniki Mitunga v. Belgium (First Section) ECHR 2006-XI App. no. 13178/03   310
Muños Díaz v. Spain (Third Section) ECHR 2009 App. no. 49151/07   308
N v. the United Kingdom (GC) ECHR 2008 App. no. 26565/05   308
Öcalan v. Turkey (First Section) App. no. 46221/99 (ECtHR, 12 March 2003)   280, 329–31
Öcalan v. Turkey (GC) ECHR 2005-IV App. no. 46221/99   280, 330

O'Keefe v. Ireland (GC) App. no. 35810/09 (ECtHR, 28 January 2014)   306
Pichkur v. Ukraine (Fifth Section) App. no. 10441/06 (ECtHR, 7 November 2013)   294, 321, 332
Pla and Puncernau v. Andorra (Fourth Section) ECHR 2004-VIII App. no. 69498/01   293, 302
Pretty v. the United Kingdom (Fourth Section) ECHR 2002-III App. no. 2346/02   281
Rantsev v. Cyprus and Russia (First Section) App. no. 25965/04 (ECtHR, 7 January 2010)   275, 283, 310, 326, 331–2, 337, 343
Rees v. the United Kingdom (Plenary) (1986) Series A no. 106 App. no. 9532/81   7, 287, 291, 316, 320, 322, 324, 341–2
Riad and Idiab v. Belgium (First Section) App. nos. 29787/03, 29810/03 (ECtHR, 24 January 2008)   310
RMT v. the Netherlands (Fourth Section) App. no. 31045/10 (ECtHR, 8 April 2014)   330
Sandra Janković v. Croatia (First Section) App. no. 38478/05 (ECtHR, 5 March 2009)   310
Schalk and Kopf v. Austria (First Section) ECHR 2010 App. no. 30141/04   286–7, 318, 326, 328, 331, 333–4, 337, 342
Schwizgebel v. Switzerland (First Section) ECHR 2010 App. no. 25762/07   293, 315, 317
Scoppola v. Italy (No. 3) (GC) App. no. 126/05 (ECtHR, 22 May 2012)   295–6, 312
Selmouni v. France (GC) ECHR 1999-V App. no. 25803/94   282, 310
Sheffield and Horsham v. the United Kingdom (GC) ECHR 1998-V App. no. 22985/93, 23390/94   287, 291, 322, 324, 341, 342
Sigidur A. Sigurjónsson v. Iceland Series A no. 264 App. no. 16130/90   291, 328, 333
Siliadin v. France (Second Section) 2005-VII App. no. 73316/01   305, 310
Sitaropoulos and Giakoumopoulos v. Greece (GC) ECHR 2012 App. no. 42202/07   279, 295, 317
Sitaropoulos and others v. Greece (First Section) App. no. 42202/07 (ECtHR, 8 July 2010)   295, 304, 316, 318, 327, 333
Société Colas Est and others v. France ECHR 2002-III App. no. 37971/97   287, 326, 342
Soering v. the United Kingdom (Plenary) (1989) Series A no. 161 App. no. 14038/88   280, 302, 314, 326, 328–9, 334
Sommerfeld v. Germany (GC) ECHR 2003-VII App. no. 31871/96   338
Stafford v. the United Kingdom (GC) ECHR 2002-IV App. no. 46295/99   305
STEC and others v. the United Kingdom (GC) (Decision) ECHR 2005-X App. no. 65731/01, 65900/01   295, 304, 308, 326, 329
Stoll v. Switzerland (GC) ECHR 2007-V App. no. 69698/01   279, 290, 311, 315, 321, 327
Stummer v. Austria (GC) ECHR 2011 App. no. 37452/02   283, 304, 315, 328, 332–4
Sukhovertskyy v. Ukraine (Second Section) ECHR 2006-VI App. no. 13716/02   316
Sutherland v. the United Kingdom (Judgment) (1997) App. no. 25186/94   294, 322
T v. the United Kingdom (GC) App. no. 24724/94 (16 December 1999)   282

Tanăse v. Romania (Third Section) App. no. 5269/02 (ECtHR, 12 May 2009)   282
Ternoviskis v. Latvia (Fourth Section) App. no. 33637/02 (ECtHR, 29 April 2014)   306, 337
Tyrer v. the United Kingdom (Chamber) Series A no. 26 App. no. 5856/72   281-2, 301-4, 320, 337, 355
V v. the United Kingdom (GC) ECHR 1999-IX App. no. 24888/94   282
Van der Mussele v. Belgium (Plenary) (1983) Series A no. 70 App. no. 8919/80   305
Vilho Eskelinen and others v. Finland ECHR 2004-VIII App. no. 63235/00   285-6, 306
Villianatos and others v. Greece (GC) App. nos. 29381/09 and 32684/09 (ECtHR, 7 November 2013)   294
Vo v. France (GC) ECHR 2004-VIII App. no. 53924/00   281
Witold Litwa v. Poland, ECHR 2000-III App. no. 26629/95   310
X and others v. Austria (GC) App. no. 19010/07 (ECtHR, 19 February 2013)   307, 310, 317, 319, 321, 332
X, Y and Z v. the United Kingdom (GC) ECHR 1997-II App. no. 21830/93   287, 337
Young, James and Webster v. the United Kingdom (1981) Series A no. 44 App. nos. 7601/76, 7806/77   275, 291
Zaunegger v. Germany (Fifth Section) App. no. 22028/04 (ECtHR, 3 December 2009)   203
Zolotukhin v. Russia (GC) ECHR 2009 App. no. 14939/03   296, 326, 331

International Court of Justice

Admissibility of Hearings of Petitioners by the Committee on South West Africa (Advisory Opinion) [1956] ICJ Rep 23   27, 217
Admissions of a State to the United Nations (Charter Article 4) (Advisory Opinion) [1948] ICJ Rep 57   248-9, 265
Aegean Sea Continental Shelf Case (Greece v. Turkey) (Judgment) [1978] ICJ Rep 3   222, 234, 239, 243, 251, 254
Aerial Incident of 10 August 1999 (Pakistan v. India) (Jurisdiction of the Court) [1999] ICJ Rep 12   234
Anglo-Iranian Oil Case (United Kingdom v. Iran) (Judgment) [1952] ICJ Rep 93   218-19, 234-5, 248, 269
Application of the Convention on the Prevention and Punishment of the Crime of Genocide (Bosnia Herzegovina v. Yugoslavia (Serbia and Montenegro)) (Order) [1993] ICJ Rep 3   223
Application of the Convention on the Prevention and Punishment of the Crime of Genocide (Bosnia Herzegovina v. Serbia and Montenegro) (Judgment) [2007] ICJ Rep 43   247-9
Barcelona Traction, Light and Power Company, Limited, Case Concerning (Belgium v. Spain) (Preliminary Objections) [1964] ICJ Rep 6   224, 247
Certain Expenses of the United Nations (Advisory Opinion) [1962] ICJ Rep 115   232, 236, 264-5

Colombian–Peruvian Asylum Case (Colombia v. Peru) (Judgment) [1950] ICJ Rep 266   234, 267
Competence of the General Assembly for the Admission of a State to the United Nations (Advisory Opinion) 1950 ICJ Rep 5   248–9, 258, 265
Continental Shelf (Tunisia v. Libyan Arab Jamahiriya) (Judgment) [1982] ICJ Rep 18   232
Corfu Channel (United Kingdom of Great Britain and Northern Ireland v. Albania) (Judgment) [1949] ICJ Rep 39   248
Dispute Regarding Navigational and Related Rights, Case Concerning (Costa Rica v. Nicaragua) (Judgment) [2009] ICJ Rep 213   246, 250, 252, 254–6, 258–9, 263–4, 268–70, 354
Fisheries Jurisdiction (Federal Republic of Germany v. Iceland) (Merits) [1974] ICJ Rep 175   221–2
Fisheries Jurisdiction (Spain v. Canada) (Jurisdiction of the Court) [1998] ICJ Rep 432   225–6, 234, 240, 258, 269
Fisheries Jurisdiction (United Kingdom v. Iceland) (Merits) [1974] ICJ Rep 3   221, 232–3
Frontier Dispute (Burkina Faso v. Republic of Mali) (Judgment) [1986] ICJ Rep 554   241
Gabčíkovo–Nagymaros Project, Case Concerning (Hungary v. Slovakia) (Judgment) [1997] ICJ Rep 7   262, 266–8, 271
International Status of South West Africa (Advisory Opinion) [1950] ICJ Rep 128   216–17, 249, 252, 257, 262–3, 269
Interpretation of Peace Treaties (Advisory Opinion, second phase) [1950] ICJ Rep 221   232
Jurisdictional Immunities of the State (Germany v. Italy: Greece Intervening) (Judgment), www.icj-cij.org/docket/files/143/16883.pdf, 3 February 2012   250
Kasikili/Sedudu Island (Botswana v. Namibia) (Judgment) [1999] ICJ Rep 1045   215, 226–7, 239–42, 252, 254–6, 259–61, 263, 268, 270
Land and Maritime Boundary between Cameroon and Nigeria, Case Concerning (Cameroon v. Nigeria: Equatorial Guinea Intervening) (Judgment) [2002] ICJ Rep 303   227, 240, 247–8, 250
Land, Island and Maritime Frontier Dispute (Judgment) [1992] ICJ Rep 351   232
Legal Consequences for States of the Continued Presence of South Africa in Namibia (South West Africa) notwithstanding Security Council Resolution 276 (1970) (Advisory Opinion) [1971] ICJ Rep 16   221, 233, 238, 253, 258, 263–5
Legal Consequences of the Construction of a Wall in the Occupied Palestinian Territory (Advisory Opinion) [2004] ICJ Rep 136   228, 255
Legality of the Threat or Use of Nuclear Weapons (Advisory Opinion) [1996] ICJ Rep 226   224, 250, 259, 261, 263, 269, 271
Legality of the Use of Force (Serbia and Montenegro v. Belgium) (Preliminary Objections) [2004] ICJ Rep 279   215, 223, 257, 262
Oil Platforms, Case Concerning (Islamic Republic of Iran v. United States of America) (Judgment) [2003] ICJ Rep 161   235

Pulp Mills on the River Uruguay Case (Argentina v. Uruguay) (Judgment) [2010] ICJ Rep 14   229–30, 250, 264, 269
Questions of Interpretation and Application of the 1971 Montreal Convention Arising from the Aerial Incident at Lockerbie, Case Concerning (Libyan Arab Jamahiriya v. United Kingdom) (Preliminary Objections) [1998] ICJ Rep 9   224
Reparations for Injuries Suffered in the Service of the United Nations (Judgment) [1949] ICJ Rep 174   234
Reservations to the Convention on the Prevention and Punishment of the Crime of Genocide (Advisory Opinion) [1951] ICJ Rep 15   248–9
Rights of Nationals of the United States of America in Morocco (France v. United States of America) (Judgment) [1952] ICJ Rep 176   217–18, 234–5, 267–8, 354
South West Africa Cases (Ethiopia v. South Africa; Liberia v. South Africa) (Preliminary Objections) [1962] ICJ Rep 319   250, 252, 255, 261, 264, 267
South West Africa (Ethiopia v. South Africa; Liberia v. South Africa) (Second Phase) [1966] ICJ Rep 6   221, 237, 245–6, 254, 256, 265, 267–8
Temple of Preah Vihear, Case Concerning (Cambodia v. Thailand) (Merits) [1962] ICJ Rep 6   210, 219, 242, 260, 269
Voting Procedure on Questions Relating to Reports and Petitions Concerning the Territory of South-West Africa (Advisory Opinion) [1955] ICJ Rep 67   217
Whaling in the Antarctic (Australia v. Japan) (Order) www.icj-cij.org/docket/files/148/17268.pdf 6 February 2013   258

Arbitration

Interpretation of the air transport services agreement between the United States of America and France (United States v. France) (1963) 16 RIAA 5   43
Island of Palmas Case (Netherlands v. USA) (1928) RIAA 829   31, 178–9, 348

United States Supreme Court

M'Culloch v. State, 17 US 316 (1819); 17 US 316 (Wheat.) 122   24

Canadian Supreme Court

Edwards v. Attorney-General of Canada [1930] AC 124, 136 (PC)   302

PART I

Definitions, assumptions and method

1

Two paths to interpretative method

At the outset of this study lies the observation that there is an increase in evolutive interpretations in international law[1] as well as a rising scholarly awareness of that phenomenon. My ambition is to inquire into how an interpreter of international treaties ought to deal with the choice between static and dynamic interpretation. This is a question of *interpretative method*, i.e. the rules guiding interpreters in the process of interpretation.[2]

1.1. What we are talking about: interpretative method and methodology

In international law, the general rule of treaty interpretation is laid out in a treaty, the Vienna Convention on the Law of Treaties.[3] This treaty on treaties,[4] which has been described as 'constitutional',[5] contains a general rule on interpretation in its Arts. 31 and 32. The treaty does not only show a very high participation among member states,[6] it is almost universally recognised by international courts as determining interpretative method in international law.[7] To find out whether and how the content of treaties

---

[1] Nolte, 'Between Contemporaneous and Evolutive Interpretation' 1679; Nolte, 'Treaties over Time: Introductory Report'.
[2] This is based on Hart's distinction of primary and secondary norms. Hart, *The Concept of Law* 81. Certain of those norms are extended to norms about interpretation.
[3] Vienna Convention on the Law of Treaties (adopted 23 May 1969, entered into force 27 January 1980) 1155 UNTS 331 (VCLT).
[4] Kearney and Dalton, 'The Treaty on Treaties' 495.
[5] As reported by Verosta, 'Die Vertragsrechts-Konferenz der Vereinten Nationen 1968/69 und die Wiener Konvention über das Recht der Verträge' 687.
[6] Currently, it is ratified by 114 states: see http://treaties.un.org/Pages/ViewDetailsIII.aspx?src=TREATY&mtdsg_no=XXIII~1&chapter=23&Temp=mtdsg3&lang=en (accessed 31 December 2014).
[7] For an overview, see Gardiner, *Treaty Interpretation* 114–26. With regard to its customary status, see Villiger, 'Articles 31 and 32 of the Vienna Convention on the Law of Treaties in

can be changed, we will have to travel into the deeper layers of interpretative method. This will lead us in two directions: That of doctrinal reflection or methodology, and that of interpretative practice. And this for a good reason: These two perspectives have been the poles whose interaction created the concepts we denote as interpretative method.[8] It is their mutual influence, which creates and alters interpretative method. *Interpretative practice* is the use of method in real life. Practice is a source but at the same time an application of method. Courts for example interpret treaties. Courts use interpretative method, but the way they do it also has a bearing upon the rules. We could say that interpretative method materialises in interpretative practice. The reflection of international legal method by legal scholars is called *methodology*.[9] Methodology influences method in two ways. On the one hand, it restates the practice as method, but it restates it in a defined way, giving it a certain structure and form. It, therefore, changes it slightly. It is mirrored interpretative method. Methodology and practice, material and mirror are magical: They aim to reproduce interpretative method but they also create it. This is a kind of magic we can observe in many areas of life: Conceptual historians like Quentin Skinner or Reinhard Koselleck tell us that some concepts like sovereignty not only describe but make history.[10] The philosophical current of pragmatism has highlighted that the utterance of words has more

---

the Case Law of the European Court of Human Rights' 118. For a detailed account of the acceptance of the rules by the ICJ, see Torres Bernárdez, 'Interpretation of Treaties by the International Court of Justice Following the Adoption of the 1969 Vienna Convention on the Law of Treaties', see also Gardiner *ibid.* 13.

[8] This runs parallel to the criteria Koskenniemi uses to describe international legal method: normativity and concreteness. Koskenniemi, 'Methodology of International Law'. Yet, the distinction of methodology and practice is more focused on the institutional perspective than on criteria for the admissibility of legal argument.

[9] For this distinction, see Schröder, 'Juristische Methode' 1449. Looking not only on interpretative method but on method and methodology in a broader sense, some authors have been able to avoid the rather refined and possibly a bit pedantic distinction I assume: Focarelli, *International Law as a Social Construct* 92. He sees the function of method as well as methodology in the ascertainment of law and attributes a broader scope of means to methodology. A similar notion is assumed by Bos, *A Methodology of International Law* 1–2. Bleckmann defined methodology by enumerating different areas of the methodology, Bleckmann, *Grundprobleme und Methoden des Völkerrechts* 33. For our purposes, the term *logos* enshrined in methodology suggests that it is a reflective practice. If we define method as rules regulating legal activity, methodology cannot be the same but must be the reflection of that activity. For an example in which both terms are exclusively used in relation to legal scholarship, see Bankowski and others, 'On Method and Methodology'.

[10] Skinner, 'Retrospect: Studying Rhetoric and Conceptual Change'; Koselleck, 'Die Geschichte der Begriffe und Begriffe der Geschichte'.

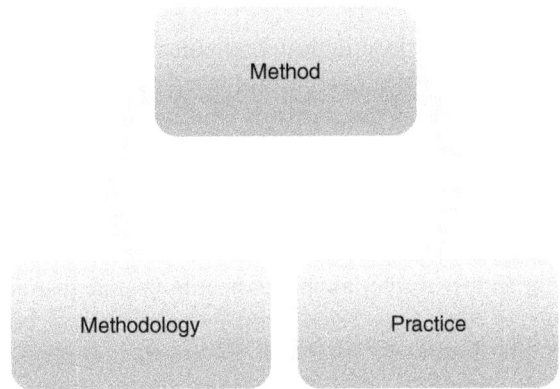

Figure 1 Method in context

consequences than solely to restate their lexical meaning.[11] Those insights might not seem spectacular to a lawyer from a practical point of view.[12] Legal concepts and their use alter reality every day: couples are married, houses are sold, and criminals are imprisoned. Whenever there is an argument about what the text ought to mean, lawyers resort to certain rules guiding their conduct even though lawyers are often not actively aware of how these rules operate. In the case of interpretation, we call the rules guiding the practice interpretative method. Figure 1 summarises the way in which interpretative method is related to interpretative practice as well as to methodology. To find out whether and how the meaning of treaties can be changed through interpretation, we have to consider legal practice as well as legal methodology. In the latter case, the present inquiry will plod through legal doctrine over time. The research on interpretative practice is limited to the practice of international courts. The scope of the study ought to be explained before defining what evolutive treaty interpretation actually is.

1.2. Who we are talking about: international courts

Disputes before international courts lie at the heart of this study.[13] We are awaiting the next wave of rising judicial practice that could

---

[11] See the classical account of Austin, *How to Do Things with Words*.
[12] Yet, there is much to be gained through the theoretical insights as shown by Ingo Venzke, *How Interpretation Makes International Law*.
[13] For accounts focusing on judicial practice, see Gerald Fitzmaurice, 'The Law and Procedure of the International Court of Justice: Treaty Interpretation' 1; Gerald Fitzmaurice,

substantiate a trend towards evolutive interpretation:[14] while there has been a '[l]onging for international adjudication' in the past,[15] international adjudication is definitively an achieved reality today.[16] Moreover, an 'explosion'[17] of judicial mechanisms leading to their 'multiplication' and 'proliferation' can be observed.[18] This means that there is a great increase in new judicial institutions, the number of which comes close to 125,[19] 24 of which can be classified as international courts.[20] They produce an increasing amount of decisions. Therefore, one might say that the structure of international law has not only moved from co-existence to cooperation, as Wolfgang Friedmann has termed it,[21] but also from diplomacy to adjudication.[22] International courts complement states as actors on the international stage. This move towards more adjudication on the international plane might entail good and bad consequences:[23] More mechanisms promise more effectiveness since disputes are decided in a final, binding and objective manner.[24] But more mechanisms might also lead to competing claims about jurisdiction.[25] This might tempt

'The Law and Procedure of the International Court of Justice 1951–4' 203; Yambrusic, *Treaty Interpretation*; Nolte, 'Second Report for the ILC Study Group on Treaties over Time'.

[14] For that trend, see Nolte, 'Between Contemporaneous and Evolutive Interpretation' 1679; Nolte, 'Treaties over Time'. See also Binder, *Die Grenzen der Vertragstreue im Völkerrecht* 83.
[15] Venzke, *How Interpretation Makes International Law* 140.
[16] Nolte, 'Introduction' 1; Alter, *The New Terrain of International Law* 68–69.
[17] Alford, 'The Proliferation of International Courts and Tribunals' 160.
[18] Buergenthal, 'Proliferation of International Courts and Tribunals' 267; Dupuy, 'The Danger of Fragmentation or Unification of the International Legal System and the International Court of Justice' 795; Paulus, 'International Adjudication' 218.
[19] Venzke, *How Interpretation Makes International Law* 135, referring to 'Project on International Courts and Tribunals', www.pict.pcti.org (accessed 15 May 2013).
[20] Alter, *The New Terrain of International Law* 70–6.
[21] Friedmann, 'The Changing Dimensions of International Law' 1147.
[22] Cohen, 'International Law's Erie Moment' 257. At the centre of his attention is the nature of the law which he describes as shifting from diplomatic to judicial. Yet, one could very well argue that this shift has even more implications.
[23] Dupuy, 'The Danger of Fragmentation or Unification of the International Legal System and the International Court of Justice' 795; Alford, 'The Proliferation of International Courts and Tribunals'; Buergenthal, 'Proliferation of International Courts and Tribunals'.
[24] Dupuy, 'The Danger of Fragmentation or Unification of the International Legal System and the International Court of Justice' 796; Nolte, 'Introduction' 1.
[25] Oellers-Frahm, 'Multiplication of International Courts and Tribunals and Conflicting Jurisdiction – Problems and Possible Solutions' 78ff; Dupuy, 'The Danger of Fragmentation or Unification of the International Legal System and the International Court of Justice' 796; Buergenthal, 'Proliferation of International Courts and Tribunals' 272.

courts to overstretch their competence, ability, legitimacy and expertise. One of the most pressing questions in this context will be how to rebalance theoretically as well as practically the relationship between states, judicial mechanisms and other actors. If there is an increasing body of judicial decisions, the likelihood increases that judicial decisions are overturned. In other words, if there is a tendency towards more decision-making there will be more instances to re-evaluate previous decisions. This could explain or substantiate the 'trend towards evolutive interpretation':[26] if courts like the ECtHR have to deal with an increasing amount of cases, they will have to revisit and adapt their jurisprudence: The fact that transsexuals had no right to have their birth certificate be corrected in 1986[27] does not mean that the same has to apply in 2003.[28] If there is an increasing number of courts dealing with similar issues, this might result in competing interpretations of the very same issue or even case.[29] Another explanation for the 'trend towards evolutive interpretation' is that aging treaties, many of which stem from the last century or, more precisely, the last millennium, might also increase the need for reinterpretation.

The changing structure of international law comes about as it is viewed and practised from a completely different perspective: if international legal argument is made not only in diplomatic lounges but also in the courtroom, this shapes the conduct of actors but also the content of law.[30] At high-level diplomatic discussions, the law is sometimes left in a fuzzy state for the sake of achieving agreement. Not all deliberations are accessible for the general public. Textbook authors can then only guess whether and how the agreed conduct could be explained legally. Before a court, on the other hand, decisions must be reached. What is even more significant for this study is that arguments before a court are transparent, and there is a real discussion between the parties and a response by the

---

[26] For that phrase and the general trend, see Nolte, 'Between Contemporaneous and Evolutive Interpretation' 1679.
[27] *Rees v. the United Kingdom* (Plenary) (1986) Series A no. 106 App. no. 9532/81 [38–47].
[28] *Christine Goodwin v. the United Kingdom* (GC) ECHR 2002-VI App. no. 28957/95 [71–93].
[29] Interesting examples are mentioned by Rheinisch, 'The Proliferation of International Dispute Settlement Mechanisms' 114.
[30] Cohen, 'International Law's Erie Moment' 271; for a more cautious approach on judicialisation, see Kingsbury, 'International Courts: Uneven Judicialisation in Global Order'. For an assessment of the judicialisation of international law on national law, see Alter, *The New Terrain of International Law*.

court. The pattern of argumentation before and of courts is more stable as compared to arbitral tribunals. Quantitatively, court decisions might constitute only a small part of all interpretations.[31] But qualitatively, there is no better context to study the 'art of interpretation'.[32] So there is a real need to examine court practice in the wake of its 'explosion'; at the same time, such practice also provides better material for the study of changing interpretations. Before ruminating the intricate problems of interpretative method, we have to know what evolutive interpretation actually means.

1.3. Interpretation

1.3.1 What interpretation is

To define interpretation is very easy and very difficult at the same time. It is the aim of this section to give a workable definition of interpretation representing what lawyers do when they interpret and at the same time to provide a basic model of interpretation that is open to incorporate different insights from different theoretical currents and disciplines. It is first important to understand that the topic of interpretation is relevant in many contexts. Texts, pictures, gestures, actions, films, objects are interpreted.[33] We can potentially interpret everything we sense in one way or another. In some academic disciplines, interpretation has a special importance:[34] a pianist as well as a musicologist might interpret Beethoven's 'Für Elise',[35] a priest and a scholar of theology a text from the Bible. Or, as Hans Kelsen has termed it, '[o]ne interprets the Bible as well as Shakespeare, primitive paintings as well as Goya'.[36] This study focuses on lawyers and legal texts. The interpretation of texts is a great part of what lawyers do in their professional life. Lawyers are familiar with what legal interpretation is. Unsurprisingly, legal academia often

---

[31] Rosenne, 'Conceptualism as a Guide to Treaty Interpretation' 417; Gardiner, *Treaty Interpretation* 110.
[32] Waibel, 'Demystifying the Art of Interpretation' 572.
[33] For a similar introduction, see Klabbers, 'Virtuous Interpretation' 17.
[34] For an account comparing legal interpretation with interpretation in other disciplines, see Greenwalt, *Legal Interpretation*.
[35] Bagatelle No. 25 in A minor (WoO 59 and Bia 515).
[36] Kelsen, *Legal Technique in International Law: A Textual Critique of the League Covenant* 12.

conveys a clear picture of what interpretation really is. Interpretation relates to the Latin expression *pretium*, which translates as meaning, price or value.[37] Therefore, interpretation could be explained as the activity of assessing, pricing or evaluating. In the legal context, it is mostly defined as the attribution of meaning to a set of signs.[38]

Since it is not the aim to give an all-encompassing and full account of all the problems of interpretation, it will suffice to focus on the context we are actually dealing with, that is, proceedings before and decisions of international courts. When international courts interpret a provision, they do it in the context of deciding a dispute and dealing with rival claims. The parties to a case disagree about the meaning of a provision or individual words in it. In such situations, those claims are based on texts, and the court in question has to choose between different readings of those texts. In the justification of their decision, courts frame their argument by basically replicating the Aristotelian deductive logic: They look at the text, rephrase the decisive words to define them more precisely and compare their elaboration of the text to the facts of the case.[39] Whether the deductive logic can[40] or cannot[41] be upheld in the light of today's theoretical insights is not of central importance. The process of handing down a decision is not envisaged to replicate the epistemological process.[42] It is rather a restatement of the result the interpreter arrived at, it is an activity or a social practice of courts. They communicate how they think a text of a treaty determines real world problems. In conclusion, when lawyers interpret, they circumscribe a legal text in different words to make it more comprehensible and to prepare the application of the text and they present arguments for their reading of the text.

While it is easy to make this observation, it is much harder to say what actually happens when a human being reads a legal text and to understand and communicate whether and how the text aims to shape

---

[37] Tammelo, *Treaty Interpretation and Practical Reason* 5. Kolb, *Interprétation et création du droit international* 27–8.
[38] Wróblewski, 'Legal Language and Legal Interpretation' 243; Herdegen, 'Interpretation in International Law' [1]; Remy, 'Techniques interpretatives et systemes de droit' 329; Villiger, 'The Rules on Interpretation: Misgivings, Misunderstandings, Miscarriage? The "Crucible" Intended by the International Law Commission' 106.
[39] An accessible explanation and defence of deductive reasoning is offered by MacCormick, *Rhetoric and the Rule of Law* 32ff.
[40] Von Bogdandy and Venzke, 'Beyond Dispute' 986. They stress the justificatory function of deductive reasoning.
[41] For a general critique of syllogistic logic and an alternative account, see Toulmin, *The Uses of Argument* 100–5.
[42] Von Bogdandy and Venzke, 'Beyond Dispute' 986.

the conduct of human beings. The question what meaning actually is, is disputed in many academic disciplines such as the philosophy of language, theology, linguistics, literary studies or cognitive sciences. Most of the disagreements circle around the question of the nature of meaning and its relation to the process of using language. In literary science, a manifest dispute over the right aim of interpretation can be witnessed, in which some favour the intention of the author as the aim of interpretation while others proclaim the 'death of the author'[43] and that the meaning is dependent upon the reader or the interpretative community[44] he or she belongs to. An important stream of the philosophy of language aimed at representing language in an abstract way with logical signs, while another influential current thinks of utterances as actions and tries to derive consequences from this.[45] Linguists have built upon those theories to develop several practical models of the use of language in general and meaning in particular.

All disciplines and areas have made significant progress and gained important insights, particularly in the twentieth century. Some groundbreaking theories in the philosophy of languages starting from the early twentieth century have been very productive and led to the rethinking of many problems. Yet, one should be mindful that the topic of language and communication is so complex that Alland might be right in his scepticism about whether any theory can really explain the whole process sufficiently.[46] Until very recently, it was also hard to test those theories apart from their internal consistency and their appropriateness in relation to the obvious features of language. Even though there are many promising advances in cognitive sciences, the theoretical riddles have not been solved either, so that any researcher writing about interpretation has to be mindful of the remaining riddles. One way of avoiding this uncertainty is to ignore the insights from other disciplines. Another is to take sides and to assume that one voice in the discourse is right and to spell out what would be true if the assumption was right. The present study tries to find a middle ground in many respects. This consists of focusing on a legal problem and the way lawyers deal with it but still being open for the insights from other disciplines. These insights are to be included in a way appreciating the explanatory potential of

---

[43] Barthes, 'Death of the Author'.   [44] Fish, 'Is There a Text in This Class'.
[45] For a good overview, see Lycan, *Philosophy of Language*; Martinich and Sosa (eds.), *The Philosophy of Language*.
[46] Alland, 'L'Interprétation de droit international public' 54.

theories without excluding any specific view that has not been substantially falsified.

On this basis, the following insights about interpretation in the legal context ought to be considered: The object of interpretation is a legal text. To be more precise, different entities within a text can be interpreted. The objects of interpretation can be single words, sentences (or parts thereof) and also entities comprising more than one sentence such as articles or sections. The operative parts of legal texts mostly follow a certain structure: They either define parts of the text or prescribe behaviour in specific conditions. The prescriptive sentences regularly describe the conditions in which the norm becomes operable and in a second step the consequences the norm has. Both parts of a norm can refer to a multitude of situations or possible actions in real life. To give just one example for a simple norm: 'Whosoever kills a person shall be liable to imprisonment of not less than eight years.' This norm becomes operable when one person kills another person. The consequence of this norm is to imprison the perpetrator for no less than eight years. One could say that a part of the norm refers to such occurrences. In a way, the norm also refers to that future instance. It is helpful to have a model in order to better understand such occurrences of reference.

The semiotic triangle, a standard model in modern linguistics, helps us to understand this basically referential process.[47] It comprises three entities in the corners of the triangle: The sign, the meaning and the referent. It shows the relationship between a sign, its meaning and potentially also a referent. In our context, a *sign* is a part of the text of a treaty that is to be understood as meaning something. If there is something in the real world to which this sign is applicable, we call this the *referent*. Yet, the relationship between the sign and the referent in the real world is not direct but established through the *meaning*. As previously mentioned, international lawyers regularly refer to interpretation as finding or determining the meaning of a legal text. It has also been mentioned that there have been many attempts to determine what meaning actually is and there are also many disputes in that regard.[48]

---

[47] This triangle is today a standard model in linguistics and semiotics: Nöth, *Handbook of Semiotics* 89–90. It goes back to Ogden and Richards, *The Meaning of Meaning*. For an application of the model to international law, see Carvalho, *Semiotics of International Law* xxiii. As will be explained soon, it has been slightly modified to illustrate the actions of interpretation and modification.

[48] For overviews of different attempts, see Nöth, *Handbook of Semiotics* 92ff; and Lycan, *Philosophy of Language* 75ff; for a perspective from the cognitive sciences, see Caplan and Gould, 'Language'; Pulvermüller, *The Neuroscience of Language*.

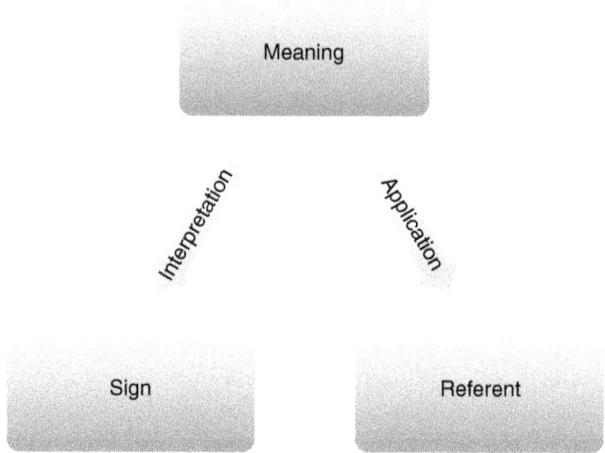

Figure 2   Semiotic triangle modified

Lawyers regularly construct it either as subjective or objective, which refers to the idea that meaning is either an internal state of certain people that can claim authority or something that has an objective existence. It is at this stage not necessary to take sides with any of the theories but just to acknowledge Gottlob Frege's basic insight that words carry a meaning that does not link them permanently to objects in the real world. Leaving the question open, we are open for each of the alternatives and state that meaning is something 'between a mental image, a concept and a psychological reality'.[49] The semiotic triangle adapted to legal interpretation is shown in Figure 2.

Looking at this triangle, we can recall some of the most basic insights from linguistics and the philosophy of language. First, the text is not directly and inherently connected to any real world object.[50] Sign and referent are linked indirectly through meaning. One central insight is that the relationship between text and meaning is arbitrary and conventional.[51] It is arbitrary in that there is no preconceived relationship

---

[49] This is the summary of Saussure's concept by Eco, *A Theory of Semiotics* 14–15. See Chandler, *Semiotics* 16.
[50] De Saussure, *Cours de linguistique générale* 38.
[51] Finegan, *Language* 7; Joseph, *Limiting the Arbitrary* 93ff; Chandler, *Semiotics* 39.

between sign and meaning, this relationship is dependent upon use and, therefore, choice.[52] Yet, once this choice is made, there is a stable and shared practice to attribute the meaning to a particular set of signs, so that it is also conventional.[53] Both notions mutually reinforce each other but are also distinct.[54] The conventionality stresses the fact that the use is constant and customary, the arbitrariness the contingency of the relationship between sign and meaning and the choice exercised by the community by employing a certain use. We can conceptualise interpretation between these two poles: To a certain extent, it is about following conventions established by others, but in another sense it is about establishing the meaning in an arbitrary manner.[55]

In the process of interpretation, the interpreter can follow conventions. But he or she might also be inclined or forced to create the meaning him or herself.[56] The standard semiotic triangle has been slightly modified to show to what activity interpretation refers to in the process: Interpretation works in-between the sign and its meaning. In the judicial context, we see that the courts first define certain parts of the text of a treaty: They rephrase words through other words. We will call the process of relating the meaning to a referent in the real world 'application'.[57] This model of the way in which courts display their reading helped to picture interpretation as attribution of meaning to a sign. To deepen our understanding of the process of interpretation, we might also look at what interpretation is not.[58]

---

[52] Finegan, *Language* 7. [53] Joseph, *Limiting the Arbitrary* 93ff; Chandler, *Semiotics* 39.
[54] On the relationship, see Keller, *A Theory of Linguistic Signs* 138; Nerlich, *Change in Language* 52.
[55] The exact relationship between these two elements will depend upon the specifics of the question. We will see in due course that the distinction between arbitrariness and convention lies at the heart of denoting interpretation of treaties as an art not a science. It will be amply discussed that this distinction, based on Aristotelian thinking was most probably introduced into international law by Vattel and is a common phrase. An art is conventional, there is a certain way, sometimes called *lege artis* to exercise it. Yet, there is also freedom and room for creativity. For further discussion, see 143.
[56] Female and male designations are used in a post-gender manner mentioning both sexes and determining their order by accident.
[57] It has been contended many times most forcefully and convincingly that those two processes cannot be separated. See for example generally Gadamer, *Truth and Method*; Habermas, *Between Facts and Norms* 199–200. The fact that they influence each other does not prohibit separating them analytically, especially when it is done for the sake of describing the mutual influence and their interrelation.
[58] This phrase is borrowed from Stone, 'Focusing the Law'.

1.3.2 What interpretation is not

1.3.2.1 Application

The modified semiotic triangle constructed application as a distinct activity relating the meaning to the real world. Interpretation, in contrast, denotes looking into the meaning of a text. Many share this view,[59] yet it is also often criticised.[60] So the assumption that interpretation is something different from application needs to be explained and justified. For a very long time, it was assumed that words necessarily relate to the real world. Under this view, there could not be a difference between interpretation and application because the text could point to nothing but the real world. In the early twentieth century, Gottlob Frege developed a very interesting line of argument showing that there was no necessary relation between texts and reality.[61] Meaning, or '*Sinn*' in Frege's terminology, was distinct from reference or '*Bedeutung*'. In this line of thought, it was argued that there are words and sentences that carry a meaning, while it is not possible to apply them. If meaning and reference are different processes, however, it is hard to contend that the processes of making or ascertaining the meaning cannot be distinguished.[62] The critiques denying the difference between applying and interpreting would have to show that it is impossible to interpret a legal text without applying it. While it can be true that in most situations both processes will be intertwined,[63] this does not mean that they cannot be distinguished in a useful way. This can be seen in academic but also in legal practice: If one were to write a commentary or an encyclopaedic entry, is it strictly necessary to apply the text in any way? A good example in which the distinction between application and interpretation even has institutional consequences is Art. 267 of the Treaty on the Functioning of the European

---

[59] Kolb, *Interprétation et création du droit international* 27; Kadelbach, 'Interpretation of the Charter' 72 para. 1.
[60] Pulkowski, *The Law and Politics of International Regime Conflict* 276.
[61] To mention just two illustrative arguments: the morning star has the same reference as the evening star, yet the meaning of the terms is different. For further critique, see Lycan, *Philosophy of Language* 7.
[62] This is made explicit by Austin when he describes how utterances are made and understood. He describes the process of communication as conventional. If a convention is invoked, it has to comply with two rules: first, that it existed and was accepted. The second rule 'is that circumstances in which we purport to invoke this procedure must be appropriate for its invocation'. Austin, 'Performative Utterances' 237.
[63] For the context of international law, see Gardiner, *Treaty Interpretation* 27. A broad reflection for the context of understanding is provided by Gadamer, *Truth and Method*.

Union. It provides that the Court of Justice of the European Union has the competence to interpret European Union law and obliges national courts to refer questions of interpretation to the Court of Justice. Yet, the national courts remain competent to apply European law to the national setting. This indicates that, despite the several interconnections between the processes of interpretation and application, it is still possible to separate them analytically as well as practically.

1.3.2.2 Evidence

It is obvious that the process of interpretation has to be distinguished from the process of taking evidence, since the latter is only about establishing the facts and reformulating them in words.[64]

1.3.2.3 Amendment and modification

To distinguish interpretation from modification is very simple and at the same time very hard.[65] If one constructed amendment and modification as processes as they are generally defined in the VCLT, they have the attribute of changing the text of a treaty.[66] This will in all probability have the result of changing the meaning of the text as a whole. Only through interpretation could the meaning be changed without changing the text.

Despite this clear analytical distinction between the two processes, it is in concrete cases conceived of as blurred,[67] and rightly so. This relates to the possible effects of the two processes.[68] The process of interpretation can also result in changes of the meaning,[69] but it is often contended that there ought to be limits. These limits are derived from the

---

[64] Visscher, *Problèmes d'interprétation judiciaire en droit international public* 31–5.
[65] A clear distinction in an analytical manner is drawn by Hafner, 'Subsequent Practice and Agreements' 114. Nolte, 'Treaties over Time: Introductory Report'. See also Kolb, *Interprétation et création du droit international* 27.
[66] It is also possible to give a more general meaning to those terms and denote just the effect. Amendment and modification would then be synonymous with change and there would not be any need to discuss them here since they could be the result of many processes such as changing the text or interpretation.
[67] Bernhardt, *Die Auslegung völkerrechtlicher Verträge insbesondere in der neueren Rechtsprechung internationaler Gerichte* 44; Bernhardt, 'Völkerrechtliche und verfassungsrechtliche Aspekte konkludenter Vertragsänderungen' 17; Gross, 'Treaty Interpretation' 108; Jennings, 'Treaties' 144; Arato, 'Subsequent Practice and Evolutive Interpretation' 465; Nolte, 'Treaties over Time: Introductory Report' 200.
[68] See Feldman, 'Evolving Treaty Obligations' 670. He distinguishes between 'effects' and 'process'.
[69] Murphy, 'The Evolution of Treaty Obligations in International Law' 88.

meaning itself[70] or from the rules of interpretation,[71] i.e. legal method. If interpreters, in particular judges, transgress this imagined line, this is called judicial legislation or judicial law-making.[72] Even within this activity, there might be a line beyond which the conduct of judges might be considered as judicial activism.[73] The problem of whether the establishment of meaning in the process of interpretation has limits is indeed a question of legal methodology, and it is certainly one of the key questions in doctrinal discourse. While the implications of modifications to and amendments of treaties in the context of the VCLT will be revisited later,[74] it suffices at this stage of the inquiry to state that amendment and modification as processes can be clearly distinguished from interpretation in that they alter the text of the treaty.

1.3.2.4 Balancing

In international law, we see more and more areas in which balancing is required: These range from determinations of necessity and proportionality in the context of the use of force and Art. 51 UN Charter[75] and proportionality in the context of international humanitarian law,[76] to the assessment of admissible countermeasures in world trade law[77] and the assessment of what could be considered as fair and equitable treatment in international investment law.[78] In human rights law, interferences are

---

[70] See Schwarzenberger, 'Myths and Realities of Treaty Interpretation' 8. He alleges that an interpretation works retrospectively whereas a revision would only operate as from the present. Strongly opposed with a structured account of the question is Venzke, 'The Role of International Courts as Interpreters and Developers of the Law' 115.

[71] Pauwelyn, *Conflict of Norms in Public International Law* 246. He states that an interpretation according to new law cannot go against the 'clear meaning' of the terms if it is not warranted by the subsequent practice of the parties.

[72] Bernhardt, 'Anmerkungen zur Rechtsfortbildung und Rechtsschöpfung durch internationale Gerichte' 13. The term law-making is used by von Bogdandy and Venzke, 'Beyond Dispute' 988. For an argument that interpretation necessarily contains law-making, see von Bogdandy and Venzke, *In Whose Name?* 12–14 and 102–5.

[73] See for example Bratza, 'Living Instrument or Dead Letter' 118.

[74] See pp. 193ff below.

[75] Gardam, *Necessity, Proportionality and the Use of Force by States* 138–86. For an interesting discourse on the matter, see Kretzmer, 'The Inherent Right to Self-Defence and Proportionality in Jus Ad Bellum' 235; Nolte, 'Multipurpose Self-Defence, Proportionality Disoriented' 283.

[76] Gardam, *Necessity, Proportionality and the Use of Force by States* 85; Nolte, 'Thick or Thin Proportionality in International Humanitarian Law' 245.

[77] Franck, 'Proportionality in International Law' 237.

[78] Schill, 'Fair and Equitable Treatment' 169.

frequently justified only when the legitimate aim is proportionate.[79] When we read words like 'necessary' and 'fair and equitable' in treaties, we accord some meaning to them. Lawyers engaging in the determination whether a certain activity is necessary or fair and equitable do more than just apply the concepts to the facts of the case: They actively engage in the process of balancing which is structured by proportionality.[80] This entails the weighing and pondering of different considerations, looking at the legal principles at stake, at the consequences, at experience, at values or interests.[81] In those situations, there is a structure to the process of balancing, which is indicated by words like 'proportionate' and 'necessary'. Yet, the outcome of balancing is not directly related to the literal meaning of those words. Assessing proportionality is not assessing the word but a certain case in real life and a question that ought to be decided. Several considerations are related to each other, weighted and pondered. It is certainly not important whether the considerations of the case would fall under the definition of words like proportionality. One could say that balancing and proportionality structure discourses in international law.[82] There have been attempts to classify different ways to assess proportionality. There have been categories such as external and internal[83] or thick and thin[84] proportionality. Proportionality is a consideration of different arguments, their weighing, and a final decision based on those arguments. Legal precepts such as the principle of proportionality then work in a way to structure this discourse. Interpretation, in contrast, is concerned with the establishment of the meaning of terms. It is this aim that distinguishes it from the process of balancing.[85]

---

[79] Harris and others, *Harris, O'Boyle and Warbrick Law of the European Convention on Human Rights* 13 with further references in n. 96.
[80] Kleinlein, 'Judicial Lawmaking by Judicial Restraint?' 1175.
[81] An excellent analysis of the process of balancing is provided for by Riehm, *Abwägungsentscheidungen in der praktischen Rechtsanwendung* 57–103. For a concise definition of balancing and proportionality, see Klatt and Meister, *The Constitutional Structure of Proportionality* 7–10.
[82] On the notion of proportionality as a discourse, see Franck, 'On Proportionality of Countermeasures in International Law' 715.
[83] Cannizzaro, 'The Role of Proportionality in the Law of International Countermeasures' 899.
[84] Nolte, 'Thick or Thin Proportionality in International Humanitarian Law' 250.
[85] For accounts of the differences between the two processes, see Schauer, 'Balancing, Subsumption, and the Constraining Role of Legal Text' 42. If we were to look at the whole issue in an even more precise manner, we would have to acknowledge that balancing is the broader category and that the process of balancing can be part of the process of interpretation: if we suppose that there are, in a given situation, more than one

1.4. Evolutive interpretation

1.4.1 What evolutive interpretation is

The term 'evolutive', which seems to have been first used in 1823,[86] is explained as meaning '[r]elating or tending to evolution or development; (also) promoting evolution.'[87] While the notion of evolution itself dates back to the seventeenth century,[88] the term 'evolutive' was coined at a time when scientists were trying to explain the development of species. The old Aristotelian notion of immutable and stringent categories was succinctly altered by different models that resulted in Charles Darwin's famous theory, which centred around variation and change.[89] Change was the central mechanism by which the struggle for existence as well as adaptation to the environment could be accomplished. The notion of change is also central to the use of the term evolutive in our context: interpreting evolutively means to read a text differently. The meaning of a text is reversed from one state to the next.[90] Instead of trying to transfer Darwin's theory, which happened to apply to a completely different context, it is better to stress that changes in the meaning of texts are a part of a more general phenomenon: A whole sub-discipline of linguistics looks at the different ways in which language can change and the different reasons for language change.[91] Amongst the many things that can change, such as the grammar, the sounds or syntax, is the so-called semantic change. If the relationship between text and meaning is

---

meaning to a term, the interpreter has to choose a meaning. In this process, he can balance different arguments to ground his decision. Riehm, *Abwägungsentscheidungen in der praktischen Rechtsanwendung* 16. On the difference between interpretation and balancing, see Röhl, 'Grundlagen der Methodenlehre II' paras. 34–51.

[86] See entry on 'evolutive' in Oxford University Press, *Oxford English Dictionary: the Definitive Record of the English Language*.

[87] Ibid.   [88] See entry on 'evolution' in *ibid*.

[89] For brief historical overviews, see Ruse, *Darwinism and Its Discontents* 6–17; Shanahan, *The Evolution of Darwinism* 11–36. For a brief application of Darwin's theories to the present context, see Dupuy, 'Evolutionary Interpretation of Treaties' 123.

[90] If we take the literal description of words as metaphor, we could say that one reformulation is replaced by another.

[91] Chambers, Trudgill and Schilling-Estes (eds.), *The Handbook of Language Variation and Change*; Campbell, *Historical Linguistics*; Hock and Joseph (eds.), *Trends in Linguistics*; Luraghi and Bebenik (eds.), *The Continuum Companion to Historical Linguistics*. I am grateful to Michael Fischer and Alejandro Rodiles for drawing my attention to the discipline of historic linguistics.

arbitrary and conventional, the meaning attached to a set of signs can change.[92] The notion of 'evolutive' also indicates that the change occurs after a lapse of time,[93] although this might be marginal.[94] This general phenomenon in the context of treaty interpretation is what we call evolutive interpretation: The words in the treaty stay the same, their meaning is altered.[95] It is not required that the interpreter makes the evolution explicit, for an implicit change can just as well amount to an evolutive interpretation.[96] It is then for the observer to compare the state of the law before and after the decision to discover the evolution. As for cases of overruling precedents, it does not seem necessary to require that the interpreter intended the evolution of the law.[97] An unintended change in the law may not be persuasive as the interpreter will be likely not to give reasons for the change. This cannot, however, affect the fact that the meaning of the law as it previously stood was altered through interpretation.[98]

In historical linguistics, several explanations for this kind of semantic changes are offered: Sometimes, it is tried to classify words and relate a certain type of changes to them,[99] changes could also be explained by other factors.[100] The purpose of the present study is far more modest: It is to inquire how international legal method as it is codified in the VCLT deals with questions of whether to change the interpretation of treaties and what this means in practice. But before doing that, it is necessary

---

[92] Luján, 'Semantic Change' 287. He also stresses that one can take the opposite perspective and look at how the meaning changes its signifiers.
[93] Bleckmann, *Grundprobleme und Methoden des Völkerrechts* 102; Brems, *Human Rights* 396.
[94] As evidenced by Crawford and Viles, 'International Law on a Given Day'.
[95] For the context of international law, see Elias, 'The Doctrine of Intertemporal Law' 292; Arato, 'Subsequent Practice and Evolutive Interpretation' 456; Ganshof van der Meersch, 'Quelques apercus de la methode d'interpretation de la Convention de Rome du 4 Novembre 1950 par la Cour Europeenne des droit de l'homme' 220; Gardiner, 'The Vienna Convention Rules on Treaty Interpretation'. Crema puts it as follows: 'An interpretation is dynamic when a term or an expression takes on a different meaning than the one originally agreed upon by the parties': Crema, 'Subsequent Agreements and Subsequent Practice within and outside the Vienna Convention' 22.
[96] See for changes in jurisprudence Kähler, *Strukturen und Methoden der Rechtsprechungsänderung* 20.
[97] See for example Probst, *Die Änderung der Rechtsprechung* 143–5.
[98] As we will later see, it is hard to prove this, which is why those changes have largely been omitted from the empirical analysis.
[99] Burling, *Patterns of Language* 79–80.
[100] An overview is provided by Luraghi, 'Causes of Language Change'.

to clarify that many expressions are used synonymously in academic discourse. The fact that there is a change of meaning prompts some authors to speak about 'reinterpretation'.[101] The terms 'evolutionary'[102] and 'evolutive'[103] seem to be used synonymously.[104] The same applies to 'evolutional' interpretation.[105] 'Progressive' interpretation is used in the same sense.[106] Another term, which is often used, is that of 'dynamic' interpretation.[107] This term also entails movement and change and would, therefore, be apt to describe the phenomenon. However, some authors associate a certain progressive mindset with this term.[108] As there is nothing to be gained from giving a second name to the subject of research, the term evolutive interpretation will generally be used.[109]

It will help to understand the different forms evolutive interpretation can take in international law if we distinguish *referential* and

---

[101] See Waldock, 'The Evolution of Human Rights Concepts and the Application of the European Convention on Human Rights' 545; Orakhelashvili, *The Interpretation of Acts and Rules in Public International Law* 289.

[102] For the use of this term, see Helfer, 'Consensus, Coherence and the European Convention on Human Rights' 135; Trindade, 'The Merits of Coordination of International Courts on Human Rights' 309; Boyle, 'Further Development of the Law of the Sea Convention: Mechanisms for Change' 567; Verhoosel, 'The Use of Investor–State Arbitration under Bilateral Investment Treaties to Seek Relief for Breaches of WTO Law' 504; Milanovic, 'The ICJ and Evolutionary Treaty Interpretation'; Dupuy, 'Evolutionary Interpretation of Treaties'; Bjorge, *The Evolutionary Interpretation of Treaties*.

[103] For authors using the term evolutive, see Pree, *Die evolutive Interpretation der Rechtsnorm im Kanonischen Recht*; Martin, 'L'Interprétation dite évolutive de termes insérés dans des traités internationaux'; Frowein, 'Die evolutive Auslegung der EMRK'; Bernhardt, 'Evolutive Treaty Interpretation' 11; Prebensen, 'Evolutive Interpretation of the European Convention on Human Rights'; Malgosia Fitzmaurice, 'Dynamic (Evolutive) Interpretation of Treaties, Part I' 101; Rigaux, 'Interprétation consensuelle et interprétation évolutive'; Arato, 'Subsequent Practice and Evolutive Interpretation'; Dzehtsiarou, 'European Consensus and the Evolutive Interpretation of the European Convention on Human Rights'; Crawford, *Brownlie's Principles of Public International Law* 379; Nolte, 'Between Contemporaneous and Evolutive Interpretation'.

[104] See for example the index to Gardiner, *Treaty Interpretation* 400.

[105] See Dzehtsiarou, 'European Consensus and the Evolutive Interpretation of the European Convention on Human Rights' 1732.

[106] Crawford, *Brownlie's Principles of Public International Law* 379.

[107] See for example Milej, 'Rechtsquellen' 80; Gross, 'Treaty Interpretation' 174; Stein and von Buttlar, *Völkerrecht* 25; Heintschel von Heinegg, 'Die völkerrechtlichen Verträge als Hauptquelle des Völkerrechts' 415.

[108] Matscher, 'Methods of Interpretation of the Convention' 70; Matscher, 'Wie sich die 1950 in der EMRK festgeschriebenen Menschenrechte weiterentwickelt haben' 441; Bernhardt, 'Evolutive Treaty Interpretation' 12.

[109] When alternative terms are being used, they are meant to mean the same.

contential[110] evolution. Contential evolution is easier to picture: A word means something at one point in time, later the meaning is changed. Referential evolution is not exactly an evolution in that sense. It describes the influence of changing referents on the meaning. The question of interpretation is then whether the meaning is tied to one certain point in time or whether it follows the course of things. Imagine for example the following sentence in a treaty: 'Those preferential rights apply subject to rights granted in other treaties.' Focusing on the word 'treaties', a contential evolution arises when this word is interpreted differently. Suppose that we would depart from the standard definition in Art. 2(a) VCLT and would take into account not only treaties between states but also between multinational companies or add unilateral declarations to that definition. This would be a change in the very concept of a treaty in international law (contential evolution). If the concept of a treaty were to stay the same, we could still ask to what point in time this clause refers: Is it only treaties which had been agreed at the time of the conclusion of the clause or can subsequently agreed treaties also be included? If we interpret the treaty in the latter sense, we speak of a referential evolution: More treaties – with varying content – exist in 2013 than in 1913. The abstract meaning of the word 'treaty' stays the same, it is still about treaties between states. But in its relation to the process of application, the meaning is changed. Rudolf Carnap's way of analysing semantic meaning might help to understand the distinction made between contential and referential evolution:[111] He distinguished the intension and the extension of semantic meaning. He states generally that '[w]e take as the extension of a predicator the class of those individuals to which it applies, and, as its intention, the property which it expresses'.[112] So the meaning can be analysed in two ways: first, regarding its intension describing properties, qualities or characteristics in an abstract manner.[113] Regarding its extension, the question is to which objects in the real world it refers, be it classes of things like humans or individual things.[114] This rather tricky distinction will be of great avail in analysing the jurisprudence of the ICJ.

---

[110] This is intended to mean 'regarding content or regarding the content'. For a similar distinction, see Böckenförde, 'Anmerkungen zum Begriff Verfassungswandel' 9.
[111] This concept is generally referred to in linguistics: see Danesi, *The Quest for Meaning* 17. For a similar distinction, see Keller, *A Theory of Linguistic Signs* 73.
[112] Carnap, *Meaning and Necessity* 1.   [113] Ibid. 19.   [114] Ibid. 17, 33.

1.4.2 What evolutive interpretation is not

The quest for a concise definition can better be successfully achieved if we continue to sharpen our analytical knife. Having established that evolutive interpretation means interpretative change, it is of the utmost importance to clarify and assume the place of evolutive interpretation in legal method. We will assume for the purposes of this study that evolutive interpretation is a result of interpretation. Evolutive interpretation is not a *means* of interpretation.[115] If we look at a text, we can use certain means to arrive at an interpretative result. An established system of means we shall call interpretative method.

Figure 3 exemplifies the distinction between means and results of interpretation. Looking at a text, the interpreter uses the means of interpretation to arrive at the meaning of the text. Means of interpretation include presumptions, maxims or interpretative principles. Using means, the interpreter establishes a certain meaning. This study will first assume that evolutive interpretation is a class of results of interpretation and not a means.[116] The means establish the result, but there is, *a priori*, no necessary connection between certain means and certain results. So, as a general first definition, evolutive interpretation is not tied to means like the principle of effectiveness or the object and purpose of the treaty. To interpret a treaty evolutively consequently describes the class of interpretative results in which the meaning of the text is changed through interpretation. The easiest case to be distinguished from evolutive interpretation is *static* interpretation. This is the antonym of evolutive interpretation and designates the class of interpretative results that do not alter the meaning even though such a change was in issue. This could also be called 'stable' interpretation. If the interpretation has not changed from the time the treaty entered into force, it is also to be called 'original' or 'contemporaneous' interpretation.[117]

---

[115] Ibid.
[116] See Greschek, *Die evolutive Auslegung völkerrechtlicher Verträge am Beispiel des GATT* 33. It is of course possible to argue that evolutive interpretation is a means of interpretation. Yet, this requires showing what the means of interpretation actually are.
[117] A certain tendency becomes evident by the fact that many international lawyers use the word 'contemporaneous' synonymously with 'contemporaneous with the conclusion of the treaty'. This tendency does not attach to individual scholars but reveals a general attitude. I will, therefore, try always to outline the object of contemporaneity.

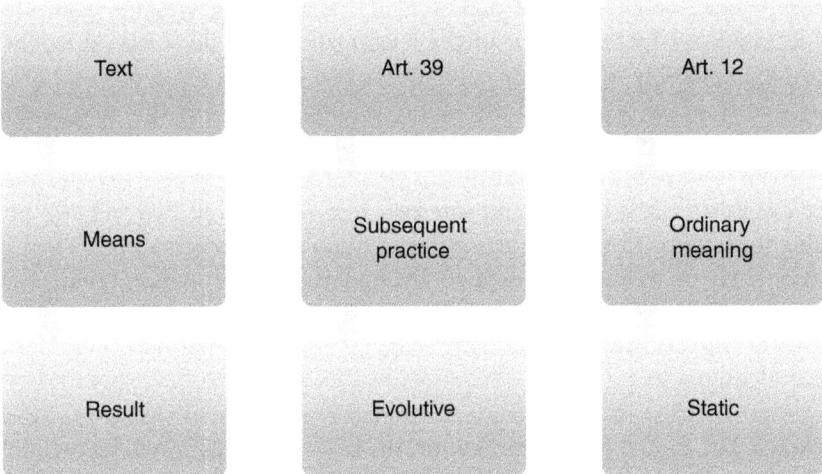

Figure 3 Distinction between means and results of interpretation

Evolutive interpretation is not *specification*. To specify is to clarify and define the meaning for the first time, since previously it was unclear. To interpret evolutively means to change. These categories are mutually exclusive. If we were to think about interpretation as adding words to explain a set of words,[118] we would add new words if we specified the meaning. To change the interpretation would mean to replace some of the words previously used in the explanation of other words. This formal and analytical distinction helps to capture the essence of evolutive interpretation. Both classes of results might be categorised under a bigger heading and be described as 'law-making activity'[119] or as '*Rechtsfortbildung*'. Yet, the analytical distinction is not only possible but also useful and necessary. Almost any interpretative problem entails a question of specification, the number of problems of stasis and evolution is much smaller. What is more, the interpretative questions in the respective situations are of a totally different quality. If an interpreter is competent to interpret and apply a legal norm, she or he will have to specify it, for the meaning would otherwise be left unclear and no decision can be made. But the competence to interpret does not necessarily imply the

---

[118] Wittgenstein, *Philosophical Investigations* 345 para. 201.
[119] Accounts in general jurisprudence are provided for by Schneider, *Richterrecht, Gesetzesrecht und Verfassungsrecht* 26; Dworkin, *Law's Empire* 6; Vogenauer, *Die Auslegung von Gesetzen in England und auf dem Kontinent* (vol. 1) 142.

competence to change the meaning. If the meaning was for example previously set by the author of the legal text or a higher court, it might prove impossible for a lower court to change it. Since the *problématique* in questions of stasis and evolution is quite different, this analytical distinction is not a *fin en soi* but as fundamental as important.

Even if we approach the problems of interpretation from a perspective of pragmatics and understand interpretations as actions, we will still be able to describe how some actions are similar while others differ. Therefore, even in treatments inspired by that theoretical stream, evolutive interpretation is discussed as a separate phenomenon.[120] To specify means that a norm develops its previously undetermined meaning without changing it.

Another class of interpretative results are *necessary implications*. This entails that, due to other stipulations, the law necessarily implies a certain meaning that is not obvious from the text. The most frequently used form of necessary implications is the concept of *implied powers*.[121] This concept is a form of necessary implication in the context of the competences of a state or an international organisation. To fulfil the functions, the subjects assume competences that are not expressly mentioned. Necessary implications and implied powers are interpretative results; they basically describe that a meaning has been given to a text that is not obvious from its words. It is possible to interpret a treaty in a manner such that the unexpressed meaning was originally implied or that it ought to be implied only later in the face of new circumstances.[122] Those concepts are distinct from the concept of evolutive interpretation in that they are not necessarily related to changes of the meaning, they can also

---

[120] Venzke, *How Interpretation Makes International Law* 230.

[121] For further elaboration on this concept, see Makarczyk, 'The International Court of Justice on Implied Powers of International Organizations'; Blokker, 'International Organizations or Institutions, Implied Powers' para. 10; Gillich, *Konsens und Evolutive Vertragsauslegung* 87–9. On inherent powers of courts, see Brown, *A Common Law of International Adjudication* 54–7. For early uses of the concept, see Heffter, *Das europäische Völkerrecht der Gegenwart* 175; Fiore, *Le Droit international codifié et sa sanction juridique* 406; Taylor, *Treatise on International Public Law* 397 para. 386; Hall, *A Treatise on International Law* 395.

[122] On this distinction, see Skubiszewski, 'Implied Powers of International Organizations' 856. The possibility of change by interpretation is envisaged by Blokker, 'International Organizations or Institutions, Implied Powers' 20. The doctrine of implied powers stems from the constitutional law of the United States see *M'Culloch v. State*, 17 US 316 (1819); 17 US 316 (Wheat.), stating that it was impossible for the framers to specify all powers for the future.

arise when it is only specified. Other than in the case of specifications, necessary implications could also coincide with evolutive interpretations.

Analogies are similar to results of necessary implications. The term analogy describes the application of a rule to circumstances which are not determined by that rule but come within its *ratio legis* and from a common law perspective[123] when the facts of a case fall within the *ratio decidendi* of a precedent but were technically not within the scope of the precedent.[124] Irrespective of the possibility of analogies in international law,[125] analogies are clearly distinct from evolutive interpretation: They can lead either to a specification or to an actual change in the interpretation.[126]

The principle of *equity* can become operational in international law in different forms:[127] In the sense of the narrow definition as *ex aequo et bono*, which is used in Art. 38(2) ICJ Statute,[128] equity allows the court to decide independently of the law and based only upon notions of justice and right reason.[129] Concerning the wider principle of equity, it is common to distinguish between equity *infra legem* and equity *praeter legem*.[130] Whereas equity *infra legem* deals with the interpretation of international legal acts, equity *praeter legem* is utilised when it comes to areas of international law that are within the scope of the law but lack specific regulation.[131] Equity *infra legem* informs the interpreter of international rules how to exercise his or her discretion with notions of justice and fairness.[132] Equity *infra legem* can prompt a change in the interpretation, but it does not necessarily lead to such a change. The same holds true for equity *praeter legem*, which might result in a change as well as a

---

[123] Lamond, 'Precedent and Analogy in Legal Reasoning'.
[124] For a detailed discussion of analogies in international law, see Bleckmann, 'Analogie im Völkerrecht' 161; Bleckmann, 'Die Rechtsanalogie im Völkerrecht' 353; Vöneky, 'Analogy in International Law'.
[125] Analogies were used very early in international law by Heffter, *Das europäische Völkerrecht der Gegenwart* 175.
[126] Von Arnauld, 'Möglichkeiten und Grenzen dynamischer Interpretation von Rechtsnormen' 465.
[127] See generally Kolb, *Interprétation et création du droit international* 861.
[128] Statute of the International Court of Justice (24 October 1945), Annex to the UN Charter.
[129] Lowe, 'The Role of Equity in International Law' 54.
[130] *Ibid.* 56; Francioni, 'Equity in International Law' para. 7.
[131] Pellet, 'Art. 38' 793 para. 162 with further references.
[132] Lapidoth, 'Equity in International Law' 164. For a critique of the notion of equity *infra legem*, see Lowe, 'The Role of Equity in International Law' 57.

first application of the rules of equity to an area that was not explicitly regulated by law previously.

The first use of a term, a definition or another legal figure could be called *innovation*.[133] As with the previous notions, innovation does not directly correspond to evolutive interpretation. If there was no legal position before the innovation was made, one must not speak of change. On the contrary, change through innovation is possible. While innovation and evolutive interpretation seem to be independent of each other, it can also be suggested that evolutive interpretation could often be regarded as legal innovation as new solutions have to be found.[134] The same can be stated with regard to *judicial creativity*. This term refers to the attitude of judges of assuming a law-making function and actively developing the law.[135] Creativity can result in overruling a precedent or changing the meaning in a way that was unforeseen by the lawmaker.[136] Like the term innovation, a creative interpretation might result in an evolutive interpretation, but it does not necessarily do so.[137]

This leads to the concept of *Rechtsfortbildung*, which could be translated as 'development of the law'. This notion found its way from German scholarship to the realm of public international law.[138] *Rechtsfortbildung* could be defined as process, which makes it possible to achieve interpretative results that cannot be achieved in the process of interpretation.

---

[133] Koch and Trapp, 'Richterliche Innovation – Begriff und Begründbarkeit' 84; Kähler, *Strukturen und Methoden der Rechtsprechungsänderung* 23. However, Schlink defines innovation as unexpected judicial pronouncement. His definition comes, therefore, much closer to evolutive interpretation. Schlink, 'Probleme und Ansätze einer Entscheidungstheorie der richterlichen Innovation' 19.

[134] Thomas, *The Judicial Process* 353; Kähler, *Strukturen und Methoden der Rechtsprechungsänderung* 23. It is less convincing to construct evolution and innovation as mutually exclusive as is done by Klappstein, *Die Rechtsprechungsänderung mit Wirkung für die Zukunft* 41.

[135] Peck, 'Comments on Judicial Creativity' 1.

[136] Tate, 'New Judicial Solution' 914; Sackville, 'Continuity and Judicial Creativity – Some Observations' 149; Shahabuddeen, 'Judicial Creativity and Joint Criminal Enterprise' 185.

[137] This is well illustrated by Mowbray, who regards the living-instrument approach of the ECtHR as part of its creative approach but does also include the practical and effective interpretation of the Court which would not signify any change in the law: Mowbray, 'The Creativity of the European Court of Human Rights' 57.

[138] Scheuner, 'Die Fortbildung der Grundrechte in internationalen Konventionen durch die Rechtsprechung: zur Rechtsprechung des Europäischen Gerichtshofs für Menschenrechte'; Bernhardt, 'Rechtsfortbildung durch den Europäischen Gerichtshof für Menschenrechte'; Kolb, *Interprétation et création du droit international* 775. This notion is discussed by von Bogdandy and Venzke, 'Beyond Dispute' 988.

It allows the extension or restriction of the meaning of clauses or words and the use of analogies. Like the last four concepts we have looked at, this may or may not entail an evolutive interpretation.

The concept of *approximate application* has similarities to but also differences from evolutive interpretation.[139] It was defined by Judge Lauterpacht in a separate opinion in the following terms:

> It is a sound principle of law that, whenever a legal instrument of continuing validity cannot be applied literally owing to the conduct of one of the parties, it must, without allowing that party to take advantage of its own conduct, be applied in a way approximating most closely to its primary object.[140]

So this concept actually concerns the situation in which the interpretation of a treaty is clear, but, due to the conduct of one party, the application of the meaning to the circumstances is impossible. Now, the treaty is applied differently. This difference makes the concept similar to evolutive interpretation. Conversely, this application is not based on the terms of the treaty but on a vague notion of its purpose and the result to be achieved. It is not an interpretation in the established sense of the term but something like a 'second best' and 'hypothetical' interpretation. It is in the very nature of the concept of approximate application that the result of that application cannot be achieved by the process of interpretation. This is why this concept is also distinct from evolutive interpretation.

To sum up, an evolutive interpretation arises when the meaning attaching to a part of the text of the treaty changes. Now that there is a clear definition on the interpretative result we are looking at, we can examine whether and how international legal method allows reaching those results. For this reason, we ought to look in Arts. 31 and 32 VCLT. On their face, those articles give no guidance how to determine those issues. Therefore, we turn to legal doctrine to see how those questions are dealt with.

---

[139] For a discussion of this concept, see Dupuy, 'On the "Doctrine" of Approximate Application of Treaties in International Law'.

[140] Admissibility of Hearings of Petitioners by the Committee on South West Africa (Advisory Opinion) Separate Opinion of Judge Lauterpacht [1956] ICJ Rep 46.

2

Suggested solutions

2.1. Suggested solutions after the coming into force of the VCLT

As there is no obvious guidance in Arts. 31 and 32 VCLT on how to deal with questions of interpretative change, legal scholarship continues to answer them in one way or another. To give a structured account of the approaches, it will be helpful to categorise the solutions into those staying within the confines of the Vienna Convention, those based on but going beyond the Vienna Convention and those outside the Vienna Convention.

First, it is argued that the problems could be solved *with the rule of interpretation contained in the Vienna Convention*.[141] Georg Nolte, the ILC Special Rapporteur on subsequent agreement and subsequent practice in relation to treaty interpretation, has stated that evolutive interpretation 'is not a separate method of interpretation but rather the result of a proper application of the usual means of interpretation'.[142] It has been stressed that there should be no exception for evolutive interpretation but that the normal factors of interpretation should apply.[143] Those would generally allow taking into account later developments, and, therefore, necessarily change the law.[144] The Institut de Droit

---

[141] Grover, 'A Call to Arms' 581; McLachlan, 'The Principle of Systemic Integration and Article 31(3)(c) of the Vienna Convention' 317; Orakhelashvili, *The Interpretation of Acts and Rules in Public International Law* 290.

[142] Nolte, 'Between Contemporaneous and Evolutive Interpretation' 1683. See also the first report of Georg Nolte as special rapporteur on subsequent practice and subsequent agreement in relation to treaty interpretation, reprinted in ILC, 'Report of the International Law Commission on the work of its sixty-fifth session (6 May–7 June and 8 July–9 August 2013)', UN Doc. A/CN.4/L.813187, para. 62.

[143] Gardiner, *Treaty Interpretation* 254; Orakhelashvili, *The Interpretation of Acts and Rules in Public International Law* 290; Matscher, 'Methods of Interpretation of the Convention' 65; Crema, 'Subsequent Agreements and Subsequent Practice within and outside the Vienna Convention' 22.

[144] Jacobs, 'Varieties of Approach to Treaty Interpretation' 331.

International discussed this and similar issues. Max Sørensen acting as Rapporteur provided for an in-depth analysis of this and related questions and came to the conclusion that the process of interpretation was in fact open to changes.[145] Sørensen, as well as the subsequent resolution, favoured the possibility of evolutive interpretations which should be determined by the ordinary means of interpretation.[146] Several techniques mentioned in the Vienna Convention have been specifically related to evolutive interpretation. Regarding the ordinary meaning,[147] the concept of *generic terms* has attracted attention. Some contend that those questions could be decided by looking at the nature of the terms in question. Some terms could be qualified as generic, which would mean that they are susceptible to evolutive interpretation.[148] The linguistic nature of those terms could be deduced from their use in the practice of courts.[149] If no generic term was used, the treaty would have to be interpreted as it stood at the time of its conclusion. If a generic term was used, it would be susceptible to evolution. Evolutive interpretation is sometimes linked to the object and purpose.[150] Subsequent practice has been adduced as a reason why the VCLT was to be considered as open for changing interpretation, also due to the fact that the preparatory works were 'only' considered as supplementary

---

[145] Sørensen, 'Exposé préliminaire' 64 para. 38; Sørensen, 'Le Problème dit du droit intertemporel dans l'ordre international' 16.

[146] Sørensen, 'Exposé préliminaire' 64 para. 38.

[147] In favour of 'housing' evolutive interpretation in the ordinary meaning, see Peanson, *Manual of the Terminology of Public International Law* 294; Simma, 'Miscellaneous Thoughts on Subsequent Agreements and Practice' 48. The ILC has, in its draft conclusions, framed the whole problem of evolutive interpretation in terms of whether a term was 'given a meaning which is capable of evolving over time'. 'Text of draft conclusions 1–5 provisionally adopted by the Drafting Committee', ILC (n. 142) Draft Conclusion 3.

[148] Higgins, 'Time and the law – international perspectives on an old problem' 518; Gardiner, *Treaty Interpretation* 173. Examples such as 'public policy', 'the protection of morals', 'domestic jurisdiction', 'territorial sea' or 'the continental shelf' are given by Sinclair, *The Vienna Convention on the Law of Treaties* 139. 'Territorial sea', 'the high seas' and 'continental shelf' are mentioned by Yasseen, 'L'Interprétation des traités d'après la Convention de Vienne sur le droit des traités' 67.

[149] Linderfalk, 'Doing the Right Thing for the Right Reason' 136.

[150] Thienel, 'The Living Instrument Approach in the ECHR and Elsewhere' 178; he then goes on to distinguish treaties as to their objects. Von Arnauld, *Völkerrecht* 93; Desierto and Gillespie, 'Evolutive Interpretation and Subsequent Practice' 557; Peters, *Völkerrecht Allgemeiner Teil* 111; Rietiker, 'The Principle of "Effectiveness" in the Recent Jurisprudence of the European Court of Human Rights' 260; Mahoney, 'Judicial Activism and Judicial Self-Restraint in the European Court of Human Rights' 57; Bratza, 'Living Instrument or Dead Letter' 120.

means.[151] The priority of this technique over the *travaux* is taken as evidence that the VCLT is open to evolution.[152] On the other hand, it was considered to be an alternative to evolutive interpretation.[153] Evolutive interpretation is also used to describe an interpretation that is based on techniques other than subsequent practice.[154] It has been emphasised that some means like Art. 31(3)(c) VCLT have a special dynamic function.[155]

Several approaches seek to complement the rules of the VCLT and, therefore, to *go beyond* them. These approaches have in common that they all depart from the Vienna Convention without limiting themselves to the interpretation of the Convention but instead adding new elements to it. The ILC Working Group on Fragmentation has taken as its point of departure the principle of contemporaneity and provided for certain exceptions which it grounded either in the evolutionary use of the terms of the treaty or in a very general drafting of obligations,[156] 'thus operating a kind of *renvoi* to the state of the law at the time of its application'.[157] It would also be possible to rely on a *presumption* in favour of a contemporaneous interpretation.[158] Oliver Dörr has started by setting out two approaches as a solution. While the static approach would interpret the treaty at the time of its conclusion, the dynamic approach 'seeks to establish the meaning of a treaty at the time of its interpretation'.[159] Inquiring into the jurisprudence on the matter, he bases his solution on the static approach and provides for a 'two-tier process'.[160] First, one would have to examine whether the term was intended to be

---

[151] Kadelbach, 'Interpretation of the Charter' 77 para. 5.
[152] Letsas, 'Intentionalism and the Interpretation of the ECHR' 257.
[153] Desierto and Gillespie, 'Evolutive Interpretation and Subsequent Practice' 557.
[154] Gardiner, *Treaty Interpretation* 242; Böth, *Evolutive Auslegung völkerrechtlicher Verträge* 28–41. Evolutive interpretation is said to be grounded in the object and purpose and the relevant rules of international law by Arato, 'Subsequent Practice and Evolutive Interpretation' 446.
[155] Peanson, *Manual of the Terminology of Public International Law* 294; Villiger, *Commentary on the 1969 Vienna Convention on the Law of Treaties* 432. An attempt to limit evolutive interpretation to these cases is undertaken by Böth, *Evolutive Auslegung völkerrechtlicher Verträge*.
[156] ILC, Report of the Study Group of the International Law Commission Finalized by Martti Koskenniemi, 'Fragmentation of International Law: Difficulties Arising from the Diversification and Expansion of International Law' in 'Reports of the International Law Commission on the work of its 42nd session' (1 May–9 June and 3 July–11 August 2006) UN Doc. A/CN.4/L.682', 242 ('ILC, Fragmentation Report').
[157] Ibid. 243.
[158] Dawidowicz, 'The Effect of the Passage of Time on the Interpretation of Treaties' 207.
[159] Dörr, 'Art. 31' 533 para. 23.   [160] Ibid. 535 para. 26.

interpreted evolutively or whether the term is 'from the outset' evolutionary.[161] The second step would then be to look at whether there actually was an evolution. Christian Tomuschat has argued that 'the original act of acceptance, which provided the treaty concerned with democratic legitimacy, fades away into the past and is progressively reduced to a pure formality which has no actual influence on the actual running of the treaty system'.[162]

Looking at approaches *outside* the Vienna Convention, the so-called *intertemporal law* has played an important part. It has been famously defined '[a]s regards the question which of different legal systems prevailing at successive periods is to be applied in a particular case' by Judge Max Huber in the *Island of Palmas Case*.[163] This case concerned the question of title to territory.[164] Intertemporal law was seen as a principle or a doctrine,[165] as an ensemble of principles and rules[166] and as a theory.[167] The Netherlands and the United States argued over sovereignty of an island, which was discovered by Spain in the late Middle Ages. While Spain ceded all its possessions in the area to the United States in 1899, the Netherlands exercised sovereignty over the island from 1677. Both parties could claim to have acquired a right. The question was now which time was determinative. In this instance, Max Huber, acting as arbitrator, introduced his famous formula:

> As regards the question which of different legal systems prevailing at successive periods is to be applied in a particular case (the so-called intertemporal law), a distinction must be made between the creation of rights and the existence of rights. The same principle which subjects the act creative of a right to the law in force at the time the right arises, demands that the existence of the right, in other words its continued manifestation, shall follow the conditions required by the evolution of law.[168]

There have been several attempts to apply this doctrine to the present problem. Authors have tried to transfer the whole rule directly to questions of changing interpretations.[169] Anthony D'Amato has regarded only the first part of the doctrine providing for the interpretation of

---

[161] *Ibid.* [162] Tomuschat, 'Pacta sunt servanda' 1055.
[163] *Island of Palmas Case* (Netherlands v. USA) (1928) RIAA 829.
[164] A very good explanation of the relevant issues is given by Khan, 'Max Huber as Arbitrator' 158. For a critical discussion, see Jessup, 'The Palmas Island Arbitration' 735.
[165] Grant and Barker, *Parry and Grant Encyclopaedic Dictionary of International Law*.
[166] Salmon, *Dictionnaire de droit international public*.
[167] Friedmann, *The Changing Structure of International Law* 131.
[168] *Island of Palmas Case* (1928) RIAA 845.
[169] Elias, 'The Doctrine of Intertemporal Law' 296; Kotzur, 'Intertemporal Law'; Heintschel von Heinegg, 'Weitere Quellen des Völkerrechts' 505.

treaties as they stood at the time of their conclusion as determinative.[170] He has framed this in the words of the maxim *contemporanea expositio*. Malgosia Fitzmaurice has linked the intertemporal doctrine to 'not only the time element, but social, ethical and political conditions as well'.[171] She, therefore, includes *extraneous factors* into the determination of stability and change in international law.

A similar suggestion is to frame the problem in terms of competing *principles*.[172] Consequently, there would be on the one hand the principle of contemporaneous interpretation and on the other hand the principle of evolutive interpretation, the respective principle applying in the case at hand would determine how the treaty ought to be interpreted. It has also been argued that evolutive interpretation was a form of *'purpose oriented'* interpretation or belonged to the *principle of effectiveness*.[173] James Crawford has seen it as part of a *teleological approach* that would, in cases of doubt, give preference to the object and purpose of a treaty.[174] Evolutive interpretation is also seen as distinct method.[175]

The dependence of evolutive interpretation on structural features of treaties or single provisions has also been highlighted. Inferences are drawn from either the nature, the classification or the area of the treaty or the respective provision. The *structure* comprises all institutional features of the treaty. The way in which treaties are interpreted evolutively could depend on the question whether and how a judicial mechanism was established by the treaty. Whereas the provision of an *ad hoc* consent would favour an inquiry into the intention of the parties, in the case of automatic jurisdiction the court could develop the law dynamically.[176] Similarly, the establishment of a permanent judicial process has

---

[170] D'Amato, 'International Law, Intertemporal Problems' 1324.
[171] Malgosia Fitzmaurice, 'Dynamic (Evolutive) Interpretation of Treaties, Part I' 113.
[172] Pauwelyn, 'The Nature of WTO Obligations'. He later emphasised the search for the intentions of the parties: Pauwelyn, 'The Role of Public International Law in the WTO' 574. *Gerald Fitzmaurice* regarded solely contemporaneity with setting up the treaty as a principle: Gerald Fitzmaurice, 'The Law and Procedure of the International Court of Justice 1951–4' 225.
[173] Grabenwarter and Pabel, *Europäische Menschenrechtskonvention* 36; Peters and Altwicker, *Europäische Menschenrechtskonvention* 25.
[174] Crawford, *Brownlie's Principles of Public International Law* 379.
[175] Van Damme, *Treaty interpretation by the WTO Appellate Body* 284.
[176] Dupuy, 'Evolutionary Interpretation of Treaties' 125. For an explanation of the relationship between the dynamism in treaty interpretation and the jurisdiction of a judicial institution, see Ruffert and Walter, *Institutionalised International Law* 64.

been seen as favouring evolutive interpretation.[177] Inferences were also drawn from structural elements of the treaty. So it has been suggested that evolutive interpretation could be linked to *multilateral* treaties,[178] especially those *creating international organisations*.[179] Another suggestion is to allow evolutive interpretation for treaties of long or unlimited duration.[180] It is also possible to structure the problem inductively in the sense that the question whether to interpret evolutively as well as the intertemporal question are dealt with depending on the *nature of the treaty or provision* one is dealing with.[181] Rosalyn Higgins employs this approach with regard to human rights, which, according to her, might fall into a 'special category' with regard to intertemporal law.[182] Other categories have been added to the list of exceptions such as international economic law or the law of the sea to make them also susceptible to evolutive interpretation.[183] Malgosia Fitzmaurice has refined the system of categories depending on the object and purpose.[184] Human rights had to meet moral standards and were, therefore, to be interpreted evolutively.[185] For multilateral environmental agreements, however, this was permissible only to the extent that gaps are filled by analogy and the efficiency of the instrument is secured.[186] She relates that to the nature of

---

[177] Herdegen, *Völkerrecht* 134.
[178] *Ibid.* 124; Bernhardt, 'Evolutive Treaty Interpretation' 21.
[179] *Ibid.* 21; Greig, 'The Time of Conclusion and the Time of Application of Treaties as Points of Reference in the Interpretative Process' 215; Herdegen, *Völkerrecht* 134; Dupuy, 'Evolutionary Interpretation of Treaties' 131.
[180] For that assumption, see for example McLachlan, 'The Evolution of Treaty Obligations in International Law' 74.
[181] Yasseen, 'L'Interprétation des traités d'après la Convention de Vienne sur le droit des traités' 66.
[182] Higgins, 'Some Observations on the Inter-Temporal Rule in International Law' 174; Higgins, 'Time and the law – international perspectives on an old problem' 518. For the suitability of human rights treaties to evolutive interpretation, see also Bernhardt, 'Evolutive Treaty Interpretation' 21; Herdegen, *Völkerrecht* 124. Careful agreement by Nolte, 'Between Contemporaneous and Evolutive Interpretation' 1681; Binder, *Die Grenzen der Vertragstreue im Völkerrecht* 84; Besson, 'Getting over the Amour Impossible between International Law and Adjudication'.
[183] Waldock, 'The Evolution of Human Rights Concepts and the Application of the European Convention on Human Rights' 536.
[184] Malgosia Fitzmaurice, 'Dynamic (Evolutive) Interpretation of Treaties, Part II' 15. For her, 'the formal rules of interpretation must reflect substantive principles and foundations of a treaty regime'.
[185] *Ibid.* 16. The author makes a notable exception and excludes environmental rights from this analysis.
[186] *Ibid.* 30.

the treaty as well as the nature of the obligations (*reciprocal/erga omnes partes*)[187] and to the status as self-contained regime.[188] Another inference could be drawn from the *structure of the treaty*. One could distinguish between *traité loi* or *law-making treaties* and *traité contrat*.[189] Based on this distinction, one could contend that law-making treaties would be susceptible to evolution while contracts are not.[190] It was also argued that treaties being a constitution ought to be interpreted evolutively.[191]

It has also been suggested that the approach one takes to the question is dependent on the so-called *schools of interpretation* one adheres to.[192] So it is argued that textualists, purposivists and intentionalists could all explain the reinterpretation of a treaty provision.[193] However, the approaches would answer the intertemporal question in different ways and, consequently, lead to different results. It is argued that a purposive interpretation could be based not only on the circumstances of the conclusion of the treaty but also on later circumstances while a textual as well as an intentional interpretation had to be based on the point in time when the treaty was concluded.[194] Consequently, the approach taken in that regard will influence the outcome. Others look to the *intentions*[195]

---

[187] *Ibid.* 17.   [188] *Ibid.* 19.
[189] Matscher, 'Methods of Interpretation of the Convention' 66. For the similar category of normative treaties, see Brölmann, 'Law-Making Treaties' 393. See also E. Klein, *Statusverträge im Völkerrecht* 343–4, who generally favours a case-by-case analysis but allows for a categorisation of treaties taking the form of a rebuttable presumption. A similar argument in relation to 'regulatory regimes' is made by Kotzur, 'Non-Retroactivity and Its Discontents' 155.
[190] A long time before the Vienna Convention came into force, it was remarked that, with regard to law-making treaties, all states could be presumed to have accepted in advance the 'adaption to changing circumstances': see Wright, 'The Interpretation of Multilateral Treaties' 101.
[191] Bleckmann, *Grundprobleme und Methoden des Völkerrechts* 97; Fassbender, *The United Nations Charter As the Constitution of the International Community* 63.
[192] Greig, 'The Time of Conclusion and the Time of Application of Treaties as Points of Reference in the Interpretative Process' 165. For a general view on the different schools of interpretation, see pp. 102–4 below. On the notion of schools, see Fassbender, 'Denkschulen im Völkerrecht'.
[193] Greig, 'The Time of Conclusion and the Time of Application of Treaties as Points of Reference in the Interpretative Process' 171.
[194] *Ibid.* 165.
[195] Bjorge, *The Evolutionary Interpretation of Treaties* 1. The importance for the intentions as a starting point is stressed by Arato, 'Subsequent Practice and Evolutive Interpretation' 444. For an in-depth inquiry into the problems posed by such approaches, see Alland, 'L'Interprétation de droit international public' 201–22.

SUGGESTED SOLUTIONS

or the *will*[196] of the parties to a treaty. If it could be established that the parties intended that the terms follow the evolution of the law, evolutive interpretation was possible.[197] This could, according to Dupuy, be 'justified by notions and concepts in the terms of the treaty from which it may be inferred that the text is open to considerations of factual or legal evolution after the conclusion of the treaty'.[198] Courts and tribunals are seen to principally and generally depart from an evolutive or static approach.[199] In both cases, exceptions to these general approaches might be warranted. Bruno Simma has taken a rather external perspective and explained evolutive interpretations of the UN Charter by highlighting the extraneous context.[200] All solutions can be mapped as shown in Figure 4.

This review of the approaches taken on the issue reveals the disagreement and disunity in international legal scholarship about the process of static or evolutive treaty interpretation. There is no agreement in the first place on whether one should deal with that issue within, beyond or outside the Vienna Convention. But even within those three categories, there are different approaches, which seem to be incompatible with each other. Is it compatible with the VCLT to resort to maxims, principles, presumptions or schools of interpretation? And are those means of interpretation compatible with each other? What rule should prevail? It should also be mentioned that the structured account given has substantially simplified the actual solution, since many authors have not only used different means but have also put them in a special systematic order. What is striking about the current discourse in academia is that hardly anyone justifies the approaches developed. Mostly, authors just propose an approach without discussing alternatives or arguing why this approach ought to be followed. This discourse can be described as perfect *polyphony*: there are many voices singing different tunes that are harmonic in themselves but not in relation to each other. If there is no agreement from the coming into force of the Convention until today, there might have been an agreed solution of those who drafted the Convention.

---

[196] Waldock, 'The Evolution of Human Rights Concepts and the Application of the European Convention on Human Rights' 536; Binder and Zemanek, 'Das Völkervertragsrecht'.
[197] Jiménez de Aréchaga, 'International Law in the Past Third of a Century: General Course' 48.
[198] Dupuy, 'Evolutionary Interpretation of Treaties' 131.
[199] Brown, *A Common Law of International Adjudication* 46.
[200] Simma, 'NATO, the UN and the use of force' 17.

36 DEFINITIONS, ASSUMPTIONS AND METHOD

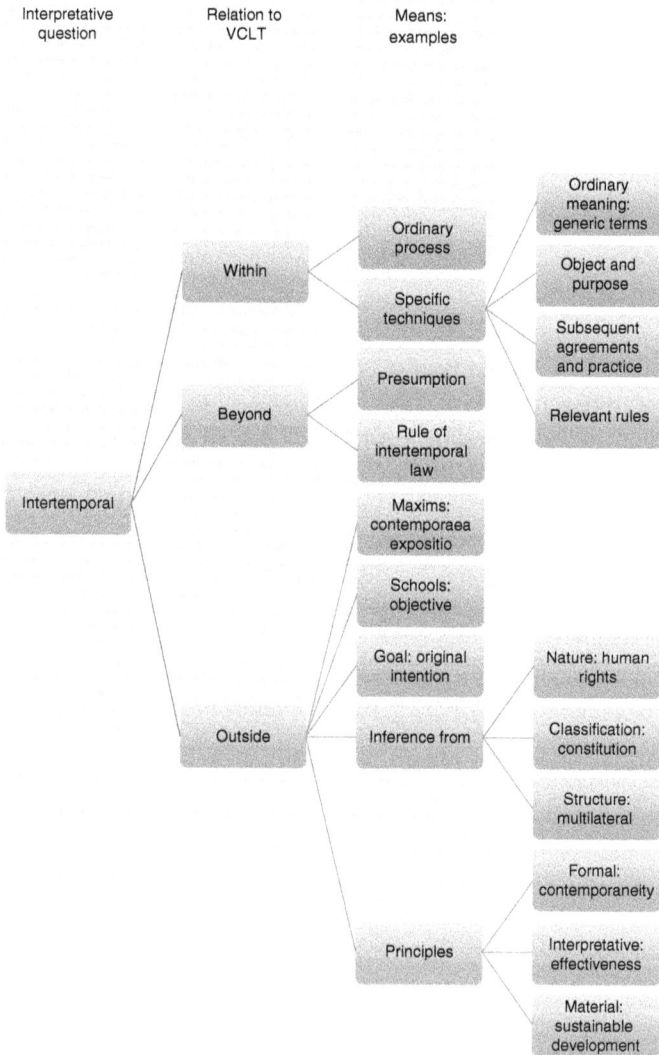

Figure 4 Discursive map: Suggested solutions to the intertemporal question

2.2. Discussion within the ILC and at the Vienna Conference

The Vienna Convention on the Law of Treaties is one of the major achievements of the International Law Commission. After about seventeen years of deliberation and discussion of several drafts under the guidance of four Special Rapporteurs,[201] the Commission submitted Draft Articles to the General Assembly and states parties assembled in Vienna to negotiate on this basis 'a treaty on treaties'.[202] The topic of interpretation was dealt with only by the last Special Rapporteur, Sir Humphrey Waldock.[203] He anticipated the problem and tried to deal with it in an article on intertemporal law.

2.2.1 Draft article on intertemporal law

This article reads

ARTICLE 56. – THE INTER-TEMPORAL LAW

1. A treaty is to be interpreted in the light of the law in force at the time when the treaty was drawn up.
2. Subject to paragraph 1, the application of a treaty shall be governed by the rules of international law in force at the time when the treaty is applied.[204]

Waldock's original idea was that this general rule was to be applied in the context of interpretation through the separate means of interpretation: the first branch of intertemporal law, which required a static meaning, was included in the part dealing with the relevant rules as well as implicitly in the ordinary meaning. The treaty ought to be interpreted

---

[201] See overview in Klabbers, 'Virtuous Interpretation' 17.
[202] This expression is used by Kearney and Dalton, 'The Treaty on Treaties'.
[203] Materials and overviews are provided by Wetzel and Rauschning, *The Vienna Convention on the Law of Treaties*; Rosenne, *The Law of Treaties*. More specifically, in relation to treaty interpretation, see Gardiner, *Treaty Interpretation* 69; Villiger, *Commentary on the 1969 Vienna Convention on the Law of Treaties* 415–18, 423–5. The history of the Draft Article is discussed by do Nascimento e Silva, 'Le Facteur temps et les traités' 266; Klabbers, 'Reluctant Grundnormen' 145; Greig, *Intertemporality and the Law of Treaties* 3–5.
[204] The importance of the article makes it necessary to state it here. See also do Nascimento e Silva, 'Le Facteur temps et les traités' 266.

'in the context of the rules of international law in force at the time of the conclusion of the treaty'.[205] The static ordinary meaning was assumed even though it was not explicitly mentioned in the text.[206] According to Waldock, there were three exceptions to this general static first limb:

> (a) emergence of a rule of customary law outside the treaty but affecting its subject-matter; (b) the conclusion of a later agreement between parties to the treaty; and (c) development of a subsequent practice in the application of the treaty which evidences a tacit agreement amongst the parties to extend or modify the treaty.[207]

The ILC discussed this topic in a most controversial manner. It is hard to imagine how there could have been more disagreement between the members of the Commission. There were competing views on almost every single point. It was unclear whether Draft Art. 56 would apply only to the technique of the relevant rules that can now be found in Art. 31(3)(c) VCLT,[208] to the law of treaties[209] or to international law in general.[210] Some held that the distinction between interpretation and application could not be upheld,[211] while others[212] stressed its usefulness.[213] Looking more specifically at interpretation, there were members taking a strict static approach tying interpretation to the will of the parties.[214] Others contemplated the possibility of evolutive interpretation generally[215] or under specific circumstances.[216] Consequently, there were

---

[205] Report of the International Law Commission on the work of its 16th session (11 May to 24 July 1964)', UN Doc. A/CN.4/167 and Add.1–3, Third Report of the Special Rapporteur, Sir Humphrey Waldock, *ILC Ybk* 1964 II, 54 para. 5. ('Waldock, Third Report') 52.
[206] *Ibid.* 56 para. 15.   [207] *Ibid.* 61 para. 32.
[208] Statement of Mr Amado, ILC, 'Report of the International Law Commission on the work of its 16th session' (11 May–24 July 1964) UN Doc. A/CN.4/SER.A/1964 38 para. 47.
[209] Statement of Mr Lachs, ILC, *ibid.* 39 para. 53.
[210] Statement of Mr Elias, ILC, *ibid.* 36 para. 14.
[211] Statement of Mr Verdross, ILC, *ibid.* 33 para. 6; statement of Mr Jiménez de Aréchaga, *ibid.* 34 para. 11.
[212] Statement of Mr de Luna, ILC, *ibid.* 37 paras. 27–8; statement of Mr Briggs, *ibid.* 38 paras. 38–40.
[213] On this part of the discourse, see Klabbers, 'Reluctant Grundnormen' 145.
[214] Statement of Mr Paredes, ILC (n. 208) 34 paras. 12–13; statement of Mr Pal, *ibid.* 35 paras. 4–5.
[215] Statement of Mr Bartos, ILC, *ibid.* 36 para. 20. See statement of Mr Ago, *ibid.* 39 para. 50, who took a careful stance and interestingly mentioned subsequent practice as an argument for the general possibility of evolutive interpretations.
[216] Statement of Mr Tsuruoka, ILC, *ibid.* 36-7 para. 24, who distinguished between expressed and implied wills; statement of Mr Jiménez de Aréchaga, *ibid.* 34 para. 10; see McLachlan, 'Investment treaties and general international law' 371.

proposals to eliminate the first,[217] but also the second section,[218] of Draft Art. 56. In the face of this stark disagreement, Waldock dropped the general rule on intertemporal law but retained the static focus of the relevant rules in Art. 69 of the revised Draft. This article stated that interpretation shall be in line with 'the rules of general international law in force at the time of the conclusion'.[219] This concerned only the first limb insofar as it applied to the process of interpretation.[220] The discussion around this certainly shows that the distinction drawn by the Special Rapporteur was problematic. Yet, the important point he was making was not really appreciated by the ILC.

Draft Art. 56 would make sense if one were to relate the first section to contential evolution and the second section to referential evolution.[221] Referential evolution takes place when the meaning of a term refers to the circumstances as they currently are: The term 'rights conferred by international law' for example could refer to rights as they currently stand or evolve. In cases of contential evolution, in contrast, the abstract meaning of the term changes: While the notion of rights might 100 years ago have been only understood as rights of states, it is agreed that individuals can today also be the bearers of international rights and duties. This is an example for a contential evolution. From the perspective of the present study, a distinction between interpretation and application could refer to the distinction between contential and referential evolution. While it is presumed that the abstract meaning (extension) stays the same, the concrete relation of the terms to reality (intension) would always refer to present circumstances. This would have been a way to make sense of the distinction, yet the ILC could reach no consensus on the matter.

Governments showed the same great reluctance towards the rule. In the context of the relationship between customary law and treaties, the

---

[217] Statement of Mr Tabibi, ILC, *ibid.* 35 para. 7.
[218] Statement of Mr Paredes, ILC, *ibid.* 34 paras. 12–13; statement of Mr Pal, *ibid.* 35 paras. 4–5.
[219] Greig, *Intertemporality and the Law of Treaties* 3; Klabbers, 'Reluctant Grundnormen' 146.
[220] Klabbers, 'Reluctant Grundnormen' 146. The government of Israel made the interesting remark that modification through practice, which will be inquired into below, could be considered as a second and dynamic limb: ILC, 'Report of the International Law Commission on the work of its 18th session' (4 May–19 July 1966), UN Doc. A/CN.4/SER.A/1966/Add.1 Annex: Law of Treaties: Comments by governments on the draft articles on the law of treaties drawn up by the Commission at its fourteenth, fifteenth and sixteenth session, UN Doc. A/CN.4/182 and Corr.1&2 and Add.1, 2/Rev.1&3, *ILC Ybk* 1966 II, 300 summary at 87–8.
[221] This distinction is also explained at *ibid.* 19.

United States government remarked that there was a 'long-recognized principle that treaties are to be applied in the context of international law and in accordance with the evolution of that law'.[222] The Israeli government said that the intertemporal problem was not limited to other rules of international law but that the ordinary meaning of terms could also change.[223] While the Syrian delegation supported the static solution,[224] the Greek delegation mentioned rather neutrally that the Draft Art. 69 would make evolution impossible.[225] This prompted the Netherlands government to call for an amendment to open up the process of treaty interpretation for the evolution of the law and leave the exact determination of the issue to good faith.[226] So the governments that commented directly on the issue were one against, one in favour and one neutral towards the possibility of changing interpretations.

Waldock agreed with the Netherlands government, which, as already stated, proposed that the question should be left open and to be interpreted in good faith.[227] He generally agreed, and deleted the respective part. Yet, he made the suggestion that, as a matter of good faith, intertemporal law had to be reintroduced in the process of interpretation, but in a different manner: he shifted the focus from the relevant rules to the ordinary meaning, and suggested that the ordinary meaning should generally be taken to be static, i.e. tied to the conclusion of the treaty.[228] Yet, he indicated that there could be exceptions. As examples, he mentioned the terms 'bay' and 'territorial waters'.[229] The meaning of the treaty 'may change with the evolution of the law if the parties used it in the treaty as a general concept and not as a word of fixed content'.[230] In the face of the diverging positions within the ILC and the states commenting upon the Draft, Waldock made a clever move: He left the question open but emphasised another aspect that had attracted attention before.[231] This idea, to generally regard the meaning as being static and to provide for exceptions for special terms, is in fact the embryonic state of the approach later taken by the ICJ.[232] What he described as a 'general' term was later called a 'generic term', another phrase used was terms which were by definition evolutionary, which is the same as the phrase 'not as a word of

---

[222] ILC (n. 220) 358; see also the short summary at 88 and 90.
[223] *Ibid.* 300, see also the short summary at *ibid.* 92.   [224] *Ibid.* 94.   [225] *Ibid.* 93.
[226] *Ibid.* 92.   [227] *Ibid.* 95–6 para. 7.   [228] *Ibid.*   [229] *Ibid.*   [230] *Ibid.*
[231] See statement of the government of Israel (n. 220) and Statement of Mr Bartos, ILC (n. 208) 192 para. 89.
[232] The ICJ later departed from a static meaning and made exceptions for terms that are by definition evolutionary or for so-called generic terms. See at 253.

fixed content'.²³³ So while the idea of intertemporal law as Waldock imagined it became relevant for international law in practice,²³⁴ the intertemporal question was generally left open in the VCLT.

The deletion of the temporal focus was warmly welcomed by the Commission, four members of which seemed to favour the more flexible approach²³⁵ while only one member still took a strictly static stance.²³⁶ In the light of the discussion, the deletion of the article can be seen as nothing other than an agreement to disagree. But the discussion was not yet over.

At the Vienna Conference, the topic of intertemporal law was brought up by a Delegate of Czechoslovakia, Mr Mysilil, who stated that the relevant rules were susceptible to change.²³⁷ Based on this observation, he put forward an approach that would also take into account the relevant rules that came into existence after the conclusion of the treaty. It does seem that the delegate regarded this as being the solution chosen by the Draft before him. The other delegations did not take up this point and the then Expert Consultant at the conference Waldock just re-emphasised at the end of his concluding statement that there 'were immense difficulties in any treatment of the subject with respect to interpretation', one of which was the complex relationship between treaties and customary international law.²³⁸ In this area, the ILC developed a norm that had the potential to at least partly deal with the evolution in treaties.

2.2.2   Modification through practice

The question whether evolutive interpretation of the law is possible under the rules of the Vienna Convention was highlighted in particular with

---

[233] ILC (n. 220) 95–6 para. 7.
[234] His later writing also confirms that he stood by the rule of intertemporal law: Waldock, 'The Evolution of Human Rights Concepts and the Application of the European Convention on Human Rights' 535.
[235] Statement of Mr Briggs, ILC, 'Report of the International Law Commission on the work of its 18th session' (4 May–19 July 1966), UN Doc. A/CN.4/SER.A/1966 187 para. 33; statement of Mr Reuter, *ibid.* 188–9 paras. 43 and 50; Statement of Mr Jiménez de Aréchaga, *ibid.* 190 paras. 71–2; Statement of Mr El-Erian, *ibid.* 196 para. 31.
[236] Statement of Mr Luna, ILC, *ibid.* 185 para. 10.
[237] 'Summary records of the plenary meetings and of the meetings of the Committee of the Whole' United Nations Conference on the Law of Treaties, First Session (Vienna 26 March–24 May 1968) 182 para. 54. ('First Vienna Conference').
[238] *Ibid.* 184 para. 74.

regard to Draft Art. 38 of the Final Draft of 1966.[239] This article allowed for the modification through subsequent practice.[240] Had this rule been adopted, there would have been at least one explicit mechanism in the VCLT to change the meaning of treaties without changing the rest of the text.

In the final version of the VCLT, modification is defined as *inter se* change of the text.[241] Draft Art. 38 employed a broader notion of the term modification which also includes changes through interpretation. The commentary on the ILC Draft also stressed that the processes of interpretation and modification were distinct.[242] Subsequent practice formed part of the techniques of treaty interpretation,[243] but modification through subsequent practice could go beyond what the normal process of interpretation allowed. Modification through practice could be considered as a process of informal modification since it did not follow the rules of amendment which are either provided for in the treaty in question or generally in what is now Arts. 54ff VCLT. It was a separate process that required consistent practice. Under Draft Art. 38, subsequent practice could outweigh all other techniques of treaty interpretation: Irrespective of the ordinary meaning and the other parts of Art. 31 VCLT, subsequent practice would have always prevailed through the process of modification in which the other techniques played no role.

Art. 73 of Waldock's original draft stated that the interpretation shall take account of '(c) any subsequent practice in relation to the treaty evidencing the consent of all the parties to an extension or modification of the treaty'.[244] In the subsequent draft, Art. 69A stated that '[t]he operation of a treaty may also be modified ... (b) by a subsequent practice of the parties in the application of the treaty establishing their tacit agreement to an alteration or extension of its provisions'.[245] After

---

[239] ILC, 'Report of the International Law Commission on the work of its 18th session' (4 May–19 July 1966) UN Doc. A/CN.4/Ser.A/1964/Add.1 'Final Draft Articles on the Law of Treaties', *ILC Ybk* 1966 II, 219 ('Final Draft Articles') 187ff.

[240] For a full discussion of the matter, see Nolte, 'Treaties over Time: Introductory Report' 200; and Kohen, 'Keeping Subsequent Agreements and Practice in Their Right Limits' 35–7.

[241] Odendahl, 'Art. 39' 699 para. 1, referring to ILC, Final Draft Articles (n. 239) 232 para. 3.

[242] ILC, Final Draft Articles (n. 239).   [243] *Ibid.* Art. 70(3).

[244] Waldock, Third Report (n. 205) 53.

[245] ILC, 'Report of the International Law Commission on the work of its 16th session' (11 May–24 July 1964) UN Doc. A/CN.4/1964 and Add.1–3, 309.

the debate within the ILC, the Draft Article was only slightly changed to the effect that 'the operation of a treaty may also be modified ... (b) By subsequent practice of the parties in the application of the treaty establishing their agreement to an alteration or extension of its provisions'.[246]

In all of the stages of deliberation by the ILC, subsequent practice was regarded as a technique of interpretation so that the combination with Draft Art. 38 led to a double function: It was a mechanism of interpretation as well as of modification. At the First Vienna Conference, Draft Art. 38 was the only provision that was rejected by the Committee of the Whole by fifty-three votes in favour of its deletion to fifteen against its deletion with sixteen abstentions.[247] This majority found expression in the discussion of the Committee of the Whole which was addressed by 30 delegates as well as the Expert Consultant Humphrey Waldock. Twenty-three delegates supported the deletion of the Draft Article, two favoured an amendment reducing the scope of the Draft Article substantially while five delegates supported it. The arguments centred around four major issues: the question whether Art. 38 ILC Draft was a rule of positive customary international law, issues of drafting and consistency of the Vienna Convention, consequences in internal law and the question of the adequate degree of formalism concerning interpretation and modification of treaties. With regard to the sources, the Commentary quoted a famous phrase contained in an arbitral case between the United States and France,[248] stating that:

> [t]his course of conduct may, in fact, be taken into account not merely as a means useful for interpreting the Agreement, but also as something more: That is, as a possible source of a subsequent modification, arising out of certain actions or certain attitudes, having a bearing on the juridical situation of the parties and on the rights that each of them could properly claim.[249]

Nine delegates contended that there had not been sufficient authority to regard the rule in Art. 38 of the ILC Draft as a rule of positive

---

[246] Ibid. 198.
[247] First Vienna Conference (n. 237) 215. Kohen has analysed the vote in detail and remarked that the opposition was 'not divided along traditional political and regional lines. They represented all regions of the world': Kohen, 'Keeping Subsequent Agreements and Practice in Their Right Limits' 36.
[248] *Interpretation of the air transport services agreement between the United States of America and France* (United States v. France) (1963) 16 RIAA 5.
[249] Ibid. 62–3.

international law.[250] Eight delegates asserted that there was authority to the contrary without specifying what it was.[251] The French delegation proposed limiting the scope of the provision.[252] So the opinion on this issue was almost equally split.

The drafting was criticised on several bases, the most important of which related to the notion of practice.[253] It was contended that it was unclear how consistent the practice ought to be.[254] Especially with regard to the consistency, the Expert Consultant indicated that the notion of 'all the parties' might satisfy cautious states that would also have to take into consideration the phrase 'establishing the agreement of the parties to modify its provisions'.[255] Some delegations contended that a modification by subsequent practice was superfluous since a change of interpretation could, up to a certain point, also be achieved by the means of interpretation.[256] Others pointed to the problem of distinguishing interpretation from modification.[257] The difficulties concerning the relationship of customary law and the law of treaties were mentioned.[258] It was argued that the formal rules of amending treaties contained in the VCLT as well

---

[250] First Vienna Conference (n. 237), Delegate Fujisaki (Japan) 208 para. 58; Delegate Carmona (Venezuela) 208 para. 59; Delegate Grishin (Union of the Soviet Socialist Republics) 210 paras. 1–2; Delegate Ruiz Varela (Colombia) 211 para. 21; Delegate Miras (Turkey) 212 para. 27; Delegate Alvarez (Uruguay) 212 para. 36; Delegate Maliti (Tanzania) 212 para. 38; implicitly Delegate Kramer (Netherlands) 213 para. 47; Delegate Zourek (Czechoslovakia) 214 para. 52.

[251] Ibid. Delegate Yasseen (Iraq) 211 para. 8; Delegate Maresca (Italy) 211 para. 22; Delegate Verosta (Austria) 33 para. 212; Delegate Chea Den (Cambodia) 213 para. 49; referring to the writings of McNair and Visscher Delegate de la Guardia (Argentina) 214 para. 51; Delegate Ruegger (Switzerland) 213–14 para. 50; Makarewicz (Poland) 211 para. 14, contending that it was a rule of international law which was outside the scope of the Convention.

[252] Ibid. Delegate de Bresson (France) 208–9 para. 64; Martinez Caro (Spain) 209 para. 66.

[253] Ibid. Delegate Martinez Caro (Spain) 209 para. 70.

[254] Ibid. Delegate Martinez Caro (Spain) 209 paras. 72–3; Delegate Wershof (Canada) 210 para. 77.

[255] Ibid. Expert Consultant Waldock, 214 para. 55.

[256] Ibid. Delegate Castrén (Finland) 207–8 para. 57; Delegate Carmona (Venezuela) 208 para. 59; Delegate Phan-Van-Thinh (Vietnam) 208 para. 61; Delegate Miras (Turkey) 211 para. 28; Delegate Kramer (Netherlands) 213 para. 44, who tried to capture the limits of how far one could go with interpretation. It was also contended that the effects were basically the same: see Delegate Rosenne (Israel) 213 para. 48.

[257] Ibid. Delegate Wershof (Canada) 210 para. 77. As an answer to this, it was proposed to base the difference on the distinction between a declaratory act and a constituent instrument: see Delegate Yasseen (Iraq) 211 para. 11.

[258] Ibid. Delegate Castrén (Finland) 207 para. 57; Delegate Martinez Caro (Spain) 209–10 para. 72; Delegate Grishin (Union of the Soviet Socialist Republics) 210 para. 3.

as in the treaties themselves would be undermined.[259] It was seen as inconsistent that unwritten treaties were originally excluded from the scope of the Convention.[260]

With regard to internal law, many concerns were expressed that informal change could affect the law and institutions on the national plane.[261] Since the conclusion as well as the modification of treaties required parliamentary consent, it was highlighted that it would be difficult to provide for such consent in those situations.[262] This could have had implications for the integrity of the treaty since in dualist systems the modified part might not even be applicable in internal law.[263] Another argument was that even within the executive branch of government there would be problems since the practice of relatively minor officials could modify treaties without the knowledge of the government.[264] This, it was argued, would go against the provisions in the Convention, which provide for the capacity of state officials to negotiate or conclude treaties.[265] In response to the constitutional argument, Waldock suggested that these problems had not yet materialised.[266]

The issue that was used by both sides as an argument was the adequate balance between formal and informal changes. Delegates favouring the inclusion of Art. 38 of the ILC Draft argued that this would give an opportunity to be closer to social reality and to account for what actually happens with treaties since they were in practice often applied in a manner that departed very far from their wording and their immediate context.[267] The Italian delegation linked Draft Art. 38 to 'the fact that law

---

[259] *Ibid.* Delegate Carmona (Venezuela) 208 para. 60; Delegate Phan-Van-Thinh (Vietnam) 208 para. 62; Delegate de Bresson (France) 208 para. 63; Delegate Martinez Caro (Spain) 209 para. 70; Delegate Ruiz Varela (Colombia) 211 para. 21; Delegate Kramer (Netherlands) 213 para. 44. This was also acknowledged by the Italian delegation which consequently voted in favour of the French amendment: see Maresca (Italy) 211 para. 25.

[260] *Ibid.* Delegate Kramer (Netherlands) 213 para. 45.

[261] *Ibid.* Generally Makarewicz (Poland) 211 para. 17.

[262] *Ibid.* Delegate Fujisaki (Japan) 208 para. 58; Delegate de Bresson (France) 208 para. 63; Delegate Grishin (Union of the Soviet Socialist Republics) 210 para. 4; Delegate Ruiz Varela (Colombia) 211 para. 21; Delegate Miras (Turkey) 211–12 para. 27; Regala (Philippines) 213 para. 43.

[263] *Ibid.* Delegate Alvarez (Uruguay) 212 para. 36; the opposite problem would arise for states which automatically apply treatise in domestic law: see Delegate Alvarez Tabio (Cuba) 213 para. 40.

[264] *Ibid.*, see especially Delegate Kearny (United States of America) 210–11 para. 6; Delegate Martinez Caro (Spain) 209 para. 68; Delegate Alvarez (Uruguay) 212 para. 35.

[265] See for example *ibid.* Martinez Caro (Spain) 209 para. 68.   [266] *Ibid.* 214, para. 56.

[267] *Ibid.* Maresca (Italy) 211 paras. 22–4.

could evolve as the need arose'.²⁶⁸ It was contended that the rules of attribution would provide for sufficient legal certainty;²⁶⁹ more certainty could be achieved by a clause providing for judicial settlement.²⁷⁰ On the opposite side, it was stressed that this would endanger legal certainty and security.²⁷¹ Essential parts of the treaty could be undermined.²⁷² In particular, states would be given opportunities to evade treaty obligations. This could destabilise treaty relations²⁷³ and change the whole climate of international relations.²⁷⁴ Frequently, the problems were seen with regard to multilateral treaties.²⁷⁵ It was suggested that groups of states might, by inter se agreements, threaten the integrity of the treaty as a whole.²⁷⁶ But independent of the nature of the treaty, third states might have a legitimate interest in knowing the content of the treaty.²⁷⁷ It could be seen as deviation from the general policy of formalising and codifying international law.²⁷⁸ This could potentially affect the rules on treaty making.²⁷⁹ Some delegations summarised their argument with the principle of *pacta sunt servanda*.²⁸⁰

---

²⁶⁸ Ibid. Maresca (Italy) 211 paras. 22–4.
²⁶⁹ Ibid. Delegate Yasseen (Iraq) 211 para. 9, who also thought attribution to be a remedy for practice of minor state officials.
²⁷⁰ Ibid. Delegate Ruegger (Switzerland) 213–14 para. 50.
²⁷¹ Ibid. Delegate Phan-Van-Thinh (Vietnam) 208 para. 62; Delegate Alvarez (Uruguay) 212 para. 37; Regala (Philippines) 213 para. 43; Delegate Zourek (Czechoslovakia) 214 para. 52.
²⁷² Ibid. Delegate Martinez Caro (Spain) 209 para. 70, termination is briefly discussed in para. 71. See also Delegate Alvarez (Uruguay) 212 para. 35, also suggesting that certain types of treaties could not be considered.
²⁷³ Ibid. Delegate Zourek (Czechoslovakia) 214 para. 52.
²⁷⁴ Ibid. Delegate de Bresson (France) 208 para. 63; Hu (China) 211 para. 18; Delegate Miras (Turkey) 211 para. 28; Delegate Thiam (Guinea) 212 para. 31.
²⁷⁵ Ibid. Delegate Thiam (Guinea) 212 para. 31; Delegate Alvarez (Uruguay) 212 para. 36; Delegate Crucho de Almeida (Portugal) 213 para. 42.
²⁷⁶ Ibid. Martinez Caro (Spain) 210 para. 73; see also with addition of the problem of an *ex-post facto* information Delegate Kramer (Netherlands) 213 para. 46.
²⁷⁷ Ibid. Delegate Zourek (Czechoslovakia) 214 para. 53, mentioning the most-favoured-nations clause as an example.
²⁷⁸ Ibid. Delegate Alvarez Tabio (Cuba) 213 para. 40.
²⁷⁹ Ibid. Delegate Martinez Caro (Spain) 209 para. 67; Delegate Ruiz Varela (Colombia) 211 para. 21.
²⁸⁰ See for example *ibid*. Delegate Martinez Caro (Spain) 209 para. 69, Delegate Vargas (Chile) 210 para. 74; Delegate Alvarez Tabio (Cuba) 213 para. 40; Delegate Thiam (Guinea) 212 para. 30; Delegate Alvarez (Uruguay) 212 para. 35; Delegate Crucho de Almeida (Portugal) 213 para. 42. This is, as the Expert Consultant and another delegate mentioned, not an entirely correct use of the phrase since the violation of a treaty could only be ascertained when one had determined the proper content of the treaty: see 214

The arguments of the delegates in Vienna about the degree of formalism were the arguments most frequently used by the supporters of Art. 38 of the ILC Draft, while it also formed part of the argument of delegates favouring the deletion of the provision. The issue was how formal the rules of modification ought to be. The choice between formality and informality was not a question of all-or-nothing but rather a question of degree. As a result, the Draft Article was dropped. Yet, it could be argued that there is an identical rule of customary international law or that the VCLT has to be interpreted in that regard due to systematic considerations. The deliberations show also that this proposal is the closest the international community of states ever got to determining issues of stasis and evolution at least partially. Draft Art. 38 would have worked as a rule and provided for one mechanism on how to deal with intertemporal problems; it was supported by the Commission and by a significant number of states.

The analysis of the preparatory works of the VCLT shows that there was no agreed solution amongst the drafters how to deal with intertemporal problems. It is interesting that the dissent among the members of the ILC as well as among the state representatives was almost perfectly symmetrical: Whenever someone tried to argue for a general static approach, another discussant would voice exactly the opposite opinion. The Special Rapporteur Waldock tried to deal with the question in Draft Art. 56, which was widely criticised by members of the Commission. But even its supporters could not agree what Art. 56 actually meant. An attempt was made to delete the static as well as the evolutive section of the Draft Article, and in the face of this stark disagreement the whole Draft Article was dropped. States quarrelled over the static reference in Draft Art. 69, some favouring static and others evolutive interpretations. After that, the static part in Draft Art. 69 was deleted as well. Draft Art. 38, which would at least partly have regulated the problem was later not adopted by the Committee of the Whole at the Vienna Conference. Every attempt to regulate the question failed. There was almost perfect disagreement about how to deal with those questions, and views directly opposed each other. The proceedings leading to the VCLT left the intertemporal question open and undetermined as does the final text of Arts. 31 and 32 VCLT. The only possibility that is now left is to look for a traditional agreement preceding the discourse about the VCLT.

para. 56. See also the critique of Delegate Yasseen (Iraq) 211 para. 10 and Delegate Verosta (Austria) 212 para. 13.

2.3. Suggested solutions prior to drafting the VCLT

While one might think that problems of evolution in treaties are rather recent and a modern concern, there was a very early awareness of the problems posed by evolutive interpretation and the intertemporal question. Possibly the oldest account of the problem stems from Alberico Gentili. In the chapter on territory and postliminium in his book *De jure bellis libri tres*, he dealt with territorial questions and the effect of peace treaties in these matters. Discussing some cases, he mentioned three examples, including one concerning the Treaty of Granada dividing Naples between the Kings of France and Spain.[281] He recounted that the boundaries 'were designated by names which signified one thing in early times and another later'.[282] The Spanish solicited the modern meaning while the French relied on the prior meaning of the names. Gentili opted for the interpretation at the time the treaty was made.[283] This is a clear question of referential evolution: The abstract meaning of the treaty stays the same; the question was to what point in time the names refer. Gentili discussed an example stemming not from antiquity but from state practice dating back just a little over 100 years before the publication of his book. This suggests that such problems could arise also in the treaty practice of his time.

In his treatise on the rules of treaty interpretation, Hugo Grotius also dealt with problems of evolutive interpretation. He mentioned that, if the same phrases were used on different occasions, they could be taken to mean the same thing.[284] From this, one could conclude that there is a general stability of law over time. Commenting upon literal interpretation, he stated: 'If there is no implication which suggests a different conclusion, words are to be understood in their natural sense, not according to the grammatical sense which comes from derivation, but according to current usage, to whose behest belong the law and rule of speech.'[285]

In cases of doubt, Grotius answered the intertemporal question with regard to literal interpretation in an evolutive manner. If there was no suggestion to the contrary, the current use of the term was to be taken up. He dealt with the question whether the term 'allies'[286] in a treaty would only refer to allies at the time of the conclusion of the treaty or also

---

[281] Gentili, *De jure bellis libri tres* 384 (original 629–30, Book III, Chapter XVII).
[282] Ibid.   [283] Ibid.
[284] Grotius, *De jure belli ac pacis libri tres* 409–10 (original 276, Book II, Chapter XVI, II).
[285] Ibid. 409 (original 276, Book II, Chapter XVI, II).
[286] Ibid. 415 (original 278, Book II, Chapter XVII, XIII).

parties that later had become allies in the context of an antique treaty between Rome and Carthage.[287] While he denied a broad interpretation and for that reason an evolutive interpretation of the word 'allies',[288] he expressly acknowledged the possibility of interpreting terms evolutively. He also gave an example of an evolutive interpretation in the case of an agreement establishing the obligation that a place should not be surrounded by walls at a time in which there is no other form of fortification.[289] If it could be established that the reason for the prohibition was the hindrance of fortification, an earthwork will be prohibited even if it was not in the mind of the parties to the agreement at the time of the conclusion of the agreement.[290] This evolutive interpretation was effectively justified with the purpose of the treaty. Most interestingly, Grotius was ready to go beyond the ordinary meaning of the words. He also permitted transgressing the original intention of the parties.[291]

While Grotius explicitly acknowledged that terms could be interpreted in an evolutive as well as an original sense, Thomas Rutherforth[292] was rather careful in his approach to the question. Although he stated very clearly that the meaning depends on the common use, Rutherforth privileged the interpretation as it stood at the time of the conclusion of the treaty. The meaning of ambiguous terms could be determined by going back to the context of the treaty, i.e. the circumstances of its conclusion.[293] He acknowledged that one can draw inferences from the contemporary use. Apart from that, the context comprised only actions of the parties to the treaty 'in the times immediately after the making of

---

[287] Ibid. For a detailed discussion on the basis of Grotius' theory and with a differing result, see Johann Textor, *Synopsis juris gentium* 259-61 (Book II, Chapter XVII, paras. 13-15).

[288] The antique treaty in question between Rome and Carthage provided for respect for allies of the other party. The Romans regarded the treaty as also applicable to future parties; consequently, they asserted a breach of the treaty. This probability of treaty breach was for Grotius an odious matter; he, therefore, in this case opted for a narrow, i.e. original, interpretation of the terms of the treaty. It has to be emphasised that the concrete interpretative decision does not mean that an evolutive interpretation was generally barred.

[289] Grotius, *De jure belli ac pacis libri tres* 422 (original 282, Book II, Chapter XVII, XIII).

[290] For a discussion of that example, see Textor, *Synopsis juris gentium* 263-4 (Book II, Chapter XVII, paras. 25-6). The example is also taken up by Vattel, *The Law of Nations or the Principles of Natural Law* 209 (Book 2, Chapter 17, mn 290).

[291] Grotius, *De jure belli ac pacis libri tres*.

[292] While dealing mostly with Grotius, Rutherforth applied his rules on interpretation not only to international treaties but also to internal laws, private contracts and wills.

[293] Rutherforth, *Institutes of Natural Law* 417 (Book II, Chapter VII, para. IX).

it'.²⁹⁴ So in relation to intertemporal problems of interpretation, Rutherforth based the interpretation mostly on the original understanding of the terms of the treaty. Like Grotius, he allowed either a broad or narrow meaning that could go against the clear terms of the treaty.²⁹⁵

Emer de Vattel contended that:

> [l]anguages are constantly varying in form; the force and meaning of terms change in the course of time. When we have to interpret a very old treaty we must know the common use of the terms at the time the treaty was drawn up, and we can discover what that use was from deeds of the same period and from contemporary writers, by a careful process of comparison.²⁹⁶

Vattel relied on the point in time at which the treaty was drawn up and concluded.²⁹⁷ With regard to unforeseen cases, which were to him cases that the author did not and could not foresee, he stated that 'we must be guided rather by his [the author's] intention than by his words, and we must interpret the document as he himself would interpret it, if he were present, or as he would have done it if he had foreseen the circumstances as they are now'.²⁹⁸

So although the meaning of the terms is to be determined with reference to the time when the treaty was drawn up, a change in the circumstances could evoke an interpretative change if this could be presumed to be the intention of the author of the treaty.²⁹⁹ And this even despite the clear wording of the treaty. Even though Vattel's approach to the intertemporal question was to look at the time of the conclusion of the treaty, it is interesting that, discussing the interpretation of the term 'allies', he did not regard the treaty as odious and, accordingly, arrived at the conclusion that the term ally should be interpreted evolutively so that present allies were included.³⁰⁰ The fact that Vattel referred not only to the potential interpretation of the party to the treaty but also its

---

[294] Ibid. 417 (Book II, Chapter VII, para. IX).
[295] Ibid. 427 (Book II, Chapter VII, para. XI).
[296] Vattel, *The Law of Nations or the Principles of Natural Law* 202 (Book 2, Chapter 17, mn 272).
[297] Ibid.   [298] Ibid. 212 (Book 2, Chapter 17, mn 297).
[299] See also his general remark that new cases had to be dealt with by inferences from the intention of the contracting party or the legislator: *ibid.* 199 (Book 2, Chapter 17, mn 262).
[300] Ibid. 217–18 (Book 2, Chapter 17, mn 309). Taking a static approach in general, he reached an evolutive outcome while Grotius employed generally a dynamic approach but reached a static outcome on the very same question.

potential behaviour as a standard for the action of the interpreter establishes a wide discretion in the interpretation of the treaty. While still sticking to the original intention of the parties, this view is deprived of its rigidity by the fiction that the parties could have foreseen later developments. A determinative guide in that regard was for Vattel the purpose of the treaty, which, if established properly, could allow going beyond the wording of the treaty.[301]

A very detailed account of the problems in question is given by Phillimore. In the context of authentic interpretation, he mentioned that instruments of the parties subsequent to the conclusion of the treaty could also influence the interpretation of the agreement.[302] He acknowledged that this case would not amount to an interpretation but a conclusion of a new treaty, but stated explicitly that subsequent treaties could also influence the process of interpretation.[303] As he was very concerned with the problems of the application of abstract rules to potentially indefinite concrete cases, he was sensitive to the situation in which a general term encompassed a situation that was not foreseen by the parties. Citing Pothier, he remarked that '[w]hen the object of the agreement is universally to include everything of a given nature the general description will comprise all particular articles, although they may not have been in the knowledge of the parties'.[304]

Right at the outset, he mentioned the possibility that the parties did not foresee specific cases 'which may fall under the principle but which are not provided for by the letter of the law or contract'.[305] Here, he implied that it could be upon the interpreter to go beyond the meaning of the words in the process of interpretation. So again, Phillimore saw some room for evolutive interpretation.[306] In interpreting restrictively and extensively, Phillimore placed limitations upon the interpreter that had a specific relevance for evolutive interpretation, which should not be substituted by inference or analogy, 'in which case it is clear, that the expression is not rectified by being brought into unison with the idea, but that a new idea is substituted by the interpreter in the place of that which was present to the mind of the framers of the Treaty'.[307] So he stressed

---

[301] Ibid. 209 (Book 2, Chapter 17, mn 290).
[302] Phillimore, *Commentaries upon International Law* 82 (Chapter VIII, para. LXVIII).
[303] Ibid. 87 (Chapter VIII, para. LXXIII). [304] Ibid. 98 (Chapter VIII, para. LXXXVI).
[305] Ibid. 79 (Chapter VIII, para. LXIV).
[306] See also Ludwik Ehrlich, 'L'Interprétation des traités' 31.
[307] Phillimore, *Commentaries upon International Law* 80 (Chapter VIII, para. LXXXIII).

the framers' intention at the time of the conclusion of the treaty. This general view was to be modified if the framers did not foresee or provide for a specific case and interpretation in that regard had become necessary. In such a situation it would be the task of the interpreter to 'conduct that interpretation as nearly as possible in accordance with what the party would have done if the circumstance which has now happened had been foreseen'.[308]

It is interesting to see that the first modern authors on public international law dealt with problems of intertemporality and evolution at comparatively great length. What certainly has to be acknowledged is that neither evolution of treaties through interpretation nor the intertemporal problem can be really said to be new problems: They have been dealt with by several authors from the beginning of modern public international law.

Amongst the later authors, there were several that did not deal with evolutive interpretations or related questions.[309] Others such as Fiore explicitly stated that the passage of time could even render the treaty ambiguous and call for reinterpretation.[310] Beginning with the twentieth century, there was a trend towards focusing on the time of the conclusion of the treaty.[311] In line with this conception, the question whether the interpretation of a treaty is to be changed in the face of changed circumstances depends on the assumed will of the parties at the time of the conclusion of the treaty. Ehrlich remarked that the parties always had the opportunity to change the law if they wished.[312] But this approach also has a bearing on the means of interpretation. Insofar as interpretative evidence is admitted stemming from the time after the conclusion of the treaty, it is either restricted to evidence that is in close temporal

---

[308] *Ibid.* 88 (Chapter VIII, para. XCI).
[309] No mention of intertemporal or evolutive matters is made by Lawrence, *The Principles of International Law* 326–7; Hall, *A Treatise on International Law* 390ff; Hershey, *The Essentials of International Law and Organization* 445ff.
[310] Fiore, *Le Droit international codifié et sa sanction juridique* 402.
[311] Wildman, *Institutes of International Law* 113; Adler, 'The Interpretation of Treaties' 62–91, 164–71 and 75; Stockton, *Outlines of International Law* 258–9; Hyde, *International Law Chiefly as Interpreted and Applied by the United States* (2nd edn) 1472. Dealing with analogies in the face of changed conditions, Heffter referred to the intentions of the parties at the time of the conclusion of the treaty: see Heffter, *Das europäisches Völkerrecht der Gegenwart* 207. A presumption for taking this point in time as the decisive point was presented by Ehrlich, who will be considered to belong to the codificatory phase, Ludwik Ehrlich, 'L'Interprétation des traités' 130.
[312] Ludwik Ehrlich, 'L'Interprétation des traités' 67.

connection with the conclusion of the treaty, or only insofar as it elucidated the intentions of the parties at the time of the conclusion of the treaty.³¹³ However, it was at times explicitly stated that the subsequent practice of parties could alter the original interpretation at the time of the conclusion of the treaty.³¹⁴

Gerald Fitzmaurice deduced six principles from the jurisprudence of the ICJ that should guide the interpretation of treaties. Amongst those principles the 'principle of contemporaneity' was included in an article published in 1957.³¹⁵ This principle was seen as a qualification to the principle of natural and ordinary meaning.³¹⁶ He concluded that the doctrine of intertemporal law required interpreting treaties 'according to the meaning they possessed ... at the date when the treaty was entered into'.³¹⁷ Fitzmaurice also acknowledged that there was a principle of subsequent practice, and he anticipated the problem that such a subsequent practice might possibly lead to a change of the meaning of a treaty.³¹⁸ In his opinion, this principle could not change the meaning of the treaty in the process of interpretation but only through revision of the treaty.³¹⁹ Therefore, it was not possible to depart in the process of interpretation from the original meaning. A very different view was held by Alejandro Alvarez who proposed a new method of interpretation so as to bring international law into line with the developments in international society.³²⁰ He explicitly called for changes in interpretation and sought to enable such changes by favouring the object and purpose of the treaty over its text.³²¹

Even doctrine predating the VCLT cannot contribute to the solution of the question whether and how international treaties could be interpreted

---

³¹³ Adler, 'The Interpretation of Treaties' 70; Ludwik Ehrlich, 'L'Interprétation des traités' 130.
³¹⁴ Hyde, *International Law Chiefly as Interpreted and Applied by the United States* (2nd edn) 1501.
³¹⁵ A previous article did not contain this principle: Fitzmaurice, 'The Law and Procedure of the International Court of Justice: Treaty Interpretation'.
³¹⁶ Fitzmaurice, 'The Law and Procedure of the International Court of Justice 1951–4' 212.
³¹⁷ Ibid. 225.   ³¹⁸ Ibid. 224.   ³¹⁹ Ibid.
³²⁰ Alvarez, *Le Droit international nouveau dans ses rapport avec la vie actuelle des peuples* 497–9. For a general discussion of the theories of Alvarez, see Aust, 'Alejandro Álvarez'. Alvarez developed his thoughts further in some of his opinions given as a judge of the ICJ which are discussed at 248–9.
³²¹ Alvarez, *Le Droit international nouveau dans ses rapport avec la vie actuelle des peuples* 498.

evolutively: It offers diametrically opposed approaches and no real discourse between them. Take for example the stances of Grotius and Vattel. Grotius was generally in favour of the recent meaning of words, while Vattel opted generally for a departure from the original intentions. When both were dealing with the treaty between Rome and Carthage, Grotius reached a static result even though he generally favoured evolutive outcomes. Vattel, on the contrary, interpreted the treaty evolutively despite the fact that he favoured static interpretations in general. This clearly shows how even the very early scholars of modern international law dissented when it came to questions of stasis and evolution. When scholars later focused on the intentions of the parties, some of them took this to be the intentions at the time the treaty was concluded while others also looked at later intentions.

2.4. Transferring solutions from other jurisdictions

When one is faced with a problem that cannot be solved easily, one tends to look to other jurisdictions. This classical function of comparative law[322] could also help in our case and indeed, there have been voices pointing to the American discourse around originalism[323] and the French discourse[324] concerning the interpretation of the *Code Civil*. So we should revisit the doctrinal construction of those approaches to see if they offer enlightenment on the problem of stasis and evolution.

2.4.1 *Originalism and non-originalism*

The debate on originalism in the context of the Constitution of the United States is certainly one of the richest, most elaborate as well as most passionate debates addressing changes through interpretation. What makes it even more interesting is that it has been debated on completely different levels. Judges have disagreed on the issue while dealing with

---

[322] For a general account of how comparative law can assist in the resolution of legal problems, see e.g. Andenas and Fairgrieve, 'Intent on making mischief: seven ways of using comparative law'.
[323] Milanovic, 'The ICJ and Evolutionary Treaty Interpretation'.
[324] Statement of Mr Bartos, ILC (n. 208) 202 para. 53, who explicitly mentioned one of the most important scholars in that discourse during his discussion of intertemporal problems. Interestingly, the discourse about the interpretation of the *Code Civil* was mentioned at the First Vienna Conference (n. 237) Delegate Verosta (Austria) 212 para. 13.

concrete cases.[325] Yet, judges also gave statements outside the judicial context.[326] The stance taken towards this issue has played a role in the election of Supreme Court judges and is frequently the subject of congressional hearings. In addition to that, there is a vast and rich amount of literature.[327] The basic dispute underlying the discussion is whether the interpreter is bound by the original meaning[328] of the Constitution or whether he or she can possibly assert a changed meaning. While originalists generally claim that the meaning at the time the Constitution was drafted and declared is determinative, non-originalists maintain that the meaning of the Constitution can be changed by subsequent interpreters even if the original meaning had been different. The labels of 'originalism' and 'non-originalism' designate, however, a great variety of different approaches and arguments that can only roughly be described here. The terms 'originalism' and 'originalist' are *neologisms* that have been coined by Paul Brest, who began his famous refutation of originalism in the following manner:

> By 'originalism' I mean the familiar approach to constitutional adjudication that accords binding authority to the text of the Constitution or the intentions of its adopters ... The most widely accepted justification for originalism is simply that the Constitution is the supreme law of the land ... Originalism may be supported by more instrumental rationales as well: Adherence to the text and original understanding arguably constrains the discretion of decision-makers and assures that the Constitution will be interpreted consistently over time. The most extreme forms of originalism are 'strict textualism' (or literalism) and 'strict intentionalism.' A strict textualist purports to construe words and phrases very narrowly and precisely. For the strict intentionalist, 'the whole aim of construction, as applied to a provision of the Constitution, is ... to ascertain and give effect to the intent of its framers and the people who adopted it'.[329]

---

[325] The way in which the US courts deal with the matter is discussed by Horwitz, 'Foreword' 30; Gillman, 'The Collapse of Constitutional Originalism' 191; Fassbender, *The United Nations Charter as the Constitution of the International Community* 22–6.

[326] See especially the speeches cited in the first part of Calabresi and Scalia, *Originalism*.

[327] See further references in Falk, 'On Treaty Interpretation and the New Haven Approach' 1085; Goldford, *The American Constitution and the Debate over Originalism*; Huscroft and Miller (eds.), *The Challenge of Originalism*.

[328] The term meaning is used in that context as comprising both the original intent as well as the original understanding.

[329] Brest, 'The Misconceived Quest for the Original Understanding' 204. See the discussion of the inception of the doctrine but also the previous use of the terms original meaning and original intention, see Goldford, *The American Constitution and the Debate over Originalism* 108.

This summary and conceptualisation of different approaches to constitutional interpretation represents the major shift that was happening in the 1980s in originalist thinking. The focus at this time was not on original understanding but on the original intention. Traditionally, interpretation focused on the original intentions either of the framers of the Constitution or its ratifiers or both.[330] Later, the focus shifted to the original understanding, i.e. the way in which the Constitution was understood in public. In contrast, non-originalists regard the Constitution as a living instrument. It was the task of interpreters, particularly judges, to make the text fit for the circumstances of the time of interpretation. A strict form of originalism would contend that ambiguities and gaps have to be determined by political actors and not by the courts.[331] Certainly, changes in meaning through interpretation are possible if one starts out from originalist premises: the clearest of those cases is where there is an original intention that the term in question was to change its meaning. Yet, other approaches found other ways to accommodate change.[332] Keith Whittington, amongst others,[333] developed a particular concept of construction.[334] According to him, construction is distinct from interpretation in that it is a political as well as creative enterprise that is, nevertheless, subordinate to the text.[335] Construction can only happen in the face of ambiguities or gaps in the text. But even within those confines, there is room for flexibility and change.[336] In the field of construction, the law is not merely adapted to societal circumstances, it is a tool in the hands of the interpreter: 'The Constitution empowers political actors to alter their social and institutional environment. The meaning of the Constitution is also a very real prize of political struggle.'[337] The power of the courts is, however, limited to interpretation.[338]

An interesting attempt to bridge the gap between originalism and non-originalism is the use of the metaphor of translation, which was

---

[330] Solum, 'What Is Originalism?' 32.
[331] Bork, 'Neutral Principles and Some First Amendment Problems' 11.
[332] A summary of those strategies is given by Strang, 'Originalism and the "Challenge of Change"' 927.
[333] Solum, 'The Interpretation-Construction Distinction' 95.
[334] There are of course different concepts. For another interesting approach which defines interpretation rather as what was termed application in the international legal discourse, see *ibid.*
[335] Whittington, *Constitutional Construction* 3–8.   [336] *Ibid.* 14.   [337] *Ibid.* 18.
[338] Whittington, *Constitutional Interpretation* 12.

elaborated by Lawrence Lessig.[339] He basically tries to include originalist thinking into a method to update the Constitution. For him, the elements of interpretation comprise the text and the context. The problem of whether to change meanings arises in particular when the context changes and departs from the original textual meaning.[340] Lessig describes originalism as a one-step process aiming at the original meaning in its original context. He, however, adds a second step in which he 'translates' the meaning into the new context.[341] Translation denotes the adaptation from one context to another.[342] The authority of the interpreter rests on changes in the context, which necessitate a change in the rules.[343] This approach he describes as follows:

> [T]he practice of translation moves in two stages: First, understanding the contexts between which the translator must move; and second, locating something called equivalence between the two contexts. In finding equivalence, the practice must first specify the sense in which translations for that practice are equivalent; it must acknowledge the necessity of creativity; and finally, it may have reasons to constrain creativity with an ethic of humility.[344]

While construction departs from an originalist premise, translation is rather non-originalist. Both theories try to integrate the opposite approach into their view to achieve a balance. Both try to set out conditions under which the meaning of the law ought to change. Since those theories are rather directly opposed, it is necessary to have a look at the arguments that are advanced for and against the positions.[345] Those arguments can be categorised as doctrinal and normative.[346] Doctrinally, it is in fact originalism that is at the centre of the discussion. With regard to original intentions, it is contended that there is nothing like a collective intention and, even if there was one, it would be impossible to ascertain it.[347] With

---

[339] Lessig, 'Fidelity in Translation' 1165; Lessig, 'Understanding Changed Readings' 395; Lessig, 'Reading the Constitution in Cyberspace' 896; Lessig, 'Fidelity and Constraint' 1365.
[340] See the summary at Lessig, 'Fidelity in Translation' 1214.
[341] On the notion of translation, see Lessig, 'Fidelity and Constraint' 1371.
[342] Lessig, 'Fidelity in Translation' 1189.   [343] Ibid. 1193.   [344] Ibid. 1211.
[345] For attempts to summarise the arguments, see Farber, 'The Originalism Debate'; Goldford, *The American Constitution and the Debate over Originalism*.
[346] This is based upon but not entirely consistent with the structure of Farber, 'The Originalism Debate'.
[347] Brest, 'The Misconceived Quest for the Original Understanding' 213; Farber, 'Disarmed by Time' 178. An attempt to rebut those arguments is made by Kay, 'Adherence to the Original Intentions in Constitutional Adjudication' 236.

regard to the original understanding, there are methodological problems in connection with historical evidence, which is said to be uncertain and inconclusive.[348] These arguments try to show that originalism could not effectively limit the discretion of judges and create the alleged interpretive fidelity. An interesting argument tries to beat originalism at its own game and to contend that the drafters of the Constitution did not intend to give an originalist meaning to the Constitution but to make change possible.[349] If one starts to look for the historical intentions of the framers of the Constitution in that regard, this could of course also provide arguments in favour of originalism.[350] Non-originalism has attained less coherence, which is used as a conceptual critique against it, since it is not clear how it would replace originalism. There are many different opinions on how to read the law and what factors or values could be recognised in the process of treaty interpretation.[351] Even though there are different strands of originalism, one could say that non-originalism is even more diverse and fails to provide even a roughly coherent framework. Bruce Ackerman, to name just one important and influential example, develops the concept of a dualist democracy and distinguishes ordinary from higher law-making.[352] He sees changes in the original meaning justified if there was consent of the public sovereign. David Strauss in contrast wants to base the living constitution approach on the common law method, which he sees as part of American doctrine.[353] This would allow for legal certainty but also for a certain amount of creativity since the judge could take into account notions of equity and justice. Others stress that law ought to follow the evolution of society or moral standards, but do not set out how those circumstances should be taken account of in the legal system. In essence, there is no agreed way or method that would explain how and under which circumstances the Constitution evolves and, further, no way to justify such a result legally.

---

[348] An account is given by Farber, 'The Originalism Debate' 1087. For a discussion of other problems, see Farber, 'Disarmed by Time' 175.
[349] This position is argued in great detail by Powell, 'The Original Understanding of Original Intent' 885.
[350] See the arguments made by Lofgren, 'The Original Understanding of Original Intent' 77.
[351] Scalia, 'Originalism: The Lesser Evil' 855.
[352] Ackerman, *We the People* 6–7. See the discussion by Strang, 'Originalism and the "Challenge of Change"' 941.
[353] Strauss, *The Living Constitution* 46, 80.

Several normative arguments are put forward in favour of originalism. The most important argument, however, is the defence of originalism with reference to democratic constitutionalism and legitimacy. The arguments are, first, based on the notion that the making of the Constitution was the foundational act by which people exercised their sovereignty to provide for the basic rules of politics. This is the reason why one would always look first to the meaning as it stood at this time. Originalists believe that changes of this meaning should be reserved for the democratic process as it is defined in the constitutional provisions on amendment.[354] From this point of view, changes which are made by the judiciary would in effect circumvent and weaken the democratic process since, arguably, there has never been any agreement to give a changed meaning to the Constitution and judges would, therefore, violate public sovereignty.[355] This is why originalists would regard judicial activity that knowingly or unknowingly goes beyond the original meaning of the Constitution as illegitimate. This is based upon the premise that judicial activity would then replace what was considered to be the agreed process of modification of the Constitution. In this sense, originalism purports to reinforce the political process by constraining the judiciary. This contention is of course disputed on various grounds. The most important counter-argument is that there is a need to update the Constitution, which is sometimes expressed with the metaphor that the American society should not be 'governed by the dead hand of the past'.[356] The argument that there are needs of society actually works in two ways: first, it is argued that, for reasons of justice or for mere social needs, the text of the Constitution has to be updated.[357] On the other hand, it is alleged that this was a way to ensure that the Constitution itself retains its force to be the guiding document for the determination of the basic political questions within society.[358]

We can see from this debate, which is summarised by Table 1, that the choice of the temporal focus is decisive. If one allows for updates, there is

---

[354] Rehnquist, 'Notion of a Living Constitution' 407.
[355] Embedding this argument in the role of the courts to limit the powers of the executive as well as the legislative power: Bork, *The Tempting of America* 139–41.
[356] Grano, 'Judicial Review and a Written Constitution in a Democratic Society' 52. A variety of perspectives in relation to this problem is developed at the special Symposium introduced by Rosen, 'Introduction' 1081.
[357] Miller, 'Notes on the Concept of the Living Constitution' 884.
[358] Strang, 'Originalism and the "Challenge of Change"' 933; Goldford, *The American Constitution and the Debate over Originalism* 57.

Table 1 *Discourse on originalism*

	Originalism	Non-originalism	VCLT
Goal	Original intent/ original understanding	Current meaning	Is there a fixed temporal focus?
Methodological problems	Ascertainment	Agreed method	Under what circumstances can the interpretation change?
Middle views	Construction	Translation	

also the question of how those updates can be achieved. While the whole debate on originalism broadens our understanding, it hardly solves the issue. Therefore, we should revisit the second discourse.

2.4.2 Méthode scientifique *and* méthode evolutive: Ways of re-reading the French Code Civil

In the considerations concerning intertemporal law, there was a direct reference to a famous French legal discourse.[359] This discourse directly concerning the question of changes through interpretation was taking place at the beginning of the twentieth century. The *Code Civil* was one of the most influential codifications of civil law in legal history. At the outset, the interpretation of the Code by judges as well as by academic treatise was based on a mere logical and systematic understanding.[360] Basic concepts were defined and distinguished from other concepts. There was a strong belief that all legal questions could be answered in this deductive fashion.[361]

Changing social conditions, however, called this method of interpretation into question. Industrialisation and the beginning of mass production

---

[359] Statement of Mr Bartos, ILC (n. 208) 202 para. 53, who explicitly mentioned one of the most important scholars in that discourse during his discussion of intertemporal problems. Interestingly, the discourse about the interpretation of the *Code Civil* was mentioned at the First Vienna Conference (n. 237) Delegate Verosta (Austria) 212 para. 13.

[360] Vogenauer, *Die Auslegung von Gesetzen in England und auf dem Kontinent* (vol. 1) 476; Fikentscher, *Methoden des Rechts: Frühe und religiöse Rechte - Romanischer Rechtskreis* (Vol. 1) 436–7.

[361] Vogenauer, *Die Auslegung von Gesetzen in England und auf dem Kontinent* (vol. 1) 476.

saw a departure from many social facts assumed by the *Code Napoleon*. François Gény, a legal scholar, was very aware of the need to adapt law to changing social conditions and considered this as a major task of jurisprudence. He observed that the *Code Civil* represented a merger of different legal acts, customs and traditions into one single document, which was only interpreted based on the literal meaning and the relation to the other terms.[362] Gény deconstructed this approach to interpretation. Referring to Rudolf von Jhering,[363] he gave a precise description of the existing legal method, which he related to the codification movement.[364] Since the traditional reasoning was based only on logical deduction, he argued that it failed to account for social reality as well as the requirements of justice.[365] This had a consequence for the capacity of the law to adapt and change.[366] Hence, his key argument ran as follows:

> En substituant aux éléments, vraiment subtantiels de la vie du droit, aux motifs moraux, psychologiques, économiques, politiques et sociaux, qui animent le monde juridique, des notions techniques, abstraites, froides et vides de réalité féconde, notre interpretation s'est fait un système, tout entier en formules et en catégories pures; et, combiné avec l'excès d'influence attribué à la codification moderne, ce système a rendu la jurisprudence scientifique, non pas seulement stérile, mais, souvent même, irrèmèdiablement rebelle au progrès.[367]

Gény went on to identify analogy and exclusion as basic logical processes underlying the methods of doctrinal interpretation.[368] If a question of interpretation arose, both of these processes would be available, but the doctrinal rules of interpretation could give no guidance as to which of the processes ought to be chosen.[369] In these situations, the interpreter would have to look at the different elements of social life and inquire into the moral, political and economic implications in order to arrive at a decision.

To provide for such possibilities, Gény offered an alternative model for the process of interpretation, which he structured in three steps.[370] The

---

[362] Gény, *Méthode d'interprétation et sources en droit privé positif: Essai critique* (vol. 1) 22-3.
[363] See for example the following references: *ibid.* 125, 178-9 and 336. For a general comparison of the doctrines, see Fikentscher, *Methoden des Rechts: Frühe und religiöse Rechte – Romanischer Rechtskreis* (vol. 1) 483.
[364] Gény, *Méthode d'interprétation et sources en droit privé positif: Essai critique* (vol. 1) 72.
[365] *Ibid.* 188.   [366] *Ibid.* 148.   [367] *Ibid.*   [368] *Ibid.* 194.   [369] *Ibid.* 199.
[370] Vogenauer, *Die Auslegung von Gesetzen in England und auf dem Kontinent* (vol. 1) 331.

first step is the ordinary process of interpretation. If there was no result within that process, the interpreter had, second, to look to customary law. If this in turn did not help, it was then permissible to engage in what he called free scientific inquiry ('*libre recherche scientifique*'). As to the process of interpretation, Gény departed from a subjective understanding and sought to establish the intentions of the drafters of the Code.[371] In the absence of an ascertainable will of the legislator,[372] the interpreter had to look for customary law which was reintroduced by Gény as a formal source.[373] Jurisprudence as well as doctrine gained great importance at the third step, the free scientific inquiry. In this process, the judge would act as a legislator and fill gaps in the existing law through an act of balancing. He would consider the autonomy of the individual, public order and the just balance between competing interests.[374] He was constrained by scientific methods,[375] but there was a certain element of choice since he was to act like a legislator in that he created completely new rules and did not ascribe meanings to terms in legal instruments.[376] Those methods would lead him to objectively ascertainable truths, which could also not be ignored by legislators.[377]

A similar approach was put forward by Raymond Saleilles, who also saw that there was a need for change in the methods of interpretation of the Code.[378] In a foreword to Gény's famous book, he puts it very vividly:

> Et il fallait que le droit se pliât à ce monde nouveau, qu'il donnât satisfaction à cette justice nouvelle, dont le principe reste immuable, amis qui, pour rester la justice, doit se plier elle-même aux transformation économiques et sociales qui se produisent![379]

However, Saleilles had a different conception which he based upon the notion of evolution.[380] He stressed that the act of interpretation was an

---

[371] Gény, *Méthode d'interprétation et sources en droit privé positif* (vol. 1) 266, 293.
[372] *Ibid.* 300.   [373] *Ibid.* 316ff.
[374] *Ibid.* (vol. 2) 90–2; Vogenauer, *Die Auslegung von Gesetzen in England und auf dem Kontinent* (vol. 1) 332.
[375] Gény, *Méthode d'interprétation et sources en droit privé positif* (vol. 1) 78 and (vol. 2) 78.
[376] *Ibid.* (vol. 1) 188 and (vol. 2) 188.   [377] *Ibid.* (vol. 2) 102.
[378] On this topic generally, see the very concise summary by Vogenauer, *Die Auslegung von Gesetzen in England und auf dem Kontinent* (vol. 1) 334.
[379] See the introduction to Gény, *Méthode d'interprétation et sources en droit privé positif* (vol. 1) xv.
[380] See the introduction to *ibid.* (Vol. 1) xix; Gaudemet, 'L'oeuvre de Saleilles et l'oeuvre de Gény en méthodologie juridique et en philosophie du droit' 6.

objective inquiry. In this inquiry, it was the task of the judge to update the meaning of the text in accordance with evolving social standards. On a rather theoretical level, he achieved this by relying on a dynamic understanding of Stammler's changing natural law.[381] Emphasising the separation of law and morals, he had to link his ideas to legal method in a way that made extra-legal considerations ascertainable. To achieve this aim, he structured the process of interpretation in two steps. The first step consists of the literal and systemic interpretation. If this did not yield useful results, the judge then had, in the second step, three choices. He could resort to analogies, to the collective legal consciousness or to comparative law.[382] Comparative law would function to make the common law of mankind (*'droit commun de l'humanité civilisée'*) visible, through which one could arrive at universal legal principles.[383]

Saleilles used the notion of a collective juridical conscience, which he equated with the public opinion, in particular as means for the law to follow economic and societal transformations.[384] In his opinion, analogies were not based upon the will of the legislator but upon an external purpose which he calls practical purpose or purpose of equity.[385] These purposes functioned as the ultimate justification of analogous application of the law.[386] Calling his approach *libre évolution scientifique*, he explicitly rejected Gény's approach. On a more general level, he saw Gény as embracing rather universal values.[387] Methodologically, he accused him of giving too much discretion to judges.[388] Saleilles sought in contrast to base his three methods of evolution on objectively ascertainable social facts. Stefan Vogenauer has convincingly shown that the approaches of Gény and Saleilles are closer than Saleilles was ready to admit.[389] Gény also structured the scientific research in a preconceived process of balancing, so the interpreter was not totally free.[390] As compared to Saleilles, he added customary law as another layer the interpreter would have to take account of. His concept of custom in essence fulfilled the same function as Saleilles's collective juridical consciousness.[391] On the other hand, it cannot be denied that deductions from public morality or comparative law will in practice allow a great leeway for interpreters.

---

[381] Saleilles, 'École historique et droit naturel' 97.   [382] Ibid. 106.   [383] Ibid. 111.
[384] Ibid. 108.   [385] Ibid. 106.   [386] Ibid. 107.   [387] Ibid. 90.   [388] Ibid. 102.
[389] Vogenauer, *Die Auslegung von Gesetzen in England und auf dem Kontinent* (vol. 1) 334.
[390] Gény, *Méthode d'interprétation et sources en droit privé positif* (vol. 1) 151ff; Gény, *Méthode d'interprétation et sources en droit privé positif* (vol. 2) 151ff.
[391] Ibid. (vol. 2) 80.

In the end, the difference might have only been the emphasis of freedom or restraint in the process of interpretation. While the model developed by Saleilles influenced the jurisprudence of French courts,[392] Art. 1 of the Swiss Code could be seen as codification of the approach developed by Gény.[393]

In order to summarise, it is first interesting that both depart from different notions of the goals of interpretation. It could be asked also in the context of the Vienna Convention whether the goal of interpretation was to ascertain the intentions of the parties or the purpose of the law. Both approaches include various means of interpretation such as comparative law or free scientific inquiry. The fact that there are different means of interpretation suggests that we ought to look to the VCLT to find out what kinds of means were employed there. It is also significant that both authors envisaged interpretation as a multi-step process and created a hierarchy between the means of interpretation. The choice of means also determines to what extent the process is open to extra-legal considerations. According to Gény, almost everything could be included in the process of treaty interpretation while Saleilles was much more conservative in that regard. Again the comparison with the French discourse of the last century, which is summarised in Table 2, is very enlightening, but instead of providing a solution, it adds to the uncertainty as to how to deal with those problems in accordance with the Vienna Convention.

---

[392] Vogenauer, *Die Auslegung von Gesetzen in England und auf dem Kontinent* (vol. 1) 335.
[393] Swiss Civil Code of 10 December 1907 (Status as on 1 January 2012) available at www.admin.ch/ch/e/rs/210/index.html (accessed 16 October 2012).

Article 1
A. Application of the law
   1 The law applies according to its wording or interpretation to all legal questions for which it contains a provision.
   2 In the absence of a provision, the Court shall decide in accordance with customary law and, in the absence of customary law, in accordance with the rule that it would make as legislator.
   3 In doing so, the Court shall follow established doctrine and case law.

Interestingly, it was Saleilles, who introduced Gény's book to Eugen Huber who played a very important part in the making of the Swiss Civil Code and he acknowledged in a letter that Gény would influence the first part of the code: see Aragoneses, *Recht im Fin de siècle* 37–8.

Table 2 Méthode scientifique et méthode évolutive

	Gény: *méthode scientifique*	Saleilles: *méthode evolutive*	Questions to the VCLT
Goal	Intentions of the parties	Purpose	What is the goal of interpretation according to the VCLT?
Process	Three steps: interpretation custom free scientific inquiry	Two steps: interpretation *opinio communis*	Is there a hierarchy amongst the means of interpretation?
Further means of interpretation	Free act of balancing	Objective material considerations	Can there be further means of interpretation?

2.4.3 Concluding outlook: Discourses in the UK and Germany

The discourses that were referred to so far enhance the comprehension of the problem to be dealt with, yet no clear-cut solution is provided. Two further examples show that the issue is still under consideration in other jurisdictions. There can be a general disagreement on whether the meaning of a legal text can be changed through interpretation. Bjorge points to the disagreements on the intertemporal question in the common law.[394] While Baroness Hale acknowledges that the common law allows for evolutive interpretation,[395] Lord Neuberger considers the interpretative practice of changing meanings as transgressing previous limits on interpretation which could, therefore, not be considered as belonging to the common law method of interpretation.[396] On the other hand, there has been a longstanding discourse in German academia on how constitutional change comes about.[397] It is interesting that, from early on,

---

[394] Bjorge, *The Evolutionary Interpretation of Treaties* 107 n. 336.
[395] Hale, 'Common Law and Convention Law' 534.
[396] Neuberger, 'The Role of Judges in Human Rights Jurisprudence' 5–6 paras. 12–13.
[397] The discussion is focused around the term '*Verfassungswandel*'. For summaries, see Badura, 'Verfassungsänderung, Verfassungswandel, Verfassungsgewohnheitsrecht' 63–5; von Arnauld, 'Möglichkeiten und Grenzen dynamischer Interpretation von Rechtsnormen' 488.

the discussion was not about whether such interpretative change was allowed.[398] The discourse rather circled around the question what the central concept of '*Verfassungswandel*' ought to mean,[399] what implications that concept could and should have,[400] which actors were relevant,[401] or how to deal with situations in which changes of the constitution through interpretation are in issue.[402] This problem has led scholars to rethink the whole process of interpretation in a very productive way.[403] These examples substantiate the findings of the review of the current discourse in international law as well as its historical forerunners and comparable discourses from several national jurisdictions.

From Alberico Gentili until right before the Vienna Convention, authors dealt with problems of stasis and evolution. What we have found for the discourse after the Vienna Convention is also true for the prevailing discourse: the approaches are diametrically opposed and there is no real discussion and argument about the best approach but only assertions. The discourse is, therefore, polyphonic. In comparative law, we came across proper discourses that justified as well as attacked different stances on interpretation. Yet, this increased the uncertainty whether and how we can deal with questions of stasis and evolution in international law. Therefore, we need another way to find out how to deal with those issues.

---

[398] Laband, *Die Wandlungen der deutschen Reichsverfassung*. See also the early descriptive and comparative treatment by Jellinek, *Verfassungsänderung und Verfassungswandlung*.

[399] For a narrow construction of the term, see Böckenförde, 'Anmerkungen zum Begriff Verfassungswandel' 3; for a wider understanding, including what is conceived here as referential evolution see Walter, 'Hüter oder Wandler der Verfassung' 524–8.

[400] Voßkuhle, 'Gibt es und wozu nutzt eine Lehre vom Verfassungswandel?' 450.

[401] Walter, 'Hüter oder Wandler der Verfassung' 531–49; Mayer, 'Verfassungswandel durch Annäherung? Der Europäische Gerichtshof, das Bundesverfassungsgericht und das Grundgesetz'.

[402] Byrde, *Verfassungsentwicklung* 283–94; Hesse, 'Grenzen der Verfassungswandlung' 136–41.

[403] Häberle, 'Zeit und Verfassung' 111; Müller, *Juristische Methodik* 140. See also the discussion by Folke-Schuppert, 'Verfassungswandel im Kontext' 346; and Byrde, *Verfassungsentwicklung*.

3

Mode of inquiry: functional reconstruction

3.1. The problem of circularity

In academic discourse there is no agreement as to how to deal with questions of stasis and evolution; the only thing agreed is the text of Arts. 31 and 32 VCLT. Looking deeper into the VCLT, we have to face a very complex and difficult question: How do we interpret the rules on interpretation?[404]

Given that the VCLT is an international treaty, the first inclination could be to apply the rules of interpretation to the treaty containing those rules.[405] We would then interpret it like any other treaty norm. To apply the rules of interpretation to themselves is not feasible because there is a manifest danger that it results in an infinite circle or in complete arbitrariness on the part of the interpreter.[406] The danger of circularity has been observed by a delegate at the Vienna Conference and later by authors.[407] Koskenniemi reframed the problem in relation to tacit consent and interpretation, he pointed to the

---

[404] On the fact that the rules on interpretation have to be interpreted, see Dworkin, *Law's Empire* 49; Villiger, 'The 1969 Vienna Convention on the Law of Treaties' 63; Bianchi, 'Textual Interpretation and (International) Law' 48; Gardiner, *Treaty Interpretation*.

[405] See for example Schwarzenberger, 'Myths and Realities of Treaty Interpretation' 6; Wetzel and Rauschning, *The Vienna Convention on the Law of Treaties* 19; Greschek, *Die evolutive Auslegung völkerrechtlicher Verträge am Beispiel des GATT* 53.

[406] For the problem that the rule on interpretation is itself ambiguous, see Pehar, 'International Law of Interpretation'.

[407] This was already observed at the first Vienna Conference by the delegate Kripsis (Greece) First Vienna Conference (n. 237) 170 para. 7. See also Klabbers, 'International Legal Histories' 270. For a general account of the problem of self-applicability in the Convention, see Villiger, 'The 1969 Vienna Convention on the Law of Treaties' 38. The problem of self-applicability in relation to rules of amendment is discussed by Suber, *The Paradox of Self-Amendment*. For a general account of the problem of how to end processes of argumentation, see Habermas, *Between Facts and Norms* 226–7.

infinite regress if the 'problem solver' was to look to the tacit consent 'behind' the tacit consent.[408]

To give just one example,[409] suppose that there is a problem of treaty interpretation of a treaty like the UN Charter. To determine this problem on the first level, we look into the VCLT for guidance. In the course of reading Art. 31 VCLT, the question comes up how the words 'object and purpose' in Art. 31(1) VCLT should be interpreted. So we have a problem on the second level and move to the third level by applying the VCLT to itself. We could look at the preparatory works of the treaty and see whether we can derive conclusions concerning the object and purpose from them. Then, we could also look to today's social exigencies and the challenges the treaty faces in the present. Going back to the Vienna Convention to interpret the notion of object and purpose, we would inquire into the different techniques contained therein. We could look at how subsequent practice, as provided for in Art. 31(3)(b) VCLT, evolved on that question. While doing that, the question might arise whether we can only take into account the practice of states or also the practice of international organisations. This would then be a question on the third level. To determine this, we would have to go back to the Vienna Convention, dealing with it from the perspective of the fourth level and continue to do this every time a question arises. It can very well happen that this leads to an endless chain of questions.

---

[408] Koskenniemi, *From Apology to Utopia* 344–5. It reads: 'But such strategy leaved unexplained why the interpretation of the content of this rule by Y was given preference to the interpretation of it by X. To be sure, it was argued that X had consented, albeit tacitly. But how do we justify the point that its conduct was such as to allow this presumption? This could be done if there existed a rule to the effect that a certain conduct, namely that adopted by X during the negotiations, is deemed to express consent. Quite apart from the fact that no such rule exist – as the same conduct might have a different meaning in a differing context – even if it existed it would still have to receive ascending justification from both X and Y. But also this rule could be challenged. The problem solver would then need to construct a tacit consent also behind it. And so on, *ad infinitum*.' It is not possible to do full justice to Koskenniemi's whole chapter on interpretation, yet, in the present context and the pages before the quote, two observations ought to be made. The first is that no mention is made of the VCLT. Even though the VCLT does not solve the problem of circularity, it changes it significantly as there is now a rule. Instead, Koskenniemi relies heavily on the distinction between subjective and objective interpretation, even though he deconstructed that distinction in the very beginning.

[409] For a similar example concerning the preparatory works, see Briggs, 'The Travaux Préparatoires of the Vienna Convention on the Law of Treaties' 707.

Among the many authors interpreting the rules on interpretation,[410] the most structured and elaborate analysis is provided for by Richard Gardiner.[411] He determines the meaning of each part of the provision by using the rule contained in the Vienna Convention as he understands it. As an argument against the danger of circularity, he alludes to the fact that the rules contained in the Vienna Convention are also part of customary law.[412] This important observation does not solve the riddle we are facing: if there was a rule in customary law, this rule can be ambiguous and, therefore, subject to interpretation.[413] The same problem would arise. Even if we suppose that the rule of customary law had a different content than the rule in the VCLT, the problem would be only solved if the other term was perfectly determinate and clear and could decide every question. Unless it is proven that there is such a norm, there will always be the danger of circularity. To cut a long story short, the problem of circularity applies to all rules of interpretation; the problem in the Vienna Convention is only representative of a wider issue.

As *Ludwig Wittgenstein* showed in his *Philosophical Investigations*, the mere interpretation of words with other words would result in an infinite regress without ever solving the problem what the rules guiding language are.[414] As an analogy to this consequence, we could assume that the rules

---

[410] See for example Sorel and Eveno, 'Art. 31 VCLT'; Bouthillier, 'Art. 32' 234; Villiger, 'The 1969 Vienna Convention on the Law of Treaties' 113.

[411] Gardiner, *Treaty Interpretation* 9.   [412] *Ibid.* 9.

[413] On the interpretation of customary law, see Bleckmann, 'Zur Feststellung und Auslegung von Völkergewohnheitsrecht' 504.

[414] Wittgenstein, *Philosophical Investigations* para. 201. The respective para. reads:

> This was our paradox: no course of action could be determined by a rule, because every course of action can be made out to accord with the rule. The answer was: if everything can be made out to accord with the rule, then it can also be made out to conflict with it. And so there would be neither accord nor conflict here. It can be seen that there is a misunderstanding here from the mere fact that in the course of our argument we give one interpretation after another; as if each one contended us at least for a moment, until we thought of yet another standing behind it. What this shows is that there is a way of grasping a rule which is *not* an *interpretation*, but which is exhibited in what we call 'obeying the rule' and 'going against it' in actual cases.

For an ample discussion of that argument in the legal context, see Stone, 'Focusing the Law' 51. For an application to the rule of interpretation in international law, see *ibid.* 107. For a contextualisation of this and related argument in the context of the ascertainment of sources, see D'Aspremont, *Formalism and the Sources of International Law* 198–201. A discussion of the argument generally is provided for by Fogelin, *Taking*

of interpretation cannot themselves be interpreted. They are part of the activity of interpretation, and the interpreter acts upon and through them. The only way out of this would be to allow interpreters having the competence to interpret treaties with binding force to determine the content of the VCLT without justifying their result. They would not go beyond the second level. This would actually work insofar as there is one interpreter that has the ultimate competence to decide. If this is not the case, rival claims could oppose each other and it would – in the absence of any argument – be impossible to determine the correct result.

Interpreting the rule of interpretation, we face harsh consequences: Such an exercise would be either circular or trivial: circular since there is an indefinite need to interpret the rules; trivial because the only way out of this is an assertion without arguments. In the absence of anyone determining the rules authoritatively, those assertions could be opposed without any possibility to be resolved. International courts and tribunals merely cite the rules of interpretation and act upon them. It is hard to find an example in which the rules of interpretation have been interpreted themselves properly and in a controversial manner outlining different alternatives. Even if there were such cases, those cases would be in the absolute minority. This is practically reasonable in the judicial context: Courts have the authority to interpret, and the parties need to adapt to their method of interpretation. If a court would deliberate extensively on how the rules on interpretation are to be interpreted, this would be perceived as a sign of indecisiveness and weakness and would offer one more opportunity to disagree with the court. In essence, legal, theoretical and practical considerations show that the interpretation of rules is either not feasible or not to be recommended. The alternative would be to observe the practice of courts and tribunals and to see what they make out of the rules. Yet, this could be unsatisfactory since there would be no way to criticise them if the exact meaning of the rules cannot be determined. International courts and tribunals would be free to use the rules of interpretation in any way they liked. We have seen that the suggested solutions on the intertemporal question exactly fitted the scheme developed here: They are either observations of justificatory patterns used in judicial practice or assertions that are sensible but not backed up by arguments. In this way, the methodological discourse has evaded the pitfalls of circular interpretation. The lack of argument has,

Wittgenstein at His Word 15–21. This intricate relationship between interpretation and application is also observed by Gadamer, *Truth and Method* 305.

however, prohibited an agreed-upon solution among the many interesting and workable suggestions.

Yet, analytical jurisprudence might offer a way out of this dilemma: H. L. A. Hart distinguished between the different perspectives a legal scholar takes: 'the "external" and the "internal points of view"'.[415] The internal view would be the perspective of those to whom the rules apply, while the external perspective is the perspective of an observer who looks only at the conduct of interpreters such as judges. Instead of choosing one of the views, Hart alludes to how difficult it is 'to remember the presence of both points of view and not to define one of them out of existence'.[416] Koskenniemi has framed a similar observation and opposed formalists and realists.[417]

If we apply this distinction to our problem, we can associate the process of interpretation with the internal perspective: Determining the meaning in a certain manner. The extreme external perspective leaves rules aside and just focuses on the agent who interprets; by contrast, the extreme internal perspective looks only at the rules and ignores the agent.[418] As called for by Hart, we seek to mitigate between the two extremes, and to do so, we turn to functional reconstruction.[419]

3.2. Functional reconstruction

The question to be dealt with here arises out of the context of legal interpretation. Even though it does sound similar and is certainly inspired by other dichotomies such as facts and norms[420] or normativity and concreteness,[421] it is different in that it aims to bring together doctrinal reflection and legal practice about the method of interpretation. This means the question how the rule of interpretation is appreciated and how it is applied.[422]

---

[415] Hart, *The Concept of Law* 89. For an analysis of the fruitfulness of this distinction for issues of interpretation, see Moore, 'Interpreting Interpretation' 26.
[416] Hart, *The Concept of Law* 91.   [417] Koskenniemi, 'Introduction' xi.
[418] For the same dialectic, see Bankowski and others, 'On Method and Methodology' 19.
[419] *Ibid.*
[420] For the respective chapter on interpretation, see Habermas, *Between Facts and Norms* 132. He reconstructs hermeneutical, positivist and realist streams of interpretative methodology.
[421] Koskenniemi, *From Apology to Utopia* 521-2.
[422] D'Aspremont has in a similar manner inquired into norm ascertainment by combining a 'source thesis' which operated with rules with a 'social thesis' which looked at social practice. While he treats a similar problem, there are differences: he talks about the

To achieve this aim, we will have recourse to functional reconstruction. This *Denkbewegung* (movement of thought/way of thinking/ approach) will allow us to achieve a proper account of the rules of treaty interpretation. This requires a structured account of what we will do when we reconstruct the rule contained in the VCLT functionally. Therefore, we will first inquire into the general *Denkbewegung* of reconstruction, apply it to our object, the rules of treaty interpretation, introduce function as guide to the reconstruction, and outline the results of the reconstruction.[423]

Reconstruction is described here as a *Denkbewegung* because it is a certain programme that can be found in different scientific disciplines with common features as well as differences. In linguistics, a reconstruction is undertaken 'not merely to explain historical relationships between present-day languages but in order to find out what the earlier languages themselves were actually like'.[424] In theology, it has been used to distinguish the reading of text from a certain perspective (interpretation) from the historical contextualisation of texts (reconstruction).[425]

The closest approaches to the present endeavour are reconstructions in the theory of sciences, social philosophy, and reconstructions of law and legal theory. In the same way that we reconstruct the method of interpretation and its doctrinal reflection, theorists of science have reconstructed other scientific disciplines.[426] Rudolf Carnap pursued the programme to reconstruct theories with new terms in order to render them more concise and correct.[427] This aptly describes what reconstruction is intended to do: It analyses its object and reframes it in its own terms. Instead of a mere replication, the object is reproduced based on deeper insights and a thorough understanding of the matter.[428] This form of

---

ascertainment of the rules of ascertainment. In the context of the VCLT we have an ascertainable valid legal rule that needs to be interpreted. Yet, our question is also more complex since we have not only one set of practice but two: the interpretive practice in the application of method and the reflection of method by academia (methodology). While D'Aspremont indeed combines both approaches that could also be termed as internal and external perspective, his approach ultimately comes down as an internal perspective: in the end, he reconstructs the practice in order to resolve ambiguities and to finally arrive at formal criteria of law ascertainment: D'Aspremont, *Formalism and the Sources of International Law* 12.

[423] For a general overview of reconstruction, see Scholtz, 'Rekonstruktion' 890.
[424] Fox, *Linguistic Reconstruction* 3.   [425] G. Klein, *Rekonstruktion und Interpretation*.
[426] For an overview, see Mittelstrass, 'Scientific Rationality and its Reconstruction' 89.
[427] Mittelstrass, 'Rationale Rekonstruktion der Wissenschaftsgeschichte' 90.
[428] Habermas, 'What is Universal Pragmatics?' 11.

thinking has been applied to the law and legal science several times. Legal methodology does the very same thing with legal method: understanding what happens when the law is applied and then reframing this understanding in a way that is supposed to be more consistent and coherent than the method that had been applied.

The *Denkbewegung* of reconstruction has also gained ground in legal and social philosophy and legal theory. Law and legal theory have been reconstructed as between the poles of facts and norms[429] or rather normatively guided by freedom as the decisive value.[430] A broad and in-depth study in comparative law on statutory interpretation edited by Neil MacCormick and Robert Summers aimed at carving out parallels and differences between the respective jurisdictions and reconstructed this practice in a more practical sense.[431] Constitutionalism in international law could be seen as another form of reconstructing the international legal order.[432] With regard to interpretation, previous studies have reconstructed interpretative methodology,[433] meaning theoretical accounts of interpretative method. Interpretative methods have also been reconstructed in a comparative manner.[434] What is more, approaches to reconstructing legal arguments in the practice of interpretation have been reviewed and developed by Feteris.[435] From all this, we can conclude that the concept of reconstruction is something which seems to be based on a paradox: To describe something differently without really changing it. It is about reorganising and restating something that is already there in a faithful manner so that it can be better dealt with. This is often the first logical step in comparative activities. It also underlies the process of codification, since it is about reframing existing rules in a systematic way. It could be said that legal doctrine reconstructs the law. The object of the present reconstruction is interpretative method. The question is only how this method ought to be reconstructed.

---

[429] Habermas, *Between Facts and Norms* 132.   [430] Honneth, *Das Recht der Freiheit.*
[431] For them, rational reconstruction justification involves presenting it as 'consisting of structured types of arguments which all belong within a coherent mode of justificatory reasoning'. Bankowski and others, 'On Method and Methodology' 19.
[432] Kleinlein, *Konstitutionalisierung im Völkerrecht* 5. Kleinlein, who elegantly reconstructs the reconstructions, mentions amongst others Peters, 'Compensatory Constitutionalism' 605. For a very similar methodology, see Fassbender, *The United Nations Charter As the Constitution of the International Community* 52.
[433] Habermas, *Between Facts and Norms* 132.
[434] Bankowski and others, 'On Method and Methodology'.
[435] See for the general approach Feteris, *Fundamentals of Legal Argumentation* 10–11.

While the afore-mentioned attempts to reconstruct legal theory or the legal system all resulted in reconstruction, their guiding principles differed. Reconstruction has been understood as mirroring a self-description of the modern law[436] with the aim of establishing its meaning.[437] The law has been analysed under the premises of the principle of freedom.[438] Different national interpretative methodologies have been compared as to their consistency and rationality.[439] These examples show that some reconstructions have something like a guiding principle, a perspective or a certain way of looking at things: They are mostly either rational or normative.[440] Rational reconstructions in the original sense are better descriptions of already existing social facts. Yet, a reconstruction can also have a normative perspective which can uncover the normative sense and the unused normative potential in social practices.[441] Whether to choose a rational or normative perspective is deliberate but not arbitrary. As a starting point, we should remember that there are largely two perspectives on interpretative method.[442] First, there is the perspective of those interpreting in practice, mainly judges using method as a guide in the process of interpretation. Then, there is the methodological perspective of scholars reviewing the practice and re-establishing legal method.[443] In their relation to legal method, those two perspectives carry different expectations towards interpretative method. We shall call them *rule-of-lawyers considerations* and *rulers-of-law considerations*.[444] Those

---

[436] Habermas, *Between Facts and Norms* 82.
[437] Ibid. 132. Yet, Habermas uses reconstruction on several levels. For an overview, see Jørgen Pedersen, 'Habermas' Method: Rational Reconstruction' 457.
[438] Honneth, *Das Recht der Freiheit*.
[439] MacCormick and Summers (eds.), *Interpreting Statutes: A Comparative Study*.
[440] Scholtz, 'Rekonstruktion' 890.
[441] This is mentioned in the second of two very instructive interviews published at www.theorie-blog.de (accessed 19 June 2013). As he admits in the first of those interviews, his book contains no exposition but only justification of his normative reconstruction. This makes the interviews that contain an in-depth discussion of his method even more interesting.
[442] Those two perspectives have been developed in accordance with typical actor perspectives on the matter. Yet, they resemble the general dichotomy of requirements for arguments introduced by Koskenniemi: they ought to be normative and concrete. Koskenniemi, 'Methodology of International Law' 1.
[443] This is, of course, a simplification since interpreters also influence the method significantly. As will become apparent, this simplification is not detrimental for the two perspectives that are being developed to derive from them a guide for interpretation.
[444] Those considerations are attributed to different legal cultures by Vogenauer, *Die Auslegung von Gesetzen in England und auf dem Kontinent* (vol. 1) 223. The decisive difference to Koskenniemi's distinction is that both sets of considerations could be

considerations are regularly value-backed arguments that require first certain features of the method and in a second step certain values. Legal methodology typically advances interpretative method in order to further the rule-of-lawyers considerations. These are to achieve coherence, integrity and clarity of the law, reasonableness of arguments and predictability of the outcomes of interpretation.[445] The considerations do not focus on the single decision but on the legal system as a whole (system-oriented). They are system-oriented in that they advance the rationality of the process. Rulers-of-law considerations are more focused on the case to be decided and the reality on the ground. They stress practicability, workability, flexibility and effective guidance.[446] They aim to achieve a just and satisfactory solution of the single case and justify it *lege artis* (goal-

---

framed as normative and concrete. Compare Koskenniemi, 'Methodology of International Law'. It should also be noted that the notion of practice differs here from Koskenniemi. A practitioner in our context is a person professionally engaged in the interpretation and application of international law outside the academic context. It is not an academic with an interest in practice. This is why the assumed interests here differ from Koskenniemi: 'Introduction' xv.

[445] Those considerations are typically put forward by voices from academia such as Adler, 'The Interpretation of Treaties' 26; Ludwik Ehrlich, 'L'Interprétation des traités' 51; McDougal, 'The International Law Commission's Draft Articles upon Interpretation: Textuality Redivivus' 992; MacCormick, 'Argumentation and Interpretation in Law' 467; Bankowski and others, 'On Method and Methodology' 19; Cremer, 'Regeln der Konventionsinterpretation' 183; Orakhelashvili, *The Interpretation of Acts and Rules in Public International Law* 305; Waibel, 'A Uniform Regime of Treaty Interpretation'.

[446] During the drafting of the VCLT, those considerations were voiced on several levels by practitioners: commenting upon a draft of the ILC, general concerns about a lack of flexibility were voiced by Hungary, ILC, 'Report of the International Law Commission on the work of its 18th session' (4 May–19 July 1966), UN Doc. A/CN.4/SER.A/1966/Add.1 91; The rigidity of the Convention in relation to a specific issue of drafting was criticised by the Netherlands government, ILC, *ibid*. 92. Those concerns were taken up by the Special Rapporteur who emphasised that the rule of interpretation was flexible and that this was important to it, *ibid*. 92. At the first Vienna Conference, the question of rigidity and flexibility was the recurrent theme and one of the most discussed issues in the process. Statements on the issue include 'Summary records of the plenary meetings and of the meetings of the Committee of the Whole' United Nations Conference on the Law of Treaties, First Session (Vienna 26 March–24 May 1968) 182 para. 54. First Vienna Conference (n. 237): Statement of Delegate McDougal (USA) 168 paras. 46–9; Statement of Delegate Jiménez de Aréchaga (Uruguay) 170 para. 66; statement of Delegate Maliti (Tanzania) 173 para. 14; Statement of Delegate Martinez Caro (Spain) 174 para. 32; Statement of Delegate Sinclair (United Kingdom), 177 para. 2; Statement of Delegate Zemanek (Austria) 178 para. 12; Statement Delegate Ruda (Argentina) 180 para. 23; Statement Delegate Ruegger (Switzerland) 180 para. 27; Statement of Delegate Alvarez Tabio (Cuba) 182 para. 43; Delegate Crucho de Almeida (Portugal) 183 para. 57; Statement of Delegate Baden-Semper (Trinidad and Tobago) 183 para. 58.

oriented).[447] Both perspectives are focused on the effect of interpretative method on interpretative practice. One could say that they are focused on the function of interpretative method. Function generally is taken to mean 'contribution of any social practices or institutions to others with which it is interdependent or in which it plays a part'.[448] The function of legal rules plays a great role for comparative method.[449] In this context, it is used as a means of comparing certain rules that seem to be different but have the same effects in the respective jurisdiction.[450] Functional analysis is not foreign to international legal scholarship either: There have been accounts of the function of law in the international community or of the judiciary in international law.[451] Yet, the task of the present inquiry is not to understand the function of law or certain institutions but of interpretative method. In this context, function denotes the effect and utility of that method for the practice of interpretation. Rulers-of-law consideration and rule-of-lawyers considerations provide for the criteria with which we ought to assess the function of interpretative method.

3.3. Functional reconstruction in practice

But first, we have to understand the function of the rule of interpretation. This makes it necessary to describe it precisely. Previous attempts to explain international interpretative method have mostly focused on the terms of Arts. 31 and 32 and interpreted them like any treaty norm. While this produced very valuable insights that are essential for the present study, they often failed to describe three things.

First, there was nothing to contrast the rule of interpretation with. Consequently, it was hard to determine its main features. Second, an explanation of the words in the treaty failed to explain the process of interpretation that is envisaged by the rule. Third, ambiguities in the rule

---

[447] See generally Schneider, *Richterrecht, Gesetzesrecht und Verfassungsrecht* 15. See in relation to justice and evolutive interpretations French, 'Treaty Interpretation and the Incorporation of Extraneous Legal Rules' 286.
[448] Entry on function in Calhoun, *Dictionary of the social sciences* 179.
[449] For a detailed discussion, see Graziadei, 'The Functionalist Heritage'.
[450] Örücü, 'Methodology of comparative law' 562.
[451] Lauterpacht, *The Function of Law in the International Community*; von Bogdandy and Venzke, 'On the functions of International Courts' 49. On early accounts of functional analysis of international law, especially in France, see Koskenniemi, *The gentle civilizer of nations* 274–84. For the social function of international law, see Allott, 'The Concept of Internaional Law'.

MODE OF INQUIRY: FUNCTIONAL RECONSTRUCTION 77

of interpretation cannot be decided conclusively. To determine whether and how changes in interpretation can be justified under the VCLT, it will be necessary to address all of those issues.

The first step of the functional reconstruction will compare the current interpretative method with its historical forerunners. This will point out the main features and the basic structural elements of the VCLT which we will call 'cardinal cores'. Focusing on the cardinal cores, we will try to figure out how the rule of interpretation structures the process of interpretation. The next step will be to take a conventional look at the means of interpretation as described in the text. However, ambiguities will consciously be left open. They will be described as 'interpretative knots', borrowing the use of the term 'knot' from Wittgenstein.[452] The study will then look to all other parts of the Convention for further insights. After establishing the cardinal cores of the rule of interpretation, it will be possible to assess how to deal generally with intertemporal problems. After dealing with the text of the rule, we can see how the different ambiguities play out for questions of stasis and evolution. We can then try to guess which of the suggested solutions fits the function of the rule best. We will then be able to compare the reconstructed rule with the practice of two courts, the International Court of Justice and the European Court of Human Rights. Their jurisprudence will be reviewed closely to arrive at a profile of the respective court.

There is a long way to go and it is necessary to retain the utmost analytical clarity. Therefore, we should lay out the *Denkbewegung* of reconstruction. It results either in the establishment of cardinal cores or of interpretative knots. As previously described, both results are derived from the observation of actual practice. Coinciding practice is termed as a 'cardinal core'. Differing practice will be denoted as an 'interpretative knot'.

Cardinal cores describe the basic structural elements of the rule of interpretation. What makes them basic structural elements is a certain conceptual necessity and regular observance in practice. Conceptual necessity entails the notion that it is a distinguishing feature, a necessary component that needs to be decided and characterises the concept. A method of interpretation is for example characterised by the type of means it uses such as presumptions, principles or maxims. A cardinal core can only be acknowledged as such when there is a consistent

---

[452] Wittgenstein, *Philosophical Remarks* 184 para. 156.

practice in that regard. If we assume that the quality of the rules is also a cardinal core and certain rules are designated as legal rules, the rules' legality could not be taken as cardinal core if they are flatly disobeyed by all interpreting actors. *Interpretative knots* refer to situations in which the internal participants disagree about an interpretation of the rules of interpretation. The competing views, taken separately, might all be consistent but lead to diametrically opposed results. Were we to apply the process of interpretation, we would choose one of the two solutions and give reasons for that. Such a decision is, however, not possible in the process of reconstruction. On the contrary, it is most important to map the disagreement and as far as possible inquire into its underlying structure. If we detect such a problem that has more than one possible outcome, we will call it a 'knot'. The reconstructing observer is faced with the problem that the internal actors are actively pulling the different ends of the ropes. So he or she can study the knot, but cannot unravel it. Looking at the notion of subsequent practice, it is, to give just one of many examples, unclear to what type of actors Art. 31(3)(b) VCLT refers. Is it only state practice, or practice attributable to the state or any kind of practice, no matter who is acting? This problem will be called an 'actor

Table 3 *Possible modes of inquiry*

	Interpretation	Reconstruction	Observation
Goal	Determination of correct and single meaning	Determination of the structure underlying the rules	Determination of patterns of conduct
Method	Rules of interpretation: Arts. 31 and 32 VCLT	Combination of the methods	Quantitative and qualitative methods to assess the behaviour
Nature of methods	Legal rules	Legal as well as scientific methods	Scientific methods
Object of inquiry	Legal text	Interaction between text and behaviour	Behaviour of the actors
Result	Correct meaning	Cardinal cores and interpretative knots	Pattern of behaviour

knot'. The different possible meanings will be shown, and they will be compared as to how they relate to the question of this study.

In the end, we will arrive at a description of the process of interpretation as envisaged by the Convention and the uncertainties attaching to this process. This will allow us to derive from this the function of the Convention. The function will in turn be helpful to see how to deal with the uncertainties, most importantly of course the intertemporal question.

PART II

The rule of interpretation in the VCLT: method and methodology

4

Historical account of the means of interpretation

The first part of the reconstruction aims at reconstructing international interpretative method from a methodological perspective. This means nothing more than looking at doctrinal discourse about how treaties ought to be interpreted. In contrast, we will look in the next part of this book at how the method is used in practice. According to functional reconstruction, we will first identify the cores of the Convention, i.e. how the process is structured. In a second step, we will look at the knots, i.e. doctrinal disputes and uncertainties concerning the techniques of interpretation.

Yet, the first task will be to identify the crucial issues. For this reason, we will be looking into the history of interpretative methodology and contrasting it with the rule of interpretation contained in the VCLT. This will result in a description of the cardinal cores of the process of interpretation as envisaged by the VCLT. We will then have a look at the specific techniques of the VCLT and identify its interpretative knots. After looking at the cardinal cores of the Convention, we will be able to identify the function of the rule of interpretation and relate it to the intertemporal question. After identifying the interpretative knots, we will be able to see the various existing ways of construction. It will then be possible to choose amongst the different possible suggested solutions the one that is in line with the function of the rule of interpretation. In the end, we will look at other provisions of the VCLT and see how those do and can impact upon the process.

4.1. Functional reconstruction in historical perspective

A functional reconstruction can go back further in history than is possible in the ordinary process of treaty interpretation. It cannot only look into the *travaux préparatoires* covering the material leading to the treaty but also the history long before the treaty in question was concluded. This chapter aims at giving a structured account to the history of treaty interpretation, a morphology establishing different layers that also relate to the development of international law as a discipline.[1] Before the Vienna Convention came into force, the task of reflecting interpretative method was fulfilled by doctrinal treatises. They were mainly contained in general textbooks on international law. It was only in the twentieth century that the literature on interpretation began to proliferate and was also contained in journal articles as well as specialised books.[2] The analysis of this material can sharpen our understanding of the rule of interpretation we are actually dealing with. As Bederman puts it emphatically and elegantly: 'Principled methods of treaty construction will triumph only when the mystery fades, but to fashion a unified theory of treaty interpretation, we must revive older canons of construction.'[3] To contrast the other approaches to treaty interpretation with what actually became the rule will guide us to the cardinal cores of the rule contained in the VCLT. We can see that those academic reflections evolved in three phases, namely, the mechanical phase, the flexible phase and the codificatory phase.[4] While the mechanical phase continued throughout the seventeenth and eighteenth century, the flexible phase

---

[1] Weiler defines this as an instrumental and structuralist approach to the history of law: Weiler, 'The Geology of International Law' 547, 548.

[2] Appert, 'De l'interprétation des traités diplomatiques au cours d'un procès' 433; Adler, 'The Interpretation of Treaties'; Hyde, 'Concerning the Interpretation of Treaties' 46; Yü, *The Interpretation of Treaties*; Ludwik Ehrlich, 'L'Interprétation des traités'; Wright, 'The Interpretation of Multilateral Treaties'; Hyde, 'The Interpretation of Treaties by the Supreme Court of the United States' 824.

[3] Bederman, 'Revivalist Canons and Treaty Interpretation' 955.

[4] Klabbers structures the layers similarly, referring first to Grotius and Vattel, then to a phase in which there was less attention and then to codificatory efforts by the ILC: see Klabbers, 'Book Review' 718. Another structure is provided for by Greig, *Intertemporality and the Law of Treaties* 26; Degan, *L'Interprétation des accords en droit international* 27ff. Degan distinguishes between classical and modern approaches. The classical approaches are divided into a first period, comprising Grotius, Pufendorf, Barbeyrac and Ortega which are said to consider the intention of the parties; a second period comprising Wolff and Vattel, taking as a 'point of departure the text of the treaty'; and a third phase, comprising Rutherforth and Phillimore, which distinguished within the process of interpretation between grammatical and logical interpretation. While this study is similar to the distinction made by Degan with regard to his third phase, the first and second phases are comprised as one phase. Bederman distinguished Grotius and his followers from the Anglo-American reception, Bederman, *Classical Canons*. Gardiner highlighted single methodologies: The Greco-Roman era, Grotius, Pufendorf and Vattel, the Harvard Draft Convention, the PCIJ, the Institut de Droit International, the practice of the ICJ before the Vienna Convention, the ILC and the Vienna Conference: see Gardiner, *Treaty Interpretation* 51. Ehrlich gave special attention to the conceptions of Gentili and Grotius and then took a chronological approach, treating the seventeenth and eighteenth after the nineteenth and twentieth centuries. Ludwik Ehrlich, 'L'Interprétation des traités' 12.

endured from the nineteenth into the twentieth century and overlapped with the codificatory phase beginning in the middle of the nineteenth century and ending with the final codification of the VCLT. Like layers, those phases are not rigid, but they share common features that are to be outlined. Samples of how authors framed treaty interpretation in international law are given in Appendix 1 below.[5] Several of those authors that were considered to be representative for their phase and influential for the development of treaty interpretation are analysed in depth. The approaches of the authors are summarised in schemes of interpretation. The way in which the analysis is conducted owes much to Bederman who has used schemes and has transferred this approach from rhetorics to the study of the history of treaty interpretation in international law.[6] While these schemes capture the systems of interpretation in all relevant detail, we will now focus on the general and important points.

4.2. The mechanical phase

Assuming that the modern international law and its scientific reflection began in the seventeenth century, this should also be taken as the starting point for the inquiry into the approaches to the means of interpretation.[7] Those first approaches were later referred to as 'technical'[8] and 'mechanical'.[9] We shall call them mechanical.[10] The authors tried to invent a mechanism that would guide the interpreter towards a certain meaning. Strict rules and a rather refined system are relied on to establish the meaning of the treaty. This is achieved by a strong reliance on the literal meaning as well as some standard rules and in particular presumptions in cases of favourable or odious obligations. Thereby, the author arrives at the assumed intentions of the parties.

The founding father of modern interpretative methodology was Francisco Suárez.[11] His rules of interpretation of laws were very influential on

---

[5] See pp. 359ff below.   [6] Bederman, *Classical Canons* 11.
[7] For an account of treaty-making and interpretation in classical antiquity, see *ibid.* 46ff.
[8] Phillimore, *Commentaries upon International Law* 94; Wheaton, Boyd and Lawrence, *Elements of International Law* (vol. 2) 323.
[9] Hudson, *The Permanent Court of International Justice* (2nd edn) 641.
[10] Both terms can be used synonymously; we will later rely on the so-called techniques of interpretation.
[11] Suárez, *Tractatus de legibus ac deo legislatore: in decem libros distributes*. For his general importance, see Azevedo Alexandrino Fernandes, *Die Theorie der Interpretation des Gesetzes bei Francisco Suárez* 83.

later scholars. Since he thought of international law as customary, he did not apply his rules of interpretation explicitly to the law of treaties, yet his work had a substantial impact upon interpretative methodology in international law. The first important feature was that he was the first to develop a system of interpretative methodology independent from rhetorics.[12] It is also significant that Suárez managed to capture the notion of interpretation for his time very aptly: it was not only about finding the significance of words but could also result in changing the meaning of words.[13]

Possibly his most original contribution was that he generally distinguished between three types of interpretation: Authoritative interpretation, interpretation by usage and doctrinal interpretation.[14] While authoritative interpretation was limited to an act that had the same quality as the act to be interpreted, interpretation by usage – which seems to be conceptualised by him for the first time outside canonical law – was reserved to the interpretation by those competent to apply the law. He could legitimately be termed as one of the forefathers of the technique of subsequent practice as enshrined in Art. 31(3)(b) VCLT.

Gentili, for whom the principle of good faith played an important role,[15] derived from this principle that treaties should not be deliberately misinterpreted in war times.[16] For him such an interpretation had to be preferred over an interpretation according to the strict letter of the law.[17] This reliance on good faith is also mentioned at the outset by Grotius.[18]

---

[12] Schröder, *Recht als Wissenschaft*.
[13] For a good summary, see Azevedo Alexandrino Fernandes, *Die Theorie der Interpretation des Gesetzes bei Francisco Suárez* 77–80.
[14] See Suárez, *Tractatus de legibus ac deo legislatore: in decem libros distributes* Book 6 Chapter 1 para. 1.
[15] Ludwik Ehrlich, 'L'Interprétation des traités' 12. Ehrlich describes Gentili's approach in detail and adds some examples.
[16] Gentili, *De jure bellis libri tres* 361 (original 591–2, Book III, Chapter XIV); Here, Gentili expressed his view that reliance on good faith supersedes entering into the 'subtle discussions on fine points of law'. Bederman inferred from this section that Gentili rejected all rules on interpretation, Bederman, *Classical Canons* 137. Whether this inference is totally correct might be doubted as Gentili on another occasion for example spoke about a decision which he describes as follows: 'many things which may be said about the use of words and the manner and method of their interpretation', Gentili, *De jure bellis libri tres* 384 (original 629–30, Book III, Chapter XVII). Bederman is certainly correct in that Gentili offered no structured account of the methods of interpretation.
[17] Gentili, *De jure bellis libri tres* 145–8 (original 232–9, Book II, Chapter IV).
[18] Grotius, *De jure belli ac pacis libri tres*, 409 (original 275, Book II, Chapter XVI, I. 1). Interesting insights about the context in which the rules of interpretation are embedded is provided for by *ibid*.

He is acknowledged to be the first to deal with the rules on treaty interpretation in a systematic fashion.[19] This is why his conception should be explained in greater detail as it will also form the basis for the discussion of later authors. His general approach to interpretation was the inference of intent from the most probable indicators.[20] As can be derived from his argumentative scheme, Grotius developed a very refined system,[21] in which he distinguished two general modes of interpretation, namely, literal interpretation and interpretation going beyond the wording of the treaty. The first category is again divided into three subcategories, namely, literal interpretation of words, the use of conjectures and inferences from the nature of the obligation whether to employ a broad or narrow meaning. The means allowing to go beyond the literal meaning are again structured as to whether they extend or restrict that meaning. Many prescriptions he made have become very influential for other authors: To give just one example, he said that terms are to be understood in their plain sense[22] whereas technical terms are to be interpreted according to their technical meaning.[23] Later authors also took up the presumtions he inferred from the nature of the obligation: A broad interpretation for favourable clauses or a narrow interpretation for odious clauses. Although the structure laid out looks rather rigid and categorical, the famous scholar and diplomat tried to retain a certain flexibility. He presumed that no other means of interpretation will be resorted to when the literal meaning is clear, except if the other means provide for an evident conclusion.[24] As the literal meaning can be overcome by other means, it is intelligible that there can be something like a restrictive and extensive interpretation. He also allotted special importance to the purpose of the treaty, distinguishing it from the intention.[25] While the ultimate goal would be to arrive at the intention of the parties, Grotius construed them rather objectively: Several presumptions guided the interpreter.[26]

---

[19] Ludwik Ehrlich, 'L'Interprétation des traités' 16. The fact that he managed to synthesise those rules in an apt manner is stressed by Bederman, *Classical Canons* 113.
[20] Grotius, *De jure belli ac pacis libri tres* 409 (original 275, Book II, Chapter XVI, I., 2.).
[21] See Appendix 1 below.
[22] Grotius, *De jure belli ac pacis libri tres* 409–10 (original 276, Book II, Chapter XVI. II).
[23] *Ibid.* 410 (original 276, Book II, Chapter XVI, III). It is interesting that the Vienna Convention employs a similar dichotomy: it opposes the ordinary meaning in Art. 31(1) with the special meaning in Art. 31(4).
[24] *Ibid.* 409–10 (original 276, Book II, Chapter XVI. II).
[25] *Ibid.* 412–13 (original 277, Book II, Chapter XVI, VIII).
[26] *Ibid.* 425ff (original 284ff, Book II, Chapter XVI, XVIIff).

In sum, Grotius provided for a rather refined system of interpretation that structured the means in different categories while trying to preserve some flexibility. The means used can be categorised as literal means, further means (attached to the treaty such as motives and effects), presumptions deriving from the nature of the treaty, and other inferences as to the intent of the parties.

Samuel Pufendorf saw himself much in the tradition of Grotius,[27] he structured his treatise in the same fashion: He first dealt with the literal meaning in its common usage and its special meaning,[28] and then went on to discuss conjectures or presumptions in the case of ambiguities or contradictions.[29] While his discussion is much more detailed at points, his general scheme very much equals that of Grotius.[30]

Like Grotius, Emer de Vattel first gave reasons for dealing with the rules on interpretation. As with Grotius, the imperfect nature of language and the impossibility of having 'perfectly clear, definite and precise' terms was a reason to provide for rules of interpretation.[31] But Vattel was also very concerned with inconsistencies in treaties and the misuse of interpretation and even drafting. To resolve these problems, Vattel provided for several rules which should be applied in a combined and balanced fashion.[32] The means can be put into three categories: General precepts, rules and presumptions. The general precepts, which are derived from reason and equity, are introduced to repress and prevent fraud in the process of interpretation.[33] The five precepts employ an objective approach to interpretation. The first precept states that it was 'not permissible to interpret what has no need of interpretation'.[34] The rule that has become famous as 'Vattel's maxim' reaffirms that terms can have a clear and objective meaning. The only qualification made is that the clear meaning must not lead to obscure results.[35] The second, third and fourth general precepts deal with questions of expressing the will of the

---

[27] See the introductory statement, Samuel Pufendorf, *De jure naturae et gentium* Book 5, Chapter 1, para. 1.
[28] Ibid. (original 541–2, Book 5, Chapter 1, paras. 3–4).
[29] Ibid. 805–15 (original 549–55, Book 5, Chapter 1, paras. 11–19).
[30] Ludwik Ehrlich, 'L'Interprétation des traités' 21. For details, see Bederman, *Classical Canons* 129.
[31] Vattel, *The Law of Nations or the Principles of Natural Law* 199 (Book 2, Chapter 17, para. 262). Interesting remarks on the nature of language are also made at paras. 272 and 299.
[32] Ibid. 199 (Book 2, Chapter 17, para. 262).
[33] Ibid.
[34] Ibid. 199 (Book 2, Chapter 17, para. 263).
[35] Ibid.

parties and the impossibility of mental reservations.[36] According to those precepts, only expressed evidence can be regarded as the intention of the parties. The fifth general precept stresses the need to interpret according to fixed rules.[37] Those precepts are general guides as to when interpretation is necessary and which emanations of the will are generally to be taken into account. As those rules are 'founded upon right reason and are consequently approved and prescribed by the Law of Nature', they are also binding upon states.[38] By stressing the need for fixed rules of interpretation, he introduces his second category, namely, that of rules. Vattel emphasises that the 'sole object of a lawful interpretation is to discover the intention of the maker or makers of the treaty'.[39] His general rule of interpretation was that only when there is a need for interpretation, had the interpreter to seek the probable intention of the parties and interpret the treaty accordingly.[40] Although the precepts emphasised the objective nature of the law, the actual meaning of the treaty is equated with the intention of the parties. This finds expression in the fact that he refers to the probable intention, which denotes that the rules do not look for the real but only the expressed intention.[41] Vattel then stated a number of rules which he did not categorise further but which have a certain order. First came rules on literal interpretation of the word or phrase in question,[42] then rules dealing with the treaty and its context,[43] with the possible consequences of interpretation,[44] rules concerning coherence and harmonious interpretation inside and outside the treaty,[45] and interpretation based upon the purpose of the treaty.[46] Regarding the purpose of a treaty, Vattel made some observations that have later been forgotten: The purpose can give rise to arguments relating to the consequences of an interpretation.[47] At the same time, he saw that purposive interpretations can also restrict the scope of a clause.[48]

---

[36] Ibid. 199–200 (Book 2, Chapter 17, paras. 264–6).
[37] Ibid. 200–1 (Book 2, Chapter 17, para. 268).
[38] Ibid. 200–1 (Book 2, Chapter 17, para. 268).
[39] Ibid. 201 (Book 2, Chapter 17, para. 270).   [40] Ibid.
[41] It is significant that he uses cases of succession as examples as they concern instances in which the author of the statement is dead and cannot express his real intention: ibid.
[42] Ibid. 202–3 (Book 2, Chapter 17, paras. 272–9).
[43] Ibid. 204–5 (Book 2, Chapter 17, paras. 280–2).
[44] Ibid. 205–6 (Book 2, Chapter 17, paras. 282–3).
[45] Ibid. 206–7 (Book 2, Chapter 17, paras. 284–6).
[46] Ibid. 207–10 (Book 2, Chapter 17, paras. 287–92).
[47] Ibid. 210–11 (Book 2, Chapter 17, para. 294).
[48] Ibid. 210–11 (Book 2, Chapter 17, para. 294).

After dealing with special problems,[49] Vattel came to cases in which the terms of the treaty were unclear and would allow for a narrower or wider interpretation but the rules previously stated gave no indication as to the intention of the parties.[50] In this context, he took up the approach of Grotius and aimed to decide these interpretative questions based on the nature of the obligation, which could be either favourable or odious.[51] From this distinction, it could be inferred whether to interpret its provisions narrowly or broadly.[52] Thus, Vattel employed a gradual approach and first established some general precepts describing the process, then general rules to discern the intention of the parties, and if that is not successful, presumptions of narrow or broad interpretation in cases of a favourable or odious character of the treaty.

Rutherforth set out a theory of interpretation of all kinds of legal acts that in many respects followed the ideas of Grotius. He almost employed the same scheme of interpretation, but it is significant that he did not include presumptions that relate to the question whether the promise was favourable or odious.[53] He inquired more deeply into what we today call the object and purpose of the treaty. He found that the object and purpose, if not explicitly stipulated by the parties, is in itself found through interpretation.[54] He also stipulated that the effect of interpretation is linked to its purpose as an unintended effect of the treaty could be determined if the effect of an interpretation went against the object of the instrument.[55] Like the other authors, Rutherforth had certain preferences for literal interpretations but followed Grotius in contending that there could be interpretations that went beyond the clear wording of the treaty. However, Rutherforth stressed that the parties could explicitly rule out such a possibility if they provided so in fixed terms.[56]

---

[49] *Ibid.* 212 (Book 2, Chapter 17, paras. 297–8). The second case concerned problems in which the conduct of a party might violate the terms of the treaty but not necessarily its object and purpose. Vattel here favoured the wording over the alleged purpose of the treaty.

[50] *Ibid.* 212–13 (Book 2, Chapter 17, paras. 299–300).

[51] *Ibid.* 213–14 (Book 2, Chapter 17, paras. 300–1).

[52] The whole issue is dealt with at *ibid.* 213–18 (Book 2, Chapter 17, paras. 300–10).

[53] Bederman sees the main difference in the triad of literal, rational and mixed interpretation. This represents for him a dialectic between intention and purpose: see *ibid.* 146.

[54] Rutherforth, *Institutes of Natural Law* (vol. 2) 417 (Book II, Chapter VII, para. IX).

[55] *Ibid.* 414 (Book II, Chapter VII, para. VIII).

[56] *Ibid.* 434 (Book II, Chapter VII, para. XIII).

The approaches of Grotius, Pufendorf, Vattel and Rutherforth[57] are similar in several respects. At the outset, they rely on good faith in the interpretation of treaties.[58] Their aim is to arrive at the assumed intentions of the authors. They all show a great reliance on literal interpretation and certain rather technical rules that could determine ambiguous cases. It could be argued that especially the presumptions relied on by the authors are a very good means in the hand of the parties to the treaty, as they would instantly and intuitively know whether an obligation is odious or favourable to them. This feature of interpretation shows that the means of interpretation were specifically designed to be used by parties to the treaty and not by a third party like a tribunal. This could also be shown by the great reliance on good faith. The approach is mechanical since it relies on certain rules establishing a procedure that will rather automatically produce the interpretative results that form the assumed intentions of the parties. Interpretative method claims to guide the interpreter to the correct result and to foresee the eventualities by constructing different layers of guidance. The interpreter can and has to apply interpretative method to arrive at the right result. The expositions of interpretative method in the mechanical phase are clearly in a hermeneutical tradition of interpretative methodology that has its roots in the Middle Ages.[59] This tradition departed from the idea that there is one right and ascertainable result that was often linked to the will of good, nature or reason. Methodology provided for a set of rules the observance of which made this right ascertainable.[60]

4.3. The flexible phase

In the phase described here as flexible, one can observe a significant development of the rules of interpretation: The doctrine tried to free itself from the complex and mechanical rules and to establish a rather free inquiry into the will of the states. The work of Robert Phillimore can be

---

[57] Textor was omitted here as he did not add anything relevant in the context. The same applies to Bynkershoek.
[58] The very convincing argument that the reliance on good faith can be traced back to the treaty practice of the ancient Greeks is made at *ibid.* 136.
[59] Schröder, *Recht als Wissenschaft* 52–3.
[60] *Ibid.* The *topoi* were in contrast rather in the rhetorical tradition that departed from an obvious meaning and provided for arguments that allowed for further inferences. Even though hermeneutic and rhetorical interpretative methodologies could be based on the same means, their general endeavour and the respective process differs substantially.

considered in many respects to represent a transition between the two phases.[61] He upholds the claim that the rules of interpretation are based on 'right reason and rational equity' but he acknowledges that the rules of interpretation are 'formed into law'.[62] So he sets out a system of interpretation like the scholars since Grotius, mentions literal interpretation and inferences from the context of the treaty as well as inferences that would lead to broad or narrow interpretations.[63] But for him, the most important means do not relate to the literal meaning: he refers to authentic interpretation, which makes reference to the interpretation through separate treaties[64] and usual interpretation, which means the interpretation through the custom of the parties, which he thought to be 'the best of all interpreters between nations'.[65] Phillimore is indicative of a general move occurring in the flexible phase: States were in the limelight.[66] This altered the whole perception of the rules of treaty interpretation. One of the differences transpires from a quote of John Westlake who said that:

> [t]he interpretation of treaties has been considered at much length by many writers on international law, and rules on it have been suggested which in our opinion are not likely to be of much practical use ... The important point is to get to the real intention of the parties, and that enquiry is not to be shackled by any rule of interpretation which may exist in a particular national jurisprudence but is not generally accepted in the civilised world.[67]

It was typical for this approach that interpretation was now a quest for the real intentions of the parties.[68] Unlike in the mechanical phase, the real intentions instead of the assumed intentions were at the centre of attention.

---

[61] Phillimore, *Commentaries upon International Law* 94.
[62] *Ibid.* 94. Ehrlich points out that interpretative methodologies from internal law had a great influence on Phillimore: Ludwik Ehrlich, 'L'Interprétation des traités' 30.
[63] Phillimore, *Commentaries upon International Law* 98ff. [64] *Ibid.* 97.
[65] *Ibid.* 98. This is also mentioned by Ludwik Ehrlich, 'L'Interprétation des traités' 31.
[66] Von Blumerincq, *Das Völkerrecht oder das internationale Recht* 304; Fauchille, *Traité de droit international public* (vol. 1) 373.
[67] Westlake, *International Law* (vol. 1) 282.
[68] Phillimore, *Commentaries upon International Law* 97. He was, however, ambiguous in that regard: see *ibid.* 95. The intentions are also mentioned by Oppenheim, *International Law* (vol. 1) 582; Fauchille, *Traité de droit international public* (vol. 1) 373ff; Hershey, *The Essentials of International Law and Organization* 445; Stockton, *Outlines of International Law* 258–60.

HISTORICAL ACCOUNT OF THE MEANS OF INTERPRETATION   93

This of course also changed the nature of the rules. It was hard to see why an interpreter should be constrained by doctrinal rules to arrive at what the states really thought.[69] This evoked a stream of extreme scepticism. Some scholars denied the existence of rules on interpretation altogether and, consequently, also omitted to state any rule on treaty interpretation.[70] Most of the authors continued to state the methods of interpretation, but they acknowledged that those rules were subject to the expressed will of states, be it that the rules were legal in nature[71] and, therefore, changeable by states, be it that they were only subsidiary to the expressed intentions of states,[72] or that there was no judiciary to enforce them.[73] Yet, not only the general nature but also the rules themselves changed.

Means of interpretation that could be related to the intention of the parties were not only mentioned but also held to be more important than other means. This applies to the *travaux préparatoires* which could shed light on what the parties originally intended.[74] Although recourse could not be had to the legislative history for the purposes of statutory interpretation in the English domestic legal system, English scholars had no problem using the *travaux* as means of interpreting treaties.[75] Yet, the *travaux* were not only an admissible means of interpretation but were sometimes considered to be able to override even the clear wording of the treaty.[76] Those means were even accorded the function of effectively amending the treaty.[77] Subsequent practice and subsequent agreements[78] that had previously been referred to only indirectly or irregularly now became one of the most frequently stressed means of treaty interpretation.[79] In analogy to municipal law, they were called authentic

---

[69] McNair, *The Law of Treaties* 366.
[70] Bonfils, *Manuel de droit international public* 459ff; Lawrence, *The Principles of International Law* 326.
[71] Phillimore, *Commentaries upon International Law* 94.
[72] Oppenheim, *International Law* (vol. 1) 582; Wilson, *International Law* 221.
[73] Smith and Wylie, *International Law* 101.
[74] Despagnet, *Cours de droit international public* 483; Hyde, *International Law Chiefly as Interpreted and Applied by the United States* (2nd edn) 1471.
[75] McNair, *The Law of Treaties* 411. For an explanation of the general difference, see Westlake, *International Law* (vol. 1) 282.
[76] Oppenheim, *International Law* (vol. 1) 584.
[77] Phillimore, *Commentaries upon International Law* 97.
[78] For agreements, see for example Klüber, *Europäisches Völkerrecht* 187; von Ullmann, *Völkerrecht* 282; Oppenheim, *International Law* (vol. 1) 582.
[79] Phillimore, *Commentaries upon International Law* 97. Although critical on many other rules, McNair found himself on 'solid ground' as he was dealing with a 'judicial practice worthy to be called a rule': see McNair, *The Law of Treaties* 424.

interpretation.[80] The specific importance attached to them is exemplified by several authors: we have already touched upon the special importance conferred on the means of interpretation by Phillimore.[81] Charles Hyde argues that in the case of a common practice of the parties to a treaty there could not even be a question as to the interpretation of treaties in the strict sense.[82] Paul Fauchille stressed that it was within the competence of states to interpret the treaty.[83] Arnold McNair accords to subsequent practice a high probative value.[84] This is all the more significant since especially subsequent practice is a distinctive feature of international interpretative methodology that cannot be found in national law.

The increasing importance of the so-called authentic means of interpretation resulted in a diminishing importance of literal interpretation.[85] The latter had enjoyed a predominant status in the mechanical phase but was now deprived of some of its importance as it was considered to stand on the same level as the authentic means at best.[86] For many authors it was clear that the literal sense would have to give way to the agreed intentions of the parties.[87] This can be easily explained by the fact that it was the meaning the parties had in mind that was the goal of the flexible approaches to treaty interpretation, which expresses a preference for the particular over the common, the subjective over the objective. How far these approaches went in detaching themselves from a common and objective meaning is also displayed by a very popular rule for the construction of multilingual treaties: authors held the view that in cases

---

[80] Von Blumerincq, *Das Völkerrecht oder das internationale Recht* 304; Oppenheim, *International Law* (vol. 1) 583.

[81] Phillimore, *Commentaries upon International Law* 98. He called subsequent practice 'usage'. Of the same opinion was von Blumerincq, *Das Völkerrecht oder das internationale Recht* 304.

[82] Hyde, *International Law Chiefly as Interpreted and Applied by the United States* (2nd edn) 1501. He went on to explain that this would 'close the door of judicial construction at variance' with subsequent practice or agreements: see *ibid*.

[83] Fauchille, *Traité de droit international public* (vol. 1) 373.

[84] McNair, *The Law of Treaties* 424.

[85] For a general comparison to English law, see Westlake, *International Law* (vol. 1) 282.

[86] See for example Hall, *A Treatise on International Law* 390ff; Hyde, *International Law Chiefly as Interpreted and Applied by the United States* (2nd edn) 1469. Oppenheim preferred the reasonable over the literal sense: Oppenheim, *International Law* (vol. 1) 583.

[87] Hyde, *International Law Chiefly as Interpreted and Applied by the United States* (2nd edn) 1468, 1470, 1499; McNair, *The Law of Treaties* 367. For a contrary view, see Hall, *A Treatise on International Law* 390.

of ambiguity that were caused by more than one authentic language versions of the treaty, each state shall apply the treaty in its own language concerning its territory.[88] This was clearly indicative of the fact that the parties favoured the intention of each party over the integrity of the treaty and its objective meaning.

Another typical view concerned presumptions which had been a major invention in the previous mechanical phase. Mostly, it was argued that any general inference would be out of touch with what the parties actually agreed upon as presumptions were not attached to a specific treaty but to the whole system of international law at large and presumptions were, therefore, discarded.[89] The only presumption that has often been referred to was the presumption in favour of interpretations that would least affect the sovereignty of the parties to the treaty, which is often referred to as *in dubio pro mitius* or the principle summarising the fundamental legal rights of the states.[90] The fact that this was one of the very few presumptions that was mentioned at all is again indicative of the material bias of the means of treaty interpretation at that time. They were clearly sovereignty-oriented. The doctrine of liberal interpretation of international treaties advocated by the US Supreme Court was met with suspicion and criticism.[91] This shows that there was a preference towards following the will of the states and their interest in the process of interpretation. Yet, what changed were not only the means themselves but also their mutual relation.

The mechanical nature of the prior approaches to interpretation was severely attacked. Hall remarked that the rules developed earlier are 'unsafe in their application' or 'of doubtful applicability' and, therefore, not apt to contribute to the resolution of disputes.[92] Lawrence pointed to

---

[88] Oppenheim, *International Law* (vol. 1) 586; Hall, *A Treatise on International Law* 392.

[89] Hyde, *International Law Chiefly as Interpreted and Applied by the United States* (2nd edn) 1468–9, 1500.

[90] See for example Taylor, *Treatise on International Public Law* 397; Oppenheim, *International Law* (vol. 1) 584; Hall, *A Treatise on International Law* 394; Hershey, *The Essentials of International Law and Organization* 447. For recent reflections on restrictive interpretation, see Crema, 'Disappearance and New Sightings of Restrictive Interpretation(s)'; Crawford, 'Sovereignty as a Legal Value' 122.

[91] McNair, *The Law of Treaties* 386. Liberal interpretation was also described as 'imputation of good faith and high purpose to the executive branch of the government': see Hyde, *International Law Chiefly as Interpreted and Applied by the United States* (2nd edn) 1500.

[92] Hall, *A Treatise on International Law* 390. He distanced himself from earlier authorities although he cites Grotius and Vattel as accounts 'on the whole subject of interpretation', ibid. 395 n. 2.

the tautological nature of many of the mechanical rules of interpretation and resorted openly to irony when he said that 'ordinary words must be taken in an ordinary sense' and 'technical words must be taken in a technical sense'.[93] The rules were held to have 'inconsiderable' value[94] and be contradictory.[95] If one adhered to the logic of the real intention of states, preconceived logical rules must have been conceived as a delusion and an obstruction to achieving that aim. In the first edition of his famous treatise, Lassa Oppenheim asserted that there were neither customary nor conventional rules on interpretation,[96] so one had to refer like 'Grotius and the latter authorities' to Roman law insofar as the respective precepts are 'full of common sense'.[97] Subject to the express will of states, there was still a place for rules as far as they could be derived from general jurisprudence.

The process of interpretation was imagined as being free and flexible, as long as the aim of arriving at the real intentions of the parties was achieved.[98] This new preference also explains the shift in the way the authors argued and the authorities they used. There was a substantial shift towards citing state practice[99] more frequently and towards attributing more authority to it.[100] The old style of alluding to classical authors and antique stories was abandoned,[101] instead scholars relied almost exclusively on rather contemporaneous state practice. Yet, the importance accorded to stating the rules on interpretation substantially decreased.

---

[93] Lawrence, *The Principles of International Law* 326.
[94] Phillipson, *Smith's International Law* 146. Similarly Smith and Wylie, *International Law* 101.
[95] McNair, *The Law of Treaties* 365.   [96] Oppenheim, *International Law* (vol. 1) 582.
[97] Ibid. We have seen that at least Grotius would have objected if it was said that he had 'applied the rules of Roman Law respecting interpretation in general to interpretation of treaties'. The authors were certainly influenced by antique sources in general and Roman law in particular, as shown extensively by Bederman, *Classical Canons* 113ff. It is suggested that the conjectures (i.e. presumptions) he uses avail of a particular originality.
[98] Phillimore, *Commentaries upon International Law* 94; Despagnet, *Cours de droit international public* 483; Hyde, *International Law Chiefly as Interpreted and Applied by the United States* (2nd edn) 1472; McNair, *The Law of Treaties* 366.
[99] See for example von Ullmann, *Völkerrecht* 282; Hall, *A Treatise on International Law* 390; McNair, *The Law of Treaties* 364ff.
[100] De Martens, *Traité de droit international* 556; Fauchille, *Traité de droit international public* (vol. 1) 373. Arbitral awards are expressly treated as subsidiary in Bonfils, *Manuel de droit international public* 459.
[101] An example of an approach between the two phases is Phillimore, *Commentaries upon International Law* 116.

While previously ample space was provided to the topic (Grotius for example dedicated twenty pages to the issue),[102] it was now dealt with often in less than a page even in large treatises.[103] Sometimes it was not mentioned at all.[104] Authors did not aim to develop a system of interpretation but rather confined themselves to indicating some means of arriving at the true intentions of the parties.[105] The primary actors of interpretation and sources of the rules of interpretation were to be the states themselves. Lawrence summarises this approach best:

> But since states have no common superior to adjust their differences and declare with authority the real meaning and force of their international documents, it is clear that no rules of interpretation can be laid down which are binding in the sense that the rules followed by a court of law in constructing a will or a lease are binding on the parties concerned. 'There is no place for the refinements of the courts in the rough jurisprudence of nations.'[106] When states get into controversy about the interpretation of a treaty, they often make a new agreement, clearing up the disputed points in the way that seems most convenient at the time, which is not always the way pointed out by strict rules of interpretation.[107]

The changes in the aim of interpretation, in the nature of its rules, in the rules themselves, their relation to each other and in the authorities used, those changes mark the flexible phase. While there were still many authors strongly rooted in this tradition, a new trend arose of treating international law differently and codifying it. This also affected the doctrinal approaches to interpretation that are here summarised as the phase of codification.

4.4. The phase of codification

One of the greatest minds of his time, Jeremy Bentham, coined the phrase 'codification' for the process of turning customary law into a code which

---

[102] Grotius, *De jure belli ac pacis libri tres* in Book II, Chapter XVI.
[103] See Despagnet, *Cours de droit international public* 483; Phillipson, *Smith's International Law* 146. Despagnet could be taken as an example, as he devotes only one paragraph out of 723 pages to treaty interpretation. See also Bonfils, *Manuel de droit international public* 460. This observation was made for example by Fauchille, *Traité de droit international public* (vol. 1) 375.
[104] See for example von Liszt, *Das Völkerrecht* 171–81.
[105] See for example Fauchille, *Traité de droit international public* (vol. 1) 373ff; Oppenheim, *International Law* (vol. 1) 582.
[106] Quoting Hall, *A Treatise on International Law* 2.
[107] Lawrence, *The Principles of International Law* 326.

would provide written rules for customary law, thereby removing gaps, as well as unclear or outdated rules.[108] Interestingly, Bentham envisaged also the codification of international law.[109] However, he came to set out only a very general code containing some principles to guide states in their mutual relations.[110] The challenge was taken up subsequently by authors like Caspar David Bluntschli or David Dudley Field, by private institutions such as the Institut de Droit International or the International Law Association, by diplomatic conferences such as the Hague Peace Conferences of 1899 and 1907 and by organs of international organisations such as the Preparatory Committee for the Codification Conference within the League of Nations or the International Law Commission in the system of the United Nations.[111] Codification attempts by authors mostly tried to provide a code that would deal with the whole body of public international law,[112] while collective bodies or diplomatic conferences only dealt with particular issues.[113] It is significant that the codification movement arose at the time when the rules on interpretation were on the decline.

While some attempts at codification did not contain any rules on interpretation,[114] others tried to set out rules in that regard. This could result in two different approaches: Compilation or synthesis. Compiling meant to collect all possible means of interpretation. Jerome Internoscia for example relied on the old distinction between grammatical and logical interpretation.[115] He then managed to accommodate several different presumptions and rules in those categories. Pasquale Fiore offered a wide variety of different means of interpretation.[116] Others tried to

---

[108] The first mention of the word was made in the title of Bentham (ed.), *Papers Relative to Codification and Public Instruction*.

[109] Bentham, *The Principles of International Law*. See Watts, 'Codification and Progressive Development of International Law' para. 4.

[110] Bentham, *The Principles of International Law* 537.

[111] For an historical overview of the different actors and attempts to the codification of public international law, see Nys, 'Codification of International Law' 871; Dhokalia, *The Codification of Public International Law* 37–143.

[112] See for example Internoscia, *New Code of International Law*; Fiore, *Le Droit international codifié et sa sanction juridique*.

[113] A good example is provided by the Brussels Conference of 1874 discussing a draft for the laws of war on land. Dhokalia, *The Codification of Public International Law* 84.

[114] Bluntschli, *Das moderne Völkerrecht der civilisirten Staten* 245, 253; Field, *Draft Outlines of an International Code* 311, 507. See also the only institutional rules in Duplessix, *La Loi des nations* 142 para. 383.

[115] Internoscia, *New Code of International Law* 138.

[116] Fiore, *Le Droit international codifié et sa sanction juridique* 402.

frame the rules in a more coherent and systematic way. Ludwik Ehrlich tried to structure the process of interpretation according to different methods and laid down a series of presumptions for each method. It is significant that single authors used to collect and compile these materials. Collective efforts resulted in synthesising the material. 'A landmark in the progression towards the codification of international law' was the Harvard Draft Convention, as it structured the means of interpretation in a completely new way.[117] It influenced the rules on interpretation in the VCLT significantly.[118] The Convention provided for the first time for a coherent system based upon what was called factors of interpretation: It laid out a non-exhaustive list of factors that ought to be taken into account in the process of interpretation.[119] To understand this new approach, one can also consider the methodological reflection of Manley Hudson. He had organised and directed the research project and his approach to interpretation, while writing on the PCIJ, showed a great resemblance to the approach of the Harvard Draft.[120] Hudson very clearly emphasised the important conceptual shift underlying the Convention: The 'function of interpretation' (*sic*!) was not to arrive at 'a pre-existing meaning'.[121] He stressed that the interpreter was 'giving' a meaning to the text.[122] Hudson stressed that the interpreter had to think about the consequences of his action rather than to look for certain inferences.[123] This clearly evidences that there was a shift from a mere hermeneutical to a justificatory and argumentative exercise, which can also be derived from the Harvard Draft: 'the so-called rules of interpretation' were only *ex post facto* descriptions or justifications or decisions arrived at by mental processes more complicated than the mere mechanical application'.[124] This shift also made it necessary to structure the process of interpretation differently.

---

[117] Gardiner, *Treaty Interpretation* 56. See the text at p. 365 below. [118] *Ibid.* 57.
[119] Harvard Law School, 'Harvard Draft Convention on the Law of Treaties' 937.
[120] Onofrio, *Missouri Biographical Dictionary* (vol. 1) 332.
[121] Hudson, *The Permanent Court of International Justice* (1st edn) 551; Harvard Law School 'Harvard Draft Convention on the Law of Treaties' 946; Hudson, *The Permanent Court of International Justice* (2nd edn) 641.
[122] Hudson, *The Permanent Court of International Justice* (1st edn) 551; Hudson, *The Permanent Court of International Justice* (2nd edn) 641; Harvard Law School 'Harvard Draft Convention on the Law of Treaties' 946.
[123] Hudson, *The Permanent Court of International Justice* (1st edn) 551; Hudson, *The Permanent Court of International Justice* (2nd edn) 642.
[124] Harvard Law School, 'Harvard Draft Convention on the Law of Treaties' 947.

The authors of the draft clearly saw the impossibility of collecting all rules of interpretation previously pronounced upon.[125] In trying to codify the different rules, the Draft not only enumerated the different means of interpretation, but tried to synthesise them systematically. It explicitly rejected what it called 'maxims' or 'canons'. Instead, it introduced the technique or factor approach as a central feature of the process of interpretation, which was laid out in Art. 19(a) of the Draft.[126] It is significant that interpretation in the light of the general purpose is mentioned as the first technique and literal interpretation is not mentioned at all.[127] Although the general purpose is just one amongst other factors in Art. 19(a), its central importance is stressed in the commentary, which underlines that 'the function of interpretation is to discover and effectuate the purpose which a treaty is intended to serve'.[128] Like the equation of the actual meaning with the intention of the parties by Vattel, the Harvard Draft equates the purpose of the treaty with its meaning. The approach taken by the Draft is to give 'considered attention to a number of factors which may reasonably be regarded as likely to yield reliable evidence of what ... [the] purpose is and how it may best be effectuated under prevailing circumstances'.[129]

The Draft gives no indication how those 'factors' would influence the actual result of interpretation; they only serve as reminders for the interpreter but will not apply in every case. The Draft sought to solve the key weakness it detected in the mechanical rules of interpretation: the Draft aimed to formulate rules that are as sensitive as possible to the meaning of the treaty and would not preoccupy the mind of the interpreter so that she or he would be already biased when approaching his or her task.[130] Stressing the active nature of the decision the interpreter had to make in the face of the imprecise and ambiguous meaning of language and the impossibility of foreseeing all future circumstances that were to be regulated by the treaty, the interpreter had to look for the best possible means to discern the meaning of the treaty. An interpretation only determined by factors leaves discretion to the interpreter for 'investigation, weighing of evidence, judgment and foresight'.[131]

This particular approach was taken up in all subsequent attempts at codification. The general idea to formulate factors instead of other means

---

[125] *Ibid.* 940.   [126] See Box 6 in Appendix 1 below.
[127] The Draft specifies that 'no importance is to be attached to the order in which they [the factors enumerated in Art. 19(a)] are named': see *ibid.* 938.
[128] *Ibid.* 937.   [129] *Ibid.* 938.   [130] *Ibid.* 946.   [131] *Ibid.*

of interpretation was from then on deeply engraved in international legal method and international legal methodology.

This is particularly true for the discussion of the Institut de Droit International. There were several drafts which were getting shorter and more concise in the course of the deliberations: Lauterpacht's first draft was comparable to the summary of a chapter in a textbook.[132] This was – for the next draft – in a slightly abbreviated form, turned into six articles.[133] Those articles were further condensed by Gerald Fitzmaurice, the new Rapporteur.[134] In the end, the two-page text with many prescriptions was boiled down to two articles, forming the final resolution which divided the rules into, first, rules of general application and, second, additional means of interpretation only applicable in the judicial context.[135] This distinction between rules of general applicability and rules for international tribunals made in the resolution also indicates another important shift regarding the addressees of the rules of interpretation. While the said resolution still reflects the flexibility and independence of states regarding the interpretation of treaties, the codifications show a clear trend towards a general system that would apply to all actors interpreting treaties. This applies in particular to international courts. One of the features that might have added to the success of the method of codification in collective decision-making processes was that those codes were developed and designed by collective bodies themselves. If the rule was adopted by a collective body, it was more likely to assist in the decision-making of a judicial body that was organised similarly. This might be an explanation why the rules of treaty interpretation were re-generalised. This generalisation as well as the 'factor'-approach could be said to be the distinctive features that were added to the means of treaty interpretation in the codificatory phase.

Beginning with the twentieth century, there were also some attempts specifically looking at the interpretative practice of national courts.[136]

---

[132] Lauterpacht, 'De l'interprétation des traités'.
[133] Lauterpacht, 'Nouveau projet définitif de résolutions'.
[134] Gerald Fitzmaurice, 'De l'interprétation des traités'.
[135] Only then was the second Article applicable: see Box 7 in Appendix 1 below.
[136] Appert, 'De l'interprétation des traités diplomatiques au cours d'un procès'; Hyde, *International Law Chiefly as Interpreted and Applied by the United States* (vol. 1, 1st edn); Hyde, *International Law Chiefly as Interpreted and Applied by the United States* (2nd edn); McNair, 'L'Application et l'interprétation des traités d'après la Jurisprudence Britannique' 263. For a clear view that national courts can apply their method only as far as it complies with general jurisprudence, see Stockton, *Outlines of International Law* 259–60.

Yet, there is no evidence that those approaches impacted upon the relevant codifications in international law. There were also some tendencies contrary to the flexible phase. A less intentionalist current can be found in the American attempts at codifying the law of treaties. The American Institute of International Law drafted a code on the law of treaties[137] and forwarded it to the International Commission of Jurists,[138] which then modified it. After further modification, the Havana Convention, a draft convention on the law of treaties, was drawn up.[139] The various drafts do not say very much about interpretation,[140] but they all contain a significant move towards formalism regarding intentionalist means: the subsequent drafts considered that, subject to the wishes of the parties, the interpretation[141] or in the case of the Havana Convention the authentic interpretation[142] must be in writing. This can be seen as a cautious attempt to formalise and possibly also to domesticate authentic interpretations by the parties. But the ideas were subsequently not taken up. Another draft stated: 'rules governing interpretation in domestic law are applicable to the interpretation of international conventions in so far as said rules are common to the legal systems of the parties to the controversy.'[143] This would have made the rules of interpretation completely relative to the respective national laws and could have resulted in severe difficulties especially in cases of multilateral treaties.

Yet, the codificatory phase is also marked by a continuing disagreement about the goals of interpretation. This discourse was summarised as representing several schools of interpretation.[144] Schools set out a certain

---

[137] American Institute of International Law, 'Project No. 21'.
[138] International Commission of Jurists, 'Project No. IV: Treaties'.
[139] Convention on Treaties (adopted 20 February 1928) (1928) 22 *AJIL Supplement* 138.
[140] On the whole process, see Orellana Zabalza, *The Principle of Systemic Integration* 150.
[141] International Commission of Jurists, 'Project No. IV: Treaties'.
[142] Convention on Treaties (adopted 20 February 1928) (1928) 22 *AJIL Supplement* 138, Art. 3.
[143] Seventh International Conference of American States, reprinted in (1935) 29 *AJIL Supplement* 1225.
[144] Gerald Fitzmaurice, 'The Law and Procedure of the International Court of Justice 1951–4' 204. For recent accounts, see Bederman, 'Revivalist Canons and Treaty Interpretation' 964; Greig, 'The Time of Conclusion and the Time of Application of Treaties as Points of Reference in the Interpretative Process' 163; Jonas and Saunders, 'The Object and Purpose of a Treaty' 577. For a general account of the notion of schools in public international law with an English summary, see Fassbender, 'Denkschulen im Völkerrecht'.

goal of interpretation and weight the means accordingly.[145] Thus the textual, the purposive and the intentional schools have been distinguished.[146] Another way to frame the discourse was to talk about objective and subjective approaches.[147] Authors termed the purpose of interpretation in a certain way and then described the means to arrive at that purpose.[148] If a school was framed as textual, this does not, of course, mean that the text of the treaty was the only means available.[149] However, the text of the treaty was accorded a special status within the other means of interpretation.[150] So the essence of the discourse was not to establish which means of interpretation was the only relevant one but rather to provide for an aim of interpretation from which the means of interpretation and their importance could be derived.[151] The so-called schools of interpretation achieved that by framing the goal of interpretation in a certain way. Textualists suggested that the goal of interpretation was to arrive at the meaning of the words of the treaty.[152] The purposive school contended that the ultimate aim was to find out what the purpose of the agreement was.[153] Intentionalists would look for the intention of the parties, thereby regularly giving more

---

[145] See a more detailed treatment at p. 147 below.
[146] Sinclair, *The Vienna Convention on the Law of Treaties* 70. Distinguishing between subjective, textual and purposive approaches, see Jacobs, 'Varieties of Approach to Treaty Interpretation' 319.
[147] Bernhardt, *Die Auslegung völkerrechtlicher Verträge insbesondere in der neueren Rechtsprechung internationaler Gerichte* 15; Quoc Dinh, *Droit international public* 247; Karl, *Vertrag und spaetere Praxis im Voelkerrecht* 25ff; Schweisfurth, *Völkerrecht* 174. Linking these approaches to national jurisprudence is Cassese, *International Law* 178. A general explanation of these approaches is provided by Vogenauer, *Die Auslegung von Gesetzen in England und auf dem Kontinent* (vol. 1) 141.
[148] Schwarzenberger, 'Myths and Realities of Treaty Interpretation' 8. For a distinction between aim and means of interpretation, see Cremer, 'Regeln der Konventionsinterpretation' 176.
[149] It could also imply that certain other means are not available: see Köck, *Vertragsinterpretation und Vertragsrechtskonvention* 82–3. For the unavailability of the *travaux préparatoires*, see Neuhold, 'Die Wiener Vertragsrechtskonvention' 28.
[150] See for example Liacouras, 'The International Court of Justice and Development of Useful Rules of Interpretation in the Process of Treaty Interpretation' 164.
[151] Gerald Fitzmaurice, 'The Law and Procedure of the International Court of Justice: Treaty Interpretation' 4.
[152] See for example McNair, *The Law of Treaties* 365. Interestingly, he himself used the intention of the parties, while he nevertheless accorded special importance to the text which he found to be the best means to arrive at the intention of the parties. In a similar fashion, see Dörr, 'Art. 31' 522 para. 3.
[153] See for example McDougal, 'Some Basic Theoretical Concepts about International Law' 353. See also Alvarez, *Le Droit international nouveau dans ses rapport avec la vie actuelle*

interpretative weight to means like the *travaux préparatoires* or the subsequent practice of the parties.[154] In the alternative classification, subjective approaches relying on the true will of the parties which should emanate from means like the *travaux*, were opposed to objective approaches which relied more on the wording or the purpose of the system of the treaty.[155] All of these rather abstract notions are constructs which are themselves uncertain and more the result of the process of interpretation. So for example the intention of the parties is based on the fiction that the parties develop a common will that guides the process of interpretation.[156] Yet, there was a dispute as to which of the goals ought to prevail. No codification gives better evidence about this struggle than the *Restatement Second of the American Law Institute*.[157] It stated that the basic function of interpretation was to 'to ascertain the meaning intended by the parties'[158] but said at the same time that interpretation aimed to 'ascertain and give effect to the purpose of the international agreement'[159] and in turn defined that purpose as appearing 'from the terms used by the parties, it was intended to serve'.[160] So we see that every school managed to anchor its keyword in the text so that the process of interpretation could have been said to have four goals. If asked which of the schools has actually won the battle for the *Restatement Second*, the answer would be most likely the textual school. To understand why this is the case, we need to look at the function a goal of interpretation can have.

The function of this discourse can be explained by the fact that the rules of interpretation were in flux at that time. By stressing a rather abstract goal, one implicitly also emphasised certain means of interpretation.[161] As we have already seen, there is a connection between the real

---

des peuples 498. He contended that the object and purpose would always trump the wording of the treaty. For a general purposive account, see also the Harvard Draft.

[154] In relation to the *travaux* this was most openly argued on different occasions by Lauterpacht, 'Les travaux préparatoires et l'interprétation des traités' 713; Lauterpacht, 'De l'interprétation des traités'. For the importance of subsequent practice, see McNair, *The Law of Treaties* 424.

[155] Köck, *Vertragsinterpretation und Vertragsrechtskonvention* 82.

[156] Ludwik Ehrlich, 'L'Interprétation des traités' 66; Nicol, 'Original Intent and the ECHR' 154. One problem with this notion is for example that common intention is called into question when new parties accede to the treaty: see Cremer, 'Regeln der Konventionsinterpretation' 185.

[157] American Law Institute, *Restatement of the Law Second: Foreign Relations Law of the United States* 449ff.

[158] Ibid. § 146. [159] Ibid. § 147(1). [160] Ibid.

[161] For a general account that the intention is just a frame that amounts to correct meaning, see MacCormick, *Rhetoric and the Rule of Law* 137.

intentions approach and means like the preparatory works or subsequent practice. This connection is even more obvious between the objective or purposive school and the object and purpose of the treaty. By stressing one goal of interpretation, one means of interpretation is brought to the fore. If we look again at the *Restatement Second*, it provides that all the factors can be resorted to in order to illuminate the meaning of the treaty.[162] The only exception it makes is that the ordinary meaning always has to be considered. So irrespective of the fact that all goals are mentioned, the textual school has actually won the day since the text is the only means in the *Restatement Second* that always has to be considered. Of course, the big contests were yet to come. What we can take away from the discourse between the schools is that its function was to establish a predominant means of interpretation. This has been a useful endeavour as long as the relationship between the means of interpretation has not been fixed.

In the course of discussion in the codificatory phase, one current of thought entered the arena of international legal doctrine that deserves special mention. The policy science approach managed to transfer a specially adapted American realist thinking into the international sphere.[163] The 'New Haven School' is particularly associated with Myres McDougal, who was also a member of the US delegation at the First Vienna Conference. His approach aimed to study the process of treaty interpretation from the perspective of communication.[164] Consequently, it introduced the 'shared expectations of the parties as another goal in the discourse'.[165] While shared expectations are similar to an imagined common will, they seem to be more rational and objective than intentionalist approaches. The policy science approach sought to alter the whole method of interpretation and to turn it to an interdisciplinary scientific endeavour. Rejecting a legalistic approach to interpretation, it answered calls for a scientific method of interpretation in American legal

---

[162] See American Law Institute, *Restatement of the Law Second: Foreign Relations Law of the United States*, § 146.
[163] Falk, 'On Treaty Interpretation and the New Haven Approach: Achievements and Prospects'. The realist thinking emerges from McDougal, 'Some Basic Theoretical Concepts about International Law: A Policy-Oriented Framework of Inquiry'.
[164] McDougal, Lasswell and Miller, *The Interpretation of Agreements and World Public Order* xi–xix, 35–9.
[165] *Ibid*. 82.

doctrine.¹⁶⁶ It also provided for a complex system of material and procedural principles to structure the inquiry of the interpreter.¹⁶⁷ In this scientific endeavour, legal norms and restrictions were considered as hampering the necessary activity of the interpreter; the rule of interpretation was severely criticised.¹⁶⁸

The New Haven approach leads back to the essentials we have found in the codificatory phase: There was a significant movement towards synthesising the prescription of legal argument and to provide for abstract and generalised factors of interpretation. The remaining question was which factors ought to be included and whether some of them were to be preferred over others. The determination of the hierarchy as between the actors gave rise to a discourse and certain schools of interpretation which formulated goals. Yet, those goals had only the function to stress certain factors of interpretation over others. This applies to all goals except the shared expectation of the parties. This goal of interpretation not only stressed certain means of interpretation but sought to open the process of interpretation up completely and to transform it to a rather realist and scientific inquiry. As we have seen, there are many similarities between the approaches to codifying the method of treaty interpretation, but many problems remained unresolved and had to await their solution through the final codification in the Vienna Convention. Before we look at the rule of interpretation contained therein, we shall briefly summarise what we learned while drilling deep into the methodological layers of treaty interpretation in international law.

4.5. Summary and explanation

As previously expressed, international interpretative method has developed significantly in the course of the centuries. What was termed here as the mechanical approach included a strong emphasis on literal interpretation which was distinct from other means of interpretation

---

[166] Yü, *The Interpretation of Treaties* 37; Harvard Law School, 'Harvard Draft Convention on the Law of Treaties' 956.

[167] McDougal, Lasswell and Miller, *The Interpretation of Agreements and World Public Order*.

[168] McDougal, 'The International Law Commission's Draft Articles upon Interpretation: Textuality Redivivus'. For a criticism on the New Haven approach, see Gerald Fitzmaurice, 'Vae Victis or Woe to the Negotiators! Your Treaty or Our "Interpretation" of It?' 358.

followed by some rather mechanical rules in the sense that they were conjectures drawn from certain preconceived features of the treaty. In the flexible phase, literal interpretation was put on the same level as the other means of interpretation and what have been termed mechanical rules were replaced by a more flexible handling, while a significant stream rejected the necessity or existence of rules of interpretation at all. In contrast, in the codificatory phase, the approaches all operated from the basis of the existence of legal norms on interpretation and tried to define a consistent approach which often resulted in the description of certain factors that would guide the process of interpretation.

One can describe this development as linear in the sense: Rules of interpretation constantly improved over time. Another view would be to tie the rules of interpretation to the structure of the international community and its underlying theory. The international family/community/society changed significantly over time and the rules of interpretation might have reacted to that: The mechanical phase to an increasing treaty practice after the Peace of Westphalia. The flexible phase to a more autonomous treaty practice of states. And the codificatory phase to the emergence of tribunals and later courts. For the mechanical phase, the work of Grotius is exemplary in many regards. Using antique sources, his theories were at least partly based on natural law, which allowed him to create a very diverse canon of treaty interpretation. It has been in many senses a quest to infer the right rules from reason. The more international legal scholarship was influenced by positivist thinking, the more the approaches lacked prescriptions that did not relate to the will of the parties but to general rules like material prescriptions and actual presumptions. There was a decrease in the rules of treaty interpretation that led some authors to deny the existence of rules on interpretation. Other authors tried to adapt the rules of treaty interpretation to positivistic thinking, which often resulted in a very strong emphasis on the authentic means of treaty interpretation such as the *travaux préparatoires* and subsequent practice. It was also often thought that the rules of treaty interpretation would only be subsidiary to the agreed interpretation of the states. Yet, while judicial actors approached the stage of international law, codificatory approaches were developed and resulted ultimately in a new category of means of treaty interpretation, namely, the 'factor' approach. In codifying, the practice of states and international courts was taken into account but framed in a particular way. The codificatory efforts ultimately resulted in the codification of the rule of interpretation in Arts. 31 and 32 VCLT. The review of the history of the method of interpretation before the coming into force of the VCLT has given us the scope to reflect on the current method and to work out its determinative features. What we can see from the different phases of treaty interpretation is that they all took a stance on the quality of the rules on interpretation.[169] They employed several different means of interpretation.[170] They established their goals of interpretation[171] and envisaged a certain process of interpretation.[172] They accounted for the relation between the various means. The historical analysis has provided us with the possibility to highlight certain questions and problems. Those questions are as follows:

- What is the nature of the rules of the VCLT?
- What type of means does the VCLT use?
- What is the relation between those means and how does the process of treaty interpretation operate?
- What limits are there to interpretation?
- What is the goal of interpretation?
- What can the specific means used in the Convention tell us about the intertemporal question?

Whenever a question is subject to dispute, we have found an intertemporal knot. The inquiry will then be limited to outlining the different approaches one can take towards a question. Intertemporal knots are likely to arise whenever we interpret the text of the convention directly. Cardinal cores are the features underlying the rule of interpretation. They mostly tell us how the rule on interpretation works and mostly will relate to the process of interpretation, i.e. the way in which the process proceeds. While looking at the cardinal cores and the interpretative knots, it will be important not only to explain them but to see how they play out regarding the intertemporal question.

---

[169] Be they legal, derived from natural law or non-existent.
[170] Examples include maxims, presumptions and inferences.
[171] Such as the real intentions, the assumed intentions, the shared expectations or the object and purpose.
[172] See for example the shift from the pre-existing meaning to an *ex post* justification.

5

Cardinal cores of the rule: features of the process

5.1. The nature of the rule core: legality

A cardinal core of the Vienna Convention that sometimes receives less attention is the fact that the rules on interpretation have a legal character.[173] This is not a necessary feature of a legal system; in jurisdictions like Germany or the United States, the rules of interpretation are not legal in nature, whereas the Acts Interpretation Act in Australia provides for rules of construction.[174] The legal status of the international rule of interpretation is seldom doubted today.[175] As with so many social facts, their legal nature is easy to acknowledge but very hard to understand. Two questions are striking in that context: The first is what nature the rules of interpretation had before being codified. The second is what effect their legal nature has.

Looking at the legal nature of the rule before codification, the first point of reference would be Art. 38(1) ICJ Statute. Indeed, it has been contended in doctrine[176] as well as in jurisprudence[177] that the rule of interpretation is also customary in nature. What is significant is that this assertion lacks justification. As is well known, customary international law is formed by general practice accepted as law, i.e. there has to be state practice as well as *opinio juris sive necessitatis* for a customary international rule. It is striking that neither the Draft Articles of the

---

[173] But cf. the extensive treatment by Haraszti and Decsenyi, *Some Fundamental Problems of the Law of Treaties* 195–218.
[174] An overview is provided by Vogenauer, 'Statutory Interpretation' 831. For an overview of the rules on interpretation for contracts in private law, see Herbots, 'Interpretation of Contracts' 424.
[175] See, however, the sceptical remarks in Brownlie, *Principles of Public International Law* 631.
[176] For an account of the customary status of the rule after the coming into force of the Vienna Convention, see Villiger, 'The 1969 Vienna Convention on the Law of Treaties' 132; Dörr, 'Art. 31' 523–5 para. 6.
[177] See the references in Villiger, 'The Rules on Interpretation: Misgivings, Misunderstandings, Miscarriage? The "Crucible" Intended by the International Law Commission' 118.

ILC nor the discussions at the First Vienna Conference contain an analysis of the elements of customary international law. While state practice is mentioned at some points in a rather general and abstract manner,[178] the ILC Commentary mainly relies on judgments and awards as authority but also uses doctrine. Yet, the sources used do not really quote state practice. Thus, it is hard to contend that the nature of the rules was really customary. Yet, it might have been possible to deduce general principles of law recognised by civilised nations as set out in Art. 38(1)(c) ICJ Statute. It is very clear that the ILC did not inquire into national methodologies. The Seventh International Conference of American States at least tried to draft a rule based on national methods.[179] The draft states in its Art. 1 that the 'rules governing interpretation in domestic law are applicable to the interpretation of international conventions in so far as said rules are common to the legal systems of the parties to the controversy'.[180] Neither of those ways to construct an international method through national methods gained much attention.[181] There might be other sources of international law such as structural principles.[182] Before entering those uncharted waters, it might be helpful to reconsider what the ILC actually did when drafting the rules.

It has often been argued that there is no strict line between codification and progressive development, as the abstraction of the rules often entails creative elements.[183] The opinion amongst authors is split on the question.[184]

---

[178] See for example Waldock's general remarks as an expert consultant 'Summary records of the plenary meetings and of the meetings of the Committee of the Whole' United Nations Conference on the Law of Treaties, First Session (Vienna, 26 March–24 May 1968) 184 para. 66 ('First Vienna Conference').

[179] See above (n. 143).   [180] Ibid.

[181] For an account that this was not very promising, see Ludwik Ehrlich, 'L'Interprétation des traités' 10.

[182] Goldmann, 'On the Comparative Foundations of Principles in International Law'.

[183] Brierly, 'The Future of Codification' 1; Jacobs, 'Innovation and Continuity in the Law of Treaties' 509; Roberts, 'Traditional and Modern Approaches to Customary International Law' 763; Treves, 'Customary International Law' 13 para. 69; In the seventh section of the preamble to the Vienna Convention, the contracting parties show their general belief that the Vienna Convention as a whole has been progressive development as well as codification.

[184] The customary nature before 1969 is supported by Köck, Vertragsinterpretation und Vertragsrechtskonvention. Amongst those who favour terming the rules on interpretation as progressive development are Merrills, 'Two Approaches to Treaty Interpretation' 58; Villiger, 'The 1969 Vienna Convention on the Law of Treaties' 133; Zemanek, 'Vienna Convention on the Law of Treaties' 2; Klabbers, 'Virtuous Interpretation' 29; Sbolci, 'Supplementary Means of Interpretation' 149.

Waldock himself contended to codify existing practice.[185] But he also admitted that every possible maxim of interpretation could be found in judicial practice.[186] This indicates that there was a creative element in the way the rules were framed. This consideration weakens the idea that the rules existing before codification still matter today.

This position becomes totally uncertain if we consider how the nature of the rules evolved in the course of time. While the initial position was that rules on interpretation could be derived from right reason or the law of nature,[187] later approaches added as possible other sources Roman law[188] as well as rules stemming from the national legal systems,[189] especially the domestic analogies derived from statutory construction or the interpretation of private law contracts[190] or both.[191] But the rise of positivistic approaches to international law subjected those rules to the will of the states in the flexible phase of interpretation. At the outset lay the observation that the rule of interpretation could have no source in international law as they had no basis in customary or treaty law.[192] Some approaches accepted rules as subsidiary to the explicit emanation of states, although the rules on interpretation belonged to doctrine and not to the body of international law.[193] During the flexible phase of interpretation, more radical approaches evolved that denied the existence of a rule of interpretation completely.[194] Speaking of '[s]o-called rules of

---

[185] ILC, 'Report of the International Law Commission on the work of its 16th session (11 May to 24 July 1964)', UN Doc. A/CN.4/167 and Add.1-3, Third Report of the Special Rapporteur, Sir Humphrey Waldock, *ILC Ybk* 1964 II, 54 para. 5 ('Waldock, Third Report'). It is noteworthy that he did not review any state practice but only referred to Chapters 20-2 in McNair, *The Law of Treaties*.

[186] Waldock, Third Report (n. 185) 54.

[187] See for example Vattel, *The Law of Nations or the Principles of Natural Law* 200-1 (Book 2, Chapter 17, para. 268).

[188] Phillimore, *Commentaries upon International Law* 98-110.

[189] *Ibid.* 98ff (Chapter VIII, para. LXVI, LXXV, LXXVII, LXXX and LXXXIII).

[190] Woolsey, *Introduction to the study of international law* 173; Pergler, *Judicial interpretation of international law in the United States* 174.

[191] Taylor, *Treatise on International Public Law* 395 para. 377. He stresses that those principles had to be adapted to the peculiarities of international law.

[192] Adler, 'The Interpretation of Treaties' 63; Oppenheim, *International Law* (vol. 1) 582.

[193] Oppenheim called it 'scientific grounds ... provided by jurisprudence'. Oppenheim, *International Law* (vol. 1) 582.

[194] See Klabbers, 'Virtuous Interpretation' 28. Such a position was taken by Lawrence, who asserted at the top of the one page he devoted to that topic that '[a] vast amount of misplaced ingenuity has been expended on this subject'. Lawrence, *The Principles of International Law* 326.

interpretation',[195] Charles Hyde rejected any rule obstructing the interpreter from collecting the evidence offering guidance on the design of the treaty, meaning the will of the parties.[196] But at the same time that these radical approaches were developed and the traditional rules of interpretation became subject to doubts, increasing attempts were made at codifying the rules of treaty interpretation. These at times contained no rules of treaty interpretation;[197] the question whether there should be legal norms was controversially discussed by the Institut de Droit International,[198] which finally decided to take rather a soft-law approach as the preamble to its resolution stated that interpreters could be 'inspired' by the rules, which suggests that they were not meant to be rigid legal norms. From this short overview of the three phases of interpretation, we can easily see that the ontology as well as the nature of the rules was in a state of flux. In view of the intertemporal question, it is tempting to take a stance: If there was a separate source, a solution to the intertemporal problem could flow from it. Yet, it is impossible to categorise those rules in one form or the other.

A better solution would consequently be to take their legal status for granted and use the assumed customary nature to extend the applicability of the rules. Yet, the focus ought to be shifted on the real, i.e. legal, nature of the rule. The fact that the interpretative method would acquire such a status was far from clear. The third Special Rapporteur Gerald Fitzmaurice came up with the idea just to provide a code for the law of treaties.[199] However, this approach was rejected by the fourth Special Rapporteur Humphrey Waldock who was generally of the opinion that the law of treaties should be regulated by a treaty. He felt a particular need to justify this decision in his commentary in the case of the rule of interpretation.[200] While Waldock conceded that the rule

---

[195] Hyde, *International Law Chiefly as Interpreted and Applied by the United States* (2nd edn) 1468.
[196] *Ibid.* 1468. He had developed this thought already in Hyde, 'Concerning the Interpretation of Treaties' 55. See also Klabbers, 'Virtuous Interpretation' 28.
[197] Bluntschli, *Das moderne Völkerrecht der civiliesirten Staten* 245, 253. Restricting himself to referring to good faith when it comes to treaty interpretation, see Field, *Draft Outlines of an International Code* 311, 507. He deals only with the interpretation of contracts in private international law.
[198] Gerald Fitzmaurice, 'De l'interprétation des traités' 325ff.
[199] ILC, 'Report of the International Law Commission on its 8th session' (23 April–4 July 1956), UN Doc. A/CN.4/104, Report of the Special Rapporteur, Sir Gerald Fitzmaurice, *ILC Ybk* 1956 II, 106–7 para. 9.
[200] Waldock, Third Report (n. 185) 53–4.

of interpretation comprised a certain degree of flexibility, he nevertheless thought that it should be codified as legal norm.[201] And indeed the usefulness of a legally binding rule was called into question at different stages of its preparation such as in the deliberations of the ILC[202] as well as in the discussions of the First Vienna Conference.[203] But Waldock's vision prevailed.

This aspect of the evolution of the VCLT recalls that it is far from common to frame the rule of interpretation as a legal norm, it is conversely interesting and surprising in many respects. Is it addressed only to states, or, also to international organisations and their organs, such as courts?[204] Or even to individuals?[205] Klabbers pointed out this issue, which is not at all clear. He also remarked that it is unclear what the result of a breach of the rule of interpretation would be:[206] Could there be a breach of the Convention separately from the breach of the treaty to be interpreted? Suppose that a court justifies its interpretation only with reference to the *travaux* and the circumstances at the time of the conclusion of the treaty without mentioning any other technique of interpretation. This could be considered as breach of the rule of interpretation. Yet, if the means enshrined in Art. 31 VCLT point in the same direction, the treaty would certainly not be violated. So, there can be a breach of the rule of interpretation without violating the treaty. Yet, Klabbers is right to contend that such legalistic consequences can hardly be assumed to be the functions of the legal nature of the rules. This function can be seen by highlighting a feature of legal norms as opposed to other alternatives such as professional guidelines or soft law: A legal norm provides for clearness, distinctness, and transparency. It might also

---

[201] Ibid.
[202] See for example the comments of Mr Verdross, ILC, 'Report of the International Law Commission on the work of its 16th session' (11 May–24 July 1964) UN Doc. A/CN.4/1964 and Add.1-3, Summary Record of the 726th meeting, *ILC Ybk* 1964 I, 21.
[203] See for example the remarks of Delegate McDougal, First Vienna Conference (n. 178) 167, as well as of Delegate Dadzie (Ghana), *ibid.* 170 para. 68, as well as the remarks of Delegate Krispis (Greece), *ibid.* 170 para. 7.
[204] The view that it is addressed to states and courts is held by Crema, 'Subsequent Agreements and Subsequent Practice within and outside the Vienna Convention' 27.
[205] Klabbers, 'Virtuous Interpretation' 24.
[206] This problem has been raised by Klabbers, *ibid.* 30. He rightly distinguishes rules of interpretation from other norms, and contends that only other norms regulate behaviour. On this point, one could stress that the rules of interpretation also seek to regulate behaviour, i.e. the behaviour of interpreters.

decrease the flexibility and changeability of the rule in Arts. 31 and 32 VCLT, since the rule of interpretation is enshrined in legal norms. Yet, it has a stark disciplining effect. Even if a breach has no real consequences, the legal nature of the rules will increase their visibility and, consequently compliance with them. This very effect will also make it difficult to go beyond the rules since this would mean a violation of the law. This is then also important for questions of stasis and evolution, since we are required by law to look first to the Vienna Convention.

It can be concluded that rules of interpretation stemming from another source cannot be ascertained. The legal nature of the rules forms a core of the Convention, which is essential for dealing with questions of stasis and evolution: This reinforces the need to apply the Vienna Convention in the process of interpretation.

5.2. The means core: techniques

The term 'means' has been used in this study to comprise different ways to interpret. We have seen that, in the mechanical phase, there was not just one but many ways to interpret: Single systems contained presumptions, principles and maxims. In the flexible phase, this variety diminished and the means of interpretation relating to the intention of the parties came to the fore. We have also seen that the Harvard Draft synthesised and reduced the means of interpretation to so-called 'factors'. As the observation of national approaches to interpretation show, there are many ways to construct a coherent system of interpretation.[207] Since the VCLT opted for the consistent use of one kind of means, the difference between different means is rarely stressed nowadays.[208] The consistent use of techniques of interpretation is a cardinal core and also one that is of the utmost importance. Especially when it comes to questions of changing interpretation of treaties, several doctrinal solutions relied on other means of interpretation. This is why we should have

---

[207] For a comparative view on statutory interpretation, see MacCormick and Summers (eds.), *Interpreting Statutes: A Comparative Study*; Vogenauer, *Die Auslegung von Gesetzen in England und auf dem Kontinent* (vol. 1); Vogenauer, 'Statutory Interpretation'. For a comparative view on the interpretation of contracts, see Herbots, 'Interpretation of Contracts'.

[208] Remy, 'Techniques interpretatives et systemes de droit' 329. For the distinction between means of interpretation and rules, see Daillier, Forteau and Pellet, *Droit international public* 284.

a closer look at the concept of techniques of interpretation. It is important to see how the other means compare to techniques of interpretation and how they can be applied to questions of stasis and evolution. This will clarify the polyphony of approaches regarding the intertemporal question to a certain extent.

5.2.1 Techniques of interpretation

In his introduction to the first commentary on the proposed rules on interpretation, Waldock stated that there were many principles and maxims frequently used in international practice.[209] As examples for this form of interpretation he mentioned maxims such as *ut res magis valeat quam pereat, contra proferentem, eiusdem generis, expressio unius est exclusio alterius* and *generalia specialibus non derogant*.[210] From these principles and maxims, Waldock distinguished what he called 'methods' of interpretation. In his conception, those means were not exclusive, and their application depended to a certain extent on the discretion of the interpreter.[211] Although he did not mention it explicitly in this context, he actually followed the 'factor' approach of the Harvard Draft Convention. It would also be possible to denote the methods as arguments or canons.[212] But recently, the rules of treaty interpretation have been referred to as containing techniques of interpretation.[213] Techniques have been defined as means allowing the interpreter to determine the meaning of a text through arguments.[214] We should expand upon this definition: the term *téchne* signifies a craft of an author, sculptor or rhetorician exercised according to a certain set of rules.[215] This evidences

---

[209] Waldock, Third Report (n. 178) 55.
[210] Ibid. 54 para. 5; see the further examples in Kolb, 'Les Maximes juridiques en droit international public' 407. For a general overview of maxims from Roman law, see Broom, *A Selection of Legal Maxims, Classified and Illustrated*.
[211] Waldock, Third Report (n. 178) 54 para. 5.
[212] Vogenauer, *Die Auslegung von Gesetzen in England und auf dem Kontinent* (vol. 1) 6.
[213] Schwarzenberger, 'Myths and Realities of Treaty Interpretation' 9; Kuijper, 'The European Courts and the Law of Treaties' 260; Arato, 'Subsequent Practice and Evolutive Interpretation' 452; Corten, 'Les Techniques reproduites aux Articles 31 à 33 des Conventions de Vienne' 351; Remy, 'Techniques interpretatives et systemes de droit'. See also the other contributions in the same issue.
[214] Remy, 'Techniques interpretatives et systemes de droit' 329.
[215] Lege, 'Was Juristen wirklich tun: Jurisprudential realism'.

an interesting feature of techniques: they make some prescriptions, yet they also leave some freedom to the craftswomen or craftsmen.

The first important feature of how techniques work is that they relate to procedure rather than to content.[216] One could alternatively say that the rules on interpretation are 'adjectival' rather than 'substantive'.[217] This is very important since it means that they do not carry any meaning that would materially influence the process of interpretation. The only thing that they do, and this marks the second important feature, is that they *validate* considerations.[218] So, a consideration that matches the requirement of a technique can be imported to the process of interpretation under the head of this technique. They work like gatekeepers. This leads us to the third feature, their *generality*. This works in two ways: First, the techniques are themselves general arguments. All considerations that can possibly comprise the object and purpose of the treaty can fall under this heading. Consequently, they establish a certain class of argument. This is most important since it also means that the considerations established by a technique can always work both ways. They are *flexible*. So they are also indifferent and general towards the interpretative outcome of the question.

5.2.2 Maxims

This can be contrasted with what Waldock called maxims. These rules often go back to Greek rhetoric and Roman law and are included in commonly accepted phrases that provide for standard arguments, which are also called *topoi* or *loci*.[219] They are 'born of the observation of the manner in which language is used'.[220] These maxims derive

---

[216] Binder and Zemanek, 'Das Vertragsrecht' 72. For the distinction of questions of content and procedure, see McDougal, Lasswell and Miller, *The Interpretation of Agreements and World Public Order* 46.

[217] ILC, 'Report of the International Law Commission on its 8th session' (20 April–26 June 1959), UN Doc. A/CN.4/104, Fourth Report of the Special Rapporteur, Sir Gerald Fitzmaurice *ILC Ybk* 1959 II, 39.

[218] In relation to arguments based on canons, see Alexy, *A Theory of Legal Argumentation* 238–9, 245. In relation to the VCLT rules, this is expressed by Kadelbach, 'Interpretation of the Charter' 74–5 para. 5.

[219] Viehweg, *Topik und Jurisprudenz*; Kolb, 'Les Maximes juridiques en droit international public'. A frequent use of maxims to explain the interpretation of treaties in international law is provided by Wildman, *Institutes of International Law* 113ff.

[220] Graham, 'In Defence of Maxims' 66.

their authority from their common usage as well as from their tradition. An interpreter using maxims will build on their 'deceptive elegance and simplicity'.[221] On the other hand, they are described as 'stereotyped formulae' that had to be applied mechanically and unvaryingly.[222] Maxims pretend to be derived from legal logic.[223] Yet, different maxims can produce contradictory results and the question is then which maxim to apply in which context. Like rhetorical figures, they depend upon their suitability in the specific context,[224] and they do not derive from logical imperatives.[225] There can even be contradictory maxims like the *expressio unius* maxim[226] which leads to the opposite result as compared to the use of the *a fortiori*[227] maxim.[228] The two maxims apply in the same circumstances, namely, that something is expressed in a rule while another is not. In those circumstances, the *expressio unius* rule would provide that there is no gap in the law but an omission that ought to remain while the *a fortiori* maxim would suggest exactly the opposite conclusion. The maxims themselves provide no guidance for the interpreter in one or the other direction. This shows that maxims leave broad discretion to the interpreter but do not oblige him or her to justify the use of one maxim or the other with the particularities of the treaty.[229] Unlike techniques, maxims do not describe a structured way of arriving at the meaning of a text but present standard arguments that have often been applied and, therefore, carry certain relevance. Techniques are in comparison more abstract, describing the general way in which a provision is to be interpreted. The use of techniques does not rule out maxims. The maxims mentioned above could be used under the heading of the context of the treaty as established by Art. 31(1) VCLT. Other maxims could help to establish the ordinary meaning. The classical maxim in regard to stasis and evolution in interpretation of texts is *contemporanea expositio est*

---

[221] Gordon, 'The World Court and the Interpretation of Constitutive Treaties' 795.
[222] Harvard Law School, 'Harvard Draft Convention on the Law of Treaties' 938.
[223] Schachter, *International Law in Theory and Practice* 54; Graham, 'In Defence of Maxims' 46, 70.
[224] Graham, 'In Defence of Maxims'.
[225] Broom, *A Selection of Legal Maxims, Classified and Illustrated* 17.
[226] The maxim *expressio unius exclusio alterius* can be translated as the express mention of one thing excludes all others not mentioned.
[227] Which could be translated as argument derived from stronger reason.
[228] McDougal, Lasswell and Miller, *The Interpretation of Agreements and World Public Order* 332.
[229] Yü, *The Interpretation of Treaties* 72.

optima et fortissima in lege which Broom translates as 'the best and surest mode of expounding an instrument is by referring to the time when, and circumstances under which, it was made'.[230] The fact that the maxim refers only to the best and surest mode means that the maxim is in no way absolute. This maxim could be understood as establishing a strong presumption in favour of static interpretations. This leads straight to the second means under consideration.

5.2.3 Presumptions

Presumptions indicate an interpretative result unless the requirements of an exception are fulfilled. Presumptions were relied on by Grotius, but were later subject to severe criticism, while Ehrlich tried to codify the law of treaties nearly exclusively by using presumptions.[231] The Vienna Convention contains several of them,[232] and also uses this approach for the interpretation of multilingual treaties in Art. 33(3) VCLT. It states that the 'terms of the treaty are presumed to have the same meaning in each authentic text'. This shows us how presumptions actually work: They set out certain requirements, and in the case of fulfilment indicate an interpretative result.

There were also attempts by states to amend the general rule of interpretation with presumptions by delegations commenting on the reports of the Special Rapporteur.[233] However, the ILC did not include

---

[230] Broom, *A Selection of Legal Maxims, Classified and Illustrated* 152.

[231] The American Law Institute, *Restatement of the Law Second: Foreign Relations Law of the United States*.

[232] Explicit presumptions with regard to the intention of a state are formulated in Art. 20(4)(b) and Art. 36(1). In other cases, the Vienna Convention presumes certain solutions unless they are not provided for in the treaty: see Art. 16, Art. 20(1), (3), (4), (5), Art. 22(1), (2), (3), Art. 25, Art. 28, Art. 29, Art. 33, Art. 36, Art. 37, Art. 40(1), Art. 41(2), Art. 44(1), Art. 55, Art. 56(1), Art. 58(2).

[233] The Czechoslovakian government proposed a presumption that the text is the authentic expression of the intentions of the parties, ILC, 'Report of the International Law Commission on the work of its 18th session' (4 May–19 July 1966), UN Doc. A/CN.4/SER.A/1966/Add.1 Annex: Law of Treaties: Comments by governments on the draft articles on the law of treaties drawn up by the Commission at its fourteenth, fifteenth and sixteenth session UN Doc. A/CN.4/182 and Corr.1&2 and Add.1, 2/Rev.1 & 3, *ILC Ybk* 1966 II, 91. Stressing the intention of the parties, the Hungarian government suggested that the text should be presumed to be the intention of the parties: see *ibid*. Waldock stressed the congruence between the Czechoslovakian position and the approach of the ILC but also showed that both approaches were different in nature as it would not be clear in what cases the presumption could be rebutted and what would be the relation to other elements of interpretation: *ibid*. 94.

presumptions of any kind in the general rule of interpretation. The necessary attribute of presumptions is that they indicate a certain interpretation and, consequently, influence the result of the interpretative exercise. In contrast, techniques do not indicate what the result of the interpretation should look like but only classify and distinguish the arguments that could possibly lead to a certain result.

As to the intertemporal question, presumptions can prescribe evolutive or static interpretations if certain criteria are fulfilled. As established above, there is a view suggesting that there should be a presumption in favour of static interpretation, with some exceptions for dynamic interpretation. Such an exception could be derived from the nature of the treaty.

5.2.4 Inferences from the nature of the treaty

The nature of the treaty refers to the areas of law to which the treaty is assigned. Those areas of treaties are contingent.[234] This means that certain treaties are grouped in a certain category such as human rights or environmental law. Such designation can play a role in the process of interpretation when a certain interpretative outcome is assigned to a certain nature. This type of interpretation is used in Art. 56(1)(b) VCLT as well as in Art. 62(2)(a) VCLT. In the first case, the nature of a treaty is used as a requirement to rebut the presumption that there is no right of withdrawal and renunciation. It is left to the interpreter to decide what kind of treaties would be fit to rebut the presumption. Art. 62(2)(a) VCLT in contrast excludes treaties with a certain nature from the scope of Art. 62 VCLT.[235] Both provisions show in which circumstances the nature of the

---

[234] Koskenniemi, 'The Fate of Public International Law' 26. See for the term 'öffentliches Recht' (public law) Grimm, *Das öffentliche Recht vor der Frage nach seiner Identität* 2. See also generally Djeffal, 'Neue Akteure und das Völkerrecht' 14.

[235] The nature of treaties has also been prominently used in the ILC Draft articles on the effects of armed conflicts on treaties, ILC, 'Report of the International Law Commission on its 63rd session' (4 July–12 August 2011) *ILC Ybk* 2011 II 2. According to Art. 5, the question of termination, withdrawal or suspension ought to be regulated according to the rules of treaty interpretation. The draft articles, however, continue to be more specific. Art. 5 contains further factors that are relevant for the determination. Subsection (a) mentions 'the nature of the treaty, in particular its subject-matter, its object and purpose, its content and the number of parties to the treaty'. Art. 7 then includes an indicative list that provides for treaties, which, by their nature, continue to exist. This is another example of the use of the nature of treaties very similar to Art. 56(1)(b) and Art. 62(2)(a) VCLT.

treaty typically works as a self-standing means of interpretation: Those are questions about the very existence of the treaty or its applicability to the parties. From the nature, it can be derived whether this class of treaties continues to exist or whether they are susceptible to termination. Since the class of treaties is linked to a certain interpretative outcome, the distinction works in a binary fashion. This leads us to the major differences in comparison to techniques: Techniques are flexible and context dependent, they are not tied to a particular interpretative outcome. On the other hand, techniques can account for the substantive arguments inherent in the nature of the treaty: the technique of object and purpose explicitly mentions the object of the treaty; this will certainly include its nature.[236]

5.2.5 Inferences from the classification of the treaty

Inferences as to the interpretation of the treaty could also be derived from the classification of the treaty. There is a longstanding distinction between *traité loi* and *traité contrat*, i.e. law-making and ordinary treaties.[237] A significant trend in international legal scholarship sees the development of the notions of constitutionalism or constitutionalisation in international law.[238] So it would also be possible to accord to a certain treaty, such as the UN Charter,[239] the status of a constitution or to several specific treaties[240] the status of constitutive elements of the international legal order.

The distinction between *traité loi* and *traité contrat* builds on the assumption that there are elements of public as well as of private law in international law in general and in the law of treaties in particular.[241]

---

[236] For an account excluding inferences from the nature of a treaty from the accepted methods of interpretation, see Haraszti and Decsenyi, *Some Fundamental Problems of the Law of Treaties* 80.

[237] Reglade, 'De la nature juridique des traités internationaux et du sens de la distinction des traités-lois et des traités-contrats' 507; Wright, 'The Interpretation of Multilateral Treaties' 100; Bederman, 'Revivalist Canons and Treaty Interpretation' 955.

[238] Peters, 'Compensatory Constitutionalism'; Fassbender, *The United Nations Charter As the Constitution of the International Community*; Kleinlein, *Konstitutionalisierung im Völkerrecht*.

[239] Fassbender, *The United Nations Charter As the Constitution of the International Community*.

[240] Brölmann, 'Specialized Rules of Treaty Interpretation' 516.

[241] For that distinction, see Bederman, 'Revivalist Canons and Treaty Interpretation' 955. A very early distinction between the public and private law nature is provided by Gentili, *De jure bellis libri tres* 191–2.

There were also several attempts to apply this distinction to the law of treaties. So it was for example contended that the respective rules of interpretation could be derived from different domestic analogies such as analogies from the law of contract for *traité contrat* and analogies from statutory interpretation for *traité loi*.[242] Others have stated that lawmaking treaties may not be interpreted restrictively.[243]

The term constitution is not used in the Vienna Convention, although the Vienna Convention has been referred to as part of a constitution itself.[244] In relation to the intertemporal question, the effects derived from the distinction could be compared to those of the distinction between *traité loi* and *traité contrat*. As already mentioned, a more dynamic interpretation could be attached to this class of instruments.

The way in which inferences from the classification of a treaty work is essentially the same as the nature of the treaty. Like inferences, techniques are more flexible and not tied to a certain interpretative outcome. The distinction between law-making and other treaties was included in a draft of Special Rapporteur Gerald Fitzmaurice,[245] although he refused to derive from it consequences for the interpretation of treaties.[246] The ILC later agreed that this distinction should have no relevance for its rule of interpretation.[247]

5.2.6 Inferences from the structure of the treaty

Another possibility would be to draw inferences from the structure of the treaty. These could include the level of participation (bilateral/multilateral/universal), the question whether the treaty grants subjective

---

[242] See Wright, 'The Interpretation of Multilateral Treaties' 101; Oppenheim, *International Law* (vol. 1) 586. The interpretation of law-making treaties is equated with constitutional interpretation by Doehring, *Völkerrecht* 171.

[243] *Ibid.*

[244] Verosta, 'Die Vertragsrechts-Konferenz der Vereinten Nationen 1968/69 und die Wiener Konvention über das Recht der Verträge' 689.

[245] Art. 8 in ILC, 'Report of the International Law Commission' (n. 199) 108.

[246] Waldock, Third Report (n. 185) 55.

[247] ILC, 'Report of the International Law Commission on the work of its 18th session' (4 May–19 July 1966) UN Doc. A/CN.4/Ser.A/1964/Add.1 'Final Draft Articles on the Law of Treaties', *ILC Ybk* 1966 II, 219 (Final Draft Articles). For critical remarks, see Doehring, *Völkerrecht* 172; Matscher, 'Methods of Interpretation of the Convention' 66. Of the opinion that no inferences from this distinction can be drawn are Tavernier, *Recherches sur l'application dans le temps des actes et des règles en droit international public* 207; McNair, *The Law of Treaties* 366.

rights or obligations to non-state actors such as individuals or enterprises, the nature of the obligation (*erga omnes partes*/reciprocity). Other inferences could be drawn from the fact that the treaty establishes an international organisation or a judicial mechanism, possibly with automatic jurisdiction.

The VCLT indeed sometimes distinguishes between different levels of participation.[248] Yet, no distinction of that kind can be found in Arts. 31 and 32 VCLT. Art. 5 VCLT could modify the rule of treaty interpretation as it sets out that the VCLT 'applies to any treaty which is the constituent instrument of an international ... organization and to any treaty adopted within an international organization without prejudice to any relevant rules of the organization'. In such cases, the structure of the treaty can influence not only the process of interpretation of a certain provision but the process of interpretation as a whole as the rules of treaty interpretation could be replaced by the rules of the respective international organisation.[249] But, unless there are such rules, the rule of interpretation in the VCLT applies. This reinforces the fact that the ordinary rule of interpretation applies to the constituent instruments of international organisations. Inferences from the structure work like inferences from the nature or the classification of the treaty and not like techniques: They can influence questions of interpretation only in a binary fashion by attaching one feature to one interpretative result.

5.2.7 Principles

The relevance of principles in international law is growing.[250] One formal source of principles is Art. 38(1)(c) ICJ Statute. Yet, it could be possible

---

[248] Bilateral treaties are referred to in Art. 60(1) VCLT, multilateral treaties are mentioned in Art. 2(1)(d), Art. 3(c), Art. 19–23, Art. 54(b), Art. 55, Art. 58, Art. 60(2), Art. 66(3), Art. 69 and Art. 79(2).

[249] Possible modifications are discussed by Peters, 'Subsequent Practice and Established Practice of International Organizations' 637; Dörr, 'Art. 31' 537 para. 31.

[250] The term 'principle' is of course often used in the non-technical and descriptive sense. Examples include Kelsen, *Principles of International Law*; Brownlie, *Principles of Public International Law*. They used principle in the sense of foundation or source, although for example Kelsen was very opposed to the use of material principles in public international law. Employing this strict terminology and distinguishing principles from other means of interpretation, the use of the term 'principle' by *Gerald Fitzmaurice* is a little misleading, as he points to six techniques which he then called principles: see Fitzmaurice, 'The Law and Procedure of the International Court of Justice 1951–4'.

to provide for principles in treaties or through custom or to derive them from the international legal system as a whole.

For our purposes, it is helpful to distinguish formal and material principles. Formal principles like the principle of restrictive interpretation or the principle of effective interpretation[251] express general results of the process of treaty interpretation.[252] They are derived from the nature of international law as such and the assumed manner in which international law should be interpreted.[253] Material principles are, by contrast, not only applicable to interpretation but have a general impact. Examples are the principle of sovereignty[254] or the principle of sustainable development.[255] Material principles influence the result of the interpretation.[256] Like techniques, principles are not hard and fast rules but flexible and elastic and can be balanced. Unlike techniques, principles are not neutral: while techniques are always dependent on the respective treaty, principles carry their material content in themselves.

5.2.8 Scientific method

A scientific method determines a result in a manner that allows other scientists to reach the same result by using the method.[257] The notion of a method depends on its exactness and the fact that different persons reach the same results after applying the method independent of each other. Some of the approaches in the mechanical phase came close to claiming

---

[251] See Lauterpacht, 'Restrictive Interpretation and the Principle of Effectiveness in the Interpretation of Treaties' 48; Crema, 'Disappearance and New Sightings of Restrictive Interpretation(s)'. The term formal is not to designate that these principles stem from the formal source as minuted in Art. 38(1)(c).

[252] For a critical account, see Visscher, *Problèmes d'interprétation judiciaire en droit international public* 87; Brownlie, *Principles of Public International Law* 631. The latter argues that restrictive or effective interpretations are only the result of the interpretative processes and cannot influence it. He is closer to the manner of interpretation used by the Vienna Convention than to the logic of a principled interpretation.

[253] Of course, there are also formal principles that do not deal with interpretation. They will, however, hardly affect the process of interpretation.

[254] De Fernàndez Casadevante Romani, *Sovereignty and Interpretation of International Norms*; Crawford, 'Sovereignty as a Legal Value'.

[255] Voigt, *Sustainable Development as a Principle of International Law*; Lowe, 'Sustainable Development and Unsustainable Arguments'.

[256] Letsas has applied *Dworkinian* thought to international law and argued that there are principles underlying the ECHR, Letsas, *A Theory of Interpretation of the European Convention on Human Rights*.

[257] For a similar distinction, see Dörr, 'Art. 31' 522 para. 2.

to be a method, which allowed for finding the assumed intentions of the parties. Techniques in contrast allow for some leeway for the interpreter.

5.2.9 Techniques as means of the VCLT

The fact that the Vienna Convention is binding and opts for a certain form of interpretation leads to the conclusion that problems of evolutive interpretations are to be resolved by techniques of interpretation. The techniques of interpretation contained in Art. 31 VCLT are the ordinary meaning of the text, the context, the object and purpose, subsequent agreements, subsequent practice and the relevant rules. Apart from the obligation to interpret in good faith, they are not material but rather procedural or formal as they only concern the process of interpretation.

As previously shown, Hudson and the Harvard Draft envisaged an interpretative method that was apt to function also in the *ex post* justification. Yet, Waldock as well as the ILC taking up the approach had only partly reflected what the inclusion of techniques meant. Interpretative method was based on rhetorical *topoi*, standardised schemes for arguments. This was of course generally in line with the rhetorical approaches of Theodor Viehweg and Chaim Perelman.[258] In this line of thinking, Friedrich Kratochwil has linked the rule of interpretation to rhetorical *topoi*.[259] Yet, he discussed it in relation to Aristotelian *topoi*, which do not really match the way in which the VCLT is framed. Therefore, I would like to submit that we take into account what later has been called '*Port Royal Topics*':[260] those are general *topoi* that are not attached to any specific argument but only classify arguments.[261] This classification does not help the interpreter to make an actual argument since classifications cannot influence the result. They exclude certain considerations from the process of interpretation, but apart from this their main function lies in structuring it. This helps the interpreter while making and justifying his decision. It helps also other actors to apprehend the justification of the interpreter. So techniques or general *topoi* in

---

[258] Viehweg, *Topik und Jurisprudenz*; Perelman and Olbrechts-Tyteca, *The New Rhetoric*.
[259] Kratochwil, *Rules, Norms, and Decisions* 234–6.
[260] Arnauld and Nicole, *Logic Or the Art of Thinking*. This approach is aptly described by Walton, Macagno and Reed, *Argumentation Schemes* 296–300.
[261] Arnauld and Nicole, *Logic Or the Art of Thinking* 188ff; Walton, Macagno and Reed, *Argumentation Schemes* 297.

the Port Royal Tradition are not only aids in the understanding and *ex-post facto* justification. They are also tools to understand the process of justification itself. We could say that they can also help to reconstruct argumentations after the argument was made. Yet, in the process of interpretation itself, they first function to validate an argument.

Techniques as they are used in the Convention are generally intertemporally open. The temporal perspective of the Convention is flexible; it is tied neither to the past nor to the present. This can be based on two observations: First, some of the techniques are open regarding their temporal applicability. When we take account of the ordinary meaning of the text, it is unclear whether this refers to the ordinary meaning at the time of the conclusion or the ordinary meaning at the time the treaty is interpreted. We have seen that the ordinary meaning of words can change and that a whole sub-discipline of linguistics focused on those aspects.[262] The same applies to parts of the context, the object and purpose and the relevant rules. There are, however, also techniques tied to a certain point in time.

The second important observation is that the temporal focus of the techniques differs. The preparatory works mentioned in Art. 32 VCLT are tied to the time before the treaty was concluded. Agreements relating to the treaty and unilateral instruments according to Art. 31(2)(a), (b) have a necessary temporal 'connection with the conclusion of the treaty'. Subsequent practice and subsequent agreements stem from the time after the treaty was made. If arguments from each of those times can be acknowledged, there is no fixed temporal point of reference in the Convention. Therefore, the techniques used in the VCLT can be presumed to be open intertemporally. In American legal scholarship, the schools of originalism and non-originalism have fixed their temporal stances, the techniques of the VCLT remain open. They can relate to several points in time. If one allows for arguments from different points in time, the interpretative result may differ over time since the arguments derived by the techniques evolve.

When we have ascertained those arguments, i.e. validated them through techniques, the next question is what to do with them. International lawyers contend that they use those techniques to put the considerations into a 'crucible'. It is time to unravel this mysterious metaphor.

---

[262] See for example Campbell, *Historical Linguistics*.

5.3. The activity core: balancing and weighing

As we have seen, the process of interpretation had been structured differently in different times: In the mechanical phase, the aim was to establish a system which had only to be applied and which would operate automatically to reach a certain result. In the flexible phase, the will of the parties was decisive and could not be constrained in any way. In the codificatory phase, the Harvard Draft established a compromise between both approaches: On the one hand, there were straightforward and binding rules, on the other hand, the interpreter was flexible in how to use them to arrive at a conclusion. The factor approach developed by the Harvard Law School was the first to state this in a consistent and coherent manner: The process of interpretation was envisaged as an *ex-post facto* justification of the interpretative result. Art. 19 Harvard Draft contained only factors, which the interpreter had to use in the case before him or her. It is interesting to see that the ILC Draft Articles evolved in a similar fashion in a very short period of time. Waldock's first draft was much more complex and contained several 'rules' of interpretation.[263] After the intervention of states[264] the drafting was simplified,[265] three articles were merged into two. In this context, the Special Rapporteur also clarified how he imagined the process of interpretation. There was not 'any intention of creating an order in which a series of rules should be successively applied; the Commission's idea was rather that of a crucible in which all the elements of interpretation would be mixed: The result of that mixing would be the correct interpretation'.[266] This metaphor of a *crucible* found its way into the commentary of the Final Draft Articles, which referred to an 'interaction' of elements.[267] In a much quoted phrase, *Waldock* described it as a 'single combined operation'.[268] The result of all techniques is to be taken together to achieve a final result. This could be related to a remark *Vattel* made right at the end of his chapter concerning interpretation in which he stated as follows:

---

[263] Waldock, Third Report (n. 185) 52–3.
[264] See for example delegation of the United States, ILC, Report of the International Law Commission (n. 233) 93; and Delegation of Greece, *ibid*.
[265] See Waldock, ILC, Report of the International Law Commission (n. 233) 94ff.
[266] Comment by Special Rapporteur Waldock, ILC, 'Report of the International Law Commission on the work of its 18th session' (4 May–19 July 1966), UN Doc. A/CN.4, UN Doc. A/CN.4/1964 and Add.1-3, Summary Record of the 883rd meeting, *ILC Ybk* 1966 I 2, 267 para. 96.
[267] Final Draft Articles (n. 247) 219–20. [268] *Ibid*.

> All the rules contained in this chapter should be combined together, and the interpretation of the law or treaty should be made in accordance with them to the extent to which they are applicable in the given case. When they appear to conflict they mutually counterbalance and limit one another according to their force and importance and according how they apply more particularly to the case in hand.[269]

So if the techniques of interpretation suggest differing results, the interpreter has to decide between those different solutions.[270] This is achieved by a process of weighing and balancing, another cardinal core of the Convention describing the activity of the interpreter. Waldock's metaphor of the crucible stands for the two steps to be taken in the process of balancing:[271] weighing and balancing. When a consideration has passed the test of a technique and could be inserted into the process of interpretation, it is first necessary to assess the *weight* of the consideration, i.e. to assess its relative importance. This is very much the question of how much of the consideration we can put into the crucible. Then comes the act of *balancing*: The right proportion has to be struck between the different considerations or arguments.[272] We put the things into the crucible and mix them. It could be said that after putting things into the crucible and mixing, we taste to check if we have achieved the right result concerning the *goût* and the consistency.

The most important feature we can derive from the process of balancing is the *discretionary* nature of the process.[273] The VCLT entails an obligation to merely interpret 'in accordance with' and to 'take into account'. It makes only *procedural* but no substantive prescriptions. The techniques are formulated in a way that they have only procedural effects.[274] Validation through techniques as well as weighing and balancing only guide the process and not the outcome. Both parts of the process are visualised in Figures 5 and 6.

---

[269] Vattel, *The Law of Nations or the Principles of Natural Law* 202–3 (Book 2, Chapter 17, para. 271).
[270] One could also speak of rival outcomes and 'intercategorical conflicts': see Vogenauer, *Die Auslegung von Gesetzen in England und auf dem Kontinent* (vol. 1) 139.
[271] Gardiner rightly stresses that the crucible is opposed to an examination in isolation: Gardiner, *Treaty Interpretation* 10.
[272] For general accounts, see Vogenauer, *Die Auslegung von Gesetzen in England und auf dem Kontinent* (vol. 1) 155; MacCormick, *Rhetoric and the Rule of Law* 137.
[273] Nolte says that the interpreter had 'some latitude': Nolte, 'Introduction' 2.
[274] Wolfrum, 'Obligation of Result Versus Obligation of Conduct' 363.

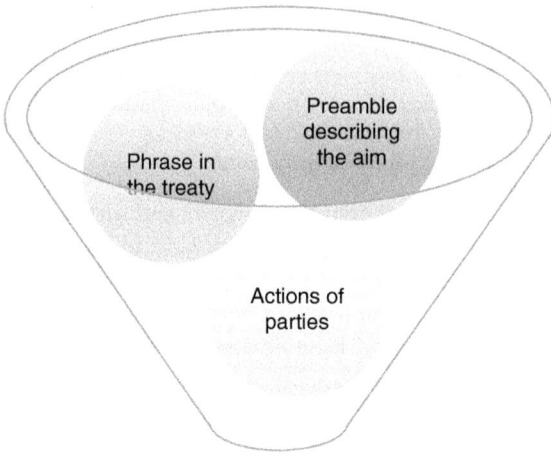

Figure 5 Techniques as filters

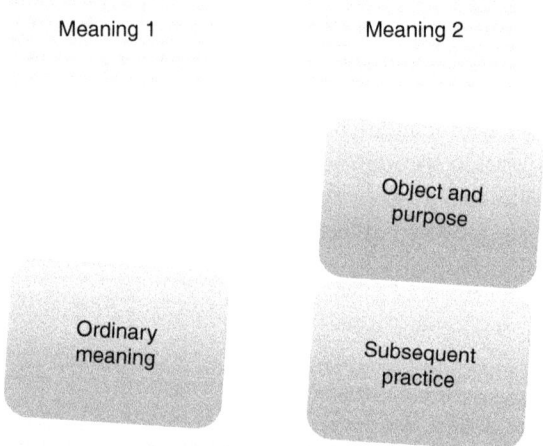

Figure 6 Weighing and balancing

5.4. The core of argumentative weight and hierarchy: 2.5 steps

We have seen so far that the VCLT aims at structuring an argumentative process. From this, it follows that the hierarchy as contained in the VCLT is not absolute and mechanical but rather aimed at attributing more weight to the arguments derived from certain techniques. This is achieved by the drafting of Art. 32 VCLT, which allows for recourse to subsidiary means only to confirm the meaning resulting from the application of Art. 31 or if after the application of Art. 31 the meaning remains ambiguous and obscure or if Art. 31 leads to a manifestly absurd or unreasonable result. The fact that supplementary means are only allowed to influence the process of interpretation in these rather narrow and exceptional circumstances shows that arguments stemming from supplementary means are not completely excluded but carry less weight than arguments derived from the techniques in Art. 31 VCLT.[275] Hierarchies in interpretative methodology have a long history in international law. We have seen that scholars tried in the mechanical phase to account for complete systems of interpretation in which the means were sorted on three or more levels, mostly with the text at the centre of attention in accordance with Vattel's maxim.[276] In the flexible phase, means that were linked to the intentions of the parties were at the top of the hierarchy. In the codificatory phase, there was no clear trend. Sometimes, there was only a slight preference as in the *Restatement Second of the American Law Institute*;[277] sometimes, the hierarchy was abolished completely, as in the Harvard Draft.[278]

Hierarchy in international interpretative method has been criticised for a long time.[279] The argument states that the inclusion of hierarchy

---

[275] Mortenson tries to broaden the scope of Art. 32 by contending that supplementary means that confirm the meaning of a treaty can also be those which do not confirm the meaning of a treaty: Mortenson, 'The *Travaux* of *Travaux*' 787.

[276] Vattel, *The Law of Nations or the Principles of Natural Law* 199 (Book 2, Chapter 17, para. 263).

[277] See Box 8 in Appendix 1 below. [278] See Box 6 in Appendix 1 below.

[279] For this argument, see Yü, *The Interpretation of Treaties* 44; Gerald Fitzmaurice, 'The Law and Procedure of the International Court of Justice: Treaty Interpretation' 5; McNair, *The Law of Treaties* 372; Haraszti and Decsenyi, *Some Fundamental Problems of the Law of Treaties* 93; Delegate McDougal (United States) First Vienna Conference (n. 178) 167 para. 41. For a deeper inquiry into that problem, see Meder, *Mißverstehen und Verstehen* 17ff; Schott, '"Interpretatio cessat in claris" – Auslegungsfähigkeit und Auslegungsbedürftigkeit in der juristischen Hermeneutik'. A general account of the circularity is given by Vogenauer, *Die Auslegung von Gesetzen in England und auf dem Kontinent* (vol. 1) 162, 299.

into systems of interpretation would be circular. The hierarchy in interpretative method in essence works as follows. Initially only some of the means of interpretation could be used in the first step, the other means only in a second step.[280] It is now asserted that the question whether the meaning is sufficiently determined on the first level is in itself a question of interpretation. Therefore, such a construction could never work.

However, this argument disregards the fundamental function of hierarchy in interpretative method.[281] This argument has some force if the process is imagined as a sequence of rules that indicates a determinative meaning. Yet, we have seen that the ILC had, after the criticism of states, clarified its approach with the metaphor of the crucible. If we assume that the interpreter has discretion in the process of justification which allows him to balance several considerations, there can be no hierarchy in the strict sense of the term. Exercising the discretion, the interpreter could circumvent any hierarchy easily just in the way the circularity suggests. Assuming the *ex-post facto* justification model, the only reasonable function a hierarchy can have is to confer differing weight on the arguments that are validated by different techniques. It is of course not impossible to include arguments into the crucible through techniques that are ranked lower in the hierarchy.[282] Yet, it is harder to argue that they prevail in the process of balancing since the other arguments will, without consideration of the concrete case, carry more weight. Even if hierarchy is understood to determine only the argumentative weight of techniques, this issue goes right to the heart of the dichotomy between rulers-of-law considerations and rule-of-lawyers considerations: To introduce hierarchy and argumentative weight to the process seeks to determine the process in a certain way and to make it more secure. This is the methodological perspective which lawyers will put forward. The practical position of the rulers of the law will emphasise flexibility and

---

[280] This is similar to Vattel's maxim; Vattel, *The Law of Nations or the Principles of Natural Law* 199 (Book 2, Chapter 17, para. 263).

[281] The ILC commentary has made a distinction between the means, since the supplementary means should not be 'alternative autonomous means' but mere aids to the interpretation: Final Draft Articles (n. 247), 223. A difference in value ('Auslegungswert') of the 'factors' (Faktoren) is assumed by Karl, *Vertrag und spaetere Praxis im Voelkerrecht* 187. A similar argument in relation to the English golden rule of statutory interpretation, which resembles very much the rules here in issue is given by MacCormick, 'Argumentation and Interpretation in Law' 478; MacCormick, *Rhetoric and the Rule of Law* 138.

[282] For a slightly different explanation framing the rule of interpretation as containing 'two analytical processes', see Mortenson, 'The *Travaux* of *Travaux*' 786.

freedom of the interpreter. It is not surprising that those issues caused controversy also at the First Vienna Conference.[283]

Interestingly, Myres McDougal, being part of the American delegation at the First Vienna Conference, put forward a proposal to change the Convention and to enumerate all means of interpretation in the same manner. This would have abolished the distinction between Art. 31 and Art. 32 VCLT.[284] Contrasting the proposal with the Vienna Convention in force, we can see that there is an interpretative hierarchy that makes all means not contained in Art. 31 VCLT supplementary, thereby lessening their argumentative weight and value while increasing the obstacles standing in the way of the interpreter having resort to them. Art. 31 VCLT contains several prescriptions for the interpreter. The interpreter has to interpret the treaty 'in accordance with' the textual means of interpretation but also 'in the light of its object and purpose'. Subsequent agreements, subsequent practice and the relevant rules 'shall be taken into account together with the context'.

To interpret in accordance with a certain technique seems to require more faithfulness and, therefore, attribute more argumentative weight to the text of the treaty and its immediate context. The term 'in accordance with' can be interpreted either rather narrowly, meaning that it should not go against something, or more broadly, meaning that it has to be actually in line with something.[285] Both meanings, however, suggest that

---

[283] For this discourse, see Pehar, 'International Law of Interpretation'; Djeffal, 'Establishing the Argumentative DNA of International Law' 130–7; Mortenson, 'The *Travaux* of *Travaux*'.

[284] To mention just some positions taken in the discussion: While Delegate Jiménez de Aréchaga (Uruguay) contended that there was no hierarchy between the means in Arts. 31 and 32 (see First Vienna Conference (n. 178) 170 para. 66), the British delegate, Mr Sinclair, departed from the assumption that there is not equal weight: see *ibid*. 184 paras. 67–9. Humphrey Waldock, acting as expert, also stressed that the Commission regarded the techniques in Art. 31 as authentically binding as opposed to the supplementary means: *ibid*. Records 170 and 184 paras. 67–9. See also Delegate of France, Mr Bresson, *ibid*. 175 para. 44.

[285] One can see the different scope of the expression 'in accordance with' in the advisory opinion in *Accordance with International Law of the Unilateral Declaration of Independence in Respect of Kosovo* (Advisory Opinion) [2010] ICJ Rep 407. The General Assembly put forward the question: 'Is the unilateral declaration of independence by the Provisional Institutions of Self-Government of Kosovo in accordance with international law?' The Court interpreted this to mean whether this action breaches any rule of international law: see *ibid*. 21 para. 56. This is criticised by Judge Simma who takes a rather broad approach and would look into what international law has to say about that question: *ibid*. 479 para. 4.

an interpretation could not go against the ordinary meaning to be given to their terms in their context. With regard to the object and purpose, more flexibility seems to be accorded to the interpreter as he would only have to see it in the light of the object and purpose, which does not seem to suggest that the interpreter would actually need to follow the object and purpose. To take the techniques outlined in Art. 31(3) VCLT 'into account' sounds like an obligation of conduct in the sense that the interpreter would have to deal with the arguments although he or she would not necessarily have to follow them. This can be seen by the commentary of the fourth Special Rapporteur who said that the phrase was deliberately used instead of the phrase 'be subject to' to leave open the result of the interpretation.[286] While this cannot finally determine the weight accorded to the techniques in Art. 31(3), it does give an indication that there has been awareness in the process of drafting of the different weights that could be accorded to the techniques contained in Art. 31 VCLT.

Another possibility to accord a special status to certain techniques of interpretation is to refer to their authenticity. An authentic interpretation is generally an interpretation stemming from the same legal source as the act interpreted.[287] Without altering the wording of an act of parliament or an international treaty, a new act stemming from the same source is introduced. This new act adds something to the determination of the meaning of the text to be interpreted.[288]

Historically, authentic interpretations were designed to allow legislative authorities to retain control over the judiciary.[289] In the same sense, international lawyers distinguished authentic, doctrinal and judicial interpretations.[290] In national as well as in international law, the concept has been broadened to include also judgments of courts which are binding upon states parties or other courts.[291] Another use of the term is to denote certain means of interpretation as authentic means or

---

[286] Waldock, Third Report (n. 185) 61 para. 32.
[287] See the very detailed treatment of those questions in the field of national law by Grabau, *Über die Normen zur Gesetzes- und Vertragsinterpretation* 102.
[288] *Ibid.*   [289] *Ibid.* 103.
[290] Ludwik Ehrlich, 'L'Interprétation des traités' 34; Verdross and Simma, *Universelles Völkerrecht* 490 para. 774; Benavides Casals, *Die Auslegungsmethoden bei Menschenrechtsverträgen* 19–20.
[291] Schweisfurth, *Völkerrecht* 173; Grabau, *Über die Normen zur Gesetzes- und Vertragsinterpretation* 105. In these cases, there is also a suggestion to call such interpretation authoritative: Kadelbach, 'Interpretation of the Charter' 89 para. 47.

techniques. Subsequent agreements and practice and the preparatory works could in particular be seen as authentic interpretation,[292] since the parties concluding the treaty also interpret it. As we will see, these techniques are special and particular and in themselves very important techniques that will attract much attention in the process of treaty interpretation. However, the question is whether we should denote these techniques as being authentic. The similarity of the processes of amendment and the techniques concerning subsequent agreements and practice seem to point in favour of this conclusion: In all of those cases, the main actors are the same, mostly states. There are, however, also differences between the processes: The question how many parties must have participated in the subsequent conduct for it to establish the agreement of the parties is at least not clear. What is more, there is a distinction between the representatives of the state acting in the processes of interpretation and treaty formation or amendment. As Art. 7 VCLT shows, the capacity of persons to act for states in these processes is limited and defined. According to Art. 39 VCLT, the same applies in the process of amendment. But in the process of interpretation, any representative of the state could potentially act in a way that is relevant.[293] It is also true that the term authentic has a special meaning in the VCLT. Arts. 2(1)(c), 7(1) and 10 VCLT, amongst others, make it clear that authenticity means that the text is 'unique and identifiable'.[294] This sense is much more limited than in the case of interpretative techniques.[295] If one were to accept that certain techniques are authentic, attempts will certainly be made to designate some of the techniques as being authentic. So the textual technique has been called authentic.[296] Yet, the seemingly most apt approach was taken by the fourth Special Rapporteur who said that all techniques now contained in Art. 31 VCLT are authentic and binding.[297] Possibly in the same spirit, Georg Nolte has remarked in his capacity as Special Rapporteur that, in the case of subsequent agreements and subsequent practice, parties are 'often, but not necessarily always ...

---

[292] See for example Bleckmann, *Grundprobleme und Methoden des Völkerrechts* 94 and 96.
[293] For this reason, authentic interpretation has been distinguished from practical interpretation. See Haraszti and Decsenyi, *Some Fundamental Problems of the Law of Treaties* 142.
[294] Thouvenin, 'Art. 10 VCLT' 185.   [295] See Arts. 7 and 10 VCLT.
[296] Final Draft Articles (n. 247) 187ff; Waldock, Third Report (n. 185) 94.
[297] First Vienna Conference (n. 178) 184; See Villiger, 'The 1969 Vienna Convention on the Law of Treaties' 128.

particularly important factors for the interpretation of treaties'.[298] An extrinsic general alteration of the argumentative weight by the standard of the authenticity of the means should be omitted. Instead of applying this concept to some techniques of interpretation, it would be preferable to determine under which circumstances and for what reasons special weight should be accorded to certain techniques.

In conclusion, we have seen that the rule of interpretation establishes a 2.5-step hierarchy in the sense that it generally accords more argumentative weight to some of the techniques. This is clear in the case of the techniques mentioned in Art. 31 as opposed to the supplementary means of interpretation. A slight preference for the ordinary meaning could be derived from the drafting of Art. 31 VCLT. Yet, there is no absolute hierarchy, so questions are generally open. This reinforces the previous finding that the intertemporal question is also generally open.

5.5. The core of openness: broad and treaty related

The openness of the process of interpretation refers to the variety of techniques that can be taken into account. Are only means relating to the text of the treaty admissible? Has the practice of the parties any significance? Or can extra-textual aspects such as the economic rationality also play a role? A canon of interpretation can take different attitudes towards that question. The openness of the process is, however, a question of degree.[299]

A feature closing the Convention is its slight hierarchy through the differentiated argumentative weight: Only the considerations validated by one of the techniques in Art. 31 VCLT will enter the process of balancing. This hierarchy closes the process for all other considerations since they have less argumentative weight. This is mitigated by the fact that the interpreter has discretion in the process of balancing. It is open to him or her to introduce other considerations if she or he undertakes to give reasons for that decision. Yet, the fact that the techniques mentioned in Art. 31 VCLT have more weight is even more apt to close the system of interpretation since we have seen that all of those techniques are related to the treaty. Again, this does not apply to the supplementary means.

---

[298] Nolte, First Report on Subsequent Agreements and Subsequent Practice, ILC, 'Report of the International Law Commission on the work of its Sixty-fifth session (6 May–7 June and 8 July–9 August 2013), UN Doc. A/CN.4/L.813187, para. 30 ('Nolte, First Report').
[299] Gross, 'Treaty Interpretation' 110.

Here, the Convention is very open and allows for a generally unlimited number of means to enter the process of interpretation. Art. 32 mentions as one of two examples the circumstances of the conclusion of the treaty. This is a technique that could import all kinds of considerations, be they political, economic or societal. A further indicator of openness can be found in Art. 31(3)(b) VCLT: Subsequent practice is indeed a very open feature, allowing legal reality to enter the process of treaty interpretation. In the process of treaty interpretation it is necessary to look at how the treaty is practised in real life and not only at the words therein. Yet, there are also very closed techniques such as the context. Art. 31(2) shows that the notion refers to written context that relates directly to the treaty. We shall describe this particular mix with the phrase *broad and treaty related*. The fact that the outcome of the deliberations was such a mix is no accident: it is the result of a controversial discussion on several levels.

The different streams are denoted as textualist and contextualist.[300] Those approaches which mainly relied on the ordinary meaning of the words of the treaty were called textualist whereas contextualist approaches stressed that 'the decision-maker should employ techniques designed to bring all potentially relevant content to the focus of his attention in the order best adapted to exhibiting actual relevance'.[301] Recently, the debate has also been reframed in a formalist account distinguishing legal and non-legal considerations.[302] American views, in particular, pointed to extrinsic evidence. Hyde for example remarked that 'interpretation was a fact-probing endeavour to ascertain the actual sense in which the parties used the words of their choice'.[303] The use of extrinsic and circumstantial

---

[300] Liacouras, 'The International Court of Justice and Development of Useful Rules of Interpretation in the Process of Treaty Interpretation' 164; Sharma, 'The ILC Draft and Treaty Interpretation with Special Reference to Preparatory Works' 367; Haraszti and Decsenyi, *Some Fundamental Problems of the Law of Treaties* 112; Yambrusic, *Treaty Interpretation* 242.

[301] The quote stems from McDougal, Lasswell and Miller, *The Interpretation of Agreements and World Public Order* 273. A similar account is given in Liacouras, 'The International Court of Justice and Development of Useful Rules of Interpretation in the Process of Treaty Interpretation' 164. For a discussion of the same problem in modern jurisprudence, see Martens, 'Rechtliche und außerrechtliche Argumente' 145.

[302] Orakhelashvili, *The Interpretation of Acts and Rules in Public International Law*. This is, however, made in the face of the rules of the Vienna Convention which allow distinguishing between the techniques which are provided for by law and those which are not explicitly mentioned. It is not clear, however, how the distinction between law and non-law could play out to distinguish between the different techniques *a priori*, i.e. without referring to already preconceived rules.

[303] Hyde, 'Judge Anzilotti on the Interpretation of Treaties' 503.

evidence was also the reason why those scholars referred to scientific methods.[304] This culminated in the approach developed by the New Haven School and in particular Myres McDougal with regard to treaty interpretation.[305] The aim of the proposals was to open up the process of treaty interpretation for any consideration that could be relevant to highlight the shared expectations of the parties, as Myres McDougal termed it. On a rather theoretical level, McDougal together with Harold Lasswell and James C. Miller elaborated a refined methodology of interpretation. In this system, the rules as established by the Vienna Convention were only a small piece in a much broader picture. So the interpreter should for example also look into the value position of the parties.[306] However, Myres McDougal had also a very practical influence on the formation of the Vienna Convention as he represented the United States at the Vienna Conferences. In this function he proposed an amendment which would rephrase the rules as they were proposed by the ILC which was rejected by sixty-six to eight votes with ten abstentions.[307] This proposal tried to open up the process of interpretation in three ways. First, it abolished any explicit hierarchy or attribution of argumentative weight between the techniques of treaty interpretation.[308] To arrive at the meaning of the wording of the treaty, however, was mentioned as an aim of the process but not as a technique of interpretation. The reduction of hierarchy is also reinforced by the fact that the various means of interpretation are not in a certain progressive order that assumes that one technique is at the centre of interpretation while the others are more remote.[309] This had the particular consequence that the preparatory works as well as other techniques not enumerated in Art. 27 of the final ILC Draft would have gained more importance.[310] But so would the other

---

[304] See the very early account by Yü, *The Interpretation of Treaties* 139. The commentary on the Harvard Draft also declared that 'scientific interpretation of the treaty must take into account its complete setting': see Harvard Law School, 'Harvard Draft Convention on the Law of Treaties' 956.

[305] McDougal, Lasswell and Miller, *The Interpretation of Agreements and World Public Order*.

[306] *Ibid.* 193.   [307] First Vienna Conference (n. 178) 185 para. 75.

[308] This was explicitly stressed by Delegate McDougal (United States), *ibid.* 168 para. 46.

[309] The progressive order has been mentioned by the Delegate of Uruguay Mr Jiménez de Aréchaga, *ibid.* 170 para. 65. For a similar thought, namely, the circles of context, see Kolb, *Interprétation et création du droit international* 459.

[310] This was also a decisive point of discussion in the deliberations of the Institut de Droit International, which led Rosenne to describe the discourse also in terms of textualism and contextualism: see Shabtai Rosenne, 'Interpretation of Treaties in the Restatement and the International Law Commission's Draft Articles' 229.

techniques of interpretation, which were not exclusively enumerated in the list. Every technique the interpreter would have found useful could have been introduced into the process on the same level as the other techniques of interpretation.

By introducing these shifts, the US delegation tried to mitigate some of the critique regarding textualism, which said that the real reasons for disagreement could then not be dealt with in the process of interpretation. It is interesting that textualists as well as contextualists basically use the same argument against the respective other side: Such a method would lead to a situation in which the proper meaning could not be ascertained. The contextualists argue that this effect comes about since the interpreter had not enough techniques at her or his disposal to argue for the right solution.[311] Even if the right conclusion was reached, the interpreter could not express the real reasons for her or his decision.[312] But if the interpreter had too many possibilities, this might also blur his or her view, especially in processes of negotiation: Endless arguments could lead to an endless conversation.[313] The interpreter would have to face a much greater complexity.[314] This exchange of arguments shows why a middle view as the one taken by the VCLT might be advisable. Yet, any choice will greatly impact upon questions of stasis and evolution. The more closed the system is, the harder it will be to achieve change,[315] the more open it is, the

---

[311] Liacouras, 'The International Court of Justice and Development of Useful Rules of Interpretation in the Process of Treaty Interpretation' 164; Merrills, 'Two Approaches to Treaty Interpretation' 72. Calling for the disclosure of the operative reasons is also Schwarzenberger, 'Myths and Realities of Treaty Interpretation' 12. This approach has been reinforced lately in relation to the obligation of judges to make explicit the principles they pursue: see von Bogdandy and Venzke, 'On the Democratic Legitimation of International Judicial Lawmaking' 1349. The critique on textualism is also summarised by Jacobs, 'Varieties of Approach to Treaty Interpretation' 340. An account of both approaches is given by Yambrusic, *Treaty Interpretation* 242. The way in which these dangers could be avoided is discussed by the Swedish delegate, Mr Eek, First Vienna Conference (n. 178) 179 para. 19.

[312] Lissitzyn, 'The Law of International Agreements in the Restatement' 108.

[313] See the statement of the delegate of Uruguay, Jiménez de Aréchaga, First Vienna Conference (n. 178) 170 para. 65. See also the statement of the then Expert Consultant Humphrey Waldock stressing the need to provide for the integrity of the treaty, ibid. 184. See also Orakhelashvili, *The Interpretation of Acts and Rules in Public International Law* 293.

[314] Merrills, 'Two Approaches to Treaty Interpretation' 65.

[315] Liacouras, 'The International Court of Justice and Development of Useful Rules of Interpretation in the Process of Treaty Interpretation' 164.

easier it will be to establish changes. In sum, one can say that the VCLT is open but treaty-related.

Assessing the rules in the Vienna Convention in these terms, it would have to be stressed that rules on interpretation will not easily be categorised as either textual or contextual but will include both elements to a certain extent.[316] Features closing the Convention are the 2.5-step hierarchy, the narrow notion of context and the treaty-relatedness of all primary techniques. Features opening the Convention are the inclusion of the techniques of subsequent conduct, the unlimited inclusion of supplementary means and the discretion of the interpreter.

5.6. Synthesis: art not science

As an introduction to the rule of interpretation, Humphrey Waldock wrote the lines that have been quoted many times: 'In other words, recourse to many of these principles is discretionary rather than obligatory and the interpretation of documents is to some extent an art, not an exact science.'[317] The process of legal interpretation was already denoted as an art by Vattel.[318] From then on, international lawyers have constantly used it when describing the process of interpretation.[319] The very same process has been described in terms of five cardinal cores. This description of the process of interpretation as an art and not a science will be used to reflect what was established so far. Gadamer aptly describes the dichotomy of art and science in classical philosophy, culminating in the Aristotelian distinctions of knowledge: he contrasted *techne*, the practical knowledge with *episteme*, the theoretical knowledge which was unchangeable and subject to objective proof.[320] This distinction

---

[316] Merrills, 'Two Approaches to Treaty Interpretation' 56; Gross, 'Treaty Interpretation' 120; Villiger, 'The 1969 Vienna Convention on the Law of Treaties'.

[317] Waldock, Third Report (n. 185) 54 para. 6; Commentary to Final Draft Articles (n. 247) 218 para. 4.

[318] Vattel, *The Law of Nations or the Principles of Natural Law* 199 (Book 2, Chapter 17, para. 262).

[319] For further references, see Haraszti and Decsenyi, *Some Fundamental Problems of the Law of Treaties* 197; Klabbers, 'International Legal Histories' 272; Koskenniemi, *From Apology to Utopia* 340 n. 6. For an account that the VCLT is both, an art and a science: see Merkouris, 'Introduction: Interpretation Is a Science, Is an Art, Is a Science'.

[320] Gadamer, *Truth and Method* 309.

is helpful in understanding the difference between art and science in the international legal discourse about interpretation.

In interpretative method, the notion of the process of interpretation as a scientific enterprise was introduced mainly by American accounts on the problem. A proper discourse on that issue can be found in the deliberations of the Institut de Droit International.

At the session in Grenada in 1956, Basdevant made the suggestion to include a preamble emphasising the non-obligatory nature of the rules of treaty interpretation.[321] De la Pradelle agreed on the approach of not using strict rules. He further stated that 'interpretation is an art that the judge has to perform taking into consideration the text he has to adhere to'.[322] This was then challenged by Guggenheim who stated that the legal nature of the rules could establish a certain hierarchy.[323] Hambro remarked that there could be rules for interpretation even if it was considered an art[324] which was reinforced by Jessup.[325] So when there are rules, why then designate the process of interpretation as art and not as science? Because the rule only guides to a certain extent and leaves some discretion to the interpreter. And indeed the aforementioned quote distinguishing art from science refers to the principles of treaty interpretation as being discretionary rather than obligatory.[326]

Why could the application of the rule of interpretation contained in the Vienna Convention be considered as art? An art, in the sense of a craft, has certain rules but also leaves some freedom to the craftswomen and craftsmen. So the VCLT provides for legal rules, but also for the discretion of the interpreter: The techniques validate considerations, but it is upon the interpreter to accord value and weight to them. There is a hierarchy, but it only accords more argumentative weight to certain techniques. This renders the process of interpretation open to a certain extent, but also limits the process through the distribution of argumentative weight and the fact that all techniques in Art. 31 are related to the treaty. These factors cannot determine the process of interpretation definitely, but they shape the process. With this reflection in mind, we can attempt to inquire into the most important feature of this reconstruction: The function of the rule of interpretation.

---

[321] This suggestion was adopted: see also Box 7 in Appendix 1 below.
[322] Gerald Fitzmaurice, 'De l'interprétation des traités' 325.   [323] Ibid. 327.
[324] Ibid. 328.   [325] Ibid. 329.   [326] Final Draft Articles (n. 247) 218 para. 4.

5.7. Finale: the function as the core of the cores

If this was not a section on the function of the rule of interpretation but a piece of music, it could hardly be considered as a symphony for it would start with a *finale furioso*.

The function of the rule of interpretation is the core of the cores. Displayed in a formula, it could be stated as an *obligation to decide based on legal arguments relating to the interpretative issue in the treaty*.

The piece of music would change its pace to *andante*: it is an obligation since the rule of interpretation is of legal nature. But it obliges interpreters only to use a certain process of balancing: As an obligation to decide, it is a procedural obligation and not an obligation of result.[327] The use of techniques suggests that considerations are introduced into the process as arguments. The techniques also have the function of pointing the interpreter to certain arguments and of structuring the process: if there is a consideration valid according to the standards of a technique, the interpreter must take note of it. The limited openness of the process has taught us that the interpreter can consider a variety of arguments. Primary means (that is, techniques) will always have a relation to the interpretative issue in the treaty. This is why the obligation extends especially to legal arguments. This is what the cardinal cores actually tell us about the function, i.e. the general impact the Convention has on interpretative practice. There have been many doubts whether the rule of interpretation in the VCLT can fulfil any useful purpose at all,[328] yet looking at the process of interpretation, we can say that the Vienna Convention enhances legal discourse.[329] Yet, we should focus on the

---

[327] Haraszti and Decsenyi, *Some Fundamental Problems of the Law of Treaties*.
[328] Klabbers, 'Virtuous Interpretation' 31.
[329] Klabbers has very rightly remarked that a harmonisation of meanings between different subsystems of international law and the respective interpretative communities would be an optimistic vision. *Ibid.* 32. This criticism is valid, but if we define the function as it has been done here, the rule of interpretation in the VCLT does not claim to harmonise the meanings. Very significantly, it obliges interpreters to justify their decision in a way that relates to the treaties. It is also a tool to reconstruct the arguments made in the justification. So it forces interpreters from different perspectives to argue in relation to the law. I feel obliged to say that I do not have the means to show that this has a beneficial effect such as enhancing a rational discourse. Alexy has drafted some requirements for canons of interpretation which would ensure that the legal discourse is rational. Alexy, *A Theory of Legal Argumentation* 244. Amongst them is also the requirement of giving precedence to arguments deriving from the text and from preparatory works. *Ibid.* 305. Yet, Habermas criticised that this did not conclusively show that the interpretative method indeed meets the criteria of a rational discourse.

relations in which the rule of interpretation impacts on the discourse. It can play out in relation to the subject or inter-subjectively.

The rules on interpretation can help the single interpreter to understand the law or – if she or he has already made up her or his mind – to justify the decision. Those different outlooks could be termed *context of discovery* as opposed to *context of justification*[330] or as hermeneutical as opposed to justificatory function: Both relate to a subject. The hermeneutical aspect relates to the influence of interpretative method on the actual understanding of the subject. The justificatory aspect stresses the fact that the interpreter is a decision-maker and prescribes the function of the rule on interpretation in this context.[331]

It is often assumed that rules of interpretation do influence the understanding of the interpreter.[332] Especially the fact that it not only mentions but also emphasises certain techniques of interpretation warrant the assumption that it is a 'hermeneutical framework'.[333] The mere fact that the interpreter will check certain techniques in the process of assessing the question might influence him. Yet, we have also seen that in the process of balancing, discretion is accorded to the interpreter which could be read as an acknowledgment that this function has its limits. We will also see that the VCLT takes no firm stance on the goals of interpretation.[334] To define a goal of interpretation would have increased the hermeneutical guidance significantly.[335] The cautious claim of the VCLT rules in that regard is well warranted: it is indeed hard to know

---

Habermas, *Between Facts and Norms* 231. And we ought to be careful, indeed: As we have seen, the process of interpretation is only one part of the process of relating text to the real world, which is again only one part of deciding about legal arguments. When we now know more about the function of the rule of interpretation, we ought to see how it plays out.

[330] For this distinction, see Feteris, *Fundamentals of Legal Argumentation* 10. See also the application by Pulkowski, *The Law and Politics of International Regime Conflict* 276–83.

[331] This aspect of interpretation is increasingly stressed and termed as an 'existential function of interpretation': see Hollis, 'The Existential Function of Interpretation in International Law'.

[332] Kammerhofer, *Uncertainty in International Law* 87; Aust, Rodiles and Staubach, 'Unity or Uniformity?' 78–9. Yet, it is also held that rules of interpretation have 'little bearing on the process of *understanding* the meaning of a rule'. Pulkowski, *The Law and Politics of International Regime Conflict* 276.

[333] Aust, Rodiles and Staubach, 'Unity or Uniformity?' *ibid*. 77.   [334] See p. 147 below.

[335] Gadamer for example criticised the historical and intentionalist focus of romantic hermeneutics and replaced this with his hermeneutic circle that linked the past to the present. Gadamer, *Truth and Method* 172.

which factors play a role in the actual decision of an interpreter.[336] To even understand it, one would also have to take into account anthropology, cognitive psychology and empirical methods. Backed up by the consistent use of the VCLT by courts in the process of justifying their decisions, it can be asserted that the rule of interpretation impacts on and structures the process of justification. It ties it to legal arguments, diminishes the relevance of techniques like the *travaux*. It is also hard for the interpreter to ignore certain techniques, since they are explicitly and transparently mentioned. One could very well argue that the mere regulation of the justificatory process might be considered as a fig leaf, if we suppose that the interpreter already has made up her or his mind. But the process of justification necessarily calls for the *inter-subjective* perspective in which the interpreter will have to worry about whether her or his justification is accepted. This very fact might influence the decision he or she takes.

Depending on the actors involved, there can of course be different relationships of legal communication.[337] In the context of the proceedings before a court, the rule of interpretation will work as between the parties and between the parties and the court.[338] The parties argue amongst themselves and plead to the court. If the court pronounces upon a question of treaty interpretation, it has several audiences: The parties to the dispute, other interested potential parties, legal scholarship as well as the general public. In all of those relationships, the rule of interpretation structures the process of justification as described before. Yet, the rules of interpretation have also a very interesting function linking the process of treaty making to the process of treaty interpretation.[339] This concerns the relationship between legislator and judiciary. The fact that there are rules

---

[336] For a recent attempt to structure the problem, see Jonathan Crowe, 'Pre-Reflective Law' 117.

[337] McDougal, Lasswell and Miller, *The Interpretation of Agreements and World Public Order* xii.

[338] It is asserted that, in this relation, the rule of interpretation in the VCLT will work best: de Fernàndez Casadevante Romani, *Sovereignty and interpretation of international norms* 61.

[339] This relationship was stressed very early by Westlake, *International Law* (vol. 1) 282; Adler, 'The Interpretation of Treaties' 63. For the context of the Vienna rules, see Waldock, Third Report (n. 185) 54; First Vienna Conference statement of the Swedish delegate, Mr Eek, First Vienna Conference (n. 178) 179 para. 19; Hogg, 'The International Law Commission and the Law of Treaties' 12; Schwarzenberger, 'Myths and Realities of Treaty Interpretation' 226; Rosenne, *Conceptualism as a Guide to Treaty Interpretation* 421; Jacobs, 'Varieties of Approach to Treaty Interpretation' 343.

of treaty interpretation will for example have a great influence on the negotiations and the drafting. Let us suppose for example in a contra-factual manner that the *travaux préparatoires* had become the most important technique of treaty interpretation. International conferences might look a lot different since all delegations would have to consider that their behaviour might have a big impact upon future interpretations. This might prompt statements and arguments trying to influence the meaning of the treaty through the backdoor; delegates would aim at influencing future interpretations and not the text of the treaty. In relations between the contracting parties and later interpreters, it becomes evident that the minor argumentative weight of the *travaux* is a major factor in facilitating the negotiation process. There is an increased awareness that the effect of interpretation by courts in international law effectively results in a law-making capacity of courts in international law.[340] If this is true, another relation becomes important, and that is the relation between courts. Their judgment can only be considered to be something equivalent to law if accepted by other actors. That could be later courts with a changed composition or institutionally distinct courts.

If we consider the functions of the rule of interpretation in relations between different actors, the VCLT points to techniques which enhance legal discourse. Again, there is no direct impact upon the result, but indirect influences are possible: The arguments are tied to the treaty to be interpreted. As regards the interpretative hierarchy, certain techniques are more emphasised than others and the arguments deriving from them will carry more weight. This abstract determination of the importance of the means of interpretation might influence the outcome. Another important feature is that the rule of interpretation provides a structure for the discourse. The fact that the Vienna Convention classifies several techniques helps also to evaluate the justification of other actors. They can be put into a certain structure which might be the first step in a reconstruction of the arguments.[341]

At this point, it needs to be mentioned that the codification of the rules on interpretation coincided with the rise of arbitration in international law. The factor approach in turn coincided with the rise of international courts, in particular the PCIJ. This can be seen from the methodological debate of the time. In the flexible phase, the absence of

---

[340] Von Bogdandy and Venzke, 'On the functions of International Courts' 49.
[341] For the different ways to reconstruct legal arguments, see Feteris, *Fundamentals of Legal Argumentation* 10ff.

rules was particularly linked to the absence of higher courts. Lawrence said in the flexible phase that:

> since states have no common superior to adjust their differences and declare with authority the real meaning and force of their international documents, it is clear that no rules of interpretation can be laid down which are binding in the sense that the rules followed by a court of law in constructing a will or a lease are on the parties concerned.[342]

In the same vein, it was asserted that 'there is no place for the refinements of the courts in the rough jurisprudence of nations'.[343] Another author observed that, 'when states get into controversy about the interpretation of a treaty, they often make a new agreement, clearing up the disputed points in the way that seems most convenient at the time, which is not always the way pointed out by strict rules of interpretation'.[344]

This alleged freedom of states also found expression in more liberal rules of treaty construction. It is interesting to note that it was at times explicitly provided that the rules of construction would gain importance if there was a tribunal to use and enforce them.[345] With the emergence of courts and tribunals in the international arena, the structure of the international system again changed and some of the attempts at codification tried to meet the needs of courts and tribunals as new important actors in the business of treaty interpretation. This is reflected by the fact that authors in many cases did not aim at deducing their own system of interpretation but at reflecting interpretative practice of international as well as national courts.[346] Yet, the historical development as well as the relational comparison indicate that the function of the Convention works best in relation to parties before a court. Techniques validate arguments, but they also classify them. Thereby, they allow for the structuring of the process of argumentation. This function plays out well when several arguments are made and there is ultimately a possibility for an answer to be given. Techniques have no material impact upon the meaning of a treaty, this does not matter when there is a final and binding decision at

---

[342] Lawrence, *The Principles of International Law* 326.
[343] Quoting Hall, *A Treatise on International Law* 395 n. 2.
[344] Lawrence, *The Principles of International Law* 326.
[345] Phillipson, *Smith's International Law* 146.
[346] Sørensen, *Les Sources du droit international* 210–14; Gerald Fitzmaurice, 'The Law and Procedure of the International Court of Justice: Treaty Interpretation'; Gerald Fitzmaurice, 'The Law and Procedure of the International Court of Justice 1951–4'; Thirlway, 'The Law and procedure of the International Court of Justice 1960–1989, Part Three' 1.

the end and there is a close connection between those making arguments. The fact that the VCLT has no direct bearing on the outcome of an interpretative question, but rather structures and guides the process, leaves some leeway for the interpreter. Questions of interpretation mostly arise when there are competing claims. The VCLT rules on interpretation oblige all claimants to express their arguments according to the techniques of the Convention. This function works best when there is a *close communicative relationship* between the parties making the claims. The best situation is that the parties directly communicate with each other. The worst situation is where the parties deal with similar questions without addressing the other party. The fact that there is little direct guidance is not problematic since the decision of the interpretative question is, to a certain extent, open. This openness does no harm when there is a *final and binding decision at the end*. So one could say that the rule of interpretation in the VCLT works very well in proceedings before international courts. It helps the parties to structure their argument, it helps the court to understand the parties and to make the basis for its decision clear. The rule of interpretation functions best in judicial proceedings before a court.

So we have discovered the function of the VCLT, that is, the obligation to decide based on legal arguments relating to the interpretative issue in the treaty. We have also found that the ideal context in which to make this function operable is the judicial context in its various relations. What we now have to discuss is what can be derived from this function for the present question, that is, the question whether and with which justification an interpretation can be changed. We shall recall that the function of the rules on interpretation, i.e. their effect to structure the process of interpretation, has been declared to be the guiding star of this reconstruction. We have determined that an apt structure is achieved when two sets of considerations are met: Rule-of-lawyers considerations and rulers-of-law considerations. The rules need to provide for guidance, coherence and foreseeability but also for the necessary flexibility, workability and adaptability. Reflecting on intertemporal issues under those premises in judicial proceedings, it can be said on an abstract level that the VCLT first and foremost provides for intertemporal openness. Problems of stability and change ought to be decided in accordance with the best argument. Under this premise, it is impossible to tie the whole process of interpretation to one point in time. We have seen that the Vienna Convention instead meets the rulers-of-law considerations. Yet, the general preference for intertemporal openness reinforces the need to make arguments, especially before courts. This very fact might contribute to achieve the coherence of the process. What is more, it is also backed up by a discourse that has existed as long as modern international law. Never was a compromise reached by scholars. Especially when rules were elaborated in collective processes, they could never agree on a specific intertemporal focal point. Even though no general compromise can be achieved, this does not mean that this is the only way to achieve coherence. In the process of interpretation, the same mechanisms that underlie the precedential value of judgments can work to achieve those aims. The considerations produced by certain techniques will apply to different parts of one treaty or even a set of treaties: Once it is established that a treaty has a certain object and purpose, this will impact upon all of its parts. The fact that the same argument is used creates some predictability. If similar provisions in one treaty are interpreted, the previous results might be taken into account as context for the rule. In this way, rule-of-lawyers considerations will not be accounted for on a general level but the structure created by the VCLT allows taking them into account for specific contexts such as certain treaties or certain judicial mechanisms. Yet, the rule-of-lawyers considerations qualify the intertemporal openness at least in one respect. This will be called the *path-dependency argument*. Once a certain interpretation is backed up by legal justification, the interpreter has taken a certain path. Irrespective of the binding nature of precedent, the rule of interpretation as contained in the VCLT requires the interpreter to warrant a changed interpretation by a change of argument. One possibility is to say that subsequent considerations changed the interpretative equilibrium. Another possibility would be to reassess the use of a technique even though the circumstances have not really changed. Yet, if the interpretation is already backed up by a justification in accordance with the VCLT, it is necessary to mark the change. This operates as a 'burden of justification' to arrive at a changed interpretation. This section was certainly not a symphony, but it might have helped us to grasp the hidden theme that runs through the whole thesis: The obligation to decide based on arguments relating to the issues of interpretation works best in the judicial context and reinforces the intertemporal openness of the Convention. Now that we have discovered the function of the rule and especially how its techniques work in the abstract, it is time to look at them more closely. This also means that we have to move away from the foundations of the rule of interpretation, its cardinal cores, and move towards rather uncertain and interesting territories where we might find interpretive knots: Let us continue in *allegro*.

6

Interpretative knots: the system of the VCLT revisited

The establishment of the cardinal cores and the mode of inquiry will enable us to revisit the text of Arts. 31 and 32 VCLT in a new light: interpretative issues will not be decided but recognised and taken account of, especially when different solutions play out differently for intertemporal questions. Thus, we will establish interpretative knots. These knots consist of different outcomes to an interpretative question. After considering all techniques of interpretation, we will finally decide which of the suggested solutions dealing with questions of stasis and evolution ought to prevail from the perspective of a functional reconstruction. But before we can determine which comes out on top, we have to turn to the goal of interpretation.

6.1. The goal knot

We have seen that the goal of interpretation evolved substantially over time. In the mechanical phase, the aim was to arrive at the assumed intentions of the parties. In the flexible phase, the aim shifted to the real intentions. In the age of codification, a debate about the correct goal of interpretation broke out which resulted in several schools of interpretation, stressing either the intention, the purpose, the text or the neutral notion of meaning. This brings us to the problem of determining the goal of the rule of interpretation. Looking at the text, there are at least four possible goals the VCLT could have: The ordinary meaning, which is the first technique mentioned in Art. 31(1) VCLT. Conversely, the fact that the text is to be interpreted 'in the light of its object and purpose' could mean that this is the goal and the technique that leads the way. Art. 31(4) VCLT refers to the intentions of the parties. Art. 32 VCLT centres around the 'meaning' of the text, which could be considered as a neutral category between objective and subjective goals. This is not surprising as there was great disagreement about the possible goals of interpretation throughout the preparation of the Convention:

While the goal of intentions of the parties was linked to some techniques in Waldock's original draft, this was later deleted,[347] and attempts to reintroduce it at the first Vienna Convention failed.[348] Today, doctrinal opinion differs on that issue. It is interesting that the Vienna Convention has sometimes been referred to as pursuing a textual and objective approach to interpretation.[349] Some see it rather as a mixed approach with a slight textual predominance,[350] others as totally flexible.[351] The ILC has recently coined the phrase 'presumed intentions' which ought to designate the outcome of the normal use of the rule of interpretation in the VCLT.[352] Another attempt was made to denote the goal of interpretation as 'objectivised intention' of the parties.[353] Others still favour the intentions of the parties as a goal for interpretation.[354] To determine whether the subjective or the objective approach is correct would require

---

[347] See Art. 71 in Waldock, Third Report (n. 185) 52.
[348] See the introduction of the delegate of the Ukrainian Socialist Soviet Republic Makarevich, First Vienna Conference (n. 178) 168 para. 54 and the proposed amendment A/CONF.39/C.1/L.201.
[349] See with regard to the ILC Drafts McDougal, 'The International Law Commission's Draft Articles upon Interpretation' 992. With regard to the Vienna Convention, the Delegate of the United Kingdom, Mr Sinclair, First Vienna Conference (n. 178) 177 para. 3; Gottlieb, 'The Interpretation of Treaties by Tribunals' 123; Sharma, 'The ILC Draft and Treaty Interpretation with Special Reference to Preparatory Works' 386; Karl, *Vertrag und spaetere Praxis im Voelkerrecht* 186; Santulli, 'Rapport general' 304; Kempen and Hillgruber, *Völkerrecht* 72; Vitzthum, 'Begriff, Geschichte und Rechtsquellen des Völkerrechts' 47 para. 123; Heintschel von Heinegg, 'Die völkerrechtlichen Verträge als Hauptquelle des Völkerrechts' 408.
[350] Merrills, 'Two Approaches to Treaty Interpretation' 56; Herdegen, 'Interpretation in International Law' 7; Stein and von Buttlar, *Völkerrecht* 25.
[351] Yambrusic, *Treaty Interpretation* 241; Corten, 'Les Techniques reproduites aux Articles 31 à 33 des Conventions de Vienne' 356; McLachlan, 'The Principle of Systemic Integration and Article 31(3)(c) of the Vienna Convention' 291; Karl, *Vertrag und spaetere Praxis im Voelkerrecht* 141; Jonas and Saunders, 'The Object and Purpose of a Treaty' 578.
[352] For a reference to the discussion of the Drafting Committee, see the statement of its Chairman Dire Tladi of 31 May 2013, available at http://legal.un.org/ilc/sessions/65/SAPracticeDCStatement(2013).pdf (accessed 31 December 2014) 7–9. The Special Rapporteur Georg Nolte remarked that 'the "original" intent of the parties is not necessarily conclusive for the interpretation of a treaty.' Nolte, Second Report on Subsequent Agreements and Subsequent Practice, ILC, 'Report of the International Law Commission on the work of its sixty-sixth session (5 May–6 June and 7 July–8 August 2014)', A/CN.4/671, paras. 115 and 62.
[353] Bjorge, *The Evolutionary Interpretation of Treaties* 57.
[354] Yasseen, 'L'Interprétation des traités d'après la Convention de Vienne sur le droit des traités' 16; Kolb, *Interprétation et création du droit international* 607.

to conduct some basic research about the process of human comprehension and communication. The discourse in international law is less concerned with these questions but is rather pragmatic in that certain goals are advanced without further justification or reasoning. It is also paradigmatic in that the goals then frame the process of interpretation. It is important to stress that the actual choice made in that regard can have important consequences in the process of interpretation.[355] This becomes most evident in the case of intertemporal questions.[356] Subjective approaches ordinarily refer to the intentions of the parties. Consequently, in intertemporal questions of interpretation, the first point of reference for such an intentional approach is to look for the understanding at the time of the conclusion of the treaty. An objective approach would rather look at how the law is understood at the time of the interpretation of the treaty.

It is of the utmost importance to note that the rule of interpretation contained in the VCLT can also be applied without setting out a goal of interpretation. Especially the choice between a subjective and an objective approach can be left open. The rules of interpretation can work even assuming that their aim is simply to interpret the treaty and to determine its meaning. This would lead to an interpretation without any assumption attaching to the subjective and objective approaches.[357] On this reading, the rule of interpretation would transcend the old battle for the goal of interpretation.

The same result is reached when one pretends to use a subjective or objective approach but attaches to it no other significance than to represent the result of the normal process of interpretation. If one contends that the application of the rule of interpretation as contained in the VCLT would result in finding the intentions of the parties, the intentions add nothing to the process of interpretation. The use of the word 'intention' would be superfluous and insignificant. As previously mentioned, Koskenniemi pointed to the circularity of objective and subjective approaches.[358] The danger inherent in defining certain goals simply as the result of the process of interpretation is that some of the assumptions underlying this approach are read into the VCLT even though they are not really grounded in the rule of interpretation. So for

---

[355] For a very interesting analysis, see Pauwelyn and Elsig, 'The Politics of Treaty Interpretation' 450.
[356] For a very interesting analysis, see *ibid*. 454.   [357] For this critique, see at 68 n. 408.
[358] *Ibid*.

example when one defines the intentions as what results from the Vienna Convention, there is a risk that the interpreter ties the interpretation to the time of the conclusion of the treaty in the first place even though nothing in Arts. 31 and 32 supports this outcome.

Summing up, the VCLT does not prescribe what the goal of interpretation is. It is possible to apply it with a subjective or an objective mindset. It is also possible to take no stance in that regard and simply look for the meaning of the treaty by complying with the rule of interpretation as contained in the VCLT.

6.2. Interpretation in good faith

This obligation is linked to the *pacta sunt servanda* principle enshrined in Art. 26 VCLT. Despite the general agreement concerning its fundamental importance, the concept is fuzzy and cannot be defined easily.[359] It is 'related to honesty, fairness and reasonableness' and the application of the rules derived through it 'is determined at any particular time by the compelling standards of honesty, fairness and reasonableness'.[360] In the context of Art. 31 VCLT it can be broadly described as 'acting honestly, without fraud or intent to deceive'.[361] Yet, in modern times, examples of the practical application of the principle are rare.[362] Most examples in Gentili's treatise relied almost exclusively on good faith. Some of those examples will give us a good understanding of what this principle is actually aimed at:

> Therefore Pericles acted criminally when he agreed to spare the enemy if they would lay aside all iron, and then slew them because they had kept the iron clasps in their cloaks ... The Plataeans were in the wrong when they agreed to surrender their prisoners, but gave them back dead; as if corpses were prisoners or a corpse were a man. Alexander was wrong when he allowed the defenders of a town to withdraw from it in safety, but gave orders that they be put to death when they had gone a short distance ... Dercyllidas, Thibron, and Paches acted unjustly when they

---

[359] For a more detailed and general discussion, see Gardiner, *Treaty Interpretation* 147ff.
[360] O'Connor, *Good Faith in International Law* 124.
[361] Gardiner, *Treaty Interpretation* 150.
[362] Aust mentions as one example the implicit change of the interpretation of Art. 23(1) UN Charter when the People's Republic of China replaced the Republic of China which was mentioned in the text. Aust, *Modern Treaty Law and Practice* 235. A mix of abstract examples that could be considered as good faith obligation is provided by Villiger, *Commentary on the 1969 Vienna Convention on the Law of Treaties* 425.

promised the besieged a return into the beleaguered city, if they would come to them, and then threatened them with death unless they surrendered their city, and when they had done so granted them a return to the surrendered town. The city was not surrendered at the time when they agreed to let the inhabitants return to it ... The Campanians were in the wrong when they pledged themselves to leave to the enemy a half of their arms, but cut them all up and left a half of them in that condition ... The Romans were unjust again when they promised that Carthage should be free, but transferred the language of the agreement to the citizens, maintaining that they were the city and not its walls and the buildings, which they ordered to be destroyed ... The Locrians acted wickedly when they agreed upon a perpetual peace, so long as they should tread that land and carry those heads upon their shoulders. For they shook off some earth which they had previously placed upon their heels and some onion heads that they had secretly put upon their shoulders, and began hostilities.[363]

Those examples show us the common essence of good faith claims: in every case, it is alleged that the interpretative result is a possible, but wrong, interpretation of the words. So, good faith prevents the misconduct of the interpreter.[364] Both parts of this definition show the great difference between good faith and techniques as previously defined: Techniques can indicate a result but not exclude another one. The obligation to interpret in good faith in contrast has a material component: It can establish that a certain interpretation is wrong. We could also say that it does not validate considerations and arguments but interpretative results.[365] So it is different from the techniques in nature.

---

[363] Gentili *De jure bellis libri tres* 145–8 (original 233–8, Book II Chapter IV).
[364] Expressing the same thought as relationship between interpretation and performance of the treaty *ibid.* 425.
[365] Interestingly, Gardiner in his extensive and learned treatment of good faith in the process of treaty interpretation suggests that good faith is intrinsically linked to the principle of effectiveness, and he finds evidence for that view in a statement of the ILC: see Gardiner, *Treaty Interpretation* 150. The Commentary says that '[w]hen a treaty is open to two interpretations one of which does and the other does not enable the treaty to have appropriate effects, good faith and the objects and purposes of the treaty demand that the former interpretation should be adopted'. Final Draft Articles (n. 247) 219 para. 6. It is suggested here that one could possibly read this in the sense that the good faith element only comes in when the interpretation would have the 'appropriate effects'. So while the effects would rest on the technique of assessing the object and purpose, this reading would not materially change the rules on interpretation but would keep the obligation to interpret in good faith apart from the techniques of interpretation. The latter seems to be important as it can very well be that an interpretation based on good faith obliges an interpreter to stick to the text of the treaty even though the object and purpose might lead beyond the text. The same opinion is advocated by Villiger, *Commentary on the 1969 Vienna Convention on the Law of Treaties* 425 para. 7; Dörr,

Yet, there is also a tension with the techniques contained in the Convention: Art. 31(3)(a) and (b) oblige the interpreter to take into account subsequent conduct (agreements and practice) in the application of the treaty. This, however, does not depend on a certain quality of the conduct or the interpretative results it leads to. From the obligation of good faith, in contrast, it would be possible to strike out certain conduct as irrelevant.[366] So the obligation to interpret in good faith is a component different from the techniques enshrined in Arts. 31 and 32 VCLT. Yet, it has been part of the interpretative method of international law ever since. The real examples of application of the obligation, however, indicate that the obligation operates rather in bilateral disputes between two parties. And this is especially so when one party of the dispute has power over the other: Then, the obligation to interpret in good faith is like a call to act virtuously.[367] What this exactly means is of course subject to the discretion of the auto-interpreter. Gentili suggests that a way out would be to imagine an objective point of view, in the sense of a common understanding.[368] The judicial process will by its very self-understanding assume such an objective view.[369] Independence is one of the essential features attributed to courts, which is sometimes expressed by a blindfolded woman representing *Justitia*. From this, we can derive that the principle of good faith has no relevance in the modern judicial context.[370] This conclusion must not be misinterpreted: interpretation concerns understanding and justifying; rules of interpretation aim to facilitate legal communication. In this relationship, the notion of good faith represents a wider issue that has been viewed from many different perspectives: any communication can only work if the parties to it have a certain mindset

---

'Art. 31' 540 para. 35; Jacobs, 'Varieties of Approach to Treaty Interpretation' 333. The latter, however, attaches good faith not to the process of interpretation but to the obligation contained in the terms of the treaty themselves. This effectively means that good faith would allow going beyond the words of the treaty. If one understands this obligation as an obligation upon the interpreter, this obligation could direct the interpreter to stick to the wording in certain cases and in other cases to give more weight to other techniques of interpretation. It is hard to see why an interpretation according to good faith should always go against the wording of the treaty.

[366] In the ordinary process of interpretation, this can happen when subsequent practice is outweighed by other techniques.
[367] Klabbers, 'Virtuous Interpretation'.
[368] Gentili, *De jure bellis libri tres* 146 (original 235, Book II Chapter IV).
[369] Thirlway, 'The Law and Procedure of the International Court of Justice 1960–1989, Part Three' 17. Generally agreeing, Gardiner, *Treaty Interpretation* 153.
[370] Dupuy, 'Evolutionary Interpretation of Treaties' 128.

and openness towards the process. This is part of Donald Davidson's principle of charity, which is envisaged as a necessary requirement to make all communication possible.[371] From a legal perspective, Jan Klabbers has lately called for 'a virtuous approach to interpretation', shifting the view from external to internal standards.[372] If it is the task of a scholar to improve international law, it would certainly be good to promote virtues in the academic and professional community. But the obligation to interpret in good faith is not the only way to do so. An obligation to argue might further virtuous interpretation since the parties are forced to be transparent about their reasons. And this even though the obligation to interpret in good faith has no apparent function in that process. If one were to rely on good faith, it is of course possible that this warrants an evolutive interpretation,[373] yet good faith can also indicate a static result.[374]

If that is true, it is hard to see why the fourth Special Rapporteur would have said that 'at root the application of the intertemporal law to interpretation is a matter of good faith'.[375] Considering the actual function that the obligation to interpret in good faith plays, this can only mean that the decision is to be left to the ordinary process of treaty interpretation, which was for Waldock the doctrine of intertemporal law.

6.3. Ordinary and special meaning of the terms of the treaty

Art. 31 prescribes that a treaty ought to be interpreted in accordance with the ordinary meaning of the text. This is taken to mean that, if we look at a text, the first thing we take into account is its general meaning. It could be rephrased as the meaning a word has to a person 'reasonably informed in that subject'.[376] The ascertainment of the ordinary meaning is actually a linguistic reconstruction of the use of the words, in practice, the interpreter would have to show evidence of the use. The most common way to do so is the use of dictionaries.[377]

It is of the utmost importance that the VCLT is not based on the premise that words have an essential meaning. Quite to the contrary. The very fact that a term has an ordinary and a special meaning entails

---

[371] Davidson, 'Radical Interpretation' 314. [372] Klabbers, 'Virtuous Interpretation' 35.
[373] Bjorge, *The Evolutionary Interpretation of Treaties* 70-1.
[374] Dahm, Delbrück and Wolfrum, *Völkerrecht* (vol. 1/3) 641.
[375] Waldock, Third Report (n. 185) 96.   [376] Gardiner, *Treaty Interpretation* 174.
[377] Ibid. 166.

the assumption that there might be different meanings to a text. As was stressed by the fourth Special Rapporteur himself,[378] the rule of interpretation does not rely on the premise that there is just one, necessary and general meaning to each term. The rule of interpretation might be called textualist in that it attaches some argumentative weight to that meaning. To say that it is based upon a necessary connection of signs to their referents would be a conscious misinterpretation.

We have already seen that there are temporal variances in the ordinary meaning of words. Yet, this is not the only way in which the meaning varies: The very same signs can also mean different things to different groups. Determinants could be age, class, generation, regional descent. Upon hearing the term 'damage', lawyers will immediately think about contracts and torts and related matters while for example young Bavarians of my age group associate it with hangovers. The same words can mean different things to different people. This might have been the reason why the Vienna Convention followed the old traditional interpretative method to opt for the ordinary meaning as a technique of interpretation. This leads us to the question what role the special meaning in Art. 31(4) VCLT has.

There is indeed a debate about how the special meaning is related to the ordinary meaning[379] and whether this clause establishes a presumption in favour of the ordinary meaning.[380] The cardinal core can shed light on these differences: The crucial fact is that Art. 31(4) VCLT does not establish any technique of interpretation. Viewed as a technique, the ordinary meaning suggests nothing different since it is only one factor amongst many.[381] So Art. 31(4) VCLT establishes no separate technique but is just a reminder that the meaning of the text to be interpreted can result in a meaning which is not the ordinary meaning.[382] In a previous draft, some techniques were attributed to the special meaning.[383] The ordinary meaning of the text is an interpretative technique; by contrast, special meaning, as used in Art. 31(4) VCLT, is a class of interpretative

---

[378] Waldock, Third Report (n. 185) 57 para. 16.
[379] This disagreement is summarised by the commentary to the Final Draft Articles (n. 247) 222 para. 17. A full discussion is provided by *ibid.* 291.
[380] In favour of a presumption: Aust, *Modern Treaty Law and Practice* 244; Dörr, 'Art. 31' 540 para. 35; Gardiner, *Treaty Interpretation* 295. Against the presumption: Villiger, *Commentary on the 1969 Vienna Convention on the Law of Treaties* 435.
[381] Gardiner, *Treaty Interpretation* 294.
[382] It is obvious from the foregoing that the clause is actually redundant.
[383] Art. 71(2) Waldock, Third Report (n. 185) 52.

results comparable to static or evolutive interpretations. It is subject to the ordinary process of interpretation, whether the interpretation results in a departure from the ordinary meaning. In essence, Art. 31(4) VCLT only clarifies the obvious: The ordinary meaning must not always prevail.

As historical linguistics tell us, the ordinary meaning of words change.[384] This was also acknowledged at the First Vienna Conference.[385] This also means that the technique of ordinary meaning can possibly suggest more than one meaning and that the meanings differ in their temporality.[386] It can suggest that the term was commonly understood one way at the time of the conclusion of the treaty but another way at present times. Since the techniques are intertemporally open, both versions are valid considerations.[387] They can be assessed in the process of balancing, and other means will help to suggest which meaning is to be preferred.

Regarding questions of stasis and evolution, attempts have been made to establish whether certain classes of words could favour a certain interpretative result. So, it could be contended that only 'generic terms' are susceptible to change their interpretation.[388] It could also be contended that the changeability relies on the flexible criterion of specificity.[389] These opinions are based on experience and observation of legal disputes but also entail a claim that only a certain category of terms can change their meaning. Whether this observation is correct empirically will be assessed later. There is no agreement upon the use of the adjective generic. In a rather narrow interpretation, it would denote a certain class of words that can be interpreted evolutively. But this definition does not tell us when a term is generic. One could allude to previous use in other treaties. Yet, there seems to be no reason why it should be impossible to attribute a meaning open to change in one treaty, while the meaning is

---

[384] See for example Luján, 'Semantic Change'; Luraghi and Bebenik (eds.), *The Continuum Companion to Historical Linguistics.*

[385] The fact that the meaning of words can change was also observed and mentioned at the Vienna Conference: see the statement of the Delegate of Greece, Mr Krispis, First Vienna Conference (n. 178) 172 para. 8.

[386] For the fact that the terms of a treaty can have more than one meaning at the same time, see Gardiner, *Treaty Interpretation* 170.

[387] Peanson, *Manual of the Terminology of Public International Law (Law of Peace) and International Organizations*, 294. Compare Gillich, *Konsens und Evolutive Vertragsauslegung* 80. Yet, she does not explain why she thinks that changes in the ordinary meanings of the terms could not be considered in the process of interpretation.

[388] *Ibid.* 173.

[389] Nolte, 'Between Contemporaneous and Evolutive Interpretation' 1679.

fixed in another treaty if this was clear from the context. Consequently, this narrow definition of 'generic terms' is useful insofar as it creates categories for the practice of courts and tribunals. This designation is only relevant if there is a practice of actually believing that there are generic terms. A broad view of generic terms would define it as '[b]elonging to or designating a genus (as opposed to a species) or a class, group or kind'.[390] It could be contended that this class of terms can be interpreted evolutively whereas other classes of terms such as names cannot. This very question is the subject of a heated debate in the philosophy of language.[391] Yet, the category of terms carrying a fixed meaning is much narrower than only those terms which are not generic.[392] The present study cannot go into details of that discourse, therefore, it ought to be assumed that every class of terms can be interpreted evolutively. Yet, we will keep the distinctions made in the back of our heads since they are relevant in interpretative practice.

Linderfalk has tried to categorise the terms in relation to whether they are 'referring expressions'.[393] Methodologically, this category has been derived from the observation of the practice of courts and tribunals.[394] Insofar as this is based on a simple observation of the actual practice, the distinction does not classify terms but only restates the practice and takes for granted that the terms are rightly classified by courts and tribunals. We have previously established that there is a referential evolution when the terms are open for changes concerning the things they are referring to. So the word 'treaties' could refer to all treaties in force at the time of the conclusion of the treaty or all treaties at present times. It is important to state that if referential evolution is possible, this does not attach to the term as such. If we decide that the term treaties is tied to the point in time of the conclusion of the treaty, this does not have to be extended to that term in all treaties.[395] The past practice of courts might be a good indicator but is far from being a safe inference.

---

[390] McArthur, *Concise Oxford Companion to the English Language*.
[391] A good overview, referring mainly to Kripke and Putnam, is given by Lycan, *Philosophy of Language* 50.
[392] See *ibid*.   [393] Linderfalk, 'Doing the Right Thing for the Right Reason' 134.
[394] *Ibid*. 136.
[395] Just for the sake of completeness it has to be stated that another possible distinction Linderfalk could have meant is that between terms that have a referent and terms that only have a meaning. Yet, there is no reason to believe that one or the other category cannot change their meaning.

The fact that we cannot really classify terms might be an advantage for the rather broad notion of specificity.[396] It could be used on a sliding scale as a categorisation of terms indicating a certain probability of stasis or evolution without indicating definite results. We can conclude that the ordinary meaning imports the general language use into the process of treaty interpretation. There can be different ordinary meanings for a text at the same time or at different points in time. The change of language can raise an intertemporal question which is to be answered in the normal process of interpretation considering the results achieved by the other techniques as well. Attempts to classify terms can give indications if the patterns are observed in actual interpretative practice. Yet, no preconceived determination can be securely derived from the classification of the terms.

6.4. Context

The context of the treaty comprises according to Art. 31(2) VCLT *inter alia* the preamble and annexes to the treaty. This clearly shows that the VCLT employs a rather defined vision of the context: The context is not comprised of general circumstances of the treaty such as economic, political or social conditions; it has somehow to be related to the text of the treaty.

A rather refined question in that regard is whether other provisions in the same treaty apart from the terms to be interpreted shall also comprise the context. The text of the VCLT as well as the status of the means contained therein as techniques clearly point to the affirmative: Art. 31(2) VCLT includes other texts 'in addition to the text' from which it can be derived that the text necessarily belongs to the context. What is more, this is in line with regarding the means contained in Arts. 31 and 32 VCLT as techniques. Provisions in the context of the terms to be interpreted are acknowledged in their current meaning and not only in their ordinary meaning. This is why it might be necessary to interpret another provision before it can be taken into account in the process of interpretation. Yet, it is essential that one can take into account the ordinary meaning of the words to be interpreted on the one hand and the full meaning of the provisions in the context of those words on the other. There is no need to think about this question as a knot.

---

[396] For this criterion, see Nolte, 'Between Contemporaneous and Evolutive Interpretation' 1679.

The definition of context in Art. 31(2) shows the narrowness of the concept of context in the Vienna Convention.[397] Instead of referring to the wider surrounding of the treaty such as its economic, political or social context, Art. 31(2) limits the significance of context to other texts that relate to the treaty.[398] This of course also limits the ability of the interpreter to take into account changes outside the legal context. In fact, this narrow construction of context then also plays out quite differently with regard to the intertemporal question. As has already been mentioned, the technique of contextual interpretation as far as Art. 31(2)(a) and (b) are concerned require an instrument to be connected temporarily to the conclusion of the treaty. Yet, those features do not necessarily mean that the context is tied to the conclusion of the treaty. It does seem that the temporal focus rather distinguishes subsequent conduct (agreements and practice) from the features belonging to the context. If the context is another part of the text in the treaty, it would also be possible to interpret according to the rules on interpretation.[399] Different meanings can result from the context. In the interpretation of Art. X, Art. Y can suggest one solution while Art. Z suggests another.

6.5. Object and purpose

The Vienna Convention also provides that the terms have to be seen in the light of the object and purpose of the treaty. This phrase refers to the reason or *telos* of the treaty. Whereas Waldock's first draft contained this means of interpretation as a rather material principle,[400] it was subsequently changed to a technique.[401] Since the object and purpose is to be considered as a technique, it is not possible to associate it with evolutive interpretation. The status of this means as a technique means that it is to be considered separately from the result of interpretation. Regarding intertemporal questions, we can conclude that the object and purpose can also call for a static interpretation. This is an important insight not to

---

[397] McDougal, 'The International Law Commission's Draft Articles upon Interpretation' 997.
[398] See Villiger, *Commentary on the 1969 Vienna Convention on the Law of Treaties* 427.
[399] To avoid the problem of circularity, it would be necessary to exclude the text that was to be interpreted first from the process of interpretation. If Art. A is to be interpreted in the context of Art. B, Art. B cannot be interpreted in the context of Art. A. Again, this is not a question of the definition of the technique but only a problem in its application.
[400] See Art. 72 in Waldock, Third Report (n. 185) 52.
[401] ILC, Final Draft Articles (n. 247) 217.

be underestimated: from the perspective of the techniques of interpretation, an evolutive interpretation is not by definition a purposive interpretation.

The first interpretative question concerns the status of the technique itself: It could be contended that the notions of object and purpose are taken to denote one technique,[402] yet, it could also be contended that there is actually two separate techniques.[403]

There is a tendency amongst French-speaking scholars to regard this as two distinctive notions and, consequently, as two distinctive techniques. Whereas the object would be something material relating to the content of the treaty, the purpose was something instrumental relating to the intended result.[404] The latter view would then construe the object of the treaty as being its substance in the sense of a core of the treaty, whereas the purpose would be its function, the social aim the treaty is made to achieve.[405] Our previous reconstruction of the cardinal cores of interpretation can help us to determine these questions: As we have seen also in the case of other techniques, they cannot only produce one but several arguments that point to different meanings. There is no need to separate both notions since one can introduce arguments that would fall under both the object and the purpose in the very same act of balancing. In the end, all the results achieved by the techniques are thrown into the 'crucible', whether we take them together or separate them. So the separation of object and purpose is enlightening as to the several aspects this technique can have, but it leads to the same results. The Convention is not very clear as to what the object and purpose refers to. The most probable subject is the treaty as a whole. Yet, it would also be possible to look at the object and purpose of parts of the treaty, of single provisions

---

[402] Villiger, *Commentary on the 1969 Vienna Convention on the Law of Treaties* 271; Linderfalk, *On the Interpretation of Treaties* 209; Jonas and Saunders, 'The Object and Purpose of a Treaty' 578; Crnic-Grotic, 'Object and Purpose of Treaties in the Vienna Convention on the Law of Treaties' 143.

[403] See the extensive treatment of this question by Buffard and Zemanek, 'The "Object and Purpose" of a Treaty' 322. See also Crnic-Grotic, 'Object and Purpose of Treaties in the Vienna Convention on the Law of Treaties' 173; Boisson de Chazournes, La Rosa and Mbengue, 'Art. 18 VCLT' 387; Pellet, 'Art. 19 VCLT' 449; Yasseen, 'L'Interprétation des traités d'après la Convention de Vienne sur le droit des traités' 55.

[404] Boisson de Chazournes, La Rosa and Mbengue, 'Art. 18 VCLT' 387; Pellet, 'Art. 19 VCLT' 449.

[405] Compare the French wording, 'object et but'.

or sections or even subsections.[406] This uncertainty will be called the *subject knot*.

The most important interpretative knot in that regard is, however, the *ascertainment knot*.[407] Like the context, the object and purpose ought to be ascertained, but the VCLT does not stipulate how this ought to be done. This also impacts upon other provisions in the Convention which rely on the same or a similar notion. There are different possible views of how the object and purpose can be ascertained. A very narrow notion would be to look exclusively at the intention of the parties and to use the *travaux* and the text to arrive at those intentions. While this is possible, it seems self-contradictory to accord to the *travaux* only a supplementary role but to include them indirectly into the primary means. The widest possible notion would be to include all possible considerations into this technique. Account could be taken of social, economic, political and all other possible circumstances in which the treaty operates.[408] This would again import considerations into the process of interpretation that would normally be considered as supplementary means.

Dealing with this question in its 'Guide to Practice on Reservations to Treaties', the ILC proposed the following solution to the problem:

> The object and purpose of the treaty is to be determined in good faith, taking account of the terms of the treaty in their context, in particular the title and the preamble of the treaty. Recourse may also be had to the preparatory work of the treaty and the circumstances of its conclusion and, where appropriate, the subsequent practice of the parties.[409]

The ILC seems to have departed from the rule of interpretation, while modifying it significantly. Most considerably, the preparatory works and the circumstances of the conclusion of the treaty are not subsidiary as in Art. 32 VCLT, but on the same level as the other techniques of

---

[406] For an account that a treaty might have many objects and purposes, see Linderfalk, *On the Interpretation of Treaties* 211; Villiger, *Commentary on the 1969 Vienna Convention on the Law of Treaties* 427. In favour of a single object and purpose, Jacobs, 'Varieties of Approach to Treaty Interpretation' 337.

[407] It is argued that there actually is no common meaning of the terms object and purpose in the Vienna Convention: see Jonas and Saunders, 'The Object and Purpose of a Treaty' 608.

[408] This can be linked to effectiveness since this refers to the reality in which the treaty operates. On effectiveness, see Linderfalk, *On the Interpretation of Treaties* 220.

[409] ILC, Guide to Practice on Reservations of Treaties, 'Report of the International Law Commission on the work of its 63rd Session' (26 April–3 June and 4 July–12 August) *ILC Ybk* ILC 2011 Vol. II 2, 359, Guideline 3.1.5.1 ('ILC, Guide on Reservations').

interpretation. On the other hand, the means of interpretation are not as open as in Art. 32 VCLT which refers to the general and open expression 'subsidiary means of interpretation' possibly providing for an indefinite list of means of interpretation. Subsequent practice according to the ILC comprises the elements mentioned in Art. 31(2)(a) and (b) as well as Art. 31(2) and (3); it is significant that the ILC added the phrase that those means of interpretation could only be resorted to 'where appropriate'. As explained above, the use of techniques mentioned in the Vienna Convention is not automatic but the interpreter has to determine their significance in every single case. So he or she will take into account any technique of interpretation only where it is appropriate. So it is perfectly in line with the ordinary method of interpretation.

This particular guideline is justified by the ILC with a review of court practice in that regard.[410] As in the case of the rule of interpretation, the ILC developed this formula as a mix of codifying judicial practice and progressively developing it. The guideline of the ILC is a very authoritative view amongst all other possible solutions. This reinforces the idea of thinking of the object and purpose as an interpretative knot: different approaches by interpreters are possible, but a definite ascertainment remains an 'enigma'.[411]

The choice concerning the ascertainment of the object and purpose impacts in several ways upon intertemporal questions: A stronger reliance on the *travaux* might favour static interpretations, a very open approach point in favour of changing interpretations. Since the object and purpose of the treaty ought to be ascertained, there is also the question of whether the object and purpose are themselves susceptible to change.[412]

One way to assess the importance of this technique for the present context would be to contrast rigid answers to the intertemporal question and to choose between the object and purpose that the parties wished to attribute to the treaty at the time of its conclusion with a rather emergent purpose.[413] The latter notion accounts for changes in the object and purpose. The question of how the object and purpose can change does

---

[410] *Ibid.* 360–1.   [411] Buffard and Zemanek, 'The "Object and Purpose" of a Treaty'.
[412] ILC, Guide on Reservations (n. 409) 362 para. 7 Guideline 3.1.5.1.
[413] See Fitzmaurice, 'Hersch Lauterpacht – The Scholar as Judge – Part III' 141; Crnic-Grotic, 'Object and Purpose of Treaties in the Vienna Convention on the Law of Treaties' 158.

depend upon its ascertainment. Narrow and broad solutions will produce changes under different circumstances.

One element that has to be mentioned is the expected duration of treaties. This can enter the process of interpretation through several techniques: It can be seen from the object and purpose as well as from the context. It is commonly assumed that treaties concluded for a very long or unspecified time are more likely to be interpreted evolutively.[414] While this is certainly not a necessary condition, a long duration of a treaty could indeed be one factor to argue for its adaptation by interpretation.

The object and purpose technique can also take account of the specific features of the treaty.[415] Its nature, such as human rights or international economic law, its classification, such as constitution or law-making treaty but also its structure, such as the bilateral–multilateral–universal distinction can be acknowledged. The important difference is that those considerations are pondered in the process of balancing. They do not favour static or dynamic interpretations automatically but only insofar as they relate to the context at hand. They have to stand the test of the technique and are to be ascertained individually.

6.6. Subsequent agreements and practice

Subsequent practice has for a very long time been an element in the interpretation of treaties in international law. As compared to many national jurisdictions, it is a distinguishing feature of international legal method. In national jurisdictions, it is at times discussed whether to accord some special weight to the practice of actors.[416] Especially in constitutional law, there is the sentiment that the way the participants live and interpret the constitution can hardly be grasped with a four-corner interpretation. To give just two examples from the German

---

[414] See the general observations by Bernhardt, 'Evolutive Treaty Interpretation' 24.
[415] See *ibid.* 65 for the specific case of human rights. Bernhardt's view is apt to explain how the VCLT can work in different circumstances. Bjorge detects a methodological flaw, as different treaties are compared by Bernhardt instead of interpreting them: Bjorge, *The Evolutionary Interpretation of Treaties* 36. Yet, it is hard to see why such a comparison was impossible in order to make a general statement about the interpretation of human rights treaties under the VCLT.
[416] For general overviews of the debate about agency interpretation in US administrative law, see Scalia, 'Judicial Deference to Administrative Interpretations of Law' 511; Mashaw, 'Norms, Practices, and the Paradox of Deference' 501.

discourse: Rudolf Smend distinguished between constitutional law and the constitution and developed a methodological approach stemming from the humanities.[417] Christian Tomuschat inquired into the topic of whether there was a customary constitutional law.[418] Subsequent agreements are more specific to international law since they provide for formal or informal agreements of the contracting parties.[419] Yet, subsequent agreements and practice taken as a whole are specific to international legal method. They show that the international interpretative method has not only transplanted its national counterparts but also moved beyond them in some respects. Especially subsequent practice is a very important external factor that ought to be acknowledged in the process of treaty interpretation.[420] Even McDougal, a fierce opponent of the Vienna rule, had to admit that subsequent practice imported a part of legal reality.[421] It has been stated that one of the key challenges of legal method is to show to what extent it can guide legal practice.[422] On the one side, a strict legalistic methodology risks being out of touch with reality. On the other side, a complete openness to any kind of consideration would deprive the legal process of its effectiveness and distinctiveness. Subsequent practice is the perfect technique of interpretation to mitigate between the two extremes. It imports legal reality, but only insofar as it concerns the application of the treaty. This can also be reinforced from a particular stream in international legal scholarship:[423] the study of pragmatics focuses on what actors actually do with words. It is obvious that subsequent practice is to be distinguished from this rather theoretical concept of practice,[424] but it has also to be emphasised that looking at the practice to a great extent meets the calls of pragmatic views.[425]

This is all the more important in the present context since subsequent conduct necessarily arises after the conclusion of the treaty and evidences

---

[417] Smend, *Verfassung und Verfassungsrecht*.
[418] Tomuschat, *Verfassungsgewohnheitsrecht*.
[419] Chanaki, *L'Adaptation des traités dans le temps* 275–84.
[420] Visscher, *Problèmes d'interprétation judiciaire en droit international public* 50; Sinclair, *The Vienna Convention on the Law of Treaties* 76.
[421] McDougal, 'The International Law Commission's Draft Articles upon Interpretation' 994.
[422] Krawietz, 'Ausdifferenzierung von Praxis und Theorie in juristischer systemtheoretischer Perspektive' 345; Morlok and Kölbel, 'Rechtspraxis und Habitus' 304.
[423] Venzke, *How Interpretation Makes International Law*. [424] Ibid. 325.
[425] Bianchi, 'Law, Time, and Change' 137.

the intertemporal openness of the Convention.[426] While it could be contended that practice is only backward looking in that it can illuminate the will of the parties at the time of the conclusion of the treaty,[427] there is nothing in the Vienna Convention to support this assumption.[428] Subsequent practice also gives evidence of later occurrences that were unheard of at the time when the respective treaty was set up. It is maybe the most prolific dynamic element in the context of the Vienna Convention.

If one were to follow a rather linear approach to the history of the method of treaty interpretation, one could say that the so-called 'authentic' means of interpretation lost their predominance after the flexible phase turned into the codificatory phase. The morphological approach suggests something else: The geology of interpretation is not comprised of only one layer, different layers are visible at different places. In the face of the multiplication and proliferation of international courts and tribunals, there is a significant shift in international governance: Many questions will now not be exclusively decided by government officials. By using the technique of subsequent practice, judicial actors can avail themselves of the legitimacy and expertise of those law-appliers. While we cannot say that subsequent practice and subsequent agreements trump automatically all other techniques of interpretation, they are special, important and particular means of interpretation that will play an important if not perhaps decisive role in many disputes. This is a very good reason to see how they operate.

Art. 31(3)(a) and (b) provide that the interpreter shall take into account beyond the context also subsequent practice and subsequent agreements. First, the Vienna Convention does not explain the exact meaning of the term 'subsequent'. The final commentary stipulates that this ought to be construed as subsequent to the conclusion of the treaty.[429] It has rightly been remarked that this can either mean the process of conclusion as well as the result of the conclusion.[430] However, in the aftermath of conclusion, there exist also the contextual elements as provided for in Art. 31(2) VCLT. Although a strict distinction does not

---

[426] Haraszti and Decsenyi, *Some Fundamental Problems of the Law of Treaties* 141; Greig, *Intertemporality and the Law of Treaties* 50; Dupuy, 'Evolutionary Interpretation of Treaties' 127; Linderfalk, *On the Interpretation of Treaties* 171 with further references.
[427] For the possibility of backward-looking practice, see Kolb, *Interprétation et création du droit international* 489.
[428] Orakhelashvili, *The Interpretation of Acts and Rules in Public International Law* 355; Nolte, 'Introduction' 1.
[429] Final Draft Articles (n. 247) 221 para. 14.
[430] Nolte, 'Treaties over Time: Introductory Report' 189.

seem to be necessary since the actual agreements and practice can be taken into account in the process of interpretation either way,[431] it does seem preferable to resort to the means of interpretation only after the treaty entered into force.[432] Only then can one speak of a practice in the application of the treaty as the treaty does not apply before it enters into force.[433] No matter at which point in time one would think a practice and agreements can be considered to be 'subsequent', it is undisputed that practice and agreements shall be taken into consideration after the treaty entered into force and as long as it is in force. This has of course very important repercussions for the intertemporal question. If the rules on interpretation allow for the consideration of conduct after the treaty came into force, those necessarily can alter the interpretation as it stood at the time of the conclusion of the treaty.

With regard to subsequent agreements, it is important to note that the term 'agreement' can mean anything from a formal treaty to an informal agreement.[434] One of the most interesting disagreements is the question whose practice ought to be considered. This will be called the *actor knot*.[435] All agree that the practice of states will certainly qualify as subsequent practice. It is often assumed that subsequent practice ought to be state practice.[436] The question is whether other actors can be considered as well. In spite of this, Art. 31(3) VCLT does not expressly limit subsequent practice to states. So a very wide interpretation would be to take into account the practice of every actor that is actually competent under the rules of the treaty to apply the treaty.[437] That could possibly include international organisations and courts.[438] A solution that seeks

---

[431] *Ibid.*
[432] In favour of taking the point in time in which the treaty was established as definite: see Linderfalk, *On the Interpretation of Treaties* 163.
[433] We will have to exclude the provisional application as envisaged in Art. 18 from this observation.
[434] Gardiner, *Treaty Interpretation* 217; Nolte, 'Third Report for the ILC Study Group on Treaties over Time Subsequent Agreements and Subsequent Practice of States outside of Judicial or Quasi-Judicial Proceedings' 309.
[435] See also Venzke, *How Interpretation Makes International Law* 238.
[436] Schermers and Blokker, *International Institutional Law* 844; implicitly Boisson de Chazournes, 'Subsequent Practice, Practices and "Family Resemblance"' 55ff. She employs the concept of familiarity in relation to other actors which in turn could mean that she regards subsequent practice as genuine state practice.
[437] So for example Gardiner discusses the inclusion of international courts as well as organs of international organisations: see Gardiner, *Treaty Interpretation* 229.
[438] For international organisations, see *ibid.* 230. On the general possibility that the practice of other natural and legal persons is acknowledged, see Nolte, 'Third Report for the ILC

the middle ground between a very narrow and a very wide interpretation might be to rely on the attributability of the practice to a state.[439] Another solution would be to determine the actors by looking at who is empowered by the treaty to apply it in real life and to extend subsequent practice respectively.

Another question is what practice establishes the agreement of the parties as set out in Art. 31(3)(b) VCLT. This shall be called the *quantitative agreement knot*: it could be required that a practice is common, concordant and consistent.[440] The other extreme approach would be to let the practice of only one party to the treaty suffice in the absence of a rejection by the other parties. This would mean that a one-off practice would not suffice.[441] A contested question that concerns both agreements and practice arises when only some of the parties have participated and claimed that the treaty has been modified between them. While this is explicitly allowed in some treaty regimes, the general implicit possibility of such an *inter se* interpretation is at least not explicitly provided for in the Convention.[442]

There is, however, also a *qualitative agreement knot*. This concerns the question of the evidence that shows the agreement of the parties in the application of the treaty.[443] There are two interpretative problems involved. The first concerns the phrase 'in the application of the treaty'. One could read this possibly either as 'in the process of applying the

---

Study Group on Treaties over Time Subsequent Agreements and Subsequent Practice of States outside of Judicial or Quasi-Judicial Proceedings' 309–10.

[439] Bleckmann, *Grundprobleme und Methoden des Völkerrechts* 95, describing a scenario in which the absence of a protest of a state against the conduct of individuals could be considered as subsequent practice; Gardiner, *Treaty Interpretation* 235; Chanaki, *L'Adaptation des traités dans le temps* 323.

[440] See for example Yasseen, 'L'Interprétation des traités d'après la Convention de Vienne sur le droit des traités' 48; Sinclair, *The Vienna Convention on the Law of Treaties* 137; Gardiner, *Treaty Interpretation* 227. A good overview of the evolution of this requirement is given by Nolte, 'Subsequent Practice as a Means of Interpretation in the Jurisprudence of the WTO Appellate Body' 141.

[441] Yasseen, 'L'Interprétation des traités d'après la Convention de Vienne sur le droit des traités' 48; Sinclair, *The Vienna Convention on the Law of Treaties* 137.

[442] In favour of the possibility are Orakhelashvili, *The Interpretation of Acts and Rules in Public International Law* 357; Gardiner, *Treaty Interpretation* 235. The availability of such an interpretation is made conditional upon whether parties the legal position of whom is not part of the interpretation would be affected: see Gillich, *Konsens und Evolutive Vertragsauslegung* 93. In favour of a classification under Art. 32 for subsequent agreements is Nolte, First Report (n. 298) para. 83.

[443] See Gardiner, *Treaty Interpretation* 239. For an account on attribution, see Nolte, 'Second Report for the ILC Study Group on Treaties over Time' 304.

treaty' or as 'within the scope of application of the treaty'.[444] The other ambiguous part is the establishment of the agreement of the parties. One extreme position would be to require behaviour that establishes the agreement on the facts. This would refer to state actions that could be taken as silently agreeing on a certain interpretation. The other extreme would be a completely objective version: The mere fact that a treaty applies to a situation which is tolerated by the parties.[445] A possible middle view would be to accept that the practice of some parties would suffice if the circumstances indicate that the other parties consented.[446] The ILC has recently in its Draft Guideline 9 agreed on the following rule: 'Silence on the part of one or more parties can constitute acceptance of the subsequent practice when the circumstances call for some reaction.'[447]

6.7. Relevant rules of international law

Art. 31(3)(c) VCLT has been the subject of much attention in recent years.[448] It provides that account should be taken of any relevant rules

---

[444] The first solution is exclusively relied on by Dörr, 'Art. 31' 562 para. 94; Ungern-Sternberg, 'Die Konsensmethode des EGMR' 327. The latter author relies, however, mainly on the non-authentic German version of the text and argues also against taking into account international treaties which would normally fall under Art. 31(3)(c) VCLT. Kohen, 'Keeping Subsequent Agreements and Practice in Their Right Limits' 41–2.

[445] Then reliance is not placed on the parties applying the treaty but on the fact that the treaty applies to the factual situation.

[446] Yasseen, 'L'Interprétation des traités d'après la Convention de Vienne sur le droit des traités' 48; Linderfalk, *On the Interpretation of Treaties* 167; Nolte, 'Third Report for the ILC Study Group on Treaties Over Time Subsequent Agreements and Subsequent Practice of States Outside of Judicial or Quasi-Judicial Proceedings' 344. This was also the understanding of the commentary to the Final Draft Articles (n. 247) 222 para. 15; for a view that practice ought to be included that was 'opposable to all parties', see Crawford, 'A Consensualist Interpretation of Article 31(3) of the Vienna Convention on the Law of Treaties' 30.

[447] See 'Texts and titles of draft conclusions 6 to 10 provisionally adopted by the Drafting Committee' in ILC, 'Report of the International Law Commission on the work of its Sixty-sixth session' UN Doc. A/CN.4/L.833 (5 May–6 June and 7 July–8 August 2014) Conclusion 9(2).

[448] ILC, Report of the Study Group of the International Law Commission Finalized by Martti Koskenniemi, 'Fragmentation of International Law: Difficulties Arising from the Diversification and Expansion of International Law' in 'Reports of the International Law Commission on the work of its 42nd session' (1 May–9 June and 3 July–11 August 2006) UN Doc. A/CN.4/L.682, 242 (ILC, Fragmentation Report); McLachlan, 'The Principle of Systemic Integration and Article 31(3)(c) of the Vienna Convention'; French, 'Treaty Interpretation and the Incorporation of Extraneous Legal Rules'.

applicable to the parties. This technique is sometimes referred to as the principle of harmonisation or systemic integration.[449] As we have seen already, techniques of interpretation are not attached to any interpretative result. Consequently, Art. 31(3)(c) VCLT is not linked to an outcome that harmonises the treaty to be interpreted with other norms of international law.[450] It is of course true that harmonious results might be desirable if we interpret the law in a responsible manner. This lies within the appreciation of the interpreter. The relevant-rules-technique allows the interpreter to reach exactly the opposite result and to contrast the treaty with the relevant rules. Like every technique, it can work either way. This does not preclude, however, that a principle of harmonisation, if it existed, could enter the process of treaty interpretation through Art. 31(3)(c) VCLT. There is no reason to believe that this principle necessarily attaches to the Convention. To give just one illustrative example: If we are looking at a term in a human rights treaty and compare it to a term in a treaty of regional economic integration, there might be good reasons to interpret the very same term in a different manner, even if that provokes a norm conflict.

Art. 31(3)(c) VCLT is a model regarding its intertemporal openness. A look to the drafting history of the provision evidences its importance for the topic under review: During the drafting, a substantial shift in the formulation and the position of this technique was evident. In a former version of the draft, only the relevant rules 'at the time of the conclusion of the treaty' were included.[451] The VCLT now contains no explicit temporal provision in that regard. It is, therefore, intertemporally open:[452] The rules as they stood at the time of the conclusion of the treaty are covered by the provision. The rules as they exist at the time of interpretation can be accounted for in the same manner.[453] If the rules at different points in time differ as to their meaning, an intertemporal question arises.

Yet, ambiguities give rise to different knots. The *source knot* refers to the possible sources that can be considered to be relevant rules. The term 'relevant' will hardly constrain the interpreter since he or she could

---

[449] McLachlan, 'The Principle of Systemic Integration and Article 31(3)(c) of the Vienna Convention' 309. He regards this as an unexpressed principle.
[450] Orakhelashvili, *The Interpretation of Acts and Rules in Public International Law* 367.
[451] See Art. 71 in Waldock, Third Report (n. 185) 52.
[452] Greig, *Intertemporality and the Law of Treaties* 45.
[453] Linderfalk, *On the Interpretation of Treaties* 179; Villiger, *Commentary on the 1969 Vienna Convention on the Law of Treaties* 432 para. 24.

decide what rule is relevant. It is agreed that the term 'international law' will generally include all legal norms stemming from the sources mentioned in Art. 38(1) ICJ Statute.[454] It would be possible to limit it to customary law or to law-making treaties.[455] On the other hand, it would also be possible to interpret Art. 31(3)(c) very broadly. If one would regard this as outside the scope of Art. 38(1) ICJ Statute, secondary law of international organisations such as decisions of the UN Security Council could fall under this provision.[456] It is also possible to regard soft law as falling into this category.[457] This is indeed another instance in which the question of law-ascertainment becomes relevant.[458]

No matter whether one interprets the relevant rules of international law broadly or narrowly, this does not predetermine the question of when the relevant rule of international law applies between the parties. This we shall call the *participation knot*. There are various ways of construction.[459] It would be possible to require that the treaty is applicable between all the parties. Conversely, it could also suffice that the treaty is only applicable between two parties or at least the two parties in dispute. Possible middle views would be to require that most of the parties to the treaty to be interpreted are parties to the relevant treaty and the others can be said to have implicitly accepted the treaty.[460] Further exceptions could be made if the treaty effectively codifies general customary international law or treaties which have a bilateral implementation structure as opposed to a structure of obligations *erga omnes partes*.[461] The determination of those two knots will impact upon the

---

[454] See Linderfalk, *On the Interpretation of Treaties* 178; Villiger, *Commentary on the 1969 Vienna Convention on the Law of Treaties* 433, with further references to statements concerning the discussion of the International Law Commission.
[455] For a discussion and rejection of these alternatives, see Gardiner, *Treaty Interpretation* 262.
[456] For the inclusion of secondary law of international organisations, see for example Dörr, 'Art. 31' 562 para. 94.
[457] Decidedly against the inclusion of soft law, Villiger, *Commentary on the 1969 Vienna Convention on the Law of Treaties* 433.
[458] For a recent take on the issue, see D'Aspremont, *Formalism and the Sources of International Law*.
[459] For the different constructions, see McLachlan, 'The Principle of Systemic Integration and Article 31(3)(c) of the Vienna Convention' 314; Linderfalk, 'Who Are the Parties' 343; Dörr, 'Art. 31' 566 para. 100.
[460] Gardiner, *Treaty Interpretation* 265. He considers that it could concern parties that have an interest in the interpretation.
[461] For the last view, see Dörr, 'Art. 31' 566 para. 100.

intertemporal questions indirectly since they open the Convention for other potential subsequent rules.

6.8. *Travaux préparatoires*

As already mentioned, the *travaux préparatoires* belong only to the supplementary means of interpretation, recourse to this technique is allowed under specific circumstances by which a certain argumentative hierarchy is introduced into the process of interpretation. As recourse to the supplementary means 'may be had', the use of these means is within the discretion of the interpreter. This has of course major repercussions for the possibility of change through interpretation. The *travaux* are necessarily attached to the time before the conclusion of the treaty. The fact that this technique is of relatively minor importance increases the probability of changes since it indicates that the original intention of the negotiating parties does not carry so much weight.[462] It has to be stressed that, therefore, this feature of the temporal structure of the VCLT favours changes in the interpretation. The *travaux* can of course also favour changing interpretations in the broader sense as they could be used as evidence that parties have not considered a problem or that certain assumptions during the negotiations have proven wrong or that the parties simply intended the treaty to be interpreted in line with later developments. All these instances can warrant a rather dynamic reading of the treaty.[463] Despite this possible double function, the fact that the *travaux* are accorded only a reduced importance are again an expression of the fact that the Vienna Convention is not necessarily focused on the interpretation as it stood at the time of the conclusion of the treaty but has a broad temporal focus that goes beyond that point in time and is temporally flexible.[464] It could be even said that by restricting the

---

[462] This observation was in general made by Beckett, 'Comments' 444. He described this in vivid terms, remarking that the text of a treaty would 'assume ... a life of its own ... To hark back to the *travaux préparatoires* for the purposes of interpretation may operate like bringing a dead hand from the grave or subjecting a grown mature man to the paternal injunctions of his boyhood.'

[463] A subjective approach relying heavily on the *travaux* but also on 'creative interpretation' was argued already by Lauterpacht, 'Restrictive Interpretation and the Principle of Effectiveness in the Interpretation of Treaties' 52. On the general point, see also Kolb, *Interprétation et création du droit international* 518; Klabbers, 'International Legal Histories' 283.

[464] It should be stressed that the *travaux* relate not exactly to the point in time of the conclusion of the treaty. Nevertheless, there is a strong and direct connection.

applicability of *travaux*, this shifted the temporal focus towards the time of interpretation as opposed to the time of the conclusion of the treaty. Since the *travaux* are subsidiary means, their function to validate arguments is not decisive. Knots concerning the *travaux* are not essential. Yet, the concept is very broad, so it can cover the various ways of treaty-making.[465] It would be possible to construe an actor knot in relation to the *travaux* or to discuss accessibility and transparency and consent of the statements.[466]

6.9. Circumstances of the conclusion of the treaty

As another example, Art. 32 VCLT explicitly refers to the circumstances of the conclusion of the treaty. These can be any factual state of affairs at the time when the treaty was concluded. Circumstances refer to 'objective (external) conditions and not to subjective (internal) motives, attitudes or expectations of the parties'.[467] Possibly, there can be taken into account social, political, cultural and economic circumstances.[468] As techniques of interpretation in the context of evolution, the circumstances of the conclusion are important in two ways. Like the *travaux*, the circumstances of the conclusion of the treaty necessarily illuminate the meaning of the terms as they were contemporaneous with the conclusion of the treaty. The fact that this technique is mentioned as a supplementary means of interpretation again shows that the Vienna Convention does not accord a primary importance to the point in time this technique is referring to. So this is again an example of the intertemporal openness and flexibility of the Convention. Yet, like the *travaux*, the circumstances of the conclusion of the treaty can also play a special role in arguing for changes in interpretation since it can very well be that there is a change of circumstances.

It is left open what relation the circumstances have to have in relation to the conclusion of the treaty. The possibilities range from a mere temporal coincidence to a causal relationship in which the circumstances ought to be factors for the conclusion of the treaties, for example in the cases of Art. 62 which explicitly requires that 'the existence of those

---

[465] Linderfalk, *On the Interpretation of Treaties* 240.
[466] *Ibid.* 241; Dörr, 'Art. 32' 575–7 paras. 14–18.
[467] See in the context of Art. 62 Giegerich, 'Art. 62' 1080 para. 36.
[468] Villiger, *Commentary on the 1969 Vienna Convention on the Law of Treaties* 445 para. 4; Dörr, 'Art. 32' 578–80 paras. 21–2.

circumstances constituted an essential basis of the consent of the parties to be bound by the treaty'.[469] In the case of a rather wide understanding, it would still be possible to vary the argumentative weight in relation to the importance of the circumstances for the conclusion of the treaty. Of course, the interpreter would have to consider the wider implications of Arts. 27 and 63, which limit the significance of a change of circumstances when it relates to the severance of diplomatic and consular relations or national law.[470] Considering that the circumstances are only supplementary means of interpretation, there is no need to form a knot: If we exclude the wide understanding, it could just form its own supplementary means of interpretation.

6.10. Other supplementary means of interpretation: facing the intertemporal knot

Art. 32 VCLT refers to other supplementary means which 'include' the *travaux* and the circumstances of interpretation but are by no means exhausted by them.[471] In what way these supplementary means impact on questions of interpretative changes depends very much on the interpretation of the term. First, it is important to determine the term 'means'. This could refer to the means used in Art. 31 VCLT, i.e. techniques.[472] On the other hand, the widest possible meaning would be to open up the process of interpretation for any possible means of treaty interpretation, irrespective of whether it relates to techniques of interpretation or not.[473] This is of crucial importance to our question. We have seen that, in doctrinal discourse, there were many suggestions to solve the intertemporal question by means other than techniques. Art. 31 contains no means other than techniques (if good faith is left aside); from this it could be inferred that this should also apply to supplementary means.

---

[469] For this problem, see Linderfalk, *On the Interpretation of Treaties* 246. The word 'factor' is used by Villiger, *Commentary on the 1969 Vienna Convention on the Law of Treaties* 445 para. 4.

[470] For details on Art. 27 VCLT, see p. 193 below; for details on Art. 63 VCLT, see p. 198–9 below.

[471] Sbolci, 'Two Approaches to Treaty Interpretation' 159.

[472] Karl, *Vertrag und spaetere Praxis im Voelkerrecht* 187; Linderfalk, *On the Interpretation of Treaties* 255ff; Dörr, 'Art. 32' 581 para. 25; Briggs, 'The Travaux Préparatoires of the Vienna Convention on the Law of Treaties' 708. The latter later disagrees with the solution reached by the Vienna Convention.

[473] So other means are mentioned by Villiger, 'The Rules on Interpretation' 112.

This argument is indicative but has no decisive force. Another indication is given by the ILC Commentary which provided that 'the word "supplementary" emphasizes that Article 28 [which is now Art. 32] does not provide for alternative, autonomous, means of interpretation but only for means to aid an interpretation governed by the principles contained in Article 27 [which is now Art. 31]'. The fact that they are not alternative could point in the direction that supplementary means have the same nature as a technique. Again, this is not determinative.

Therefore, we will have to address the question of whether the other means of interpretation should enter the process of interpreting intertemporal questions at this stage. Even though different outcomes are possible, we will in this case take the functional perspective that has been established above. At this point, we have to face the intertemporal knot and approach the suggested solutions from the perspective of the function of the rule of interpretation.

The *maxim* that static interpretation is the best and fitting interpretation is, like all other maxims, more a proposition than an argument. It is based on experience. Since the maxim stems from ancient times, it is unclear whether this experience is still valid today. Unless the proposition in the maxim can be backed up by present-day knowledge, the maxim should not be introduced into the process of interpretation.[474]

One could also try to attach the rules of interpretation to a certain *school* in order to come closer to a solution. This could either be done on a rather abstract level referring to objective or subjective schools or rather specifically with schools favouring one interpretative outcome (static/dynamic) or one technique of interpretation (ordinary meaning/subsequent practice/object and purpose). Regarding schools of interpretative outcomes, it has been established at great length that it is not possible at the moment to put the rules of interpretation into one or the other category. The same applies to the distinction between subjective and objective. The VCLT combines both elements. Regarding schools attaching to certain techniques of interpretation, this would have the effect to diminish the discretion of the interpreter and to introduce a certain hierarchy and, therefore, to disrespect cardinal cores of the rule of interpretation. Schools have had their function to structure the discourse about interpretation, yet no school could establish the superiority of a

---

[474] Maxims are termed as supplementary means by Villiger, 'The 1969 Vienna Convention on the Law of Treaties' 126. The author is, however, himself sceptical of the utility of those.

certain technique over all others. This might be due to the fact that we cannot generalise and tell for all cases which interpretative technique ought to prevail. This will very much rely on the question and the circumstances, the way in which a certain technique applies to a question and the discretion of the interpreter. To favour generally one technique over all others is like saying that a hammer is the most important tool in the world. If you want to repair your computer and you desperately need a screwdriver instead of a hammer, you will certainly rethink that argument. The construction of the VCLT is consequently based on valid arguments which strongly disfavour the reintroduction of schools.

Third, there could be a *presumption* in favour of or against evolutive interpretation. We have seen that some favour a presumption in favour of static interpretation and make subsequent exceptions to that presumption. From the perspective of the VCLT, a presumption is in itself part of the result of interpretation. The only thing a presumption effectively does is that it shifts the burden of argument in a certain direction. This favours a certain interpretative outcome. This makes it easier for the interpreter to achieve this outcome, since possible counterarguments can be discarded without the same argumentative effort.

Yet, reducing the need to argue goes against the function of the Convention as specified here. It is hard to establish a workable system that provides for the circumstances of rebuttal of the presumption. The interpretative process is subject to the discretion of the interpreter so that the only possible result would be to relieve him or her from arguing for certain results. The problem with the presumption often lies in its exceptions. With regard to additional exceptions suggested in international legal doctrine, this ought to be discussed together with inferences from the *nature*, the *structure* or the *classification* of the treaty.

All of those inferences work in the same way: They link one feature of the treaty to a certain interpretative outcome: Human rights treaties, multilateral treaties, constitutional treaties and *traités loi* are to be interpreted evolutively; treaties of sale, bilateral treaties, *traités contrat* and non-constitutional treaties are to be interpreted statically. This characterisation is appealing, especially in the academic context. All those suggestions might rely on correct empirical observations. Yet, to draw inferences from them entails two major flaws: Those inferences are unworkable and undesirable. They are unworkable because they are either not complex enough to deal with intertemporal problems or indeed too complex to deal with them. If those distinctions establish merely a binary system, they leave open many questions. Does the fact that the Charter could be called a constitution mean that HIV can be considered as a threat to the peace according to Art. 39 UN Charter? Suppose that a human rights treaty regulates the time limits for applications to the court or the minimum age for judges. Must these questions be reassessed through interpretation after some time? If those inferences allow for an evolutive interpretation, they hardly lay out the requirements according to which this is possible. An evolutive answer to every intertemporal question would be the result. Yet, the inferences are also contingent in many cases. Take the connection between human rights or the constitution and an evolutive outcome as an example. As will be shown, there are examples of drafts of human rights treaties containing strong static elements.[475] As we have seen in the discourse about originalism, one can very well argue that democratic constitutions do favour originalism.[476] This can be explained with the preferences of the interpreter, but not with the essence of a constitution.[477] Another contingency is evident if we look at treaties that are supposed to be static. It is very questionable that they would always have to be interpreted this way.[478] Consider that treaties of a long duration are more likely to be interpreted evolutively. It is hard to understand why a treaty of a short duration should always be interpreted in a static manner: Even in the context of the *clausula rebus sic stantibus*, which has much greater consequences, the ILC acknowledged that treaties of a short duration can terminate.[479] Binary inferences from different features of the treaty are not complex enough to deal with questions of evolution: To designate whole treaties as

---

[475] See p. 185 below.
[476] Goldsworthy, 'The Case for Originalism'; Scalia, 'Originalism: The Lesser Evil'.
[477] A simple question might illuminate this point: would we regard a basic law of a state, containing basic human rights and regulating the process of law-making, as a constitution if it contains a clause which provided that (a) it can be changed by interpretation, or (b) it cannot be changed by interpretation but only by constitutional amendment? If the answer in good faith to both of those questions is yes, then the intertemporal focus of a constitution does not determine its classification as a constitution. Yet, evolutive interpretation could be linked to constitutionalism as a broader phenomenon. Such a theory might summarise the change of times, yet, as has been shown, it is more an overall description than a workable interpretative method.
[478] Bernhardt, 'Evolutive Treaty Interpretation' 21.
[479] This has been outlined in the discussions concerning fundamental change of circumstances: see Final Draft Articles (n. 247) 259 para. 8. *A maiore ad minus*, the same reasoning could be applied to evolutive interpretation.

static or evolutive is just not flexible enough for the scope of regulation of modern treaties.

This could tempt scholars to refine the system and to create exceptions and look not at the treaty but at individual provisions to classify them. So it could be said that human rights treaties are to be interpreted evolutively, but not their procedural provisions. The problem is that there might be procedural provisions essential for the effective implementation, such as the territorial jurisdiction. Should an exception be introduced for this provision? And what if treaties fulfil more than one feature: A bilateral investment treaty, conferring individual rights, a multilateral sales contract between states. Which of the features ought to prevail? If legal doctrine tried to solve all these issues in advance, this would result in interpretative systems much more complex than anything we have seen in the mechanical phase of interpretation. It is very likely that those systems, binary or complex, will be unworkable. Or that they fail to draw attention to the real legal issue: It has been suggested that the UN Charter was Janus-headed and had a contractual as well as a constitutional face.[480] Depending on the issues one deals with, one head or the other would prevail. This distinction could be transferred to questions of static and evolutive interpretation. And indeed, this solution would be more flexible, but it also omits to answer the decisive question which is: Under which circumstances is a clause *constitutional*? This would have to be determined in a process of interpretation.[481] This is in itself no problem as the techniques in the VCLT might require interpretation as well, such as the object and purpose.[482] Yet, even if this method was accepted generally, it is far from clear how this ought to be done. The delimitation of concepts might be very complex in concrete cases. It is for example hard to come up with a workable definition of *traité loi*.[483]

This leads to the second critique questioning the desirability: Mechanical inferences seem to give orientation, but they fail to provide for the essential function performed by the VCLT: to link the arguments to the issue of interpretation. The fact that a multilateral constitutional treaty is interpreted is interesting, but the essential question is why it should make a difference for the interpretative issue at hand. This is a blind spot of

---

[480] Fassbender, *The United Nations Charter as the Constitution of the International Community* 63.
[481] Kadelbach, 'Interpretation of the Charter' 82 para. 23.   [482] Compare *ibid*.
[483] Tavernier, *Recherches sur l'application dans le temps des actes et des règles en droit international public* 207; Wright, 'The Interpretation of Multilateral Treaties' 101.

inferences from features of the treaty. On the other hand, the rule of interpretation contained in the VCLT has no quarrels with taking into account the considerations of the structure, the nature or the classification of the treaty: They will regularly either form part of the context or even be considered as its object and purpose. Yet, those techniques validate those considerations only insofar as they relate to the interpretative issue. If the rule of interpretation can import all necessary considerations but the inferences from the different features of the treaty cannot fulfil the function of the Convention, the rule of interpretation is to be preferred from the perspective of its function.

The fact that the function of the VCLT cannot be fulfilled by introducing a distinction is also based on the fact the underlying inference seems rather contingent. First, as previously mentioned, it cannot be inferred from the notion that a constitutional norm must be interpreted evolutively. What is more, it is even harder to conclude that contractual norms must not be interpreted evolutively. There are many cases in which constitutional courts interpret ordinary legal acts evolutively in order to make them compatible with constitutional norms. In the light of this, it does seem to be preferable and more in line with the function of the VCLT to use techniques instead of inferences from the nature, the structure or the classification of the treaty.[484]

---

[484] Linked to the argument distinguishing the rules of interpretation according to their nature is the discourse about fragmentation in international law. From the perspective taken in this book, it would be very well possible to introduce a norm adapting, altering or replacing the general rule of interpretation. In fact, the VCLT contains several of those rules that guide the interpretation in specific circumstances with different means such as Art. 56. There has been a feeling that the rule of interpretation is not sufficient to accommodate all international treaties. Weiler, 'The Interpretation of Treaties – A Re-examination: Preface' 507. The fact that the way the rule of interpretation works is similar to if not the same as interpretative method in many national jurisdictions indicates the opposite. To rebut this indication, some further research would be necessary. It has also been mentioned that the rules avail themselves of a high level of generality: Waibel, 'A Uniform Regime of Treaty Interpretation' 410. The research conducted in this book helped to spot the generality built into the rule of interpretation: the interpreter has some discretion to weigh and balance the considerations deriving from the different techniques, what is more, there are also interpretative knots where the rule is not determined. If one were to criticise the generality, one ought to be careful not to attribute a function to the rule that it obviously does not have. The rule of interpretation is obviously not capable of automatically guiding the interpreter to the right result. Yet, it can enhance and structure legal discourse about interpretation. Looking at that function, the rule of interpretation as contained in the VCLT is rather specific. See similarly Çali, *Specialized Rules of Treaty Interpretation*.

The same applies to other possible solutions. It could for example be contended that this gap is to be closed by other provisions that are applied by analogical reasoning. A similar provision could be seen in Art. 33(3) VCLT which deals with the question of differing authentic versions of treaty texts. It provides that in the case where the issue cannot be solved by the ordinary means of interpretation, the rule favouring the object and purpose ought to prevail. We could now compare the differing meanings of two authentic versions of the treaty to the differing meaning at two points in time in which the treaty applied. So the meaning favouring the object and purpose should prevail. If the question was left open intertemporally, other means such as the *travaux* can be resorted to. If there is really a cardinal core providing for balancing and discretion of the interpreter, there can hardly be a situation in which the interpreter cannot decide: She or he has to use the arguments available to reach a result. A decision is necessary in any case.

Another possibility might be to transfer the *rule on intertemporal law* in a direct manner to the problem at hand. It has been famously defined '[a]s regards the question which of different legal systems prevailing at successive periods is to be applied in a particular case' by Judge Max Huber in the *Island of Palmas Arbitration*.[485]

> As regards the question which of different legal systems prevailing at successive periods is to be applied in a particular case (the so-called intertemporal law), a distinction must be made between the creation of rights and the existence of rights. The same principle which subjects the act creative of a right to the law in force at the time the right arises, demands that the existence of the right, in other words its continued manifestation, shall follow the conditions required by the evolution of law.[486]

The doctrine of intertemporal law is not about the evolution of the law but about acquired rights in international law. The rules on territorial acquisition are norms of customary law. The arbitrator assumed that those rules had changed over time. He held that the right of the United States had been created according to the rules in force at an earlier time. He further stated that, after the rules changed, the Netherlands acquired a right of their own which meant that the United States lost their right.

---

[485] *Island of Palmas Case* (1928) RIAA 829. See also at p. 31 below.   [486] *Ibid.* 845.

Let us draw a parallel to the law of treaties. If prescription was regulated in a universal treaty, a party might, after the conclusion of the treaty, acquire a right to a certain territory on the basis of the treaty. If the treaty was changed subsequently through interpretation or amendment, another party could claim sovereignty over the very same territory on the basis of the changed treaty. If we assumed those rights to be mutually exclusive such as title to territory, the question would then be whether the party could retain its right or whether the second party had acquired it. The parallel makes it very obvious: The law on the issue changed. The question is only whether the legal position that was obtained under the old law was still valid after the change. This gives us no hint for the determination of questions of stasis and evolution. It is rather a question of delimiting the temporal scope of the old and the new treaty provision. The fact that the arbitrator acknowledged a change in customary law can hardly have an impact upon the question whether treaties are susceptible to change. From this, we can conclude that the intertemporal rule does not determine questions of stasis and evolution. Any other attempt to transfer the doctrine will only result in expressing a certain intertemporal preference. Those preferences would, however, conflict with the intertemporal openness of the Convention.

Regarding *principles*, we have to recall first that there are formal and material principles. As formal principles impacting upon the intertemporal question, one could oppose the principle of contemporaneity and the principle of evolutive interpretation. These principles operate on a high level of abstraction. They describe the changeability of the law as a general feature of the international legal system which could be termed as paradigms. Opposing those principles is an interesting way to summarise on what basis international legal scholars and decision-makers act. But once all participants accept that there is at least the possibility of both interpretative results, the opposing principles lose some of their explanatory force. The choice between contemporaneity and evolution would then not be made for international law as a whole but only in relation to single interpretative questions. Formal principles would then only work if one looked into their grounds such as the underlying precedents or supporting material principles. This would, however, lead the interpretative process away from formal principles.

Of course, this is different with material principles such as sustainability and development. Those principles include substantive considerations of the process of interpretation which actually helps in the process of justification. The rule of interpretation as contained in the VCLT has many open doors through which principles can enter the process of interpretation. They can be taken into account as context if they are mentioned in a way similar to Arts. 1 and 2 UN Charter. They can be acknowledged as object and purpose of the treaty or as deriving from the relevant rules or even from the subsequent practice. The only thing the interpreter would have to do is to justify the principles in a way so as to make them legally relevant. By doing this, he or she fulfils one of the key functions of the VCLT. Part of this function is to link the process of justification to the treaty which limits the leeway of the interpreter in justifying his or her result. If there are competing principles, they have to be balanced against each other. Since the rule on interpretation also results in a process of balancing, this again poses no problem for the inclusion of principles into the process. In conclusion, formal principles play no role in the process of justification while material principles can be included as far as they meet the criteria of the VCLT.

This openness requires the interpreter to look into all techniques contained in Art. 31 VCLT and appreciate the arguments derived therefrom. If he or she feels that the question cannot be determined, Art. 32 would certainly allow the interpreter to consult any other technique possible: Arguments from the preparatory works, from any other science, considerations that do not meet the requirements of the techniques of Art. 31 VCLT. It is hardly imaginable that he or she will not find a consideration providing for a sustainable justification. From the perspective of the present inquiry, the intertemporal knot is the biggest interpretative knot of all. Many have tried to unravel it by pulling one string or the other. It is suggested here that those voices, including the ILC and the Institut de Droit International, that advocated leaving the question to be determined by the interpreter in the concrete case are to prevail. This does not mean that the other solutions proposed are not valuable or workable, quite to the contrary. They are all well reasoned and interesting, yet from the perspective here taken, the solution to leave the question open seems to enhance the function of the Convention.

This solution is the one that is the most fitting in relation to the function of the Convention: It reinforces the intertemporal openness of the Convention and motivates the interpreter to find the best justification and, therefore, the best solution for the question he or she is dealing with. The function of the Convention cuts through the mighty intertemporal knot as King Alexander cut the Gordian knot with his sword. And under the knot appears the core of intertemporal openness. Interpreters are free to determine questions of stasis and evolution if they stick to the process described in the VCLT.

6.11. Executive summary

International law has a meaning beyond the law of nations: It can also be the law of conflicts. That is apparent in the notion of private international law. When a case could be dealt with in several jurisdictions, private international law regulates which of the competing provisions is applied. When there is an alleged change in the law, one could construe this as a conflict of laws stemming from different times. There is a little flaw in that comparison when it comes to interpretation: In those situations we do not know whether the law really has changed. Yet, there can still be an intertemporal problem. The present study has shown that the VCLT accords discretion to the interpreter to deal with interpretative questions. The VCLT also contains ambiguities which have been called interpretative knots. While scholars have a general distaste for those ambiguities, there is also something good about them: They allow interpreters to choose their version of the VCLT and to adapt to their needs without violating it. If we suppose that no such choice was made and we applied the rule of interpretation to an intertemporal problem as if it was the first time, the solution could look like this:

For an intertemporal problem to arise, it will at least be necessary to have one technique pointing to an old and one to a changed meaning. The interpreter will point out the different possibilities and look at whether they can be backed up by arguments that stand the test of Art. 31 VCLT and its techniques. Two things have to be emphasised while using the techniques: The first is that every technique can produce changing results over time. We are more familiar with those outcomes while using subsequent agreements and practice since they are subsequent by nature. Yet, this also applies to the relevant rules, the ordinary meaning, the context and the object and purpose. Especially the ordinary meaning refers to general language use which evolves over time. The context is subject to interpretation and the object and purpose has to be ascertained. This is why those techniques can produce evolving results. This leads to a second important point: Techniques validate arguments. Every technique can produce any result in relation to intertemporal problems. The ordinary meaning can suggest changes in the law, the object and purpose as well as the subsequent practice of the parties can potentially reinforce an original meaning. The interpreter will consider all arguments thoroughly and, if he or she feels that more justification is needed, Art. 32 VCLT allows resorting to an unlimited arsenal of techniques. Limitless considerations can enter the process of treaty interpretation this way as long as they relate to the treaty. In essence, the intertemporal problem is solved in the ordinary process of treaty interpretation according to the rule of interpretation enshrined in Art. 31. We must not forget that the VCLT has no clear preference regarding the intertemporal question, yet it also contains no prohibition for interpreters to have certain interpretative preference insofar as they are competent to interpret treaties. This is, again, the second face of the intertemporal openness of the Convention. If a certain court establishes a certain case law in one direction or the other and the cases have some precedential value for the court, it is free to resort to those practices. This specific stance is binding insofar as the interpreter is competent to interpret. The stances can also be changed if the rules of the court allow for it. In the absence of such a specific stance, the problems can still be resolved by Art. 31 VCLT and the function of this process is to trigger a decision based on legal arguments relating to the interpretative issue in the treaty.

7

Shout of encore: evolutive interpretation in the context of the VCLT

In the preceding chapter, we reconstructed the rule of interpretation in the VCLT and tried to see how far it deals with questions of temporal variances in the process of interpretation. However, Arts. 31–33 are not the only prescriptions that can have a possible impact upon those matters. In its eight Parts, the VCLT provides *inter alia* for Observance, Application and Interpretation of Treaties (Part III); Amendment and Modification of Treaties (Part IV); and Invalidity, Termination and Suspension of Treaties (Part V). Those rules can illuminate the issues dealt with here in two ways. They could give an indication as to the intertemporal issues raised in general, i.e. they could contribute to illuminating the intertemporal focus of the VCLT. They can also highlight problems of evolutive interpretations in specific situations. In those situations, the rules on interpretation possibly need to be modified by other rules. We will, therefore, first look into whether other parts of the Convention can assist in resolving international problems and second whether intertemporal problems can assist in that context.

While this will allow us to go beyond the rules of treaty interpretation as expressed in Arts. 31–33 VCLT, this analysis will not deal with the issues explicitly excluded from the scope of the VCLT in Art. 73. It cannot be denied that cases of state succession,[487] state responsibility as well as the outbreak of hostilities[488] could have impacts upon the interpretation

---

[487] When treaties continue after the succession of states, certain provisions will have to be reinterpreted, such as most obviously the name of the respective states. So those treaties will often be reconsidered. In the course of those considerations, it is questionable whether certain techniques of interpretation will have to be modified. So it could be asked whether the subsequent practice or subsequent agreements of a colonial power can always be attributed to the later decolonised state. It could well be argued that the *travaux préparatoires* might under such circumstances be even less valuable.

[488] For a general overview, see Vöneky, 'Armed Conflict, Effect on Treaties'. There can be issues of interpretation in these situations. Art. 5 of the ILC Draft Articles on the

of treaties in the course of time, but those issues are left to the specific consideration which they deserve.

7.1. Express regulation

A general feature of the Vienna Convention is that most provisions are dispositive and subject to explicit provisions in treaties.[489] A general exception is provided for in Art. 5 VCLT, which gives priority to the relevant rules of international organisations.[490] Since we could find no clear regulation of the matter within the VCLT, it would be still possible to provide for those issues in specific treaties. Supposing that a clause in a treaty gives some guidance on the interpretation of treaties, it could be considered a *lex specialis* rule. This is, however, not necessary for two reasons. The rule of interpretation takes account of the context of interpretation since it imports also the text in the context. When a different rule of interpretation can be imported into the process of treaty interpretation, there is no norm conflict but a direct reference through the means of interpretation. Second, since those clauses in treaties are mostly not fully fledged systems, they are themselves subject to the process of interpretation. In this case, the rules contained in the Vienna Convention apply.[491]

In essence, interpretative questions can be determined through clauses in treaties, annexes, preambles or other regulations in the text or context of the treaty. This can possibly include the determination of questions of stasis and evolution. These clauses are well known in private commercial

---

Effects of Armed Conflicts on Treaties provides that 'the rules of international law on treaty interpretation shall be applied to establish whether a treaty is susceptible to termination, withdrawal or suspension in the event of an armed conflict'. While the ILC envisaged factors for such a determination in the subsequent articles, it is interesting to see that all of those questions had to be determined by interpretation. It is imaginable that questions like the termination of certain treaties in cases of hostilities cannot be settled once and for all but the provision of such a right could arise or expire in the face of certain changing circumstances being relevant factors in the process of interpretation.

[489] See for example Arts. 28, 29, 40(5) and 60(4) VCLT.
[490] On those questions, see Peters, 'Subsequent Practice and Established Practice of International Organizations'.
[491] The issue of circularity does not have the same quality since rules of interpretation in one treaty are of limited application and cannot be considered an all-encompassing rule. Without being circular, they can be determined by the Vienna Convention.

law.[492] There are similar clauses in treaties between investors and host states, which provide to '"freeze" the law of the host state with respect to the investment project over the life of the project'.[493] Those freezing clauses prohibit change through amendment but also changes through interpretation. The practice in international law is rather limited. A proposal for such a provision has been made in the context of the negotiations leading up to the ECHR. The Draft Convention prepared by members of the European Movement, which formed the basis of the negotiations leading to the ECHR, contained the following provision:

Article 6
(a) Until the conclusion of such Supplementary Agreement every State a party to this Convention shall be bound to guarantee the human rights enumerated in Articles 1 and 2 only to the extent that [they] were secured by the constitution, laws and administrative practice existing in each country at the date of the signing of the Convention.
(b) Any additions to the above-mentioned rights which may be effected after the signing of this Convention as a result of changes in law or administrative practice shall, as from the date of such changes, be guaranteed in the same manner as the rights existing at the date of the signing of this Convention by the State concerned.[494]

This provision, which Bates termed a 'freezing provision',[495] clearly evidences that the content of the rights should be tied to the situation as it existed at the time of the conclusion of the treaty.[496] It is, therefore, to be regarded as express regulation prescribing a static interpretation of the treaty. However, the static effect is only partial since section (b) clearly shows that the Convention could evolve, if the law in the member states was changed. The direction in which the evolution of the law is possible is, however, fixed: The law can only

---

[492] These clauses mostly determine a certain point in time of the past as determinative. For an overview, see Wu, 'Timing the Choice of Law by Contract' 401; and Sandrock, '"Versteinerungsklauseln" in Rechtswahlvereinbarungen für internationale Handelsverträge'.
[493] Ruggie, 'Stabilization Clauses and Human Rights' vii.
[494] European Movement, 'Draft European Convention on Human Rights' (INF/5/E/R). See also the accompanying explanation at 14 of the draft.
[495] Bates, *The Evolution of the European Convention on Human Rights* 55.
[496] The rationale behind this was of course to prevent the abolishment of the human rights standards as they stood since totalitarianism was perceived as a great threat. On the other hand, it should be a provisional step in the construction of a European Union. This provision was, however, never really discussed and implicitly dropped during the negotiations leading to the ECHR. See *ibid*.

change to guarantee more rights. It could be inferred that the preamble to the ECHR suggests a similar effect since it considers that 'the aim of the Council of Europe is the achievement of greater unity between its members and that one of the methods by which this aim is to be pursued is the maintenance and further realisation of human rights and fundamental freedoms'. It is true that the notions of greater unity and further realisation suggest a development,[497] but it is equally true that the preamble cannot necessarily be taken to command the achievement of that development through the means of interpretation.[498]

A clearer example is included in Art. 16(2) of the Agreement of Free Movement between Switzerland and the EU and reads as follows:[499]

> Insofar as the application of this Agreement involves concepts of Community law, account shall be taken of the relevant case law of the Court of Justice of the European Communities prior to the date of its signature. Case law after that date shall be brought to Switzerland's attention. To ensure that the Agreement works properly, the Joint Committee shall, at the request of either Contracting Party, determine the implications of such case law.[500]

This clause is aimed at freezing the state of the law and not allowing the CJEU to develop the law further.[501] It does not rule out, however, that a change of interpretation is prompted by other techniques.[502] In this sense, it is only an 'imperfect' freezing clause. An example for a clause which freezes not the whole treaty but only a certain material part of it can be found in the VCLT. Art. 56 provides for the requirements for an implied right of denunciation or withdrawal.[503] Paragraph (1)(a) of that article states as one of two alternative requirements that it ought to be 'established that the parties intended to admit the possibility of

---

[497] Similarly Drzemczewski, 'The Sui Generis Nature of the European Convention on Human Rights' 60.
[498] Cremer expresses similar doubts carefully but convincingly: see Cremer, 'Regeln der Konventionsinterpretation' 184.
[499] For a detailed discussion, see Burri, 'Workers and Case Law as Vehicles for the European Hegemon' 119. And Burri and Pirker, 'Stromschnellen im Freizügigkeitsfluss' 165.
[500] Agreement between the European Community and its Member States, of the one part, and the Swiss Confederation, of the other, on the free movement of persons (entry into force 30 April 2002), OJ L114/6 cap.
[501] See Burri, 'Workers and Case Law as Vehicles for the European Hegemon' 121.
[502] On the practical implications, see *ibid.*; and Burri and Pirker.   [503] See p. 196 below.

denunciation or withdrawal'. As explained in more detail below, the interpreter can meet the requirements of this clause only by showing that the parties at the time of the conclusion of the treaty intended such a right. So this section fixes the point in time at which the treaty is to be interpreted regarding an implied right of denunciation or withdrawal. The reverse perspective would be that a clause determines that it will have no effect on the interpretation of previous treaties. An example of this can be found in Art. 80 UN Charter which states that 'nothing in this Chapter shall be construed in or of itself to alter in any manner the rights whatsoever of ... existing international instruments'. Even though the clause had only a limited effect,[504] it clearly stipulates that a respective part of one treaty shall have no intertemporal effect on other treaties.

But treaties can not only freeze but also 'fluidify' treaties if they explicitly prescribe changing interpretations. Art. 2(1) of the International Covenant on Economic, Social and Cultural Rights cannot be read as explicitly allowing for evolutive interpretation.[505] It provides that

> [e]ach State Party to the present Covenant undertakes to take steps, individually and through international assistance and co-operation, especially economic and technical, to the maximum of its available resources, with a view to achieving progressively the full realization of the rights recognized in the present Covenant by all appropriate means, including particularly the adoption of legislative measures.

It is true that this provision obliges states to progressively develop the human rights standards in their states. But from a progressive realisation of the rights enshrined in a treaty it does not necessarily follow that the norms entailing those rights also evolve.[506] Furthermore, the phrase 'rights recognised' indicates that the rights have been recognised at some point in time. Whether or not those rights evolve through interpretation is not clear.

A comparable norm that clearly favours an evolutive interpretation is to be found in Wilson's Draft of the Covenant of the League of Nations. Art. III reads:

---

[504] Burri, 'Workers and Case Law as Vehicles for the European Hegemon'.
[505] International Covenant on Economic, Social and Cultural Rights (adopted 16 September 1966, entered into force 3 January 1976) 993 UNTS 3.
[506] Compare Desierto and Gillespie, 'Evolutive Interpretation and Subsequent Practice' 562–3.

> The Contracting Powers unite in guaranteeing to each other political independence and territorial integrity; but it is understood between them that such territorial readjustments, if any, as may in the future become necessary by reason of changes in present racial conditions and aspirations or present social and political relationships, pursuant to the principle of self-determination, and also such territorial readjustments as may in the judgment of three fourths of the Delegates be demanded by the welfare and manifest interest of the peoples concerned, may be effected, if agreeable to those peoples.[507]

This draft article allows for affecting territorial readjustments in two sets of circumstances, the first of which relates to 'racial conditions' and 'present social and political relationships'. It is, therefore, to be regarded as an explicit prescription of an interpretation that takes into account later developments. Another example of an explicit prescription of the evolution of a term is Art. 37 ICJ Statute. This provision could either account for a reinterpretation or a modification of treaties providing for the jurisdiction of the PCIJ. It has the purpose to establish the jurisdiction of the ICJ.[508]

States explicitly discussed the question of evolutive interpretation in the process of drafting the UNCITRAL Rules on Transparency in Treaty-Based Investor–State Arbitration ('Rules on Transparency').[509] This instrument prescribes transparency standards for investment arbitrations and, therefore, complements many investment treaties that were concluded before the Rules on Transparency came into force and several that will come into force after 1 April 2014. States negotiating the rules argued over the question whether already existing treaties would and could be interpreted dynamically or whether the inclusion of the rules would be subject to the express consent of states.[510] Some states emphasised that the rules should only be applicable upon express state consent.[511] Other states argued that evolutive interpretation should be at least available for treaties containing a dynamic clause.[512] In the end, the states agreed that

---

[507] 'Wilson's First Draft' in Miller (ed.), *Drafting of the Covenant* (vol. 2) 12.
[508] Simma and Richemond-Barak, 'Art. 37' 713.
[509] United Nations Commission on International Trade Law, Rules on Transparency in Treaty-Based Investor–State Arbitration and Arbitration Rules (as revised in 2010, with new article 1, para. 4, as adopted in 2013), UNGA A/Res/109(LXVIII) (16 December 2013) Supplement No. 17.
[510] UNCITRAL, Report of its forty-sixth session (8–26 July 2013), Report of Working Group II (Arbitration and Conciliation) on the work of its fifty-seventh session (Vienna, 1–5 October 2012), UN Doc. A/CN.9/760, 23–4 paras. 135–40.
[511] *Ibid.* 23 para. 135.   [512] *Ibid.* 24 paras. 138–40.

the rules on transparency would only be applicable to investment treaties predating them upon express consent of the parties.[513]

Initially, it was stipulated that the rules ought to apply 'as may be revised from time to time'.[514] The parties then disagreed on whether the envisaged revisions would be read into existing investment treaties.[515] Some delegations feared that this could be a threat to legal security since it would insert 'dynamic language' into the treaty. Other states opposed this view, and argued that there should be still a possibility to update treaties. The parties first agreed to retain the 'dynamic language' while expressly stressing the possibility of states to issue a reservation.[516] The phrase 'as may be revised from time to time' was subsequently eliminated.

In conclusion, the intertemporal question as well as the question of static or evolutive interpretation can be subject to express regulation in treaties.[517] Treaty practice has not yet brought forward an all-encompassing clause prescribing static or evolutive interpretation of a whole treaty. Most of the respective clauses were only contained in drafts. Yet, this practice has shown that those clauses do not need to result in all or nothing solutions. They can be limited to certain parts of the treaty. Freezing clauses can be softened with exceptions, and fluidifying clauses be restrained by conditions that are to be fulfilled before they operate.

7.2. Reservations

The VCLT grants states the right to exclude or modify the legal effect of certain treaty provisions by a unilateral statement. If, in contrast, states only 'specify or clarify the meaning or scope of a treaty or of certain of its provisions', this would amount to an interpretative declaration.[518] While the influence of an interpretative declaration has to be assessed

---

[513] See Art. 1(2). If the investment treaty is concluded after the coming into force of the Rules on Transparency, the applicability of the rules is assumed, which means that states would only have the possibility to opt out according to Art. 1(1).

[514] UNCITRAL, Forty-seventh session (7–25 July 2014), Report of Working Group II (Arbitration and Conciliation) on the work of its fifty-ninth session (16–20 September 2013) UN Doc. A/CN.9/794, 11 para. 51.

[515] Ibid. 16–17 paras. 91–5.   [516] Ibid. 16–17 para. 93.

[517] One has to be careful not to assume such an express regulation too easily. Not every term that can refer to present-day conditions is automatically to be interpreted evolutively. This requires an act of interpretation. Cf. Thienel, 'The Living Instrument Approach in the ECHR and Elsewhere' 183–4.

[518] ILC, Guide on Reservations (n. 409).

by the rules laid down in Arts. 31 and 32 VCLT, the permissibility of reservations is dealt with in Arts. 19–21 VCLT. Both types of instruments are unilateral declarations and, therefore, subject to interpretation, both can themselves have an impact on the interpretation of treaties.[519] We will in turn encounter how interpretative declarations, reservations and conditional interpretative declarations can influence questions of intertemporality. Then we will briefly revisit under what circumstances this would be acceptable. Third, we will have a look at the possible effects of those reservations.

As to their impact on treaty interpretation, interpretative declarations will normally form part of the context, mostly in accordance with Art. 31(2)(b) VCLT, but could – if it was accepted – even become part of a subsequent agreement or subsequent practice.[520] An interpretative declaration issued at the time of the conclusion of the treaty can expressly regulate the temporal focus of the treaty.

Reservations are by their definition in Art. 2(1)(d) VCLT tied to the point in time 'when signing, ratifying, formally confirming, accepting, approving or acceding to a treaty'.[521] This stance has, yet, no bearing upon the solution of intertemporal questions. But reservations could be used to determine the focus of interpretation in an exact manner. Such reservations could state that the treaty provision concerned is – with respect to the party – to be interpreted as it stands at the time of its conclusion or, conversely, at the time of interpretation. If the treaty took a temporal stance different from that in the reservation, its legal effects would indeed be altered. To give one example, when a human rights treaty is to be interpreted evolutively, a state could issue a reservation

---

[519] The law of reservations offers no hint as to whether treaties ought to be interpreted statically or evolutively.
[520] ILC, Guide on Reservations (n. 409) 70 paras. 24–6.
[521] While sticking to the original definition in the Vienna Convention, the ILC has indicated that declarations after the relevant point in time could still be considered as reservations. According to Guideline 2.3, they could not be considered, 'unless the treaty otherwise provides or none of the other contracting States and contracting organizations opposes the late formulation': ILC, Guide on Reservations (n. 409) 173. This has led to a general criticism of the definition of reservations. So it is contended that reservations ought to be defined only by their effect and not by the point in time at which they are issued and that so-called 'late reservations' could also be considered to be reservations. For that account, see Müller, 'Reservations and Time: Is There Only One Right Moment to Formulate and to React to Reservations?' 11–15. If the author was correct, this would mean that the Convention was one more time intertemporally open rather than tied to the time specified in Art. 2(1)(d).

accepting the treaty only as it stands at this point in time. Looking at the previous practice, such reservations are not amongst the types mentioned by the ILC.[522] But this typology is only a review of the current practice and, therefore, does not exclude any possible reservation. Yet, based upon one type of reservation, it might be possible to provide for an interesting analogy: as reservations can limit the territorial application of treaties,[523] it might also be possible to limit their temporal application, more specifically to the temporal focus of their interpretation. Again, one could either reserve the right to interpret the treaty statically or evolutively.

If a party reserved the right to interpret a term, a provision or a whole treaty evolutively instead of statically, it could effectively enlarge the obligations of the treaty with respect to other parties. Reservations enlarging the scope of the obligation are called 'extensive reservations'.[524] They do not qualify as a reservation within the meaning of Art. 2(1)(d) VCLT.[525] Therefore, reservations that provide that a treaty is to be interpreted evolutively and not statically face a particular problem: Evolutive interpretations can have both an increasing as well as a limiting effect on the obligations. To qualify as reservations, those declarations will have to limit their effect to changes in interpretation restricting the obligations of the parties. This will be a necessary requirement for those reservations. While this is technically possible, the opposite case that states reserve their right to apply the treaty as it stood at the time of conclusion is much more probable.

Reservations of both kinds could be problematic from a strategic point of view as their issuers might be seen as implicitly acknowledging the interpretative stand they wish to evade. As we have seen, most treaties are open in that regard. Filing such a reservation could be seen as admitting that the treaty is to be interpreted differently. In such situations, a conditional interpretative declaration might be the better solution.[526] This declaration expresses the parties' understanding of a clause like a normal interpretative declaration and might influence the interpretation of the treaty. But this declaration contains a condition: If the treaty is interpreted differently, the state will not be bound by the provision.[527]

---

[522] ILC, Guide on Reservations (n. 409) 41–2 para. 18.   [523] Ibid. 2 para. 1.1.3 and 1.1.4.
[524] Ibid. 45–7 paras. 4–12 (Guideline 1.1.1).
[525] See Sinclair, *The Vienna Convention on the Law of Treaties* 54. ILC, Guide on Reservations (n. 409) 45–7 paras. 4–12 (Guideline 1.1.1). In favour of the possibility of extensive reservations, see Szafarz, 'Reservations to Multilateral Treaties' 294.
[526] Two sample reservation clauses can be found at Appendix 2 below.
[527] ILC, Guide on Reservations (n. 409) 3–4 (Guideline 1.4).

The interpretative declaration will only turn into a reservation if the material condition is fulfilled, that means if the treaty is interpreted differently as assumed by the interpretative declaration. So an interpretative declaration will only operate as a reservation when it favours an evolutive interpretation while the treaty is to be interpreted statically and *vice versa*. It is of course true that a condition can also be included in a proper reservation. Then the party can not avail itself of the potential of the interpretative declaration to influence the process of interpretation. But could such a reservation or a conditional interpretative declaration ever be permissible?

Cases in which the reservation is prohibited outright or is not amongst the enumerated reservations permitted by the treaty or, more importantly, where it is incompatible with the object and purpose of the treaty, leave two options: Either the reservation will be invalid or the state will cease to be a party.[528] In many cases, it could be argued that reservations that freeze or fluidify the treaty could go against the object and purpose of the treaty. Yet, it is impossible to determine this in the abstract.

Art. 20 VCLT, regulating the conditions of acceptance and objection, could be applied to those reservations. According to Art. 21(1) VCLT, the reservation will generally modify the treaty as between the parties. In the case of an objection, the reservation would apply between the issuing and the objecting state according to Art. 21(3) VCLT. Since it has been established that the effect of the reservation can be solely to limit the obligation, the temporal focus as provided for in the reservation will apply as between the issuing and the objecting state. In practice, there does not yet seem to have been a reservation that would directly impact upon the temporal dimensions of treaty interpretation.[529]

7.3. Temporal applicability

Art. 28 VCLT deals with the temporal applicability of a treaty. It contains the presumption that a treaty does not apply to 'any act or fact which took place or any situation which ceased to exist before the date of the entry into force of that treaty'. This is, however, in no way conclusive for the question of the content of the treaty. No conclusion can be derived for the purposes of the Vienna Convention.

---

[528] *Ibid.* 25 (Guideline 4.7).
[529] This is why two sample reservation clauses have been included: see Appendix 2 below.

7.4. Internal law

Art. 27 VCLT prescribes that the non-performance of treaties cannot be justified with the invocation of provisions of internal law. This also extends to changes in internal law.[530] The *ratio* of this norm is to protect the integrity of treaties and to make it independent of the disposition of the law of individual states.[531] The provision serves to make the validity of treaties independent of national law, which can be seen as a consequence of the principle of *pacta sunt servanda*.[532] As we have already seen, the interpretation of treaties can be influenced by internal law, which can be included into the process of treaty interpretation through Art. 31(3)(b) VCLT as subsequent practice of the parties. Art. 27 VCLT, therefore, has no relevance for the determination of intertemporal questions.

7.5. Amendment

As previously stated, interpretation and amendment have to be interpreted as being categorically different regarding their processes, while they can possibly have the same effects, both can alter the meaning.[533] Both can also specify or perpetuate the meaning. In the normal course of things, the meaning of signs is specified by acts of interpretation and altered by acts of amendment. It is, yet, also possible to specify or perpetuate the meaning in the process of modification. Changes in meaning are the very subject of this book. Considering the relationship between amendment and interpretation, it is first interesting to see what intersections both processes potentially have and second, whether some of the rules concerning amendments can also impact upon the process of evolutive interpretation. The provisions on amendment raise two issues that can become pertinent in the interpretation of treaties.

Art. 40(5) VCLT presumes that if a state accedes to a treaty before it enters into force, the state is considered as being party to the treaty as amended. In the case of changes in interpretation, states acceding to the treaty might be considered to accept the treaty as it currently stands. The interesting question would be whether they would have the right to reject

---

[530] See in the context of treaty termination Giegerich, 'Art. 62' 1082.
[531] Schmalenbach, 'Art. 27' 453.
[532] Villiger, *Commentary on the 1969 Vienna Convention on the Law of Treaties* 375.
[533] See p. 15.

changes in the interpretation of the treaty. An interpretative declaration will not suffice. However, states are free to file a reservation.

Art. 41 VCLT sets out the possibility for states parties to a treaty to modify a multilateral treaty between some of the parties only. A rather refined question is whether an evolutive interpretation *inter se* would also be possible in the process of interpretation. This will normally not be the case since the meaning of the terms will apply to all parties. Yet, if the treaty allows for deviations in certain relationships, the subsequent conduct could possibly alter the meaning only in these relationships. In that vein, Art. 47(2)(b) of the Vienna Convention on Diplomatic Relations provides that states might in their bilateral relations allow for a more favourable treatment by custom or agreement.[534] When treaties take this or related forms, an evolutive or static *inter se* interpretation seems to be possible.[535]

7.6. Norm conflict

Art. 30 VCLT deals with norm conflicts between treaties. In cases of conflict, one of the treaties will be considered inapplicable. Dealing with successive treaties, it clearly entails an intertemporal element. The relevance for interpretation is linked to Art. 31(3)(c) VCLT.

Art. 30(3) VCLT provides that, in cases of conflict between two treaties relating to the same subject-matter,[536] the later treaty prevails over the earlier. This imports the *lex posterior* maxim into the VCLT. Can we draw a conclusion for the determination of differing meanings of successive treaties that have to be considered in the process of interpretation? Is the latest treaty always to be preferred in the process of interpretation the same way it is to be preferred when a conflict of norms arises? While it would be possible to derive a general argument in favour of evolutive interpretations from this *lex posterior* rule, there are also weighty arguments against it: Norm conflicts concern the application of the treaty, the process of application ought to be distinguished from the process of interpretation. To interpret a treaty, i.e. to ascertain its meaning, is a

---

[534] Nolte, 'Third Report for the ILC Study Group on Treaties over Time Subsequent Agreements and Subsequent Practice of States outside of Judicial or Quasi-Judicial Proceedings' 326.

[535] Vienna Convention on Diplomatic Relations (adopted 18 April 1961, entered into force 24 April 1964) 500 UNTS 95.

[536] ILC, Fragmentation Report (n. 448) 47–9 paras. 85–7.

necessary corollary to the establishment of a norm conflict. Before we know how the norms are to be interpreted, we cannot know whether they conflict. While no firm conclusion can be reached on that matter, it can be stated that one can at least not conclude cogently that Art. 30(3) VCLT generally requires evolutive interpretation. This cannot be considered as part of the general structure unquestionably underlying the Convention. The same applies to another ground for termination, Art. 59 VCLT. This provision is also an expression of the *lex posterior* maxim.

If a treaty provides that it ought to prevail over other subsequent treaties, this could prohibit an evolutive interpretation based on the meaning of those treaties. The UN Charter will for example have a great impact upon other treaties due to its supremacy as expressed in Art. 103 UN Charter. But its meaning cannot easily be changed by other treaties due to its supremacy over them. Regarding norm conflicts beyond the Vienna Convention, it could be argued that certain preferences in the case of conflict ought to influence the process of interpretation. Drawing upon the jurisprudence of the ICJ as well as prominent doctrinal opinion, the ILC argued that there is an informal hierarchy between the sources that gives treaties preference over customary international law and general principles.[537] Without prejudice to the truth of this or other contentions, it can be said that even an alleged hierarchy would not necessarily have to play out in the process of treaty interpretation.

So in conclusion, it can be stated that we cannot derive a definite answer to questions of evolution from the rules of norm conflict.

7.7. Invalidity, termination and suspension

The rules on invalidity, termination and suspension allow the parties to free themselves in specific circumstances from a treaty or parts of it treaty. Necessarily, those provisions strike a delicate balance between the stability of treaty relations and the need to end treaties under specific circumstances. Some of those provisions require the parties to resort to interpretative means other than those mentioned in Art. 31 VCLT to determine specific questions. We can contrast these methods with the methods of evolutive interpretation. Other provisions react to changes such as the change of circumstances. We can compare both aspects with the rule of treaty interpretation.

---

[537] *Ibid.* 129–34 paras. 253–66.

7.7.1 Contractual right of denunciation and withdrawal

The Vienna Convention limits the grounds for termination and suspension in the abstract and accords exclusivity to the grounds which are mentioned in the VCLT. Yet, for the scope of its application, it acknowledges in Art. 54 VCLT that the parties generally have the right to provide for denunciation and withdrawal in the respective treaties or by agreement of the parties. But even if a treaty grants no express possibility of denunciation or withdrawal, there is a possibility for implicit regulation, which is described in Art. 56 VCLT. This, however, only applies if the treaty provides neither for the termination nor (cumulatively) for denunciation or withdrawal.[538] In these cases, the provision contains a general presumption against such an implicit right which can be rebutted in two circumstances: first, where it can be established that the parties intended to admit such a possibility; second, where the nature of the treaty might imply such a right.[539] Both refer to a special way of interpreting the treaty. It has been contended that the two options can be termed as subjective in the case of the intention of the parties and objective in the case of the nature of the treaty.[540]

With respect to Art. 56(1)(a) VCLT, the most consistent way to determine the existence of such an implied right would be to depart from Arts. 31 and 32 VCLT, but to modify their techniques respectively. It is agreed that all techniques of interpretation are apt to establish the intention of the parties. To arrive at the conclusion that 'the parties provided for such a possibility', two modifications will have to be made.[541] First, the wording suggests focusing on the point in time of the conclusion of the treaty. Second, this makes it necessary to take into account the *travaux préparatoires* as well as the circumstances at the conclusion of the treaty. Those techniques are adequate for the determination of what the parties intended.[542] There is consequently no justification in according less argumentative weight to them. On the contrary, they have to be treated on the same level as the other techniques of interpretation. As to

---

[538] Villiger, *Commentary on the 1969 Vienna Convention on the Law of Treaties* 701; Giegerich, 'Art. 56' 975.
[539] For a detailed consideration of interpretation by inferences from the nature of the treaty, see pp. 119–20, 174–7 below.
[540] See Christakis, 'Art. 56 VCLT' 1266.
[541] An unmodified application of the Articles seems to be preferred by *ibid*. This is quoted by Giegerich, 'Art. 56' 976.
[542] In relation to the *travaux*, see Villiger, *Commentary on the 1969 Vienna Convention on the Law of Treaties* 701.

the first point, Art. 56(1)(a) requires that it ought to be 'established that the parties intended to admit the possibility' implicitly. This formulation suggests that in the relevant point in time is the time up to the conclusion of the treaty since the phrase is clearly formulated in the past tense. So, subsequent conduct (agreements and practice) is only admissible as far as it illuminates the intentions of the parties at the time of the conclusion of the treaty. The relevant rules as defined in Art. 31(3)(c) VCLT can only be considered if and as they existed at the time of the conclusion of the treaty. Due to this temporal focus, there seems to be no reason to regard the *travaux* as well as the circumstances at the conclusion of the treaty only as supplementary means. They can be resorted to in the same manner as the techniques mentioned in Art. 31 VCLT.[543]

In essence, Art. 56 VCLT alters the ordinary process of interpretation as to its means which has potentially an intertemporal effect. Art. 56(1)(a) seems to be fixed in time and alters some of the methods of interpretation such as the *travaux*. Most importantly, the determination of the interpretative question is tied to the original meaning. The VCLT here uses the static approach. Art. 56(1)(b) introduces an alternative means of interpretation: It resorts to 'the nature of the treaty'. The inferences we draw from the nature of a treaty can change, similar to the object and purpose of a treaty. Yet, it can be assumed that the nature of a treaty remains stable most of the time.

7.7.2 *Material breach and material impossibility*

The two grounds for termination and suspension contained in Arts. 60 and 61 VCLT are again an expression of the intertemporal structure of the Convention and the fact that it can take into account later changes. Interestingly, both contain also a part of the *pacta sunt servanda* rule which includes that a party cannot profit from its own wrong.[544] Art. 60 VCLT makes an exception to the right to terminate a treaty as a consequence of a material breach when it concerns a treaty of humanitarian character the provisions of which relate to the protection of human

---

[543] It is true that Art. 31(4) VCLT uses almost the same phrase but is considered here to be a mere reminder that the ordinary meaning can be supplemented. This difference in treatment is due to the fact that Art. 56 is entirely outside the context of Art. 31.

[544] The Latin expression of which would be: *Nullus commodum capere potest ex sua injuria propria*.

persons. The same static approach in relation to the interpretation of treaties protecting human persons can hardly be warranted.

7.7.3 Fundamental change of circumstances

Art. 62 VCLT allows for the termination of the treaty when its circumstances have changed fundamentally. This provision can also be understood as striking a balance between stability and change, between the preservation of treaties and the need to adapt to new circumstances.[545] In a broad sense, this provision shows that the Vienna Convention does deal with intertemporal questions and changing circumstances. An interpretative change will not need to meet the requirements set out in Art. 62 VCLT. Yet, it is interesting that Art. 32 VCLT also mentions the circumstances of the conclusion of the treaty as a supplementary means of interpretation. This means that they are only secondary for the determination of the content of the treaty. It is agreed that Art. 62 VCLT establishes a high threshold for the termination of a treaty.[546] This might at least indirectly increase the pressure for renegotiation or evolutive interpretation. This will especially apply to treaties establishing a border, which are totally excluded from the scope of the provision according to Art. 62(2)(a) VCLT.

7.7.4 Severance of diplomatic and consular relations

Art. 63 VCLT establishes another ground for termination or suspension.[547] While it generally provides that the severance of diplomatic and consular relations does not impact upon treaties, it allows an exception in case those relations are 'indispensable for the application of the treaty'. However, it is again an expression of the fact that, if the exception applies, subsequent developments can possibly impact on the treaty. The severance of diplomatic relations might be taken into account in

---

[545] See similarly Giegerich, 'Art. 62' 1068.
[546] Rabl Blaser, *Die clausula rebus sic stantibus im Völkerrecht* 338.
[547] In the latter sense, Villiger, *Commentary on the 1969 Vienna Convention on the Law of Treaties* 788. This is also suggested by the Special Rapporteur's statement during the discussion of the draft articles, in which he said that the severance of diplomatic relations was a matter different from the preceding articles and should, therefore, be placed after them: see ILC, 'Report of the International Law Commission on the work of its 18th session' (4 May–19 July) UN Doc. A/CN.4/SER.A/1966, 332 para. 94.

the process of interpretation in the context of Art. 32 VCLT. One might draw a parallel and contend that the interpretation of treaties will generally not be affected by the circumstances unless the exception laid out in Art. 63 VCLT applies.

7.7.5 Peremptory norms of general international law

Arts. 53 and 64 deal with the effect of peremptory norms of general international law on the law of treaties. With regard to peremptory norms and evolutive interpretation, two questions arise: first, how a peremptory norm can trigger an evolutive interpretation of another treaty norm; and, second, how a peremptory norm contained in a treaty can itself be interpreted evolutively.[548]

Like any other norm, peremptory norms of general international law ought to be taken into consideration in the process of interpretation since they will automatically fulfil the criteria set out in Art. 31(3)(c) VCLT.[549] If a norm having peremptory character is to be included in the process of interpretation, this technique will either trump the other techniques or a conflict of norms will arise in which the peremptory norm would necessarily prevail. A peremptory norm can either trigger or prohibit an evolutive interpretation. If a new peremptory norm comes into being, treaties might have to be reinterpreted to fit the new standards.

In turn, the question arises whether and under which circumstances norms that are non-derogable could then be interpreted evolutively. A treaty norm can have peremptory status.[550] Suppose that there is a norm in a treaty that qualifies as a norm of general international law and is deemed to be non-derogable, this norm will be interpreted according to Art. 31 VCLT. As we have already seen, the content of norms can change not only in the process of modification but also by

---

[548] A third most interesting question is whether *jus cogens* can be applied retroactively and not, as envisaged by the Vienna Convention, only to circumstances contemporaneous with it. This question is dealt with by Bjorge, *The Evolutionary Interpretation of Treaties* 161.

[549] For the sake of completeness, it ought to be mentioned that, if a peremptory norm is enshrined in the same treaty as the norm to be interpreted, it would of course be part of the context of the treaty.

[550] See Schmalenbach, 'Art. 53' 920; Villiger, *Commentary on the 1969 Vienna Convention on the Law of Treaties* 670; Lagerwall, 'Art. 64 VCLT' 1468. For a different account limiting *jus cogens* to customary international law, see Raffeiner, 'Wege der Konstitutionalisierung im Völkerrecht' 50.

interpretation.⁵⁵¹ The ILC itself stated that 'it would clearly be wrong to regard even rules of *jus cogens* as immutable and incapable of modification in the light of future developments'.⁵⁵²

Art. 53 VCLT, however, prescribes that a non-derogable norm 'can be modified only by a subsequent norm of general international law having the same character'. The rationale of this last bit of the definition of *jus cogens* is to preserve the special status of these norms and the acceptance of the international community of any changes.⁵⁵³ Had it not been for that effect, *jus cogens* would prevail in norm conflicts but could easily be changed by amendment or modification. This might call for some caution when changing *jus cogens* through interpretation. On the other hand, if *jus cogens* is enshrined in treaties, a total prohibition of change through interpretation might render the norm ineffective and superfluous despite its very high normative status.

A possible way out of this tension would be to require that an evolutive interpretation will have to meet special requirements in these cases. Effectively, through the use of the techniques of interpretation it will have to be shown that the interpretation is equivalent to a modification by a norm having *jus cogens* character. So the interpretation ought to show that those norms have been 'accepted and recognised by the international community of states as a whole as a norm from which no derogation is permitted'. How can we show this in the process of treaty interpretation? We ought to look for two techniques that equal the requirements of *jus cogens*. The question would then be how states could show after the conclusion of the treaty that they accepted and recognised a changed interpretation. It could only be through the means contained in Art. 31(3) VCLT. Subsequent conduct (agreements and practice) as well as the relevant rules can be ways in which states act and show that the meaning has shifted. Yet, the valid application of those techniques does not guarantee the derogable status of the interpretation. This element of the formula contained in Art. 53 VCLT can be equalled by the object and purpose of the treaty: From the interpretation it must transpire that there can be no derogation.⁵⁵⁴ If it is possible to establish those

---

⁵⁵¹ The question would of course only arise when the content of the treaty provision is literally changed; a further specification of the meaning or an application to new circumstances will not be problematic.

⁵⁵² Final Draft Articles (n. 247) 248 para. 4.   ⁵⁵³ Schmalenbach, 'Art. 53' 918.

⁵⁵⁴ Raffeiner, who constructs the matter in the terms of customary international law, talks about a double requirement of *opinio juris*. Raffeiner, 'Wege der Konstitutionalisierung im Völkerrecht' 51. The object and purpose is in effect equivalent to the second requirement extending beyond mere legal bindingness to the non-derogatory status of norms.

two elements in the process of interpretation, a change of *jus cogens* through interpretation is possible.

In conclusion, it can be said that *jus cogens* norms can provide for mandatory reasons to change the interpretation of treaty norms in order to avoid norm conflict. Under the system of the Vienna Convention, peremptory norms cannot avail themselves of any retrospective effect. In order to interpret a peremptory norm evolutively, it is necessary to establish that the changed interpretation is accepted and recognised by the community of states and that the new interpretation is also intended to have mandatory character.

7.8. Conclusions and reflection on intertemporal openness

In general, it can be stated that different provisions in the VCLT refer to different points in time. As in the case of Art. 56(1)(a) VCLT, it is sometimes the time of the conclusion of the treaty which is determinative. In other cases, such as the *lex posterior* rule as established in Arts. 30(3) and 59, or grounds of termination due to changed circumstances as expressed in Arts. 62 and 63, other points in time are relevant. The Vienna Convention, consequently, tries to achieve a stable but adaptable system. On the other hand, express regulation in the treaty, the preamble or possibly also through reservations allows the parties to deal with the issue. The same would be achievable under certain circumstances by reservations to treaties. Resort to changes in interpretation are more difficult if the object of interpretation is a *jus cogens* norm. In these instances, the process of treaty interpretation will have to be modified in such a way as to meet the requirements for the amendments of those norms as laid out in Art. 53 VCLT. These are the most important scenarios that can arise under the Vienna Convention. The fact that there are many points in focus reinforces the idea that the Convention as a whole is intertemporally open.

The concept of intertemporal openness has been a steady companion throughout the argument made in this study, and the things we discovered about this principle deserve to be summarised at the very end of Part II. The concept of intertemporal openness is no general principle but a description of the intertemporal stance the rule of interpretation takes in the VCLT with regard to static and evolutive interpretations. It is open in two ways: First regarding the interpretative result, and second regarding possible stances the interpreter can take. The openness regarding the interpretative result means that the VCLT allows for both static and evolutive results. This can be concluded from techniques that are by their nature subsequent to the conclusion of the treaty and by the openness of other techniques that can include arguments that trigger change. Subsequent practice is for example always subsequent, the relevant rules as provided for in Art. 31(3)(c) VCLT can also be included in the process of interpretation when they become applicable only after the conclusion of the treaty. The rule of interpretation of course also allows for static results. Yet, it entails no rule that favours an evolutive or static result over the other. This is the first sense in which it is intertemporally open.

The second sense in which intertemporal openness works is that, even though it takes no stance and provides for a workable solution, it leaves room for interpreters to take a stance. We have seen that the goal of interpretation in the VCLT is something between a core and a knot. The goal of interpretation according to the VCLT is most likely the neutral notion of meaning. Yet, other goals like purpose or the intention of the parties are also possible. It is for the interpreter to define her or his goal and, consequently, the intertemporal stance. Focusing on the intention of the parties, one will in the first place resort to the time of the conclusion of the treaty. Focusing on the purpose of the treaty, it will be more important how the treaty works in present circumstances. If an interpreter has the competence to render binding interpretations, others will take his or her interpretative stance when communicating legally. Yet, the stance of one interpreter is not to be generalised for the VCLT. It is maybe one of the secrets of the success of the VCLT that it is quite definite and binding on the one hand but flexible on the other. This allows not only for different interpretative stances of different interpreters but also for single institutions like courts to adapt their stance on interpretation over time. The intertemporal openness of the convention allows the rule of interpretation to fulfil its function without running the risk of being outdated and ineffective. This is the function of intertemporal openness.

PART III

Court practice

8

Profiling courts: a framework of analysis

The rule of interpretation contained in the VCLT leaves questions of stasis and evolution open. It is within the margin of appreciation of the interpreter to decide those questions in a process of balancing the arguments corresponding to the respective techniques. The rule of interpretation gives effect to rulers-of-law considerations like flexibility and adaptability since it envisages the process as basically discretionary and argumentative. But it also provides interpreters with tools to materialise rule-of-lawyers considerations like coherence and foreseeability since it forces interpreters to make their reasons known and explicit. This stabilises the interpretation since changes will have to be justified while taking into account the previous reasoning. The Convention leaves it also open for interpreters to take an intertemporal stance and to tie the process to the intentions at the time of the conclusion or to the time of interpretation. Interpretation as envisaged by the Convention depends much on the interpreter, which makes it all the more interesting to reconstruct interpretative method not only from the perspective of methodology but also from the practical perspective.

The aim of this reconstruction is the profiling of courts:[1] this means carefully analysing their behaviour in relation to the relevant question. The general aim of the profiles is to collect all relevant information illuminating how the actors deal with those questions. The end is to have all relevant data enabling one to know how the respective court sees and uses interpretative method, what arguments it would accept and how it would argue. It could also be put like this: let us imagine that a law firm wants to specialise in intertemporal disputes before international courts

---

[1] The methodology of profiling was inspired by different accounts of profiling interpretation, yet with different outlooks. On the one hand, and primarily, the reports of the then chairman of the working group of treaties over time, which can be found in Nolte (ed.), *Treaties and Subsequent Practice*. See also on the other hand the close and structured observation of the interpretative practice of the ICJ by Yambrusic, *Treaty Interpretation*.

and, therefore, develop a scheme that would help it to deal with all possible questions and desires parties before those courts had. What data would this law firm collect? It would probably first need to know about the institutional facts of the judicial mechanism, then look to all intertemporal instances that have been collected by a stocktaking, look at the general stance of the judicial mechanism as well as at the justificatory patterns in detail and resort to a summary putting the views of the judicial mechanism into certain perspectives.

In the first place, it would need some *institutional facts* as background. These include the way in which the judicial mechanism works. On the one hand, the composition of the judicial mechanism as well as its different procedures would need to be explained, this is important for understanding the basic conditions in which decision-makers fulfil their duties. On the other hand, the basis of its jurisdiction and the value which is accorded to precedent would also be important. The rules of jurisdiction shed light on how frequently and under which circumstances courts can deal with questions; the doctrine of precedent indicates how and under which circumstances the jurisprudence of a body can be changed.[2] Second, it would be helpful to have an overview of as many cases as possible dealing with stasis and evolution. A *stocktaking*[3] of those cases would be a necessary requirement for other considerations. It would be useful for the specialist lawyers to have a good knowledge of all the cases for they could compare individual cases and also derive further conclusions from those cases. The stocktaking briefly sets out the cases in which intertemporal questions arose and the terms of the treaties that gave rise to the issues. The interpretative result and a short overview of the justification would have to be included. From this, a preliminary overview concerning the approach of the respective court is possible. But it would also be possible to derive in a third step the *general stance* towards intertemporal questions. The specialist lawyers need to know how the court generally thinks about the problem so they can assess the chances of success of a claim and how the court would generally react to it. This would include issues like whether the court

---

[2] Unfortunately, the full scope of this topic could not be inquired into. It is most interesting that the use of precedents is far from automatic. While it might be possible to derive certain patterns, its use might seem chaotic in other instances. A very interesting set of ideas in that regard is developed by Burri, 'Do Lawyers Knead the Dough? – How Law, Chaos, and Uncertainty Interact' 371.

[3] This was particularly inspired by Yambrusic, *Treaty Interpretation*.

addressed intertemporal issues directly or only implicitly, whether it has taken an originalist or dynamic focus or whether it remained generally open towards intertemporal questions. It would also look at how the court generally constructed the problem. The general stance would then lead to an inquiry into the *justificatory patterns* of the court. This concerns the question of how the court justified the stance but also the decisions. This is an essential part for lawyers arguing in intertemporal disputes since they would need to know how to argue and to please the court. The interpretation is mostly done in line with the VCLT but other forms of justifications must not be omitted from the analysis. The use of precedent is another important factor in the process of justification. The use of the Vienna Convention in those disputes will be reviewed from a quantitative and a qualitative perspective. The quantitative perspective gives indications as to the frequency of the use and the correlation of the results suggested by the techniques with the results of interpretation. The qualitative analysis indicates which stance the courts took in relation to the interpretative knots. After this review, the specialist lawyers would have all the relevant legal information, but it would be good if they had at least a broader idea of the issues they were dealing with and were able to see them in a bigger context. The lawyers would need not only to argue before courts, they would also have to take strategic business decisions. To take those decisions, it is necessary to know about the general trends from other fields that might enable them to foresee impacts on their fields. This is why the *summary* of the approaches will be linked to three indicators, namely, *power, pace,* and *perception*. Those indicators help to describe the different approaches of courts, but they also translate the knowledge gained to other scientific discourses. Before the indicators are explained in greater depth, the selection of courts and the selection of relevant cases need to be addressed.

This study focuses on the International Court of Justice and the European Court of Human Rights. An in-depth review has been opted for instead of a general review of more courts; this made it necessary to select courts. There are several reasons for the selection. First, these courts are amongst the oldest and most traditional judicial institutions. The ICJ deals with a wide range of issues and is not limited to one area of international law. Consequently, there is diverse material to look at. The ECtHR, in contrast, is limited to the ECHR but has a great output, deciding tens of thousands of cases every year. Consequently, there is more material to analyse. Another reason is that both courts played a significant role in openly acknowledging evolutive interpretations which we will encounter in due course. All the reasons mentioned speak in favour of the two courts. The fact that other courts are excluded from the inquiry is less significant since the discretionary and intertemporally open nature of the VCLT limits the normative significance to the respective mechanism. To put it differently: Unless there is one court competent for exclusive interpretation of the Convention, each court can legitimately have its own stance.

In the process of reviewing the case law, intertemporal questions had to be identified. This study only acknowledges cases in which courts explicitly addressed the question or no other interpretation from the facts seems possible. This excludes 'actively hidden' evolutive interpretations, in which courts interpret evolutively without addressing the issue in their decision. It is hard to establish such an actively hidden evolutive interpretation as one would have to prove the changes in the meaning. Those cases are themselves subject to interpretation and dispute. They cannot be assumed as clear cases in the process of reconstructing the behaviour. What is more, the focus of the whole study is the justificatory behaviour of courts. If the courts did not assume to interpret evolutively, there is no use in reviewing their behaviour apart from stating that the courts have not assumed to interpret evolutively. This is why actively hidden evolutions will be mentioned in the context of this study without trying to give an extensive account of them. What also needs to be explained are the indicators power, pace and perception.

8.1. Power: the actor dimension

Many scholars have linked issues of interpretation to power.[4] If we define power as an exercise of (legal) supremacy,[5] rendering binding interpretations comes under that definition since it authoritatively states what the law ought to mean. If we look at the VCLT, all techniques of

---

[4] See e.g. Roberts, 'Power and Persuasion in Investment Treaty Interpretation' 181; Roberts, 'Subsequent Practice'; Klabbers, 'Book Review'.

[5] For a similar definition, see Buchanan, *Justice, Legitimacy and Self-Determination* 235; see also the delimitation of power and legitimacy by Bodansky, 'Legitimcy in International Law and International Relations'.

interpretation relate to the treaty and can be said to be grounded in the consent of the parties. Yet, different techniques can be shaped by different actors. To give the two most prominent examples: The object and purpose can be explicitly defined by the drafters but also be subject to an interpretative effort of those interpreting the treaty. In contrast, subsequent practice and subsequent agreements rely on those who apply the law in practice. This is why the pattern of justification tells us also something about power. It can possibly indicate on which actor the interpretation is based. Yet, we must not forget that we can only observe in the context of justification, i.e. the patterns of referring to certain actors. This is different from the actual power relation in that it only concerns what one actor says in order to justify its interpretation. This is particularly relevant for evolutive interpretations for they entail change. The empirical analysis can help to clarify this issue. The results this perspective offers can feed into discourses about the legitimacy of the exercise of power through law.[6] Those discourses are first and foremost concerned with fleshing out normative standards or observing standards of relevant actors, yet they also have the potential for application: On their basis, proposals for reform are developed.[7] This is all the more important since we have already seen that the number of international courts and tribunals as well as their output is vastly increasing. This might be a reason for the increased interest in treaty interpretation in recent years.[8] But it will certainly also further academic reflection, justification and critique of power through interpretation. An analysis based on the VCLT can feed into these discourses since it visualises to a certain extent how interpreters communicate power relations in the context of their justification. The way in which a certain technique is used or the frequency of its use has the potential to indicate certain power relations. Since there is no fixed hierarchy within the VCLT, the results based on it will hardly grant a special status to one set of actors in the process of interpretation. But it might indicate that there is a *primus inter pares*.

---

[6] See just two of many examples: Wolfrum and Röben (eds.), *Legitimacy In International Law*; and Meyer (ed.), *Legitimacy, Justice and Public International Law*.
[7] Von Bogdandy and Venzke, 'In Whose Name? An Investigation of International Courts' Public Authority and Its Democratic Justification' 24ff.
[8] For this and similar observations, see Nolte, 'Introduction' 1; Klabbers, 'Book Review'. See also the review of recent literature by Waibel, 'Demystifying the Art of Interpretation'.

8.2. Perception: the material dimension

The criterion of perception aims at the distinction between the legal and the non-legal in the process of interpretation. This distinction lies at the heart of the process of rule ascertainment.[9] It is also significant when it comes to issues of interpretation.[10] In this context, it basically sets apart certain considerations or means of interpretation that are not considered to be legal and not allowed to be acknowledged in the process of interpretation. In the context of drafting the VCLT, this has been aptly described as a feud between textualists and contextualists.[11] Textualists wanted to allow fewer means of interpretation and tried to tie them to the text, while contextualists asked for a broader arsenal of interpretative means. We have seen that the VCLT determines these questions up to a certain point but there is also room for manoeuvre.[12] It was established that the Convention is generally broad but techniques all relate to the treaty. A closer look at the techniques revealed knots impacting on questions of openness and closure of the rule: in the case of subsequent practice, the different strings of the awareness knot can limit the technique to silent and implicit agreements but also extend it to mere practice irrespective of who is acting or whether the parties are aware of it. The ascertainment knot can limit the object and purpose to the ordinary means of interpretation but also extend it to broad social, political or economic considerations. Depending upon the strings we pull, i.e. the interpretations we choose, the Convention will be more open or more closed. The stance the VCLT and interpretative practice have taken constitutes and determines the relationship between the law as a societal system and its environment.

The relationship between the law and its environment will become more important because the areas of international regulation are increasing vastly: International environmental law and international investment law could be named as important new or expanding areas. New areas as well as new developments can mean that international law has to answer

---

[9] For a general account, see D'Aspremont, *Formalism and the Sources of International Law*. For customary international law, see Kammerhofer, *Uncertainty in international law*.

[10] For an account of interpretation as a broader phenomenon based on this distinction, see Orakhelashvili *The Interpretation of Acts and Rules in Public International Law*.

[11] *Case Concerning the Temple of Preah Vihear (Cambodia v. Thailand)* (Merits) [1962] ICJ Rep 6 16.

[12] So, on the basis of the Vienna Convention, Orakhelashvili has developed a strict legal approach whereas Kolb managed to take into account several extra-textual factors such as values. Kolb, *Interprétation et création du droit international* 281ff.

new questions and is put under pressure. On the one hand, it has to be open for new developments, but also to retain its specific legal rationality. This tension underlying, in particular, questions of stasis and evolution by interpretation found expression in sociology.

It has been famously outlined that the adaptability of a social institution determines to a significant extent whether it functions in society.[13] If the law is considered to be more open, it will harmonise better with the other systems like politics and the economy. On the other hand, it has been asserted that a certain closure of a system is necessary for it to constitute itself and to mark the distinction between the system and its environment.[14] This does not mean that there are no connections between the law and its environment; on the contrary, those connections require that a system like the legal system is constituted and closed to a certain extent.[15] Adaptability and operational closure represent only two approaches in a very rich and wealthy social science literature that takes different stances on questions of openness and closure that are crucial to international law in many respects: The question of whether law and morals are to be separated or inherently intertwined, or the question to what extent the law ought to follow economic rationalities. The analytical framework of the VCLT regarding the cardinal cores and the knots has been laid out already. The following analysis will assess whether courts showed awareness of the problem of openness and how their justifications related to that issue. The approaches taken can indicate where the actors are situated in practice and might to a certain extent enable the explanatory force of the theories to be tested.

8.3. Pace: the temporal dimension

The criterion of pace seeks to point out the temporal awareness of the judicial actors and the question of how fast changes can and do happen. It has been shown that the Vienna Convention is intertemporally open: This means that change through interpretation is possible. Yet, the particular stances taken with regard to interpretative knots will determine how fast the law can change.

---

[13] Parsons, *The Social System* 428–79.
[14] For a general account, see Luhmann, *Soziale Systeme* 242ff; Luhmann, *Das Recht der Gesellschaft* 124ff.
[15] Luhmann, *Soziale Systeme* 242ff.

We are witnessing a vast acceleration of processes in society. The sociologist Peter Borscheid has given a historical account of the acceleration in different parts of society.[16] He concludes his overview with a final epoch, starting in 1950 in which technological acceleration reached all parts of society.[17] He observes factors of acceleration ranging from industrial production to genetics, enabling the acceleration in the process of evolution.[18] At the end of the twentieth century, the Internet had another huge impact, accelerating again all parts of society, from communication to production.[19] In the face of this development, there has been a trend towards linking the phenomenon of acceleration to modernity.[20] Sociologists have tried to describe and explain the constant acceleration.

Hartmut Rosa has developed a systematic narrative of our society as being subject to increasing social acceleration. This means that in many aspects society changes faster and more often than before. Defining three forms of acceleration, their driving forces and their interconnectedness, he seeks to show how this is a systematic pattern of the world we live in. The first category is technological acceleration, which he defines as 'goal-directed processes of transport, communication, and production'.[21] The incentive to make these processes faster is seen in capitalism, which has the aim to increase productivity and effectiveness. Time is crucial in the process of production, many factors of which depend on time such as wages and salaries. The second form looks at social change, i.e. 'change of social constellations and structures as well as patterns of action and orientation'.[22] Social change can possibly affect 'attitudes and values as well as fashions and lifestyles, social relations and obligations as well as groups, classes, or milieus, social languages as well as forms of practice and habits'.[23] This would lead to an effect of 'concentration of the present' since the present was the time span in which 'horizons of experience and expectation coincide'.[24] Those are distinct from technological acceleration in the sense that they can be influenced by it but they can be a source of influence themselves. Referring to Niklas Luhmann, he

---

[16] Borscheid, *Das Tempo Virus*. [17] Ibid. 345. [18] Ibid. 346. [19] Ibid. 362.
[20] See a general overview by Rosa, *Acceleration: A New Theory of Modernity* 46; Rosa, *Weltbeziehungen im Zeitalter der Beschleunigung* 185–9. Citing *inter alia* the two exemplary quotes: 'Modernity is about the acceleration of time' by Conrad, *Modern Times, Modern Places* 9. And '[m]odernity is speed' by Erikson, *Tyranny of the Moment* 159.
[21] Rosa, 'Social Acceleration: Ethical and Political Consequences of a Desynchronized High-Speed Society' 3, 6.
[22] Ibid. 7. [23] Ibid. [24] Ibid.

sees the driving force of the acceleration of social change in functional differentiation of the society.[25] The increasing complexity within society is perceived as a lack of time which then again leads to social differentiation. Certain processes function only to follow one rationale such as legal or illegal; external rationales such as moral, religious or political expectations are excluded from the process.[26] The third category is that of the pace of life, which means rather subjectively the experience of time by the individual and objectively measuring the time used for certain tasks as well as the combination of tasks sometimes referred to as multitasking.[27] This kind of acceleration is triggered by a growing notion that a good and fulfilled life requires many experiences and acquired skills, which Rosa terms as the cultural motor. Those three areas of acceleration mutually influence each other. The interesting observation Rosa makes is that on all levels of society the pace of change increases. The concept of pace highlights the central importance of the awareness of the temporal dimension in stability and change. It is crucial to understand how fast the law reacts to social changes. If it is true that those developments such as the digital revolution will increase the pace of society, this might call for responses in the legal system. In national law, it was observed that the executive could speed up the process of norm production if it is enabled to create norms outside the ordinary parliamentary process. Such procedures were once called 'motorised legislation'.[28] Yet, evolutive interpretation might also prove to be an important tool for the adaptation of the law to new developments. It could become even more frequent when the assumptions about social acceleration are correct. There are of course also other ways to provide for an increased pace in the legal system, including lowering the requirements for amendment and modification of treaties or the possibility of providing for so-called secondary law, especially in the context of international organisations.

Undertaking a comparison of several courts will make it possible to designate them as fast and slow. Comparing the courts to other actors in society, the pace will indicate whether they are at the front, provoking societal development, or at the back, forming its critical mass.

---

[25] Ibid. 14.   [26] Rosa, *Acceleration: A New Theory of Modernity* 185–6.
[27] Rosa, 'Social Acceleration: Ethical and Political Consequences of a Desynchronized High-Speed Society' 8.
[28] Schmitt, 'The Motorized Legislator' 66.

9

The International Court of Justice: peacemakers and disputants

The International Court of Justice is not only a principal organ of the United Nations, it could also be considered as the standard setter for public international law. Its decisions are quoted by other international courts and tribunals, national courts as well as legal scholars.[29] As shown above, the jurisprudence of the ICJ had also a great influence on the rules of treaty interpretation. These examples indicate that the ICJ could be considered as one of the best examples of the law-making function of international courts and tribunals. Dissenting and separate opinions indicate that some issues are disputed. We will see that one of those issues has been the intertemporal question. From the very first years until the present day, there has been constant disagreement on how to deal with those questions. There was a manifest dispute amongst judges. Yet, some of the issues concerned the high-profile cases the ICJ dealt with as well as the most politically sensitive cases. The ICJ had to act in a manner to solve very controversial disputes involving imminent risks. This might be the reason for avoiding rigidity in its intertemporal stance and for building up a flexible approach that was apt to deal with the intertemporal questions. The ICJ acted as peacemaker. This important function is attributed to it also institutionally.

9.1. Institutional aspects

The International Court of Justice is the principal judicial organ of the United Nations (Art. 92 UN Charter) and consists of fifteen members who are elected by the General Assembly and the Security Council and should represent 'the main forms of civilization and of the principal legal

---

[29] For a detailed overview of the impact of the Court, see Amr, *The Role of the International Court of Justice as the Principal Judicial Organ of the United Nations*. For a short overview, see Shaw, *International Law* 1113–1114.

systems' (Art. 9 ICJ Statute).[30] The ICJ regularly decides as a full court,[31] there is, however, the possibility for chamber decisions.[32] The ICJ decides contentious cases and gives advisory opinions. Whereas only states have standing before the Court in contentious cases, organs of the United Nations can request advisory opinions which answer abstract questions. In contentious cases, only states can be parties before the ICJ. Art. 38 ICJ Statute shows that potentially every possible international treaty can be invoked before the Court. Consequently, the Court deals with diverse matters, ranging from labour law disputes and border delimitations to questions of war and peace. It has over the years established its reputation as an effective instrument for the settlement of disputes.[33] Being a principal organ, the Court rendered principled decisions, but being responsible for potentially any matter that can arise in inter-state dispute resolution, a certain degree of flexibility has been required. The same tension arises when one looks at the jurisdiction of the Court. The hope that permanent submissions to the jurisdiction would solve all issues was realised only in part and was seriously hampered by reservations. Since all routes envisaged in Art. 36 ICJ Statute play a part, the Court remains a hybrid between an *ad hoc* arbitral tribunal and a court having automatic jurisdiction.

The ICJ has repeatedly applied the VCLT directly as a reflection of the rules as enshrined in customary law in cases in which the Convention was not applicable in its temporal[34] or personal[35] scope. The fact that the ICJ itself applies the rules on interpretation retrospectively makes it plausible to reconstruct the arguments used by the Court in the same manner in cases in which the Vienna Convention was not in existence or

---

[30] In practice, the distribution of the membership in relation to the regional groups corresponds to that in the Security Council, which means Africa 3, Latin America and the Caribbean 2, Asia 3, Western Europe and other States 5, Eastern Europe 2: see Registrar of the International Court of Justice, 'Members of the Court'.

[31] In contentious cases, there is of course the possibility to appoint *ad hoc* judges or to declare a judge as prejudiced.

[32] See Arts. 26–29 ICJ Statute.

[33] Schulte, *Compliance with Decisions of the International Court of Justice*.

[34] *Legality of the Use of Force (Serbia and Montenegro v. Belgium)* (Preliminary Objections) [2004] ICJ Rep 279 318 para. 100; *Case Concerning the Dispute Regarding Navigational and Related Rights (Costa Rica v. Nicaragua)* (Judgment) [2009] ICJ Rep 213 237 para. 47. For a critical remark as to the retroactive application of the rules of interpretation, see Greig, *Intertemporality and the Law of Treaties* 108.

[35] *Kasikili/Sedudu Island (Botswana v. Namibia)* (Judgment) [1999] ICJ Rep 1045 1059 para. 18; *Case Concerning the Dispute Regarding Navigational and Related Rights (Costa Rica v. Nicaragua)* (Judgment) 237 para. 47.

not applied by the Court. Some interpretations of the ICJ were made before the VCLT came into force, in some cases the ICJ did not mention the Convention. Yet, the rule of interpretation in the VCLT was a reconstruction of ICJ practice. So the VCLT will be applied in the analysis of interpretations as long as the jurisprudence of the Court is consistent with it. Even though Art. 59 provides that the Court only decides *inter partes*, the Court has generally developed a practice of referring to previous decisions and regarding them as authoritative but not binding.[36] What does not transpire from this very brief institutional overview is that the ICJ as an institution has a very long history and is the most prestigious court in the international sphere. There is a very particular institutional culture at the ICJ that also extends to the way the parties plead and the Court argues. Many of the traditions and patterns at the Court are only visible if the Court is closely observed.

9.2. Stocktaking

9.2.1 Intertemporal instances

Not long after its establishment, the ICJ had to deal with intertemporal issues, and those issues have arisen constantly ever since. Building upon previous reviews,[37] all of those instances will be reviewed as to the intertemporal issues they are raising and the arguments they made in that regard.

In the advisory opinion on the *International Status of South-West Africa*, the General Assembly asked the ICJ amongst other things to determine the status of South-West Africa and the obligations of the Union of South Africa regarding South-West Africa.[38] Those obligations derived from South Africa's mandate agreement that was concluded according to Art. 22 of the Covenant of the League of Nations. Without expressly determining the exact status of the mandate, the Court held that the mandate continued to exist even though the League of Nations had ceased to exist.[39] This mandate provided for certain obligations of

---

[36] Guillaume, 'The Use of Precedent by International Judges and Arbitrators' 5, 11.
[37] General overviews of ICJ case law are provided by E. Klein, *Statusverträge im Völkerrecht* 341–2; Linderfalk, 'Doing the Right Thing for the Right Reason' 112; Malgosia Fitzmaurice, 'Dynamic (Evolutive) Interpretation of Treaties, Part I'; Böth, *Evolutive Auslegung völkerrechtlicher Verträge* 28–41.
[38] *International Status of South-West Africa* (Advisory Opinion) [1950] ICJ Rep 131.
[39] Ibid. 132.

the Union of South Africa regarding South-West Africa and their supervision by the League of Nations.[40] The Court referred in particular to the obligations 'to submit to the supervision and control of the Council of the League and the obligation to render to it annual reports in accordance with Article 22 of the Covenant and Article 6 of the Mandate'.[41] After an extensive discussion, the ICJ came to the conclusion that the General Assembly ought to take over the supervisory function of the League of Nations.[42] By replacing the Council of the League of Nations with the General Assembly, the Court interpreted the mandate evolutively. Since this changed the content of the norm, we have to regard it as contential evolution. It also held that the General Assembly 'should conform as far as possible to the procedure followed in this respect by the Council of the League of Nations'.[43] The Court considered the ordinary meaning of the Covenant as well as the UN Charter as an argument against this solution.[44] Yet, it found also arguments in favour of this solution such as the object and purpose, as derived from the intentions of the framers of the Covenant and the UN Charter as well as Art. 80 UN Charter[45] and Art. 10 UN Charter,[46] which will have to be considered as a relevant rule in the sense of Art. 31(3)(c) VCLT. It also adduced the subsequent agreement of the Assembly of the League of Nations as well as the subsequent practice of the General Assembly.[47] The Court upheld this evolutive interpretation in several decisions.[48]

In the case *Concerning Rights of Nationals of the United States of America in Morocco*, the ICJ had to decide upon the scope of the consular jurisdiction of the United States in Morocco. The question was whether the term 'dispute' as contained in Art. 20 of the Treaty of Peace and Friendship of 1836 could be interpreted as including civil and criminal

---

[40] Ibid. 133.   [41] Ibid. 136.

[42] Judge McNair disagreed and provided a detailed discussion of the arguments made by the Court. See *International Status of South-West Africa* (Advisory Opinion), Separate Opinion Judge McNair [1950] ICJ Rep 159–62. For a dissent without reference to the means of interpretation, see *International Status of South-West Africa* (Advisory Opinion), Separate Opinion Judge Read [1950] ICJ Rep 164.

[43] *International Status of South-West Africa* (Advisory Opinion) 138.   [44] Ibid. 136.

[45] Ibid. 136.   [46] Ibid. 137.   [47] Ibid.

[48] *Voting Procedure on Questions Relating to Reports and Petitions Concerning the Territory of South-West Africa* (Advisory Opinion) [1955] ICJ Rep 72; *Admissibility of Hearings of Petitioners by the Committee on South West Africa* (Advisory Opinion) [1956] ICJ Rep 27–8. See also Dugard, 'The Opinion on South-West Africa ('Namibia')' 464. Since these decisions also repeat the arguments advanced by the ICJ and relate to the very same question, they will not be mentioned in the quantitative analysis.

matters as it was interpreted originally or whether the situation had changed in the sense that the United States would only have consular jurisdiction over civil matters. The Court decided to read this referential provision statically and to favour the meaning at the time of the conclusion of the treaty without giving any further reasons for its decision.[49] The Court then went on to determine the actual meaning of the term. Yet, there was a second question regarding static and evolutive interpretation.[50] The ICJ implicitly gave an evolving meaning to a most-favoured-nations clause contained in Arts. 14 and 24. The United States had argued that the most-favoured-nations clause had to be interpreted statically: It conferred on the United States all rights that existed at the time of the conclusion of the treaty no matter whether they still remained in existence.[51] The ICJ acknowledged that there were two ways to construe the most-favoured-nations clause: Either as 'drafting by reference', i.e. statically, as the United States had contended, or as a 'method for the establishment and maintenance of equality of treatment without discrimination amongst the various countries concerned', i.e. dynamically.[52] The argument of the United States was rejected by the ICJ which held that the most-favoured-nations clause would always apply to the rights that currently existed.[53] So the mechanism of incorporation in the most-favoured-nations clause was interpreted evolutively rather than statically. This represents a case of referential evolution. The Court argued with reference to the ordinary meaning of the terms of the treaty[54] and the treaty practice[55] which would be today considered as an argument according to Art. 31(3)(c) VCLT.

In the same year, the ICJ decided the *Anglo-Iranian Oil Case*. The ICJ had to deal with two possible readings of a reservation.[56] This reservation excluded from the courts jurisdiction 'disputes arising after

---

[49] *Rights of Nationals of the United States of America in Morocco (France v. United States of America)* (Judgment) [1952] ICJ Rep 188. This case is mentioned by Greig, *Intertemporality and the Law of Treaties* 49.

[50] The Court then relied on the ordinary meaning of the treaty and the relevant rules, i.e. the treaty practice at the time. Since those arguments were tied to the point in time of the conclusion of the treaty and the intertemporal issue was resolved before the arguments came into play, they will not be counted in the quantitative analysis.

[51] *Rights of Nationals of the United States of America in Morocco (France v. United States of America)* (Judgment) 191.

[52] Ibid.   [53] Ibid. 192.   [54] Ibid. 191.   [55] Ibid. 192.

[56] Reservations are texts to be interpreted; since this case was quoted by the Court as precedent also in the context of treaty interpretation, it has to be included in the stocktaking.

the ratification of the present declaration with regard to situations or facts relating directly or indirectly to the application of treaties or conventions accepted by Persia and subsequent to the ratification of this declaration'.[57] The question before the Court was whether the phrase 'subsequent to the ratification' referred to 'facts' or 'treaties and conventions'. Before deciding the case based on grammatical arguments, the Court took the following stance regarding interpretation:

> But the Court cannot base itself on a purely grammatical interpretation of the text. It must seek the interpretation which is in harmony with a natural and reasonable way of reading the text, having due regard to the intention of the Government of Iran at the time when it accepted the compulsory jurisdiction of the Court.[58]

So the Court took a static stance. This played, however, no role in the actual process of interpretation. The Court also did not justify the static stance it took.

In the *Preah Vihear Case*, Thailand and Cambodia disagreed about who had sovereignty over a temple in the border area. Art. 1 of the Treaty of 13 February 1904 determined that the watershed line between the basins of the Nam Sen and the Mekong and the Nam Moun should constitute the border. This treaty was concluded between Thailand and France, the latter being colonial power and the former being a protectorate. The parties then undertook steps to determine the exact borderline with the help of a commission.[59] In the course of those proceedings, France produced maps which it brought to the attention of Thailand. The Court held that Thailand had acquiesced in those maps.[60] Through those maps, a borderline different from the real watershed line was established.[61] The question was how this map impacted on the original treaty. The Court held that the inclusion of the map did not depart from or violate the terms of the treaty.[62] The Court held that the parties in 1908 interpreted the treaty settlement provided for in the Treaty of 1904 in such a way that the line on the map would 'prevail' over the watershed line provided for in the treaty.[63] While the Court seemed to indicate that the watershed line is altered through a conflicting norm, it explicitly stated that the same result could have been achieved in the

---

[57] Translation from the French original found in *Anglo-Iranian Oil Case (United Kingdom v. Iran)* [1952] ICJ Rep 103.
[58] Ibid. 104. This case is discussed by Greig, *Intertemporality and the Law of Treaties* 35.
[59] *Case Concerning the Temple of Preah Vihear (Cambodia v. Thailand)* (Merits) 16.
[60] Ibid. 23. [61] Ibid. 21. [62] Ibid. 33–4. [63] Ibid. 34.

process of treaty interpretation.[64] The Court went on to discuss the object and purpose of the Treaty of 1904[65] which went against a static meaning and the treaty practice of the parties, which could be said to fall under Art. 31(3)(c) VCLT.[66] So the Court arrived at the conclusion that the subsequent practice of the parties could alter the watershed line which was supported by the other techniques. The way the ICJ construed it, the new line was rather a contential than a referential evolution: The map determined the border in a final manner irrespective of whether it related to the real watershed line or not. The Court could leave the question open as to whether it would have to refer to the watershed line as it stood in 1904 or as it evolved due to changes of the respective rivers.[67] This would, in contrast, have been a question of referential evolution.

Ethiopia and Liberia instituted proceedings against South Africa after it had failed to cooperate in relation to Namibia.[68] Both relied upon the mandate agreement. In the preliminary phase of the *South West Africa Cases*, the ICJ had to deal with the question whether the applicants would fall under the jurisdictional clause of Art. 7(2) of the mandate being an agreement between the League of Nations and the mandatory South Africa. This clause provided that 'another Member of the League of Nations' had standing before the Court. Referring to the dissolution of the League of Nations in 1946, the Court held that the meaning of the term evolved and that the applicants had standing.[69] The Court found that the ordinary meaning of the terms would speak in favour of a static interpretation.[70] Yet, the object and purpose,[71] the context of the provision[72] as well as the subsequent agreement of the Assembly of the League of Nations[73] would favour an evolutive interpretation that would also apply to members of the United Nations.

---

[64] *Ibid.* 34. [65] *Ibid.* [66] *Ibid.* [67] *Ibid.* 35.
[68] On the background to the case, see Heyns and Killander, 'South West Africa/Namibia (Advisory Opinions and Judgments)' [31–3].
[69] *South West Africa Cases (Ethiopia v. South Africa; Liberia v. South Africa)* (Preliminary Objections) [1962] ICJ Rep 335–42. Critique on the substance and the general argumentative weight of the arguments used by the Court was made by *South West Africa Cases (Ethiopia v. South Africa; Liberia v. South Africa)* (Preliminary Objections), Dissenting Opinion Judges Spender and Fitzmaurice [1962] ICJ Rep 504–46; *ibid.* Dissenting Opinion Judge van Wyk [1962] ICJ Rep 319.
[70] *South West Africa Cases (Ethiopia v. South Africa; Liberia v. South Africa)* (Preliminary Objections) 336.
[71] *Ibid.* [72] *Ibid.* 336. [73] *Ibid.* 338.

In the second phase of the case, the Court held that, even though the parties had standing, they could not avail themselves of a subjective right conferred by the mandate. In the course of the argument, the Court took a very strict static approach centring on the time of the institution of the mandate.[74] Since no rights of members of the League had existed then, no right could subsequently come into existence. Arguments for the static interpretation came from the context,[75] the ordinary meaning[76] and the *travaux*.[77]

In the *Namibia opinion*, the Court once again revisited the question whether the supervision as provided for in the mandate continued after the dissolution of the League of Nations. The Court again came to the conclusion that the system of supervision continued and ought to be effected by the General Assembly. Yet, the Court for the first time explicitly stressed that it would interpret the mandate in an evolutive manner.[78] It mainly relied on the ordinary meaning[79] and the relevant rules at the time it determined the question of interpretation.[80]

A quasi-evolutive treaty interpretation was conducted in the *Fisheries Jurisdiction (The United Kingdom v. Iceland & Germany v. Iceland) Cases*. The ICJ first established that there was a customary rule of preferential fishing rights of coastal states, which existed if the coastal state was dependent on the fishing and the interests of other states were accounted for. The ICJ found the custom established in actual state practice as well as the practice of states in bilateral and multilateral treaties.[81] It also took account of an amendment to a draft treaty that later failed to come into existence but nevertheless supported the customary nature of the rule in the draft amendment.[82] Discussing this rule, the ICJ held that the

---

[74] *South West Africa (Ethiopia v. South Africa; Liberia v. South Africa)* (Second Phase) [1966] ICJ Rep 23 para. 16.
[75] *Ibid.* 23–5; 28.   [76] *Ibid.* 25.   [77] *Ibid.* 27.
[78] *Legal Consequences for States of the Continued Presence of South Africa in Namibia (South West Africa) Notwithstanding Security Council Resolution 276 (1970)* (Advisory Opinion) [1971] ICJ Rep 31 para. 53.
[79] The terms 'strenuous conditions of the modern world', 'the well-being and development' and 'sacred trust' in Art. 22 of the Covenant of the League of Nations were by definition evolutionary. *Legal Consequences for States of the Continued Presence of South Africa in Namibia (South West Africa) Notwithstanding Security Council Resolution 276 (1970)* (Advisory Opinion), Dissenting Opinion Judge Fitzmaurice [1971] ICJ Rep 31 para. 53.
[80] The Court refers to the UN Charter as well as custom, which is likely to be a reference to the right of self-determination: see *ibid.* 31 paras. 52, 53.
[81] *Fisheries Jurisdiction (United Kingdom v. Iceland)* (Merits) [1974] ICJ Rep 26 para. 58.
[82] *Ibid.* 25–6 para. 57.

requirement of dependence was not to be interpreted statically but had to be assessed at the time of interpretation.[83] Technically, the source of this term was customary, but the interpretative question ran parallel.

In the *Aegean Continental Shelf Case*, the Court had to determine its jurisdiction concerning a case brought by Greece against Turkey under the General Act for the Pacific Settlement of International Disputes of 1928. Turkey invoked a reservation of Greece to its acceptance on the basis of reciprocity. The Court dealt with four intertemporal issues, the first of which it left open. Discussing whether the phrase '*et notamment*' was to be understood in a cumulative or alternative sense, the Court seemed to follow the contention of Greece to look for the 'current' ordinary meaning,[84] but then also looked for the intention of Greece in the past.[85] So this intertemporal issue was not really determined by the Court.

The most important intertemporal issue concerned the phrase 'domestic jurisdiction' in the same reservation: It was questionable whether it would apply to continental shelves. The continental shelf had been attributed to the territory of a state only since 1945.[86] This indicates that the time difference between 1931 and 1978 really mattered. In this context, the Court held that this phrase was to be interpreted so as to follow the development of international law. So, the Court opted for an evolutive interpretation.[87] Since the very concept of territory changed and continental shelves came under its definition, this is again a contential evolution. The Court relied mainly on historical evidence, especially the ordinary meaning of the text,[88] the context,[89] the *travaux*,[90] and the treaty practice around the time the declaration was issued.[91] In the course of the argument, the Court noted that Greece itself had interpreted the term 'rights' in Art. 17 of the General Act of 1928 in an evolutive manner and explicitly acknowledged that this had to be read evolutively.[92] This

---

[83] *Ibid.* 30 para. 70. Consider also the parallel case, *Fisheries Jurisdiction (Federal Republic of Germany v. Iceland)* (Merits) [1974] ICJ Rep 199 para. 62. As these cases concern the determination of custom and not the interpretation of treaties, they were not included in the further analysis concerning the techniques of interpretation. The fact that the static interpretation of concepts was explicitly mentioned warrants at least an explanation.

[84] See the contention of Greece: *Aegean Sea Continental Shelf Case (Greece v. Turkey)* (Judgment) [1978] ICJ Rep 22 para. 51. The Court acknowledged this implicitly: *ibid.* 22 paras. 52, 54.

[85] *Ibid.* 23 para. 56.   [86] Crawford and Viles, 'International Law on a Given Day'.

[87] *Aegean Sea Continental Shelf Case (Greece v. Turkey)* (Judgment) 33–4 para. 80.

[88] *Ibid.* 31 para. 74.   [89] *Ibid.* 30 para. 73, 33 para. 79.   [90] *Ibid.* 30 para. 73.

[91] *Ibid.* 30–1 paras. 73–4.   [92] *Ibid.* 33 para. 79.

could be considered as the second evolutive interpretation in that case since it did not concern the reservation but the treaty. The Court had previously also mentioned that the phrase 'domestic jurisdiction' was to be interpreted so as to follow the law as it presently stands.[93] It is significant that the Court managed to interpret three phrases evolutively in this case.

In two cases before the ICJ, the question arose under what circumstances the ICJ was open to states not being party to its Statute. According to Art. 35(2) ICJ Statute, the conditions for access of states not parties to the treaty shall be laid down by the Security Council, 'subject to the special provisions contained in treaties in force'. The question before the Court was now, to which point in time the exception referred. Since Art. 35 ICJ Statute was based upon a similar provision in the PCIJ Statute, the Court had to choose between three points in time: The entry into force of the PCIJ Statute, the entry into force of the ICJ Statute or the time when the dispute arose. In an Order concerning provisional measures of the *Application of the Convention on the Prevention and Punishment of the Crime of Genocide Case* the ICJ first decided *prima facie* that Art. 35 ICJ Statute would have to be interpreted dynamically and that the Genocide Convention would qualify as a treaty in force.[94] The Court later held in the *Legality of the Use of Force Cases* that Art. 35 ICJ Statute was to be interpreted statically so as to include only treaties in force at the time when the ICJ Statute entered into force.[95] The Court found that the ordinary meaning of the treaty was generally open,[96] the context was considered to point in the direction of an evolutive interpretation[97] while the object and purpose went against this conclusion.[98] The Court then resorted to the *travaux* which warranted an evolutive interpretation.[99]

---

[93] Ibid. 25 para. 59. The Court also reinforced this finding: *ibid*. 33 para. 79. This is a case of referential evolution since it refers to the issues that are currently not determined by international law.

[94] *Application of the Convention on the Prevention and Punishment of the Crime of Genocide (Bosnia Herzegovina v. Yugoslavia (Serbia and Montenegro))* (Order) [1993] ICJ Rep 14 para. 19.

[95] *Legality of the Use of Force (Serbia and Montenegro v. Belgium)* (Preliminary Objections) 324 para. 113. This finding was objected to by Judge Elaraby who aimed at including peace treaties after the Second World War as well as treaties 'redressing violations of *jus cogens*'. *Legality of the Use of Force (Serbia and Montenegro v. Belgium)* (Preliminary Objections) Separate Opinion Judge Elaraby [2004] ICJ Rep 363 paras. 16–18.

[96] *Legality of the Use of Force (Serbia and Montenegro v. Belgium)* (Preliminary Objections) 318 para. 101.

[97] Ibid. 319 para. 101.   [98] Ibid. 319 para. 102.   [99] Ibid. 319.

As shown by the Court, similar problems could arise in the context of Arts. 36 and 37 ICJ Statute.[100] Yet, the Court had, without further discussion, affirmed for example in the preliminary objections of the *Case Concerning Questions of Interpretation and Application of the 1971 Montreal Convention Arising from the Aerial Incident at Lockerbie* in which Art. 36 ICJ Statute was implicitly interpreted so as to follow the evolution of the law.[101] All of the cases mentioned in this section concerned referential evolutions.

In its opinion *Legality of the Threat or Use of Nuclear Weapons*, the ICJ was asked by the General Assembly whether the threat or use of nuclear weapons would be permitted under any circumstances in international law. The Court looked into different provisions to see whether it could find a prohibition in that regard. In this context, the Court discussed the Martens Clause. While this clause can be found in different treaties and forms part of customary humanitarian law, the ICJ relied upon the ordinary meaning of Art. 1(2) Additional Protocol.[102] The Court dealt with the problem that 'these principles and rules had evolved prior to the invention of nuclear weapons', while later treaties did not deal with nuclear weapons.[103] The Court concluded that the 'newness of the weapons' could not prohibit the applicability of humanitarian law.[104] The Court justified this evolutive reading with the 'intrinsically humanitarian character of the legal principles' applying to 'all forms of warfare and to all kinds of weapons, those of the past, those of the present and those of the future'.[105] This could be qualified as argumentative

---

[100] The following case is mentioned in *ibid*. 319 para. 101. The Court adduced Art. 37 ICJ Statute as an example. Yet, this provision will logically only apply when treaties have been both in force at the time of the Statute entering into force and the time of interpretation. It is hardly conceivable that a treaty referring to the Permanent Court of Justice would be concluded after the ICJ Statute entered into force on 26 June 1945. The case quoted by the ICJ is not an example to the contrary. *Case Concerning the Barcelona Traction, Light and Power Company, Limited (Belgium v. Spain)* (Preliminary Objections) [1964] ICJ Rep 28.

[101] *Case Concerning Questions of Interpretation and Application of the 1971 Montreal Convention Arising from the Aerial Incident at Lockerbie (Libyan Arab Jamahiriya v. United Kingdom)* (Preliminary Objections) [1998] ICJ Rep 16 para. 19. The Court also mentions Art. 37 ICJ Statute.

[102] *Legality of the Threat or Use of Nuclear Weapons* (Advisory Opinion) Concurring Opinion Judge Vereshchetin [1996] ICJ Rep 257 para. 78. It is true that the Court not only interpreted the respective treaties but at the same time determined the content of the respective customary law.

[103] *Ibid*. 259 para. 85.   [104] *Ibid*. 259 para. 86.   [105] *Ibid*.

technique relating to the object and purpose. As a second argument, the Court cited several statements of states during the proceedings, which could be qualified as subsequent state practice.[106] This is considered as a referential evolution of the Martens Clause as laid out in several treaties.

In the *Case Concerning the Gabčíkovo-Nagymaros Project*, the ICJ had to decide on the validity or termination of the obligations arising out of the Treaty of 16 September 1977 concerning the construction and operation of the *Gabčíkovo-Nagymaros* System of Locks. While discussing whether there might be a conflict of norms, the Court found that three provisions of that treaty incorporated environmental standards, even if those standards arose or changed after the conclusion of the treaty.[107] The Court held that the three provisions would follow the evolution of the law. Therefore, they avoided a conflict between the treaty and later environmental norms since the norms would refer to the environmental standards as they developed.

In the jurisdictional phase of the *Fisheries Jurisdiction (Spain v. Canada) Case*, the Court interpreted a reservation 'having due regard to the intention of the State concerned at the time when it accepted the compulsory jurisdiction of the Court'.[108] Again, this case is only interesting with regard to the general intertemporal stance taken since the Court from then on only interpreted statically: it took into account the circumstances at the time of the issuance of the reservation, especially 'ministerial statements, parliamentary debates, legislative proposals and press communiqués'.[109] The Court used all those materials to arrive at the 'intention which underlay the adoption of that text'. It effectively derived from the circumstances the object and purpose of the reservation, which was to protect the Canadian coastal fisheries legislation and used this

---

[106] *Ibid*. 259–60 para. 86. It is of course questionable whether the statements quoted would really qualify as subsequent practice. If one were of that opinion, one could justify that with the wide participation of many states in the proceedings and the possibility of all states to react to statements issued in the proceedings.

[107] *Case Concerning the Gabčíkovo-Nagymaros Project (Hungary v. Slovakia)* (Judgment) [1997] ICJ Rep 67–8 paras. 112–13.

[108] *Fisheries Jurisdiction (Spain v. Canada)* (Jurisdiction of the Court) [1998] ICJ Rep 454 para. 49.

[109] *Ibid*. For a critique stemming from a very narrow reading of the terms 'at the time', see *Fisheries Jurisdiction (Spain v. Canada)* (Jurisdiction of the Court), Dissenting Opinion of Judge Vereshchetin [1998] ICJ Rep 580–1 para. 22. According to *Judge Vereshchetin*, it should not be allowed to include into the considerations a bill that was discussed at the time but passed only one year later.

result for the interpretation of the term 'measures'[110] as well as the term 'conservation and management measure'.[111]

The *Kasikili/Sedudu Case* concerned the delimitation of a boundary between Namibia and Botswana around the Kasikili/Sedudu Island. The claim was based *inter alia* on a treaty dating back to 1890.[112] The Court had to deal with three interpretative issues. The Court had to determine whether the words in the authentic English and German versions 'centre of the [main] channel' and *'Thalweg des Hauptlaufes'* had the same or a different meaning. The Court acknowledged that the term *'Thalweg'* could have different meanings,[113] but it found that the parties to the treaty had used it interchangeably with the English expression.[114] Taking a static reading and referring to the 'time of the conclusion of the treaty', the Court held that the ordinary meaning of the term *'Thalweg'* was open so that it 'may be that the terms ... were used interchangeably'. Yet, the decisive argument for the synonymous use was found in the *travaux* which were the last technique to be considered.[115] Nevertheless, the Court clearly expressed a static preference in the process of treaty interpretation.

Once it was established that *'Thalweg des Hauptlaufes'* effectively meant the same as *'centre of the main channel'*, the Court went on to ascertain the criteria for the determination of the centre of the main channel. Most interestingly, 'to illuminate the meaning of the words agreed upon in 1890' the Court took into account 'present-day scientific knowledge'.[116] This evolutive reading is confirmed by the fact that the Court used present-day dictionaries to determine the ordinary meaning of the term.[117] In effect, the Court developed and applied criteria that must have been foreign, unknown and inapplicable to the parties at the time of the conclusion of the treaty.[118] Those criteria have subsequently

---

[110] *Fisheries Jurisdiction (Spain v. Canada)* (Jurisdiction of the Court) 460 para. 66.
[111] *Ibid.* 462 para. 71.
[112] *Kasikili/Sedudu Island (Botswana v. Namibia)* (Judgment) 1058 para. 17. For a full discussion of the case, see p. 239 below.
[113] *Ibid.* 1061–1062 para. 24. [114] *Ibid.* 1061–2 paras. 25–8.
[115] *Ibid.* 1062 para. 25 with reference to 1074–5 para. 46. [116] *Ibid.* 1060 para. 20.
[117] *Ibid.* 1064 para. 30.
[118] It is significant that the criteria elaborated by the Court form part of the meaning and are not methods of interpretation. They are in effect part of the meaning that is later subsumed. For the discussion of the criteria, see *ibid.* 1065 para. 32. Judge Rezek dissented on that point and found that there should be only criteria that would have been known to the parties at the time of the conclusion of the treaty. See *Kasikili/Sedudu Island (Botswana v. Namibia)* (Judgment), Dissenting Opinion of Judge Rezek [1999]

formed part of the meaning of the words, which means that there has been a contential evolutive interpretation.[119]

The Court, third, inquired into possible changes through subsequent agreement and subsequent practice but found in each case that the meaning of the treaty and, thereby, the border, had not been altered. The most contentious question was whether the presence of certain tribes people on the island could be regarded as subsequent practice which was denied by the Court.[120]

In the *Case Concerning the Land and Maritime Boundary between Cameroon and Nigeria*, the Court had to determine how the term 'mouth' of a river in a bilateral treaty concluded by a joint declaration and a subsequent exchange of notes[121] ought to be interpreted.[122] The Court held that it had to 'seek to ascertain the intention of the parties at the time'.[123] With the help of two maps from the time in question, the Court could ascertain the position of the mouth at the time of the conclusion of the treaty.[124] The Court later had to determine what the parties meant when they referred to the river 'Kohom'. The provision in question referred to that river as having its source in a mountain

---

ICJ Rep 1234 para. 4. For a similar critique of Judge Weeramantry, see *ibid*. Dissenting Opinion of Judge Weeramantry [1999] ICJ Rep 1175 para. 67. See also *ibid*., Separate Opinion Judge Oda [1999] ICJ Rep 1132-3 paras. 37-8. And *ibid*., Declaration Judge Higgins [1999] ICJ Rep 1114-15 para. 6.

[119] The evolutive interpretation rendered by the ICJ must be distinguished from a mere false application. This happens if the meaning of a term stays the same but the parties are only subsequently able to apply the treaty correctly. Let us suppose that states delimit their territory and refer for that purpose to the deepest point in a lake. If the parties due to technical insufficiencies choose the wrong point and only later find a deeper point with the help of new technical methods, the meaning in the treaty has not changed. The treaty would still refer to the deepest point, i.e. the point that is closest to the centre of the earth. The interpretative question concerning the main channel is different. The term 'main' is subject to interpretation; certain criteria determine its meaning. If the criteria change, there is necessarily a change in the meaning. This is what happened in this case. For details, see p. 247 below.

[120] *Kasikili/Sedudu Island (Botswana v. Namibia)* (Judgment) 1094ff paras. 73ff. The Court also rejected three arguments reinforcing its finding as being subsequent practice: a report from 1912 had not been made known to the other party, *ibid*. 1077 para. 55. Another joint report issued in 1947 was rejected since it was intended only to be factual, *ibid*. 1087 para. 63. A third report from 1985 was held not to establish the agreement of the parties, *ibid*. 1091 para. 68.

[121] *Case Concerning the Land and Maritime Boundary between Cameroon and Nigeria (Cameroon v. Nigeria: Equatorial Guinea Intervening)* (Judgment) [2002] ICJ Rep 332 para. 34.

[122] *Ibid*. 345-6 paras. 58-9.   [123] *Ibid*. 346 para. 59.   [124] *Ibid*. 346 paras. 59-61.

(Mount Ngossi) while the river Kohom has its source somewhere else. Taking a static approach, the Court went on 'to determine where the drafters ... intended the boundary to run in this area when they described it as following the course of a river called "Kohom"'.[125] The context of that phrase was inconclusive since none of the villages and localities mentioned could be found by the Court.[126] So the Court resorted to a map which it held showed the circumstances of the conclusion of the agreement and with the help of which it established 'what the intention of the Parties was at the time'.[127] With the help of that map the Court established that what the parties meant by river Kohom was actually the river Bogaza.

In the *Wall Opinion*, the ICJ had to determine whether the General Assembly acted *ultra vires* and specifically against Art. 12 UN Charter by dealing with issues of peace and security while the Security Council remained occupied with the matter. The Court, however, found that the practice of the organs of the United Nations had evolved in that regard and determined a change in the interpretation of the treaty in the sense that Art. 12 would now not prohibit the involvement of the General Assembly in those situations.[128] This clearly denoted a contential evolution. The Court indicated that the Security Council had often dealt with the hard issues of peace and security while the General Assembly then addressed the wider implications of the conflict such as 'humanitarian, social and economic aspects', but it did not put this in a way that would restrict the General Assembly to dealing with those issues.[129]

In the *Navigational and Related Rights Case*, Costa Rica and Nicaragua argued over sovereignty and the right to ship on the San Juan river.[130] These questions were governed by the Treaty of Limits of 15 April 1858

---

[125] *Ibid.* 366 para. 100.   [126] *Ibid.* 366 para. 101.   [127] *Ibid.* 367 para. 101.

[128] *Legal Consequences of the Construction of a Wall in the Occupied Palestinian Territory* (Advisory Opinion) [2004] ICJ Rep 148–50 paras. 25–8. This case has been taken to be an evolutive interpretation. It is of course true that the *Court* only stated that the practice evolved and not the law itself. Nevertheless, this case is counted as explicit evolutive interpretation for several reasons. First, the *Court* also refers to a precedent from which it seems that under the previous state of the law, there was no such exception, *ibid.* 148–9 para. 26. Secondly, the *Court* has stressed the responsibility of the organs of the United Nations to interpret the UN Charter. So an evolution in the organ's practice could be said to represent an evolution in the law.

[129] *Ibid.* 150 para. 27.

[130] For discussions of the intertemporal aspects, see Tanaka, 'Navigational Rights on the San Juan River' 215; Dawidowicz, 'The Effect of the Passage of Time on the Interpretation of Treaties' 201; Nolte, 'Between Contemporaneous and Evolutive Interpretation'.

which stipulated in its Art. VI that Nicaragua had sovereignty over the river while Costa Rica retained the right to ship on the river 'con objetos de comercio', which was translated by the Court to mean 'for the purposes of commerce'.[131] The question was now whether commerce would include shipping tourists on the said river. The Court did not decide on Nicaragua's contention that the notion of commerce only referred to trade in goods at the time but held that even if there was a difference in meaning, the current meaning which would include tourism prevailed. The Court held that the term 'comercio' was generic and adaptable to new developments and had in fact changed in the sense that tourism, which might not have been included in 1858, would now fall under the respective provision of the treaty.[132] The Court relied on the ordinary meaning of the treaty,[133] second on its context,[134] and third on its object and purpose.[135] Interestingly, the Court did mention but did not use the technique of subsequent practice even though two judges showed that the same conclusion could have been arrived at by relying on this technique.[136]

In the *Pulp Mills on the River Uruguay Case*, Argentina claimed that the authorisation of one pulp mill and the actual construction of another by Uruguay on the river Uruguay, which is the boundary between the two states, violated international law.[137] Both parties had concluded a treaty in 1975 that implemented several obligations and an international organisation with legal capacity.[138] In the context of the proceedings, an intertemporal question of interpretation arose.[139] Argentina claimed that

---

[131] *Case Concerning the Dispute Regarding Navigational and Related Rights (Costa Rica v. Nicaragua)* (Judgment) 240 para. 56.
[132] *Ibid.* 244 para. 70.   [133] It denoted the term as being *generic ibid.* 243 para. 67.
[134] Here, it is referred to the rest of the text of the treaty which does not provide for a date of termination. *Ibid.* 243-4 paras. 67, 69.
[135] *Ibid.* 243 para. 68.
[136] *Case Concerning the Dispute Regarding Navigational and Related Rights (Costa Rica v. Nicaragua)* (Judgment) Separate Opinion Judge Skotnikov [2009] ICJ Rep 285 paras. 8–10.
[137] *Pulp Mills on the River Uruguay Case (Argentina v. Uruguay)* (Judgment) [2010] ICJ Rep 14.
[138] Vienna Convention on the Law of Treaties (adopted 23 May 1969, entered into force 27 January 1980) 1155 UNTS 331 (VCLT). Statute of the River Uruguay (signed 26 February 1975, entered into force 18 September 1976) 1295 UNTS 340 ('1975 Statute').
[139] Another intertemporal issue was raised, yet, not decided. Art. 60 of the 1975 Statute established the jurisdiction of the ICJ for '[a]ny dispute concerning the interpretation or application of the treaty'. Argentina claimed that this would encompass other

Table 4 *Frequency of intertemporal instances at the ICJ*

	Total	Static	Evolutive
Intertemporal instances	25 (100%)	9 (36%)	16 (64%)
Unjustified interpretations as compared to interpretations in total	10 (40%)	6 (66.67%)	4 (25%)

Uruguay had violated Art. 41(a) of the 1975 statute which obliged the parties 'to protect and preserve the aquatic environment and, in particular, to prevent its pollution, by prescribing appropriate rules and [adopting appropriate] measures in accordance with applicable international agreements and in keeping, where relevant, with the guidelines and recommendations of international technical bodies'.[140] The Court agreed with the parties that this provision also entailed an obligation for an environmental impact assessment and clarified the intertemporal question lying behind this assumption. Citing the *Dispute Regarding Navigational and Related Rights*, the ICJ held that Art. 41(a) ought to be interpreted evolutively and that an environmental impact assessment ought to be read into the obligation.[141] The Court argued with the practice of states which resulted in a customary international obligation to make environmental impact assessments.[142]

This exercise of stocktaking offers interesting insights from the perspective of frequency, which is summarised in Table 4.[143] Twenty-five intertemporal issues have been counted; 16 have been decided evolutively and 9 statically. In 4 out of 16 (25 per cent) the Court resorted to evolutive

---

environmental norms not contained in the treaty applicable to the River Uruguay. Argentina relied on Arts. 1 and 41 of the 1975 Statute as well as on Art. 31(3)(c) VCLT in order to show that the treaty actually did refer to norms outside of the treaty. Had the ICJ decided that there actually was such a reference, an intertemporal question could have arisen. Yet, the ICJ denied that there was a reference, and consequently no intertemporal question arose. See *ibid*. paras. 48–66.

[140] *Pulp Mills on the River Uruguay Case (Argentina v. Uruguay)* (Judgment).
[141] *Ibid*. 83 para. 204.
[142] *Ibid*. Even though the Court mentioned the practice of states, in the context of its statement it becomes clear that it did not use the technique of subsequent practice as enshrined in Art. 31(3)(b) VCLT. The Court referred to the general practice of all states and not to the parties to the 1975 Statute.
[143] The numbers given are not statistically significant for the interpretative results but are only meant to illustrate the findings.

interpretations without making any arguments while the Court did not argue in 6 out of 9 (66.67 per cent) static interpretations. In the evolutive cases, the Court resorted 8 times to referential and 8 times to contential evolution. As to the static results, the Court interpreted 2 times statically in questions of referential evolution and 2 times in questions of contential evolution; 5 times the Court only asserted that it would interpret statically without opening up an intertemporal question. Regarding the nature of the treaty, we can see that border treaties have been interpreted 5 times statically and 4 times evolutively. The ICJ Statute and the Act of Peaceful Settlement of Disputes have been interpreted 3 times dynamically and once statically. Reservations to treaties have been interpreted both ways twice. The mandate agreement concerning South West Africa has been interpreted 3 times in an evolutive manner and once statically. The UN Charter and international humanitarian law have been interpreted evolutively once. Regarding the participation of states, the ratio between static and evolutive interpretations is '2:2' for unilateral declarations, '5:6' for bilateral, '1:5' for multilateral, and '1:3' for universal treaties.[144] These numbers indicate that the structure and classification of the treaty are at least not decisive factors for those questions. One interesting observation is that the majority of static interpretation was assumed without any argument whereas the majority of evolutive interpretations required arguments by the parties.[145]

9.2.2 *Related forms of interpretation*

Some interesting cases do not fall within the confines of this study, yet knowledge of similar cases will increase the appreciation of intertemporal questions: there are first possible interpretations in accordance with the law of the future, fuzzy decisions in which a change in the interpretation is unclear and interpretations that merely ascertain the meaning of treaties or in which the termination of treaties is at issue.

While static interpretations look backwards, the Court has also had to deal with the question whether it could take into account the law as it will

---

[144] The mandate agreement as well as the First Additional Protocol were counted as multilateral treaties.
[145] This could be taken as an indication that the path-dependency argument is backed up by the argumentative practice of the Court. The path-dependency argument assumed that if the state of the law was backed up by arguments at a certain point in time, it would need at least one argument in order to arrive at a change of meaning. Therefore, there was a burden of reasoning for evolutive interpretations.

stand in the future.[146] This may sound adventurous, but the Court has in effect already considered this idea. But the ICJ has in contentious cases regularly declined to do so. It has insisted 'to render a judgment on the basis of the law as it exists at the time of its decision'.[147] When Tunisia and Libya empowered the Court through a special agreement to take account of 'new accepted trends in the Third Conference on the Law of the Sea',[148] the Court was asked by one of the parties to take into account those trends as factors in the interpretation of treaties.[149] The Court pursued two ways of incorporating those trends: Either to the degree that they became part of customary international law[150] or through the interpretation of the special agreement of the parties.[151] The Court looked into the extent to which the parties accepted the new trends as accepted rules, but did not find anything significant for the resolution of the case.[152] This way, the Court reinforced its general approach not to look for possible future events such as the ratification of the trends already expressed at the conference but included the results as far as it could through the ordinary methods of international law.

Subsequent agreements or subsequent practice can have the function of changing the meaning in treaties. But they can also be used as arguments to illuminate the meaning without changing it.[153] Even when the practice goes beyond or against the ordinary meaning, no intertemporal questions need necessarily arise.[154] The fuzzy cases are those in which we cannot say whether the Court has changed the law or not. To do so would in itself amount to an interpretation. One example is the advisory opinion *Interpretation of Peace Treaties*: The articles in question provided for the establishment of a commission for the settlement of disputes.[155] While it was for the parties to select one commissioner, the Secretary General was competent to select the third in the absence of further agreement of the parties. The question before the Court was

---

[146] *Fisheries Jurisdiction (United Kingdom v. Iceland)* (Merits) 23–4 para. 53.
[147] Ibid. 19 para. 40.
[148] *Continental Shelf (Tunisia v. Libyan Arab Jamahiriya)* (Judgment) [1982] ICJ Rep 23 para. 4.
[149] Ibid. 38 para. 24.   [150] Ibid.   [151] Ibid. 48–9 para. 48.   [152] Ibid. 48 para. 48.
[153] *Certain Expenses of the United Nations* (Advisory Opinion) [1962] ICJ Rep 160. The practice was considered to be 'consistent with the plain meaning of the text'. No change in the interpretation was at issue.
[154] See for example *Land, Island and Maritime Frontier Dispute* (Judgment) [1992] ICJ Rep 586 para. 380. Here the ordinary meaning of the text of the treaty was considered to be more important than the subsequent practice.
[155] *Interpretation of Peace Treaties* (Advisory Opinion, Second Phase) [1950] ICJ Rep 227.

whether the Secretary General also had the right to select the third commissioner without one party having selected its commissioner. One could ask whether the case of one party not having selected a commissioner amounts to an unforeseen circumstance. The ICJ, however, dealt with the issue as if it was within what the parties envisaged. Consequently, no change can be established. There are also some examples of rendering norms more concrete. In the already mentioned *Namibia opinion*, the Court had to decide whether Resolution 284 (1970) of the Security Council was valid. Art. 27(3) UN Charter provides that '[d]ecisions of the Security Council on all other matters shall be made by an affirmative vote of nine members including the concurring votes of the permanent members'; but two permanent members had abstained from voting. The ICJ held that due to the generally accepted organ practice an abstention could be regarded as an affirmative vote.[156] The Court framed the practice as consistent and uniform so it left the question open whether there was a change or whether this was to be considered as the correct interpretation from the outset.[157] In the *Frontier Dispute Case*, a treaty referred back to a decision of a state official determining a border, and the question before the Court was whether this decision was amended by something like subsequent practice.[158] Since the decision is not an international treaty, this falls outside of the scope of the present inquiry even though it resembles questions of stasis and evolution in many ways.[159] In the *Fisheries Jurisdiction Case*, the ICJ had to determine its jurisdiction which seemingly went beyond the ordinary meaning of the agreed terms. The ICJ looked to the subsequent conduct of the parties but also affirmed the meaning via the preparatory works.[160] Again, the meaning is ascertained and not changed.

The ICJ has for example assumed the legal personality of the United Nations as implied competences given to the organisation in the *Reparations for Injuries Case*. Yet, in its reasoning it made clear that those powers were conferred upon the Organisation from the beginning of

---

[156] *Legal Consequences for States of the Continued Presence of South Africa in Namibia (South West Africa) Notwithstanding Security Council Resolution 276 (1970)* (Advisory Opinion) 22 para. 23.
[157] *Ibid.*
[158] *Frontier Dispute (Burkina Faso/Niger)* 2013 www.icj-cij.org/docket/files/149/17306.pdf (accessed 10 June 2013) 37 paras. 77–9.
[159] *Ibid.* 37 para. 77.
[160] *Fisheries Jurisdiction (United Kingdom v. Iceland)* (Merits) 21 para. 47.

its existence.¹⁶¹ There was no change in the interpretation of the UN Charter. The Court has on several occasions had to deal with necessary implications, in particular in the context of competences. In the *Asylum Case*, the Court had to answer the question whether one state could define the respective crimes unilaterally.¹⁶² The Court denied the necessary implication of such a competence.¹⁶³

Changes in the circumstances can not only lead to changed interpretations but also to claims of termination and obsolescence. These affect not exclusively the meaning of terms but the validity of a part of a treaty. In the *Aerial Incident Case*, the Court had to deal with the question whether a reservation restricting jurisdiction in cases in which the other party is a commonwealth country is obsolete after the demise of the commonwealth. Pakistan had claimed that the historical reasons for the insertion of this clause were a plan to provide for a system of adjudication between those countries.¹⁶⁴ It argued that after the demise of the commonwealth, this clause was obsolete. Taking a static approach, the Court argued that the text made specific provisions for the reservation and did include former members of the commonwealth.¹⁶⁵ Under these circumstances, the Court rejected that a change in the circumstances could change the meaning of the terms that Pakistan had included in its four subsequent reservations.¹⁶⁶

9.3. General approaches

When faced with a question of evolution and stasis, the ICJ very generally asserts that it would inquire into the intentions of the parties to the treaty.¹⁶⁷ What the Court effectively does to achieve that aim has varied

---

[161] *Reparations for Injuries Suffered in the Service of the United Nations* (Judgment) [1949] ICJ Rep 178.
[162] *Colombian-Peruvian Asylum Case (Colombia v. Peru)* (Judgment) [1950] ICJ Rep 266.
[163] Ibid.
[164] *Aerial Incident of 10 August 1999 (Pakistan v. India)* (Jurisdiction of the Court) [1999] ICJ Rep 26 para. 30.
[165] Ibid. 31 para. 44.   [166] Ibid. 31 paras. 43–4.
[167] See for example *Rights of Nationals of the United States of America in Morocco (France v. United States of America)* (Judgment) 191; *South West Africa (Ethiopia v. South Africa; Liberia v. South Africa)* (Second Phase) [1966] ICJ Rep 23 para. 16. For unilateral instruments such as reservations, see *Aegean Sea Continental Shelf Case (Greece v. Turkey)* (Judgment) 32 para. 77; *Fisheries Jurisdiction Case (Spain v. Canada)* (Judgment) [1998] ICJ Rep 454 paras. 48–9; *Anglo-Iranian Oil Case (United Kingdom v. Iran)* (Judgment) [1952] ICJ Rep 104. For the use of the more neutral term 'meaning' in

and did develop significantly over time. First, static and dynamic approaches coexisted peacefully, when the Court stressed its static approach openly and interpreted dynamically only implicitly. Then came a clash between two groups of judges at the Court and the Court changed its intertemporal stance twice in a very short period of time. There was a camp of judges that would further a static interpretation while the other camp at least acknowledged the possibility of evolutive interpretations. This clash resulted in the first openly acknowledged evolutive interpretation. In a third phase, the jurisprudence slowly but steadily opened up towards a more dynamic stance.

9.3.1 Peaceful coexistence: Rights of US Nationals in Morocco

A very good example for the 'peaceful co-existence approach' is the case *Concerning the Rights of Nationals of the United States in Morocco*. The ICJ referred to a static interpretation as 'necessary' without any argument supporting it.[168] As previously described,[169] the Court held that the most-favoured-nations clause would evolve, which was held to apply always to present circumstances. Given that the ICJ interpreted the most-favoured-nations clause evolutively, one would have expected the Court to make more efforts to justify the static interpretation. Yet, it did what it usually did in that time: affirming the static approach openly and interpreting evolutively without stating it openly. There is a certain irony in the fact that a case that also contained an evolutive interpretation is today widely considered as a landmark case for static interpretation.

In the *Anglo-Iranian Oil Case*, the Court held that reservations are to be interpreted with a focus on the time of their issuance even though this was not crucial for deciding the case. The Court found that the readings of both parties were grammatically possible. After asserting that the Court would have regard to the intention of the declaring state at the time the declaration was made, the Court went on to make grammatical arguments: It mentioned the conjunction '*et*' as well as the proximity of the words achieved in one possible construction which seemed more 'natural' to the Court.[170] The reasons adduced by the court are valid,

---

another context, see for example *Case Concerning Oil Platforms (Islamic Republic of Iran v. United States of America)* (Judgment) [2003] ICJ Rep 206 para. 96.

[168] *Rights of Nationals of the United States of America in Morocco (France v. United States of America)* (Judgment) 188.

[169] *Anglo-Iranian Oil Case (United Kingdom v. Iran)* (Judgment) 104.   [170] Ibid. 104.

yet they have no intertemporal significance: They had the same force in 1932, when the government of Persia issued the reservation as in 1952 when the Court decided the case. This clearly shows that the intertemporal stance taken by the ICJ was rather to be taken as an *obiter dictum*.

The bottom line and the constant approach of the ICJ is very well captured by Judge Spender:[171] interpretation was generally the inquiry into the meaning as it stood at the time of the conclusion of the treaty. This meaning could only be modified by the object and purpose. No mention is made of an explicit evolution. This allowed the Court to settle all disputes peacefully and give way to the evolutive interpretations where necessary. Yet, there was an inherent tension since the problem of evolution was never explicitly mentioned. Therefore, the question when and how it could be justified remained undetermined. The danger of a clash was evident. This actually happened in the *South West Africa Case*, when two African states instituted proceedings against South Africa, the mandate power in Namibia.

9.3.2 The clash: From South West Africa to Namibia

The situation in South West Africa had occupied the Court previously, yet in the *South West Africa Case* it was very hard for the Court to reach agreement. In the first judgment concerning admissibility, the Court held that the mandate agreement allowed standing for the two states by an eight to seven majority.[172] To do that, it had to interpret this mandate agreement evolutively. In the merits phase, the Court held that the mandate agreement conferred standing upon the states but no subjective rights so that their claim would necessarily be ill-founded. The Court reached this decision with the judges being equally split so that the decision depended on the casting vote of President Spender. Instead of acknowledging at least implicitly that evolutive interpretation was possible, the Court endorsed the real intentions of the parties and tied the interpretation to the time of the conclusion of the mandate and the

---

[171] *Certain Expenses of the United Nations* (Advisory Opinion) Separate Opinion of Judge Spender [1962] ICJ Rep 186.
[172] *South West Africa Cases (Ethiopia v. South Africa; Liberia v. South Africa)* (Preliminary Objections). In relation to the voting patterns, see Bernhardt, 'Homogenität, Kontinuität und Dissonanzen in der Rechtsprechung des Internationalen Gerichtshofs' 6.

Covenant. The approaches taken are as contradictory as they could have been.

In the judgment during the preliminary phase, the Court did not make it explicit that it would effectively be changing the meaning but clothed the general question whether only members of the League of Nations had *locus standi* in different terms. It framed this question as a weighing exercise between the 'natural and ordinary meaning' and 'spirit, purpose and context' of the clause.[173]

In the second phase, the Court went exactly in the opposite direction and employed an extremely static approach. To answer the questions of interpretation before the Court it found that:

> [the Court] must place itself at the point in time when the mandates system was being instituted, and when the instruments of the mandate were framed. The Court must have regard to the situation as it was at that time, which was the critical one, and to the intentions of those concerned as they appear to have existed, at or are reasonably inferred, in the light of that situation. Intentions that might have been formed if the Mandate had been framed at a much later date, and in the knowledge of circumstances, such as the eventual dissolution of the League and its aftermath, that could never originally have been foreseen, are not relevant. Only on this basis can a correct appreciation of the legal rights of the Parties be arrived at.[174]

This can be regarded as an extremely static stance. The Court really put itself in the shoes of the parties at the relevant point in time and proposed to act as if its knowledge was limited to the point in time when the relevant instruments were drawn up. Even though it allows some scope for the intentions that are reasonably to be assumed, it is not even allowed to depart from the knowledge of the parties at the particular point in time. But it then happened that a similar question came before the Court one more time, when asked by the Security Council for an advisory opinion on Namibia.

In this case, the Court could have evaded the question of stasis and evolution since the question of the subjective rights of certain states was not before it and the question of the continuation of the mandate system had been decided several times.[175] Nevertheless, the Court decided to

---

[173] *South West Africa Cases (Ethiopia v. South Africa; Liberia v. South Africa)* (Preliminary Objections) 336.

[174] *South West Africa (Ethiopia v. South Africa; Liberia v. South Africa)* (Second Phase) 23 para. 16.

[175] Dugard, 'The Opinion on South-West Africa ('Namibia')' 464.

reconsider the question.[176] After setting out the general development of the law, it used the opportunity to change its stance again and endorse a change through interpretation openly and expressly:

> Mindful as it is of the primary necessity of interpreting an instrument in accordance with the intentions of the parties at the time of its conclusion, the Court is bound to take into account the fact that the concepts embodied in Article 22 of the Covenant – 'the strenuous conditions of the modern world' and 'the well-being and development' of the peoples concerned – were not static, but were by definition evolutionary, as also, therefore, was the concept of the 'sacred trust'. The parties to the Covenant must consequently be deemed to have accepted them as such. That is why, viewing the institutions of 1919, the Court must take into consideration the changes which have occurred in the supervening half-century, and its interpretation cannot remain unaffected by the subsequent development of law, through the Charter of the United Nations and by way of customary law. Moreover, an international instrument has to be interpreted and applied within the framework of the entire legal system prevailing at the time of the interpretation.

It is significant that the Court departed from the intentions of the parties, but held that the certain terms had an evolutive nature and were susceptible to evolution. They could not be interpreted differently. So the parties were 'deemed' to have accepted that meaning. It was not their real intention but their intention was necessarily implied. A close reading, therefore, reveals a ping-pong argument that is very well explicable by the context of the two preceding judgments concerning South West Africa. In the first place, this was a very clear and open move towards open and explicit changes in the interpretation of treaties. It was a clear rejection of the previous explicit static approach that could only be overcome implicitly by the object and purpose. But this move by the Court was not a radical break from its previous stance in all respects. Moreover, the Court tried to find a middle ground between the two extreme positions. It sought compromise.

The evolution of the law was tied to the intentions of the parties as they could be ascertained at the time of the conclusion of the treaty. So the starting point was static, but the Court asserted the power to overcome this static approach since it could necessarily infer an evolutive

---

[176] *Legal Consequences for States of the Continued Presence of South Africa in Namibia (South West Africa) Notwithstanding Security Council Resolution 276 (1970)* (Advisory Opinion) 27.

outcome from the use of certain terms. If it is accepted that the terms were 'by definition evolutionary', no further arguments are necessary. Since the Court did not really explain how it ascertained the nature of the terms, this seemed to rest within the discretion of the Court. So after the clash, the Court endorsed evolutive interpretation openly but in a balanced manner.

9.3.3 Cooperation: between the Aegean Continental Shelf and the Kasikili/Sedudu Islands

In the *Aegean Continental Shelf Case*, the Court looked first at the intention of Greece when issuing its reservation to the General Act of 1928. After considering all techniques of interpretation, it established that Greece had used a 'generic term'. When such terms were used, a presumption in favour of evolutive interpretation would 'necessarily' arise.[177] If so, there was a strong presumption in favour of an evolutive interpretation. In comparison to the previously discussed *Namibia opinion*, the notion of generic terms developed the concept used in Namibia that some terms were by definition evolutionary: The generic nature of the term is at least in part conferred by the party and does not attach to the nature of the term.[178] In a way, the Court stressed the idea that the meaning of some terms can be developed while a certain class of terms resisted such changes. It reinforced the compromise of first looking at the intentions of the parties at the time when the treaty was drafted and only then looking at whether the parties allowed for a departure through interpretation. As shown above, the Court interpreted three different terms as to their present-day conditions and explicitly mentioned this. As in the case of the term 'rights' contained in Art. 17 of the Act of Settlement of 1928, the Court showed how natural and self-evident it is that some terms necessarily follow the evolution of the law or other circumstances. No one would object that such a jurisdictional clause could also apply to future treaties. The increased focus on the intentions[179] might be explained by the fact that the case concerned a unilateral declaration or as a small concession to the originalist camp. There is still a possibility to distinguish this precedent from the ordinary rules of

---

[177] *Aegean Sea Continental Shelf Case (Greece v. Turkey)* (Judgment) 32 para. 77.
[178] *Ibid.*
[179] This refers to the dependence of generic terms on the intentions of the parties.

treaty interpretation.[180] Yet, the case also showed that evolutive interpretation must not always produce results that could be considered as 'progressive internationalist'. The changed reading of the reservation widened its scope and limited the jurisdiction of the ICJ itself. This might have been the perfect setting for the 'originalist camp' to tolerate an evolutive interpretation. Under these circumstances, the 'evolutive camp' used the moment so that the Court in this case resorted to evolutive interpretation on three different occasions. This perfect setting might be the reason why this case became the *locus classicus*, whereas we will see that the *Namibia opinion* is rarely cited by the Court. The fact that the Court found a good compromise could also be reinforced by the *Case Concerning the Gabčíkovo-Nagymaros Project*. The ICJ found that the parties had included 'evolving provisions' that would 'require the parties ... to take new environmental norms into consideration'.[181] Again, it departed from the intentions of the parties[182] but found that they themselves included a dynamic element which could justify changes through interpretation.

The ICJ also took this stance when dealing with border treaties. In these instances, it departed from a static starting point and departed from the original meaning only when indicated by subsequent practice[183] or to resort to silent evolution. The *Kasikili/Sedudu Case* is a good example for such a silent evolution: while the ICJ established the mouth of a river with maps contemporaneous with the conclusion of the treaty,[184] and also looked at this point in time to see whether the term 'main channel'

---

[180] This actually was stressed in *Fisheries Jurisdiction (Spain v. Canada)* (Jurisdiction of the Court) 453. The Court held that the provisions ought to apply 'analogously to the extent compatible with the *sui generis* character of the unilateral acceptance of the Court's jurisdiction'. This was in the case of a unilateral reservation.

[181] *Case Concerning the Gabčíkovo-Nagymaros Project (Hungary v. Slovakia)* (Judgment) [1997] ICJ Rep 67 para. 112.

[182] The Court emphasised that it was the parties that 'recognised' the evolution of the treaty by inserting evolving provisions. *Case Concerning the Gabčíkovo-Nagymaros Project (Hungary v. Slovakia)* (Judgment) [1997] ICJ Rep 67 para. 112.

[183] For the general possibility, see *Case Concerning the Land and Maritime Boundary between Cameroon and Nigeria (Cameroon v. Nigeria: Equatorial Guinea Intervening)* (Judgment), Dissenting Opinion Judge Ajibola [2002] ICJ Rep 580 para. 132.

[184] *Case Concerning the Land and Maritime Boundary between Cameroon and Nigeria (Cameroon v. Nigeria: Equatorial Guinea Intervening)* (Judgment) 346 paras. 59-61. Another interesting and parallel case worth mentioning is the Frontier Dispute Case. The Court had to interpret several administrative orders that became relevant for international law as the internal French border was internationalised according to the principle of *uti possidetis* in the process of decolonisation. In the course of its argument,

meant the same as 'Thalweg', it used present-day scientific methods to determine what centre of the main channel meant. The Court had to pick one of two channels. While it was assumed that the geographical situation had not changed,[185] the Court defined the term with several factors that were themselves to be determined by scientific methods. Some of the factors such as the width[186] of the channel could have also been determined by the parties at the time of the conclusion of the treaty; others like the flow[187] and aerial photography[188] would not have been available to the parties. If we reconsider the semiotic triangle,[189] 'main channel' is the sign while the factors established by the respective scientific methods are to be taken as the meaning of the term. The two channels are the possible referents. Since the very criteria that constituted the concept of 'main channel' changed, it is necessary to define this as evolutive interpretation. The judgment shows how answering the question of evolutive interpretation can be the crucial part in a decision, as the changed treaty refers to a different object.

The materials before the Court show that the parties would have approached the determination of the main channel in a much less refined way. The Court cites a letter from the British Secretary of State for the Colonies dated 14 July 1911 in which information is requested that can also be used before an arbitral tribunal.[190] Yet, the Secretary of State refers only to a map and measurement of the streams. This evidence indicates that the determination of the border with the means available at the time of the conclusion would have resulted in a different line. And

the Court took a rigorously static approach that can be contrasted very well with the subsequent approach in the *Kasikili/Sedudu Case*.

> *It takes as a starting-point of its reasoning the fact, attested by Order 2728 AP, that in 1935 the administrative authorities were aware of the existence, close to the boundary between the cercles of Mopti and Ouahigouya, of four villages bearing the names of Dioulouna, Oukoulou, Agoulourou and Koubo. At this stage the Chamber must remain solely within the context of 1932 (the reference date in the 1947 law for the purpose of defining the boundaries of Upper Volta) and 1935; it is not required to consider whether the villages in question still exist today, or whether they still bear the same names. Similarly, in order to ascertain the intentions of the Governor-General in 1935, it has to consider only such maps and documents as existed at the time.*

Frontier Dispute (Burkina Faso v. Republic of Mali) (Judgment) 605 para. 95.
[185] *Kasikili/Sedudu Island (Botswana v. Namibia)* (Judgment) 1065 para. 31.
[186] *Ibid.* 1066 para. 33.   [187] *Ibid.* 1066–7 para. 34.   [188] *Ibid.* 1069.
[189] See pp. 11–12 below.   [190] *Ibid.* 1077 para. 53.

indeed the Court came to the conclusion that the parties drew the line differently until 1948,[191] when a joint report and the availability amongst other things of an aerial photograph offered more information to the parties.[192] Had the Court really stuck to the approach of looking at the intentions of the parties, it would have had to take account of a factual joint report by the parties which came to the conclusion that this is not ascertainable since a flood might have changed the course of the river.[193] The way the Court construed the meaning of the term 'centre of the main channel' but also the facts the Court applied it to show that the Court as well as the parties departed not only from what the parties could have meant but also from the factual situation the parties faced. It is hard to contend that this does not amount to an evolutive interpretation.[194] Even though this case is often cited as a precedent for static results, it also contains an instance of evolutive interpretation. On the other hand, the Court has openly acknowledged that border treaties can be changed through interpretation if subsequent practice was used.

As the *Preah Vihear Case* shows, border treaties can be open to evolution since the chosen method of delimitation – using the watershed line – did not have the purpose and was considered to be 'insufficient by itself to achieve certainty and finality'.[195] So the Court allowed for the possibility to change the border through interpretation. It is significant that the evolution happens in the context of the subsequent practice of the parties. This is reinforced by the third interpretative question in the *Kasikili/Sedudu Case* in which the Court in the context of a border treaty clearly acknowledged that the meaning of a treaty could be altered by interpretation and in particular by the techniques of subsequent practice and subsequent agreement.[196] Since the Court was unable to find any practice and agreement, the meaning of the treaty was not being altered.[197] Subsequent practice as well as a border treaty played

---

[191] *Ibid*. 1086 para. 62 conclusion (2). This conclusion is also reinforced later by several maps that regarded the other route as the main channel until 1948.
[192] *Ibid*. There were several aerial photographs taken, starting from 1925: see *ibid*. 1065 para. 31.
[193] *Ibid*. 1088–9 para. 64. Yet, the Court as well as both parties assumed that the course of the river was not changed, *ibid*. 1065 para. 31.
[194] See also the critical remarks by *Kasikili/Sedudu Island (Botswana v. Namibia)* (Judgment) Declaration Judge Higgins 114 paras. 3–4.
[195] *Case Concerning the Temple of Preah Vihear (Cambodia v. Thailand)* (Merits) 34.
[196] See the extensive analysis in Nolte, 'Treaties over Time: Introductory Report' 183, 199.
[197] *Kasikili/Sedudu Island (Botswana v. Namibia)* (Judgment) 1095 para. 75.

significant roles in the *Navigational and Related Rights Case* in which a slight but important shift in approach can be detected.

9.3.4 Beyond cooperation: the Navigational and Related Rights Case

In the *Navigational and Related Rights Case*, the approach of the Court resembles the approaches in *Namibia* and the *Aegean Continental Shelf Case*: Departing from the intentions of the parties at the time of the conclusion of the treaty, the Court provides for two exceptions. At the outset, it stresses that 'the terms used in a treaty must be interpreted in the light of what is determined to have been the parties' common intention, which is, by definition, contemporaneous with the treaty's conclusion'.[198] However, the Court also identifies two situations in which the interpreter could go beyond original meaning: either the subsequent practice as described in Art. 31(3)(b) VCLT or 'situations in which the parties' intent upon conclusion of the treaty was, or may be presumed to have been, to give the terms used – or some of them – a meaning or content capable of evolving, not one fixed once and for all'.[199] While the first alternative will allow a variation of the perceived original meaning, the second looks for the original meaning and tries to determine whether the parties at the time of the conclusion of the treaty intended to give the term a potentially evolving meaning.

Three features of the general approach taken by the Court deserve special mention: these are the use of subsequent practice, the opposition of subsequent practice and evolutive interpretation and the shift of the Court's goal towards the assumed intentions of the parties.

The Court acknowledges that one way to depart from the original intentions of the parties is the use of subsequent practice. While the Court had implicitly acknowledged this before, it now incorporated this possibility into its general approach and increased the visibility and the general importance of subsequent practice. Yet, it is very interesting that the Court seems to distinguish subsequent practice from evolutive interpretation.

This effectively splits subsequent practice from the other techniques of interpretation. The ICJ seems to transgress the single combined approach: The formula indicates that there are two rules instead of one

---

[198] *Case Concerning the Dispute Regarding Navigational and Related Rights (Costa Rica v. Nicaragua)* (Judgment) 242 para. 63.
[199] *Ibid.* 242 para. 64.

rule of interpretation for intertemporal questions, namely, subsequent practice and evolutive interpretation. From the perspective of the present study, the ICJ could be said to rightly lay emphasis upon two distinctive features of subsequent practice. First, it directly relates to the behaviour of those applying the treaty – often the parties to the treaty – which might possibly increase its argumentative weight. In the terms of the ICJ, one could say that it 'can result in a departure from the original intent on the basis of a tacit agreement between the parties'.[200] The other fact is that subsequent practice is necessarily subsequent. This technique can by definition not be used in the way it stood at the time the treaty was set up. While these special features distinguish subsequent practice from the other means of interpretation, this does not necessarily mean that it has to be separated in the process of treaty interpretation. Suppose for example that it was not entirely clear whether the parties intended to include a generic term or whether they wanted to fix the meaning. Why should one not also look at their subsequent practice and throw it into the crucible with all the other arguments? Other techniques can have the same or an even stronger argumentative value and, therefore, be said to be linked to the intention of the parties. The relevant rules as defined in Art. 31(3)(c) VCLT are also linked to the parties; they can also be taken into account when they come into existence after the rule to be interpreted. So the distinctive features in no way make it necessary to separate the process of interpretation. In this light, the distinction drawn by the ICJ seems artificial at best and misleading and wrong in the worst case. Yet, the Court adhered to its 'two rules' construction and did not inquire into subsequent practice even though the use of this technique would have reinforced the result the Court reached. This attracted the criticism of two dissenting judges, one of whom explained the attitude with the rather 'mechanical application of the jurisprudence'.[201] There is also another explanation: The dispute between the two camps might have moved beyond cooperation, and the discourse at the bench might have changed its centre: Whereas the discourse previously centred around whether to interpret evolutively or not, the judges at the Court now disagree about the question how to interpret evolutively. While one camp tries to establish justification based on the nature of the terms and the object and purpose, the other camp leans more towards subsequent

---

[200] Ibid.
[201] *Case Concerning the Dispute Regarding Navigational and Related Rights (Costa Rica v. Nicaragua)* (Judgment) Separate Opinion Judge Skotnikov 284 para. 6.

practice. Like the schools of interpretation in the codificatory phase, the camps at the bench try to emphasise certain means of interpretation. In this light, cutting out subsequent practice might not have been a mechanical application of precedents but a move to build up precedents of evolutive interpretations based on the ordinary meaning and the purpose. What is more, there is also another significant shift in the approach of the Court.

The fact that the Court finds the interpreter to be competent to 'presume' the parties' intent shows that the parties must not have made their intention explicit. The fact that the ICJ refers here not only to the intention but to the presumed intention must not be underestimated: It effectively allows the Court to assume itself to be in the position of the legislator but also assume an increased and updated knowledge. The question is then what the legislator would have done, had it known of subsequent developments. The difference between real intentions and presumed intentions was clearly seen by the Judges Spender and Fitzmaurice, who opposed the idea of presumed intentions.[202] In the same line, Judge van Wyk distinguished 'true intentions' from implications, and stressed that only the true intentions could be the legitimate aim of interpretation.[203] His conclusions then indeed arrive at the 'truth' about what the parties really contemplated.[204] Judge Tanaka explicitly defines and discusses the concept of 'reasonably assumed intentions'.[205] Theoretically, this concept would link voluntarism with the inclusion of social necessities.[206] This concept explicitly departs from the 'psychological intention' and is wider in the sense that the quest for this kind of intention allows for all kinds of factors to be included, be they legal or extra-legal.[207] The difference between real intentions and assumed intentions looks small on paper. The historical reflection of interpretative method in international law suggests however that this shift in goals can have a significant impact upon interpretation: In the mechanical phase, the canons purported to arrive at the assumed intentions which

---

[202] *South West Africa Cases (Ethiopia v. South Africa; Liberia v. South Africa)* (Preliminary Objections), Dissenting Opinion Judges Spender and Fitzmaurice 814.
[203] *South West Africa (Ethiopia v. South Africa; Liberia v. South Africa)* (Second Phase) Individual Opinion Judge van Wyk [1966] ICJ Rep 84–5.
[204] *Ibid.* 89.
[205] *South West Africa (Ethiopia v. South Africa; Liberia v. South Africa)* (Second Phase), Dissenting Opinion Judge Tanaka [1966] ICJ Rep 277–8.
[206] *Ibid.* 278.   [207] *Ibid.*

gave them room to envisage residual rules of interpretation. In the flexible phase, the quest for the real intentions gave priority to means such as the *travaux*. In this time, the real intentions were projected to the time of the conclusion of the treaty, which had the potential to limit all techniques of treaty interpretation.[208] This evidences that the difference between real intentions and assumed intentions has a bearing upon intertemporal questions since the latter is more flexible and dynamic. The new formula used in the *Navigational and Related Rights Case* clearly endorses the 'assumed intentions' and softens the tougher intentionalist approach in previous cases. This observation can be reinforced by two smaller arguments.

The Court declared that it would interpret 'in accordance with the intentions of its authors as reflected by the text of the treaty and the other relevant factors in terms of interpretation'.[209] Although the Court relies on the intentions of the parties, it rather distances itself in two respects from those: First, 'in accordance' with the intentions is not equivalent with the intentions themselves. This expression offers some scope for the interpreter. Second, the intentions of the parties are effectively related to the VCLT as they need to be reflected in the ordinary meaning and the other factors of interpretation. So the intentions are to be found by the techniques as envisaged by the VCLT.

It has moved from a rather strict intentionalist approach that would not make evolutions in the law explicit, to looking for the assumed intentions of the parties, which is much more dynamic.

9.3.5 Epilogue: two camps at the bench

The inquiry has shown that the approach of the ICJ significantly shifted over time: Static and evolutive interpretations first coexisted peacefully under the condition that the Court endorsed the static approach openly and changed the meaning only silently. This finally resulted in a clash of two camps in which the Court shifted its approach twice in less than ten years. The result of this clash was a compromise with a static starting

---

[208] *South West Africa (Ethiopia v. South Africa; Liberia v. South Africa)* (Second Phase) 23 para. 16.
[209] *Case Concerning the Dispute Regarding Navigational and Related Rights (Costa Rica v. Nicaragua)* (Judgment) 237 para. 48.

point and exceptions allowing for evolutive interpretations. It could be argued that this position shifted again towards evolutive interpretation.

It has to be emphasised that at every step of the development of the jurisprudence, the Court retained some flexibility: When the approaches coexisted peacefully, the Court allowed for silent evolutions; when there was coordination, the Court balanced the approaches with a static starting point and dynamic exceptions. While the importance of the parties was weakened by the move from true to assumed intentions, they were brought back by including subsequent practice as another and independent exception that can lead to evolutive interpretation. So at each stage of the development, there has been a static and a dynamic element. This flexibility is essential for the peaceful and sustainable resolution of disputes. At the same time, the changing approach gives evidence of two camps at the Court, one tending to originalism, the other tending to dynamism. Whether the struggle between judges about the possibility of evolutive interpretations was really decided after the *Navigational and Related Rights Case* cannot be predicted. Yet, it could very well be that the discourse shifted to a struggle over which should be the determinative technique to solve the intertemporal problem. Be that as it may, the judges from the two camps kept pronouncing upon those issues in separate and dissenting opinions. This is of particular interest since they also developed solutions for intertemporal questions, some of which should be taken account of.

Judge Koroma favoured a static interpretation in accordance with the rules of international law applicable at the time the treaty was concluded.[210] In a joint declaration with Judge Shi, they stressed that several times.[211] Judges Spender and Fitzmaurice also showed a clear originalist preference.[212] Four judges affirmed this in dissenting and separate opinions without further arguments.[213] Especially in the first phase when

---

[210] *Case Concerning the Land and Maritime Boundary between Cameroon and Nigeria (Cameroon v. Nigeria: Equatorial Guinea Intervening)* (Judgment), Dissenting Opinion Judge Koroma [2002] ICJ Rep 479 para. 15.

[211] *Application of the Convention on the Prevention and Punishment of the Crime of Genocide (Bosnia Herzegovina v. Serbia and Montenegro)* (Judgment), Joint Declaration of Judges Shi and Koroma [2007] ICJ Rep 279-80, 282.

[212] *South West Africa Cases (Ethiopia v. South Africa; Liberia v. South Africa)* (Preliminary Objections), Dissenting Opinion Judges Spender and Fitzmaurice 521, 540, 546.

[213] *Case Concerning the Barcelona Traction, Light and Power Company, Limited (Belgium v. Spain)* (Judgment, Preliminary Objections), Dissenting Opinion Judge Armand-Ugon [1964] ICJ Rep 140; *South West Africa Cases (Ethiopia v. South Africa; Liberia v. South Africa)* (Preliminary Objections), Dissenting Opinion Judge van Wyk 577; *Case*

evolution was not made explicit, there must have been many more judges favouring static interpretations that felt no need to emphasise this since it was the standard position.

Judges favouring evolutive interpretations seemed to have more reason to make their reasoning explicit. This applies especially to Judge Alvarez, whose conception needs to be considered in greater detail.[214] He contended that there was a time shift that necessarily would change the law of nations.[215] In this context, he found that a new theory and technique of interpretation was necessary. Rejecting analogies to contractual interpretation in private law,[216] the old rules of interpretation had to be modified in four ways.[217] First, he introduced a system of categorising treaties. Peace treaties, 'treaties creating principles of international law' and treaties establishing an international organisation had 'a political and a psychological character'.[218] Those treaties were 'not to be interpreted literally, but primarily by having regard to their purposes'.[219] The Charter of the United Nations was designated as 'constitutional' and, therefore, to be interpreted rather broadly.[220] Second, he insisted upon not giving much argumentative weight to the text. It had to be 'vivified' to keep up with new developments.[221] The purpose of a treaty as well as 'new conditions of international life' could trump even

---

Concerning the Land and Maritime Boundary between Cameroon and Nigeria (Cameroon v. Nigeria: Equatorial Guinea Intervening) (Judgment) Separate Opinion Judge Mbaye [2002] ICJ Rep 518 para. 63.

[214] See generally Aust, 'Alejandro Álvarez'; Nolte, 'Between Contemporaneous and Evolutive Interpretation' 1681–2.

[215] *Corfu Channel (United Kingdom of Great Britain and Northern Ireland v. Albania)* (Judgment) Individual Opinion Judge Alvarez [1949] ICJ Rep 39.

[216] *Reservations to the Convention on the Prevention and Punishment of the Crime of Genocide* (Advisory Opinion) Separate Opinion Judge Alvarez [1951] ICJ Rep 53.

[217] *Competence of the General Assembly for the Admission of a State to the United Nations* (Advisory Opinion), Dissenting Opinion of Judge Alvarez [1950] ICJ Rep 16. For a similar restatement, see *Anglo-Iranian Oil Case (United Kingdom v. Iran)* (Judgment), Dissenting Opinion Judge Alvarez [1952] ICJ Rep 126.

[218] *Competence of the General Assembly for the Admission of a State to the United Nations* (Advisory Opinion), Dissenting Opinion of Judge Alvarez 16.

[219] Ibid. 17.

[220] *Admissions of a State to the United Nations (Charter Article 4)* (Advisory Opinion), Individual Opinion of Judge Alvarez [1948] ICJ Rep 70. He designated more universal treaties as having constitutional character. See *Reservations to the Convention on the Prevention and Punishment of the Crime of Genocide* (Advisory Opinion) Separate Opinion Judge Alvarez 51.

[221] *Competence of the General Assembly for the Admission of a State to the United Nations* (Advisory Opinion), Dissenting Opinion of Judge Alvarez 18.

the clear ordinary meaning of the text. Third, he aimed at generally excluding the preparatory works from the process, especially for treaties establishing international organisations.[222] In this context, he made it very clear that he would not take an originalist position but always look at the time of interpretation since the text acquired 'a life of its own' and should be 'in harmony with the new conditions of social life'.[223] This led, fourthly, to his idea that '[t]he interpretation of treaties must not remain immutable; it will have to be modified if important changes take place in the matter to which it relates.'[224] Judge Alvarez clearly rejected the notion of immutable texts and favoured what is here called evolutive interpretation.[225] While his methods were not exclusively aimed at effecting changes in the law, he stressed the interdependence of his proposal for a new method and the desired possibility of changes in interpretation.

In connection with changes in interpretation, he believed it to be the function of the ICJ to provide for the progressive development of the law.[226] He developed a theoretical account to justify his methods. Therefore, he 'reconstructed' international law as a 'law of social interdependence' which is the 'outcome, not of theory, but of the realities of international life and of the juridical conscience of the nations'.[227] The basic arguments triggering this are rather sociological and might play a role as principled arguments. One characteristic of that 'law of social interdependence' was that it 'adjusts itself to the necessities of international life and evolves together with it; accordingly, it is in harmony with policy'. Policy, serving for him as a key term, is defined not to be 'selfish and arbitrary' but 'collective or individual policy inspired by the general interest'.[228] He tried to think of law as being open to influences from other societal spheres and marked the law as something 'not of an exclusively juridical character' but to have 'also political, economic, social, and psychological characteristics'.[229]

---

[222] See also *Reservations to the Convention on the Prevention and Punishment of the Crime of Genocide* (Advisory Opinion) Separate Opinion Judge Alvarez 53.

[223] *Competence of the General Assembly for the Admission of a State to the United Nations* (Advisory Opinion), Dissenting Opinion of Judge Alvarez 18.

[224] *Ibid.* [225] *Ibid.* 19.

[226] *Competence of the General Assembly for the Admission of a State to the United Nations* (Advisory Opinion), Dissenting Opinion of Judge Alvarez 12; *International Status of South West Africa* (Advisory Opinion) [1950] ICJ Rep 176.

[227] *Admissions of a State to the United Nations (Charter Article 4)* (Advisory Opinion), Individual Opinion of Judge Alvarez 69.

[228] *Ibid.* 70. [229] *International Status of South West Africa* (Advisory Opinion) 176.

This approach had many followers at the bench: Judge Bustamante favoured an evolutive interpretation and described law as 'a living phenomenon which reflects the collective demands and needs of each stage of history'.[230] Judge Cançado Trindade also generally favoured evolutive interpretations.[231] Judge Al-Khasawneh criticised the rule of intertemporal law, which he associated with a rather static approach and showed that this rule was neither followed by the ICJ, nor in international criminal law nor by the ECtHR.[232] He concluded that intertemporal law was 'a perplexing idea that was incapable of finding a place in the 1969 Vienna Convention'[233] and 'a confusing concept the status of which as a rule, or principle, or doctrine or rule of interpretation, is steeped in controversy'.[234] All in all, he favoured overcoming static interpretations but did not give a precise account of how to do this.

There are, however, also mitigating voices such as Judge *ad hoc* Guillaume, who took an intentionalist approach but allowed for evolutive interpretation if such an intention of the parties could be established.[235] A similar system is established by *Judge Bedjaoui* in his Separate opinion to the *Case Concerning the Gabčíkovo-Nagymaros Project*.[236] Generally,

---

[230] *South West Africa Cases (Ethiopia v. South Africa; Liberia v. South Africa)* (Preliminary Objections), Dissenting Opinion Judge Bustamante [1962] ICJ Rep 351.

[231] *Jurisdictional Immunities of the State (Germany v. Italy: Greece Intervening)* (Judgment), Dissenting Opinion Judge Cançado Trindade 5–6. See also his statement in *Pulp Mills on the River Uruguay Case (Argentina v. Uruguay)* Separate Opinion Judge Cançado Trindade (Judgment) 172 para. 99: 'Yet, treaties are living instruments, and the development of international law itself may have effect upon the application of the treaty at issue; such a treaty ought then to be considered in the light of international law at the moment its interpretation is called for.'

[232] *Case Concerning the Land and Maritime Boundary between Cameroon and Nigeria (Cameroon v. Nigeria: Equatorial Guinea Intervening)* (Judgment), Dissenting Opinion Judge Al-Khasawneh [2002] ICJ Rep 502–4 paras. 15–17. It has to be mentioned that those remarks are made in general, while he applied them not to the process of treaty interpretation but to the question whether a treaty has the status of an international treaty.

[233] *Ibid.* 503 para. 15.   [234] *Ibid.* 503 para. 17.

[235] *Case Concerning the Dispute Regarding Navigational and Related Rights (Costa Rica v. Nicaragua)* (Judgment) Declaration of Judge *ad hoc* Guillaume [2009] ICJ Rep 296–7 paras. 14–15.

[236] *Case Concerning the Gabčíkovo-Nagymaros Project (Hungary v. Slovakia)* (Judgment) Separate Opinion Judge Bedjaoui [1997] ICJ Rep 7. However, in a later advisory opinion, *Judge Bedjaoui* argued that the principle of sovereignty has evolved due to developments such as 'supranationalism' and 'globalisation' and that this changed the old *Lotus* principle: see *Legality of the Threat or Use of Nuclear Weapons* (Advisory Opinion) Declaration President Bedjaoui [1996] ICJ Rep 270 paras. 12–13.

he favoured an interpretation in line with Art. 31 VCLT.[237] He understood the first instance of evolutive interpretation not as a general paradigm shift that would mean that all words would necessarily have to follow the evolution of the law.[238] For him, the method of interpretation could lead to evolutive as well as static results. Departing from the intentions of the parties, Judge Bedjaoui thought that treaties had to be interpreted as the parties understood them originally.[239] The terms would primarily have to be interpreted statically and only secondarily dynamically.[240] Interestingly, Judge Castro supported his theory of static interpretation with a comparative law argument. Looking at laws on how to interpret treaties in private law, he found that '[l]egal tradition settles the matter logically'.[241] He distinguished the rules of interpretation for contracts and laws in the sense that the latter would be susceptible to evolutive interpretation.[242] Drawing an analogy between the interpretation of laws and law-making treaties, which he exemplified with the UN Charter, he held the view that those law-making treaties would be susceptible to evolutive interpretation.[243]

All in all, we can say that there is a constant dispute at the bench amongst judges favouring evolutive and those favouring static interpretation. The Court has been moving constantly towards more evolution, while static interpretation is very common especially in cases of border treaties. It is true that the Court had from the very beginning interpreted provisions evolutively, yet the *Namibia opinion* was the first explicit endorsement of evolutive interpretation. The subtle but slow move towards an 'assumed intention' approach is another sign of the increasing evolutive approach.

9.4. Justificatory patterns

9.4.1 Rule of interpretation

It is interesting to see that the duty to interpret in good faith had played no role in any case relating to static and evolutive interpretations. When the Court mentioned good faith in the context of intertemporal

---

[237] *Case Concerning the Gabčíkovo–Nagymaros Project (Hungary v. Slovakia)* (Judgment) Separate Opinion Judge Bedjaoui 121 para. 5, 124 para. 18.
[238] *Ibid.* 122 para. 10. [239] *Ibid.* 122 para. 9. [240] *Ibid.* 123 para. 13.
[241] *Aegean Sea Continental Shelf Case (Greece v. Turkey)* (Judgment) Separate Opinion Castro [1978] ICJ Rep 65 para. 5.
[242] *Ibid.* [243] *Ibid.* 68–9 para. 14.

questions, it solely addressed the compliance of or implementation by the parties.[244]

The ICJ seems to follow the order as set out in the VCLT. Mostly, the Court has not afforded special weight to any technique of treaty interpretation, while it sometimes stresses the particular importance of certain techniques. It is significant that from a very early stage, the Court was prepared to go beyond the ordinary meaning of the terms. This was made explicit when it stated in the *International Status of South West Africa* Opinion that 'doubts might arise from the fact that the supervisory functions of the League with regard to mandated territories not placed under the new Trusteeship System were neither expressly transferred to the United Nations nor expressly assumed by that organisation'.[245]

Using almost all other techniques of interpretation, the Court was, however, able to overcome the text.[246] In the preliminary phase of the *South West Africa Cases*, the ICJ favoured an interpretation against the 'ordinary meaning of the words employed by the provision'.[247] It stated accordingly that '[w]here such a method of interpretation results in a meaning incompatible with the spirit, purpose and context of the clause or instrument in which the words are contained, no reliance can be validly placed on it'.[248]

In the *Kasikili/Sedudu Case*, the Court interestingly afforded special weight to the ordinary meaning of the text[249] as well as to subsequent agreements and practice.[250] Taking into account that the Court regularly

---

[244] *Case Concerning the Dispute Regarding Navigational and Related Rights (Costa Rica v. Nicaragua)* (Judgment) 242 para. 63; *Case Concerning the Gabčíkovo–Nagymaros Project (Hungary v. Slovakia)* (Judgment) [1997] ICJ Rep 68 para. 112. This reinforces the findings made above: see p. 152 below.

[245] *International Status of South-West Africa* (Advisory Opinion) 136.

[246] *Ibid.* 136. The primacy of the text was upheld by *South West Africa Cases (Ethiopia v. South Africa; Liberia v. South Africa)* (Preliminary Objections), Dissenting Opinion Judges Spender and Fitzmaurice 512. The supplementary nature of object and purpose was asserted by *South West Africa Cases (Ethiopia v. South Africa; Liberia v. South Africa)* (Preliminary Objections), Dissenting Opinion Judge van Wyk 590.

[247] *South West Africa Cases (Ethiopia v. South Africa; Liberia v. South Africa)* (Preliminary Objections) 336.

[248] *Ibid.*

[249] In the *Kasikili/Sedudu Case*, the ICJ made the following observation concerning the weight of the ordinary meaning of the text in the process of interpretation: 'Interpretation must be based above all upon the text of the treaty.' *Kasikili/Sedudu Island (Botswana v. Namibia)* (Judgment) 1060 para. 20.

[250] The ICJ quoted the following excerpt from the commentary to the ILC draft: '[A]n agreement as to the interpretation of a provision reached after the conclusion of the

gives no special preference to any technique of interpretation, those exceptional observations reinforce the pragmatic stance of the judges: Special weight is accorded to a technique when it fits while it is also always possible to decide against a technique. A quantitative analysis of the use of the means of interpretation reveals that the frequency of the use of the techniques in the cases is as follows:

- ordinary meaning: 12
- object and purpose: 8
- subsequent practice as well as relevant rules: 6
- context: 4
- subsequent agreement: 2

The Court held that a technique produced no conclusive result for the matter in the case of the ordinary meaning (3 times) and the context (once). The Court also once held that the requirements of subsequent practice were not fulfilled. If the Court used a technique, this always coincided with the interpretative result apart from the ordinary meaning (2 out of 9 correlation at 77.78 per cent) and the context (1 out of 3 correlation at 66.67 per cent). While these numbers are certainly not significant in the statistical sense, they indicate that the Court is willing to disregard the rather 'literal' techniques like the ordinary meaning and the context and base interpretations either on the object and purpose or the subsequent agreements and practice of the parties. Yet, this is only a quantitative indication, and we should continue to review the qualitative use of the techniques.

Looking at how the ICJ has used the VCLT qualitatively, several points are of note. With regard to the *ordinary meaning* of the text of the treaty, the key question for the Court is whether the term in question is 'generic'/'evolving' or static. The Court has held that the terms 'strenuous conditions of the modern world', 'the well-being and development' and 'sacred trust' in Art. 22 of the Covenant of the League of Nations were by definition evolutionary.[251]

The court qualified other norms such as provisions for the protection of water quality or obligations to take into account environmental norms

---

treaty represents an authentic interpretation by the parties which must be read into the treaty for purposes of its interpretation.' *Ibid.* 1075 para. 49.

[251] *Legal Consequences for States of the Continued Presence of South Africa in Namibia (South West Africa) Notwithstanding Security Council Resolution 276 (1970)* (Advisory Opinion), Dissenting Opinion Judge Fitzmaurice 31 para. 53.

as intrinsically evolutive without giving an explanation for the evolving nature of the terms.[252] The Court spoke about generic terms in relation to the notion of 'commerce' in the Treaty of Separation since this would amount to a 'class of activity'.[253] It also indicated that notions like 'territorial status' and 'fixed jurisdiction' will generally be interpreted evolutively.[254] Judge Higgins defines generic terms in the abstract as 'a known legal term, whose content the parties expected would change through time'.[255] She uses the narrow concept whereas the ICJ has defined it broadly as 'a class of activity'.[256] Yet, a 'known legal term' might be known if there are precedents for its dynamic use. It is indeed sometimes assumed that there is a certain category of terms being 'dynamic' in nature.[257] This suggests that some terms by their nature changed their meaning. As established above, this can only be inferred from the practice of the Court. A similar critique found expression in some separate and dissenting opinions. With regard to the ordinary meaning of the treaty, Judge de Castro offers interesting insights. On the one hand, he stressed that words had 'no intrinsic value in themselves' and that their 'semantic value' depended 'on the time and the circumstances in which they were uttered'.[258] Building upon this insight, he goes on to put the notion of generic terms into context, remarking that 'the meaning of most words is in fact subject to a certain degree of flexibility, with the exception of those which refer to individual concrete objects'.[259] So, he questions the usefulness of the said category of generic terms.[260] A similar criticism came from Judge Skotnikov, who questioned the 'mechanical'

---

[252] *Case Concerning the Gabčíkovo–Nagymaros Project (Hungary v. Slovakia)* (Judgment) 67 para. 112.
[253] *Case Concerning the Dispute Regarding Navigational and Related Rights (Costa Rica v. Nicaragua)* (Judgment) 243 para. 67.
[254] *Aegean Sea Continental Shelf Case (Greece v. Turkey)* (Judgment) 32 para. 77.
[255] *Kasikili/Sedudu Island (Botswana v. Namibia)* (Judgment) Declaration Judge Higgins 1113 para. 2.
[256] *Case Concerning the Dispute Regarding Navigational and Related Rights (Costa Rica v. Nicaragua)* (Judgment) 243 para. 67.
[257] *South West Africa (Ethiopia v. South Africa; Liberia v. South Africa)* (Second Phase) Separate Opinion Judge Padilla Nervo [1966] ICJ Rep 464.
[258] *Aegean Sea Continental Shelf Case (Greece v. Turkey)* (Judgment) Separate Opinion Castro 63 para. 4.
[259] *Ibid.* 65 para. 7.
[260] Interestingly, he entertains an essentialist argument in the concrete application of the rules to the dispute at hand.

conclusion that the use of a generic term would allow for an evolutive interpretation.[261]

Instead of generic terms, *Judge Bedjaoui* distinguished between terms with fixed references and terms with mobile references. To decide whether the words provide for a fixed or a mobile reference, he looked at the terms of the treaty. In the case at hand, he affirmed a mobile reference due to the vagueness of the terms.[262] The present study has suggested that the question Judge Bedjaoui is posing is the question whether a term evolves referentially. From the perspective of the Vienna Convention, this question is subject to the ordinary process of treaty interpretation and not to the classification of terms. On the contrary, it can very well be argued that terms such as names or terms directly referring to a real world object are much less likely to be considered as changing over time.[263] This convincing argument can be compared to a similar discourse in the philosophy of language, prompted mainly by the works of Kripke and Putnam.[264]

Under the rules of the VCLT, there is no necessary connection between the classification of the terms and a static or evolutive outcome. Two examples from the jurisprudence of the Court might evidence this. In the first phase of the *South West Africa Case*, the ICJ managed to accord standing before it to members of the United Nations even though the text to be interpreted referred to members of the League of Nations.[265] This is a case in which the ICJ has reinterpreted a rather direct reference to an international organisation that went out of existence.

Another fascinating example is provided in the *Kasikili/Sedudu Case*: The Court looked at the intentions of the parties at the time of the conclusion of the treaty to determine that the term '*Thalweg*' exactly matches the other authentic expression 'centre of the [main] channel'. To determine the meaning of the latter term, the Court referred to 'present-day knowledge'. So the synonymity of the terms was established looking at the time the parties set up the treaty. Their content was established

---

[261] *Case Concerning the Dispute Regarding Navigational and Related Rights (Costa Rica v. Nicaragua)* (Judgment) Separate Opinion Judge Skotnikov 284 para. 6.
[262] *Case Concerning the Gabčíkovo–Nagymaros Project (Hungary v. Slovakia)* (Judgment) Separate Opinion Judge Bedjaoui 124 para. 17.
[263] Nolte, 'Between Contemporaneous and Evolutive Interpretation' 1679. Discussing also arbitral decisions, he categorises those as 'rather specific terms'.
[264] A good overview is given by Lycan, *Philosophy of Language* 50.
[265] *South West Africa Cases (Ethiopia v. South Africa; Liberia v. South Africa)* (Preliminary Objections) 336.

in the light of later circumstances. The synonymous terms have been interpreted statically as well as evolutively in the very same case. This reinforces the previous analysis: Features of a term such as its nature can provide for arguments to decide or justify intertemporal questions. While it can be a weighty argument, it is certainly neither the only nor a cogent argument. Arguing before the Court, one could try to show the changeability or stability of terms which derived either from their inherent nature or from the intentions of the parties. Evolutive claims will be more convincing if one can show the generality of the term and find supporting precedential decisions. Yet, we should assume that every term can possibly change its meaning or retain the same meaning.

Another issue in relation to evolutive interpretation is the use of dictionaries, since dictionaries can be said to point to the ordinary meaning at certain points in time. Here, temporal differences can become ascertainable when dictionaries from different times are being used. Sometimes, the Court referred to more than one dictionary from different points in time,[266] yet it explicitly referred to new dictionaries[267] or old dictionaries or old comparable sources.[268] This can be taken as acknowledging that it is at least possible that the ordinary meaning of a treaty varies over time. One factor favouring evolutive interpretation was the 'continuing duration' of a treaty.[269] Judge Skotnikov remarked that this would not automatically lead to an evolutive interpretation.[270] The envisaged length of the operation of the treaty can result from different techniques of interpretation. In the jurisprudence of the ICJ, the text of the treaty[271] as well as its object and purpose[272] could suggest that a treaty is operable for a long period of time.

---

[266] *South West Africa (Ethiopia v. South Africa; Liberia v. South Africa)* (Second Phase) Individual Opinion Judge van Wyk 209.
[267] *Kasikili/Sedudu Island (Botswana v. Namibia)* (Judgment) 1064 para. 30.
[268] *Kasikili/Sedudu Island (Botswana v. Namibia)* (Judgment) 1062 para. 25; *Case Concerning the Dispute Regarding Navigational and Related Rights (Costa Rica v. Nicaragua)* (Judgment) Separate Opinion Judge Skotnikov 284 para. 7.
[269] *Aegean Sea Continental Shelf Case (Greece v. Turkey)* (Judgment) 32 para. 77.
[270] In the respective case, the Judge arrived at an evolutive reading by looking at the subsequent practice of the parties to the treaty: see *Case Concerning the Dispute Regarding Navigational and Related Rights (Costa Rica v. Nicaragua)* (Judgment) Separate Opinion Judge Skotnikov 285 paras. 9–10.
[271] *Case Concerning the Dispute Regarding Navigational and Related Rights (Costa Rica v. Nicaragua)* (Judgment) 243 para. 67.
[272] Ibid. 243 para. 68.

As regards the *context*, the ICJ established that if some parts of the text ought to follow the development of the law, this supported the same conclusion for other terms in the same instrument.[273] The same could be said about the relevant rules, if the instrument to be interpreted and the rules have a close connection.[274] Like the text, the context can be generally open for static as well as evolutive interpretations. While interpreting a reservation, the ICJ was faced with the problem whether the prohibition of vague and subjective reservations in Art. 39 of the Act of Settlement would prohibit reservations following the evolution of the law. The ICJ held that this provision had no bearing upon the intertemporal question.[275]

The ICJ has stressed the need for continuity of a norm and a legal instrument, when the *object and purpose* was to protect 'not only the rights of States, but also the rights of the peoples'.[276] Art. 80(1) UN Charter provides that 'nothing in this Chapter shall be construed in or of itself to alter in any manner the rights whatsoever of any states or any peoples or the terms of existing international instruments'. The Court used this provision as an argument for replacing the Council of the League of Nations with the General Assembly. Judge McNair contended that the purpose went well beyond what was expressed in the treaty. He argued that it was not the Charter, but the dissolution of the League which altered the content of the mandate.[277] So Art. 80(1) UN Charter did not apply on its terms. The ICJ, however, saw the object and purpose in more abstract terms. Very significantly, in the *Legality of the Use of Force Cases*, the object and purpose of Art. 35 ICJ Statute favoured a static interpretation of the term 'special provisions contained in treaties in force'.[278] This is a very good example of the flexibility the Vienna Convention affords to the interpreter. Every technique can favour static as well as dynamic results. Nevertheless, also in individual opinions, the special importance of this technique for changing interpretations is very prevalent. It is interesting to look at the ICJ's ways of dealing with the

---

[273] *Aegean Sea Continental Shelf Case (Greece v. Turkey)* (Judgment) 33 paras. 78–9.
[274] *Ibid.* 33 para. 79. It has to be noted that this case concerned the interpretation of a reservation and the relevant rule was the treaty, to which the reservation applied.
[275] *Ibid.* 30 para. 73.
[276] *International Status of South-West Africa* (Advisory Opinion) 136.
[277] *International Status of South-West Africa* (Advisory Opinion), Separate Opinion Judge McNair 160.
[278] *Legality of the Use of Force (Serbia and Montenegro v. Belgium)* (Preliminary Objections) 319 para. 102.

ascertainment knot: On the one hand, in the case of unilateral declarations such as reservations, the Court takes a static approach, focusing exclusively on supplementary means such as the circumstances when issuing the declaration.[279] Judge Cançado Trindade stressed what has previously been described as emerging purpose: The object and purpose can be developed by the parties as well as by organs competent to interpret the treaty.[280] And indeed, in the *Namibia opinion*, the Court developed the object and purpose of the section on C mandates in Art. 22 of the Covenant of the League of Nations in the light of changes in international law, in particular the right to self-determination.[281] This could indeed be viewed as precedent for an emerging purpose.

Judge Azevedo stressed the 'teleological character' of the UN Charter, which he also termed to be 'a means not an end'.[282] Yet, he not only grounds this special status in the importance of the Charter but also connects it to the drafting of the Charter: Principles and aims attained a special and prominent status.[283] This would influence the techniques of treaty interpretation as one would have to 'seek the methods of interpretation most likely to serve the natural evolution of the needs of mankind'.[284] In this context, the aims, which would be called object and purpose today, ought to be preferred over the text as well as the practice.[285] At least in the context of the Charter, Judge Azevedo believed the object and purpose to be the most important, and derived from this an evolutive reading of the Charter. Judge Cançado Trindade indicated that the object and purpose would be even more important in the case of protective norms, which would safeguard human beings, the environment or the general interest.[286]

Subsequent agreements and practice have been frequently used by the ICJ. In the *Navigational and Related Rights Case*, the Court very interestingly did not inquire into the subsequent practice of the parties even

---

[279] *Fisheries Jurisdiction (Spain v. Canada)* (Jurisdiction of the Court) 456–7 paras. 58–60.
[280] *Whaling in the Antarctic (Australia v. Japan)* (Order) Separate Opinion of Judge Cançado Trindade 16 para. 55.
[281] *Legal Consequences for States of the Continued Presence of South Africa in Namibia (South West Africa) Notwithstanding Security Council Resolution 276 (1970)* (Advisory Opinion) 30–1 paras. 50–1.
[282] *Competence of the General Assembly for the Admission of a State to the United Nations* (Advisory Opinion), Dissenting Opinion of Judge Azevedo [1950] ICJ Rep 22, 23.
[283] *Ibid.* [284] *Ibid.* [285] *Ibid.* 24.
[286] *Whaling in the Antarctic (Australia v. Japan)* (Order) Separate Opinion of Judge Cançado Trindade 16 para. 55.

though the practice would have confirmed the Court's conclusion.[287] This has, however, been criticised by Judge Skotnikov and Judge *ad hoc* Guillaume.[288]

In general, there is no reason why state conduct should not be classified as agreement or practice if it fulfils the requirements of Art. 31(3)(a) or (b) VCLT. Subsequent practice is assumed by the ICJ even if the agreement is not as obvious as in the case of a subsequent agreement.[289] Regarding the *qualitative agreement knot*, the number of states participating in the practice is of particular interest. In the case of *Legality of the Threat or Use of Nuclear Weapons*, the ICJ, without explicitly classifying the argument as subsequent practice, referred to the written statements of one state while emphasising that there was no statement to the contrary.[290] In the context of the United Nations, the ICJ has referred to the practice of the organs of the United Nations instead of state practice.[291] This practice was not unanimous but had to meet only the conditions of a simple or a two-thirds majority of the members present and voting as set out by Art. 18 UN Charter. So, of the resolutions quoted in the *Wall Opinion*,[292] Resolution 1599 (XV) was accepted with 61 yes votes, 5 no votes and 33 abstentions with all 99 parties present and voting.[293]

---

[287] *Case Concerning the Dispute Regarding Navigational and Related Rights (Costa Rica v. Nicaragua)* (Judgment) 243–4 paras. 67–71.

[288] *Ibid*. Separate Opinion Judge Skotnikov 285 para. 8; *Ibid*. Declaration of Judge *ad hoc* Guillaume 298 para. 16.

[289] *Kasikili/Sedudu Island (Botswana v. Namibia)* (Judgment) 1087 para. 63.

[290] *Legality of the Threat or Use of Nuclear Weapons* (Advisory Opinion) Concurring Opinion Judge Vereshchetin 259–60 para. 86.

[291] See the very early reference to the Assembly of the League of Nations as well as to the General Assembly, *International Status of South-West Africa* (Advisory Opinion) 137. The ICJ later referred to the 'accepted practice of the General Assembly'. This could be interpreted to mean that states have accepted the practice of the organ and, therefore, the ICJ still looks at actual state practice. *Legal Consequences of the Construction of a Wall in the Occupied Palestinian Territory* (Advisory Opinion) 150 para. 28. However, in the context of Art. 12 UN Charter which delimits the competences of the General Assembly and the Security Council, it is much more probable that the practice was accepted by the Council. Pointing in the sense of the latter is also *Legal Consequences of the Construction of a Wall in the Occupied Palestinian Territory* (Advisory Opinion) Separate Opinion Judge Kooijmans [2004] ICJ Rep 224 para. 17.

[292] *Legal Consequences of the Construction of a Wall in the Occupied Palestinian Territory* (Advisory Opinion) 149 para. 27. All voting patterns are derived from http://ubisnet.un.org (accessed 19 June 2013).

[293] The situation in the Republic of Congo, UNGA A/RES/1599(XV) (15 April 1961). The Court quoted Resolution 1955 (XV). Given that there is no such resolution, it is most probable that the Court meant the resolution referred to.

Resolution 1600 (VI) was adopted with 60 yes votes, 16 no votes and 23 abstentions with all 99 members present and voting.[294] Resolution 1913(XVIII) was accepted with 91 yes votes, 2 no votes, 11 abstentions and 7 states not voting and a total voting membership of 111 states.[295] These numbers show that the ICJ will consider practice in the context of the United Nations even if it is far from unanimous. As the *Wall Opinion* shows, subsequent practice has a particular importance and an increased weight in the context of international organisations: the ICJ based an evolutive reading of Art. 12 UN Charter only on the subsequent practice of the General Assembly, without discussing other techniques of interpretation. Such an increased importance can also be found in the context of border treaties where the Court in two cases either altered the terms of the treaty or was at least open to the possibility that subsequent agreements and practice, if established, could alter the meaning: yet, the criteria concerning the qualitative agreement other than in the border cases varied: While the Court relied on acquiescence in the *Preah Vihear Case*,[296] it required full awareness and acceptance in the *Kasikili /Sedudu Case*.[297] While the Court seemed to establish a quite high threshold to establish the agreement of the parties, it took into account three surveys as 'factual findings'.[298] These findings did not – according to the Court – amount to 'subsequent practice by the parties in the interpretation of the 1890 Treaty'.[299] Two things about this part of the judgment are remarkable. First, the Court did apply a technique similar to subsequent practice. Since, however, it only used the argument derived from the technique to confirm the meaning already established, it can well be held to be a supplementary means of interpretation as provided for in Art. 32 VCLT. Second, while Art. 31(3)(b) VCLT provides that subsequent practice ought to be in the *application* of the treaty, the Court uses here

---

[294] The situation in the Republic of Congo, UNGA A/RES/1600(XV) (15 April 1961). The Court quoted Resolution 1960 (XVI). Given that there is no such resolution, it is most probable that the Court meant the resolution referred to.
[295] Territories under Portuguese administration, UNGA A/RES/1913(XVIII) (3 December 1963).
[296] *Case Concerning the Temple of Preah Vihear (Cambodia v. Thailand)* (Merits) 32. It has to be admitted that this statement was not made in the context of treaty interpretation, yet the Court shortly after stated that the same holds true if it were dealt with in that context.
[297] *Kasikili/Sedudu Island (Botswana v. Namibia)* (Judgment) 1096 para. 80.
[298] Ibid. [299] Ibid.

the term 'interpretation'. While one should not put too much emphasis on phrases, the context of the question links up to the awareness problem that has been identified above: the Court implied that the parties have to act wilfully under the treaty and to consciously interpret the treaty.[300] If they failed to do so, their practice could only be considered as 'factual' and be taken into account as supplementary means.

The fact that subsequent practice can either look back at the time of the conclusion of the treaty or alter the meaning to a certain extent was explicitly acknowledged by Judge Parra-Arranguren.[301] Yet, other judges tried to limit the effects of subsequent practice. Judges Fitzmaurice and Spender limited the impact of subsequent events[302] since they could alter the 'intrinsic legal character' of a norm that ought to be established contemporaneous with concluding the treaty.[303] In the context of custom formation, Judge Shi remarked that the practice of threatening with nuclear weapons could not be considered as relevant state practice.[304] This line of argument could be transferred to subsequent practice as defined in Art. 31(3)(b) VCLT. On the other hand, there seems no need to disregard any kind of practice from the beginning as it can still be outweighed by considerations such as the object and purpose of a treaty. An interesting account was taken by Judge Ranjeva in the *Nuclear Weapons Opinion*. He pictured evolution of the law as depending on attitudes and awareness, while 'one fact remains permanent: The final objective.'[305] On the one hand, he openly referred to legal realism as an

---

[300] In the *Kasikili/Sedudu Case*, the parties to the Treaty of 1890 issued two joint reports. It was easy for the Court to reject agreement in the first report since their report explicitly stated that it should be considered as *factual* and not to determine the legal situation. Ibid. 1079 para. 57. This is, however, much more difficult to contend for the second joint report issued in 1985. This report was explicitly made in the context of a border dispute and with reference to the Treaty of 1890, ibid. 1088 para. 64.

[301] *Kasikili/Sedudu Island (Botswana v. Namibia)* (Judgment), Dissenting Opinion of Judge Parra-Arranguren [1999] ICJ Rep 1212–13 para. 16.

[302] An expression including also the relevant rules as expressed in Art. 31(3)(c) VCLT if they came into force subsequent to the conclusion of the treaty.

[303] *South West Africa Cases (Ethiopia v. South Africa; Liberia v. South Africa)* (Preliminary Objections), Dissenting Opinion Judges Spender and Fitzmaurice 521.

[304] *Legality of the Threat or Use of Nuclear Weapons* (Advisory Opinion) Declaration of Judge Shi [1996] ICJ Rep 226, 277. For a more balanced account on the same question, see *Legality of the Threat or Use of Nuclear Weapons* (Advisory Opinion), Dissenting Opinion Judge Schwebel [1996] ICJ Rep 311ff.

[305] *Legality of the Threat or Use of Nuclear Weapons* (Advisory Opinion) Concurring Opinion Judge Ranjeva [1996] ICJ Rep 295.

approach to evolutive interpretation. He saw evolution as a one-way street pointing in one direction.[306]

The *relevant rules* as defined in Art. 31(3)(c) VCLT have often played a major part in the determination of evolutive interpretations. Regarding their use, it is interesting that the ICJ in an environmental case just stated that there are new rules but did not specify them.[307] Later, the Court summarised those developments as the concept of sustainable development.[308] By using this phrase, the Court came close to establishing a legal principle, which could also be taken to trigger change in the interpretation of treaties. In the *International Status of South West Africa Opinion*, the ICJ considered relevant rules in the interpretation of the mandate of South Africa, especially the UN Charter, since the question was whether the General Assembly should perform the functions of the Council of the League of Nations.[309] The ICJ did not only refer to the text of the Charter, but also the object and purpose of Art. 80, the *travaux* of the Charter in relation to the Trusteeship System and the subsequent practice.

Regarding the *travaux préparatoires*, their minor importance appeared from the quantitative analysis. In the *Legality of the Use of Force Cases*,[310] the interpretative question seemed fairly open. Since the context was said to speak in favour of an evolving interpretation while the object and purpose was said to speak against, the ICJ resorted to the *travaux* to reinforce its finding.[311] It then went on to explain the history of the provision using over four pages.[312] The sheer length of the argument and the way it was presented as being conclusive indicates its importance for the interpretative outcome. Yet, the Court also had recourse to these only as supplementary means. Another interesting aspect of the case is that the Court looked into the preparatory works not only of Art. 35 ICJ Statute but also of the very similar provision of Art. 35 PCIJ Statute. Since the *travaux* are only exemplary for the other supplementary means of

---

[306] *Ibid.*
[307] *Case Concerning the Gabčíkovo–Nagymaros Project (Hungary v. Slovakia)* (Judgment) 67 para. 112.
[308] *Ibid.* 78 para. 140.
[309] *International Status of South-West Africa* (Advisory Opinion) 136. The question whether the Covenant of the League of Nations is, in relation to the mandate, also a relevant rule according to Art. 31(3)(c) VCLT or rather part of the context, is complex but can be left open here.
[310] See p. 323 below.
[311] *Legality of the Use of Force (Serbia and Montenegro v. Belgium)* (Preliminary Objections) 319 para. 103.
[312] *Ibid.* 319.

interpretation, there seems to be no problem including the *travaux* of other treaties as supplementary means even if they were not considered to be *travaux* in the strict sense of the term. Interestingly, the *travaux* of the earlier treaty were used to indicate that the later treaty ought to be interpreted as it stood at the time of its coming into force. So the preparatory works did not determine the point in time – namely, of the earlier treaty – but only the static nature of the treaty. One could say that the argument derived from the preparatory works of the earlier treaty was applied to the later treaty on an analogical or even evolutive reading. In the *Kasikili/Sedudu Case*, the *travaux* have been referred to only after the other means of interpretation allowed no firm conclusion as to the meaning.[313] The preparatory works can also warrant an evolutive interpretation, especially when they are used to reinforce the object and purpose of the treaty.[314] Judge Castro employed the circumstances of the conclusion of the treaty as argument for his static approach, since those were mentioned in Art. 32 as supplementary means.[315]

9.4.2 Other arguments

The Court did not only use the rule of interpretation in the VCLT but also resorted to means of interpretation not mentioned there. Those arguments were used in a flexible manner. The Court also mentioned material *principles* at least in the context of evolutive interpretations.[316] Concerning other legal means of interpretation, the ICJ has, as already explained, sometimes resorted to *presumptions*: it generally presumed that the treaty ought to be read contemporaneously with the time of its conclusion[317] while the insertion of generic terms triggered the presumption that the meaning of the text can evolve.[318] The Court has, however, rejected the *in dubio pro mitius* principle that would presume a restrictive

---

[313] *Kasikili/Sedudu Island (Botswana v. Namibia)* (Judgment) 1062 para. 25 with reference to 1074–5 para. 46.
[314] See *International Status of South-West Africa* (Advisory Opinion) 136.
[315] *Aegean Sea Continental Shelf Case (Greece v. Turkey)* (Judgment) Separate Opinion Castro 68 para. 13.
[316] *Legality of the Threat or Use of Nuclear Weapons* (Advisory Opinion) [1996] ICJ Rep 226 259 para. 86; *Legal Consequences for States of the Continued Presence of South Africa in Namibia (South West Africa) Notwithstanding Security Council Resolution 276 (1970)* (Advisory Opinion) 28 para. 45.
[317] *Case Concerning the Dispute Regarding Navigational and Related Rights (Costa Rica v. Nicaragua)* (Judgment) 243 para. 66.
[318] *Aegean Sea Continental Shelf Case (Greece v. Turkey)* (Judgment) 32 para. 77.

interpretation.[319] Yet, it was applied by Judge Skotnikov who favoured restrictive interpretations.[320] A preference for restrictive interpretation was also expressed by Judge *ad hoc* Guillaume in the same case[321] and by Judge *ad hoc* Torres Bernárdez in the *Pulp Mills on the River Uruguay Case*.[322]

Regarding inferences from the treaty, the Court considered the *nature of the treaty*[323] and its *structure*.[324] Many judges had views on these issues: Judge Jessup stressed that in particular 'multi-partite treaties of a constitutional or legislative character' would sometimes have to react to changes in their environment.[325] Judge de Castro thought that the Vienna Convention should not apply to constituent instruments of international organisations and that they ought to be interpreted evolutively.[326] Judge Spender considered the original intentions of the parties not as important for 'multilateral treaties such as the Charter'.[327] This leads to the discussion of the UN Charter as a special treaty.[328] Beyond intertemporal

---

[319] *Case Concerning the Dispute Regarding Navigational and Related Rights (Costa Rica v. Nicaragua)* (Judgment) 237. In this latter case, the ICJ argued in a dialectical manner: it first conceded that, generally, limitations of sovereignty are not to be presumed, but then argued, that this does not mean that treaties in general ought to be interpreted in a restrictive manner. For an opposite view, see *Case Concerning the Dispute Regarding Navigational and Related Rights (Costa Rica v. Nicaragua)* (Judgment) Separate Opinion Judge Skotnikov 283–4 paras. 2–4; *Case Concerning the Dispute Regarding Navigational and Related Rights (Costa Rica v. Nicaragua)* (Judgment) Declaration of Judge *ad hoc* Guillaume 298 para. 15.

[320] *Case Concerning the Dispute Regarding Navigational and Related Rights (Costa Rica v. Nicaragua)* (Judgment) Separate Opinion Judge Skotnikov 283–4 paras. 3–4.

[321] *Case Concerning the Dispute Regarding Navigational and Related Rights (Costa Rica v. Nicaragua)* (Judgment) Declaration of Judge *ad hoc* Guillaume 297–8 para. 15.

[322] *Pulp Mills on the River Uruguay Case (Argentina v. Uruguay)* Separate Opinion Judge Cançado Trindade 236 para. 13.

[323] *Aegean Sea Continental Shelf Case (Greece v. Turkey)* (Judgment) 32 para. 77. It stressed the nature of a treaty providing for the peaceful settlement of disputes.

[324] *Ibid.* It stressed the general applicability of a treaty providing for the peaceful settlement of disputes which was applicable to all other treaties.

[325] *South West Africa (Ethiopia v. South Africa; Liberia v. South Africa)* (Second Phase), Dissenting Opinion Judge Jessup [1966] ICJ Rep 439.

[326] *Legal Consequences for States of the Continued Presence of South Africa in Namibia (South West Africa) Notwithstanding Security Council Resolution 276 (1970)* (Advisory Opinion), Dissenting Opinion Judge de Castro [1971] ICJ Rep 182–4. See reference by Greig, *Intertemporality and the Law of Treaties* 59.

[327] *Certain Expenses of the United Nations* (Advisory Opinion) Separate Opinion of Judge Spender 184.

[328] Fassbender, *The United Nations Charter As the Constitution of the International Community*.

questions, the Court has in the interpretation of the UN Charter referred to its authors[329] and even inquired into the 'minds of the drafters'.[330] While these instances do not suggest that the interpretation of the Charter is absolutely fixed temporarily, the approach to the drafters can be equated with the focus on the intentions of the parties: Only if the drafters allowed for the law to develop, this can be done by interpretation. Among the judges, there are different opinions in that regard. Some are in favour of evolutive interpretations of the Charter: Judge Azevedo managed to do this not only by referring to the process of drafting but also to 'the requirements of world peace, co-operation between men, individual freedom and social progress'.[331] Interestingly, Judge de Castro termed the UN Charter as a constitution but derived from this status that the obligations of the states were fixed.[332] Otherwise, he contended, the United Nations would be like a super state.

With regard to *extra-legal considerations* and arguments, the *South West Africa Case* is again an apt example of how far the Court can go to restrict or expand its perception. To describe the different stances taken with regard to openness, one could speak of sociological and teleological on the one side and juristic and formalistic on the other.[333]

The position of the Court in the second phase of the *South West Africa Case* was closed. It stated that:

> [t]hroughout this case it has been suggested, directly or indirectly, that humanitarian considerations are sufficient in themselves to generate legal rights and obligations, and that the Court can and should proceed accordingly. The Court does not think so. It is a court of law, and can take account of moral principles only in so far as these are given a sufficient expression in legal form. Law exists, it is said, to serve a social need; but precisely for that reason it can do so only through and within the limits of its own discipline. Otherwise, it is not a legal service that would be rendered.[334]

---

[329] *Admissions of a State to the United Nations (Charter Article 4)* (Advisory Opinion) [1948] ICJ Rep 62–3.
[330] *Certain Expenses of the United Nations* (Advisory Opinion) 159.
[331] *Competence of the General Assembly for the Admission of a State to the United Nations* (Advisory Opinion), Dissenting Opinion of Judge Azevedo 23.
[332] *Legal Consequences for States of the Continued Presence of South Africa in Namibia (South West Africa) Notwithstanding Security Council Resolution 276 (1970)* (Advisory Opinion), Dissenting Opinion Judge de Castro 341 para. 35.
[333] *South West Africa (Ethiopia v. South Africa; Liberia v. South Africa)* (Second Phase), Dissenting Opinion Judge Tanaka 276.
[334] *South West Africa (Ethiopia v. South Africa; Liberia v. South Africa)* (Second Phase) 34 para. 49.

The majority prevailing in this case made it very clear that it aimed at preserving the legal rationality of the process. This rationality was in itself a purpose and something of value that did not allow the Court to disregard its method in order to serve other purposes. In this line of thinking, the law sets the limits for the other rationales, not the other way around. The legal rationale prevailed over 'interests'[335] or 'necessities'.[336] The Court finally arrived at a static interpretation of the mandate agreement. In contrast, an evolutive result was reached in the *Case Concerning the Gabčíkovo–Nagymaros Project*, in which the Court was also very open to extra-legal considerations. The Court argued as follows:

> Throughout the ages, mankind has, for economic and other reasons, constantly interfered with nature. In the past, this was often done without consideration of the effects upon the environment. Owing to new scientific insights and to a growing awareness of the risks for mankind – for present and future generations – of pursuit of such interventions at an unconsidered and unabated pace, new norms and standards have been developed, set forth in a great number of instruments during the last two decades. Such new norms have to be taken into consideration, and such new standards given proper weight, not only when States contemplate new activities but also when continuing with activities begun in the past. This need to reconcile economic development with protection of the environment is aptly expressed in the concept of sustainable development.[337]

The social exigencies do not directly trigger the evolution of the law, but they seem to be the decisive argument why the new rules ought to be considered in the process of interpretation. Extra-legal considerations can be found in separate and dissenting opinions: Judge Bedjaoui once mentioned the pressure of international public opinion in *Case Concerning the Gabčíkovo–Nagymaros Project* that 'would have not understood had the Court disregarded the application of the new law'.[338] It is significant that he regarded pressure from public opinion as one of the motives of the Court for interpreting evolutively but regretted that the Court did not justify its decision additionally according to the rules in the VCLT.[339] Judge Weeramantry argued in the same case for the need to interpret human rights evolutively and compared provisions relating

---

[335] *Ibid.* 34 para. 50.   [336] *Ibid.* 47 para. 89.
[337] *Case Concerning the Gabčíkovo–Nagymaros Project (Hungary v. Slovakia)* (Judgment) 78 para. 140.
[338] *Case Concerning the Gabčíkovo–Nagymaros Project (Hungary v. Slovakia)* (Judgment) Separate Opinion Judge Bedjaoui 124 para. 18.
[339] *Ibid.*

to the protection of the environment with human rights.[340] From this, he concluded that those provisions would also have to be interpreted evolutively. Judge Bustamante referred to 'sociological factors' such as the 'social development', 'collective demands' and the 'social purpose' in the interpretation of mandate agreements.[341] Judge Foster has accepted that the Court would be competent to use political methods when faced with a political question.[342] Judge Tanaka has referred to 'interests' underlying the law.[343] He also argued with social institutions such as the international community that could warrant evolutive interpretations, for example replacing the League of Nations with the United Nations.[344] Judge Azevedo managed to include extra-legal factors in the process of treaty interpretation: He interpreted the Havana Convention on Asylum of 1928 'beyond the intentions of the draftsmen' for practical reasons on the one hand but then also included considerations, which he denoted 'special factors'.[345] As examples he mentioned 'race, religion, and geographical proximity'. Especially regarding rules having restricted territorial scope, 'geographical, historical and political circumstances' had to be taken into account.[346]

This rich practice shows the awareness of extra-legal factors by individual judges. The Court only seldom comments on those questions; the two reviewed cases show again its flexibility. Legal arguments outside the VCLT are only sparsely and inconsistently used by the Court.

9.4.3 Precedent

In the first phase of its jurisprudence, the ICJ did not cite any precedents neither to affirm nor to distinguish its intertemporal stance.[347] Later, the ICJ was very pragmatic in its use of precedents and cited different cases without a clear pattern. Yet, the use of precedents was discussed in

---

[340] *Case Concerning the Gabčíkovo–Nagymaros Project (Hungary v. Slovakia)* (Judgment) Separate Opinion Judge Weeramantry 114.
[341] *South West Africa Cases (Ethiopia v. South Africa; Liberia v. South Africa)* (Preliminary Objections), Dissenting Opinion Judge Bustamante 351.
[342] *South West Africa (Ethiopia v. South Africa; Liberia v. South Africa)* (Second Phase), Dissenting Opinion Judge Tanaka 481.
[343] Ibid. 252.   [344] Ibid. 270.
[345] *Colombian–Peruvian Asylum Case (Colombia v. Peru)* (Judgment), Dissenting Opinion Judge Azevedo [1950] ICJ Rep 333.
[346] Ibid.
[347] See for example *Rights of Nationals of the United States of America in Morocco (France v. United States of America)* (Judgment) 188.

separate and dissenting opinions of judges.[348] Many of the intertemporal instances mentioned above were never cited in the jurisprudence of the Court. While some might have been insignificant, others, such as those concerning South West Africa had possibly a strong political connotation. Yet, the *Rights of Nationals of the United States in Morocco Case* seems to be the only case that was mentioned twice in the same – in this case static – sense.[349] A more detailed account of the case law is provided for by Judge *ad hoc* Guillaume, who analysed several ICJ and arbitration cases. He discovered five '*contemporaneous*' and four 'evolutionary cases' while he did not count the *Navigational Rights Case*, which was an 'evolutionary case'.[350] What is interesting and in line with the outcomes of the present study is that he cited an arbitral award that contained two interpretations that resulted in a static and a dynamic reading in the very same case.[351] This finding by the judge calls into question the use of precedents by collecting Court decisions in order to show that international treaties are generally to be interpreted evolutively or statically. The critique of 'mechanical' application of precedent could in part be directed to this kind of use of precedents.[352] This is especially due to the fact that many of the cases that have been used as landmark cases for static interpretations are in fact more multifaceted: the *Rights of Nationals of the United States in Morocco* entails in fact also an instance of evolutive interpretation,[353] and so does the *Kasikili/Sedudu Island Case*.[354] Other cases determine intertemporal questions even though this was not necessary but rather superfluous for the resolution of the dispute.

---

[348] See *Case Concerning the Gabčíkovo–Nagymaros Project (Hungary v. Slovakia)* (Judgment) 67–8 para. 112. The case is distinguished by *Case Concerning the Gabčíkovo–Nagymaros Project (Hungary v. Slovakia)* (Judgment) Separate Opinion Judge Bedjaoui 122–3 paras. 10-11. In favour of a comparison are *Case Concerning the Gabčíkovo–Nagymaros Project (Hungary v. Slovakia)* (Judgment), Dissenting Opinion Judge Herczegh 178; *Case Concerning the Gabčíkovo–Nagymaros Project (Hungary v. Slovakia)* (Judgment) Separate Opinion Judge Weeramantry [1997] ICJ Rep 114.

[349] *South West Africa (Ethiopia v. South Africa; Liberia v. South Africa)* (Second Phase) 23 para. 16; *Case Concerning the Dispute Regarding Navigational and Related Rights (Costa Rica v. Nicaragua)* (Judgment) 242 para. 63.

[350] *Case Concerning the Dispute Regarding Navigational and Related Rights (Costa Rica v. Nicaragua)* (Judgment) 295 paras. 11–12.

[351] *Ibid.* 296 para. 13.

[352] *Case Concerning the Dispute Regarding Navigational and Related Rights (Costa Rica v. Nicaragua)* (Judgment) Separate Opinion Judge Skotnikov 284 para. 6.

[353] *Rights of Nationals of the United States of America in Morocco (France v. United States of America)* (Judgment) 192.

[354] *Kasikili/Sedudu Island (Botswana v. Namibia)* (Judgment) 1064 para. 30.

This applies to the *Anglo-Iranian Oil Case* for static interpretations and to the *Legality of the Threat or Use of Nuclear Weapons Opinion* as well as to the *Preah Vihear Case* for evolutive interpretations.[355] This casts doubt on whether all those cases could be used as general precedents in favour or against evolutive interpretation. Their precedential value might lie more in comparing the arguments advanced in the process of interpretation in subsequent cases with similar problems. This would result in a flexible approach that was not looking for all-or-nothing solutions.

The *Aegean Continental Shelf Case* provides an apt example for the use of precedent: The Court used the *Nationality Decrees Issued in Tunisia and Morocco Case* before the PCIJ as the only argument to accept that the term 'domestic jurisdiction' was to be interpreted evolutively in a reservation[356] but then in the very same case did not follow the precedent set in the *Petroleum Development Ltd v. Sheikh of Abu Dhabi* arbitration.[357] The *Aegean Continental Shelf Case* itself is also subject to flexible precedential use: in the *Navigational and Related Rights Case*, it was used as authority for an evolutive interpretation,[358] while it was used in the *Fisheries Jurisdiction Case* as precedent for a static view.[359] In the most recent decision with an intertemporal aspect, the ICJ cited the *Navigational and Related Rights Case*.[360]

9.5. Summary

We have seen that the Court dealt with over 20 intertemporal issues with the first case in 1950 and the last case in 2010. Cases concerned different treaties and went either way. The general approach of the Court evolved significantly over time and continued to open up towards evolutive interpretation. The Court generally departed from a static premise and then embraced changes of interpretation on different grounds. One was the use of a special type of terms, which were by definition evolutionary or generic. The Court also often used the object and purpose or the subsequent practice and agreement of the parties. The use of precedent played no significant role for the jurisprudence of the Court. Justificatory

---

[355] See above Section 2.
[356] *Aegean Sea Continental Shelf Case (Greece v. Turkey)* (Judgment) 24–5 para. 59.
[357] *Ibid.* 32 para. 77.
[358] *Case Concerning the Dispute Regarding Navigational and Related Rights (Costa Rica v. Nicaragua)* (Judgment) 241–2 para. 65.
[359] *Fisheries Jurisdiction Case (Spain v. Canada)* (Judgment) 454 para. 49.
[360] *Pulp Mills on the River Uruguay Case (Argentina v. Uruguay)* (Judgment) 83 para. 204.

patterns outside the VCLT are sparse even though the statements of judges show that such arguments might at least appeal to parts of the bench. All in all, the Court always managed to deal flexibly with the needs of the parties while there were constantly differing views on intertemporal questions.

Regarding *power*, we have seen that there has been a slow but steady shift of the Court towards evolution. This also means that the Court has succinctly assumed more responsibility to determine intertemporal questions of interpretation. The shift of its goal from real to assumed intention is the most visible expression of this trend. Amongst the three arguments that played the most important part in the process of justification, the definition of the terms and the object and purpose are clearly arguments that the Court can determine and handle. This is well known for the object and purpose, but it applies particularly to terms that are by their nature susceptible to evolution. Examples have shown that very clear referential terms have been interpreted evolutively such as 'members of the League of Nations'; on the other hand, broad terms such as jurisdiction have been interpreted statically. The competence to designate terms as evolutive or not evolutive is a powerful tool in the hands of the Court. On the other hand, subsequent agreements and practice relate mostly to state behaviour. The Court mostly used all arguments available to it, but in the *Navigational and Related Rights Case*, the technique of subsequent practice was neglected. If this pattern continues, this could be read as a further assumption of power by the Court in its justificatory behaviour.

Another aspect that links in with the indicator of power is the question of what kinds of actors are considered to be competent to count as subsequent practice of states. The fact that the practice of the Masubian tribe was not considered to be relevant in the process of interpretation[361] indicates that the ICJ does not accord much relevance to tribes and possibly also to other societal structures beyond the level of a federal government. The Court solely asked the question whether the conduct of the tribesmen could in any way be linked to the authorities; no mention was made that they might have a competence of their own.[362] This might be a sensible and responsible decision, given the problems that might arise in the alternative. Yet, it cannot be denied that the Court does not accord power to actors of that kind.

---

[361] *Kasikili/Sedudu Island (Botswana v. Namibia)* (Judgment) 1094–1095 paras. 74–5.
[362] *Ibid.* 1094 para. 74.

The flexible and pragmatic approach of the Court also allows regulating the *pace* of change. In this context, it ought to be mentioned that the Court at times has interpreted a clause evolutively but left the final resolution to the parties. In the *Case Concerning the Gabčíkovo-Nagymaros Project*, it was left to the parties to implement the new environmental norms.[363] While the Court held that the threat or use of nuclear weapons was considered illegal, the Court added an exception to the general prohibition.[364] This left a backdoor for states so that a general prohibition can only be achieved through their consent.

The Court often refrains from commenting on extra-legal arguments, which makes it hard to determine the indicator of *perception*. As has been shown in the section on other arguments, the Court took a strictly legal approach in the second phase of the *South West Africa Case* but a very open approach in the *Case Concerning the Gabčíkovo-Nagymaros Project*. In the latter case, it could be said that those environmental considerations were the only real arguments to support the evolutive interpretation of the Court. The perceptiveness of the Court can be distilled from the many separate and dissenting opinion taking up the issue. That suggests that the Court will acknowledge those arguments even though it will only in exceptional circumstances respond to them in an affirmative or non-affirmative manner.[365]

The indicators of power, pace and perception reinforce the great flexibility of the Court. While there might be principled argument inside the Court, it has always acted as a responsible peacemaker and tried to retain flexibility in intertemporal matters to effectively solve the disputes before it.

---

[363] *Case Concerning the Gabčíkovo-Nagymaros Project (Hungary v. Slovakia)* (Judgment) 67 para. 112.
[364] *Legality of the Threat or Use of Nuclear Weapons* (Advisory Opinion) 263 para. 79; *ibid.* Concurring Opinion Judge Vereshchetin 280.
[365] For a similar conclusion and a detailed analysis of the extra-legal context of the South West Africa judgments of the Court, see Higgins, 'The International Court and South West Africa' 585.

10

The European Court of Human Rights: an aging activist

Being the first binding human rights instrument, the European Convention on Human Rights has been an important milestone in the development of human rights. More than that, it gave birth to an adventurous and exciting development of an initially little known but later extremely important institution that is today even referred to as a constitutional court for Europe.[366] It is responsible for forty-seven European States and possibly soon also for the European Union. Its mechanisms have produced more than 87,000 decisions and judgments in the year 2012,[367] while there were 65,000 new applications during the same period of time.[368] It would be no exaggeration to call the Court one – if not *the* – characteristic face of Europe. A characteristic feature of the Court is its intertemporal stance.[369] But as we will see, the Court's perception of evolutive interpretation has shifted over time: When the Convention was twenty-five years old, there were active calls among the judges to allow for changes through interpretation. Some forty years later, there is a serious debate about how to limit those interpretations. In many respects, the development of the ECHR and the case law of the Court can be analysed in a dialectic fashion between expansion and limitation.

---

[366] Wildhaber, 'The European Court of Human Rights' 528; Peters and Altwicker, Europäische Menschenrechtskonvention 13.

[367] 1,678 judgments and 86,201 decisions, which together add up to 87,879 judgments and decisions in total: see European Court of Human Rights, *Annual Report* 149.

[368] 65,150: see *ibid*.

[369] This is mentioned prominently by Wildhaber, 'European Court of Human Rights' 310; Wildhaber, 'The European Court of Human Rights: The Past, the Present, the Future' 524; Grabenwarter and Pabel, *Europäische Menschenrechtskonvention* 36; Peters and Altwicker, Europäische Menschenrechtskonvention 25; Harris, O'Boyle, Buckley and others, *Harris, O'Boyle and Warbrick Law of the European Convention on Human Rights* 8–10; Raney, Wicks and Ovey, *Jacobs, White and Ovey, The European Convention on Human Rights* 73–8.

In this sense, we will encounter the Court's stance through the metaphor of an aging activist.[370]

10.1. Institutional aspects

Expansion and limitation have coined the institutional development: The adjudication machinery continued to grow, and after some time it expanded to such an extent that the Court could no longer deal with the applications and fulfil its function to safeguard human rights. This prompted substantial institutional changes. Since judgments before the institutional reforms will also be referred to, it is necessary to explain also the previous institutional arrangements. Under the original system,[371] the central actor was the European Commission of Human Rights ('Commission').[372] States and, on the condition the states agreed, individuals could file complaints to that institution.[373] If there was no friendly settlement, the Commission filed a report either with the Committee of Ministers, which was composed of the foreign ministers of the member states, or with the Court.[374] One of those two institutions decided the matter. The possibility of referrals to the Court was optional.[375] The Court sat in Plenary Sessions or in Chambers, composed of seven judges.[376] Until the coming into force of Protocol 11, there had been a substantial evolution of the system.[377] Protocol 11 was a revolution: the functions of the Commission and the Court were integrated in one single institution, the European Court of Human Rights.[378] This Court had compulsory jurisdiction for individual complaints as well as the possibility to give final and binding decisions in all

---

[370] For a discussion about the Court and activism, see Forowicz, *The Reception of International Law in the European Court of Human Rights* 13; Mahoney, 'Judicial Activism and Judicial Self-Restraint in the European Court of Human Rights' 60; Frowein, 'European Integration through Fundamental Rights' 5, 10.

[371] For accessible and concise summaries of the old system, see Raney, Wicks and Ovey, *Jacobs, White and Ovey, The European Convention on Human Rights* 8–9 and Mowbray, *Cases and Materials on the European Convention on Human Rights* (3rd edn) 10–14.

[372] On the Composition, see Arts. 20–23 of the original text of the ECHR as signed in Rome on 4 November 1950, available at www.echr.coe.int/Documents/Collection_Conventio n_1950_ENG.pdf (accessed 20 June 2015) ('original ECHR').

[373] Arts. 24–25 of the original ECHR (n. 372). For a very good overview, see Mowbray, *Cases and Materials on the European Convention on Human Rights* (3rd edn) 12.

[374] Arts. 31 and 32 of the original ECHR (n. 372).

[375] Art. 48 of the original ECHR (n. 372).   [376] Art. 43 of the original ECHR (n. 372).

[377] Raney, Wicks and Ovey, *Jacobs, White and Ovey, The European Convention on Human Rights* 9.

[378] See Art. 19 Protocol 11.

cases.[379] The workload was divided between Committees, comprised of three judges, Chambers, comprised of seven judges and the Grand Chamber, in which seventeen judges sat.[380] While the Committees could unanimously determine the inadmissibility of a complaint,[381] the Chambers were competent to decide both the admissibility and the merits of a case.[382] In cases raising 'a serious question affecting the interpretation of the Convention', this question could be referred to the Grand Chamber.[383] Not long after the Protocol came into force, the need for further reform arose.[384] And indeed, the attention paid to an individual case was severely limited with the coming into force of Protocol 14: The admissibility of complaints could thereafter be determined by 'single-judge formations'.[385] Three-judge Committees have the additional power to judge the cases that can be decided in accordance with 'well established case law of the Court'.[386] Those changes certainly increase the efficiency and pace of the system,[387] but have a limiting effect on the attention the Court can give to individual cases.

Forty-seven judges sit in Strasbourg to watch over human rights in Europe. Each state has the right to nominate three candidates,[388] who have to fulfil the highest moral and ethical standards.[389] The Assembly of the Council of Europe, which is comprised of 318 representatives from the national parliaments of the member states, selects the judges for a single nine-year term.[390]

The Court is obliged by Art. 45(1) ECHR to support its decisions by presenting arguments. According to Art. 32 ECHR, the jurisdiction of the Court comprises 'all matters concerning the interpretation and application of the Convention and the Protocols'. Art. 46(1) provides that the judgment is binding only for the state party to the proceedings. The Court assumed very early that its task was not only to decide the cases before it but to 'elucidate, safeguard and develop the rules instituted by the Convention'.[391] On other occasions, it had been more careful to state that 'in proceedings originating in an individual application, it has,

---

[379] Arts. 34 and 46 Protocol 11.   [380] Art. 27 Protocol 11.   [381] Art. 28 Protocol 11.
[382] Art. 29 Protocol 11.   [383] Art. 30 Protocol 11.
[384] Statement in that regard by the then President Wildhaber are quoted by Mowbray, *Cases and Materials on the European Convention on Human Rights* (2nd edn) 48.
[385] Art. 27 ECHR: see *ibid*. 52.   [386] Art. 28 ECHR: see *ibid*.   [387] *Ibid*.
[388] Art. 22 ECHR. See Mackenzie, Romano and Shany, *The Manual on International Courts and Tribunals* 337–8.
[389] Art. 23 ECHR. See *ibid*.   [390] Arts. 22–23 ECHR.
[391] *Ireland v. the United Kingdom* (Plenary) Series A no. 25 App. no. 5310/71 [154].

without losing sight of the general context, to confine its attention as far as possible to the issues raised by the concrete case before it'.[392]

The Court has very clearly and decidedly acknowledged that it would adhere to the rule of interpretation contained in the Vienna Convention. In the interpretation of the ECHR, the Convention was used either explicitly or implicitly as part of customary international law,[393] even though it fell outside the temporal scope of the VCLT.[394] Yet, the Court indicated at times that it might depart from the Convention. In *Golder*, the Court used Art. 5 VCLT as an exit door that would allow for the non-application of the rules,[395] this was subsequently not invoked.[396] In *Demir and Baykara*, the Court again included a cautionary note when it held that it would 'mainly' apply the VCLT.[397] Indeed, the Court departed from the Vienna Convention and developed its own methodology in many respects. The most important of those is the consensus method.[398] This evolved in the discourse of the Court centring on the availability of evolutive interpretation. To understand why the Court might be best understood as an aging activist, we will look at two high points in the discourse centring around the issue: First, a colloquy held in 1975, which asked the following question as its major theme: 'Do the rights set forth in the European Convention on Human Rights in 1950 have the same significance in 1975?'[399] The second occasion is a dialogue between judges also organised by the Court as well as the Council of Europe that asked the question: 'What are the limits to the evolutive interpretation of the Convention?'[400]

The first conference was a regular meeting to celebrate the anniversary of the ECHR. The gathering for the twenty-fifth birthday in Rome was

---

[392] *Young, James and Webster* v. *the United Kingdom* (1981) Series A no. 44 App. nos. 7601/76, 7806/77 [53].
[393] *Johnston and others* v. *Ireland* (Plenary) (Judgment) (1986) App. no. 9697/82 [51]; *Loizidou* v. *Turkey* (Preliminary Objections) (Chamber) (1995) Series A no. 310 App. no. 15318/89 [73]; *Hirsi Jamaa and others* v. *Italy* (GC) 2012 App. no. 27765/09 [170–1]; *Rantsev* v. *Cyprus and Russia*, (First Section) App. no. 25965/04 (ECtHR, 7 January 2010) [274].
[394] See Art. 4 VCLT.
[395] *Golder* v. *the United Kingdom* (1973) Series A no. 18 App. no. 4451/70 [29–30].
[396] See *Johnston and others* v. *Ireland*, (Plenary) (Judgment) [51]; *Loizidou* v. *Turkey* (Preliminary Objections) (Chamber) (1995) Series A no. 310 [73].
[397] *Demir and Baykara* v. *Turkey* (GC) ECHR 2008 App. no. 34503/97 [65].
[398] Nolte, 'Second Report for the ILC Study Group on Treaties over Time' 256–7.
[399] Council of Europe (ed.), *Proceedings of the Fourth International Colloquy about the European Convention on Human Rights*.
[400] Council of Europe (ed.), *Dialogue between Judges, European Court of Human Rights*.

frequented by judges of the Court and from member states courts, civil servants from the Council of Europe as well as from its member states, members of parliament, academics from the legal but also other sciences and practising lawyers.[401] Among the three substantive topics discussed over the course of the conference, the question of evolution of the ECHR was the only subject to which four speeches were devoted. The key note speech on the issue was presented by Max Sørensen, at that time a judge at the Court. He was Rapporteur at the Institut de Droit International and prepared a resolution on intertemporal problems of treaties. He regarded the international interpretative method to be open for evolutive interpretations.[402] His speech, which will be referred to throughout the chapter, is emblematic of what later became the approach of the Court. While the title, being formulated as a question, indicated openness, the line of his argument suggested only one answer: the Convention ought to be interpreted evolutively. His argument ran as follows. In a first step, he attested member states general changes in society after the Second World War that would put economic questions in the foreground. These changes would, however, not make civil and political rights superfluous.[403] Those rights retained their field of application and his question was whether they would be subject to change in that field. He argued that evolutive interpretations were allowed by the rules of the VCLT.[404] He used the ICJ as an authority, remarked that the ECHR employed broad standards and drew parallels with constitutional interpretation.[405] He mentioned the slow process of amendment and the need to keep up by using the process of interpretation.[406] Focusing on institutional aspects, he discussed the role of the ECtHR, the Commission and the Committee of Ministers and also the question of whether friendly settlements could be regarded as interpretations of the Convention.[407] He then came up with two mechanisms to update the Convention which he did not link to the Vienna Convention: first, international treaties,[408] and, second, the case law and practice of the member states.[409] What he envisaged here was the consensus method in its embryonic state. He was clearly friendly towards evolutive interpretation and found an approach very closely

---

[401] For a list of participants, see Council of Europe (ed.), *Proceedings of the Fourth International Colloquy about the European Convention on Human Rights* 293.
[402] Sørensen, 'Le problème dit du droit intertemporel dans l'ordre international'.
[403] Sørensen, 'Do the Rights Set Forth in the European Convention on Human Rights in 1950 Have the Same Significance in 1975?' 86.
[404] Ibid. 88.   [405] Ibid. 88.   [406] Ibid. 89.   [407] Ibid. 90.   [408] Ibid. 92.
[409] Ibid. 93.

related to constitutional interpretation. He departed from the VCLT, to which he gave a specific reading, but then developed a certain autonomous method that relied mainly on the internal law of the member states and their international obligations. He also identified the Articles in the ECHR that indeed later proved to be subject to the most changing interpretations: Art. 3 ECHR which prohibits *inter alia* degrading and inhumane treatment and punishment, Art. 8 ECHR which protects family life, as well as Art. 14 ECHR which in combination with other Articles prohibits discriminations.[410] Asserting first that 'attitudes are no longer rigid',[411] his conclusion opens with the sentence: 'the European Convention on Human Rights is a living legal instrument.' It is very probable that Sørensen is the most important founding father of the particular activist stance the Court later took while he was on the bench and which it still retains today. Looking at the list of participants which included many people who played important roles at that time as well as later,[412] it is not surprising that this approach was deeply engraved into the DNA of the Court. We will see this at every stage of our inquiry. But things have moved on since 1975 which becomes apparent when we see how the now aging activist greets the New Year.

In 2011, there was a high-level meeting between judges of the Court and other guests in Strasbourg before the Court opened the new year with a solemn hearing. The picture on the first page of the publication of this meeting conveys the impression that it was less a birthday party and more like a strategy meeting of a large enterprise. The theme was, as already mentioned, the limits of evolutive interpretation. Comparing the presentations given to those in Rome, the evolutive interpretation was not an exciting prospect but more of a pressing problem. The principal speech was given by Judge Françoise Tulkens, who briefly outlined some general features of the approach of the Court as well as two examples for its approach to evolutive interpretation.[413] But the main part of the

---

[410] *Ibid.* 96.   [411] *Ibid.* 103.
[412] To mention just a few, the list includes Rudolf Bernhardt, at that time director of the Max Planck Institute of Comparative Public Law and International Law in Heidelberg, who later became member of the ECtHR, Jochen Frowein, at that time Professor in Bielefeld and member of the Commission and Luzius Wildhaber, at that time Professor in Fribourg, who later also became judge and President of the Court.
[413] Tulkens, 'What Are the Limits to Evolutive Interpretation of the Convention?' 6. The conference is also referred to by Garapon, 'Les Limites à l'interprétation évolutive de la Convention Européenne' 439.

speech was dedicated to the critique of the particular evolutive approach of the Court: a lack of faithfulness to the text, 'concerns of "democratic legitimacy"', 'evolutive interpretation ... as a symbol of "activism" or worse, judicial imperialism'.[414] Departing from that analysis, Judge Tulkens envisaged different ways of limiting those evolutive interpretations ranging from remarks on the consensus method to institutional proposals such as the envisaged conferral of jurisdiction for these questions to the Grand Chamber.[415]

Comparing the speeches of Sørensen in 1975 and Tulkens in 2011, we can detect a substantial shift in the discourse concerning evolutive interpretation. It is not only about fighting fiercely for the possibility to interpret evolutively, but also about knowing where the limits of such interpretation are. In this sense, the story of the Court is the story of an aging activist. The activist has succeeded and achieved many of his or her goals. But he or she has also matured and developed; new questions have entered his or her life. The Court is no longer twenty-five years old, it is over sixty and the world looks very different now. It listens not only to the voices pushing for more evolution but also to the voices that call for clear limits.[416] We shall pursue this dialectic of expansion and limitation without favouring one over the other in order to see how the approach to evolutive interpretation has evolved.

10.2. Stocktaking: intertemporal instances

No less than seventy-five times did the Court discuss intertemporal questions. It is important to mention that intertemporal instances can arise in two sets of circumstances. First, in the process of *interpretation*, which arises when the Court attributes meaning to the text. The Court, like courts that are responsible for interpreting and applying human rights on the domestic or international level, also engages in the process of *balancing*. This mostly results in a proportionality test, but is regularly composed of a structured way of deciding a question in accordance

---

[414] Tulkens, 'What Are the Limits to Evolutive Interpretation of the Convention?' 8.
[415] Ibid. 9.
[416] Golsong, 'Interpreting the Convention'; Gaja, 'Does the European Court of Human Rights Use its Stated Methods of Interpretation?'.

with all considerations that are relevant for the case. Balancing is not about determining the meaning of words in a treaty. The Court resorts to balancing in four situations: First, if the Court has found an interference with a right, it establishes whether this interference is justified.[417] In these situations, the Court looks for a proportionate aim and sees whether this aim fulfils the requirements of the Convention and in this context looks for a legitimate aim and its proportionality.[418] Second, the Court looks at situations in which Art. 14 ECHR is applied together with the other rights enshrined in the Convention.[419] In these situations, the Court has to decide whether there is an unjustified discrimination.[420] Third, the Court acknowledges that certain rights have also a positive dimension in the sense that they do not only guarantee the absence of state interference, but oblige the state to protect the rights in question in an active manner.[421] Fourth, the Court at times determines the content of very vague terms through a process of balancing, in which it examines whether the terms apply on a case-by-case basis.[422] The notion of 'inhuman and degrading treatment or punishment' is one example of that category. The Court goes as far as to interpret this to require a certain severity. The severity is then determined according to all facts of the case and all possible considerations instead of establishing the abstract meaning of severity. The Court rather evaluates the situation before it in an all-encompassing manner, which can only be conceptualised as a process of balancing. Justification of interferences, establishment of discrimination and a positive obligation and the determination of very vague terms are the circumstances in which the Court balances several considerations. As we will see, the Court is also sensitive to developments. Like reinterpreting, the Court would also consider rebalancing the law if there are indications that it was necessary. To give a structured account of all cases found that makes it easy for the reader to navigate, the commentary method will be employed.[423]

---

[417] See for example *Stoll v. Switzerland* (GC) ECHR 2007-V App. no. 69698/01 [103–4].
[418] The different tests of proportionality and rationality are discussed by Frowein, 'European Integration through Fundamental Rights' 17.
[419] *Marckx v. Belgium*, (Plenary) (1979) Series A no. 31 App. no. 6833/74.
[420] *Ibid.* [41].
[421] *Christine Goodwin v. the United Kingdom* (GC) ECHR 2002-VI [71–2].
[422] *Sitaropoulos and Giakoumopoulos v. Greece* (GC) ECHR 2012 App. no. 42202/07 [71–2].
[423] For the commentary method, see Djeffal, 'Commentaries on the Law of Treaties' 1223–38.

Art. 2: right to life

1. Everyone's right to life shall be protected by law. No one shall be deprived of his life intentionally save in the execution of a sentence of a court following his conviction of a crime for which this penalty is provided.

...

Intertemporal questions in relation to the right to life touched upon the applicability to unborn life, assisted suicide and death penalties. The death-penalty question arose in a line of cases looking into whether the death penalty violated Art. 3 ECHR. This was considered to be possible only if the respective possibility as mentioned in the second sentence of Art. 2(1) ECHR could not be relied on.[424] In *Soering*, the Court had to deal with the question whether an extradition could violate the Convention when the person to be extradited faced the death penalty in the country requesting extradition.[425] The Court held that, due to Art. 2 ECHR, Art. 3 ECHR would not apply to the death penalty as the death penalty was explicitly described as an exception to the right to life.[426] In *Öcalan*, the Court indicated that the death penalty in times of peace would be contrary to the Convention.[427] In *Al-Saadoon and Mufdhi*, the Court held that the death penalty would also be contrary to Art. 3 ECHR in times of war.[428]

---

[424] In practice, this problem comes very close to the concept of desuetude or obsolescence.
[425] *Soering v. the United Kingdom* (Plenary) (1989) Series A no. 161 App. no. 14038/88. The Court found that the subsequent practice would favour an evolutive interpretation. Yet it held that the context – Art. 2(1) ECHR – and a subsequent agreement – Protocol 6 – favoured a static interpretation.
[426] *Soering v. the United Kingdom* (Plenary) (1989) Series A no. 161 [101]. In favour of a static solution the Court considered the context as well as the subsequent agreement of the parties. These techniques trumped the object and purpose as well as the subsequent practice, which was previously termed as virtual consensus but was not inserted in the process of balancing.
[427] *Öcalan v. Turkey*, (First Section) App. no. 46221/99 (ECtHR, 12 March 2003) [190–8]. The Court took the context to be an argument for static interpretation which could be overcome by subsequent agreement, subsequent practice as well as the relevant rules. While the Court left the question technically open, the whole justification suggests that the Court did interpret evolutively. The decision was reinforced by the Grand Chamber in *Öcalan v. Turkey* (GC) ECHR 2005-IV App. no. 46221/99 [164–5]. In the face of three outstanding signatures as well as sixteen ratifications, the Court held that the death penalty could not be considered to be abolished in times of war.
[428] *Al-Saadoon and Mufdhi v. the United Kingdom*, (Fourth Section) ECHR 2010 App. no. 61498/08 [115–22]. The Court considered again the context as favouring a static

Art. 2 ECHR also entails a positive obligation to protect the right to life. It is unclear, however, at what point in time this protection starts and whether a foetus is also protected. In *VO v. France*, the Court looked at this interpretative question and decided that it was within the margin of appreciation of the member states.[429] A question that had to be determined in the process of balancing as opposed to interpretation was whether there was a positive obligation for states to permit assisted suicide, which could also very briefly be termed as a right to death. In *Pretty*, the Court interpreted Art. 2 ECHR as not entailing a right to death,[430] and held that states had no positive obligation to assist in suicide.

Art. 3: prohibition of torture

> No one shall be subject to torture or to inhuman or degrading treatment or punishment.

Regarding the prohibition of torture, mainly *questions of balancing* arose. This is due to the fact that the terms 'torture' and 'inhuman and degrading treatment or punishment' were interpreted to apply if there was a certain level of severity. The question whether this level was reached in a specific case was then based on all the facts of the case. The Court, therefore, turned it into a question of balancing. It can be seen from the case law that the general standard was lowered over time: Actions that would not have been considered to violate Art. 3 ECHR were later said to fall under its terms. *Tyrer* is a very good example of this. It relied on the severity test establishing an inhuman or degrading treatment or punishment.

In this case, the Court had established that degrading treatment would require a certain level of humiliation. The Court found that this was 'relative' and, therefore, 'depends on all the circumstances of the case and, in particular, on the nature and context of the punishment itself and

---

interpretation which it overcame by stressing the subsequent agreement and the subsequent practice of the member states.

[429] *Vo v. France* (GC) ECHR 2004-VIII App. no. 53924/00 [82–5]. In the interpretation of Art. 2 ECHR, the Court found no consensus concerning the beginning of life and the protection of this form of life. Therefore, the subsequent practice as well as the relevant rules were inconclusive.

[430] *Pretty v. the United Kingdom*, (Fourth Section) ECHR 2002-III App. no. 2346/02 [39, 54]. The Court considered the ordinary meaning as well as the context.

the manner and method of its execution'.[431] In the process of balancing, the Court held that the assessment of what could be considered as degrading had to be updated.[432]

The Court also had other cases on minors. In *T v. the United Kingdom*, the Court held that Art. 3 ECHR did not apply automatically when criminal responsibility is attributed to a ten-year-old.[433] In the same case, the Court had to determine whether a public trial over a period of time of three weeks would violate Art. 3 ECHR, an assertion rejected by the Court.[434] In *MC v. Bulgaria*, the Court looked at the previously established positive obligation to punish and prosecute in rape cases. It found an evolution of the definition of rape, which could be perpetrated even in the absence of physical harm or threat, which altered the positive obligation derived from Art. 3 ECHR.[435]

While the former cases all dealt with severity as a minimum requirement to fall under the term 'inhuman or degrading treatment or punishment',[436] severity is also important to distinguish the latter concept from torture, for torture requires a higher level of severity. The Court acknowledged in *Selmouni*[437] and *Dikme*[438] that the standards for this assessment changed over time. *Selmouni* concerned a wide range of

---

[431] *Tyrer v. the United Kingdom*, (Chamber) Series A no. 26 App. no. 5856/72 [30].

[432] In that context, the Court considered the 'commonly accepted standards in penal policy' and, therefore, the practice of states as well as the practice of the part of the state acting as respondent, and found both factors to warrant a change in the balance struck by the convention: *ibid.* [31].

[433] *T v. the United Kingdom* (GC) App. no. 24724/94 (16 December 1999) [70-2]. The Court could find no consensus, neither internationally nor in the practice of states. See also the identical case of *V v. the United Kingdom* (GC) ECHR 1999-IX App. no. 24888/94 [71-80].

[434] *T v. the United Kingdom* (GC) [73-8]. While the Court detected an international trend that was also reinforced by Art. 6 ECHR, the facts of the case showed that the level of severity was not achieved.

[435] *MC v. Bulgaria*, (First Section) ECHR 2003-XII App. no. 39272/98 [154-66]. The Court considered the internal and external practice of states as well as an 'evolving understanding' of what happened to rape victims. Rape is not a legal term of the Convention, so there was no real evolutive interpretation but rather a rebalancing of the positive obligation which was held to include cases in which there was no physical harm or threat.

[436] This has the consequence for Art. 3 ECHR to apply: see *Hénaf v. France*, (First Section) ECHR 2003-XI App. no. 65436/01 [55]. See also *Tanăse v. Romania*, (Third Section) App. no. 5269/02 (ECtHR, 12 May 2009) [83].

[437] *Selmouni v. France* (GC) ECHR 1999-V App. no. 25803/94 [100-1].

[438] *Dikme v. Turkey*, (First Section) ECHR 2000-VIII App. no. 20869/92 [92-4]. Since this case only supports the finding in *Selmouni*, it will not be counted for the statistical analysis.

mistreatment by police officials including physical blows, humiliation and threats, while *Dikme* also concerned blows in interrogation sessions. Both cases were considered to amount to torture as opposed to 'only' 'inhuman or degrading treatment or punishment'.

Art. 4: prohibition of slavery and forced labour

1. No one shall be held in slavery or servitude
2. No one shall be required to perform forced or compulsory labour
3. For the purpose of this Article the term 'forced or compulsory labour' shall not include:
   (a) any work required to be done in the ordinary course of detention imposed according to the provisions of Article 5 of this Convention or during conditional release from such detention;
   ...

Like Art. 3 ECHR, Art. 4 ECHR is a non-derogable right and the Court dealt in two instances with the question whether it ought to change the interpretation of this article. In *Rantsev*, the Court had to look into whether Art. 4 ECHR would be applicable to trafficking in persons which could be described as forcing a person to be transferred for a benefit into a setting in which the person is exploited. The Court had to consider whether the provision would fall under Art. 4(1) or (2) ECHR. The Court held that trafficking would fall under Art. 4 while abstaining from qualifying it as forced or compulsory labour or slavery and concluded that Art. 4 ECHR would be applicable as if trafficking was mentioned in it.[439] So the Court added the word by interpretation. In *Stummer*, the Court considered whether the exemption from forced labour in Art. 4(3)(a) ECHR would be applicable when the labourers in a prison were not included in the national pension scheme. The Court found that the law had not changed and the exception applied.[440] There was, consequently, no violation.

---

[439] *Rantsev v. Cyprus and Russia*, (First Section) [272-82]. The Court held that the ordinary meaning did not encompass trafficking but that due to a change in the relevant rules and the rise of a new phenomenon, Art. 4 could be applied to trafficking.

[440] *Stummer v. Austria* (GC) ECHR 2011 App. no. 37452/02 [112-34]. While the relevant rules could be considered as evidence in favour of such a rule, the subsequent practice was diverse and not conclusive. The way in which the Court relied on the practice is significant: even though the practice is inconclusive, it was taken as an argument against evolution. When a technique normally produces inconclusive results, this is not taken as an argument for either side. The fact that the Court here justified the static solution

Art. 5: right to liberty and security

1. Everyone has the right to liberty and security of person. No one shall be deprived of his liberty save in the following cases and in accordance with a procedure prescribed by law:

    ...

    (b) the lawful arrest or detention of a person for non-compliance with the lawful order of a court or in order to secure the fulfilment of any obligation prescribed by law;

    ...

3. Everyone arrested or detained in accordance with the provisions of paragraph 1(c) of this Article ... shall be entitled to trial within a reasonable time or to release pending trial. Release may be conditioned by guarantees to appear for trial.
4. Everyone who is deprived of his liberty by arrest or detention shall be entitled to take proceedings by which the lawfulness of his detention shall be decided speedily by a court and his release ordered if the detention is not lawful.

The ECHR protects the freedom of the person and gave rise to three interpretative issues. In *McVeigh*, the Commission had to determine whether the detention of terrorist suspects at an airport could be justified as securing the fulfilment of an obligation prescribed by law as set out in Art. 5(1)(b) ECHR. In its previous case law, the Commission had held that there ought to be 'specific circumstances which warrant the use of detention as means of fulfilment of the obligation'.[441] In this case, the complainant had no obligation other than to submit to a questioning and interrogation. Even though this could not be considered as a sufficiently specific obligation, the Commission changed its jurisprudence due to the circumstances of the case.[442] While generally only a 'refusal or neglect to comply with an obligation' could justify detention, the Commission found that there could also be 'limited circumstances of a pressing nature which could justify such a detention'.[443] In *Mangouras*, the Court had to determine whether the bail set by a court for somebody accused of an

---

with the absence of practice will make it necessary to regard it as correlating with the interpretative result.

[441] *McVeigh and others v. the United Kingdom* (Decision) (1981) App. nos. 8022/77, 8025/77, 8027/77 [189].
[442] *Ibid.* [190–1]. The Court argued mainly with the context but also looked to terrorism as a pressing social issue.
[443] *Ibid.* [190].

environmental crime was disproportionate, which the Court answered in the affirmative.[444]

In *Lebedev*, the Court held that the right to be heard as enshrined in Art. 5(4) ECHR would also confer fair trial rights and thereby extend the scope of the provision.[445] In *Austin*, the Court determined whether the 'containment of a group of people carried out by the police on public order grounds' which is also called 'kettling' could be considered as deprivation of liberty.[446] After balancing the respective interests, the Court held that this new policing technique would fall under the scope of Art. 5 ECHR.[447]

Art. 6: right to a fair trial

1. In the determination of his civil rights and obligations or of any criminal charge against him, everyone is entitled to a fair and public hearing within a reasonable time by an independent and impartial tribunal established by law. Judgment shall be pronounced publicly but the press and public may be excluded from all or part of the trial in the interests of morals, public order or national security in a democratic society, where the interests of juveniles or the protection of the private life of the parties so require, or to the extent strictly necessary in the opinion of the court in special circumstances where publicity would prejudice the interests of justice.

...

The ECHR contains several rights which have been extended by the Court to contain general fair trial rights. In *Ferrazzini*, the Grand Chamber decided that Art. 6(1) ECHR had not evolved in the sense that tax obligations could be considered as 'civil rights and obligations' and, thereby, extended the scope of Art. 6(1) ECHR.[448] In *Vilho Eskelinen and*

---

[444] *Mangouras v. Spain* (GC) App. no. 12050/04 (ECtHR, 28 September 2010) [82–92]. The Court relied *inter alia* on 'new realities' such as the 'legitimate concern' of European states as well as internationally for the environment as well as the 'tendency' to outlaw pollution of the environment by means of criminal law.

[445] *Lebedev v. Russia*, (First Section) App. no. 4493/04 (ECtHR, 25 October 2007) [71–2].

[446] *Austin and others v. the United Kingdom* (GC) ECHR 2012 App. nos. 39692/09, 40713/09, 41008/09 [52].

[447] *Ibid.* [52–60].

[448] *Ferrazzini v. Italy* (GC) ECHR 2001-VII App. no. 44759/98 [26–31]. In favour of an evolution the Court alluded to several decisions which highlighted the subsequent practice of the parties as well as the context. The Court also referred to general societal

others, the question was whether the 'determination of civil rights and obligations' would also entail disputes about wage supplements for civil servants. The Court had previously interpreted this phrase as entailing a functional criterion that would exclude the applicability of Art. 6(1) ECHR in cases involving civil servants. The Court, however, changed the interpretation and held that there ought to be two additional criteria:[449] express exclusion of the access to the Court for that post and justification 'on objective grounds in the state's interest'. Adding these criteria to the definition, the Court interpreted Art. 6(1) ECHR evolutively.[450] The Court held in *Annoni* that the right of access to a court was also violated when the access was dependent upon payment of an unreasonable sum.[451] This meant that the Court extended the scope of fair trial rights also to economic questions that could also be considered to be regulated by the European Social Charter rather than the ECHR.

Art. 8: right to respect for private life and family life

1. Everyone has the right to respect for his private and family life, his home and his correspondence.
2. There shall be no interference by a public authority with the exercise of this right except such as is in accordance with the law and is necessary in a democratic society in the interests of national security, public safety or the economic well-being of the country, for the prevention of disorder or crime, for the protection of health or morals, or for the protection of the rights and freedoms of others.

Art. 8 ECHR, protecting the private and family life as well as the home, plays a special role in the present context. In *Schalk and Kopf*, the Court had to determine whether the notion of 'family life' applied to same-sex

---

observations, yet those could be considered as considerations of the ordinary meaning. Against change, the Court adduced another argument from the context as well as the ordinary meaning of the text.

[449] *Vilho Eskelinen and others v. Finland* ECHR 2004-VIII App. no. 63235/00 50–64. The Court referred to the consequences of the old test in the present circumstances, which could be termed as using the technique of object and purpose. It referred to the context of the rule and the relevant rules.

[450] *Ibid.* 62.

[451] *Annoni di Gussola and others* v. France, (Third Section) ECHR 2000-XI App. nos. 31819/96, 33293/96 [56, 59]. The Court considered *inter alia* the consequences for the applicants as well as the internal law.

relationships and found that it did.[452] In *Société Colas Est* the Court reversed a previous decision by holding that the right to a private home extended to rooms owned by juristic persons.[453] In *Harroudj*, the Court held that the notion of a family could also include the recognition to a certain extent of alternatives to the institution of adoption in other legal orders. So the Court held that the Islamic *kafala* had to be recognised to a certain extent.[454]

The Court also had to deal with many issues of *rebalancing* in that regard. A famous line of birth certificate cases related to the fact that it was impossible for human beings who had undertaken an operation changing their sex to have their birth certificates changed accordingly. The Court had to deal with the question of whether states had a positive obligation to recognise the gender change and in particular to reissue birth certificates for transsexuals. In *Rees*, the Court held that the respondent state would not have the obligation to issue new birth certificates.[455] The Court affirmed the state of the law in *Cossey*[456] and *Sheffield and Horsham*.[457] In *X, Y and Z*, the Court decided a related question, namely, whether a change of the sex of a transsexual must be included in the birth certificate of the child of his or her partner which the Court denied.[458] In *B v. France*, the Court reinforced that there were

---

[452] *Schalk and Kopf v. Austria*, (First Section) ECHR 2010 App. no. 30141/04 [90-5]. The Court referred to subsequent practice as well as to the relevant rules. For a different conclusion, see *Schalk and Kopf v. Austria*, (First Section), Concurring Opinion of Judge Malinverni joined by Judge Kovler ECHR 2010 App. no. 30141/04.

[453] *Société Colas Est and others v. France* ECHR 2002-III App. no. 37971/97 [40-2]. The Court mainly argued with an evolutive interpretation of another norm of the ECHR, it, therefore, argued with the context of the provision.

[454] *Harroudj v. France*, (Fifth Section) App. no. 43631/09 (ECtHR, 4 October 2012) [41, 49]. The Court argued that there was only a partial consensus, established by international treaties and the internal laws of other member states and reinforced by the respondent state's internal law, but came later to the conclusion that France had not violated the Convention. This outcome could be seen as a partial evolution.

[455] *Rees v. the United Kingdom* (Plenary) (1986) Series A no. 106 [38-47]. The Court mainly argued with the adverse consequence for the state and its administration.

[456] *Cossey v. the United Kingdom*, (Plenary) 1990 Series A no. 184 App. no. 10843/84 [37-40]. The Court reasoned that there was no scientific progress and no change in the internal practice of states.

[457] *Sheffield and Horsham v. the United Kingdom* (GC) ECHR 1998-V App. nos. 22985/93 23390/94 [51-6]. The Court found that neither the scientific knowledge on the situation or the subsequent practice had changed in a significant manner.

[458] *X, Y and Z v. the United Kingdom* (GC) ECHR 1997-II App. no. 21830/93 [41-52]. The Court again found that there was no common ground and that the consequences upon the states would be too burdensome.

no changes in the law,[459] yet, it held that the situation in France could be distinguished from the United Kingdom.[460] This enabled the Court to find a breach without changing the law.[461] Finally, the Court held in *Christine Goodwin* that the law had changed and Art. 8 ECHR had been violated.[462] In *L v. Lithuania*, the Court held that there was a positive obligation to pay for operations for transsexuals.[463]

In *KU*, the Court determined whether there was a positive obligation stemming from the duty to respect the private life for a state to require Internet providers to reveal the identity of perpetrators of crimes.[464] The Court affirmed this obligation. In *Haas*, a positive obligation to provide for a certain substance which would enable an applicant to commit suicide was denied by the Court.[465] In *Chapman*, the Court held that the obligation for gypsies to move to alternative accommodation would not be considered as unjustified interference in the rights conferred upon them by Art. 8 ECHR.[466] The Commission held in *Acmanne and others* that mandatory tests for children (including x-ray) leading to convictions of the parents in cases of failed compliance could be considered as proportionate.[467] The Court held in *Emonet*

---

[459] B v. France, (Plenary) (1992) Series A no. 232-C App. no. 13343/87 [48].
[460] Ibid. [49–51].   [461] Ibid. [63].
[462] Christine Goodwin v. the United Kingdom (GC) ECHR 2002-VI [71–93]. The Court entered into a lengthy process of balancing. Among the arguments used, it considered European as well as international state practice, medico-scientific considerations, the object and purpose of the Convention, which it found to be human dignity and personal autonomy and the consequences for the claimant as well as for the respondent state. The Court also decided the following case in an identical manner: I v. the United Kingdom (GC) App. no. 25680/94 (ECtHR, 11 July 2002). The evolutive interpretation was confirmed in Grant v. the United Kingdom, (Fourth Section) ECHR 2006-VII App. no. 32570/03 [39–44].
[463] L v. Lithuania, (Second Section) ECHR 2007-IV App. no. 27527/03 56–60. The Court mainly referred to the consequences, its own case law and the national law of the respondent state.
[464] KU v. Finland, (Fourth Section) ECHR 2008 App. no. 2872/02 [42–51]. The Court affirmed this obligation, referring amongst other things to the social views on the Internet at the material time (1999).
[465] Haas v. Switzerland, (First Section) ECHR 2011 App. no. 31322/07 [55–61]. The Court considered that there was no consensus amongst other arguments.
[466] Chapman v. the United Kingdom (GC) ECHR 2001-I App. no. 27238/95 [90–116]. The Court relied on several consequential arguments against such an obligation and found the practice within the external practice in the Council of Europe not conclusive.
[467] Acmanne and others v. Belgium DR 1984 App. no. 10435/83 Decisions and Reports 256-7. The Commission came to this conclusion despite the practice of other European countries but recognised that the situation in Belgium developed in the direction of 'present-day conditions of life'.

that the consequences for the child–parent relationship after the adoption by the partner of the parent violated a positive obligation under the Convention.[468] In *A, B and C v. Ireland*, the Court found that there was still a wide margin of appreciation to provide for restrictions on abortion so that there was no violation of the right to respect for one's private life.[469]

Art. 9: freedom of thought, conscience and religion

1. Everyone has the right to freedom of thought, conscience and religion; this right includes freedom to change his religion or belief, and freedom, either alone or in community with others and in public or private, to manifest his religion or belief, in worship, teaching, practice and observance.
2. Freedom to manifest one's religion or beliefs shall be subject only to such limitations as are prescribed by law and are necessary in a democratic society in the interests of public safety, for the protection of public order, health or morals, or the protection of the rights and freedoms of others.

In *Bayatyan*, the Grand Chamber considered that the freedom of religion enshrined in Art. 9 ECHR is applicable to conscientious objection.[470] The Third Section had previously held in the very same case that there was no evolution of the law and Art. 9 ECHR was not applicable to conscientious objection.[471]

---

[468] *Emonet and others v. Switzerland*, (First Section) App. no. 39051/03 (ECtHR, 13 December 2007) 63–87. The Court relied mainly upon the consequences and disregarded the national law of the respondent state as well as an international treaty, but also took into account a draft revision of that treaty.

[469] *A, B and C v. Ireland* (GC) ECHR 2010 App. no. 25579/05 [229–41]. The Court found that there was a consensus concerning a freer stance on abortion but that there was no consensus on when the right to life began.

[470] *Bayatyan v. Armenia* (GC) ECHR 2011 App. no. 23459/03 [98–111]. The Court first argued that one provision from the context, namely, Art. 4(3)(b) ECHR, had no bearing upon the issue. The Court then found that the subsequent practice as well as the relevant rules established a sufficient consensus. This case is not considered to be an interpretation of Art. 4(3)(b) ECHR since the question the Court asked was whether Art. 9 ECHR ought to be read in conjunction with that provision or not, which is mainly an interpretation of Art. 9 ECHR.

[471] *Bayatyan v. Armenia*, (Third Section) App. no. 23459/03 (ECtHR, 27 October 2009) [61–6]. The Court held that Art. 4(3)(b) ECHR as a provision stemming from the context leaves no room for other means such as subsequent practice or the relevant rules to change the law.

Art. 10: freedom of expression

1. Everyone has the right to freedom of expression. this right shall include freedom to hold opinions and to receive and impart information and ideas without interference by public authority and regardless of frontiers. This article shall not prevent States from requiring the licensing of broadcasting, television or cinema enterprises.
2. The exercise of these freedoms, since it carries with it duties and responsibilities, may be subject to such formalities, conditions, restrictions or penalties as are prescribed by law and are necessary in a democratic society, in the interests of national security, territorial integrity or public safety, for the prevention of disorder or crime, for the protection of health or morals, for the protection of the reputation or the rights of others, for preventing the disclosure of information received in confidence, or for maintaining the authority and impartiality of the judiciary.

In *Stoll*, the Court assessed the proportionality of an interference with the freedom of expression in Art. 10 ECHR. In this case, a journalist was punished for releasing a secret. The Court found no violation and gave more weight to the restriction of the right due to changed circumstances.[472] The Court also took into account new circumstances that were not present at the time the Convention was drafted: in *Mouvement Raëlien Suisse*, it considered the content of an Internet site when its address was displayed on a poster in the process of balancing.[473]

Art. 11: freedom of assembly and association

1. Everyone has the right to freedom of peaceful assembly and to freedom of association with others, including the right to form and to join trade unions for the protection of his interests.
2. No restrictions shall be placed on the exercise of these rights other than such as are prescribed by law and are necessary in a democratic society in the interests of national security or public safety, for the prevention of disorder or crime, for the protection of health or morals or for the

---

[472] *Stoll v. Switzerland* (GC) ECHR 2007-V [104–7]. The Court argued with a general observation of society, but supported the finding with the observation of the uniform practice of the members of the Council of Europe. The fact that this amounts to a change in the law is also reinforced by *Stoll v. Switzerland* (GC), Dissenting Opinion of Judge Zagrebelsky joined by Judges Lorenzen, Fura-Sandström, Jaeger and Popović ECHR 2007-V App. no. 69698/01 [106].

[473] *Mouvement Raëlien Suisse v. Switzerland* (GC) ECHR 2012 App. no. 16354/06 [68]. Since this was only a single question in the whole context of balancing, this instance has not been counted as an intertemporal instance.

protection of the rights and freedoms of others. this article shall not prevent the imposition of lawful restrictions on the exercise of these rights by members of the armed forces, of the police or of the administration of the State.

Two famous cases were decided in the context of the freedom of assembly and association. In *Sigurjönsson*, the Court held that the right to form and join trade unions as enshrined in Art. 11 ECHR entailed also the negative right not to join them.[474] In *Demir and Baykara*, the Court held that 'the right to form and join trade unions' entailed the right to bargain collectively which was not previously included in this provision.[475]

Art. 12: right to marry

> Men and women of marriageable age have the right to marry and to found a family, according to the national laws governing the exercise of this right.

The right to marry enshrined in Art. 12 ECHR gave rise to a line of intertemporal disputes. A disputed question of interpretation has been whether the right to marry would only cover the traditional marriage between one man and one woman or whether there was a broader concept also covering transsexuals that have changed their sex, or gay marriage. Regarding transsexuals, the Court reaffirmed in *Rees* the traditional concept of marriage.[476] In *Cossey*[477] and *Sheffield and Horsham*,[478] the Court held that transsexuals could not avail themselves of the right to

---

[474] *Sigidur A. Sigurjónsson v. Iceland* Series A no. 264 App. no. 16130/90 [33–6]. The Court referred to the *travaux* but held that the practice of the parties as well as the relevant rules would call for an evolution of the law. This issue was not determined conclusively in *Young, James and Webster v. the United Kingdom* (1981) Series A no. 44 [50–7].

[475] *Demir and Baykara v. Turkey* (GC) ECHR 2008 [147]. Using the consensus method, the Court reviewed the treaty practice of the states as well as their internal practice. Since the case concerned an interpretation, this was translated to subsequent practice and relevant rules.

[476] *Rees v. the United Kingdom* (Plenary) (1986) Series A no. 106 [49–51]. The Court mainly relied on the ordinary meaning of the text as well as its context.

[477] *Cossey v. the United Kingdom*, (Plenary) 1990 Series A no. 184 [43–8]. The Court mainly referred to the wording as well as the subsequent practice.

[478] Cotterrell, *Law, Culture and Society* paras. 66–9. Here the Court merely reiterated the previous cases, therefore, this case will not be counted in that regard.

marry. This was subsequently changed in *Christine Goodwin*.[479] In this case, the Court found a breach of Art. 12.

In *Schalk and Kopf*, the Court held that Art. 12 ECHR evolved partly but not fully in relation to gay marriage. It held that Art. 12 was applicable to the question of gay marriage, but that it would be, for the moment, left to the national authorities to decide whether the institution of marriage is also open to gay couples.[480] In *F v. Switzerland*, the Court held a three year ban of marriage after divorce to be disproportionate.[481]

Art. 14: prohibition of discrimination

> The enjoyment of the rights and freedoms set forth in this Convention shall be secured without discrimination on any ground such as sex, race, colour, language, religion, political or other opinion, national or social origin, association with a national minority, property, birth or other status.

Art. 14 ECHR prohibits discrimination in the enjoyment of Convention rights. The Court, therefore, has in a first step to look into whether the situation is within the application of a Convention right, and second whether there is discrimination, i.e. a distinction without objective and reasonable justification. Whether such a distinction has been made is to be determined by the process of balancing. Intertemporal issues mostly arose when the Court considered to rebalance situations in which Art. 8 ECHR was applicable. In *Marckx*, the Court had to deal with the question whether a situation in which the maternal affiliation of married mothers was automatically recognised while unmarried mothers had to go

---

[479] *Christine Goodwin v. the United Kingdom* (GC) ECHR 2002-VI [97–104]. The Court interpreted the ordinary meaning to be at least open to a different reading. It referred to societal and medical developments as well as to new relevant rules applicable between the parties. The Court decided the following case in an identical manner: *I v. the United Kingdom* (GC).

[480] *Schalk and Kopf v. Austria*, (First Section) ECHR 2010 [55–63]. The Court found the language to be open but the context favouring a static result. This was reinforced by the circumstances at the conclusion of the treaty. The context of Art. 8 ECHR was not held to be determinative for that question. While there was no consistent subsequent practice to support the conclusion, the relevant rules could be taken to support at least the partial evolution. For a different conclusion on this point, see *Schalk and Kopf v. Austria*, (First Section), Concurring Opinion of Judge Malinverni joined by Judge Kovler ECHR 2010.

[481] *F v. Switzerland* (Plenary) (1987) Series A no. 128 App. no. 11329/85 [30–40]. The Court referred to the law in other contracting states, the internal situation in the respondent state and the consequences. All those factors were taken to be in favour of change.

through a procedure was to be considered as illegal discrimination. It found that this amounted to discrimination against children born out of wedlock.[482] The Court had to deal with this issue several times,[483] but other family matters also involved questions of rebalancing. In *Zaunegger*, the Court held that German law discriminated against unmarried fathers as compared to divorced fathers, insofar as the former had no possibility to have custody of their children and there was no possibility for judicial review of the custody of the mother. In that context, the Court held that the wide margin of appreciation of the member states ought to be restricted regarding the question of judicial review.[484] In *Konstantin Markin*, the Court held that the omission to provide for parental leave for male soldiers was discriminatory.[485] In *Schwizgebel*, the Court was faced with the question whether an application for adoption could be made dependent upon the age of the applicant.[486] In *X v. Austria*, the Court found that a ban on adoption by the second partner of a same-sex couple would violate the Convention.[487] In *Fretté*, the Court held that the states enjoyed a margin of appreciation as to whether they allow for adoption by single homosexuals.[488] The last two cases lead us to issues relating to

---

[482] *Marckx v. Belgium*, (Plenary) (1979) Series A no. 31 [38–43]. The Court referred to an international treaty and the practice of the great majority of member states.

[483] The following cases just reiterated the changes and were, therefore, not counted: *Inze v. Austria*, (Chamber) (1987) Series A no. 126 App. no. 869579 [41]; *Brauer v. Germany*, (Fifth Section) App. no. 3545/04 (ECtHR, 28 May 2009) [40]; *Genovese v. Malta*, (Fourth Section) App. no. 53124/09 (ECtHR, 27 October 2011) [44]; *Pla and Puncernau v. Andorra*, (Fourth Section) ECHR 2004-VIII App. no. 69498/01 [62]; *Mazurek v. France*, (Third Section) App. no. 34406/97 (ECtHR, 1 February 2000) [48–55].

[484] *Zaunegger v. Germany*, (Fifth Section) App. no. 22028/04 (ECtHR, 3 December 2009) [60]. The Court argued with the European consensus on the question of judicial review, while it held that there was no consensus as to whether fathers of children born out of wedlock had the right to request custody without the consent of the mother.

[485] *Konstantin Markin v. Russia* (GC) ECHR 2012 App. no. 30078/06 [131–52]. The Court found that the practice in the several states had evolved. It found treaty obligations, consequential arguments as well as social attitudes in the respondent state inconclusive. Interestingly, the First Section had also referred to changing conditions. Yet, the fact that it cited previous judgments indicates that it found no evolution of the law: see *Konstantin Markin v. Russia*, (First Section) App. no. 30078/06 (ECtHR, 7 October 2010) [44, 58].

[486] *Schwizgebel v. Switzerland*, (First Section) ECHR 2010 App. no. 25762/07 [78–99]. The Court found no consensus in neither internal nor external practice.

[487] *X and others v. Austria* (GC) App. no. 19010/07 (ECtHR, 19 February 2013) [132–53]. The Court found no consensus among the member states but relied *inter alia* on the internal law of the respondent state.

[488] *Fretté v. France*, (Third Section) ECHR 2002-I App. no. 36515/97 34–43. The Court restricted the margin in so far as it said that states could not arbitrarily exclude

homosexuality. In *Sutherland v. the United Kingdom*, the Commission held that a different age of consent for men engaging in homosexual and heterosexual activity violated the Convention.[489] In *Schalk and Kopf*, the Court held that the absence of a right to marry for same-sex couples did not entail a discrimination relating to their rights conferred by Art. 8 ECHR.[490] In *Vallianatos*, the Court held that introducing a civil union beyond marriage had to be considered as a discrimination in relation to Art. 8.[491] In *Pichkur*, the Court found a discrimination violating Art. 14 and Art. 1 Protocol 1 in a provision granting pension claims only if the person took up residence within the state and, therefore, excluded pensioners living abroad.[492]

Art. 1 Protocol 1: protection of property

1. Every natural or legal person is entitled to the peaceful enjoyment of his possessions. No one shall be deprived of his possessions except in the public interest and subject to the conditions provided for by law and by the general principles of international law.
2. The preceding provisions shall not, however, in any way impair the right of a State to enforce such laws as it deems necessary to control the use of property in accordance with the general interest or to secure the payment of taxes or other contributions or penalties.

---

homosexuals. The Court relied on the lack of a scientific consensus as well as on a lack of consensus in state practice.

[489] *Sutherland v. the United Kingdom* (Judgment) (1997) App. no. 25186/94 [45–66]. The Commission relied mainly on new medical evidence and the practice followed in the great majority of the member states.

[490] *Schalk and Kopf v. Austria*, (First Section) ECHR 2010 [104–6]. The Court found that there was no majority for a consensus, and the subsequent developments in the law of the respondent state also had no impact upon the question.

[491] *Vallianatos and others v. Greece* (GC) App. nos. 29381/09 and 32684/09 (ECtHR, 7 November 2013) [75–92]. The Court based its reasoning on the fact that Greece could have achieved its purpose of strengthening the rights of children born out of wedlock without discriminating against same-sex couples. The Court also adduced an emerging trend which it based on the practice of certain member states and a resolution of the Council of Europe.

[492] *Pichkur v. Ukraine* (Fifth Section) App. no. 10441/06 (ECtHR, 7 November 2013) [52–3]. The Court found the ban to be disproportionate despite the fact that an ILO Convention from 1950 allowed for such discriminations as it was only on technical grounds which had become obsolete in the face of 'population mobility, the higher levels of international cooperation and integration, as well as developments in the area of banking services and information technologies'.

The protocols that have updated the Convention also provide for substantive rights that are similarly subject to evolutive interpretation. In *STEC*, the Court held that the term 'possessions' in Art. 1 Protocol 1 from then on covered a claim to a non-contributory welfare benefit.[493] Art. 1 also provided that an expropriation could be justified by the 'general principles of international law'. This was understood to apply only to non-nationals: in *James* the Court decided that the meaning of the provision had not changed in that respect.[494]

Art. 3 Protocol 1: right to free elections

> The High Contracting Parties undertake to hold free elections at reasonable intervals by secret ballot, under conditions which will ensure the free expression of the opinion of the people in the choice of the legislature.

In *Matthews*, the Grand Chamber held that the European Parliament would not fall outside the scope of Art. 3 Protocol 1 just because the drafters could not have known of such a form of governance.[495] In *Sitaropoulos*, the first Chamber determined whether a failure to implement a right to vote for citizens living abroad would be an interference that could be justified. Reversing its previous case law, the Chamber held that this constituted a violation.[496] The Grand Chamber overturned the judgment and held that there had been no change in the law and consequently no violation.[497] In *Scoppola No. 3*, the Court was faced with

---

[493] *STEC and others v. the United Kingdom* (GC) (Decision) ECHR 2005-X App. nos. 65731/01, 65900/01 [47–56]. The Court argued with the context of the provision, as well as the subsequent practice.

[494] *James and others v. the United Kingdom* (Plenary) (1986) Series A no. 98 App. no. 8793/79 [64–6]. The Court resorted to the *travaux* as well as to subsequent practice, but it found that there was no practice. This was later reinforced in *ibid.* [117–19].

[495] *Matthews v. the United Kingdom* (GC) ECHR 1999-I App. no. 24833/94 [36–44]. The Court found the wording to be inconclusive and argued mainly with the object and purpose of the provision.

[496] *Sitaropoulos and others v. Greece*, (First Section) App. no. 42202/07 (ECtHR, 8 July 2010) [35–47]. The Court used the consensus method and referred to the internal and external practice of states.

[497] *Sitaropoulos and Giakoumopoulos v. Greece* (GC) ECHR 2012 [70–81]. The Court argued that the wording did not cover the situation but a general presumption would favour the inclusion. Comparing the law to other relevant human rights instruments, no such right could be found. The Court reviewed the practice of states which pointed in this direction but, due to its diversity, left a substantial margin to the states.

the task of re-examining the illegality of a prohibition on prisoners voting. The Court found that the law had not changed.[498]

Questions of stasis and evolution also arose in relation to the other protocols of the Convention. In *Leyla Şhahın*, the Court held that the right to education enshrined in Art. 2 Protocol 1 would also apply to higher education.[499] In *Hirsi Jamaa*, the question was whether a 'removal of aliens to a third state carried out outside national territory' could be considered as collective 'expulsion' as provided for in Art. 4 Protocol 4. The Court interpreted Art. 4 Protocol 4 as well as Art. 1 ECHR in an evolutive manner and answered the question affirmatively.[500] The Court held in *Zolotukhin* that the term 'offence' in Art. 4 Protocol 7, which prohibits punishment twice for the same offence, ought to relate to the facts of the case. The prohibition of *ne bis in idem* would, therefore, applies when two charges are based on the same or almost the same facts.[501] Questions of evolution and stability arose not only in the context of the material rights but also in relation to institutional and procedural and general rules.[502]

Art. 1: obligation to respect human rights

> The High Contracting Parties shall secure to everyone within their jurisdiction the rights and freedoms defined in Section I of this Convention.

In *Banković*, the Court abstained from an evolutive interpretation in order to restrict the jurisdiction of the ECHR to the territory of its

---

[498] *Scoppola v. Italy (No. 3)* (GC) App. no. 126/05 (ECtHR, 22 May 2012) [94–6]. The Court referred to the internal practice of states which showed that there was no evolution of the law.

[499] *Leyla Şhahın* (GC) ECHR 2005-XI App. no. 44774/98 [134–42]. The Court relied mainly on the object and purpose and relevant rules, but mentioned also economic necessities.

[500] *Hirsi Jamaa and others v. Italy* (GC) ECHR 2012 [166–82]. The Court found the wording to be inconclusive, which was confirmed by the *travaux*. While no firm conclusion could be derived from the context, the object and purpose of the provision favoured an evolution of the meaning.

[501] *Zolotukhin v. Russia* (GC) ECHR 2009 App. no. 14939/03 [78–82]. While the ordinary meaning was inconclusive, the Court argued with the relevant rules as well as with the object and purpose in an abstract manner.

[502] For further procedural evolutions outside the judicial context, see Bernhardt, 'Der Übergang vom "alten" zum "neuen" Europäischen Gerichtshof für Menschenrechte' 913. This concerned in particular the way in which the individual could participate in the proceedings at the times when the commission acted on its behalf before the Court.

member states.[503] In *Loizidou*, the Court held that the ECHR would not allow the restriction of the territorial scope through a reservation.[504] The Court clearly stated that there could also be an evolution in procedural provisions.[505]

Art. 34: individual applications

> The Court may receive applications from any person, nongovernmental organisation or group of individuals claiming to be the victim of a violation by one of the High Contracting Parties of the rights set forth in the Convention or the Protocols thereto ...

The Court has interpreted Art. 34 in the sense that only direct victims, representatives or under certain circumstances indirect victims such as heirs could file an individual complaint.[506] In *Câmpeanu*, the Court broadened its jurisprudence and allowed for application by unaffected parties.[507] The Court emphasised the exceptional nature and the narrow conditions under which it operated.[508]

---

[503] *Banković v. Belgium, the Czech Republic, Denmark, France, Germany, Greece, Hungary, Iceland, Italy, Luxembourg, the Netherlands, Norway, Poland, Portugal, Spain, Turkey and the United Kingdom* (GC) (Decision) ECHR 2001-XII App. no. 52207/99 [64–5]. The Court argued with the ordinary meaning of the terms as well as with the *travaux*. In *Al Skeini*, the Court argued in a concrete case that the United Kingdom had exercised extra-territorial jurisdiction. The Court framed its judgment in a way as if it was applying previous exceptions to the case at hand: see *Al Skeini and others v. the United Kingdom* ECHR 2011 App. no. 55721/07 [130–50].

[504] *Loizidou v. Turkey* (Preliminary Objections) (Chamber) (1995) Series A no. 310 65. In favour of an evolutive interpretation, the Court invoked the context, the object and purpose and the subsequent practice of the parties. It found the ordinary meaning and other relevant rules applicable between the parties to be inconclusive.

[505] *Ibid.* [71].

[506] *Centre for Legal Resources on behalf of Valentin Câmpeanu* (GC) App. no. 47848/08 (17 July 2014) [104–14].

[507] The Court supported its finding with the object and purpose and the context: *ibid.* [105, 112–13].

[508] The Court based its finding on the following conditions: the person on behalf of whom the application was made was treated as if he had no legal capacity; he was very vulnerable and unable to take any legal steps and he had neither family nor any other legal guardian protecting his interest. During the medical and judicial proceedings the authorities also acquiesced to the fact that the applicant represented the victim: *ibid.* [108–11].

Rule 39 of the Rules of Procedure: interim measures

1. The Chamber or, where appropriate, the President of the Section or a duty judge appointed pursuant to paragraph 4 of this Rule may, at the request of a party or of any other person concerned, or of their own motion, indicate to the parties any interim measure which they consider should be adopted in the interests of the parties or of the proper conduct of the proceedings.

...

In *Cruz Varas*, the Court found that the Commission could not order binding interim measures. Rule 39, which was then Rule 36,[509] of the Rules of Procedure was held not to have changed its meaning.[510] The Court reversed this judgment in *Mamatkulov* and approved a change in the law and held that provisional measures were binding.[511]

Several interesting developments can be deduced from the cases. First, looking at interpretation proper i.e. intertemporal questions concerning the meaning of terms, the following observations deserve mention. In the 32 instances identified above, the Court has interpreted evolutively 22 times and 10 times statically. Looking at evolutive interpretations, we can see a clear trend towards evolutive interpretation:[512] from 1 change in the 1980s, to 3 changes in the 1990s we have witnessed 15 changes in the 2000s.[513] The number of intertemporal questions arising in respect of each article was as follows:

- Art. 2: 5 times (twice evolutive and three times static)
- Art. 12: 4 times (twice evolutive and twice static)
- Art. 4: 2 times (twice evolutive)
- Art. 5: 2 times (twice evolutive)

---

[509] It was amended by the Court on 4 July 2005, 16 January 2012 and 14 January 2013.
[510] *Cruz Varas and others* v. *Sweden* (Plenary) Series A no. 201 App. no. 15576/89 [94–103]. While the ordinary meaning favoured a static interpretation, the context, the subsequent practice of the states parties, the relevant rules as well as the preparatory works remained inconclusive.
[511] *Mamatkulov and Askarov* v. *Turkey* (GC) ECHR 2005-I App. nos. 46827/99, 46951/99 [108–26]. The Court relied on the changed context of the Convention (Protocol 11), its object and purpose as well as the relevant rules in that area. See the previous stage with almost identical arguments: *ibid.* [96–110].
[512] Nolte, 'Treaties over Time: Introductory Report' 185.
[513] Since the numbers of evolutive interpretations are so small, there is hardly any use in relating them to the absolute number of cases. Yet, it has to be acknowledged that the number of cases grew significantly, especially after the coming into force of Protocol 11.

- Art. 6: 2 times (split)
- Art. 8: 2 times (twice evolutive)
- Art. 9: 2 times (split)
- Art. 11: 2 times (twice evolutive)

Forty-three intertemporal questions arose in the process of balancing: 28 times the Court rebalanced issues in an evolutive manner, and 15 times it left the old balance intact. The temporal outlook on evolutive instances is again very interesting: 3 times in the 1970s, 2 times in the 1980s, 2 times in the 1990s and 16 times in the 2000s. In the process of balancing, individual articles were considered as follows:

- Art. 8: 18 times (split)
- Art. 14 together with Art. 8: 9 times (6 evolutive and 3 static)
- Art. 3: 7 times (5 evolutive and 2 static)

It is remarkable that this matches exactly what Sørensen had predicted.[514]

It is also interesting to look at the actors involved. The organisation of the Convention machinery changed over time. Today, there is the dichotomy of Grand Chambers and Sections, whereas earlier, the Plenary was opposed to Chambers. We will consider the respective parts of the Court together first, and then separately.

Tables 5 and 6 show intertemporal instances in total numbers and then give the total numbers for static and evolutive decisions. The next line gives the ratio of evolutive interpretations, i.e. the percentage of evolutive as opposed to static results. The last line informs about the decision ratio, which is the percentage of evolutive interpretations as compared to static results. The fact that we can compare the old to the new Convention enforcement system means that we can also compare how the systems changed with regard to evolutive interpretation. The numbers allow us to identify an interesting observation and one trend. The observation is that the smaller the body making the decision, the more likely it is that it renders an evolutive interpretation. Chambers in the old system as well as Sections in the new system have consistently had higher ratios of successful reinterpretations and rebalancings whereas the ratio of evolutive interpretations and balancing exercised

---

[514] Sørensen, 'Do the Rights Set Forth in the European Convention on Human Rights in 1950 Have the Same Significance in 1975?' 96.

Table 5 *Frequency of interpretative intertemporal instances at the ECtHR*

Actor/statistic	Commission	Full Court (plenary/ Grand Chamber)	Part of the Court (Chamber/Section)
All intertemporal instances	1	21 (6 + 15)	10 (1 + 9)
Static interpretations	0	8 (5 + 3)	2 (0 + 2)
Evolutive interpretations	1	13 (1 + 12)	8 (1 + 7)
Evolutive ratio[a]	100%	61.9% (16.67%/80%)	80% (100%/77.78%)
Decision ratio for Full Court[b]		67.74% (85.71%/62.45%)	

Notes [a]Percentage of evolutive interpretations as opposed to static interpretations. How many times was the intertemporal question resolved in an evolutive manner?
[b]Percentage of intertemporal interpretations determined by the Full Court (plenary or Grand Chamber). How many times did the Full Court decide as opposed to chambers/sections?

Table 6 *Frequency of intertemporal instances of balancing at the ECtHR*

Actor/statistic	Commission	Full Court (plenary/ Grand Chamber)	Part of the Court (Chamber/Section)
All intertemporal instances	2	25 (8 + 17)	16 (0 + 16)
Static interpretations	1	10 (3 + 7)	4 (0 + 4)
Evolutive interpretations	1	15 (5 + 10)	12 (0 + 12)
Evolutive ratio[a]	50%	60% (62.5%/58.82%)	75% (0%/75%)
Decision ratio for Full Court[b]		57.5% (80%/50%)	

Notes [a]Percentage of evolutive interpretations as opposed to static interpretations. How many times was the intertemporal question resolved in an evolutive manner?
[b]Percentage of intertemporal interpretations determined by the Full Court (plenary or Grand Chamber). How many times did the Full Court decide?

by the full Court[515] is constantly lower. The only exception are evolutive interpretations by the Grand Chamber and the Sections which are roughly the same, but apart from that, the ratio of change is always almost 20 per cent higher for smaller bodies. This observation could be reformulated in a hypothesis that smaller bodies are more likely to interpret the law evolutively.

The trend clearly points towards more evolutive interpretations in the new system. The fact that there is more evolutive interpretation in absolute numbers might be explained by the great rise in the number of judgments and decisions after Protocol 11. Yet, it is particularly interesting to look at the ratio of judgments. While the plenary had only interpreted 1 out of 6 cases evolutively, the Grand Chamber rendered evolutive interpretations in 11 out of 14 cases. This shows that the relation between static and evolutive interpretations has substantially shifted.

10.3. General approach

10.3.1 The living instrument doctrine

In 1975, judges and specialists met to discuss issues of stasis and evolution. It took the Court three more years to decide the first evolutive question explicitly. Indeed, *Tyrer*[516] became the landmark case on the issue and coined the most famous phrase that has been repeated in the case law of the Court as well as in academia:

> The Court must also recall that the Convention is a living instrument which, as the Commission rightly stressed, must be interpreted in the light of present-day conditions. In the case now before it the Court cannot but be influenced by the developments and commonly accepted standards in the penal policy of the member States of the Council of Europe in this field.[517]

The Court did not explain what the living instrument doctrine actually meant.[518] Yet, parts of this section have always been mentioned when the Court openly has changed the interpretation of the ECHR or when it

---

[515] The expression 'Full Court' refers to the configuration containing the most judges. This means that Grand Chamber judgments come into that category, even though not all judges sit in one Grand Chamber.
[516] *Tyrer* v. *the United Kingdom*, (Chamber) Series A no. 26.   [517] *Ibid.* [31].
[518] Letsas, 'The Truth in Autonomous Concepts' 279; Mowbray, 'The Creativity of the European Court of Human Rights' 71.

has rebalanced it. This phrase has been used in American constitutional law[519] but similar expressions like *lebendes Recht*[520] ('living law') or 'the constitution as a living tree'[521] have previously developed. As previously mentioned, Sørensen had already called the Convention a 'living legal instrument'.[522] The emphasis of the phrase is clear: The determinative point in time for the interpretation is the present and not the past. So the process of interpretation is in no way a quest for the real or assumed intentions of the parties. It is an inquiry into the content of the law as it stands at the time of interpretation. Consequently, in later judgments, the Court generally declined to look at the law from the perspective of the drafters of the Convention.[523] When it referred to the 'intentions of the drafters' while discussing possible changes in the law, it used this approach only as a starting point.[524] In *Loizidou*, it held that the provisions of the Convention 'cannot be interpreted solely in accordance with the intentions of their authors as expressed more than forty years ago'.[525] In another case, the Court started out to consider the situation 'during the preparation and subsequent conclusion of the Convention'.[526] It held that, even if national law required interpreting an instrument such as a will at the time it was made, this would have no bearing on the time of application of the ECHR.[527] Yet, in an early dissenting opinion, Judge Fitzmaurice opposed the Court's approach with his intentionalist account.[528]

When the Court said that it 'recalls', it was referring to the case law of the Commission in other cases that have been amply discussed by Sørensen in his speech in 1975.[529] In *Tyrer*, the Commission has taken another route and held that the alleged breach is not '*inhuman*' but

---

[519] McBain, *The Living Constitution*.
[520] See the many small contributions in E. Ehrlich, *Gesetz und lebendes Recht*.
[521] *Edwards v. Attorney-General of Canada* [1930] AC 124, 136 (PC) (Lord Sankey).
[522] Sørensen, 'Do the Rights Set Forth in the European Convention on Human Rights in 1950 Have the Same Significance in 1975?' 106.
[523] *Matthews v. the United Kingdom* (GC) ECHR 1999-I [39].
[524] *Soering v. the United Kingdom* (Plenary) (1989) Series A no. 161 [103].
[525] *Loizidou v. Turkey* (Preliminary Objections) (Chamber) (1995) Series A no. 310 [71].
[526] *Konstantin Markin v. Russia* (GC) ECHR 2012 [128].
[527] *Pla and Puncernau v. Andorra*, (Fourth Section) ECHR 2004-VIII [62].
[528] *Tyrer v. the United Kingdom*, (Chamber), Separate Opinion of Judge Fitzmaurice, Series A no. 26 App. no. 5856/72 14; *Marckx v. Belgium*, (Plenary), Dissenting Opinion of Judge Fitzmaurice (1979) Series A no. 31 App. no. 6833/74 [7].
[529] Sørensen, 'Do the Rights Set Forth in the European Convention on Human Rights in 1950 Have the Same Significance in 1975?' 96.

nevertheless a breach since it could be considered as 'degrading treatment'.[530] This enabled the Commission to come to the same conclusion without dealing with intertemporal issues. The context of the decision provides a number of reasons why the Court might have taken another route in the justification of its decision.

To assert evolutive interpretations openly was very much in line with the *Zeitgeist* of the 1970s. That courts could do this became evident in many jurisdictions: as previously shown, the ICJ during that time took every opportunity to stress that it changed the interpretations of certain terms.[531] Sørensen had quoted the respective part of the *Namibia opinion* abundantly.[532] He had also referred to the jurisprudence of the Supreme Court of the United States and of European constitutional courts and quoted one judge of the German Federal Constitutional Court.[533] So the judgment fitted into a broader movement in international law, Europe and at least the Western hemisphere towards activist courts that changed the meaning attached to their constitutions where necessary.

It might be a too far-reaching inference to conclude that if hard cases make bad law, easy cases make good law. Yet, it cannot be denied that *Tyrer* was a good and easy case to establish the possibility of changing interpretations. First of all, judicial corporal punishment was literally abolished everywhere except for a small island with around 45,000 inhabitants.[534] So the decision had almost no effects or consequences for any legal system, not even in the United Kingdom. The Court was clever enough to frame the question as an issue of balancing and not interpretation: It did not really try to establish a meaning of the terms 'degrading' or 'humiliation'. It looked at the specific issues of the case to decide whether a breach of Art. 3 ECHR was warranted. This also meant that the precedential value for other decisions could be limited by the mere difference in the facts of the case. Another feature of the case might indicate that the Court really wanted to decide the case: Since the applicant, when turning 18, tried to withdraw from the procedure in the Commission, the Court might have considered this as a fact that

---

[530] *Anthony M. Tyrer against the United Kingdom* Report (1976) App. no. 5856/72, Report of the Commission [32–5].

[531] *Legal Consequences for States of the Continued Presence of South Africa in Namibia (South West Africa) Notwithstanding Security Council Resolution 276 (1970)* (Advisory Opinion) 31 para. 53.

[532] Sørensen, 'Do the Rights Set Forth in the European Convention on Human Rights in 1950 Have the Same Significance in 1975?' 87.

[533] *Ibid.* 88.   [534] *Tyrer v. the United Kingdom*, (Chamber) Series A no. 26 [14].

indicated the 'solution of the matter', which would have given it the power to discontinue the present proceedings.[535] Such a discontinuation might have played into the hands of the government which would have avoided losing a case. There was a standard practice of friendly settlements in those situations.[536] All in all, *Tyrer* was an easy case at the right time to establish the living instrument doctrine. This has been the starting point for some further developments of the doctrine.

The living instrument doctrine was applied in the processes of interpretation as well as balancing. In the process of balancing, the Court would often not invoke the whole living instrument doctrine but only refer to the need to see the case 'in the light of present-day conditions'.[537] Several slight alterations were made to the living instrument doctrine as established in *Tyrer*: The Court has added the phrase 'and the ideas prevailing in democratic states today'[538] or 'in the light of the notions prevailing in democratic states'.[539] The notion of democratic states restricts and broadens the focus of the Court at the same time. On the one hand, the Court seems to look at all democratic states, not only those that are members of the Council of Europe. Yet, it stressed that it focuses on democratic standards. Undemocratic practice inside and outside the Council of Europe will, consequently, not be acknowledged. The Court tended to use this phrase in the context of the most basic and non-derogable rights such as Art. 3 ECHR. The Court also tended to mention other doctrines in the context of evolutive interpretations. In these situations, the Court also stressed that the 'Convention is designed to guarantee not rights that are theoretical or illusory but rights that are practical and effective'.[540] There is, however, no necessary link between the practical and effective doctrine on the one side and the doctrine of evolutive interpretation on the other.

The Court often referred to the living instrument doctrine where it did not seem necessary to do so. So, the Court used the formula when simply

---

[535] *Ibid.* [25].
[536] See for example Sørensen, 'Do the Rights Set Forth in the European Convention on Human Rights in 1950 Have the Same Significance in 1975?' 90.
[537] *Christine Goodwin v. the United Kingdom* (GC) ECHR 2002-VI [75].
[538] *Bayatyan v. Armenia* (GC) ECHR 2011 [102].
[539] *Stummer v. Austria* (GC) ECHR 2011 [118].
[540] *STEC and others v. the United Kingdom* (GC) (Decision) ECHR 2005-X [47]; *Sitaropoulos and others v. Greece*, (First Section) [46]. Compare also *Bayatyan v. Armenia* (GC) ECHR 2011 [98]. See also in the context of present-day conditions, *Airey v. Ireland*, (Chamber) Series A no. 41 App. no. 6289/73 [26].

reiterating changes in previous judgments.[541] It used it in *van der Mussele*, when referring to an old ILO Convention as a reminder that the law can evolve even though the definition in the ILO Convention was applied throughout the case and no evolution was in question.[542] The Court mentioned the formula even in cases in which there was no indication that the law had changed.[543] In *Stafford*, the Court mentioned the living instrument doctrine in the context of Art. 5 ECHR just to track the evolution of the internal law of the United Kingdom.[544] Changes in the internal law prompted a different evaluation: while the Court certainly changed its case law, it is not clear that it actually changed the meaning of the ECHR.[545] In *Kress*, the Court used the doctrine to argue that an institution belonging to the administrative courts system in France, which was over 100 years old, would still be susceptible to judicial review.[546] In all these instances, no harm was caused by citing the living instrument doctrine. Yet, by a measure as simple as restricting its use of the formula only to necessary cases, the Court might avoid the idea that it was interpreting evolutively to an excessive degree.

10.3.2 Retroactive application of evolutive interpretations

When the Court changes the interpretation of the Convention, the question arises at what point in time the new interpretation takes effect. The original position of the Court in *Marckx* was to limit interpretations to the future in order not to reopen already decided disputes before national courts.[547] In the interest of legal certainty, the changed law

---

[541] *Engel and others v. Sweden* (Decision) (1994) App. no. 15533/89 [2]; *Moretti and Benedetti v. Italy* (Second Section) App. no. 16318/07 (ECtHR, 27 April 2010) [64].

[542] *Van der Mussele v. Belgium* (Plenary) (1983) Series A no. 70 App. no. 8919/80 [32]. The Court referred to an evolution in the internal law only in the process of balancing: see [40].

[543] *Demades v. Turkey*, (Third Section) App. no. 16219/90 (ECtHR, 31 July 2003) [33]; *Siliadin v. France*, (Second Section) 2005-VII App. no. 73316/01 [121]. Yet, the Court also failed to mention the doctrine when the judges in the majority remarked that there was in effect an evolutive interpretation: see *Hirst v. the United Kingdom (No. 2)* (GC), Joint Dissenting Opinion of Judges Wildhaber, Costa, Lorenzen, Kovler and Jebens ECHR 2005-IX App. no. 74025/01 [6].

[544] *Stafford v. the United Kingdom* (GC) ECHR 2002-IV App. no. 46295/99 [68–82].

[545] See generally the description by Wildhaber, 'European Court of Human Rights' 313.

[546] *Kress v. France* (GC) ECHR 2001-VI App. no. 39594/98 [70].

[547] *Marckx v. Belgium*, (Plenary) (1979) Series A no. 31 [58]. On the whole problem, see Thijmen Koopmans, 'Retrospectivity Reconsidered'. An instance of a retroactive

would only apply for the future. This could be considered as a limit on the doctrine of evolutive interpretation.[548] In most cases that are referred to above, the Court changed the interpretation instantly. In one case the Court explicitly argued that otherwise no changes in case law would be possible.[549] In *Eskelinen*, the Court changed its interpretation regarding Art. 6(1) ECHR and subsequently even decided cases in accordance with its new jurisprudence that were filed before that case.[550]

The Court has not yet set out the guiding principles of its case law. There are different possibilities to resolve the tension present in the decisions. One would be to focus on whether the changes in the case law had been foreseeable for the domestic authorities at the time they took the decisions.[551] Another possibility would be to apply the jurisprudence of the Court regarding retroactive application in general to questions of 'retroactive application of evolutive interpretation'.[552]

10.3.3 Other important concepts

Distinguishing itself from the International Court of Justice, the Court had stressed that it would always have 'supervisory functions' and interpret a 'law-making treaty'.[553] Those two notions are thereby linked to evolutive outcomes. Apart from that, the Court only very rarely recalled the status of the Convention as a *law-making treaty*.[554] A tricky relationship is that of the living instrument doctrine and the *margin of appreciation*. The Court had extended the living instrument doctrine to questions in which it previously accorded a margin of appreciation to states. This doctrine generally describes that the law of the Convention applies to a certain question but the Court is not competent to render a

---

application of an evolutive interpretation is *Aoulmi v. France*, (Fourth Section) ECHR 2006-I App. no. 50278/99 [112].

[548] Tulkens, 'What Are the Limits to Evolutive Interpretation of the Convention?' 8.
[549] *Lucky Dev v. Sweden* (Fifth Section) App. no. 7356/10 (ECtHR, 27 November 2014) [50]; see also the critical Concurring Opinion of Judges Villiger, Nussberger and De Gaetano.
[550] *Ternoviskis v. Latvia* (Fourth Section) App. no. 33637/02 (ECtHR, 29 April 2014) [49] with further references.
[551] In favour of an interpretation of the Convention as it stood at the critical date, see Judge Ziemle in his Concurring Opinion in *O'Keefe v. Ireland* (GC) App. no. 35810/09 (ECtHR, 28 January 2014) [11].
[552] See the latest case law of the Court in *Janowiec and others v. Russia* (GC) App. nos. 55508/07 and 29520/09 (ECtHR, 21 October 2013) [128–51].
[553] *Loizidou v. Turkey* (Preliminary Objections) (Chamber) (1995) Series A no. 310 [84].
[554] *Leyla Şahın* (GC) ECHR 2005-XI [141].

decision.⁵⁵⁵ In these cases, the Convention provides only for the outer limits of the decision which are ultimately left for the member states to determine. A margin of appreciation can arise in different contexts: In the course of interpretation, the member states can be free to choose the exact meaning of a clause. In the context of balancing, the member states are free to weigh different interests. The fact that the states have a certain margin in one sense or the other does not mean that the margin cannot be reduced or extended. The position of the Court in that regard can change. Every change of the margin is in essence a change of the meaning or a change in the outcome of the process of balancing.⁵⁵⁶ When the margin is reduced, extended, introduced or abolished, this changes the Convention and it is natural that the living instrument doctrine is applied in that context.⁵⁵⁷ So a change of the margin can in effect be the outcome of an evolutive interpretation. Yet, the Court often resorts to the method of balancing to determine whether there is a margin of appreciation:

> Where a particularly important facet of an individual's existence or identity is at stake, the margin allowed to the State will normally be restricted. Where, however, there is no consensus within the member States of the Council of Europe, either as to the relative importance of the interest at stake or as to the best means of protecting it, particularly where the case raises sensitive moral or ethical issues, the margin will be wider.⁵⁵⁸

The Court has also extended the doctrine to *procedural* law.⁵⁵⁹ However, it distinguished *Banković* from *Loizidou* in that the latter case concerned the effectiveness of the whole Convention system and thereby warrants an evolutive interpretation while the former would only apply to the

---

⁵⁵⁵ See on this doctrine Macdonald, 'The Margin of Appreciation'; Arai-Takahashi, *The Margin of Appreciation Doctrine and the Principle of Proportionality in the Jurisprudence of the ECHR*; Greer, *The Margin of Appreciation*.

⁵⁵⁶ Similarly Mahoney, 'Judicial Activism and Judicial Self-Restraint in the European Court of Human Rights 80; Mahoney, 'Marvellous Richness of Diversity or Invidious Cultural Relativism' 5.

⁵⁵⁷ *A, B and C v. Ireland* (GC) ECHR 2010 [232]. The interrelation of the two doctrines is discussed by Mahoney, 'Judicial Activism and Judicial Self-Restraint in the European Court of Human Rights' 83; Andenas and Bjorge, 'National Implementation of ECHR Rights' 187.

⁵⁵⁸ *X and others v. Austria* (GC) [148].

⁵⁵⁹ *Cruz Varas and others v. Sweden* (Plenary), Joint Dissenting Opinion of Judges Cremona, Thór Vilhjálmsson, Walsh, Macdonald, Bernhardt, de Meyer, Martens, Foighel, Morenilla Series A no. 201 App. no. 15576/89 [5]. For a critical review of this development, see Golsong, 'Interpreting the Convention' 150.

justiciability.⁵⁶⁰ So the Court generally extended its power to change the meaning of clauses to the procedural law of the Convention, but seems to limit it to the cases in which the effectiveness of the system is at issue. But the Court also tried to include absolute limits to the Convention. Sometimes, it is asserted that evolutive interpretation had its limits where *new rights* were created.⁵⁶¹ This had also been specified by a prohibition to allow for new 'concepts and spheres of application'.⁵⁶² Another possible limitation is the fact that the Court mentions the foreseeability of the changes,⁵⁶³ which could indicate that unforeseeable changes cannot lead to an evolutive interpretation.

We generally divide international law into certain fields or *areas*, such as human rights law, international humanitarian law and international trade law.⁵⁶⁴ The field of human rights is in itself again divided into the sphere of civil and political as well as social, economic and cultural rights. While the ECHR is considered to cover civil and political rights, the Court has not abstained from deciding issues which had for example strong economic implications.⁵⁶⁵ Yet, if the Court interpreted the object and purpose of the ECHR to be the protection of civil and political rights instead of economic and social rights, this could be a means to limit an expansion of the Convention. Indeed, the Court has used such a restrictive definition of the purpose as means to limit interpretations.⁵⁶⁶

---

⁵⁶⁰ *Banković v. Belgium, the Czech Republic, Denmark, France, Germany, Greece, Hungary, Iceland, Italy, Luxembourg, the Netherlands, Norway, Poland, Portugal, Spain, Turkey and the United Kingdom* (GC) (Decision) ECHR 2001-XII [65]. While this argument appears to be valid, one is inclined to ask whether the effect of denying jurisdiction is not exactly the same as that of a reservation. If this is accepted, it is hard to contend that the same notions of effectiveness should not apply in this case.

⁵⁶¹ *Muños Díaz v. Spain*, (Third Section), Dissenting Opinion Judge Myjer ECHR 2009 App. no. 49151/07; *Cruz Varas and others v. Sweden* (Plenary) Series A no. 201 [100]; *Austin and others v. the United Kingdom* (GC) ECHR 2012 [53].

⁵⁶² *Deumland v. Germany* (Plenary), Dissenting Opinion of Judges Ryssdal, Bindschedler-Robert, Lagergren, Matscher, Sir Vincent Evans, Bernhardt and Gersing Series A no. 100 App. no. 9384/81 [24].

⁵⁶³ *Bayatyan v. Armenia* (GC) ECHR 2011 [108].

⁵⁶⁴ Koskenniemi, 'The Fate of Public International Law'.

⁵⁶⁵ See also *STEC and others v. the United Kingdom* (GC) (Decision) ECHR 2005-X [52]; *Annoni di Gussola and others v. France*, (Third Section) ECHR 2000-XI [56]. For a general account of the social rights arising out of the Convention, see *Konstantin Markin v. Russia* (GC), Partly Concurring Partly Dissenting Opinion of Judge Pinto de Albuquerque ECHR 2012 App. no. 30078/06.

⁵⁶⁶ *N v. the United Kingdom* (GC) ECHR 2008 App. no. 26565/05 [44]. See the very critical remarks by *N v. the United Kingdom* (GC), Joint Dissenting Opinion of Judges Tulkens, Bonello and Spielmann ECHR 2008 App. no. 26565/05 [6].

The Court also stressed that it was 'aware that the further realisation of social and economic rights is largely dependent on the situation – notably financial – reigning in the State in question'.[567] Yet, it also went on to interpret the Convention evolutively in cases having those implications.[568]

10.3.4 The problem of devolution

History teaches us that the human rights project, like any human endeavour, is not on a linear path towards success and full realisation but rather on a changing track with ups and downs. The Court was for example alarmed when the United Kingdom, after losing several cases in the 1970s, threatened to withdraw from the ECHR and reduced the duration of its acceptance of the Court's jurisdiction from three to two years.[569] Jochen Frowein, being a former member of the Commission, gave a lively account of the hostile environment towards the ECHR in those times.[570] If regress is possible in human rights, this could at least potentially happen through changes in interpretation. This could then be called '*devolution*'.[571] Devolution is an expression for a change of interpretation that lowers the standard of human rights instead of increasing it. There are two questions in that regard: First, whether this should be possible or whether evolutive interpretation should be regarded as a one-way street.[572] If devolution was possible, the next question was whether it is subject to the same requirements as evolution or whether special requirements apply.

Looking at the general possibility of devolution, it has been asserted on several occasions that such changes could not be made. In a dissenting opinion, Judge Bonello expressed the view that a change in interpretation

---

[567] *Airey v. Ireland*, (Chamber) Series A no. 41 [26].   [568] *Ibid.*
[569] Bates, *The Evolution of the European Convention on Human Rights* 15.
[570] Frowein, 'Die evolutive Auslegung der EMRK'.
[571] Prebensen, 'Evolutive Interpretation of the European Convention on Human Rights' 1136. See also on the issue Wildhaber, 'Rethinking the European Court of Human Rights' 215; Mahoney, 'Judicial Activism and Judicial Self-Restraint in the European Court of Human Rights' 66; Matscher, 'Wie sich die 1950 in der EMRK festgeschriebenen Menschenrechte weiterentwickelt haben' 454; Matscher, 'Methods of Interpretation of the Convention' 69. For the similar notion of 'regress', see Thienel, 'The Living Instrument Approach in the ECHR and Elsewhere' 198.
[572] Wildhaber, 'Ein Überdenken des Zustands und der Zukunft des Europäischen Gerichtshofs für Menschenrechte' 546.

could not go against the object and purpose of the ECHR and reduce the scope of its rights.[573] Judge Casadevall invoked the principle of 'non-regression' in relation to acquired rights.[574] This is very much in line with what the European Movement envisaged in its first draft of the European Convention: A safeguard of a certain standard of protection that could be only augmented but not lowered.[575] In certain cases, the Court varies the living instrument doctrine in the sense that 'the increasingly high standard being required in the area of the protection of human rights and fundamental liberties correspondingly and inevitably requires greater firmness in assessing breaches of the fundamental values of democratic societies'.[576] This formula suggests that the practice is rather unidirectional heading towards an increasing standard. This is supported and justified by the fundamental values of democratic society. A lowering of the standard is not possible under these premises. In *X and others*, the Court held that '[s]tates retain Convention liability in respect of treaty commitments subsequent to the entry into force of the Convention'.[577] The Court did not say that subsequent treaties could not generally change the Convention, but the fact that states cannot limit the liability

---

[573] *Witold Litwa v. Poland*, Concurring Opinion of Judge Bonello ECHR 2000-III App. no. 26629/95. This is cited approvingly in *Kharin v. Russia*, (First Section), Joint Dissenting Opinion of Judges Rozakis, Spielmann and Jebens App. no. 37345/03 (ECtHR, 3 February 2011) [2].

[574] *Gorou v. Greece (No. 2)* (GC), Partly Dissenting Opinion of Judge Casadevall App. no. 12686/03 (ECtHR, 20 March 2009) [8]. He did, however, make an exception for manifest mistakes.

[575] European Movement, 'Draft European Convention on Human Rights' (INF/5/E/R) 20. See also the accompanying explanation on 14.

[576] *Selmouni v. France* (GC) ECHR 1999-V [101]. See also *Mubilanzila Mayeka and Kaniki Mitunga v. Belgium*, (First Section) ECHR 2006-XI App. no. 13178/03 [48]; *A v. Croatia*, (First Section) App. no. 55164/08 [67]; *Giusto and others v. Italy*, (Second Section) (Decision) App. no. 28972/06; *Hénaf v. France*, (First Section) ECHR 2003-XI [55]; *Riad and Idiab v. Belgium*, (First Section) App. nos. 29787/03, 29810/03 (ECtHR, 24 January 2008) [97]; *Siliadin v. France*, (Second Section) 2005-VII [121]; *Beganović v. Croatia*, (First Section) App. no. 46423/06 (ECtHR, 25 June 2009); *Rantsev v. Cyprus and Russia*, (First Section) [277]. For a positive obligation deriving from Art. 8 ECHR, see *Sandra Janković v. Croatia* (First Section) App. no. 38478/05 (ECtHR, 5 March 2009) [47].

[577] *Al-Saadoon and Mufdhi v. the United Kingdom*, (Fourth Section) ECHR 2010 [128]; *X and others v. Austria* (GC) [150]. See the critical remarks by *X and others v. Austria* (GC), Joint Partly Dissenting Opinion of Judges Casadevall, Ziemele, Kovler, Jočienė Šikuta, de Gaetano and Sicilianos App. no. 19010/07 (ECtHR, 19 February 2013) [22].

suggests that the protection can only be increased.[578] This can be considered at least as a partial prohibition of devolution.

On the other hand, the issue of devolution was present from the beginning of the discourse about evolution. At the twenty-fifth anniversary in 1973, Francis Jacobs reported on this very question.[579] Some cases can be found which have effectively and sometimes also expressly reduced the scope of the Convention. In *Stoll*, the Court sitting as the Grand Chamber considered whether a journalist, who had been convicted for publishing parts of a classified diplomatic note, had suffered a violation of his right to freedom of expression. Before considering the proportionality concretely, the Court laid down its general stance and stressed the need to achieve a just balance between 'the vital role, played by the press in a democratic society'[580] and restrictions on the freedom and 'duties and responsibilities of journalists'[581] in particular their compliance with 'the ethics of journalism'.[582] Stressing the increasing importance of the media in contemporary society, the Court established that 'monitoring compliance with journalistic ethics takes on added importance' and explicitly designates this to be an evolutive interpretation.[583] This clearly rebalanced the right of free expression with legitimate aims to restrict it in such a way as to reduce the scope of the protection of the Convention. In relation to the right of education, the Court held that the 'development of the right to education, whose content varies from one time or place to another according to economic and social circumstances, mainly depends on the needs and resources of the community'.[584] This phrase suggests that the scope of the rights can be reduced as well as extended. The ECHR could, therefore, evolve in many directions. The Court also rebalanced the legitimacy of bails in criminal proceedings in the face of growing environmental concerns.[585] The Court took the view that 'the increasingly high standard being required in the area of the protection of human rights and fundamental liberties correspondingly

---

[578] The fact that evolutive interpretation was aimed at increasing the scope of the Convention was also mentioned by *Herrmann* v. *Germany* (GC), Partly Concurring and Partly Dissenting Opinion of Judge Pinto de Albuquerque (2012) App. no. 9300/07 (26 June 2012) Hunting as a social restriction on the right to property: the Chassagnou Precedent.
[579] Jacobs, 'To What Extent Have Restrictions on the Enjoyment of Freedoms Evolved?'.
[580] *Stoll* v. *Switzerland* (GC) ECHR 2007-V [102].
[581] *Ibid.* [582] *Ibid.* [103]. [583] *Ibid.* [104].
[584] *Leyla Şahin* (GC) ECHR 2005-XI [136].
[585] *Mangouras* v. *Spain* (GC) App. no. 12050/04 [87].

and inevitably requires greater firmness in assessing breaches of the fundamental values of democratic societies'.[586] This argument aims at relating the development of legitimate measures touching upon human rights to the expansion of human rights themselves.

A minority of judges accused the Court in *Hatton* of having rebalanced the equilibrium between environmental considerations and economic necessities in such a way as to reduce the protection of the Convention.[587] In *Scoppola No. 3*, the Court acknowledged that a change in the practice of states could possibly lead to a re-examination of the case law.[588] Since it found no different stance in relation to prisoners' voting rights, this inquiry remained only theoretical. A clear instance of a changing interpretation decreasing the level of human rights protection by the Commission is *McVeigh*. Here the Commission effectively introduced a new ground for the restriction of movement. It justified going beyond the scope of the words of Art. 5(1)(b) ECHR with pressing needs.[589] After establishing that the Convention ought to be interpreted in present-day conditions, the Commission equated 'organised terrorism' as a 'feature of modern life' with 'changes in social condition and moral opinion' and found that in those instances an exception had to be acknowledged.[590] This decision by the Commission is all the more interesting since it concerns not only a rebalancing but a proper reinterpretation of the ECHR. A similar result was reached in *Hassan*, in which the grounds for imprisonment in the Geneva Conventions were acknowledged even though no exception within the Convention applied.[591] As the Court explicitly stressed that it was faced with this question for the first time and nothing indicates that the law has been different prior to the judgment, this case cannot be considered as an evolutive interpretation in the proper sense of the term.[592] Nevertheless, it clearly shows that the Court

---

[586] *Ibid.*
[587] *Hatton and others v. the United Kingdom* (GC), Joint Dissenting Opinion of Judges Costa, Ress, Türmen, Zupančič and Steiner ECHR, 2003-VIII App. no. 36022/97 [5]. See generally on that issue Malgosia Fitzmaurice, 'The European Convention on Human Rights and Fundamental Freedoms and the Human Right to a Clean Environment'.
[588] *Scoppola v. Italy (No. 3)* (GC) [94–6].
[589] *McVeigh and others v. the United Kingdom* (Decision) [188].
[590] *Ibid.* [157]. Compare also in the process of balancing *Klass and others v. Germany* (1978) Series A no. 28 App. no. 5029/71 [48].
[591] *Hassan v. the United Kingdom* (GC) App. no. 29750/09 (ECtHR, 16 September 2014) [96–107].
[592] *Ibid.* in particular [99].

would also employ interpretations going beyond or against the ordinary meaning of the Convention even if that lowered the level of human rights protection.[593]

We can conclude from this that the practice of the Court is not uniform: It sometimes asserts rather implicitly that there ought to be no evolution downwards, yet there are some precedents in which the ECHR was interpreted and applied in that manner. Since these precedents exist, it is all the more interesting to see whether there are any restrictions on devolution. The former President of the ECHR, Lucius Wildhaber, has indicated three reasons why it should be possible. From this we could derive three instances in which it would be possible:[594] when the judges erred and subsequently attained a better knowledge;[595] when the law changed in other respects such as conflicting human rights; and when the values of democratic societies changed. In *Austin*, the Court, after introducing the living instrument doctrine, made the following statement:

> This does not, however, mean that to respond to present-day needs, conditions, views or standards the Court can create a new right apart from those recognised by the Convention ... or that it can whittle down an existing right or create a new 'exception' or 'justification' which is not recognised in the Convention.[596]

While this could also be read as a prohibition on reducing the scope of protection through interpretation, the Court has effectively put the same constraint on devolution as it did on evolution: it might not create new rights but it will also not restrict the rights in an unjustified manner. Yet, the exact scope of the restriction remains unclear: When is an exception new and when has the provision just evolved?

The formula of new rights gives hardly any guidance, so we might revisit the issue with the help of the general insights concerning the process of interpretation. First, it is true that an evolution downwards would be against the object and purpose of the Convention of achieving the 'maintenance and further realisation of human rights and

---

[593] See the Partly Dissenting Opinion of Judge Spano joined by Judges Nicolaou, Bianku and Kalaydjieva *ibid.* [13].
[594] Wildhaber, 'Ein Überdenken des Zustands und der Zukunft des Europäischen Gerichtshofs für Menschenrechte' 546.
[595] The exception of a manifest mistake was also mentioned by *Gorou v. Greece (No. 2)* (GC), Partly Dissenting Opinion of Judge Casadevall [8].
[596] *Austin and others v. the United Kingdom* (GC) ECHR 2012 [53].

fundamental freedoms' as expressed in the preamble.[597] We have found out that the techniques of interpretation work like general *topoi* in rhetoric: they qualify arguments and attribute a certain value to them, but no argument derived from a certain technique can claim to prevail in all circumstances. Yet, no technique is on top of the hierarchy in such a manner as to always prevail. The Court has itself acknowledged in *Soering* that it might also decide cases against the object and purpose.[598] So while the object and purpose is no absolute barrier to devolutive interpretation, there might be others.

In some cases, the Court referred to the essence of a right.[599] This is again a vague concept, but can render the formula in *Austin* at least a little more concrete: A right is whittled down when the interpretation impacts upon its essence. Rights like the prohibition of torture and slavery can avail themselves of the status of *jus cogens* norms. As pointed out earlier, these cannot be changed as easily as other norms. It requires the interpretation to be backed up by the general conduct of states as provided for in Art. 31(3) VCLT and from this conduct it must transpire that the new understanding should be non-derogable. This criterion is far from absolute, yet since those interpretations are in breach of the old understanding of *jus cogens*, it is hardly imaginable that they would in reality go against the very object and purpose of Arts. 3 and 4 which prohibit *inter alia* torture and slavery.

10.4. Justificatory patterns

10.4.1 Balancing

We have seen that the Court engaged in the process of balancing, which is separate from interpretation, in four instances: When reviewing the justification of interferences with rights, when determining discrimination, when determining a positive obligation and in exceptional cases when looking at very broad terms such as 'inhuman and degrading'. Since the Court often declared in these processes that the law has changed, the most important and typical considerations in those contexts

---

[597] Mahoney, 'Judicial Activism and Judicial Self-Restraint in the European Court of Human Rights' 67.
[598] *Soering* v. *the United Kingdom* (Plenary) (1989) Series A no. 161 [103].
[599] See for example *Christine Goodwin* v. *the United Kingdom* (GC) ECHR 2002-VI [90].

should be revisited.⁶⁰⁰ In the process of balancing, the Court sometimes stresses that it would revise the decisions of national authorities only in rare circumstances.⁶⁰¹ Nevertheless, the Court very often entered into the assessment of all circumstances of the case. This means that every consideration can be advanced and assessed by the Court. This also means that several processes might differ to a significant extent even if they concern similar issues. If the cases to be decided are very similar, the Court might feel obliged to justify a different outcome of the process of balancing by certain techniques of balancing. In these contexts, typical considerations can be the consensus method, the practice of the respondent state, social factors as well as scientific insights.

The *consensus method* is the most prominent and most important amongst them.⁶⁰² In general, the Court looks for the consensus amongst the states parties as one argument in the balancing process. In rare cases, a unanimous practice could be established.⁶⁰³ If there was only 'little common ground' and a 'diversity of practice' this would speak against an update in the process of balancing.⁶⁰⁴ In those cases the Court found no consensus. Interestingly, even no consensus can be used as an argument: If this was generally taken to disfavour changes.⁶⁰⁵ Between complete and no consensus, there are different notions of partial agreement.⁶⁰⁶ The notion of a 'virtual consensus' was used when the contracting states followed a certain practice, for example not to execute the death penalty, even though the internal law did not provide for that practice.

The weakest forms of consensus are 'emerging consensus' and 'international trends'.⁶⁰⁷ It rarely happens that trends coincide with the final

---

⁶⁰⁰ It should be emphasised that there is generally no limit to the considerations that can be introduced in the process of balancing.
⁶⁰¹ *Moretti and Benedetti v. Italy* (Second Section) [64]; *Harroudj v. France*, (Fifth Section) [42].
⁶⁰² See generally Forowicz, *The Reception of International Law in the European Court of Human Rights* 9; Nolte, 'Second Report for the ILC Study Group on Treaties over Time' 256–7; Dzehtsiarou, 'European Consensus and the Evolutive Interpretation of the European Convention on Human Rights'.
⁶⁰³ *Stoll v. Switzerland* (GC) ECHR 2007-V [107].
⁶⁰⁴ *Cossey v. the United Kingdom*, (Plenary) 1990 Series A no. 184 [40].
⁶⁰⁵ *Schwizgebel v. Switzerland*, (First Section) ECHR 2010 [92]; *Haas v. Switzerland*, (First Section) ECHR 2011 [55].
⁶⁰⁶ Bratza, 'Living Instrument or Dead Letter' 124.
⁶⁰⁷ *Christine Goodwin v. the United Kingdom* (GC) ECHR 2002-VI [84]. For a 'trend', see *Vallianatos and others v. Greece* (GC) App. nos. 29381/09 and 32684/09 [91]. Compare *Stummer v. Austria* (GC) ECHR 2011 [132].

result of the interpretation.⁶⁰⁸ The Court sometimes indicated that an 'emerging consensus' that was not shared by the majority of the states would not tip the balance. When the Court found only tendencies, it also concluded that there ought to be no change in the law.⁶⁰⁹ On the other hand, the Court held that even if a country was in an 'isolated position as regards one aspect of its legislation does not necessarily imply that that aspect conflicts with the Convention'.⁶¹⁰ But in general, the outcome of the determination plays a big role in the argument of the Court. It can influence the process of balancing in two ways: Either it establishes a presumption or the practice is itself considered in the process of balancing. In some cases, the Court just refers to the outcome of its elaboration.⁶¹¹ Most of the time, the Court would look to the internal practice as well as the external practice of states to establish whether there is a consensus amongst them. From both directions, a consensus can be established. It is remarkable how this focus on internal and external practice could already be found in Sørensen's speech in 1975.⁶¹²

The *internal practice* is evidenced by acts of parliament,⁶¹³ Court decisions⁶¹⁴ or informal or formal acts of the executive.⁶¹⁵ Sometimes reviews by other bodies such as the European Commission for Democracy through Law (Venice Commission) are considered.⁶¹⁶ The Court regularly includes a comparative section after setting out the facts of the case. As to the numbers, the Court has considered the practice of twenty-nine out of thirty-three member states to be relevant internal practice.⁶¹⁷

---

⁶⁰⁸ An example for the 'successful' use of such a trend is *Christine Goodwin* v. *the United Kingdom* (GC) ECHR 2002-VI [84–5]; *Vallianatos and others* v. *Greece* (GC) App. nos. 29381/09 and 32684/09 [91].
⁶⁰⁹ *Schalk and Kopf* v. *Austria*, (First Section) ECHR 2010 [105].
⁶¹⁰ *Vallianatos and others* v. *Greece* (GC) App. nos. 29381/09 and 32684/09 [92].
⁶¹¹ *Rees* v. *the United Kingdom* (Plenary) (1986) Series A no. 106 [37]; *X, Y and Z* v. *the United Kingdom* (GC) ECHR 1997-II [44]; *Dudgeon* v. *the United Kingdom* (Plenary) (1981) Series A no. 4 App. no. 7525/76 [60]. For a critique, see *Hirst* v. *the United Kingdom (No. 2)* (GC), Joint Dissenting Opinion of Judges Wildhaber, Costa, Lorenzen, Kovler and Jebens ECHR 2005-IX [6].
⁶¹² Sørensen, 'Do the Rights Set Forth in the European Convention on Human Rights in 1950 Have the Same Significance in 1975?' 93.
⁶¹³ *MC* v. *Bulgaria*, (First Section) ECHR 2003-XII [158–60].
⁶¹⁴ *Christine Goodwin* v. *the United Kingdom* (GC) ECHR 2002-VI [81].
⁶¹⁵ *MC* v. *Bulgaria*, (First Section) ECHR 2003-XII [162].
⁶¹⁶ *Sitaropoulos and others* v. *Greece*, (First Section) [45]. For consideration of a report by the Venice Commission, see *Sukhovertskyy* v. *Ukraine*, (Second Section) ECHR 2006-VI App. no. 13716/02 70.
⁶¹⁷ *Sitaropoulos and others* v. *Greece*, (First Section) [45].

A lack of consensus was acknowledged when the numbers were sixteen out of forty-seven member states.[618]

In general, it is to be assumed that the practice will be more conclusive, the more consistent it is and the more states participate in it. In an exceptional case, the Court overcame the rather diverse practice of European states and mentioned an international trend which it derived from two judgments from Australia and New Zealand.[619] Even if there is internal practice pointing in a certain direction, the Court has developed several strategies to render this practice inconclusive. Sometimes, only some of the states have comparable provisions. In *X and others*, the Court did not take into account the practice of states when it could look only at ten states due to the 'narrowness of this sample'.[620] Partly dissenting judges criticised on the basis that this would not be adequate since a limited sample could very well establish the lack of consensus.[621] To compare several provisions is again a matter of appreciation for the Court. The Court could come to the conclusion that the practice does not show the necessary consistency: In one case it acknowledged that several states provided for rights for expatriates to vote. The Court, however, saw that the practice of the states was very divergent as to the conditions of that right and it found that this could warrant only a partial change: There was a right to vote, but the exact modalities could be determined by the member states.[622] The same thing happened in *Vallianatos*, which was about a Greek law providing for a civil union that was not accessible for same-sex couples.[623] The Court compared the practice of Greece to that of other states that had introduced a civil union that also covered same-sex couples. From this angle, the position of excluding same-sex couples is isolated in a relation of 17:2.[624] Comparing the states that allow same-sex couples to marry or to enter into a civil union to those who do not conveys again a different picture.

---

[618] *Schwizgebel v. Switzerland*, (First Section) ECHR 2010 [27, 91].
[619] *Christine Goodwin v. the United Kingdom* (GC) ECHR 2002-VI [84–5]. Compare the reference to the US Supreme Court in the context of the discussion of the legal situation concerning the definition of rape in common law countries in *MC v. Bulgaria*, (First Section) ECHR 2003-XII [158].
[620] *X and others v. Austria* (GC) [149].
[621] *X and others v. Austria* (GC), Joint Partly Dissenting Opinion of Judges Casadevall, Ziemele, Kovler, Jočienė Šikuta, de Gaetano and Sicilianos [12–14].
[622] *Sitaropoulos and Giakoumopoulos v. Greece* (GC) ECHR 2012 [74–5].
[623] *Vallianatos and others v. Greece* (GC) App. nos. 29381/09 and 32684/09.
[624] *Ibid.* [91].

The states not allowing for recognition outnumber states officially recognising same-sex couples by 27:20. Both samples can be taken into consideration in resolving the question whether a discrimination was justifiable. Yet, stating only one perspective certainly frames the argument in a particular way.

The Court could also choose to prefer one group over another when considering different groups in respect of the same issue. For example, when discussing the discrimination in respect of servicemen not being entitled to parental leave, it found that on the one hand a 'significant number' (twenty-three against six)[625] of member states provided for parental leave for servicemen and servicewomen, while on the other hand in the civilian sector there was only a 'small minority' (three against twenty-eight)[626] of states which did not do so.[627] Even though the first group seems to be closer to the actual question before the Court, it took into account a wider comparison on a similar question. The Court also in another case disregarded a 'substantial majority' which it regarded as forming a consensus on easier access to abortion since there was no consensus on the related question of when the life of a foetus would actually begin.[628] When looking at statutes, the Court preferred the actual interpretation of a national court over what the ordinary meaning of the national laws would suggest.[629] All in all, the first limb of the consensus method is to look at the internal practice. Yet, to decide whether there is a consistent internal practice is subject to the appreciation of the Court, and the Court has found several ways to deal with this.

In the process of seeking the consensus, the Court looks into the *external practice* of the parties. While it mostly cites international treaties, it also refers to soft law, especially that of the Council of Europe.[630] Only very rarely was the practice guided by Art. 31(3)(c) VCLT.[631]

The 1975 European Convention on the Legal Status of Children Born out of Wedlock is an apt example of how the Court would take into account treaties to which the respondent state is not a party and membership of which consists only of a minority of the member states of the

---

[625] *Konstantin Markin* v. *Russia* (GC) ECHR 2012 [74].   [626] *Ibid.* [72].
[627] *Ibid.* [140].   [628] *A, B and C* v. *Ireland* (GC) ECHR 2010 [234–7].
[629] *MC* v. *Bulgaria*, (First Section) ECHR 2003-XII [130–7], [159]. It is interesting that the Court also mentions doctrine.
[630] *Sitaropoulos and others* v. *Greece*, (First Section) [44]. The practice of the Committee of Ministers was associated with state practice in *MC* v. *Bulgaria*, (First Section) ECHR 2003-XII [162].
[631] *Harroudj* v. *France*, (Fifth Section) [42, 48].

ECHR. It considered the Convention in 1979, when four out of twenty members were party to it,[632] in 1987, when nine out of twenty-one states were members[633] and in 2009 when twenty-two out of forty-seven states were members.[634] It argued with reference to the Convention in cases in which the respondent states were Belgium,[635] Germany[636] and France,[637] none of which are parties to the Convention. Indeed, in relation to the question whether the Court could rely on treaties which were not signed by the respondent state, the Court very openly asserted that 'searching for common ground among the norms of international law it has never distinguished between sources of law according to whether or not they have been signed or ratified by the respondent State'.[638] Instead, the Court used the participation of the respondent state as a special feature that would actually increase the argumentative weight of the treaty.[639] Yet, the Court also argued that the fact that a certain respondent state is not party to a treaty could also be taken as an argument for there being no consensus.[640] As in the case of internal practice, the external practice is not always conclusive for the Court: Obligations might be too broad,[641] the treaty might allow member states to expand its scope in certain questions,[642] the treaty is sometimes also interpreted differently by the Court as compared to the government.[643] In *Emonet*, the Court interestingly disregarded a treaty which was binding 'only' upon 18 Council of Europe members but found a trend in a draft revision.[644] Generally, it can be stated that factors that weaken the weight of arguments drawn from other rules are the number of ratifications as well as the conclusiveness of the interpretation of the treaty.[645]

---

[632] *Marckx v. Belgium*, (Plenary) (1979) Series A no. 31 [40].
[633] *Inze v. Austria*, (Chamber) (1987) Series A no. 126 [41].
[634] *Brauer v. Germany*, (Fifth Section) [40].
[635] *Marckx v. Belgium*, (Plenary) (1979) Series A no. 31 [41].
[636] *Brauer v. Germany*, (Fifth Section) [40].
[637] *Mazurek v. France*, (Third Section) [49].
[638] *Genovese v. Malta*, (Fourth Section) [44].
[639] *Emonet and others v. Switzerland*, (First Section) [65].
[640] *X and others v. Austria* (GC) [150]. See also the critical remarks by *X and others v. Austria* (GC), Joint Partly Dissenting Opinion of Judges Casadevall, Ziemele, Kovler, Jočienė Šikuta, de Gaetano and Sicilianos [18].
[641] *Chapman v. the United Kingdom* (GC) ECHR 2001-I [93–4].
[642] *X and others v. Austria* (GC) [150].
[643] *Konstantin Markin v. Russia* (GC) ECHR 2012 [148].
[644] *Emonet and others v. Switzerland*, (First Section) [84].
[645] *X and others v. Austria* (GC) [150].

So the Court has used the internal as well as the external practice to establish the consensus of the contracting states. It relied on state conduct but in many instances, it had to make sense of many quite different practices. The examples above show that the Court had to interpret state practice and it was quite creative in doing that. What is significant is that in many of the creative cases, the Court balanced in line with the object and purpose of the ECHR. It tried to use interpretative leeway to frame the practice in a way that would fit interpretations furthering human rights. These instances of using arguments derived from state conduct with a certain 'spin' will be called *aconsensual consensualism*. In the process of balancing, the Court can include any consideration so it will by definition have more freedom. This also becomes evident from the fact that the Court greatly relies on *the practice of only the respondent state*.

It then considers the legal situation as well as developments in the respondent state. Changes in national law can trigger an evolution of former balancing decisions. Yet, the Court has also shown some caution when taking into account national legislation since states would have to be cautious that internal reform might prompt the evolution of Court jurisprudence. So the Court has aimed at avoiding 'that government departments would become over-cautious in the exercise of their functions and the helpfulness necessary in their relations with the public could be impaired'.[646] Even if the respondent state did change its internal law later, this did not necessarily influence the process of balancing.[647] So for example a change in the legislation did not automatically mean that the very same change ought to have been inserted earlier. Yet, mere proposals for reform can constitute a tendency that is to be taken into account in the process of balancing.[648] It would favour an evolution if the law in the state evolved, but also if it was inconclusive and lacked coherence: in *X and others*, the respondent state allowed children to live with a same-sex couple but prohibited the adoption by the second partner. This partial trend in the legislation prompted the Court to

---

[646] *Rees v. the United Kingdom* (Plenary) (1986) Series A no. 106 [45]. Later, the Court made the opposite argument and referred to the incompleteness of the law to argue for a rebalancing: *Christine Goodwin v. the United Kingdom* (GC) ECHR 2002-VI [78].

[647] *Tyrer v. the United Kingdom*, (Chamber) Series A no. 26 [31]; *Genovese v. Malta*, (Fourth Section) [44].

[648] *Mazurek v. France*, (Third Section) [52].

rebalance the question.[649] Interestingly, the Court did not attach much importance to historical interpretations of national law.[650]

The Court has, however, attached weight and importance to *social factors*. It has looked to attitudes in society. A change in such attitudes does not necessarily require changes in the law.[651] But the Court has, in many instances, framed the social development as an imperative for the law to follow. It has for example referred to a 'conflict between social reality and law' placing the applicant in an 'anomalous position' in *Christine Goodwin*.[652] The Court also looked at attitudes towards the Internet in society at a certain point in time[653] or at evolving standards of sexual autonomy in society.[654] Yet, the Court found that social attitudes could not justify discrimination, so it disregarded them when they went against a higher human rights standard.[655] In *Stoll*, the Court has justified greater interferences with reference to the increased importance, influence and quantity of information with explicit mention of 'electronic media' and an 'ever growing number of players' would trigger public monitoring.[656] In *F v. Switzerland*, a unanimous consensus based upon a recent trend would have no impact 'in a field – matrimony – which is so closely bound up with the cultural and historical traditions of each society'.[657] The Court was also careful to modify conceptions which 'bring into play the existing religious, ideological or traditional conceptions ... in each community'.[658] Yet, in another case, the Court perceived 'changes in the perception of social, civil-status and relational issues'.[659] In a case concerning the denial of social welfare, the Court referred to 'population mobility, the higher levels of international cooperation and integration, as well as developments in the area of banking services and information technologies'.[660] The inclusion of social factors makes it easy for the

---

[649] *X and others v. Austria* (GC) [144].
[650] *Emonet and others v. Switzerland*, (First Section) [83].
[651] *B v. France*, (Plenary) (1992) Series A no. 232-C [48].
[652] *Christine Goodwin v. the United Kingdom* (GC) ECHR 2002-VI [77].
[653] *KU v. Finland*, (Fourth Section) ECHR 2008 [48].
[654] *MC v. Bulgaria*, (First Section) ECHR 2003-XII [165].
[655] *Konstantin Markin v. Russia* (GC) ECHR 2012 [127, 142–3].
[656] *Stoll v. Switzerland* (GC) ECHR 2007-V [104].
[657] *F v. Switzerland* (Plenary) (1987) Series A no. 128 [33].
[658] *Kroon and others v. the Netherlands*, Dissenting Opinion Judge Morenilla Series A no. 297-C App. no. 18535/91.
[659] *X and others v. Austria* (GC) [139].   [660] *Pichkur v. Ukraine* (Fifth Section) [53].

Court to render the process of balancing flexible by general observations. Not as often did the Court use *scientific insights*.

In one case, the Court took into account a 'better understanding' which it linked to increased tolerance in society and in the internal laws of the member states.[661] The Court reviewed scientific knowledge and progress in the birth certificate cases.[662] The same phrase was applied to argue that the knowledge concerning the psychological pressure on rape victims has increased.[663] In *Sheffield and Horsham*, in which the Court was confronted with one theory of a natural scientist that might have prompted a reconsideration of the case, the Court held that, since 'it cannot be said that his views enjoy the universal support of the medico-scientific profession' the fact that the respective state held an opposite view 'cannot be criticised as being unreasonable'.[664] So the Court seems to look for a certain measure of certainty and agreement in the scientific community. The Commission abundantly discussed new medical evidence concerning the age of consent for young homosexuals and found that it had to reconsider its case law on the basis of that evidence.[665]

Of course, there is an unlimited number of grounds the Court would take into account especially on the side of the aims pursued by the government, such as the consequences for the administration.[666] In the process of balancing, the Court would also refer to considerations that were not important at the time the Convention was concluded such as environmental considerations.[667] Only in rare cases has the Court referred to rather abstract notions such as 'the essence of the Convention', which it found to be 'human dignity and human freedom'.[668] These notions fulfilled the function that is ordinarily attributed to the object and purpose of the treaty.

---

[661] *Dudgeon v. the United Kingdom* (Plenary) (1981) Series A no. 4 [60].
[662] *Cossey v. the United Kingdom*, (Plenary) 1990 Series A no. 184 [40]; *Sheffield and Horsham v. the United Kingdom* (GC) ECHR 1998-V App. nos. 22985/93, 23390/94 [56]; *Christine Goodwin v. the United Kingdom* (GC) ECHR 2002-VI [81–3].
[663] *MC v. Bulgaria*, (First Section) ECHR 2003-XII [164].
[664] *Sheffield and Horsham v. the United Kingdom* (GC) ECHR 1998-V [56].
[665] *Sutherland v. the United Kingdom* (Judgment) [59].
[666] *Rees v. the United Kingdom* (Plenary) (1986) Series A no. 106 [42].
[667] *Hatton and others v. the United Kingdom* (GC) ECHR 2003-VIII App. no. 36022/97 [96–104, 116–30]. Even though those cases are interesting, they do not fall within the rather strict definition of changes in the law. Had every consideration in the process of balancing to be considered, the inquiry would be totally limitless.
[668] *Christine Goodwin v. the United Kingdom* (GC) ECHR 2002-VI [90].

10.4.2 Rule of interpretation

As previously noted, the Court generally structured its interpretation according to the Vienna Convention.[669] No importance was attributed to the obligation to interpret in *good faith*. In *Cruz Varas*, the principle of good faith was used to express that the practice of states ought not to be legally relevant.[670] Even when one government explicitly invoked the duty to interpret in good faith,[671] the Court did not react to that argument. Good faith was never applied as an obligation on the Court but only on the parties to the dispute.[672] This reinforces the previous finding that the principle of good faith operates in relations between states but not in the judicial context.

Before looking at the means of interpretation in a qualitative manner, the use of the techniques of interpretation in the 31 cases containing intertemporal questions should be reviewed quantitatively.[673] Concerning the frequency of the use, the techniques are in the following order:

- Context: 20
- subsequent practice: 18
- relevant rules: 15
- ordinary meaning: 14
- object and purpose: 9
- *travaux*: 4
- subsequent agreement: 2

Regarding the question whether the Court uses the means to justify static or evolutive interpretations, there seem to be three categories: Some techniques could be termed as 'evolutive techniques' (object and purpose, subsequent practice, relevant rules), some 'static techniques' (ordinary meaning[674] and *travaux*). The context functioned as 'open technique'

---

[669] For a general observation on the use of the techniques of treaty interpretation beyond the context of changes in interpretation, see Forowicz, *The Reception of International Law in the European Court of Human Rights* 23.
[670] *Cruz Varas and others* v. *Sweden* (Plenary) Series A no. 201 [100].
[671] *Loizidou* v. *Turkey* (Preliminary Objections) (Chamber) (1995) Series A no. 310 [67].
[672] *Hirsi Jamaa and others* v. *Italy* (GC) ECHR 2012 [179].
[673] Again, the dataset is too small to show significant relationships, yet the quantitative view is indicative of the Court and summarises its patterns of interpretation.
[674] Regarding the ordinary meaning, the data show that there is an interesting correlation: every time the Court considered the ordinary meaning but found it to be inconclusive, the interpretation resulted in an evolutive interpretation. One could derive from this that

pointing almost evenly either to static or to dynamic solutions. Regarding the success rate, i.e. the ratio in which the result of the technique was the same as the interpretative outcome, the favourite techniques of the Court seem to be the ordinary meaning, the object and purpose, subsequent agreements, and the relevant rules. The other techniques seem to belong to a second class. Yet, the consideration of techniques even though they are in the end inconclusive also indicates that the Court takes some techniques very seriously. This applies in particular to the ordinary meaning (7 inconclusive mentions) and subsequent practice (5 inconclusive mentions).[675] The frequency and success rates of the techniques are summarised by Table 7.

The *ordinary meaning* was used more often than is perceived concerning the general jurisprudence of the Court.[676] Instead of using dictionaries, the Court referred to scholarly writings to derive from them the ordinary meaning especially of legal terms.[677] An interesting example for shifts in the ordinary meanings can be derived from Art. 12 ECHR in relation to transsexuals: In the first line of cases, the marriage was linked to the concept of the family so that biological factors played a decisive part.[678] In *Christine Goodwin*, the Court changed its understanding of the ordinary meaning and argued that this was due to the fact that couples 'unable to conceive or parent a child' would not be protected by the provision.[679] It, therefore, found that the ordinary meaning of the terms was inconclusive. Only in rare cases did the Court imply the ordinary meaning of the terms to be the decisive argument.[680] Yet,

---

an inconclusive ordinary meaning might have a justificatory effect for evolutive interpretations.

[675] Another explanation would be that the parties explicitly made these arguments before the Court.

[676] See Forowicz, *The Reception of International Law in the European Court of Human Rights* 31. Special importance was attributed to that technique by *Catan and others v. Moldova and Russia* (GC), Partly Dissenting Opinion of Judge Kovler ECHR 2012 App. nos. 43370/04, 8252/05, 18454/06.

[677] See for example *Banković v. Belgium, the Czech Republic, Denmark, France, Germany, Greece, Hungary, Iceland, Italy, Luxembourg, the Netherlands, Norway, Poland, Portugal, Spain, Turkey and the United Kingdom* (GC) (Decision) ECHR 2001-XII [59].

[678] *Rees v. the United Kingdom* (Plenary) (1986) Series A no. 106 [49]; *Sheffield and Horsham v. the United Kingdom* (GC) ECHR 1998-V [66].

[679] *Christine Goodwin v. the United Kingdom* (GC) ECHR 2002-VI [100].

[680] A good example can be found in *Ferrazzini v. Italy* (GC) ECHR 2001-VII [27]. The only arguments against evolution were basically a norm from the context and the ordinary meaning of the text of the treaty. When discussing the context, the Court explicitly held that it did 'not attach decisive importance to that factor'.

Table 7 Frequency and success rates of interpretative techniques

	Ordinary meaning	Context	Object and purpose	Subsequent agreement	Subsequent practice	Relevant rules	Travaux
Total use	14	20[a]	9	2	18	15	4
Static (successful/unsuccessful)	7 (6 + 1)	9 (5 + 4)	0 (0 + 0)	1 (1 + 0)	2 (1 + 1)	0 (0 + 0)	3 (2 + 1)
Evolutive (successful/unsuccessful)	0 (0 + 0)	8 (7 + 1)	9 (8 + 1)	1 (1 + 0)	11 (8 + 3)	12 (12 + 0)	0 (0 + 0)
Inconclusive for justification	7[b]	3	0	0	5	3	
Ratio	85.71%	70.59%	88.88%	100%	69.23%	100%	66.67%

Notes [a]In two instances, the court derived two arguments from the technique of context.
[b]Interestingly, all of those seven instances coincided with evolutive interpretations.

this technique can also be inconclusive and not point to any of the suggested meanings.[681] In *Rantsev*, the Court explicitly went beyond the ordinary meaning in an analogical manner. It found that Art. 4 ECHR was applicable to trafficking in persons without attaching it to any of the alternatives contained in Art. 4 ECHR.[682] In conclusion, it can be said that the wording is like the outer frame for the Court: The Court seldom goes completely beyond the ordinary meaning, it seldom takes the wording to be the decisive factor.

The *context* of the provision must not be considered as a whole. There can also be different arguments derived from the context,[683] sometimes one argument in favour and one against evolutive interpretation. If the Court interprets one norm evolutively, this can trigger changes in other norms: building upon its jurisprudence to allow for non-pecuniary damage under Art. 41 ECHR, the Court also applied Art. 8 ECHR to companies.[684] So the context can produce spill over effects on other norms.[685] This also shows that provisions in the context are themselves subject to interpretation.[686]

The *object and purpose* is sometimes not used as technique, but asserted in a rather abstract manner suggesting that the interpretation in line with the object and purpose will be favoured.[687] It was rarely taken to be the decisive argument.[688] Yet, the Court has developed its own formula to stress the object and purpose. It frequently refers to the necessity of interpreting the right in a 'practical and effective' manner for them not to remain 'theoretical and illusory'.[689] It sometimes also referred to the 'general spirit' of the Convention.[690] Very rarely, the Court has also considered a principle of effectiveness.[691] Regarding the

---

[681] *Schalk and Kopf* v. *Austria*, (First Section) ECHR 2010 [55]; *Matthews* v. *the United Kingdom* (GC) ECHR 1999-I [40]. Mentioning that there was also a restrictive reading: *Zolotukhin* v. *Russia* (GC) ECHR 2009 [80].

[682] *Rantsev* v. *Cyprus and Russia*, (First Section) [282]. See also Moerman, 'A Critical Analysis of the Prohibition of Slavery and Forced Labour under Article 4 of the European Convention on Human Rights' 112.

[683] *Schalk and Kopf* v. *Austria*, (First Section) ECHR 2010 [55–6, 59].

[684] *Société Colas Est and others* v. *France* ECHR 2002-III [41].

[685] See also *STEC and others* v. *the United Kingdom* (GC) (Decision) ECHR 2005-X [48–9].

[686] *Bayatyan* v. *Armenia* (GC) ECHR 2011 [100].

[687] *Zolotukhin* v. *Russia* (GC) ECHR 2009 [80].

[688] But see *Matthews* v. *the United Kingdom* (GC) ECHR 1999-I [40]; *Hirsi Jamaa and others* v. *Italy* (GC) ECHR 2012 [177].

[689] *Mamatkulov and Askarov* v. *Turkey* (GC) ECHR 2005-I [121].

[690] *Soering* v. *the United Kingdom* (Plenary) (1989) Series A no. 161 [87, 103].

[691] *Mamatkulov and Askarov* v. *Turkey* (GC) ECHR 2005-I [123].

subject knot,[692] i.e. the question of to what the phrase refers, the Court is very flexible: It used the object and purpose of the whole Convention,[693] of single provisions,[694] or even of specific sections[695] in certain provisions. Concerning the ascertainment knot, i.e. the question how the object and purpose is to be ascertained, the Court has taken a broad and liberal approach: The object and purpose could also be informed by extra-legal considerations such as the economic, political or social situation.[696] This then formed the basis for a consequential argument.[697] The jurisprudence of the Court reinforces that this technique can be used to form consequential arguments which rule out certain possible meanings as to their detrimental effect on the purpose envisaged by the treaty.[698] In one case, the Court hypothetically posed the question of what would happen if it considered transfers from outside the territory not as expulsion according to Art. 4 Protocol 4: 'The consequence of that would be that migrants having taken to the sea, often risking their lives, and not having managed to reach the borders of a State, would not be entitled to an examination of their personal circumstances before being expelled, unlike those travelling by land'.[699] The situation in reality clearly shows what happens if the party does not comply with the demands of the object and purpose. This clearly forms the basis of a consequential argument. Sometimes, the consensus was taken to influence the purpose of provisions.[700] As the consensus of the states can change over time, this necessarily implies that the object and purpose can emerge as well, so that emergent purposes are possible under the system of the ECHR.

---

[692] This describes the question of what the object and purpose refers to, for example the purpose of the treaty or the purpose of just one Article.
[693] In the process of balancing, *Christine Goodwin v. the United Kingdom* (GC) ECHR 2002-VI [90].
[694] *Loizidou v. Turkey* (Preliminary Objections) (Chamber) (1995) Series A no. 310 [88]; *Matthews v. the United Kingdom* (GC) ECHR 1999-I [43].
[695] *Stoll v. Switzerland* (GC) ECHR 2007-V [61]; *Bayatyan v. Armenia* (GC) ECHR 2011 [100], considering the purpose of Art. 4(3)(b) ECHR. Outside the context of changes in the law: *Stoll v. Switzerland* (GC) ECHR 2007-V [61].
[696] *Hirsi Jamaa and others v. Italy* (GC) ECHR 2012 [176-7].
[697] A consequential argument means an argument that points to the consequences of the different meanings.
[698] *Loizidou v. Turkey* (Preliminary Objections) (Chamber) (1995) Series A no. 310 [75].
[699] *Hirsi Jamaa and others v. Italy* (GC) ECHR 2012 [177].
[700] *Sitaropoulos and others v. Greece*, (First Section) [44]. This judgment concerned the process of balancing rather than interpretation, but this does not limit its relevance in the present context.

Subsequent agreement and practice are important techniques of interpretation. With regard to the relevant actors, the Court referred to court practice. Also in the context of subsequent practice, the Court looked not only at the letter of the law but also at its application: Not only the fact whether the death penalty is forbidden by law but also the question whether it is executed was relevant for the Court.[701] The material time to assess subsequent practice is when the application was made to the Court.[702] Yet, in *Bayatyan*, the Court circumvented this by considering that the later practice reinforced the trend the Court detected.[703] It really formed an intertemporal argument. It stated that there had been originally twenty opposing states, while five were left at the moment of the application, two of which subsequently changed their legislation.[704]

Regarding the qualitative knot of agreement, the 'great majority' of the member states was held to be sufficient.[705] The Court held that a practice which was not shared by four states out of forty-seven could be relevant subsequent practice.[706] Conversely the behaviour of six out of forty-seven,[707] as well as twenty-two out of forty[708] would not establish relevant practice. Regarding the knot of agreement, it is significant that the Court in *Cruz Varas* found a unanimous practice that would have sufficed to establish the agreement between the parties but concluded from the context that this was just a 'good faith compliance' and not subsequent practice proper. Interpretations of the practice of the member states could limit the potential for evolutive interpretations. In *Loizidou*, the Court used circumstantial evidence to interpret the practice in a different manner. It found that twenty-eight out of thirty states had not filed a certain reservation and took this as evidence for the impermissibility of that kind of reservation.[709] Read on its own, the practice is hardly conclusive: From the fact that states did not file a reservation we cannot conclude that they regard such a reservation to be impermissible.[710] Yet, the Court added that five states and the Secretary General of the Council

---

[701] *Soering v. the United Kingdom* (Plenary) (1989) Series A no. 161 [102].
[702] *Bayatyan v. Armenia* (GC) ECHR 2011 [103].   [703] *Ibid.*   [704] *Ibid.*
[705] *Sigidur A. Sigurjónsson v. Iceland* Series A no. 264 [35].
[706] *Bayatyan v. Armenia* (GC) ECHR 2011 [103].
[707] *Schalk and Kopf v. Austria*, (First Section) ECHR 2010 [58].
[708] *Stummer v. Austria* (GC) ECHR 2011 [131]. In the very same case, the Court indicated that an absolute majority (thirty-seven out of forty) might suffice.
[709] *Loizidou v. Turkey* (Preliminary Objections) (Chamber) (1995) Series A no. 310 [80–1].
[710] Otherwise, states would have a strong incentive to draft all kinds of reservations they regard as being permissible.

of Europe objected to the reservation. This reinforced that the practice of the twenty-eight states had to be interpreted in a certain way.[711]

Concerning the qualitative agreement knot, the Court sometimes took into account subsequent practice even if the states did not seem to be aware that they were applying the ECHR or acting in a field which is sensitive to human rights. In *STEC*, the Court discussed the system of benefits within the legal system of the member states and the dependence of many people on those schemes.[712] Here, the practice of states had *prima facie* nothing to do with the Convention, it was only assumed that the ECHR applied to those kinds of circumstances. The question whether the states grant those benefits as human rights was only briefly mentioned. Subsequent state practice was used more to show a social necessity. In *Cruz Varas*, the Court relied on the presumed 'belief' of the states, which equals the requirement of *opinio juris*.[713]

Additional protocols have been a problematic feature. Protocols are amendments to the Convention. As such, they alter its text. Yet, they can be used as arguments in the process of interpretation before they enter into force. They can potentially be acknowledged as context, as subsequent agreement[714] or as subsequent practice. The death penalty cases provide very good examples for the different roles additional protocols can play: Protocol 6 has abolished the death penalty in times of war, Protocol 13 also in times of peace. These protocols were signed and ratified only gradually. In the meantime, the Court had to decide several times whether Art. 3 ECHR would apply to those cases. When an additional protocol amends the ECHR, this can change it and be a trigger for evolutive interpretations also in other parts of the Convention.[715]

In *Soering*, the fact that a protocol existed and was not ratified by all states was taken as an argument that the states intended to entrust the evolution of the law to the process of amendment instead of to the process of interpretation.[716] The Court explicitly stated that it was upon each and every state to decide when exactly it would become bound by the amendment. In *Öcalan*, the Court drew exactly the opposite conclusion from Protocol 6, which had been signed by all parties and ratified by

---

[711] Ibid. 81.
[712] *STEC and others* v. *the United Kingdom* (GC) (Decision) ECHR 2005-X [50].
[713] *Cruz Varas and others* v. *Sweden* (Plenary) Series A no. 201 [100].
[714] *Öcalan* v. *Turkey*, (First Section) [103].
[715] See for example *Mamatkulov and Askarov* v. *Turkey* (GC) ECHR 2005-I [122].
[716] *Soering* v. *the United Kingdom* (Plenary) (1989) Series A no. 161 [103].

all parties except three.[717] Even Protocol 13, which could not attract the same level of participation at that point in time, was taken to confirm the general trend in state practice.[718] Yet, the Grand Chamber stressed that three outstanding signatures and sixteen outstanding ratifications were a clear indicator that Protocol 13 was tending against evolution prohibiting the death penalty in times of war.[719] In *Al-Saadoon and Mufdhi*, the Court held that, with two outstanding signatures and three states having signed but not ratified, Protocol 13 together with state practice would be 'strongly indicative' that there was an amendment of the ECHR effectively prohibiting the death penalty.[720] In a later case, a Protocol was taken as evidence that the parties intended to amend the treaty instead of reinterpreting it.[721] In *Demir and Baykara*, the Court took into account the failure of an additional protocol to the social charter which aimed to increase the enforcement mechanisms.[722] This did not stop the Court detecting a tendency towards the strengthening of the enforcement system of the said treaty. The Court argued that the states accompanied their rejection of increased enforcement with statements that they would generally 'wish to strengthen the mechanism'.[723] These issues again show the readiness of the Court to interpret state practice in a way that points in the same direction as the purpose of the Convention, i.e. to increase the protection of human rights. This goes together with what was previously observed as being a softening of the requirements of the Vienna Convention.[724] The way in which the Court dealt with subsequent practice, but particularly with protocols is again indicative of its approach of aconsensual consensualism.

In any case, those judgments reinforce the great value the Court attaches to subsequent practice: It is obvious that the practice can have

---

[717] *Öcalan v. Turkey*, (First Section) [195].   [718] *Ibid.* [197].
[719] *Öcalan v. Turkey* (GC) ECHR 2005-IV [164].
[720] *Al-Saadoon and Mufdhi v. the United Kingdom*, (Fourth Section) ECHR 2010 [120].
[721] See the argument in *Bayatyan v. Armenia* (GC), Dissenting Opinion by Judge Gyulumyan ECHR 2011 App. no. 23459/03 [2].
[722] *Demir and Baykara v. Turkey* (GC) ECHR 2008 [84]. This could have also been discussed in relation to the relevant rules, the proximity to the protocols favoured to move it to subsequent practice. Generally critical towards those arguments is Richter, 'Lücken der EMRK' 445–6.
[723] *Demir and Baykara v. Turkey* (GC) ECHR 2008 [84]. Regarding the European Committee on Social Rights, the Court later also based its recognition on the fact that the members had 'generally accepted' it: *RMT v. the Netherlands* (Fourth Section) App. no. 31045/10 (ECtHR, 8 April 2014) [94].
[724] Nolte, 'Second Report for the ILC Study Group on Treaties over Time' 266–8.

the same consequences as an amendment, so it is not surprising that the Court denoted the possible effect of practice as being an amendment.[725] Subsequent practice did, however, not always prevail in the interpretation.[726] The Court in one case explicitly stated that it could not 'create new rights and obligations which were not included in the Convention at the outset'.[727] Yet, in *Loizidou*, 'uniform and consistent' subsequent practice overcame the old treaty practice that could have helped to arrive at the intentions of the parties at the time of drafting the ECHR.[728]

The leading case on the questions of *relevant rules* was certainly *Demir and Baykara*, in which the respondent government explicitly raised the issue of which relevant rules could be read into the Convention. The issues identified by the ECHR resemble some of the issues identified above: The Court pronounced upon the notion of Art. 31(3)(c) VCLT as a technique, the source knot, the knot of participation and partly rejected the international interpretative method to apply its consensus method. Regarding the source knot, the Court acknowledged all possible sources in *Demir and Baykara*: The Court held that it would also take into account general principles of international law[729] as well as the *jus cogens* status of the norms in question.[730] It acknowledged the relevant rules as they are interpreted by the relevant courts and tribunals.[731] The Court also applied secondary law, such as directives in EU law.[732]

The Court also reinforced the observation that the relevant rules operate as a technique. This means that the Convention need not be interpreted in perfect harmony with other international treaties. Different results are possible. The Court has in the abstract described this as an equilibrium between the 'special nature of the Convention as a

---

[725] *Öcalan v. Turkey*, (First Section) [191]; see also *Hassan v. the United Kingdom* (GC) App. no. 29750/09 [101].
[726] *Acmanne and others v. Belgium* DR 1984 156. Yet, in this case, the Court acknowledged that Belgium had moved in the direction of the practice of the other states.
[727] *Cruz Varas and others v. Sweden* (Plenary) Series A no. 201 [100]. Compare *Austin and others v. the United Kingdom* (GC) ECHR 2012 [53].
[728] *Loizidou v. Turkey* (Preliminary Objections) (Chamber) (1995) Series A no. 310 [82].
[729] *Demir and Baykara v. Turkey* (GC) ECHR 2008 [71].
[730] *Ibid.* [73].
[731] For a citation of the CJEU and the Inter-American Court of Human Rights, see *Zolotukhin v. Russia* (GC) ECHR 2009 [79]. For a citation of the ICTY, see *Rantsev v. Cyprus and Russia*, (First Section) [280]; Compare *MC v. Bulgaria*, (First Section) ECHR 2003-XII [163]. For reference to the United Nations Human Rights Committee, see *Bayatyan v. Armenia* (GC) ECHR 2011 [105].
[732] *Schalk and Kopf v. Austria*, (First Section) ECHR 2010 [26, 93].

human rights instrument' and the greatest possible consistency 'with the other principles of international law'.[733] So arguments derived from other relevant rules can either stress that the Court is different from other instruments or emphasise the harmony between all rules. In the abstract, the latter seems to be the usual assumption for the Court. Yet, there are exceptions. In *Pichkur*, the Court held that the Convention was not 'prevented from defining higher standards than those contained in other legal instruments' and went beyond an ILO Convention of 1952.[734] In *Loizidou*, the Court stressed differences between the Convention system and the ICJ.[735] So the Court mentioned that Art. 3 ECHR could encompass the obligation not to extradite even though it is mentioned separately in another treaty on the matter.[736] In *Rantsev*, the Court took two conventions into account even though they had nothing to do with the provision the Court was occupied with.[737] The Court only used them as an argument that international law dealt with related questions and concluded from this that Art. 4 ECHR might be applicable. Again, the relevant rules are intertemporally open and can allude to different points in time. If they precede the treaty, they can *de facto* work like *travaux*, enlightening the meaning at the time of the conclusion of a treaty.[738] Yet, the Court also limited the scope of the technique when it held that 'States retain Convention liability in respect of treaty commitments subsequent to the entry into force of the Convention'.[739]

The Court also took a soft[740] approach in relation to the knot of 'bindingness'. It consistently referred to soft-law instruments such as the Universal Declaration of Human Rights,[741] the Charter of Fundamental Rights of the European Union when it was still a soft-law

---

[733] *Mamatkulov and Askarov* v. *Turkey* (GC) ECHR 2005-I [111].
[734] *Pichkur* v. *Ukraine* (Fifth Section) [53].
[735] *Loizidou* v. *Turkey* (Preliminary Objections) (Chamber) (1995) Series A no. 310 [84]. In a different context, the Court took exactly the opposite stance towards the ICJ Statute: see *Mamatkulov and Askarov* v. *Turkey* (GC) ECHR 2005-I [117, 124].
[736] *Demir and Baykara* v. *Turkey* (GC) ECHR 2008 [82].
[737] *Rantsev* v. *Cyprus and Russia*, (First Section) [278].
[738] For an example outside the context of changes in interpretation, see *Stummer* v. *Austria* (GC) ECHR 2011 [118].
[739] *X and others* v. *Austria* (GC) [150]; *Al-Saadoon and Mufdhi* v. *the United Kingdom*, (Fourth Section) ECHR 2010 [128]. See the critical remarks by *X and others* v. *Austria* (GC), Joint Partly Dissenting Opinion of Judges Casadevall, Ziemele, Kovler, Jočienė Šikuta, de Gaetano and Sicilianos [22].
[740] For the notion of soft requirements, see Nolte, 'Second Report for the ILC Study Group on Treaties over Time' 266–8.
[741] *Rantsev* v. *Cyprus and Russia*, (First Section) [277].

instrument,⁷⁴² and non-binding instruments like resolutions of the Committee of Ministers⁷⁴³ and the Parliamentary Assembly⁷⁴⁴ and other organs such as the Venice Commission, the European Commission against Racism and Intolerance and the Committee for the Prevention of Torture and Inhuman or Degrading Treatment or Punishment.⁷⁴⁵ The Court was also very liberal when it came to issues of participation. It held that it would take into account treaties even though they have not been ratified by all parties.⁷⁴⁶ In particular, the Court applied treaties even though they were not applicable to the party in question.⁷⁴⁷ An instrument of limited participation that is regularly considered is the Charter of Fundamental Rights of the European Union.⁷⁴⁸

The *travaux* were rarely used.⁷⁴⁹ In *Johnston*, they entered the process of interpretation rather indirectly through the object and purpose.⁷⁵⁰ Yet, even indirectly, they only confirmed the meaning that was supported also by the other means of interpretation. In *Loizidou*, the Court held that the evidence as to the intentions of the authors, which is most likely to be the *travaux*, was 'not decisive'.⁷⁵¹ In *Banković*, the Court heavily relied on this technique but did not fail to stress that it only did so to confirm (*sic!*) the static result.⁷⁵² It has to be mentioned that this technique can also lead to the result that the interpretation ought to be

---

⁷⁴² *Christine Goodwin v. the United Kingdom* (GC) ECHR 2002-VI [100]; *Schalk and Kopf v. Austria*, (First Section) ECHR 2010 [61].
⁷⁴³ *Stummer v. Austria* (GC) ECHR 2011 [130]; *Bayatyan v. Armenia* (GC) ECHR 2011 [107].
⁷⁴⁴ See further references at *Demir and Baykara v. Turkey* (GC) ECHR 2008 [74]; *Bayatyan v. Armenia* (GC) ECHR 2011 [107]. Compare in the process of balancing *Sitaropoulos and others v. Greece*, (First Section) [44].
⁷⁴⁵ *Demir and Baykara v. Turkey* (GC) ECHR 2008 [75].   ⁷⁴⁶ *Ibid.* [80–2].
⁷⁴⁷ *Ibid.* [83, 149]. The Court went even further as to consider the participation of the respondent state in an international treaty as an additional reason for the state to accept the evolutive interpretation: *Bayatyan v. Armenia* (GC) ECHR 2011 [108].
⁷⁴⁸ See for example *Christine Goodwin v. the United Kingdom* (GC) ECHR 2002-VI [100]; *Bayatyan v. Armenia* (GC) ECHR 2011 [106].
⁷⁴⁹ See for example *Bayatyan v. Armenia* (GC) ECHR 2011 [100]. It is not very clear whether they played a role in *Cruz Varas and others v. Sweden* (Plenary) Series A no. 201 [95].
⁷⁵⁰ *Johnston and others v. Ireland*, (Plenary) (Judgment) [52].
⁷⁵¹ *Loizidou v. Turkey* (Preliminary Objections) (Chamber) (1995) Series A no. 310 [71]. See also *Sigidur A. Sigurjónsson v. Iceland* Series A no. 264 [35].
⁷⁵² *Banković v. Belgium, the Czech Republic, Denmark, France, Germany, Greece, Hungary, Iceland, Italy, Luxembourg, the Netherlands, Norway, Poland, Portugal, Spain, Turkey and the United Kingdom* (GC) (*Decision*) ECHR 2001-XII [65].

changed.⁷⁵³ In *James*, the Court looked almost exclusively and only briefly to the *travaux* but stressed their supplementary status.⁷⁵⁴ The *circumstances at the time of the conclusion* have only rarely been used as a technique of interpretation.⁷⁵⁵

10.4.3 The consensus method

As already mentioned, the Court included a cautionary note in its willingness to apply the rules of interpretation as enshrined by the VCLT.⁷⁵⁶ Yet, it has at times replaced the VCLT with its consensus method and looked at the internal practice⁷⁵⁷ instead of subsequent practice, and the external practice instead of the relevant rules. The Court stated in *Demir and Baykara*:

> The Court, in defining the meaning of terms and notions in the text of the Convention, can and must take into account elements of international law other than the Convention, the interpretation of such elements by competent organs, and the practice of European States reflecting their common values. The consensus emerging from specialised international instruments and from the practice of Contracting States may constitute a relevant consideration for the Court when it interprets the provisions of the Convention in specific cases.⁷⁵⁸

This is a clear example of the Court applying the *consensus method* in the process of interpretation in linking it even to vaguer notions such as values. The question whether the Court is free to use the consensus method should be revisited in turn. It is striking that the notion of consensus,⁷⁵⁹ but also the important status of treaties⁷⁶⁰ and the case

---

⁷⁵³ *Bayatyan v. Armenia* (GC) ECHR 2011 [100]. Here the *travaux* limited the scope of a provision in the context which originally was taken to support a rather static meaning. If the different stages of amendment are used to show its history, this historical recount can again be indicative of further changes. See for example *Mamatkulov and Askarov v. Turkey* (GC) ECHR 2005-I [122].
⁷⁵⁴ *James and others v. the United Kingdom* (Plenary) (1986) Series A no. 98 [66].
⁷⁵⁵ *Schalk and Kopf v. Austria*, (First Section) ECHR 2010 [55].
⁷⁵⁶ *Demir and Baykara v. Turkey* (GC) ECHR 2008 [65]; *Golder v. the United Kingdom* (1973) Series A no. 18 [29–30].
⁷⁵⁷ *Soering v. the United Kingdom* (Plenary) (1989) Series A no. 161 [102]; *Schalk and Kopf v. Austria*, (First Section) ECHR 2010 [58]; *Cossey v. the United Kingdom*, (Plenary) 1990 Series A no. 184 [46]; *Stummer v. Austria* (GC) ECHR 2011 [130-2].
⁷⁵⁸ *Demir and Baykara v. Turkey* (GC) ECHR 2008 [85].
⁷⁵⁹ Sørensen, 'Do the Rights Set Forth in the European Convention on Human Rights in 1950 Have the Same Significance in 1975?' 106.
⁷⁶⁰ *Ibid.* 92.

law and practice in the member states[761] were clearly already envisaged by Sørensen. The question of whether the Court should have a method of its own is often discussed under the label of fragmentation and unity of international law:[762] in essence, it concerns the question how autonomous rules in certain areas of international law can be, as opposed to general standards.[763] Instead of revisiting the general debate about the desirability or necessity of fragmentation or unity, we shall discuss the question of whether the autonomous stance as taken by the Court is warranted. The answer from the perspective of this study cannot be clearer: The use of the consensus method should be restricted to questions of balancing, no use should be made of it in the process of interpretation. Several arguments support this.

First, using the internal and external practice as establishing consensus has no advantage over the use of the techniques of subsequent practice and the relevant rules. All the notions basically work in parallel. The only proper effect the consensus method has is that it blurs the interpretative method. First, Art. 31(3) VCLT establishes at least some guidance for the interpreter. And even in cases in which the techniques are ambiguous, the rule of interpretation still fulfils a function: It can map disagreement between the different approaches. The present study has described these as interpretative knots. In this sense, if used consistently, the rule of interpretation contained in the VCLT makes the interpretative stance visible. We should also not forget that, in the course of establishing the consensus, the other techniques are seldom mentioned. So the consensus method fails to point for example to the ordinary meaning and the context in the same way. This is most striking in the case of the object and purpose. It is hardly mentioned when the Court establishes the consensus of the parties. Yet, a detailed analysis of the argumentative

---

[761] *Ibid.* 93.
[762] See for example Dupuy, 'The Danger of Fragmentation or Unification of the International Legal System and the International Court of Justice'; Fischer-Lescano and Teubner, *Regime-Kollisionen: Zur Fragmentierung des globalen Rechts*.
[763] For an account that is aimed at the question of interpretation, see Rietiker, 'The Principle of "Effectiveness" in the Recent Jurisprudence of the European Court of Human Rights' 252. Amongst the vast amount of literature on this issue, see for example the contributions in Buffard and Hafner (eds.), *International law between universalism and fragmentation*; ILC, Report of the Study Group of the International Law Commission Finalized by Martti Koskenniemi, 'Fragmentation of International Law: Difficulties Arising from the Diversification and Expansion of International Law' in 'Reports of the International Law Commission on the work of its 42nd session' (1 May–9 June and 3 July–11 August 2006) UN Doc. A/CN.4/L.682'.

patterns of the Court has revealed that it is very creative in interpreting and framing the practice in a certain way. These methods used by the Court may be called *aconsensual consensus* methods:[764] The Court purports to look for state conduct while it construes the practice in such a way as to follow the object and purpose. And it does so without mentioning this technique. This might explain the fact that the jurisprudence is designated as being purposive whereas the object and purpose is less frequently invoked than by the ICJ. A departure from the Vienna rules of interpretation is of course not unprecedented: The Court of Justice of the European Union has famously chosen not to apply the rule of interpretation and replaced it with its own interpretative method. As already mentioned, the VCLT enhances also the communication between different international courts interpreting similar issues. So the VCLT might have the function to facilitate communication between the ECtHR and other courts dealing with human rights and similar issues. It would make interpretations by different actors on the same subject very comparable. For all of these reasons, it would be advisable for the ECtHR to stick to the rule of interpretation in the Vienna Convention.

The review of the approach of the ECtHR has shown that the Court has taken a 'soft'[765] approach in many respects: Ascertaining the object and purpose from wider political and economic observations, taking a moderate approach concerning the consistency with regard to subsequent practice and looking to soft law as relevant rules are just some of many examples of how the Court employed the techniques in the VCLT in an extensive manner.

10.4.4 Other arguments

As we have seen, the social observations are linked to techniques of interpretation which they inform.[766] In the process of interpretation, other arguments such as social observations are resorted to less often.

---

[764] For a similar account, namely, the fact that the subsequent practice of the parties was invoked even though the parties did not consent, see Forowicz, *The Reception of International Law in the European Court of Human Rights* 42. A very interesting exposition of the consensus method is provided for by von Ungern-Sternberg, 'Die Konsensmethode des EGMR' 312; a problematique very close to the one developed here can be found at *ibid.* 334-6.

[765] Nolte, 'Second Report for the ILC Study Group on Treaties over Time' 266-8.

[766] On that relationship, see generally even though with a slightly different account Forowicz, *The Reception of International Law in the European Court of Human Rights* 69.

They partially served to reinforce the margin of appreciation of the domestic authorities.[767] Sometimes, 'social attitudes' are merely mentioned in the context of subsequent practice.[768] In the case of slavery, servitude and forced and compulsory labour, the Court also took into account wider problems such as trafficking of persons. This was considered to be an increasing 'global phenomenon'.[769] Yet, the Court has used changes in society and science also as arguments standing on their own.[770]

10.4.5 Precedent

Even in the landmark case of *Tyrer*, the Court '*recalled*' that the Convention was a 'living instrument'.[771] Yet, in other cases, citations as to static and evolutive outcomes were more explicit in the sense that concrete cases were cited. *Tyrer* remains the most cited case, irrespective of whether the issue is interpretation or balancing or which Article of the Convention is at issue.[772] Only very rarely did the Court invoke jurisprudence other than its own.[773] As to the other cases, precedents sometimes seem to correlate in relation to the respondent state.[774] It is interesting that the Court also cited cases like *X, Y and Z*[775] even though they did not really change the law.[776] Especially in the process of balancing, the Court distinguished similar cases to come to a different conclusion.[777] Yet, precedents can also be left intact while the Court distinguishes the case due to other circumstances in the respective country.[778] The living instrument doctrine has been used to signal that precedents are

---

[767] *Schalk and Kopf* v. *Austria*, (First Section) ECHR 2010 [62].   [768] *Ibid.* [93].
[769] *Rantsev* v. *Cyprus and Russia*, (First Section) [278]. The Court, however, mentioned two international conventions in that context so that it did not merely look into the said phenomenon.
[770] *Christine Goodwin* v. *the United Kingdom* (GC) ECHR 2002-VI [100].
[771] *Tyrer* v. *the United Kingdom*, (Chamber) Series A no. 26 [31].
[772] See the explicit and separate mention in *A, B and C* v. *Ireland* (GC) ECHR 2010 [234].
[773] A reference to the *Namibia opinion* of the ICJ is contained in *Ternoviskis* v. *Latvia* (Fourth Section) App. no. 33637/02 [49].
[774] *T* v. *the United Kingdom* (GC) [70].
[775] *X, Y and Z* v. *the United Kingdom* (GC) ECHR 1997-II.
[776] *Banković* v. *Belgium, the Czech Republic, Denmark, France, Germany, Greece, Hungary, Iceland, Italy, Luxembourg, the Netherlands, Norway, Poland, Portugal, Spain, Turkey and the United Kingdom* (GC) (Decision) ECHR 2001-XII [64]; *Hirsi Jamaa and others* v. *Italy* (GC) ECHR 2012 [175].
[777] *Mazurek* v. *France*, (Third Section) [52].
[778] *B* v. *France*, (Plenary) (1992) Series A no. 232-C [49–62].

overturned.[779] In the process of overruling a precedent, the Court will find a balance between 'the interests of legal certainty, foreseeability and equality before the law' and the risk of the Court becoming 'a bar to reform and improvement'.[780] If a case is merely distinguished, no such distinction ought to be drawn since the legal considerations involved are presumed to be identical and only the facts of the cases differ. This makes it possible to reach a different conclusion.[781]

10.5. Summary and outlook

We have seen that the ECtHR has managed to retain a dynamic approach that favours presentism over backward-looking intentionalism. Yet, the question came to the forefront of how this dynamism can be tempered.[782] Unlike in doctrinal or activist disputes, the aging activist might have recognised that this is not a question of black and white, of all or nothing, but rather a question of degree. We have to imagine the method and related issues like a huge mixing console at a live concert with many controls. Nobody wants the music to be too loud, nobody wants it to stop, but the aim is just to find the right tone for the band. To achieve that we can adjust different controls, each of them influencing the sound in a certain way: The bass, the heights, the definition and many other variables. Figure 7 restates the variables we have found so far.

With regard to the *stocktaking*, we have seen that there are different parts of the Court that can decide. Limitation of evolutive interpretations would be achieved if those decisions could only be made by the Grand Chamber.[783] On the other hand, one could also think that not just every part of the Court, but also national courts are competent to change the meaning of the terms of the Convention.[784] This would certainly increase the number of evolutive interpretations.

---

[779] *Mizzi v. Malta*, (First Section) ECHR 2006-I App. no. 26111/02 [132–4].

[780] *Christine Goodwin v. the United Kingdom* (GC) ECHR 2002-VI [74]; *Cossey v. the United Kingdom*, (Plenary) 1990 Series A no. 184 [35]; *Bayatyan v. Armenia* (GC) ECHR 2011 [98].

[781] *Sommerfeld v. Germany* (GC) ECHR 2003-VII App. no. 31871/96 [90–1]. This is a very apt example since the applicant had submitted that the ECHR ought to be interpreted evolutively: see *ibid.* [79–80]. The different effects and requirements are also shown in *Cossey v. the United Kingdom*, (Plenary) 1990 Series A no. 184 [31–4, 35].

[782] Different possibilities are also envisaged by Bratza, 'Living Instrument or Dead Letter' 122.

[783] Tulkens, 'What Are the Limits to Evolutive Interpretation of the Convention?' 8.

[784] Andenas and Bjorge, 'National Implementation of ECHR Rights' 188.

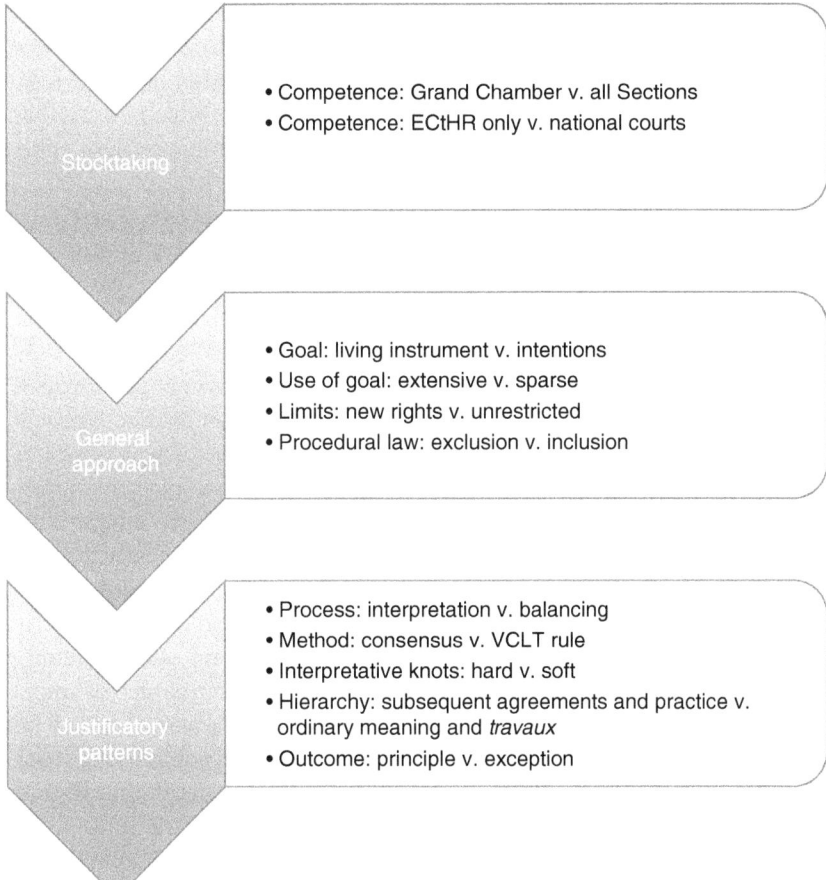

Figure 7 Mixing console: Ways of limiting and enhancing static or evolutive interpretations

Concerning the *general approach*, judgments would look more expansive the more the 'living instrument' doctrine is used while a referral to the intentions of the parties will look like a limitation of the approach.[785] Similar to the intention is the assertion that the Court could not create 'new rights' but only interpret those in the Convention. Like the notion of

---

[785] Mahoney, 'Judicial Activism and Judicial Self-Restraint in the European Court of Human Rights' 69; Jean-Paul Costa, 'What Are the Limits to Evolutive Interpretation of the Convention?'.

intentions or the distinction between interpretation and amendment, this view departs from the assumption that there is something like an essence of the Convention. This is in the opinion of the author not the case. Conversely, evolutive interpretation presupposes change which means that there necessarily has to be something new. So the formula of new rights might function as a rhetorical device appealing to the virtue of judges.

The same applies to the frequency of use of the doctrine. The Court can, on the one hand, be very liberal with invoking the doctrine in circumstances which are not evolutive interpretations proper. This would include citations of previous evolutive interpretations. On the other hand, the Court can also be very restrictive and use the doctrine only and exclusively when the meaning of the Convention is changed through interpretation. The frequency of use of the living instrument doctrine will not change the law, but it changes the perception of the jurisprudence of the Court. Regarding the question of whether to allow evolutive interpretations of procedural law, the Court seemed to have reached a middle ground between total exclusion and inclusion in that it allowed for the evolutive interpretation if the effectiveness of the whole Convention was concerned.[786] Regarding the areas of the law, one could either strictly separate civil and political rights from social, cultural and economic rights or regard them as mutually reinforcing. The techniques of interpretation, especially the relevant rules, can work both ways: They can be used as an exclusionary argument in the sense that a problem might for example be dealt with in the Social Charter in greater depth and should therefore be left out of the scope of the ECHR. In this regard, it has to be stated that, considering the expressed intention of the Court to limit the expansion of its case law, which might also be due to a significantly rising case load, in this case it might be advisable to focus on the core competencies and the core areas, i.e. political and civil rights.[787] The Court can set the tune with its general attitude, yet the arguments will be more convincing, the more they deal with the specifics of the case and the related instruments. To rely solely on one or the other position will not be particularly convincing.

In relation to the *justificatory patterns*, it is obvious that the expansive use of balancing when determining the meaning of vague phrases will

---

[786] Against any evolution of procedural norms is Golsong, 'Interpreting the Convention' 150. In favour of the general requirement of consensus in those questions is Tomuschat, 'Das Europa der Richter' 866.

[787] See for example *Demir and Baykara* v. *Turkey* (GC) ECHR 2008 [84].

make it easier to interpret evolutively while the constant use of the process of interpretation will make it harder since the means of justification are more limited. This also links to the question of the consensus method: The use of this method at least blurs the justification to a significant extent; a limitation might be achieved by using the rule of interpretation as contained in the VCLT since it allows for a comparison between the approach of the ECtHR and other courts and makes expansive uses of the rule visible. When using the rule of interpretation, it is for the Court to choose how it determines its knots. When the Court allows taking into account the subsequent practice of only a part of the states parties to the Convention or to taking into account treaties only some of the states have ratified, it will be easier to justify evolutive interpretations. The same logic applies to other arguments. The more they are included, the more likely evolutive interpretations are. The same can be said in relation to the general relationship between the techniques of interpretation. The Court currently puts much emphasis on subsequent agreement and practice. Inquiring into the *travaux*[788] or taking the ordinary meaning more seriously could also limit evolutive interpretations. These are some of the aspects with which the Court can influence its stance on evolutive interpretations. The stance it has taken can be reviewed with the indicators of power, pace and perception. Regarding the question how the Court frames the outcome, it can either frame evolutive interpretation as a general rule or restrict it and frame it only as an exception.[789] In this way, the Court can guide the application of its finding in future cases but potentially also future questions of stasis and evolution.

The birth certificate cases are a good example of the *power* exercised by the Court. Even though the Court constantly used the same techniques, the stance shifted slowly. In the initial judgment, *Rees*, three out of fifteen judges dissented. The next cases were then decided with very slim majorities: Ten to eight judges in *Cossey* and eleven to nine judges in *Sheffield and Horsham*, until it found unanimously (seventeen to nil) that there were two violations of the Convention in *Christine Goodwin*.[790] To observe the shifting stances of the Court is also interesting since one can very well compare how the processes of balancing and interpretation

---

[788] See Tulkens, 'What Are the Limits to Evolutive Interpretation of the Convention?' 8.
[789] For framing an evolution as an exception, see *Centre for Legal Resources on behalf of Valentin Câmpeanu* [112].
[790] The two dissenting opinions referred only to the calculation of the interest rates and not to substantive matters.

work in these situations. This line of cases and the reliance on the object and purpose in *Christine Goodwin* clearly show that the Court at times takes the initiative and asserts power. But in general we have seen that it pursues another policy, namely, that of aconsensual consensualism: It frames the practice of the states, be it internal or external, subsequent practice or the relevant rules, in a way that furthers human rights.[791] While it does not use purposive arguments in the justification, they clearly underlie the construction of state practice. This is a subtle way of the Court to seemingly attribute power to state consensus while remaining 'in power'.

The Court is very careful to set the *pace* of change in the Convention. It can be very quick in its actions. In *Société Colas Est*, it relied merely on a roughly similar interpretation of a procedural norm and declared that 'the time has come' to interpret evolutively.[792] Yet, the Court indicated that it will watch the developments in that field and remains occupied with the matter.[793] It even found that there was an obligation for the member states to review the situation.[794] Cases like *Schalk and Kopf* indicate that the Court sometimes prefers a very slow pace of movement over no movement at all. As previously mentioned, the Court held that Art. 12 ECHR was applicable to same-sex marriages but the issue was still within the margin of appreciation of the member states. So the Court gradually assumed competences to determine the matter. The rhetoric of the Court is framed in a way to suggest movement in a certain direction when it held that changes would 'not yet' exist or the law was in a 'transitional stage'.[795] The temporality of arguments is also used by the Court in framing trends. The Court then not only looks at the subsequent practice of states as it stands at one point in time, it also looks at how the practice developed before and after the dispute arose and tries to give a direction to the development over time.[796]

---

[791] For a similar critique, see Golsong, 'Interpreting the Convention' 158.
[792] *Société Colas Est and others v. France* ECHR 2002-III [41].
[793] *Rees v. the United Kingdom* (Plenary) (1986) Series A no. 106 [47].
[794] *Cossey v. the United Kingdom*, (Plenary) 1990 Series A no. 184 [42]; *Sheffield and Horsham v. the United Kingdom* (GC) ECHR 1998-V [60]. Such an obligation can then be used as an argument in favour of change since the states could foresee that there might be changes: see *Christine Goodwin v. the United Kingdom* (GC) ECHR 2002-VI [92].
[795] *Rees v. the United Kingdom* (Plenary) (1986) Series A no. 106 [37].
[796] *Bayatyan v. Armenia* (GC) ECHR 2011 [103].

The Court is ready to speed up the development when needed and it takes into account the temporal dimension of the law. No case exemplifies this better than *Christine Goodwin*. The Court justified its rebalancing as follows:

> *In the twenty first century* the right of transsexuals to personal development and to physical and moral security in the full sense enjoyed by others in society cannot be regarded as a matter of controversy requiring the *lapse of time* to cast clearer light on the issues involved. In short, the unsatisfactory situation in which post-operative transsexuals live in an intermediate zone as not quite one gender or the other is *no longer* sustainable.[797]

As shown above, the processes of interpretation and balancing vary to a significant extent when it comes to the issue of *perception*. In the process of interpretation, the Court will be open to developments in society or international relations, but it will be always inclined to link these developments to legal rules it can take into account according to the VCLT.[798] Yet, it opened up the VCLT to a significant extent. In the process of balancing, the Court has been open for any kind of consideration.

The Court has never betted solely on one horse. The Court has shifted its method between balancing and interpretation, consensus and the VCLT, as well as between various ways to interpret the VCLT. The aging activist now has more scope to limit or expand its evolutive stance.

---

[797] *Christine Goodwin v. the United Kingdom* (GC) ECHR 2002-VI [90] (emphasis added).
[798] *Rantsev v. Cyprus and Russia*, (First Section) [278].

PART IV

Summary and conclusions

11

Summary and conclusions

This book has focused on the question of how international lawyers are to deal with questions of static and evolutive treaty interpretation. The inquiry has been separated into three parts, each of which has addressed aspects of this question. The first part defined the problems and laid out the mode of inquiry, the second part explained the rule of interpretation and the third part described how this rule is applied in practice. In conclusion, we shall revisit the results of this inquiry and summarise the most important insights.

11.1. Part I: definition of the problem, suggested solutions, mode of inquiry

Before talking about interpretation, the concepts need to be clear: Those are interpretation, evolutive interpretation, interpretative method, practice and methodology. Definitions have no absolute truth value, but are essential nevertheless. This applies first and foremost to the notion of interpretation. The definition given here was derived from the social practice of interpreting, the activity that lawyers designate as interpretation. This is the establishment of the meaning of a treaty and can best be seen in judgments when courts first generally state how a part of the text is to be understood before they effectively apply it to the text. Even though this practice is closely related to other activities such as the application of the treaty to real-world occurrences, interpretation is at least analytically separate in the sense that we can think of it as a distinct activity as opposed to application or balancing. So, we look to lawyers who establish the meaning of legal texts, which means in the case of international law the meaning of treaties. An evolutive interpretation occurs when the meaning of the text of the treaty changes over time. The element of change is all important in that regard. It sets evolutive interpretation apart from mere specification in which the previously unknown meaning is defined for the first time. A specification answers a question for the first time, an evolutive interpretation revises an already existing answer. While specifications are mutually exclusive with evolutive interpretation, other concepts such as analogy, '*Rechtsfortbildung*', judicial creativity or approximate application cannot be directly related to evolutive interpretation: They can coincide or not, depending on the circumstances. The inquiry has consequently been limited to changes in interpretation.

How can an interpreter change the meaning of a treaty? From a legal perspective, this is a question of interpretative method, of the rules guiding the conduct of lawyers. The two major perspectives on interpretative method are interpretative practice and methodology. Methodology is the scholarly reflection of interpretative method and practice is its application. Our first aim is to look at whether methodology has solved the issue.

The result of an extensive study of the legal discourse concerning this question resulted in the finding that there is the greatest possible disagreement on this question. There are currently over 20 different views based on the VCLT that either partly complement the VCLT, or totally depart from it. Some resort to the nature of the terms and look for so-called 'generic terms'; others assume an intertemporal rule or see evolutive interpretation as a form of purposive interpretation. What is interesting is that the different approaches mostly assert a solution without many arguments and without reacting to other solutions. Going further back in time, it is interesting to see that in the whole drafting process, there was never a consensus concerning questions of static and evolutive interpretation. The only thing the parties could really agree on was to let the question be determined by the ordinary process of treaty interpretation and therefore to leave it open. In the preparation of the draft that later became the VCLT, the fourth Special Rapporteur Humphrey Waldock had included Draft Art. 56 applying Max Huber's famous *dictum* in the *Island of Palmas Case* to the question but the ILC disagreed on the interpretation of almost every point. What is more, proposals for amendments were made for the rule that had a static and a dynamic section. After the proposals tried to delete either the static or the dynamic limb, the whole provision was taken out. Draft Art. 69 stipulated that interpretation shall be in line with 'the rules of general international law in force at the time of the conclusion'. States quarrelled in the Sixth Committee over this provision and finally decided to delete it. The ILC could not agree how to solve this problem. It is interesting and significant that the Institut de Droit International took the question up again after the Vienna Convention was concluded. Yet, after the deliberations, the

Institut arrived at exactly the same result as the ILC had reached some years before: Intertemporal questions should be determined in the ordinary process of treaty interpretation.

Even if one were to go further back, there have always been opposing voices: In the nineteenth century when the intentions of the parties were emphasised, some resorted to the intentions of the parties at the time of the conclusion of the treaty while others accentuated the intentions as they presently stood. It is significant that even the first authors of international law had competing views: Hugo Grotius favoured looking at the current meaning of the terms while Emer de Vattel first looked to the intentions of the parties as they stood at the time of the conclusion of the treaty. Both discussed a treaty between Rome and Carthage which included the term 'allies' but failed to stipulate whether this applied to the allies at the time of the conclusion of the treaty or the alliances *au courant* with later interpretations. Grotius came to a static conclusion despite his evolutive preference while Vattel favoured a dynamic result despite his static preference. There was no agreement at the outset and no agreement has been reached ever since.

Even in the absence of an agreed solution, one of them might be right or at least preferable over the others. To determine which solution to pick, we need to depart from the agreed method of interpretation as enshrined in Arts. 31 and 32 VCLT. As this method does not address the intertemporal question expressly and directly, it could still cover the problem. The complex problem some scholars have described can be seen as follows: How do we interpret the rules of interpretation? There is an eminent danger of engaging in a circular exercise: If we interpret the rules of interpretation according to the same or other rules of interpretation, those rules on the higher level might need interpretation themselves. In the process of interpreting those rules with rules of an even higher order, another interpretative issue might arise. This will then lead to an endless exercise in which one problem leads to the next. To avoid this circle, one could determine the questions without any argument. But these interpretations would be arbitrary and produce a polyphony of different approaches. The question how to interpret the rules of interpretation should not be taken as mere logical or theoretical exercises; the solution of this question is in fact decisive for any statement one makes about the VCLT.

How can this problem be solved in a serious and workable manner? This book argues that this is to be done through a functional reconstruction. In contrast to ordinary interpretation, we have not explained the terms in the treaty but rediscovered the whole rule of interpretation from a certain perspective to reformulate it and to separate the things we can assert from the open points concerning its interpretation. A reconstruction is a reformulation of its object to bring out some of its defining features. The reconstruction is aimed at discovering how the Convention worked, what its function was and which points remained open. The features we can ascertain are called 'cardinal cores', the questions to be left open 'interpretative knots'. This approach concluded Part I and at the same time provided the structure for Part II.

11.2. Part II: the rule of interpretation

In practice, a functional reconstruction means to conduct some fundamental research about the Convention. It means to identify the defining as well as the open features and to try to conclude on the basis of cardinal cores and interpretative knots what functions the Convention fulfils. Looking for the defining features, it is important to have an understanding of the problems to be addressed. These can be identified by engaging in the history of interpretative method. The historical perspective allows us to see in which ways the current methodology differs from its antecedents. Interpretative method has evolved quite substantially. In its 'mechanical phase', starting with Hugo Grotius, scholars designed all-encompassing systems that tried to guide the interpreter in every possible situation to arrive at the assumed intentions of the parties. A wide array of means of interpretation was used but literal interpretation often played a decisive role. In the flexible phase, scholars took the rigidity away from the rules and set out with the goal of ascertaining the intentions of the parties. Interpreters were supposed to be flexible in how to discern the intentions of the parties, yet some means such as the preparatory works or subsequent conduct of the parties gained special importance. In the codificatory phase, codes of interpretation were drafted, but there was disagreement as to the goal of interpretation. A very important step within the codificatory phase was achieved by the Harvard Draft Convention which employed a 'factor approach' framing the means of interpretation as generalised arguments such as 'the subsequent conduct of the parties'. The Harvard Draft openly acknowledged that it was not to work as a hermeneutical guide but only as an *ex post facto* justification. The Vienna Convention has been drafted in a very similar way. Reviewing the history of international interpretative methodology from Grotius to the VCLT, we have identified certain defining features of interpretative methods differing over time. The features concern the nature of the interpretative method (for example legal or doctrinal; if legal: Treaty, custom or general principles), the type of means used (such as presumptions, techniques, maxims), the operation of the process of interpretation (balancing or application of rules) and the goal of interpretation (intention of the parties, the meaning or the object and purpose).

Taking these questions seriously, we can first determine the cardinal cores of the Convention. The rule of interpretation is enshrined in an international treaty, a hard and fast legal rule. Yet, this rule prescribes the use of techniques; these are standard arguments describing a class of considerations that is allowed to enter the process: The ordinary meaning of the text, the context, the object and purpose, subsequent agreements and subsequent practice and the relevant rules are the six techniques mentioned in Art. 31 VCLT. If a consideration matches the requirements of those techniques, it is allowed to enter the process. All the considerations standing the test are then weighted and balanced against each other. There might be a slight preference for the ordinary meaning, but generally the techniques enshrined in Art. 31 VCLT have the same force which means that the interpreter has some leeway and discretion in how to treat them. Other means of interpretation not mentioned in Art. 31 VCLT are not generally excluded, but they carry significantly less argumentative weight since the interpreter will first need to argue that he or she cannot reach a conclusion on the basis of the techniques of Art. 31 VCLT. The VCLT is relatively open to include considerations going beyond the text of the treaty such as subsequent practice. Yet, the strict notion of the context being limited to the surrounding text is emblematic that the VCLT is not open for any kind of consideration on the level of Art. 31.

Many very important points can be derived from this. The first is that the cardinal cores of the VCLT point to the general intertemporal openness of the Convention. Some techniques stem by definition from different points in time. The preparatory works mentioned in Art. 32 VCLT precede the time of the conclusion of the treaty; the context comprises agreements in connection with the conclusion of the treaty as provided for by Art. 31(2)(a) VCLT which are temporally closely related to the conclusion of the treaty. The techniques mentioned in Art. 31(3)(a) and (b) are necessarily subsequent to the conclusion of the treaty. If the interpreter has discretion to take into account results from different points in time, it is easy to see that the results can change when new developments occur matching the requirement of the techniques. However, this does not only relate to subsequent agreements and practice. Other techniques can include considerations from different points in time. The ordinary meaning is not fixed, it can be the meaning at the time of the conclusion of the treaty or at later points in time. The same applies to the relevant rules which can themselves be subject to evolutive interpretation. This feature of the process gives evidence that the Convention is intertemporally open.

From the way in which the VCLT works, we can derive its function. The features of its operation will also tell us in which circumstances the rule of interpretation can work best. In sum, the rule of interpretation in the VCLT works as an obligation to decide based on legal arguments relating to the interpretative issue in the treaty. Other than the previous interpretative methods especially in the mechanical phase, the rule of interpretation in the VCLT functions less as a hermeneutical guide for the interpreter to arrive at goals such as the intentions of the parties to the treaty. It is rather a structure for international legal argument. It classifies arguments and attaches a certain value to them and helps the interpreter to organise his or her reasoning. The discretion and the great reliance on arguments point to the increased importance of the Convention in intersubjective settings. The rule of interpretation in the VCLT is most effective when there is communication about interpretation and not when a single interpreter meditates to arrive at some preconceived notions in a text. The rule of interpretation in the VCLT does not directly impact upon the interpretative result, but if somebody has rendered a binding interpretation, the Convention requires a justification which will further the precedential value for future cases since it forces the interpreter to make his or her arguments visible. This works best when there is a mechanism like a court able to render binding decisions. The VCLT enhances legal discourse in that it forces the interpreter to make his legal arguments known in such a way that other interpreters can assess them. It is very important to keep that function in mind when dealing with open questions of interpretation because the function of the rule of interpretation can be a guide in those instances.

Yet, there are also unclear features of the Convention which have been called interpretative knots. The most important knot concerns the question of what the goal of interpretation in the VCLT actually is. The rule mentions 'intentions', 'meaning' and 'purpose', but it is far from clear whether one of those could be considered as the ultimate goal in the same ways as the intentions of the parties were considered to be the goal of interpretation in the flexible phase. Yet, the different goals also bear upon the intertemporal question: Stressing the intentions of the parties is often associated with a static outlook, while the object and purpose is often constructed dynamically. This highlights the other face of the intertemporal openness of the Convention: Interpreters can make some choices such as to take the intentions of the parties or the meaning as a goal of interpretation. While interpreters have to make choices, there is no way to determine whether the choice was right or wrong. This applies basically to every interpretative knot. Take for example the question of how the object and purpose is to be ascertained (ascertainment knot): It could be derived solely from the *travaux préparatoires*, but also from current political, social and economic conditions. These are quite extreme examples of how opposing views are possible. If an interpreter is competent to render authoritative interpretations, his ways of reading the Convention will be acknowledged, but the authority only goes as far as the competence of the respective interpreter and entails no necessary general claim.

One of the questions which cannot easily be determined is whether, in unclear intertemporal cases, the subsidiary means in Art. 32 VCLT shall include any means of interpretation such as presumptions or notions of an intertemporal law or whether it ought to be restricted to techniques. At this point, it is necessary to discuss whether the many interesting suggestions made to resolve intertemporal issues could and should be included in the process of interpretation. Principles insofar as they are legal principles can be included as relevant rules. Yet, other means like the maxim *contemporanea expositio* could only be included through Art. 32 VCLT. At this point, the function of the rule of interpretation suggests that only those means of interpretation can be used that actually enhance the process of argumentation. Those means are techniques. So the function of the Convention suggests that the interpreter should use techniques instead of other means of interpretation.

This means in effect that the VCLT is generally open for static as well as for dynamic interpretation. Interpreters have to collect arguments stemming from every technique mentioned in Art. 31 VCLT and to balance them against each other. As some of the techniques can produce arguments that had been necessarily unknown when the treaty was drafted, interpretative changes are possible. But changes must be justified. In this sense, intertemporal problems can be handled with the ordinary means of interpretation. This is the first sense of the intertemporal openness of the Convention. While the VCLT generally works best when it is open, it does not forbid interpreters competent to render binding interpretations in their jurisdiction to take certain stances. The Convention is also open in this regard.

11.3. Part III: court practice

The third part engages in the analysis of the practice of the ICJ and the ECtHR and conducts an in-depth analysis. This analysis starts with an exercise of stocktaking, a collection of all intertemporal instances that have been dealt with by the court. In a second step, the general approach towards static and evolutive interpretation is described. In a third step, the justificatory patterns of the courts are explained, in particular with regard to the VCLT. In a fourth step, the results are summarised with three indicators, namely, power, pace and perception.

The story of static and evolutive interpretation at the ICJ is the story of peacemakers and disputants at the bench. There are many indications that, from the first days of the Court until today, opinions amongst judges have been sharply divided on this issue. Possibly, there were even different 'camps' at the Court, but in its judgments, the ICJ has been very pragmatic: In the beginning, the Court was openly asserting that it would only interpret the law as it stood at the time the treaty was made. In contrast, the Court would interpret norms evolutively without explicitly saying so. The Court did so for the first time in 1950. Even decisions that were well-known precedents for static interpretations such as the *Case Concerning the Rights of Nationals of the United States in Morocco* included not only static but also evolutive interpretations. The *South-West Africa* or *Namibia* question led to a rupture in the jurisprudence of the court. Within less than eight years, the court reversed its jurisprudence twice.

In 1962, the ICJ interpreted the jurisdictional clause in the mandate agreement evolutively without expressly mentioning it. In the second phase of the proceedings in 1966, the Court held that, while the parties had standing, they could not avail themselves of a subjective right and based its decision on an extremely static approach. Only four years later, the Court for the first time openly acknowledged that it was interpreting evolutively in the *Namibia opinion*. From this time on, the Court interpreted evolutively as well as statically in many cases. Yet, in the rather recent *Navigational and Related Rights Case*, the Court opened up even more towards evolutive interpretations: It held that such evolution must not be based on the intentions but the assumed intentions of the parties.

SUMMARY AND CONCLUSIONS 355

This effectively means that the interpreter must not prove but can also assume the intentions. What is more, the Court also reinforced that the meaning of the treaty could be changed through subsequent practice.

Regarding the argumentative patterns, the techniques mostly used by the Court are the ordinary meaning of the terms, the object and purpose and subsequent practice. Apart from the ordinary meaning and the context, the Court would, however, only use a technique to support its result. It is significant that the court once used the object and purpose in favour of a static result. Another interesting observation of the jurisprudence of the ICJ is that the nature, structure and classification of the treaties did not really play a role. It interpreted unilateral declarations as well as bilateral, multilateral and even universal treaties statically as well as dynamically. Border treaties were at times interpreted evolutively and at times statically. Generally, the Court was open and flexible and also adjusted its approach over time. This flexibility can also be seen in relation to power, pace and perception. The Court sometimes assumed the competence to change the law, but sometimes abstained from changing it. It was sometimes very perceptive in having regard to broader political and societal circumstances while it was rather legalistic in other cases. On occasion it speeded up the development but sometimes left the determination of the pace to the parties. While judges in their separate and dissenting opinions often furthered principled arguments, the overall approach of the Court was very flexible.

Despite the fact that the ICJ was over time opening up towards evolutive interpretation, the ECtHR already started out with a very evolutive approach in *Tyrer* when it held that the Convention was a 'living instrument which, as the Commission rightly stressed, must be interpreted in the light of present-day conditions'. Yet, the Court later looked for ways to limit its very open stance towards evolutive interpretation. Metaphorically, we could speak of an aging activist. Yet, the ECtHR has used its 'living instrument' doctrine not only in cases of reinterpretations proper but also when engaging in the exercise of balancing. This has happened for example when determining whether there were discriminations or whether certain measures were proportionate. In cases of rebalancing, the Court has not used the rule of interpretation since it has not been constrained to include any consideration in the general process of balancing. However, it has reframed some of the techniques of interpretation as consensus method. It is then looking into the internal and external legal practice of the member states, their internal law and their international obligations. In some rare instances, the Court has also started to apply the consensus method to questions of interpretation. Since Art. 31(3) VCLT contains the techniques of subsequent practice and the relevant rules, the consensus method has no advantage but entails the danger of blurring the limits set by Art. 31 VCLT.

Despite the fact that the ECtHR is often said to follow a purposive approach, the technique of the object and purpose is only in fifth place regarding the frequency of use in intertemporal instances. The context, subsequent practice, the relevant rules and the ordinary meaning are more frequently used. In many instances, it could be suspected that the Court did not argue with the object and purpose but employed other techniques in a way as to further the object and purpose. This applies particularly to the techniques that correspond to the Courts consensus method. This is why these instances might be called 'aconsensual consensualism'. Another interesting and significant question is whether there can be an evolution downwards, i.e. a change in interpretation lowering the human rights standard. While judges on the Court disagree, the Commission rendered a devolutive judgment in the *McVeigh* case. The only legal reason limiting such devolutions is the evolutive interpretation of norms having *jus cogens* status.

The numbers of evolutive interpretations at the ECtHR are increasing. There have been many attempts by the Court and by scholars to provide for ways to limit evolutive interpretation, fourteen of which have been identified. Those include the question of the competence of Sections and Single Judges to interpret evolutively, the doctrine of the Court that it must not create new rights as well as restrictions regarding procedural law or cultural, social or economic rights. The Court mostly justified evolutive interpretations with the conduct of the parties, be it subsequent agreements, subsequent practice or relevant rules, in particular treaties concluded by the parties. This generally means that it accepted the power of the states parties to halt or trigger changes in the meaning of the Convention. Only in rare cases has the ECtHR openly assumed the power to interpret evolutively without referring to practice and further obligations of the states. In these instances, the court has been accelerating the pace of change while generally following the pace the states set. The Court has also been very perceptive regarding developments outside the law. In the process of interpretation, the Court was more inclined to relate the evolutive interpretations to legal developments than the process of application.

11.4. Intertemporal openness as the solution and not the problem

Intertemporal instances form only a tiny fraction of all interpretative questions. Many other issues are resolved much more easily. Questions of stasis and evolution, in contrast, are mostly argued over very forcefully. The beauty of looking at questions of static and evolutive interpretations is that they represent some of the crucial and existential questions of legal interpretation so that these questions are to be brought to the fore: How far can an interpreter go? How far must she or he go? And how far is his or her conduct determined by interpretative method?

This study resulted in the conclusion that the VCLT is intertemporally open and that, within this openness, interpreters can take a stance insofar as their jurisdiction is concerned. This might prove to be unsatisfactory to lawyers and legal scholars if they prefer guidance over discretion. With this mindset, intertemporal openness is a problem to be solved by a new scholarly doctrine or a solution deduced from a theoretical insight. This inquiry has taken another stance: Intertemporal openness has not been conceived as the problem but as part of the solution.

We can see from the history of interpretative methodology that attitudes towards the intertemporal question change. They have sometimes been more static and sometimes more evolutive. What is more, they have not developed in a certain direction, and neither have they departed from an original agreement of how to resolve that question. It is very probable that, even if there was an agreed way to deal with those questions, this method would need to be changed at some point in time. This can be due to hard cases that call for a treatment such as the *Namibia opinion*, but also to the general prevailing attitude towards the possibility of reinterpretation of the law. The choice between static and evolutive results is situated within competing attitudes. Those relate to different understandings of the concept of law and the temporality in law, different general political mindsets (conservative/progressive) or different philosophical standpoints on language (intentionalist/pragmatist). It is very hard to find a solution that mitigates between these views once and for all. The VCLT has taken another road; it is not filling the gap in a determinative manner but bridging it. The ILC has proven to be the perfect mechanism to provide for an overall approach to the interpretation of treaties. The process as well as the composition of the Commission unites many interesting features. The law of treaties was the work of a special rapporteur, but also of the whole Commission, and states were involved through the Sixth Committee of the General Assembly. The Commission was composed of practitioners as well as legal scholars. Yet, the practitioners often shared an interest in legal scholarship while the scholars were regularly engaged with practical matters. It is also significant that the members come from all regions of the world. Involving very different actors secured the general acceptability of the Convention. The time in which the VCLT was discussed was the time of the harshest bloc confrontation between the East and the West while decolonised states were already on the rise. It is very probable that in such a setting only a neutral rule representing the lowest common denominator could accrue. But the fact that the rule of interpretation regulated the process rather than the substance of interpretation is not necessarily to be considered as a flaw but also as a strength: The rules can be applied in different situations and between different actors. If the general rule of interpretation was formulated in such an abstract manner, it is not surprising that there was no agreement as to a specific intertemporal law. The ILC negotiated the rules during the time in which the ICJ reversed its jurisprudence in that regard two times and had three different stances in three cases. Instead of providing for definite guidance in this area of transition, the VCLT opted for providing a way to make intertemporal questions negotiable instead of trying to determine them. This is the ultimate value of intertemporal openness: Instead of resolving the questions generally, interpretative method empowers interpreters to resolve the questions themselves. Its function is then to enhance international legal discourse.

It provides for techniques that structure and organise legal argument and allow different participants in international legal dialogue. The use of the Convention is mandatory, but it leaves some leeway to the interpreter. Very little substantive considerations are enshrined in the Convention; it is rather a guide for the interpreters to extrapolate their agreed reading of the treaty. The rule of interpretation in the VCLT impacts upon intertemporal questions as on other interpretative problems: It enhances international legal discourse.

Appendix 1

Schemes of interpretation

The general structure that was used to summarise the conception of different authors regarding treaty interpretation is set out in Boxes 2 to 8 below. Within each box, the first part sets out the general statements about interpretation, and the second part sets out the means of interpretation in their given order and hierarchy. This structure follows the structure in most treaties, although, in rare cases, adjustments in the correct order might have been made. If elements of the structure are not mentioned in the respective texts, they have been omitted. The general structure of the boxes follows the template set out in Box 1.

BOX 1 TEMPLATE FOR THE SCHEMES OF INTERPRETATION

A. **General statements**
  - Definition of interpretation
  - Authorities
  - Sources
  - Legal status and quality of the rules on interpretation
  - Actors of interpretation

B. **Means of interpretation**

BOX 2 MECHANICAL CONSTRUCTION PHASE: HUGO GROTIUS

A. **General statements**
  I. Definition of interpretation
    - Aim: Assumed intentions
    - Obligations are grounded in the intention of the party as understood by the other party
  II. Authorities: Mostly antique authors and antique state practice

BOX 2 *(cont.)*

B. **Means of interpretation**
   I. Words
      1. Literal Means
         a. In the absence of other implications words are to be understood in their ordinary sense
         b. Technical words are to be understood in their technical sense
      2. Conjectures
         a. Applicability
            i. In the case of ambiguity or contradiction of words
            ii. Possibility to override even a clear meaning in cases that the other means provide for an evident result
         b. Form
            i. Subject-matter
            ii. Effect of the agreed interpretation
            iii. Connection in origin or in place (proceeding from the same will but uttered in different places or on different occasions)
            iv. From the reason of the law
      3. Presumptions as to broad and narrow meaning
         a. Favourable promises
            i. Full meaning according to current usage, broadest possible meaning
            ii. Exceptions: Absurdity, injustice, obvious disadvantage
         b. Odious promises: Restrictive interpretation
         c. Mixed promises
         d. Median promises
   II. Means leading to a result beyond the meaning of words
      1. Broadening the meaning: Reason for broadening the meaning was the sole effective cause (purpose) of the promissor
      2. Restricting the meaning
         a. Defect of original intent stemming from
            i. Absurdity
            ii. Cessation of the reason being the only motive of the intent
            iii. Defect of the subject-matter
         b. Incompatibility with the original intent based on the following implications
            i. Cases of conflict with divine or natural law
            ii. Too burdensome for one party
            iii. Conflicting meaning with words in other parts of the treaty

BOX 3 MECHANICAL CONSTRUCTION PHASE: THOMAS RUTHERFORTH

A. **General statements**
   I. Definition of interpretation: Finding out the meaning of a treaty by collection of the intention of the parties
   II. Authorities: Authors
   III. Legal status and quality of the rules on interpretation: positive law (written laws or custom)

B. **Means of interpretation**
   I. Literal interpretation: Collecting the intentions from the words only
      1. Follow words and construction in agreeable common use (not etymology or grammatical refinements)
      2. Presumption to follow the literal and grammatical sense
   II. Mixed interpretation: Collecting the intentions from words and inferences
      1. From the subject-matter
      2. As to a reasonable effect produced by the interpretation
      3. Circumstances: Stipulations connected in origin, place or time
   III. Rational interpretation: Collecting the intentions from inferences going beyond the meaning of the words
      1. Extensive interpretation: Based on the purpose
      2. Restrictive interpretation
         a. Original defect in the intention of the authors
            i. Effect: Contrary to general reason or the reason of the law
            ii. Subject-matter
            iii. Circumstances: Stipulations connected in origin, place or time
         b. Accidental defect in the intention of the authors: Derived from equity particularly when the meaning is in conflict with natural law

BOX 4 EQUITABLE CONSTRUCTION PHASE: LASSA OPPENHEIM

A. **General statements**
   I. Legal status and quality of the rules on interpretation
      1. Neither customary nor treaty law exists
      2. Preference for agreed interpretations of the states parties to a treaty either informally or through a subsequent treaty
      3. In case of disagreement between states: Scientific grounds reflecting common sense as mirrored in jurisprudence (legal theory) and applied by arbitral tribunals
      4. Possibility also to include the rules commonly applied by national courts with regard to the interpretation of laws

BOX 4 (*cont.*)

  II. Actors of Interpretation
   1. States parties to the treaty the agreed interpretation of which enjoys preference
   2. Arbitration Tribunals, which is the best mechanism in cases of disagreement
  III. Authorities: State Practice
B. **Means of interpretation: Those which 'recommend themselves on account of their suitability'**[a]
  I. Literal interpretation
   1. Preference of the reasonable over the literal sense
   2. Literal meaning on the basis of common language ('of everyday life') unless
     a. Expressly used technical meaning,
     b. other meaning derived from the context of the treaty
     c. Or one state is known to uphold a meaning 'different from the generally prevailing meaning'[b]
  II. Presumptions in cases of ambiguity
   1. For reasonable interpretation favouring the meaning in accordance with
     a. The purpose of the treaty
     b. The consistent construction of the provisions of the treaty
     c. The generally recognised principles of international law
     d. Previous treaty obligations towards third states
   2. For an interpretation favouring sovereignty (*in dubio pro mitius*): Less onerous for the obliged party, fewer interferences with the parties' territorial and personal supremacy, less restrictions upon the parties
   3. For a meaning less favourable – at the time of the negotiations – to the party proposing the stipulations
  III. Previous treaties between the parties or one of the parties and a third party alluding to the meaning[c]
  IV. Intention of the parties, derived from the *travaux préparatoires*, takes precedence over clear literal meaning; while this is clear in a case of a declaration by all the parties, it depends on the circumstances in a case where not all the parties issued the declaration.
  V. In cases of ambiguity, the meaning is to be preferred that one state made before a dispute arose unless protested by the other contracting parties.
  VI. Interpretation that does not render the stipulation meaningless is to be preferred.

BOX 4 (cont.)

VII. General obligation to interpret as to 'exclude fraud and make the operation consistent with good faith'[d]
VIII. If there is more than one authoritative language, each party is bound by the version in its language.

Notes

[a] Oppenheim, *International Law* (vol. 1) 583.
[b] *ibid.*, 585.
[c] Compare B.II.3.
[d] Oppenheim, *International Law* (vol. 1) 586.

BOX 5 CODIFICATORY PHASE: LUDWIK EHRLICH

A. **General statements**
   I. The actors of interpretation: Scientists (doctrinal interpretation), organs of the contracting parties (official interpretation), which may be authentic, quasi-authentic or particular, depending on whether all parties agree, either organs of one contracting party (unilateral interpretation) or of all parties (international interpretation), of organs of international organisations (international interpretation) which may be judicial or executive, diplomats (diplomatic interpretation as better expression for authentic interpretation) which can be either bilateral or multilateral, depending on the treaty in question.
   II. The goals of interpretation
      1. Different suggestions: Intention of the authors, meaning of the text apart from the context, consequences of certain interpretation, to establish a rule for circumstances not known to the authors of the treaty
      2. Quest to find out what the will of the parties was
   III. The methods of interpretation: Grammatical interpretation, etymological interpretation, historical interpretation (looking at historical circumstances), practical interpretation (looking at the practice of the parties), logical interpretation
   IV. Sources: Authors, state practice, judgments and awards of courts and tribunals
B. **Means of interpretation**
   1. Research into the will of the parties in the text
      a. The text
         i. Presumption that the text is the expression of the will of the parties
         ii. If there was an exchange of notes, every party is bound by the terms it used

BOX 5 (*cont.*)

    iii. If there is more than one text and there are differences in the text, presumption in favour of good faith
    iv. If there is more than one text, and if more than one text can be reconciled with good faith, then there is a presumption in favour of an interpretation that can be reconciled with all texts
    v. Presumption in favour of an interpretation in accordance with the text of the whole treaty and not just parts of it in light of, first, what the treaty is intended to accomplish; second, how the phrase in question relates to the whole treaty; and, third, how the words used in the phrase in question relate to the same expressions in other parts of the treaty
    vi. Presumption in favour of arguments derived from the preamble to the treaty
  b. The words
    i. Presumption in favour of a natural and ordinary meaning (not etymological)
    ii. Presumption in favour of the meaning afforded by the context; that presumption trumps the presumption in favour of natural meaning
    iii. Presumption in favour of the meaning at the time of the conclusion of the treaty
    iv. Presumption that every word used should mean something
  c. Grammatical interpretation
    i. Presumption that language has been used grammatically correctly and that sense could be derived from grammatical analysis
    ii. Grammatical errors should be corrected via interpretation
  d. Logical interpretation
    i. Presumption that all parts of the treaty complement each other
    ii. Presumption against contradictions or contradictory meaning
2. Research into the will of the parties outside the text
  a. *Travaux préparatoires*
    i. Generally admissible
    ii. Presumption against their use if the text is clear
  b. Subsequent practice of the parties
  c. Historical Circumstances
3. General presumptions
  a. Presumption in favour of sovereignty
  b. No presumptions in favour of the individual
  c. Presumption in favour of international solidarity / international society
  d. Presumption against the interpretation that would violate previously established rights of third states

> BOX 6 CODIFICATORY PHASE: HARVARD DRAFT
>
> **Article 19 Interpretation of Treaties**
> (a) A treaty is to be interpreted in the light of the general purpose which it is intended to serve. The historical background of the treaty, *travaux préparatoires*, the circumstances of the parties at the time the treaty was entered into, the change in these circumstances sought to be effected, the subsequent conduct of the parties in applying the provisions of the treaty, and the conditions prevailing at the time interpretation is being made, are to be considered in connection with the general purpose which the treaty is intended to serve.

> BOX 7 CODIFICATORY PHASE: INSTITUT DE DROIT INTERNATIONAL
>
> Estime que lorsqu'il y a lieu d'interpréter un traité, les Etats, les organisations et les juridictions internationales pourraient s'inspirer des principes suivants
>
> **Article premier**
> 1. L'accord des parties s'étant réalisé sur le texte du traité, il y a lieu de prendre le sens naturel et ordinaire des termes de ce texte comme base d'interprétation. Les termes des dispositions du traité doivent être interprétés dans le contexte entier, selon la bonne foi et à la lumière des principes du droit international.
> 2. Toutefois, s'il est établi que les termes employés doivent se comprendre dans un autre sens, le sens naturel et ordinaire de ces termes est écarté.
>
> **Article 2**
> 1. Dans le cas d'un différend porté devant une juridiction internationale il incombera au tribunal, en tenant compte des dispositions de l'article premier, d'apprécier si, et dans quelle mesure, il y a lieu d'utiliser d'autres moyens d'interprétation.
> 2. Parmi ces moyens légitimes d'interpréter se trouvent:
>   a) Le recours aux *travaux préparatoires*;
>   b) La pratique suivie dans l'application effective du traité;
>   c) La prise en considération des buts du traité.

> BOX 8 CODIFICATORY PHASE: RESTATEMENT SECOND OF THE AMERICAN LAW INSTITUTE
>
> **§ 146 Basic Function of Interpretation**
> The extent to which an international agreement creates, changes or defines relationships under international law is determined in case of doubt by the

BOX 8 (*cont.*)

interpretation of the agreement. The primary object of interpretation is to ascertain the meaning intended by the parties for the terms in which the agreement is expressed, having regard to the context in which they occur and the circumstances under which the agreement was made. This meaning is determined in the light of all relevant factors.

§ 147 Criteria for Interpretation

(1) International law requires that the interpretative process ascertain and give effect to the purpose of the international agreement which, as appears from the terms used by the parties, it was intended to serve. The factors to be taken into account by way of guidance in the interpretative process include:
  (a) the ordinary meaning of the words of the agreement in the context in which they are used;
  (b) the title given the agreement and statements of purpose and scope included in its text;
  (c) the circumstances attending the negotiation of the agreement;
  (d) drafts and other documents submitted for the consideration, action taken on them, and the official record of the deliberations during the course of the negotiation;
  (e) unilateral statements of understanding made by a signatory before the agreement came into effect, to the extent that they were communicated to, or otherwise known to, the other signatory or signatories;
  (f) the subsequent practice of the parties in the performance of the agreement, or the subsequent practice of one party, if the other party or parties knew or had reason to know of it;
  (g) change of circumstances, to the extent indicated in § 153;
  (h) the compatibility of alternative interpretations of the agreement with (i) the obligations of the parties to other states under general international law and other international agreements of the parties, and (ii) the principles of law common to the legal systems of the parties or of all states having reasonably developed legal systems;
  (i) comparison of the texts in the different languages in which the agreement was concluded, taking into account any provision in the agreement as to the authoritativeness of the different texts.
(2) The ordinary meaning of the words of an agreement, as indicated in Subsection (1)(a), must always be considered as a factor in the interpretation of the agreement. There is no established priority as between the factors indicated in Subsection (1)(b)–(i) or as between them and additional factors not listed therein.

Appendix 2

Sample reservation clauses

BOX 1 EXAMPLE 1

The Kingdom of X reserves its right as to the interpretation of this treaty / Article X / the term 'peace and security' in Article X. It considers its meaning to be the meaning as it stood at the time of the signature / conclusion / ratification / formal confirmation / acceptance / approval / accession of / to the treaty. This meaning is not subject to evolution or change through interpretation but can only be changed through the procedures of modification, amendment and termination as set out in the treaty and in general international law, in particular in the Vienna Convention on the Law of Treaties.

BOX 2 EXAMPLE 2

The Republic of Y reserves the right to regard the treaty / Article X / term 'peace and security' in Article X as evolutionary and, therefore, its interpretation abreast of the development of the law and present-day circumstances. A change of the meaning through interpretation can be affected in accordance with the rules of interpretation, in particular as they are codified in Articles 31–33 of the Vienna Convention on the Law of Treaties.

Appendix 3

Sample conditional interpretative declaration clauses

BOX 1 EXAMPLE 1

The Kingdom of X is of the conviction that the treaty / Article X / the term 'peace and security' in Article X is to be interpreted as it stood at the time of signature / conclusion / ratification / formal confirmation / acceptance / approval / accession of / to the treaty. If it emerges that the treaty is to be interpreted differently, the High Contracting Party reserves its right that in its relations with the other party the interpretation of the treaty is to be modified to carry the meaning as indicated above.

BOX 2 EXAMPLE 2

The Republic of Y is of the conviction that the treaty / Article X / the term 'peace and security' in Article X is to be interpreted abreast of the development of the law and present-day circumstances. A change of the meaning through interpretation can be affected in accordance with the rules of interpretation, in particular as they are codified in Articles 31–33 of the Vienna Convention on the Law of Treaties. If it emerges that a static interpretation is to be employed, the high contracting party reserves its right to apply in its relations only an interpretation as indicated above.

BIBLIOGRAPHY

Ackerman, B. A., *We the People: Foundations* (Belknap Press of Harvard University Press, 1991)
Adler, H. M., 'The Interpretation of Treaties' (1900) 26 *Law Magazine or: Quarterly Review of Jurisprudence* 62–91 and 164–71
Alexy, R., *A Theory of Legal Argumentation: The Theory of Rational Discourse as Theory of Legal Justification* (R. Adler and N. MacCormick trans., Clarendon Press, 1989)
Alford, R. P., 'The Proliferation of International Courts and Tribunals: International Adjudication in Ascendance' (2000) 94 *ASIL Proceedings* 160
Allott, P., 'The Concept of International Law' (1999) 10 *European Journal of International Law* 31
Alland, D., 'L'Interprétation de droit international public' (2014) 326 *RdC* 41
Alter, K. J., *The New Terrain of International Law* (Princeton University Press, 2014)
Alvarez, A., *Le Droit international nouveau dans ses rapport avec la vie actuelle des peuples* (Pedone, 1959)
Aly, S., *L'Interprétation évolutive en droit international public* (on file at the library of the Institut des Hautes Etudes Internationales, Geneva, Ref. HEIDS 576, 1997)
American Institute of International Law, 'Project No. 21: Treaties' (1926) 20 *AJIL* Supplement 348
Amr, M. S. M., *The Role of the International Court of Justice as the Principal Judicial Organ of the United Nations* (Kluwer, 2003)
Andenas, M., and Bjorge, E., 'National Implementation of ECHR Rights' in Føllesdal, A., Peters, B., and Ulfstein, G. (eds.), *Constituting Europe: The European Court of Human Rights in a National, European and Global Context* (Cambridge University Press, 2013)
Andenas, M., and Fairgrieve, D., 'Intent on Making Mischief: Seven Ways of Using Comparative Law' in Montaneri, P. G. (ed.), *Methods of Comparative Law* (Edward Elgar Publishing, 2013)
Appert, G., 'De l'interprétation des traités diplomatiques au cours d'un procès' [1989] *Journal du Droit International Privé* 433

Aragoneses, A., *Recht im Fin de siècle: Briefe von Raymond Saleilles an Eugen Huber (1895–1911)* (Klostermann, 2007)

Arai-Takahashi, Y., *The Margin of Appreciation Doctrine and the Principle of Proportionality in the Jurisprudence of the ECHR* (Intersentia, 2002)

Arato, J., 'Subsequent Practice and Evolutive Interpretation: Techniques of Treaty Interpretation over Time and Their Diverse Consequences' (2010) 9 *The Law and Practice of International Courts and Tribunals* 443

Arnauld, A., 'Möglichkeiten und Grenzen dynamischer Interpretation von Rechtsnormen' (2001) 32 *Rechtstheorie* 465

Völkerrecht (2nd edn, C. F. Müller, 2014)

Arnauld, A., and Nicole, P., *Logic Or the Art of Thinking* (J. V. Buroker trans., Cambridge University Press, 1996)

Aust, A., *Modern Treaty Law and Practice* (Cambridge University Press, 2007)

Aust, H., 'Alejandro Álvarez' in Fassbender, B., and Aust, H. (eds.), *Basistexte: Völkerrechtsdenken* (Nomos, 2012)

Aust, H., Rodiles, A., and Staubach, P., 'Unity or Uniformity?: Domestic Courts and Treaty Interpretation' (2014) 27 *Leiden Journal of International Law* 75

Austin, J. L., *How to Do Things with Words: [The William James Lectures Delivered at Harvard University in 1955]* (Harvard University Press, 1978)

'Performative Utterances' in Austin, J. L., *Philosophical Papers* (3rd edn, Oxford University Press, 1979)

Azevedo Alexandrino Fernandes, J. M., *Die Theorie der Interpretation des Gesetzes bei Francisco Suárez* (Peter Lang, 2005)

Badura, P., 'Verfassungsänderung, Verfassungswandel, Verfassungsgewohnheitsrecht' in Isensee, J., and Kirchhof, P. (eds.), *Handbuch des Staatsrechts der Bundesrepublik Deutschland* (Vol. 7, C. F. Müller, 1992)

Bank, R., 'Verbot von Folter' in Dörr, O., Grote, R., and Marauhn, T. (eds.), *EMRK / GG: Konkordanzkommentar zum europäischen und deutschen Grundrechtsschutz* (vol. 1, 2nd edn, Mohr Siebeck, 2013)

Bankowski, Z., and others, 'On Method and Methodology' in MacCormick, N., and Summers, R. S. (eds.), *Interpreting Statutes: A Comparative Study* (Ashgate, Dartmouth, 1991)

Barthes, R., 'Death of the Author' 5–6 (1967), www.ubu.com/aspen/aspen5and6/threeEssays.html#barthes

Bates, E., *The Evolution of the European Convention on Human Rights: From Its Inception to the Creation of a Permanent Court of Human Rights* (Oxford University Press, 2010)

Beckett, E., 'Comments' (1950) 43 I *Annuaire de l'Institut de Droit International* 435

Bederman, D. J., *Classical Canons: Rhetoric, Classicism and Treaty Interpretation* (Ashgate, 2001)

'Revivalist Canons and Treaty Interpretation' (1994) 41 *UCLA Law Review* 953

Benavides Casals, M. A., *Die Auslegungsmethoden bei Menschenrechtsverträgen: Die Rechtsprechung des Europäischen Gerichtshofs für Menschenrechte und des Interamerikanischen Gerichtshofs für Menschenrechte* (Nomos, 2010)

Bentham, J., *Papers Relative to Codification and Public Instruction: Including Correspondence with the Russian Emperor and Divers Constituted Authorities in the American United States* (J. McCreery, 1817)

'The Principles of International Law' in Bowring, J. (ed.), *Works of Jeremy Bentham* (Vol. 1, Part 2, W. Tait, 1838)

Bernhardt, R., 'Anmerkungen zur Rechtsfortbildung und Rechtsschöpfung durch internationale Gerichte' in Ginther, K., and others (eds.), *Völkerrecht zwischen normativem Anspruch und politischer Realität: Festschrift für Karl Zemanek zum 65. Geburtstag* (Duncker & Humblot, 1994)

'Der Übergang vom "alten" zum "neuen" Europäischen Gerichtshof für Menschenrechte' in Bröhmer, J., and others (eds.), *Internationale Gemeinschaft und Menschenrechte: Festschrift für Georg Ress zum 70. Geburtstag am 21. Januar 2005* (Carl Heymanns Verlag, 2005)

Die Auslegung völkerrechtlicher Verträge insbesondere in der neueren Rechtsprechung internationaler Gerichte (Carl Heymanns Verlag, 1963)

'Evolutive Treaty Interpretation, Especially of the European Convention on Human Rights' (1999) 42 *German Yearbook of International Law* 11

'Homogenität, Kontinuität und Dissonanzen in der Rechtsprechung des Internationalen Gerichtshofs: Eine Fall-Studie zum Südwestafrika / Namibia-Komplex' (1973) 33 *Zeitschrift für ausländisches öffentliches Recht und Völkerrech* 1

'Rechtsfortbildung durch den Europäischen Gerichtshof für Menschenrechte' in Ginther, K., and others (eds.), *Völkerrecht zwischen normativem Anspruch und politischer Realität: Festschrift für Karl Zemanek zum 65. Geburtstag* (Duncker & Humblot, 1994)

'Völkerrechtliche und verfassungsrechtliche Aspekte konkludenter Vertragsänderungen' in Arndt, H.-W., and others (eds.), *Völkerrecht und deutsches Recht: Festschrift für Walter Rudolf zum 70. Geburtstag* (C. H. Beck, 2001)

Besson, S., 'Getting over the Amour Impossible between International Law and Adjudication' in Romano, C., Alter, K. J., and Shany, Y. (eds.), *The Oxford Handbook of International Adjudication* (Oxford University Press, 2014)

Bianchi, A., 'Law, Time, and Change: The Self-Regulatory Function of Subsequent Practice' in Nolte, G. (ed.), *Treaties and Subsequent Practice* (Oxford University Press, 2013)

'Textual Interpretation and (International) Law Reading: The Myth of (In)Determinacy and the Genealogy of Meaning' in Bekker, P. H. F., and others (eds.), *Making Transnational Law Work in the Global Economy: Essays in Honour of Detlev Vagts* (Cambridge University Press, 2010)

Binder, C., *Die Grenzen der Vertragstreue im Völkerrecht* (Springer, 2013)

Binder, C., and Zemanek, K., 'Das Völkervertragsrecht' in Rheinisch, A. (ed.), *Österreichisches Handbuch des Völkerrechts* (Vol. 1, 5th edn, Manz, 2013)

Bjorge, E., 'Evolutionary Interpretation and the Intention of the Parties' (2012) http://ssrn.com/abstract=2159657 (accessed 8 December 2012)

The Evolutionary Interpretation of Treaties (Oxford University Press, 2014)

Bleckmann, A., 'Analogie im Völkerrecht' (1977 / 8) 17 *Archiv des Völkerrechts* 161

'Die Rechtsanalogie im Völkerrecht' (1993) 31 *Archiv des Völkerrechts* 353

Grundprobleme und Methoden des Völkerrechts (Verlag Karl Alber, 1983)

'Zur Feststellung und Auslegung von Völkergewohnheitsrecht' (1977) 37 *Zeitschrift für ausländisches öffentliches Recht und Völkerrech* 504

Blokker, N., 'International Organizations or Institutions, Implied Powers' in Wolfrum, R. (ed.), *The Max Planck Encyclopedia of Public International Law* (Oxford University Press, 2012)

Bluntschli, J. C., *Das moderne Völkerrecht der civilisirten Staten: als Rechtsbuch dargestellt* (C. H. Beck, 1868)

Böckenförde, E.-W., 'Anmerkungen zum Begriff Verfassungswandel' in Badura, P., and Scholz, R. (eds.), *Wege und Verfahren des Verfassungslebens: Festschrift für Peter Lerche zum 65. Geburtstag* (C. H. Beck, 1993)

Bogdandy, A. von, and Venzke, I., 'Beyond Dispute: International Judicial Institutions as Lawmakers' (2011) 12 *German Law Journal* 983

In Whose Name? A Public Law Theory of International Adjudication (Oxford University Press, 2014)

'In Whose Name? An Investigation of International Courts' Public Authority and Its Democratic Justification' (2012) 23 *EJIL* 7

'On the Democratic Legitimation of International Judicial Lawmaking' (2011) 12 *German Law Journal* 1341

'On the Functions of International Courts: An Appraisal in Light of Their Burgeoning Public Authority' (2013) 26 *Leiden Journal of International Law* 49

Boisson de Chazournes, L., 'Subsequent Practice, Practices and "Family Resemblance": Towards Embedding Subsequent Practice in Its Operative Milieu' in Nolte, G. (ed.), *Treaties and Subsequent Practice* (Oxford University Press, 2013)

Boisson de Chazournes, L., La Rosa, A., and Mbengue, M. M., 'Art. 18 VCLT' in Corten, O., and Klein, P. (eds.), *The Vienna Conventions on the Law of Treaties: A Commentary* (Oxford University Press, 2011)

Bonfils, H., *Manuel de droit international public* (Arthur Rousseau, 1894)

Bork, R., 'Neutral Principles and Some First Amendment Problems' (1971) 47 *Indiana Law Journal* 1

The Tempting of America (Simon & Schuster, 1997)

Borscheid, P., *Das Tempo Virus* (Campus, 2004)

Bos, M., *A Methodology of International Law* (North-Holland, 1984)

Böth, K., *Evolutive Auslegung völkerrechtlicher Verträge: Eine Untersuchung zu Voraussetzungen und Grenzen in Anbetracht der Praxis internationaler Streitbeilegungsinstitutionen* (Peter Lang, 2013)

Boyle, A. E., 'Further Development of the Law of the Sea Convention: Mechanisms for Change' (2005) 54 *International and Comparative Law Quarterly* 563

Bratza, N., 'Living Instrument or Dead Letter – The Future of the European Convention on Human Rights', [2014] *European Human Rights Law Review* 116

Brems, E., *Human Rights: Universality and Diversity* (Martinus Nijhoff Publishers, 2001)

Brest, P., 'The Misconceived Quest for the Original Understanding' (1980) 60 *Boston University Law Review* 204

Brierly, J., 'The Future of Codification' (1931) 12 *BYIL* 1

Briggs, H. W., 'The Travaux Préparatoires of the Vienna Convention on the Law of Treaties' (1971) 65 *AJIL* 705

Brölmann, C., 'Law-Making Treaties: Form and Function in International Law' (2005) 74 *Nordic Journal of International Law* 383

'Specialized Rules of Treaty Interpretation: International Organizations' in Hollis, D. B. (ed.), *The Oxford Guide to Treaties* (Oxford University Press, 2012)

Broom, H., *A Selection of Legal Maxims, Classified and Illustrated* (Lawbook Exchange, 2000 [1845])

Brown, C., *A Common Law of International Adjudication* (Oxford University Press, 2007)

Brownlie, I., *Principles of Public International Law* (Oxford University Press, 2008)

Buchanan, A., *Justice, Legitimacy and Self-Determination: Moral Foundations for International Law* (Oxford University Press, 2007)

Buergenthal, T., 'Proliferation of International Courts and Tribunals: Is It Good or Bad?' (2001) 14 *Leiden Journal of International Law* 267

Buffard, I., and Hafner, G. (eds.), *International Law Between Universalism and Fragmentation: Festschrift in Honour of Gerhard Hafner* (Martinus Nijhoff Publishers, 2008)

Buffard, I., and Zemanek, K., 'The "Object and Purpose" of a Treaty: An Enigma?' (1998) 3 *Austrian Review of International and European Law* 311

Burling, R., *Patterns of Language: Structure, Variation, Change* (Academic Press, 1992)

Burri, T., 'Do Lawyers Knead the Dough? – How Law, Chaos, and Uncertainty Interact' (2010) 4 *European Journal of Risk Regulation* 371

'Workers and Case Law as Vehicles for the European Hegemon' (2010) 3–4 *Studia Diplomatica* 119

Burri, T., and Pirker, B., 'Stromschnellen im Freizügigkeitsfluss: von der Bedeutung von Urteilen des Europäischen Gerichtshofes im Rahmen des Personenfreizügigkeitsabkommens' (2010) 20 *Schweizerische Zeitschrift für internationales und europäisches Recht* 165

Byrde, B.-O., *Verfassungsentwicklung: Stabilität und Dynamik im Verfassungsrecht der Bundesrepublik Deutschland* (Nomos, 1982)

Calabresi, S. G., and Scalia, A., *Originalism: A Quarter-Century of Debate* (Regnery Publishing, 2007)

Calhoun, C. J., *Dictionary of the Social Sciences* (Oxford University Press, 2002)

Çali, B., 'Specialized Rules of Treaty Interpretation: Human Rights' in Hollis, D. B. (ed.), *The Oxford Guide to Treaties* (Oxford University Press, 2012)

Campbell, L., *Historical Linguistics: An Introduction* (2nd edn, Edinburgh University Press, 2004)

Cannizzaro, E., 'The Role of Proportionality in the Law of International Countermeasures' (2001) 12 *EJIL* 889

Caplan, D. N., and Gould, J. L., 'Language' in Squire, L., and others (eds.), *Fundamental Neuroscience* (Elsevier, 2013)

Carnap, R., *Meaning and Necessity: A Study in Semantics and Modal Logics* (University of Chicago Press, 1947)

Cartier-Bresson, H., 'The Decisive Moment 1952' in Goldberg, V. (ed.), *Photography in Print: Writings from 1816 to the Present* (University of New Mexico Press, 1998)

Carvalho, E. M. de, *Semiotics of International Law: Trade and Translation* (Springer, 2011)

Cassese, A., *International Law* (Oxford University Press, 2005)

Chambers, J. K., Trudgill, P., and Schilling-Estes, N. (eds.), *The Handbook of Language Variation and Change* (Wiley-Blackwell, 2002)

Chanaki, A., *L'Adaptation des traités dans le temps* (Bruylant, 2013)

Chandler, D., *Semiotics: The Basics* (Taylor and Francis, 2007)

Christakis, T., 'Art. 56 VCLT' in Corten, O., and Klein, P. (eds.), *The Vienna Conventions on the Law of Treaties: A Commentary* (Oxford University Press, 2011)

Cohen, H. G., 'International Law's Erie Moment' (2013) 34 *Michigan Journal of International Law* 249

Conrad, P., *Modern Times, Modern Places* (Knopf, 1999)

Corten, O., 'Les Techniques reproduites aux articles 31 à 33 des Conventions de Vienne: Approche objectiviste ou approche volontariste de l'interprétation?' (2011) 115 *RGDIP* 351

Costa, J., 'What Are the Limits to Evolutive Interpretation of the Convention?' in Council of Europe (ed.), *Dialogue Between Judges, European Court of Human Rights: What Are the Limits to Evolutive Interpretation of the Convention?* (Council of Europe, 2011)

Cotterrell, R., *Law, Culture and Society: Legal Ideas in the Mirror of Social Theory* (Ashgate, 2006)

Council of Europe (ed.), *Dialogue Between Judges, European Court of Human Rights: What Are the Limits to Evolutive Interpretation of the Convention?* (Council of Europe, 2011)

Proceedings of the Fourth International Colloquy About the European Convention on Human Rights: Organised by the Ministry of Foreign Affairs of Italy and the Secretariat General of the Council of Europe; Rome, 5–8 November 1975 (Council of Europe, 1975)

Craven, M. C. R., Fitzmaurice, M., and Vogiatzi, M. (eds.), *Time, History and International Law* (Martinus Nijhoff Publishers, 2007)

Crawford, J., 'A Consensualist Interpretation of Article 31(3) of the Vienna Convention on the Law of Treaties' in Nolte, G. (ed.), *Treaties and Subsequent Practice* (Oxford University Press, 2013)

 Brownlie's Principles of Public International Law (8th edn, Oxford University Press, 2012)

 'Sovereignty as a Legal Value' in Crawford, J., and Koskenniemi, M. (eds.), *International Law* (Cambridge University Press, 2012)

Crawford, J., and Viles, T., 'International Law on a Given Day' in Ginther, K., and others (eds.), *Völkerrecht zwischen normativem Anspruch und politischer Realität: Festschrift für Karl Zemanek zum 65. Geburtstag* (Duncker & Humblot, 1994)

Crema, L., 'Disappearance and New Sightings of Restrictive Interpretation(s)' (2010) 21 *EJIL* 681

 'Subsequent Agreements and Subsequent Practice Within and Outside the Vienna Convention' in Nolte, G. (ed.), *Treaties and Subsequent Practice* (Oxford University Press, 2013)

Cremer, H., 'Regeln der Konventionsinterpretation' in Dörr, O., Grote, R., and Marauhn, T. (eds.), *EMRK / GG: Konkordanzkommentar zum europäischen und deutschen Grundrechtsschutz* (vol. 1, 2nd edn, Mohr Siebeck, 2013)

Crnic-Grotic, V., 'Object and Purpose of Treaties in the Vienna Convention on the Law of Treaties' (1997) 7 *Asian Yearbook of International Law* 141

Crowe, J., 'Pre-Reflective Law' in Del Mar, M. (ed.), *New Waves in the Philosophy of Law* (Palgrave Macmillan, 2011)

Dahm, G., Delbrück, J., and Wolfrum, R., *Völkerrecht* (vol. 1 / 3, 2nd edn, De Gruyter, 2002)

Daillier, P., Forteau, M., and Pellet, A., *Droit international public* (8th edn, LGDJ, 2009)

d'Amato, A. A., 'International Law, Intertemporal Problems' in Bernhardt, R., and Macalister-Smith, P. (eds.), *Encyclopedia of Public International Law* (North-Holland Publishers, 2003)

Danesi, M., *The Quest for Meaning: A Guide to Semiotic Theory and Practice* (University of Toronto Press, 2007)

D'Aspremont, J., *Formalism and the Sources of International Law* (Oxford University Press, 2011)

Davidson, D., 'Radical Interpretation' (1973) 27 *Dialectica* 314

Dawidowicz, M., 'The Effect of the Passage of Time on the Interpretation of Treaties: Some Reflections on Costa Rica v. Nicaragua' (2011) 24 *Leiden Journal of International Law* 201

de Fernàndez Casadevante Romani, C., *Sovereignty and Interpretation of International Norms* (Springer, 2007)

Degan, V., *L'Interprétation des accords en droit international* (Martinus Nijhoff Publishers, 1963)

Desierto, D., and Gillespie, C., 'Evolutive Interpretation and Subsequent Practice: Interpretative Communities and Processes in the Optional Protocol to the ICESCR' (2013) 73 *Zeitschrift für ausländisches öffentliches Recht und Völkerrech* 549

Despagnet, F., *Cours de droit international public* (L. Larose, 1899)

Dhokalia, R. P., *The Codification of Public International Law* (Manchester University Press, 1970)

Djeffal, C., 'Commentaries on the Law of Treaties: A Review Essay Reflecting on the Genre of Commentaries' (2013) 24 *EJIL* 1223

'Establishing the Argumentative DNA of International Law: A Cubistic View on the Rule of Treaty Interpretation and Its Underlying Legal Culture(s)' (2014) 5 *Journal of Transnational Legal Theory* 128

'Neue Akteure und das Völkerrecht: eine begriffsgeschichtliche Reflexion' in Berhard, T., Nikol, R., and Schniederjahn, N. (eds.), *Transnationale Unternehmen und Nichtregierungsorganisationen im Völkerrecht* (Nomos, 2013)

Doehring, K., *Völkerrecht: Ein Lehrbuch* (Müller, 2004)

Dörr, O., 'Art. 31' in Dörr, O., and Schmalenbach, K. (eds.), *Vienna Convention on the Law of Treaties: A Commentary* (Springer, 2012)

'Art. 32' in Dörr, O., and Schmalenbach, K. (eds.), *Vienna Convention on the Law of Treaties: A Commentary* (Springer, 2012)

Dörr, O., and Schmalenbach, K. (eds.), *Vienna Convention on the Law of Treaties: A Commentary* (Springer, 2012)

Drzemczewski, A., 'The Sui Generis Nature of the European Convention on Human Rights' (1980) 29 *International and Comparative Law Quarterly* 54

Dugard, J., 'The Opinion on South-West Africa ("Namibia"): The Teleologists Triumph' (1971) 88 *South African Law Journal* 460

Duplessix, E., *La Loi des nations: Projet d'institution d'une autorité internationale législative, administrative et judiciaire* (J. B. Sirey, 1906)

Dupuy, P., 'Evolutionary Interpretation of Treaties: Between Memory and Prophecy' in Cannizzaro, E. (ed.), *The Law of Treaties Beyond the Vienna Convention* (Oxford University Press, 2011)

'On the "Doctrine" of Approximate Application of Treaties in International Law' in Hafner, G. (ed.), *Liber Amicorum Professor Ignaz Seidl-Hohenveldern in Honour of His 80th Birthday* (Martinus Nijhoff, 1980)

'The Danger of Fragmentation or Unification of the International Legal System and the International Court of Justice' (1998–9) 31 *New York University Journal of International Law and Politics* 791

Dworkin, R., *Law's Empire* (Hart Publishing, 1998)

Dzehtsiarou, K., 'European Consensus and the Evolutive Interpretation of the European Convention on Human Rights' (2011) 12 *German Law Journal* 1730

Eco, U., *A Theory of Semiotics* (Indiana University Press, 1979)

Ehrlich, E., *Gesetz und lebendes Recht: vermischte kleinere Schriften* (Duncker & Humblot, 1986)

Ehrlich, L., 'L'Interprétation des traités' (1928) 24 *RdC* 1

Elias, T. O., 'The Doctrine of Intertemporal Law' (1980) 74 *AJIL* 285

Eriksen, T. H., *Tyranny of the Moment: Fast and Slow Time in the Information Age* (Pluto Press, 2001)

European Court of Human Rights, *Annual Report* (Registry of the European Court of Human Rights, 2013), www.echr.coe.int/Documents/Annual_repor t_2013_ENG.pdf (accessed 23 June 2015)

Falk, R. A., 'On Treaty Interpretation and the New Haven Approach: Achievements and Prospects' in Falk, R. A. (ed.), *The Status of the International Society* (Princeton University Press, 2015)

Farber, D. A., 'Originalism Debate: A Guide for the Perplexed' (1988) 49 *Ohio State Law Journal* 1085

  'Disarmed by Time: The Second Amendment and the Failure of Originalism' (2000) 76 *Chicago-Kent Law Review* 167

Fassbender, B., 'Denkschulen im Völkerrecht' in Fassbender, B., and others (eds.), *Paradigmen im internationalen Recht Implikationen der Weltfinanzkrise für das internationale Recht* (C. F. Müller, 2012)

  The United Nations Charter as the Constitution of the International Community (2nd edn, Martinus Nijhoff Publishers, 2009)

Fauchille, P., *Traité de droit international public* (vol. 1, Rousseau, 1926)

Feldman, A. M., 'Evolving Treaty Obligations: A Proposal for Analyzing Subsequent Practice Derived from WTO Dispute Settlement' (2009) 41 *New York University Journal of International Law and Politics* 655

Feteris, E. T., *Fundamentals of Legal Argumentation: A Survey of Theories on the Justification of Judicial Decisions* (Kluwer, 1999)

Field, D. D., *Draft Outlines of an International Code* (Diossy, 1872)

Fikentscher, W., *Methoden des Rechts: Frühe und religiöse Rechte – Romanischer Rechtskreis* (Mohr Siebeck, 1975)

Finegan, E., *Language: Its Structure and Use* (Thomson, 2008)

Fiore, P., *Le Droit international codifié et sa sanction juridique* (Charles Antoine trans., A. Pedone, 1911)

Fischer-Lescano, A., and Teubner, G., *Regime-Kollisionen: Zur Fragmentierung des globalen Rechts* (Suhrkamp, 2006)

Fish, S. E., *'Fish v. Fiss', Doing What Comes Naturally* (Duke University Press, 1989)
  'Is There a Text in This Class' in Veseer, H. A. (ed.), *The Stanley Fish Reader* (Blackwell, 1999)
Fitzmaurice, G., 'Hersch Lauterpacht – The Scholar as Judge – Part III' (1963) 39 *BYIL* 133
  'De l'interprétation des traités' (1956) 46 *Annuaire de l'Institut de Droit International* 317
  'The Law and Procedure of the International Court of Justice 1951–4: Treaty Interpretation and Other Treaty Points' (1957) 33 *BYIL* 203
  'The Law and Procedure of the International Court of Justice: Treaty Interpretation' (1951) 28 *BYIL* 1
  'Vae Victis or Woe to the Negotiators! Your Treaty or Our "Interpretation" of It?' (1971) 65 *AJIL* 358
Fitzmaurice, M., 'Dynamic (Evolutive) Interpretation of Treaties, Part I' (2008) 21 *Hague Yearbook of International Law* 101
  'Dynamic (Evolutive) Interpretation of Treaties, Part II' (2010) 22 *Hague Yearbook of International Law* 3
  'The European Convention on Human Rights and Fundamental Freedoms and the Human Right to a Clean Environment: The English Perspective' in Revesz, R. L., Sands, P., and Stewart, R. B. (eds.), *Environmental Law, the Economy and Sustainable Development: The United States, the European Union, and the International Community* (Cambridge University Press, 2008)
Fitzmaurice, M., Olufemi, E., and Merkouris, P. (eds.), *Treaty Interpretation and the Vienna Convention: 30 Years on* (Martinus Nijhoff Publishers, 2010)
Focarelli, C., *International Law as a Social Construct: The Struggle for Global Justice* (Oxford University Press, 2012)
Fogelin, R. J., *Taking Wittgenstein at His Word: A Textual Study* (Princeton University Press, 2009)
Folke-Schuppert, G., 'Verfassungswandel im Kontext. Aspekte einer Theorie des Verfassungswandels' in Hönnige, C., Kneip, S., and Lorenz, A. (eds.), *Verfassungswandel im Mehrebenensystem* (VS Verlag, 2011)
Forowicz, M., *The Reception of International Law in the European Court of Human Rights* (Oxford University Press, 2010)
Fox, A., *Linguistic Reconstruction: An Introduction to Theory and Method* (Oxford University Press, 1995)
Francioni, F., 'Equity in International Law' in Wolfrum, R. (ed.), *The Max Planck Encyclopedia of Public International Law* (Oxford University Press, 2012)
Franck, T. M., 'On Proportionality of Countermeasures in International Law' (2008) 102 *AJIL* 715
  'Proportionality in International Law' (2010) 4 *Law and Ethics of Human Rights* 230

French, D., 'Treaty Interpretation and the Incorporation of Extraneous Legal Rules' (2006) 55 *International and Comparative Law Quarterly* 281

Friedmann, W., 'The Changing Dimensions of International Law' (1962) 62 *Columbia Law Review* 1147

The Changing Structure of International Law (Stevens, 1964)

Frowein, J. A., 'Die evolutive Auslegung der EMRK' in Marauhn, T. (ed.), *Recht, Politik und Rechtspolitik in den internationalen Beziehungen* (Mohr Siebeck, 2005)

'European Integration Through Fundamental Rights' (1984) 18 *University of Michigan Journal of Law Reform* 5

Gadamer, H., *Truth and Method* (Continuum, 1975)

Gaja, G., 'Does the European Court of Human Rights Use Its Stated Methods of Interpretation?' in Capotorti, F. (ed.), *Divenire sociale e adeguamento del diritto: studi in onore di Francesco Capotorti* (A. Giuffrè, 1999)

Ganshof van der Meersch, W. J., 'Quelques apercus de la methode d'interpretation de la Convention de Rome du 4 Novembre 1950 par la Cour Europeenne des droit de l'homme' in Legros, R. (ed.), *Mélanges offerts à Robert Legros* (Ed. de l'University de Bruxelles, 1985)

Garapon, A., 'Les Limites à l'interprétation évolutive de la Convention Européenne' (2011) 87 *Revue trimestrielle de droit de l'homme* 439

Gardam, J. G., *Necessity, Proportionality and the Use of Force by States* (Cambridge University Press, 2004)

Gardiner, R., 'The Vienna Convention Rules on Treaty Interpretation' in Hollis, D. B. (ed.), *The Oxford Guide to Treaties* (Oxford University Press, 2012)

Treaty Interpretation (Oxford University Press, 2010)

Gaudemet, E., 'L'Oeuvre de Saleilles et l'oeuvre de Gény en méthodologie juridique et en philosophie du droit', in *Les Sources générales des systèmes juridiques actuels* (Recueil Sirey, 1934)

Gentili, A., *De jure bellis libri tres* (vol. II, translation of the edition originally published in 1612, Rolf, J. C. trans., Hein, 1993)

Gény, F., *Méthode d'interprétation et sources en droit privé positif: Essai critique* (vol. 1, 2nd edn, LGDJ, 1919)

Méthode d'interprétation et sources en droit privé positif: Essai critique (vol. 2, 2nd edn, LGDJ, 1919)

Giegerich, T., 'Art. 56' in Dörr, O., and Schmalenbach, K. (eds.), *Vienna Convention on the Law of Treaties: A Commentary* (Springer, 2012)

'Art. 62' in Dörr, O., and Schmalenbach, K. (eds.), *Vienna Convention on the Law of Treaties: A Commentary* (Springer, 2012)

Gillich, I.-E., *Konsens und Evolutive Vertragsauslegung* (Peter Lang, 2014)

Gillman, H., 'The Collapse of Constitutional Originalism and the Rise of the Notion of the "Living Constitution" in the Course of American State-Building' (1997) 11 *Studies in American Political Development* 191

Goldford, D. J., *The American Constitution and the Debate Over Originalism* (Cambridge University Press, 2005)
Goldsworthy, J., 'The Case for Originalism' in Huscroft, G., and Miller, B. (eds.), *The Challenge of Originalism: Theories of Constitutional Interpretation* (Cambridge University Press, 2011)
Golsong, H., 'Interpreting the Convention' in MacDonald, R. St J., Matscher, F., and Petzold, H. (eds.), *The European System for the Protection of Human Rights* (Martinus Nijhoff Publishers, 1993)
Gordon, E., 'The World Court and the Interpretation of Constitutive Treaties' (1965) 59 *AJIL* 794
Gottlieb, G., 'The Interpretation of Treaties by Tribunals' (1969) 9 *ASIL Proceedings* 122
Grabau, F., *Über die Normen zur Gesetzes- und Vertragsinterpretation* (Duncker & Humblot, 1993)
Grabenwarter, C., and Pabel, K., *Europäische Menschenrechtskonvention: Ein Studienbuch* (5th edn, C. H. Beck, 2012)
Graham, R., 'In Defence of Maxims' (2001) 22 *Statute Law Review* 45
Grano, J. D., 'Judicial Review and a Written Constitution in a Democratic Society' (1981) 28 *Wayne Law Review* 1
Grant, J. P., and Barker, J. C., *Parry and Grant Encyclopaedic Dictionary of International Law* (3rd edn, Oxford University Press, 2009)
Graziadei, M., 'The Functionalist Heritage' in Legrand, P., Munday, R., and Munday, R. J. C. (eds.), *Comparative Legal Studies: Traditions and Transitions* (Cambridge University Press, 2003)
Greenwalt, K., *Legal Interpretation* (Oxford University Press, 2010)
Greer, S. C., *The Margin of Appreciation: Interpretation and Discretion under the European Convention on Human Rights* (Council of Europe Publications, 2000)
Greig, D., *Intertemporality and the Law of Treaties* (British Institute of International and Comparative Law, 2001)
  'The Time of Conclusion and the Time of Application of Treaties as Points of Reference in the Interpretative Process' in Craven, M. C. R., Fitzmaurice, M., and Vogiatzi, M. (eds.), *Time, History and International Law* (Martinus Nijhoff Publishers, 2007)
Greschek, E., *Die evolutive Auslegung völkerrechtlicher Verträge am Beispiel des GATT* (Peter Lang, 2012)
Grimm, D., *Das öffentliche Recht vor der Frage nach seiner Identität* (Mohr Siebeck, 2012)
Gross, L., 'Treaty Interpretation: The Proper Role of an International Tribunal' (1969) 63 *ASIL Proceedings* 108
Grotius, H., *De jure belli ac pacis libri tres*, (vol. II, translation of the edition originally published in 1646, Kelsey, F. W. trans., Humphrey Milford, 1925)

Grover, L., 'A Call to Arms: Fundamental Dilemmas Confronting the Interpretation of Crimes in the Rome Statute of the International Criminal Court' (2010) 21 *EJIL* 543

Guillaume, G., 'The Use of Precedent by International Judges and Arbitrators' (2011) 2 *Journal of International Dispute Settlement* 5

Häberle, P., 'Zeit und Verfassung' (1974) 21 *Zeitschrift für Politik* 111

Habermas, J., *Between Facts and Norms: Contributions to a Discourse Theory of Law and Democracy* (William Rehg trans., MIT Press, 1996)

Habermas, J., *Faktizität und Geltung: Beiträge zur Diskurstheorie des Rechts und des demokratischen Rechtsstaats* (Suhrkamp, 1992)

   'What Is Universal Pragmatics?', *Communication and Evolution of Society* (Polity Press, 1991)

Hafner, G., 'Subsequent Agreements and Practice: Between Interpretation, Informal Modification and Amendment' in Nolte, G. (ed.), *Treaties and Subsequent Practice* (Oxford University Press, 2013)

Hale, Baroness, 'Common Law and Convention Law: The Limits to Interpretation' (2011) 5 *European Human Rights Law Review* 534

Hall, W. E., *A Treatise on International Law* (8th edn, Clarendon Press, 1924)

Haraszti, G., and Decsenyi, J., *Some Fundamental Problems of the Law of Treaties* (Akad. Kiadó, 1973)

Harris, D. J., O'Boyle, M., Buckley, C., and others, *Harris, O'Boyle and Warbrick Law of the European Convention on Human Rights* (3rd edn, Oxford University Press, 2014)

Hart, H. L. A., *The Concept of Law* (2nd edn, Oxford University Press, 1994)

Harvard Law School, 'Harvard Draft Convention on the Law of Treaties' (1935) 29 *AJIL Supplement* 937

Heffter, A. W., *Das europäische Völkerrecht der Gegenwart* (2nd edn, G. H. Schroeder, 1848)

Heintschel von Heinegg, W., 'Die völkerrechtlichen Verträge als Hauptquelle des Völkerrechts' in Ipsen, K. (ed.), *Völkerrecht* (6th edn, C. H. Beck, 2014)

   'Weitere Quellen Des Völkerrechts' in Ipsen, K. (ed.), *Völkerrecht* (6th edn, C. H. Beck, 2014)

Heisenberg, W., 'Über den anschaulichen Inhalt der quantentheoretischen Kinematik und Mechanik' [1927] *Zeitschrift für Physik* 172

Helfer, L. R., 'Consensus, Coherence and the European Convention on Human Rights' (1993) 26 *Cornell International Law Journal* 133

Herbots, J. H., 'Interpretation of Contracts' in Smits, J. M. (ed.), *Elgar Encyclopedia of Comparative Law* (2nd edn, Edward Elgar Publishing, 2012)

Herdegen, M., 'Interpretation in International Law' in Wolfrum, R. (ed.), *The Max Planck Encyclopedia of Public International Law* (Oxford University Press, 2012)

   Völkerrecht (Grundrisse des Rechts, C. H. Beck, 2013)

Hershey, A., *The Essentials of International Law and Organization* (Macmillan, 1927)

Hesse, K., 'Grenzen der Verfassungswandlung' in Ehmke, H., and others (eds.), *Festschrift für Ulrich Scheuner* (Duncker & Humblot, 1973)

Heyns, C., and Killander, M., 'South West Africa / Namibia (Advisory Opinions and Judgments)' in Wolfrum, R. (ed.), *The Max Planck Encyclopedia of Public International Law* (Oxford University Press, 2012)

Higgins, R., 'Some Observations on the Inter-Temporal Rule in International Law' in Makarczyk, J., and Skubiszewski, K. (eds.), *Theory of International Law at the Threshold of the 21st Century: Essays in Honour of Krzysztof Skubiszewski* (Kluwer, 1996)

'The International Court and South West Africa' (1966) 42 *International Affairs* 573

'Time and the Law – International Perspectives on an Old Problem' (1997) 46 *International and Comparative Law Quarterly* 501

Hilgevoord, J., and Uffink, J., 'The Uncertainty Principle', http://plato.stanford.edu/archives/spr2014/entries/qt-uncertainty (accessed 8 May 2014)

Hock, H. H., and Joseph, B. D. (eds.), *Trends in Linguistics: Language History, Language Change, and Language Relationship* (Mouton de Gruyter, 2009)

Hogg, J. F., 'The International Law Commission and the Law of Treaties' (1965) 59 *ASIL Proceedings* 8

Hollis, D., 'The Existential Function of Interpretation in International Law', http://papers.ssrn.com/sol3/papers.cfm?abstract_Fid=2330642 (accessed 31 December 2014)

Honneth, A., *Das Recht der Freiheit: Grundriß einer demokratischen Sittlichkeit* (Suhrkamp, 2011)

Horwitz, M. J., 'Foreword: The Constitution of Change Legal Fundamentality Without Fundamentalism' (1993) 107 *Harvard Law Review* 30

Hudson, M. O., *The Permanent Court of International Justice* (Macmillan, 1934)

The Permanent Court of International Justice: 1920–1942 (2nd edn, Macmillan, 1943)

Huscroft, G., and Miller, B. (eds.), *The Challenge of Originalism: Theories of Constitutional Interpretation* (Cambridge University Press, 2011)

Hyde, C. C., 'Concerning the Interpretation of Treaties' (1909) 3 *AJIL* 46

International Law Chiefly as Interpreted and Applied by the United States (1st edn, Little, Brown & Co., 1922)

International Law Chiefly as Interpreted and Applied by the United States (2nd edn, Little, Brown & Co., 1945)

'Judge Anzilotti on the Interpretation of Treaties' (1933) 27 *AJIL* 502

'The Interpretation of Treaties by the Supreme Court of the United States' [1929] *AJIL* 824

International Commission of Jurists, 'Project No. IV: Treaties' (1928) 22 *AJIL Supplement* 244

Internoscia, J., *New Code of International Law* (The International Code Company of New York, 1910)

Jacobs, F. G., 'Innovation and Continuity in the Law of Treaties' (1970) 33 *Modern Law Review* 508

  'To What Extent Have Restrictions on the Enjoyment of Freedoms Evolved?' in Council of Europe (ed.), *Proceedings of the Fourth International Colloquy About the European Convention on Human Rights: Organised by the Ministry of Foreign Affairs of Italy and the Secretariat General of the Council of Europe; Rome, 5–8 November 1975* (Council of Europe, 1975)

  'Varieties of Approach to Treaty Interpretation: With Special Reference to the Draft Convention on the Law of Treaties Before the Vienna Diplomatic Conference' (1969) 18 *International and Comparative Law Quarterly* 318

Jellinek, G., *Verfassungsänderung und Verfassungswandlung* (Goldbach, 1996 [1906])

Jennings, R. Y., 'Treaties' in Bedjaoui, M. (ed.), *International Law: Achievements and Prospects* (UNESCO, 1991)

Jessup, P. C., 'The Palmas Island Arbitration' (1928) 22 *AJIL* 735

Jiménez Aréchaga, E. de, 'International Law in the Past Third of a Century: General Course' (1978) 159 *RdC* 1

Jonas, D. S., and Saunders, T. N., 'The Object and Purpose of a Treaty: Three Interpretive Methods' (2010) 43 *Virginia Journal of International Law* 565

Joseph, J. E., *Limiting the Arbitrary: Linguistic Naturalism and Its Opposites in Plato's Cratylus and Modern Theories of Language* (John Benjamins Publishing, 2000)

Kadelbach, S., 'Interpretation of the Charter' in Simma, B., Khan, D., Nolte, G., and Paulus, A. (eds.), *The Charter of the United Nations* (3rd edn, Oxford University Press, 2012)

Kähler, L., *Strukturen und Methoden der Rechtsprechungsänderung* (2nd edn, Nomos, 2011)

Kammerhofer, J., *Uncertainty in International Law: A Kelsenian Perspective* (Routledge, 2010)

Karl, W., *Vertrag und spaetere Praxis im Voelkerrecht: zum Einfluß der Praxis auf Inhalt und Bestand völkerrechtlicher Verträge* (Springer, 1983)

Kay, R. S., 'Adherence to the Original Intentions in Constitutional Adjudication: Three Objections and Responses' (1987) 82 *Northwestern University Law Review* 226

Kearney, R. D., and Dalton, R. E., 'The Treaty on Treaties' (1970) 64 *AJIL* 495

Keith, A., 'Metamorphosis' in Weiden, B. (ed.), *Brill's Companion to Ovid* (Brill, 2001)

Keller, R., *A Theory of Linguistic Signs* (Oxford University Press, 1998)

Kelsen, H., *Legal Technique in International Law: A Textual Critique of the League Covenant* (Geneva Research Centre, 1939)
  Principles of International Law (Rinehart & Co., 1952)
Kempen, B., and Hillgruber, C., *Völkerrecht* (C. H. Beck, 2012)
Khan, D., 'Max Huber as Arbitrator: The Palmas (Miangas) Case and Other Arbitrations' (2007) 18 *EJIL* 145
Kingsbury, B., 'International Courts: Uneven Judicialisation in Global Order' in Crawford, J., and Koskenniemi, M. (eds.), *The Cambridge Companion to International Law* (Cambridge University Press, 2012)
Klabbers, J., 'Book Review' (2013) 24 *EJIL* 718
  'International Legal Histories: "Declining Importance of Travaux Préparatoires in Treaty Interpretation?"' (2003) 50 *Netherlands International Law Review* 267
  'Reluctant Grundnormen: Articles 31(3)(c) and 42 of the Vienna Convention on the Law of Treaties and the Fragmentation of International Law' in Craven, M. C. R., Fitzmaurice, M., and Vogiatzi, M. (eds.), *Time, History and International Law* (Martinus Nijhoff Publishers, 2007)
  'Virtuous Interpretation' in Fitzmaurice, M., Olufemi, E., and Merkouris, P. (eds.), *Treaty Interpretation and the Vienna Convention: 30 Years on* (Martinus Nijhoff Publishers, 2010)
Klappstein, V., *Die Rechtsprechungsänderung mit Wirkung für die Zukunft* (Duncker & Humblot, 2009)
Klatt, M., and Meister, M., *The Constitutional Structure of Proportionality* (Oxford University Press, 2012)
Klein, E., *Statusverträge im Völkerrecht* (Springer, 1980)
Klein, G., *Rekonstruktion und Interpretation* (Kaiser, 1969)
Kleinlein, T., 'Judicial Lawmaking by Judicial Restraint? The Potential of Balancing in International Economic Law' (2011) 12 *German Law Journal* 1175
  Konstitutionalisierung im Völkerrecht: Konstruktion und Elemente einer idealistischen Völkerrechtslehre (Springer, 2012)
Klüber, J. L., *Europäisches Völkerrecht* (2nd edn, Hurter, 1851)
Koch, H. J., and Trapp, R., 'Richterliche Innovation – Begriff und Begründbarkeit' in Harenburg, J., Podlech, A., and Schlink, B. (eds.), *Rechtlicher Wandel durch richterliche Entscheidung* (Toeche-Mittler, 1980)
Köck, H. F., *Vertragsinterpretation und Vertragsrechtskonvention: zur Bedeutung der Art. 31 und 32 der Wiener Vertragsrechtskonvention 1969* (Duncker & Humblot, 1976)
Kohen, M., 'Keeping Subsequent Agreements and Practice in Their Right Limits' in Nolte, G. (ed.), *Treaties and Subsequent Practice* (Oxford University Press, 2013)
Kolb, R., *Interprétation et création du droit international: Esquisses d'une herméneutique juridique moderne pour le droit international public* (Bruylant, 2006)

'Les Maximes juridiques en droit international public: Questions historiques et théoriques' (1999) 32 *Revue Belge de Droit International* 407
Koopmans, T., 'Retrospectivity Reconsidered' (1980) 39 *Cambridge Law Journal* 287
Koselleck, R., 'Die Geschichte der Begriffe und Begriffe der Geschichte' in Koselleck, R. (ed.), *Begriffsgeschichten: Studien zur Semantik und Pragmatik der politischen und sozialen Sprache* (Suhrkamp, 2010)
Koskenniemi, M., *From Apology to Utopia: The Structure of International Legal Argument* (Cambridge University Press, 2005)
  'Introduction' in Koskenniemi, M. (ed.), *Sources of International Law* (Ashgate, 2000)
  'Methodology of International Law' in Wolfrum, R. (ed.), *The Max Planck Encyclopedia of Public International Law* (Oxford University Press, 2012)
  'The Fate of Public International Law: Between Technique and Politics' (2007) 70 *Modern Law Review* 1
  The Gentle Civilizer of Nations: The Rise and Fall of International Law 1870-1960 (Cambridge University Press, 2008)
Kotzur, M., 'Intertemporal Law' in Wolfrum, R. (ed.), *The Max Planck Encyclopedia of Public International Law* (Oxford University Press, 2012)
  'Non-Retroactivity and Its Discontents' in Tams, C., Tzanakopoulos, A., and Zimmermann, A. (eds.), *Research Handbook on the Law of Treaties* (Edward Elgar, 2014)
Kratochwil, F. V., *Rules, Norms, and Decisions: On the Conditions of Practical and Legal Reasoning in International Relations and Domestic Affairs* (Cambridge University Press, 1991)
Krawietz, W., 'Ausdifferenzierung von Praxis und Theorie in juristischer systemtheoretischer Perspektive' (2001) 32 *Rechtstheorie* 345
Kretzmer, D., 'The Inherent Right to Self-Defence and Proportionality in Jus Ad Bellum' (2013) 24 *EJIL* 235
Kuijper, P. J., 'The European Courts and the Law of Treaties: The Continuing Story' in Cannizzaro, E. (ed.), *The Law of Treaties Beyond the Vienna Convention* (Oxford University Press, 2011)
Laband, P., *Die Wandlungen der deutschen Reichsverfassung* (Zahn & Jaensch, 1895)
Lagerwall, A., 'Art. 64 VCLT' in Corten, O., and Klein, P. (eds.), *The Vienna Conventions on the Law of Treaties: A Commentary* (Oxford University Press, 2011)
Lamond, G., 'Precedent and Analogy in Legal Reasoning', http://plato.stanford.edu/entries/legal-reas-prec (accessed 31 December 2014)
Lapidoth, R., 'Equity in International Law' (1987) 22 *Israel Law Review* 161
Lauterpacht, H., 'De l'interprétation des traités' [1950] *Annuaire de l'Institut de Droit International* 345

'De l'interprétation des traités' [1950] *Annuaire de l'Institut de Droit International* 366

'Les Travaux préparatoires et l'interprétation des traités' [1937] *RdC* 713

'Nouveau projet définitif de résolutions' (1950) *Annuaire de l'Institut de Droit International* 390

'Restrictive Interpretation and the Principle of Effectiveness in the Interpretation of Treaties' (1949) 36 *BYIL* 48

The Function of Law in the International Community (Clarendon Press, 1933)

Lawrence, T. J., *The Principles of International Law* (2nd edn, Macmillan, 1895)

Bouthillier, Y. le, 'Art. 32' in Corten, O., and Klein, P. (eds.), *The Vienna Conventions on the Law of Treaties: A Commentary* (Oxford University Press, 2011)

Lege, J., 'Was Juristen wirklich tun: Jurisprudential realism' in Brugger, W., Kirste, S., and Neumann, U. (eds.), *Rechtsphilosophie im 21. Jahrhundert* (Suhrkamp, 2008)

Lessig, L., 'Fidelity and Constraint' (1996) 65 *Fordham Law Review* 1365

'Fidelity in Translation' (1992) 71 *Texas Law Review* 1165

'Reading the Constitution in Cyberspace' (1996) 45 *Emory Law Journal* 896

'Understanding Changed Readings: Fidelity and Theory' (1994) *Stanford Law Review* 395

Letsas, G., *A Theory of Interpretation of the European Convention on Human Rights* (Oxford University Press, 2007)

'Intentionalism and the Interpretation of the ECHR' in Fitzmaurice, M., Olufemi, E., and Merkouris, P. (eds.), *Treaty Interpretation and the Vienna Convention: 30 Years on* (Martinus Nijhoff Publishers, 2010)

'The Truth in Autonomous Concepts: How to Interpret the ECHR' (2004) 15 *EJIL* 279

Liacouras, P. J., 'The International Court of Justice and Development of Useful Rules of Interpretation in the Process of Treaty Interpretation' (1965) 59 *ASIL Proceedings* 161

Linderfalk, U., 'Doing the Right Thing for the Right Reason – Why Dynamic and Static Approaches Should Be Taken in the Interpretation of Treaties' (2008) 10 *International Community Law Review* 109

On the Interpretation of Treaties: The Modern International Law as Expressed in the 1969 Vienna Convention on the Law of Treaties (Springer, 2007)

'Who Are the Parties: Article 31, Paragraph 3(c) of the 1969 Vienna Convention and the Principle of Systemic Integration Revisited' (2008) 55 *Netherlands International Law Review* 343

Lissitzyn, O. J., 'The Law of International Agreements in the Restatement' (1966) 41 *New York University Law Review* 96

Liszt, F. von, *Das Völkerrecht: systematisch dargestellt* (4th edn, O. Haering, 1906)

Lofgren, C. A., 'The Original Understanding of Original Intent' (1988) 5 *Constitutional Commentary* 77

Lowe, V., 'Sustainable Development and Unsustainable Arguments' in Boyle, A. E., and Freestone, D. A. C. (eds.), *International Law and Sustainable Development: Past Achievements and Future Challenges* (Oxford University Press, 2001)
    'The Role of Equity in International Law' (1988) 8 *Australian Year Book of International Law* 54
Luhmann, N., *Das Recht der Gesellschaft* (Suhrkamp, 1993)
    Soziale Systeme: Grundriß einer allgemeinen Theorie (2nd edn, Suhrkamp, 1985)
Luján, E. R., 'Semantic Change' in Luraghi, S., and Bebenik, V. (eds.), *The Continuum Companion to Historical Linguistics* (Continuum, 2010)
Luraghi, S., 'Causes of Language Change' in Luraghi, S., and Bebenik, V. (eds.), *The Continuum Companion to Historical Linguistics* (Continuum, 2010)
Luraghi, S., and Bebenik, V. (eds.), *The Continuum Companion to Historical Linguistics* (Continuum, 2010)
Lycan, W. G., *Philosophy of Language: A Contemporary Introduction* (Routledge, 1999)
MacCormick, N., 'Argumentation and Interpretation in Law' (1995) 9 *Argumentation* 467
    Rhetoric and the Rule of Law: A Theory of Legal Reasoning (Oxford University Press, 2010)
MacCormick, N., and Summers, R. S. (eds.), *Interpreting Statutes: A Comparative Study* (Ashgate, Dartmouth, 1991)
Macdonald, R. St J., 'The Margin of Appreciation' in Matscher, F., and Petzold, H. (eds.), *The European System for the Protection of Human Rights* (Martinus Nijhoff Publishers, 1993)
Mackenzie, R., Romano, C., and Shany, Y., *The Manual on International Courts and Tribunals* (Oxford University Press, 2010)
Mahoney, P., 'Judicial Activism and Judicial Self-Restraint in the European Court of Human Rights: Two Sides of the Same Coin' (1990) 11 *Human Rights Law Journal* 57
    'Marvellous Richness of Diversity or Invidious Cultural Relativism' (1998) 19 *Human Rights Law Journal* 1
Makarczyk, J., 'The International Court of Justice on Implied Powers of International Organizations' in Makarczyk, J. (ed.), *Études de droit international en l'honneur du Juge Manfred Lachs* (Martinus Nijhoff Publishers, 1984)
Martens, F. de, *Traité de droit international* (Alfred Léo trans., A. Chevalier-Marescq, 1883)
Martens, S. A. E., 'Rechtliche und außerrechtliche Argumente' (2011) 42 *Rechtstheorie* 145
Martin, A., 'L'Interprétation dite évolutive de termes insérés dans des traités internationaux. Regards sur un arrêt du Tribunal fédéral suisse' in La Faculté de Droit et des Sciences Économiques de l'Université de Neuchâtel

(ed.), *Mélanges en l'honneur de Jacques-Michel Grossen* (Helbing & Lichtenhahn, 1992)

Martinich, A., and Sosa, D. (eds.), *The Philosophy of Language* (6th edn, Oxford University Press, 2013)

Mashaw, J., 'Norms, Practices, and the Paradox of Deference: A Preliminary Inquiry Into Agency Statutory Interpretation' (2005) 57 *Administrative Law Review* 501

Matscher, F., 'Methods of Interpretation of the Convention' in Matscher, F., and Petzold, H. (eds.), *The European System for the Protection of Human Rights* (Martinus Nijhoff Publishers, 1993)

'Wie sich die 1950 in der EMRK festgeschriebenen Menschenrechte weiterentwickelt haben' in Breitenmoser, S., and others (eds.), *Human Rights, Democracy and the Rule of Law: Liber Amicorum Luzius Wildhaber* (Dike, 2007)

Mayer, F., 'Verfassungswandel durch Annäherung? Der Europäische Gerichtshof, das Bundesverfassungsgericht und das Grundgesetz' in Hönnige, C., Kneip, S., and Lorenz, A. (eds.), *Verfassungswandel im Mehrebenensystem* (VS Verlag, 2011)

McArthur, T., *Concise Oxford Companion to the English Language* (Oxford University Press, 1998)

McBain, H., *The Living Constitution* (Macmillan, 1927)

McDougal, M. S., 'Some Basic Theoretical Concepts About International Law: A Policy-Oriented Framework of Inquiry' (1960) 4 *Journal of Conflict Resolution* 337

'The International Law Commission's Draft Articles upon Interpretation: Textuality Redivivus' (1967) 61 *AJIL* 992

McDougal, M. S., Lasswell, H. D., and Miller, J. C., *The Interpretation of Agreements and World Public Order* (Yale University Press, 1967)

McLachlan, C., 'Investment Treaties and General International Law' (2008) 57 *International and Comparative Law Quarterly* 361

'The Evolution of Treaty Obligations in International Law' in Nolte, G. (ed.), *Treaties and Subsequent Practice* (Oxford University Press, 2013)

'The Principle of Systemic Integration and Article 31(3)(c) of the Vienna Convention' (2005) 54 *International and Comparative Law Quarterly* 279

McNair, A. D., 'L'Application et l'interprétation des traités d'après la jurisprudence britannique' (1933) 43 *RdC* 263

The Law of Treaties (Oxford University Press, 1961)

Meder, S., *Mißverstehen und Verstehen: Savignys Grundlegung der juristischen Hermeneutik* (Mohr Siebeck, 2004)

Merkouris, P., 'Introduction: Interpretation Is a Science, Is an Art, Is a Science' in Fitzmaurice, M., Olufemi, E., and Merkouris, P. (eds.), *Treaty Interpretation and the Vienna Convention: 30 Years on* (Martinus Nijhoff Publishers, 2010)

Merrills, J. G., 'Two Approaches to Treaty Interpretation' (1968–9) 57 *Australian Year Book of International Law* 55

Meyer, L. H. (ed.), *Legitimacy, Justice and Public International Law* (Cambridge University Press, 2009)

Milanovic, M., 'The ICJ and Evolutionary Treaty Interpretation' (2009) www.ejiltalk.org / the-icj-and-evolutionary-treaty-interpretation (accessed 15 April 2013)

Milej, T., 'Rechtsquellen' in Heintschel von Heinegg, W. (ed.), *Casebook Völkerrecht* (C. H. Beck, 2005)

Miller, A. S., 'Notes on the Concept of the Living Constitution' (1962) 31 *George Washington Law Review* 881

Mittelstrass, J., 'Rationale Rekonstruktion der Wissenschaftsgeschichte' in Janich, P. (ed.), *Wissenschaftstheorie und Wissenschaftsforschung* (C. H. Beck, 1981)
  'Scientific Rationality and Its Reconstruction' in Rescher, N. (ed.), *Reason and Rationality in Natural Science: A Group of Essays* (University Press of America, 1988)

Moerman, J., 'A Critical Analysis of the Prohibition of Slavery and Forced Labour under Article 4 of the European Convention on Human Rights' (2010) 3 *Inter-American and European Human Rights Law Journal* 86

Montaneri, P. G. (ed.), *Methods of Comparative Law* (Edward Elgar Publishing, 2013)

Moore, M., 'Interpreting Interpretation' in Marmor, A. (ed.), *Law and Interpretation: Essays in Legal Philosophy* (Oxford University Press, 1996)

Morlok, M., and Kölbel, R., 'Rechtspraxis und Habitus' (2001) 32 *Rechtstheorie* 289

Mortenson, D. J., 'The *Travaux* of *Travaux*: Is the Vienna Convention Hostile to Drafting History?' (2013) 107 *AJIL* 780

Mowbray, A. R., *Cases and Materials on the European Convention on Human Rights* (2nd edn, Oxford University Press, 2007)
  Cases and Materials on the European Convention on Human Rights (3rd edn, Oxford University Press, 2012)
  'The Creativity of the European Court of Human Rights' (2005) 5 *Human Rights Law Review* 57

Müller, D., 'Reservations and Time: Is There Only One Right Moment to Formulate and to React to Reservations?' (2012) www.JeanMonnetProgram.org (accessed 10 March 2013)

Müller, F., *Juristische Methodik* (Duncker & Humblot, 1993)

Murphy, S., 'The Evolution of Treaty Obligations in International Law' in Nolte, G. (ed.), *Treaties and Subsequent Practice* (Oxford University Press, 2013)

Nascimento e Silva, G. E. do, 'Le Facteur temps et les traités' (1977) 154 *RdC* 221

Nerlich, B., *Change in Language: Whitney, Breal and Wegener* (Routledge, 1990)

Neuberger, Lord, 'The Role of Judges in Human Rights Jurisprudence: A Comparison of the Australian and UK Experience', https://www.supremecourt.uk/docs/speech-140808.pdf (accessed 30 December 2014)

Neuhold, P., 'Die Wiener Vertragsrechtskonvention' (1971) 15 *Archiv des Völkerrechts* 1

Nicol, D., 'Original Intent and the ECHR' [2005] *Public Law* 152

Nolte, G., 'Between Contemporaneous and Evolutive Interpretation: The Use of "Subsequent Practice" in the Judgment of the International Court of Justice Concerning the Case of Costa Rica v. Nicaragua (2009)' in Hestermeyer, H. P., and others (eds.), *Coexistence, Cooperation and Solidarity* (Martinus Nijhoff Publishers, 2012)

'Introduction' in Nolte, G. (ed.), *Treaties and Subsequent Practice* (Oxford University Press, 2013)

'Multipurpose Self-Defence, Proportionality Disoriented: A Response to David Kretzmer' (2013) 24 *EJIL* 283

'Second Report for the ILC Study Group on Treaties Over Time: Jurisprudence Under Special Regimes Relating to Subsequent Agreements and Subsequent Practice' in Nolte, G. (ed.), *Treaties and Subsequent Practice* (Oxford University Press, 2013)

'Subsequent Practice as a Means of Interpretation in the Jurisprudence of the WTO Appellate Body' in Cannizzaro, E. (ed.), *The Law of Treaties Beyond the Vienna Convention* (Oxford University Press, 2011)

'Thick or Thin Proportionality in International Humanitarian Law' (2010) 4 *Law and Ethics of Human Rights* 245

'Third Report for the ILC Study Group on Treaties Over Time Subsequent Agreements and Subsequent Practice of States Outside of Judicial or Quasi-Judicial Proceedings' in Nolte, G. (ed.), *Treaties and Subsequent Practice* (Oxford University Press, 2013)

Treaties and Subsequent Practice (Oxford University Press, 2013)

'Treaties Over Time: Introductory Report' in Nolte, G. (ed.), *Treaties and Subsequent Practice* (Oxford University Press, 2013)

Nöth, W., *Handbook of Semiotics* (Indiana University Press, 1995)

Nys, E., 'Codification of International Law' (1911) 5 *AJIL* 871

O'Connor, J. F., *Good Faith in International Law* (Dartmouth, 1991)

Odendahl, K., 'Art. 39' in Dörr, O., and Schmalenbach, K. (eds.), *Vienna Convention on the Law of Treaties: A Commentary* (Springer, 2012)

Oellers-Frahm, K., 'Multiplication of International Courts and Tribunals and Conflicting Jurisdiction – Problems and Possible Solutions' (2001) 5 *Max Planck Yearbook of United Nations Law* 67

Ogden, C. K., and Richards, I. A., *The Meaning of Meaning: A Study of the Influence of Language upon Thought and of the Science of Symbolism* (Routledge & Kegan Paul, 1969)

Onofrio, J., *Missouri Biographical Dictionary* (3rd edn, Vol. 1, St Clair Shores, 2001)
Oppenheim, L., *International Law: A Treatise* (1st edn, vol. 1, Longman, 1912)
Orakhelashvili, A., *The Interpretation of Acts and Rules in Public International Law* (Oxford University Press, 2008)
Orellana Zabalza, G., *The Principle of Systemic Integration: Towards a Coherent International Legal Order* (Lit Verlag, 2012)
Örücü, A. E., 'Methodology of Comparative Law' in Smits, J. (ed.), *Elgar Encyclopedia of Comparative Law* (2nd edn, Edward Elgar Publishing, 2012)
Oxford University Press, *Oxford English Dictionary: The definitive record of the English language* (9 June 2013), www.oed.com (accessed 8 August 2013)
Parsons, T., *The Social System* (Free Press, 1951)
Paulus, A., 'International Adjudication' in Besson, S., and Tasioulas, J. (eds.), *The Philosophy of International Law* (Oxford University Press, 2010)
Pauwelyn, J., *Conflict of Norms in Public International Law: How WTO Law Relates to Other Rules of International Law* (Cambridge University Press, 2009)
  'The Nature of WTO Obligations', Jean Monnet Working Paper No. 1 / 02 (2002), New York University School of Law, Jean Monnet Center, 2002
  'The Role of Public International Law in the WTO: How Far Can We Go?' [2001] *AJIL* 535
Pauwelyn, J., and Elsig, M., 'The Politics of Treaty Interpretation: Variations and Explanations Across International Tribunals' in Dunoff, J. L., and Pollack, M. A. (eds.), *Interdisciplinary Perspectives on International Law and International Relations* (Cambridge University Press, 2013)
Peanson, I., *Manual of the Terminology of Public International Law (Law of Peace) and International Organizations* (Bruylant, 1990)
Peck, C. J., 'Comments on Judicial Creativity' (1983) 69 *Iowa Law Review* 1
Pedersen, J., 'Habermas' Method: Rational Reconstruction' (2008) 38 *Philosophy of Social Science* 457
Pehar, D., 'International Law of Interpretation: An Ambiguous Response to Ambiguity' (2006) 5 *Journal of Diplomatic Language*
Pellet, A., 'Art. 19 VCLT' in Corten, O., and Klein, P. (eds.), *The Vienna Conventions on the Law of Treaties: A Commentary* (Oxford University Press, 2011)
  'Art. 38' in Zimmermann, A., and others (eds.), *The Statute of the International Court of Justice: A Commentary* (2nd edn, Oxford University Press, 2012)
Perelman, C., and Olbrechts-Tyteca, L., *The New Rhetoric. (La nouvelle rhétorique). A Treatise on Argumentation.* (University of Notre Dame Press, 1969)
Pergler, C., *Judicial Interpretation of International Law in the United States* (F. B. Rothman, 1928)
Peters, A., 'Compensatory Constitutionalism: The Function and Potential of Fundamental International Norms and Structures' (2006) 19 *Leiden Journal of International Law* 579

Völkerrecht Allgemeiner Teil (3rd edn, Schulthess, 2012)

Peters, A., and Altwicker, T., *Europäische Menschenrechtskonvention: Mit rechtsvergleichenden Bezügen zum deutschen Grundgesetz* (C. H. Beck, 2012)

Peters, C., 'Subsequent Practice and Established Practice of International Organizations: Two Sides of the Same Coin?' (2011) 3 *Goettingen Journal of International Law* 617

Phillimore, R., *Commentaries upon International Law* (vol. 2, Butterworths, 1855)

Phillipson, C., *Smith's International Law* (J. M. Dent & Sons Ltd, 1918)

Powell, J. H., 'The Original Understanding of Original Intent' (1985) 98 *Harvard Law Review* 885

Prebensen, S. C., 'Evolutive Interpretation of the European Convention on Human Rights' in Mahoney, P., and Ryssdal, R. (eds.), *Protecting Human Rights: The European Perspective* (Carl Heymanns Verlag, 2000)

Pree, H., *Die evolutive Interpretation der Rechtsnorm im Kanonischen Recht* (Springer, 1980)

Probst, T., *Die Änderung der Rechtsprechung: eine rechtsvergleichende, methodologische Untersuchung zum Phänomen der höchstrichterlichen Rechtsprechungsänderung in der Schweiz (civil law) und den Vereinigten Staaten (common law)* (Helbing & Lichtenhahn, 1993)

Pufendorf, Samuel, *De jure naturae et gentium* (Vol. II, translation of the edition of 1688, C. H. Oldfather and W. O. Oldfather trans., Clarendon Press, 1934)

Pulkowski, D., *The Law and Politics of International Regime Conflict* (Oxford University Press, 2014)

Pulvermüller, F., *The Neuroscience of Language: On Brain Circuits of Words and Serial Order* (Cambridge University Press, 2008)

Quoc Dinh, N., *Droit international public* (LGDJ, 1975)

Rabl Blaser, C., *Die clausula Rebus Sic stantibus im Völkerrecht* (Dike, 2012)

Raffeiner, S., 'Wege der Konstitutionalisierung im Völkerrecht: Vorrang der UN-Charta und ius cogens' in Pernice, I., Müller, M., and Peters, C. (eds.), *Konstitutionalisierung jenseits des Staates: Zur Verfassung der Weltgemeinschaft und den Gründungsverträgen internationaler Organisationen* (Springer, 2012)

Raney, B., Wicks, E., and Ovey, C., *Jacobs, White and Ovey, The European Convention on Human Rights* (6th edn, Oxford University Press, 2014)

Registrar of the International Court of Justice, 'Members of the Court', www.icj-cij.org/court/index.php?p1=1&p2=2 (accessed 27 November 2012)

Reglade, M., 'De la nature juridique des Traités internationaux et du sens de la distinction des traités-lois et des traités-contrats' [1924] *Revue de Droit Public et de la Science Politique en France et à l'Etranger* 507

Rehnquist, W. H., 'Notion of a Living Constitution' (1975) 54 *Texas Law Review* 693

Reinisch, A., 'The Proliferation of International Dispute Settlement Mechanisms: The Threat of Fragmentation vs. the Promise of a More Effective System?

Some Reflections from the Perspective of Investment Arbitration' in Buffard, I., and Hafner, G. (eds.), *International Law Between Universalism and Fragmentation: Festschrift in Honour of Gerhard Hafner* (Martinus Nijhoff Publishers, 2008)

Remy, B., 'Techniques interpretatives et systemes de droit' (2011) 115 *RGDIP* 329

Richter, D., 'Lücken der EMRK' in Dörr, O., Grote, R., and Marauhn, T. (eds.), *EMRK / GG: Konkordanzkommentar zum europäischen und deutschen Grundrechtsschutz* (vol. 1, 2nd edn, Mohr Siebeck, 2013)

Riehm, T., *Abwägungsentscheidungen in der praktischen Rechtsanwendung: Argumentation, Beweis, Wertung* (C. H. Beck, 2006)

Rietiker, D., 'The Principle of "Effectiveness" in the Recent Jurisprudence of the European Court of Human Rights: Its Different Dimensions and Its Consistency with Public International Law: No Need for the Concept of Treaty Sui Generis' (2010) 79 *Nordic Journal of International Law* 245

Rigaux, F., 'Interprétation consensuelle et interprétation évolutive' in Sudre, F. (ed.), *L'Interprétation de la Convention européenne des droits de l'homme: Actes du colloque des 13 et 14 mars 1998; Organisé par l'Institut de Droit Européen des Droits de l'Homme (UMR.CNRS.5815), Faculté de Droit de l'Université de Montpellier I* (Nemesis, 1998)

Roberts, A., 'Power and Persuasion in Investment Treaty Interpretation: The Dual Role of States' (2010) 104 *AJIL* 179

'Subsequent Practice: The Battle Over Interpretive Power' in Nolte, G. (ed.), *Treaties and Subsequent Practice* (Oxford University Press, 2013)

'Traditional and Modern Approaches to Customary International Law: A Reconciliation' (2001) 95 *AJIL* 757

Röhl, K. F., 'Grundlagen der Methodenlehre II: Rechtspraxis, Auslegungsmethoden, Kontext des Rechts', www.enzyklopädie-rechtsphilosophie.net (accessed 21 March 2013)

Rosa, H., *Acceleration: A New Theory of Modernity* (J. Trejo-Mathys trans., Columbia University Press, 2013)

'Social Acceleration: Ethical and Political Consequences of a Desynchronized High-Speed Society' (2003) 10 *Constellations* 3

Weltbeziehungen im Zeitalter der Beschleunigung: Umrisse einer neuen Gesellschaftskritik (Suhrkamp, 2012)

Rosen, J., 'Introduction' (1997) 66 *George Washington Law Review* 1081

Rosenne, S., 'Conceptualism as a Guide to Treaty Interpretation' in Rosenne, S. (ed.), *An International Law Miscellany* (Kluwer, 1993)

'Interpretation of Treaties in the Restatement and the International Law Commission's Draft Articles: A Comparison' (1966) 5 *Columbia Journal of Transnational Law* 205

The Law of Treaties: A Guide to the Legislative History of the Vienna Convention (Sijthoff, 1970)

Ruffert, M., and Walter, C., *Institutionalised International Law* (C. H. Beck, Hart, Nomos, 2015)

Ruggie, J. G., 'Stabilization Clauses and Human Rights: A Research Project Conducted for IFC and the United Nations Special Representative to the Secretary General on Business and Human Rights' (2008), www.ifc.org/wps/wcm/connect/9feb5b00488555eab8c4fa6a6515bb18/Stabilization%2BPaper.pdf?MOD=AJPERES (accessed 7 June 2015)

Ruse, M., *Darwinism and Its Discontents* (Cambridge University Press, 2006)

Rutherforth, T., *Institutes of Natural Law* (vol. II, edition originally published in 1756, William and Joseph Neal, 1832)

Sackville, R., 'Continuity and Judicial Creativity – Some Observations' (1997) 20 *University of New South Wales Law Journal* 145

Saleilles, R., 'École historique et droit naturel' (1902) 1 *Revue Trimestrielle de Droit Civil* 80

Salmon, J., *Dictionnaire de droit international public* (Bruylant, 2001)

Sandrock, O., '"Versteinerungsklauseln" in Rechtswahlvereinbarungen für internationale Handelsverträge' in Jayme, E., Kegel, G., and Lutter, M. (eds.), *Ius Inter nationes* (C. F. Müller, 1983)

Santulli, C., 'Rapport general' (2011) 115 *RGDIP* 297

Saussure, F. de, *Cours de linguistique générale* (Payot, 1986 [1915])

Sbolci, L., 'Supplementary Means of Interpretation' in Cannizzaro, E. (ed.), *The Law of Treaties Beyond the Vienna Convention* (Oxford University Press, 2011)

Scalia, A., 'Judicial Deference to Administrative Interpretations of Law' (1989) 3 *Duke Law Journal* 511

  'Originalism: The Lesser Evil' (1988) 57 *University of Cincinnati Law Review* 849

Schachter, O., *International Law in Theory and Practice* (Martinus Nijhoff Publishers, 1991)

Schauer, F., 'Balancing, Subsumption, and the Constraining Role of Legal Text' (2010) 4 *Law and Ethics of Human Rights* 34

Schermers, H. G., and Blokker, N., *International Institutional Law: Unity Within Diversity* (5th edn, Martinus Nijhoff Publishers, 2011)

Scheuner, U., 'Die Fortbildung der Grundrechte in internationale Konventionen durch die Rechtsprechung: zur Rechtsprechung des Europäischen Gerichtshofs für Menschenrechte' in Münch, I. von (ed.), *Staatsrecht, Völkerrecht, Europarecht: Festschrift für Hans-Jürgen Schlochauer zum 75. Geburtstag am 28. März 1981* (De Gruyter, 1981)

Schill, S., 'Fair and Equitable Treatment, the Rule of Law, and Comparative Public Law' in Schill, S. (ed.), *International Investment Law and Comparative Public Law* (Oxford University Press, 2010)

Schlink, B., 'Probleme und Ansätze einer Entscheidungstheorie der richterlichen Innovation' in Harenburg, J., Podlech, A., and Schlink, B. (eds.), *Rechtlicher Wandel durch richterliche Entscheidung* (Toeche-Mittler, 1980)

Schmalenbach, K., 'Art. 27' in Dörr, O., and Schmalenbach, K. (eds.), *Vienna Convention on the Law of Treaties: A Commentary* (Springer, 2012)
  'Art. 53' in Dörr, O., and Schmalenbach, K. (eds.), *Vienna Convention on the Law of Treaties: A Commentary* (Springer, 2012)
Schmitt, C., 'The Motorized Legislator' reprinted in Rosa, S., and Scheuermann, W. E. (eds.), *High Speed Society: Social Acceleration, Power, and Modernity* (Pennsylvania State University Press, 2009)
Schneider, H., *Richterrecht, Gesetzesrecht und Verfassungsrecht* (Klostermann, 1969)
Scholtz, G., 'Rekonstruktion' in Ritter, J., and Gründer, K. (eds.), *Historisches Wörterbuch der Philosophie* (Vol. 8, Schwabe, 1992)
Schott, C., '"Interpretatio cessat in Claris" – Auslegungsfähigkeit und Auslegungsbedürftigkeit in der juristischen Hermeneutik' in Schröder, J. (ed.), *Theorie der Interpretation vom Humanismus bis zur Romantik – Rechtswissenschaft, Philosophie, Theologie: Beiträge zu einem interdisziplinären Symposion in Tübingen, 29. September bis 1. Oktober 1999* (Steiner, 2001)
Schröder, J., 'Juristische Methode' in Cordes, A. (ed.), *Handwörterbuch zur deutschen Rechtsgeschichte: HRG* (2nd edn, Schmidt, 2008)
  Recht als Wissenschaft (2nd edn, C. H. Beck, 2012)
Schulte, C., *Compliance with Decisions of the International Court of Justice* (Oxford University Press, 2004)
Schwarzenberger, G., 'Myths and Realities of Treaty Interpretation: Articles 27–29 of the Vienna Draft Convention on the Law of Treaties' (1968) 9 *Virginia Journal of International Law* 1
  'Myths and Realities of Treaty Interpretation' (1969) 22 *Current Legal Problems* 205
Schweisfurth, T., *Völkerrecht* (Mohr Siebeck, 2006)
Shahabuddeen, M., 'Judicial Creativity and Joint Criminal Enterprise' in Darcy, S., and Powderly, J. (eds.), *Judicial Creativity at the International Criminal Tribunals* (Oxford University Press, 2010)
Shanahan, T., *The Evolution of Darwinism: Selection, Adaptation, and Progress in Evolutionary Biology* (Cambridge University Press, 2004)
Sharma, S. P., 'The ILC Draft and Treaty Interpretation with Special Reference to Preparatory Works' (1968) 8 *Indian Journal of International Law* 367
Shaw, M. N., *International Law* (6th edn, Cambridge University Press, 2008)
Simma, B., 'Miscellaneous Thoughts on Subsequent Agreements and Practice' in Nolte, G. (ed.), *Treaties and Subsequent Practice* (Oxford University Press, 2013)
  'NATO, the UN and the Use of Force: Legal Aspects' (1999) 10 *EJIL* 1
Simma, B., and Richemond-Barak, D., 'Art. 37' in Zimmermann, A., and others (eds.), *The Statute of the International Court of Justice: A Commentary* (2nd edn, Oxford University Press, 2012)

Sinclair, I., *The Vienna Convention on the Law of Treaties* (2nd edn, Manchester University Press, 1984)
Skinner, Q., 'Retrospect: Studying Rhetoric and Conceptual Change' in Skinner, Q. *Visions of Politics* (vol. 1, Cambridge University Press, 2002)
Skubiszewski, K., 'Implied Powers of International Organizations' in Dinstein, Y. (ed.), *International Law at a Time of Perplexity: Essays in Honour of Shabtai Rosenne* (Martinus Nijhoff Publishers, 1989)
Smend, R., *Verfassung und Verfassungsrecht* (Duncker & Humblot, 1929)
Smith, K. C., and Wylie, J., *International Law* (Little, Brown & Co., J. M. Dent & Sons Ltd, 1911)
Solum, L. B., 'The Interpretation–Construction Distinction' (2010) 27 *Constitutional Commentary* 95
  'What Is Originalism? The Evolution of Contemporary Originalist Theory' in Huscroft, G., and Miller, B. (eds.), *The Challenge of Originalism: Theories of Constitutional Interpretation* (Cambridge University Press, 2011)
Sorel, J. M., and Eveno, V. B., 'Art. 31 VCLT' in Corten, O., and Klein, P. (eds.), *The Vienna Conventions on the Law of Treaties: A Commentary* (Oxford University Press, 2011)
Sørensen, M., 'Do the Rights Set Forth in the European Convention on Human Rights in 1950 Have the Same Significance in 1975?' in Council of Europe (ed.), *Proceedings of the Fourth International Colloquy About the European Convention on Human Rights: Organised by the Ministry of Foreign Affairs of Italy and the Secretariat General of the Council of Europe; Rome, 5–8 November 1975* (Council of Europe, 1975)
  'Exposé prélimaire' [1973] *Annuaire de l'Institut de Droit International* 50
  'Le Problème dit du droit intertemporel dans l'ordre international' [1973] *Annuaire de l'Institut de Droit International* 1
  Les Sources du droit international: Etude sur la jurisprudence de la Cour Permanente de Justice Internationale (Munskgaard, 1946)
Stein, T., and Buttlar, C. von, *Völkerrecht* (12th edn, Carl Heymanns Verlag, 2012)
Stockton, C. H., *Outlines of International Law* (Charles Scribner's Sons, 1914)
Stone, M., 'Focusing the Law: What Legal Interpretation Is Not' in Marmor, A. (ed.), *Law and Interpretation: Essays in Legal Philosophy* (Oxford University Press, 1996)
Strang, L. J., 'Originalism and the "Challenge of Change": Abduced-Principle Originalism and Other Mechanisms by Which Originalism Sufficiently Accommodates Changed Social Conditions' (2009) 60 *Hastings Law Journal* 927
Strauss, D. A., *The Living Constitution* (Oxford University Press, 2010)
Suárez, F., *Tractatus de legibus ac deo legislatore: in decem libros distributes* (1612)
Suber, P., *The Paradox of Self-Amendment* (Peter Lang, 1990)
Szafarz, R., 'Reservations to Multilateral Treaties' (1970) 3 *Polish Yearbook of International Law* 293

Tammelo, I., *Treaty Interpretation and Practical Reason: Towards a General Theory of Legal Interpretation* (Law Book Co., 1967)

Tanaka, Y., 'Navigational Rights on the San Juan River: A Commentary on the Costa Rica v. Nicaragua Case' (2009) 4 *Hague Justice Journal* 215

Tate, A., 'New Judicial Solution: Occasions for and Limits to Judicial Creativity' (1979) 54 *Tulane Law Review* 877

Tavernier, P., *Recherches sur l'application dans le temps des actes et des règles en droit international public: Problèmes de droit intertemporel ou de droit transitoire* (Pichon et Auzias-Durand, 1970)

Taylor, H., *Treatise on International Public Law* (Callaghan & Co., 1901)

Textor, J. H., *Synopsis juris gentium* (translation of the edition originally published in 1680, Bate, J. P. trans., Carnegie Institution, 1916)

Thienel, T., 'The Living Instrument Approach in the ECHR and Elsewhere' in Delbrück, J., and others (eds.), *Aus Kiel in die Welt: Kiel's Contribution to International Law* (Duncker & Humblot, 2014)

Thirlway, H., 'The Law and Procedure of the International Court of Justice 1960–1989, Part Three' (1991) 62 *BYIL* 1

Thomas, E. W., *The Judicial Process* (Cambridge University Press, 2005)

Thouvenin, J., 'Art. 10 VCLT' in Corten, O., and Klein, P. (eds.), *The Vienna Conventions on the Law of Treaties: A Commentary* (Oxford University Press, 2011)

Tomuschat, C., 'Das Europa der Richter' in Bröhmer, J., and others (eds.), *Internationale Gemeinschaft und Menschenrechte: Festschrift für Georg Ress zum 70. Geburtstag am 21. Januar 2005* (Carl Heymanns Verlag, 2005)

'Pacta sunt servanda' in Fischer-Lescano, A., and others (eds.), *Frieden in Freiheit: Festschrift für Michael Bothe* (Nomos, 2008)

Verfassungsgewohnheitsrecht?: Eine Untersuchung zum Staatsrecht der Bundesrepublik Deutschland (Carl Winter Universitätsverlag, 1972)

Torres Bernárdez, S., 'Interpretation of Treaties by the International Court of Justice Following the Adoption of the 1969 Vienna Convention on the Law of Treaties' in Hafner, G. (ed.), *Liber Amicorum: Professor Ignaz Seidl-Hohenveldern in Honour of His 80th Birthday* (Kluwer, 1998)

Toulmin, S., *The Uses of Argument* (Cambridge University Press, 2003)

Treves, T., 'Customary International Law' in Wolfrum, R. (ed.), *The Max Planck Encyclopedia of Public International Law* (Oxford University Press, 2012)

Trindade, A. A. C., 'The Merits of Coordination of International Courts on Human Rights' (2004) 2 *Journal of International Criminal Justice* 309

Tulkens, F., 'What Are the Limits to Evolutive Interpretation of the Convention?' in Council of Europe (ed.), *Dialogue Between Judges, European Court of Human Rights: What Are the Limits to Evolutive Interpretation of the Convention?* (Council of Europe, 2011)

Ullmann, E. von, *Völkerrecht* (J. C. B. Mohr, 1908)

Ungern-Sternberg, A. von, 'Die Konsensmethode des EGMR: Eine kritische Bewertung mit Blick auf das völkerrechtliche Konsens-und das innerstaatliche Demokratieprinzip' (2013) 51 *Archiv des Völkerrechts* 312

van Damme, I., *Treaty Interpretation by the WTO Appellate Body* (Oxford University Press, 2009)

Vattel, E., *The Law of Nations or the Principles of Natural Law*, (Vol. III, translation of the edition of 1758, Fenwick trans., W. S. Hein, 1995)

Venzke, I., *How Interpretation Makes International Law: On Semantic Change and Normative Twists* (Oxford University Press, 2012)

'The Role of International Courts as Interpreters and Developers of the Law: Working Out the Jurisgenerative Practice of Interpretation' (2011) 34 *Loyola of Los Angeles International and Comparative Law Review* 99

Verdross, A., and Simma, B., *Universelles Völkerrecht: Theorie und Praxis* (Duncker & Humblot, 1984)

Verhoosel, G., 'The Use of Investor–State Arbitration Under Bilateral Investment Treaties to Seek Relief for Breaches of WTO Law' (2003) 6 *Journal of International Economic Law* 493

Verosta, S., 'Die Vertragsrechts-Konferenz der Vereinten Nationen 1968 / 69 und die Wiener Konvention über das Recht der Verträge' (1969) 29 *Zeitschrift für ausländisches öffentliches Recht und Völkerrech* 654

Viehweg, T., *Topik und Jurisprudenz* (5th edn, C. H. Beck, 1974)

Villiger, M. E., 'Articles 31 and 32 of the Vienna Convention on the Law of Treaties in the Case Law of the European Court of Human Rights' in Bröhmer, J., and others (eds.), *Internationale Gemeinschaft und Menschenrechte: Festschrift für Georg Ress zum 70. Geburtstag am 21. Januar 2005* (Carl Heymanns Verlag, 2005)

Commentary on the 1969 Vienna Convention on the Law of Treaties (Martinus Nijhoff Publishers, 2009)

'The 1969 Vienna Convention on the Law of Treaties – 40 Years After' (2009) 344 *RdC* 9

'The Rules on Interpretation: Misgivings, Misunderstandings, Miscarriage? The "Crucible" Intended by the International Law Commission' in Cannizzaro, E. (ed.), *The Law of Treaties Beyond the Vienna Convention* (Oxford University Press, 2011)

Visscher, C. de, *Problèmes d'interprétation judiciaire en droit international public* (A. Pedone, 1963)

Vitzthum, W. Graf von, 'Begriff, Geschichte und Rechtsquellen des Völkerrechts' in Vitzthum, W. Graf von, and Proelß, A. (eds.), *Völkerrecht* (6th edn, De Gruyter, 2013)

Vogenauer, S., *Die Auslegung von Gesetzen in England und auf dem Kontinent: Eine vergleichende Untersuchung der Rechtsprechung und ihrer historischen Grundlagen* (vol. 1, Mohr Siebeck, 2001)

'Statutory Interpretation' in Smits, J. M. (ed.), *Elgar Encyclopedia of Comparative Law* (2nd edn, Edward Elgar Publishing, 2012)

Voigt, C., *Sustainable Development as a Principle of International Law: Resolving Conflicts Between Climate Measures and WTO Law* (Martinus Nijhoff Publishers, 2009)

von Blumerincq, A., *Das Völkerrecht oder das internationale Recht: Systematisch dargestellt* (Akademische Verlagsbuchhandlung, 1889)

Vöneky, S., 'Analogy in International Law' in Wolfrum, R. (ed.), *The Max Planck Encyclopedia of Public International Law* (Oxford University Press, 2012)

'Armed Conflict, Effect on Treaties' in Wolfrum, R. (ed.), *The Max Planck Encyclopedia of Public International Law* (Oxford University Press, 2012)

Voßkuhle, A., 'Gibt es und wozu nutzt eine Lehre vom Verfassungswandel?' (2004) 43 *Staat* 450

Waibel, M., 'A Uniform Regime of Treaty Interpretation' in Tams, C., Tzanakopoulos, A., and Zimmermann, A. (eds.), *Research Handbook on the Law of Treaties* (Edward Elgar, 2014)

'Demystifying the Art of Interpretation' (2011) 22 *EJIL* 571

Waldock, H., 'The Evolution of Human Rights Concepts and the Application of the European Convention on Human Rights' in Reuter, P. (ed.), *Mélanges offerts à Paul Reuter: Le droit international: Unité Et diversité* (A. Pedone, 1981)

Walter, C., 'Hüter oder Wandler der Verfassung: Zur Rolle des Bundesverfassungsgerichts im Prozess des Verfassungswandels' (2000) 125 *Archiv des öffentlichen Rechts* 524

Walton, D. N., Macagno, F., and Reed, C., *Argumentation Schemes* (Cambridge University Press, 2008)

Watts, A., 'Codification and Progressive Development of International Law' in Wolfrum, R. (ed.), *The Max Planck Encyclopedia of Public International Law* (Oxford University Press, 2012)

Weiler, J. H. H., 'The Geology of International Law – Governance, Democracy and Legitimacy' (2004) 64 *Zeitschrift für ausländisches öffentliches Recht und Völkerrech* 547

'The Interpretation of Treaties – A Re-examination: Preface' (2010) 21 *EJIL* 507

Westlake, J., *International Law* (vol. 1, Cambridge University Press, 1904)

Wetzel, R. G., and Rauschning, D., *The Vienna Convention on the Law of Treaties* (Metzner, 1978)

Wheaton, H., Boyd, A. C., and Lawrence, W. B., *Elements of International Law* (vol. 2, Stevens, 1836)

Whittington, K. E., *Constitutional Construction: Divided Powers and Constitutional Meaning* (Harvard University Press, 1999)

Constitutional Interpretation: Textual Meaning, Original Intent, and Judicial Review (University Press of Kansas, 1999)

Wildhaber, L., 'Ein Überdenken des Zustands und der Zukunft des Europäischen Gerichtshofs für Menschenrechtee' [2009] *Europäische Grundrechte-Zeitschrift* 541
  'European Court of Human Rights' (2002) 40 *Canadian Yearbook of International Law* 309
  'Rethinking the European Court of Human Rights' in Christoffersen, J., and Madsen, M. R. (eds.), *The European Court of Human Rights Between Law and Politics* (Oxford University Press, 2011)
  'The European Court of Human Rights: The Past, the Present, the Future' (2006–7) 22 *American University International Law Review* 521
Wildman, R., *Institutes of International Law* (T. & G. W. Johnson, 1850)
Wilson, G. G., *International Law* (9th edn, Silver Burdett & Co., 1935)
Wilson, W., 'Wilson's First Draft' in Miller, D. H. (ed.), *Drafting of the Covenant* (Vol. 2, G.P. Putnam, 1928)
Wittgenstein, L., *Philosophical Investigations* (G. Anscombe trans., Blackwell, 1953)
  Philosophical Remarks (Maximilian Aue trans., University of Chicago Press, 1975)
Wolfrum, R., 'Obligation of Result Versus Obligation of Conduct: Some Thoughts about the Implementation of International Obligation' in Arsanjani, M., and others (eds.), *Looking to the Future: Essays on International Law in Honour of W. Michael Reisman* (Martinus Nijhoff Publishers, 2010)
Wolfrum, R., and Röben, V. (eds.), *Legitimacy in International Law* (Springer, 2008)
Woolsey, T. D., *Introduction to the Study of International Law* (6th edn, Charles Scribner's Sons, 1891)
Wright, Q., 'The Interpretation of Multilateral Treaties' (1929) 23 *AJIL* 94
Wróblewski, J., 'Legal Language and Legal Interpretation' (1985) 4 *Law and Philosophy* 239
Wu, D., 'Timing the Choice of Law by Contract' (2011) 9 *Northwestern Journal of Technology and Intellectual Property* 401
Yambrusic, E. S., *Treaty Interpretation: Theory and Reality* (University Press of America, 1987)
Yasseen, M. K., 'L'Interpretation des traités d'après la Convention de Vienne sur le droit des traités' (1976) 151 *RdC* 1
Yü, T., *The Interpretation of Treaties* (Columbia University Press, 1927)
Zemanek, K., 'Vienna Convention on the Law of Treaties', http://untreaty.un.org/cod/avl/ha/vclt/vclt.html (accessed 2 June 2011)

INDEX

abortion, 286–9
Ackermann, Bruce, 56–8
aconsensual consensualism, 320–1, 334–6
activity core, balancing and weighing in, 126–8
actor knot, 165–6
Acts Interpretation Act (Australia), 109–14
adoption rights, ECtHR jurisprudence and, 292–4
Aegean Sea Continental Shelf case, 222–3, 239–43, 267–9
Aerial Incident case, 231–4
a fortiori maxim, 116–18
Agreement of Free Movement, 186–7
Alexy, R., 140–1n.329
Al-Khasawneh (Judge), 246–51
Alland, 10–11
Al-Saadoon and Mufdhi, 280–1, 329–31
Alvarez, Alejandro (Judge), 52–4, 246–51
amendments to treaties
    ECtHR jurisprudence and, 273–8
    interpretation and, 15–16
    VCLT provisions concerning, 193–4
American Institute of International Law, 101–2
American Law Institute, Restatement Second of, 102–4, 129–34, 365–6
analogies interpretation and, 22–7
analytical jurisprudence, circularity in treaty interpretation and, 67–71
Anglo-Iranian Oil Company case, 218–19, 235–6, 267–9
Annoni case, 285–6

Application of the Convention on the Prevention and Punishment of the Crime of Genocide case, 223–4
approximate application, evolutive interpretation and, 27
arbitration cases, 26
argumentative process
    ICJ jurisprudence and, 224–5 354–6
    weight and hierarchy in, 129–34
Aristotle, 13n.55
    categorical models of, 18–21
    deductive logic of, 8–13
    on knowledge, 138–9
    topoi of, 124–5
armed conflict, effect on treaties, 183–4n.488
arrest, ECtHR jurisprudence concerning, 284–5
art of interpretation, 138–9
ascertainment knot, 159–62
    ECtHR jurisprudence and, 326–7
    ICJ jurisprudence and, 257–8
    perception and, 210–11
Assembly of the Council of Europe, 273–8
assumed intentions, 243–6
Auerbach, Erich, xiii–xviii
Austin, J. L., 14n.62
Austin case, 284–5, 309–14
authentic interpretation
    flexibility and, 91–7
    hierarchies of interpretation and, 132–4
    historical evolution of, 51–2
    subsequent agreement and practice and, 162–7

authoritative interpretation, 85–6
Azevedo (Judge), 258, 263–7

balancing techniques. *See also*
  rebalancing; weighing
  activity core and, 126–8
  consensus and, 315–16, 334–6
  in ECtHR intertemporality, 278–301
  in ECtHR justificatory patterns, 314–22
  hierarchies of interpretation and, 129–34
  interpretation and, 16–17
Banković case, 296–7, 306–9, 333–4
Bates, E., 185–6
Bayatyan case, 289, 328–9
Bederman, D. J., 83–5
Bedjaoui (Judge), 246–51, 253–5, 263–7
Bentham, Jeremy, 97–8
Bernhardt, Rudolf, 277n.412
'better understanding' principle, ECtHR jurisprudence and, 321–2
birth certificates, ECtHR jurisprudence concerning, 286–9, 338–43
Bluntschli, Caspar David, 97–8
Bonnello (Judge), 309–14
border treaties, ICJ jurisprudence concerning, 226–30, 239–43
Borscheid, Peter, 211–13
Brest, Paul, 31–54
Broom, H., 116–18
Bustamante (Judge), 246–51, 263–7
B v. France case, 286–9

Câmpeanu case, 297
Cançado Trindade (Judge), 246–51, 257–8
cardinal cores of VCLT, 350–4
  activity core, 126–8
  argumentative weight and hierarchy core, 129–34
  functional reconstruction and, 76–8
  function as core of cores, 140–6
  means core, 114–25
  nature care, 109–14
  openness core, 134–8
  ordinary and special meaning and, 153–7
Carnap, Rudolf, 20–1, 72–3

Cartier-Bresson, Henry, xiii–xviii
Casadevall (Judge), 309–14
Case Concerning Questions of Interpretation and Application of the 1971 Montreal Convention Arising from the Aerial Incident at Lockerbie, 223–4
Case Concerning the Gabčíkovo-Nagymaros Project, 225, 239–43, 250–1, 263–7, 269–71
Case Concerning the Land and Maritime Boundary between Cameroon and Nigeria, 227–8, 240–1n.184
Case Concerning Rights of Nationals of the United States of America in Morocco, 217–18, 235–6, 267–9, 354–6
Castro (Judge), 250–1, 253–5, 262–7
categories of treaties, VCLT rules of interpretation and, 32–4
Chapman case, 286–9
Charter of Fundamental Rights of the European Union, 332–3
children's rights, ECtHR jurisprudence and, 286–9, 292–4, 320–1
Christine Goodwin case, 286–9, 291–2, 321–2, 324–6, 338–43
circularity
  in treaty interpretation, 67–71, 347–50
circumstances of the conclusion of the treaty, 171–2, 333–4
civil rights, ECtHR jurisprudence concerning, 285–6
classification of the treaty
  inferences from, 120–1
  supplementary means and, 174
clausula rebus sic stantibus principle, 174–8
Code Civil (France), *méthode scientifique* and *méthode evolutive* interpretations of, 60–5
codification approach to treaty interpretation, 97–106, 363–4
  compilation v. synthesis approaches, 98–100
collective bargaining, ECtHR jurisprudence and, 290–1

collective juridical conscience, Saleilles' concept of, 62–4
Colombian–Peruvian Asylum case, 231–4
common law
  intertemporal doctrine and, 65–6
  originalism and, 56–8
communication
  codification of interpretation and, 105–6
  functions of treaty rules and, 145–6
  treaty interpretation and, 8–13
comparative law, functional reconstruction in, 72–3
conditional interpretive declaration, 367–8
conscientious objection, ECtHR jurisprudence concerning, 289
consensus method
  ECtHR jurisprudence and, 273–8, 315–16, 334–6
  internal practice and, 316–18
constitutional interpretation
  classification of treaties and, 120–1
  ECtHR jurisprudence and, 273–8
  functional reconstruction and, 72–3
  intertemporal doctrine and, 172–81
  living instrument doctrine and, 301–5
  subsequent practice principle and, 162–7
Constitution of the United States, 31–54
construction, evolutive interpretation and, 56
consular relations
  International Court of Justice jurisprudence and, 217–18
  termination or suspension of treaties and severance of, 198–9
contemporanea expositio est optima et fortissima in lege maxim, 116–18, 350–4
contemporaneity, principle of, 52–4
  intertemporality and, 178–81
contemporaneous interpretation
  competing principles and, 32–4
  precedent and, 267–9

Rutherforth's discussion of, 49–51
VCLT rules of interpretation and, 30–5
contential evolution, 20–1, 39
context of discovery v. context of justification, 140–6
  in ICJ justificatory patterns, 251–63
contextualist approach, 135–7, 210
contract treaties (*traité contrat*), structure of, 33–4
Cossey case, 286–9, 291–2, 338–43
Court of Justice of the European Union
  competences of, 14–15
  VCLT rules and, 334–6
Covenant of the League of Nations
  International Status of South West Africa and, 216–17
  Wilson's Draft of, 187–8
crucible metaphor
  balancing and weighing in treaty rules and, 126–8
  hierarchies of interpretation and, 129–34
Cruz Varas case, 298–9, 323–34
customary law
  circularity in treaty interpretation and, 67–71
  International Court of Justice jurisprudence and, 214–16
  intertemporal doctrine and, 39–41
  legality of VCLT cardinal cores and, 109–14

D'Amato, Anthony, 31–2
Darwin, Charles, 18–21
D'Aspremont, J., 71–7n.422
Davidson, Donald, 152–3
death penalty, ECtHR jurisprudence and, 280–1, 328–9
deductive logic, treaty interpretation and, 8–13
degrading treatment, ECtHR jurisprudence concerning, 281–3, 301–5
De jure bellis libri tres (Gentili), 48
Demir and Baykara case, 273–8, 290–1, 329–32, 334–6

Denkbewegung (movement of thought/ way of thinking) approach
  evolutive interpretation and, 183–4
  functional reconstruction and, 71–6
  function in practice and, 76–8
denunciation of treaties, contractual right of denunciation and withdrawal, 196–7
detention
  devolution of rights concerning, 309–14
  ECtHR jurisprudence concerning, 284–5
devolution in interpretation, ECtHR and problem of, 309–14
dictionaries, ICJ use of, 153, 256
Dikme case, 281–3
diplomatic relations, termination or suspension of treaties and severance of, 198–9
discretionary process, balancing in interpretation and, 126–8
discrimination, prohibition of, ECtHR jurisprudence and, 292–4
discursive mapping, intertemporal doctrine and, 34–5
doctrinal argument
  history of treaty interpretation and, 83–5
  originalism and, 56–8
  Suárez's interpretive methods and, 85–6
domestic jurisdiction, International Court of Justice jurisprudence and, 222–3
Dörr, Oliver, 30–1
dualist democracy, originalism and, 56–8
Dupuy, P., 34–5
duration of treaties, 33, 162, 256

education, right to, ECtHR jurisprudence and, 295–6
effectiveness, principle of, VCLT rules of interpretation and, 32–4
Ehrlich, Ludwik, 52–4, 98–100, 118–19, 363–4

elections, right to free elections, 295–6
Emonet case, 318–19
environmental standards treaties
  devolution of, 309–14
  ECtHR jurisprudence concerning, 284–5
  ICJ jurisprudence and, 225, 253–5, 269–71
  relevant rules for, 262
equitable construction phase, 95–7, 361–3
equity, 22–7
European Commission for Democracy through Law (Venice Commission), 316–18, 333
European Commission of Human Rights, 273–8
European Convention on the Legal Status of Children Born out of Wedlock, 293, 318–19
European Court of Human Rights (ECtHR)
  additional protocols and jurisprudence of, 329–31
  consensus method and jurisprudence of, 273–8, 315–16, 334–6
  devolution and, 309–14
  institutional aspects of, 273–8
  intertemporal issues and jurisprudence of, 272–3, 278–301
  justificatory patterns in, 314–43
  legacy of, 272–3
  living instrument doctrine and, 26n.137, 301–5
  precedent in jurisprudence of, 337–8
  table of cases, 20–4
European Movement, 184–9, 309–14
European Parliament, ECtHR jurisprudence on elections to, 295–6
evidence, interpretation and, 15
evolutive interpretation
  basic principles, 18–21, 347–50
  classification of terms and, 40, 255–63
  comparative law and solutions to, 54–66
  competing principles and, 32–4
  express regulation and, 184–9
  false application and, 227n.119

historical background for, 48–54
ILC draft article on intertemporal
  law and, 37–41
intertemporality and, 178–81
invalidity, termination and
  suspension rules, 195–201
limits of, 22–7
living instrument doctrine and,
  301–5
maxims for, 116–18
méthode scientifique and *méthode
  evolutive* interpretations of *Code
  Civil* and, 60–5
norm conflict and, 194–5
ordinary and special meaning and,
  153–7
originalism and non-originalism
  and, 31–54
peremptory norms of international
  law and, 199–201
precedent and, 267–9
retroactive application by ECtHR of,
  305
VCLT rules and, 28–31, 183–202
voting rights and, 295–6
ex aequo et bono, equity as, 22–7
expressio unius maxim, 116–18
external practice, ECtHR jurisprudence
  and, 318–19, 334–6
extra-legal considerations, 31–2
  in ECtHR jurisprudence, 326–7
  in ICJ jurisprudence, 243–6, 263–7
extrinsic evidence, rules of
  interpretation and, 135–7

fair trial, right to, ECtHR jurisprudence
  concerning, 285–6
family life, right to, ECtHR
  jurisprudence and, 286–9
Fauchille, Paul, 93–4
Ferrazzini case, 285–6, 324n.680
Feteris, E. T., 72–3
Field, David Dudley, 97–8
Fiore, P., 52–4
Fiore, Pasquale, 98–100
Fisheries Jurisdiction (Spain v. Canada)
  cases, 240n.180, 267–9
  ICJ jurisprudence, 225–6, 231–4

*Fisheries Jurisdiction (United Kingdom
  v. Iceland and Germany v. Iceland)*
  cases, ICJ jurisprudence, 221–2
Fitzmaurice, Gerald, 52–4, 101, 112–14,
  120–1, 243–51, 258–62, 301–5
Fitzmaurice, Malgosia, 31–4
flexible phase of treaty interpretation
  hierarchies of interpretation and,
    129–34
  history of, 91–7, 101
fluidification of treaties, 187–8
foetus, protection of, ECtHR
  jurisprudence concerning,
  280–1
forced labour, ECtHR jurisprudence
  concerning, 283
formal principles
  legal v. non-legal interpretations,
    134–8
  properties of, 122–3
Foster (Judge), 263–7
fragmentation in international law,
  treaty interpretation and,
  177n.484
France, *méthode scientifique* and
  méthode evolutive interpretations
  of *Code Civil* in, 60–5
freedom of assembly and association,
  ECtHR jurisprudence concerning,
  290–1
freedom of expression, ECtHR
  jurisprudence concerning, 290
freedom of thought, conscience and
  religion, ECtHR jurisprudence
  concerning, 289
free elections, right to, ECtHR
  provisions concerning, 295–6
free scientific inquiry (*libre recherche
  scientifique*), Gény's concept of,
  60–2
freezing clauses, rules of interpretation
  and, 184–9
Frege, Gottlob, 11–15
Fretté case, 292–4
Friedman, Wolfgang, 5–8
Frontier Dispute case, 231–4,
  240–1n.184
Frowein, Jochen, 277n.412, 309–14

functional reconstruction in treaty interpretation, 71–6
historical account of, 83–108
practical application of, 76–8, 350–4
future law, intertemporal interpretations and, 231–4
fuzzy cases, ICJ jurisprudence and, 231–4
F v. Switzerland case, 291–2, 321–2

Gadamer, H., 13n.57, 138–9
Gardiner, Richard, 67–71, 151–2n.365
generality, techniques of interpretation and, 115–16
generic terms
  in *Aegean Sea Continental Shelf* case, 239–43
  defined, 28–31, 347–50
  in ICJ justificatory patterns, 251–63
  ordinary and special meaning and, 153–7
  in *South West Africa* cases, 236–9
genocide, ICJ jurisprudence on, 223–4
Gentili, A., 48, 65–7, 86–8, 150–3
Gény, François, 60–4
Germany, evolutive interpretation discourse in, 65–6
goal knot of interpretation, 147–50
Golder case, 273–8
good faith, 86–8, 90–1, 150–3
governments, resistance to intertemporal doctrine by, 39–41
Greece
  Aegean Sea Continental Shelf case and, 222–3, 239–43
  resistance to intertemporal doctrine in, 39–41
Grotius, Hugo, 48–9, 53–4, 84n.4
  interpretive methods of, 86–8, 90–1, 95–7, 350–4
  on presumptions in interpretation, 118–19
Guillaume (Judge *ad hoc*), 246–51, 258–69
gypsies, rights of, ECtHR jurisprudence and, 286–9

Haas case, 286–9
Habermas, J., 140–1n.329

Hague Peace Conferences of 1899 and 1907, 97–8
Hale (Baroness), 65–6
Hall, W. E., 95–7
harmonisation, international law rules and rules of interpretation, 167–9
Harroudj case, 286–9
Hart, H. L. A., 72
Harvard Draft Convention, 98–100, 124–5, 350–4
  balancing and weighing in, 126–8
  techniques of interpretation and, 115–16, 365
Hassan case, 309–14
Hatton case, 309–14
Havana Convention on Asylum, 101–2, 263–7
Heisenberg uncertainty principle, xiii–xviii
hermeneutics, 140–6
hierarchies of interpretation
  argumentative process and, 129–34
  openness core and, 134–8
Higgins, Rosalyn (Judge), 32–4, 253–5
Hirsi Jamaa case, 295–6
history of treaty interpretation
  codificatory phase of, 97–106
  flexible phase of, 91–7
  mechanical phase of, 85–91
  overview of, 83–108
homosexuality, ECtHR jurisprudence and, 292–4, 321–2
Huber, Max (Judge), 31–2, 178–81, 347–50
Hudson, Manley, O., 98–100, 124–5
human rights. *See also* specific rights, e.g. liberty and security, right to
  devolution in, 309–14
  ECtHR jurisprudence and, 296–7, 329–31
  new rights creation and, 306–9
  object and purpose of interpretation and, 162n.415, 185n.496
Hyde, Charles, 93–4, 111–12

ILO Commission, 301–5
implied powers, necessary implications and, 22–7

'in accordance with' principle,
    hierarchies of interpretation and,
    131–2
in dubio pro mitius principle
    flexible interpretative approaches
        and role of, 94–5
    ICJ rejection of, 263–7
inferences
    from classification of the treaty, 120–1
    interpretative outcome and, 174–8
    from nature of the treaty, 119–20,
        263–7
    from structure of treaties, 121–2,
        263–7
innovation, in evolutive interpretation,
    22–7
Institut de Droit International, 28–31,
    97–8, 101, 365
    art of interpretation, 138–9
    legality issues discussed by, 111–12
institutional facts, profile of
    international courts and, 205–8
intentionalist interpretation
    codification and, 102–4
    Grotius and, 86–8
    ICJ jurisprudence and, 250–1, 263–7
    Navigational and Related Rights case
        and, 243–6
    Vattel and, 88–90
interim measures, ECtHR
    jurisprudence including, 298–9
internal law
    ECtHR jurisprudence and, 273–8
    living instrument doctrine and,
        301–5
    modification of intertemporal
        doctrine and, 41–7
    Suárez's interpretive methods and,
        85–6
    VCLT provisions and, 193
internal practice, consensus and,
    316–18, 334–6
International Commission of Jurists,
    101–2
International Court of Justice (ICJ). *See
    also* specific cases
    analytical framework concerning,
        205–8

ex aequo et bono in statutes of, 22–7
    future law and, 231–4
    institutional aspects of, 214–16
    intertemporal issues and
        jurisprudence of, 216–31, 246–63,
        269–71
    justificatory patterns in, 251–69
    miscellaneous rules of interpretation
        used by, 263–7
    norm conflict and jurisprudence of,
        194–5
    peaceful co-existence approach and,
        235–6
    precedent in rulings of, 267–9
    shift to evolutive interpretation in,
        246–51
    table of cases, 24–6
    treaty interpretation and
        jurisprudence of, 52–4, 214,
        234–51, 354–6
international courts and tribunals
    circularity in treaty interpretation
        and, 67–71
    codification of treaty interpretation
        and, 101
    factor-based treaty interpretation,
        140–6
    object and purpose of treaties and,
        159–62
    profiling of, 205–8
    treaty interpretation and, 5–8
International Covenant on Economic,
    Social and Cultural Rights, 187–8
international law
    codification of, 97–106
    expansion of, 210–11
    treaty interpretation and, 5–8
International Law Association, 97–8
International Law Commission (ILC)
    balancing and weighing in draft of,
        126–8
    codification and, 97–8
    draft article on intertemporal law,
        37–41
    evolutive interpretation and, 30n.156
    intertemporal openness and, 357–8
    modification of intertemporal
        doctrine by, 41–7

International Law Commission (ILC) (cont.)
  on object and purpose of treaties, 159–62
  presumptions in interpretation and, 118–19
  reservations concerning treaties and, 190–2
  rules of treaty interpretation and, 37–47
  state practices and, 109–14
  Working Group on Fragmentation, 30–5
international legal method, evolutive interpretation and, 18–21
international organisations, creation of, 32–4
International Status of South West Africa, 216–17, 252, 262
Internoscia, Jerome, 98–100
interpretation. *See also* rules of interpretation; specific interpretive methods
  application of, 14–15
  basic principles of, 8–13, 347–50
interpretation by usage, 85–6
Interpretation of Peace Treaties advisory opinion, 231–4
interpretive declarations, reservations concerning treaties and, 189–92
interpretive knot. *See* knots of interpretation
interpretive method and methodology
  analysis of, xi–xiii
  definitions, 3–5
  means of interpretation and, 22–7
interpretive practice, defined, 3–5
intertemporal problems
  British and German discourses on, 65–6
  ECtHR and, 272–3, 278–301
  future applications of, 357–8
  goal knot of interpretation and, 147–50
  good faith in interpretation and, 152–3
  governments' resistance to, 39–41
  Grotius and, 48–9
  historical precedent for, 52–4
  ICJ jurisprudence and, 216–31, 246–63, 269–71
  ILC draft article on, 37–41
  interim measures of ECtHR and, 298–9
  international law rules and, 167–9
  knot of interpretation and, 172–81
  méthode scientifique and *méthode evolutive* interpretations of *Code Civil* and, 60–5
  modification through practice of, 41–7
  non-judicial interpretations, 231–4
  object and purpose concept and, 158–62
  pace of judicial interpretation and, 211–13
  right to life and, 280–1
  rules of interpretation and, 201–2, 350–4
  stocking concerning, 278–301
  subsequent agreement and practice and, 162–7
  summary of, 181–2
  VCLT rules of interpretation and, 30–5
intra-subjective perspective, contextual analysis of treaties and, 140–6
invalidity of treaties, 195–201
Islamic *kafala*, recognition of, 286–9
Island of Palmas case, 31–2, 178–81, 347–50
Israel, resistance to intertemporal doctrine in, 39–41

Jacobs, Francis, 151–2n.365, 309–14
James case, 294–5
Jessup, Phillip (Judge), 138–9, 263–7
Johnston case, 333–4
judicial authority
  in authentic interpretation, 132–4
  rules of interpretation and, 140–6
judicial corporal punishment, abolition of, 301–5
judicial creativity, in evolutive interpretation, 22–7

judicial mechanisms
  in ECtHR, 273–8
  originalism debate and, 31–54
  treaty interpretation and, 5–8
jus cogens
  devolution of rights and, 314
  ECtHR jurisprudence and, 331–2, 354–6
  intertemporal doctrine and, 201–2
  norm conflicts and, 199–201
justificatory function
  contextual analysis of treaties and, 140–6
  in European Court of Human Rights, 314–43
  in ICJ treaty interpretations, 251–63
  profile of international courts and, 205–8

Kasikili Sedudu case, ICJ jurisprudence in, 226–7, 239–43, 252–3, 255–6, 258–63, 269–71
Kelsen, Hans, 8–9, 122n.250
Klabbers, Jan, 112–14, 140–1n.329, 152–3
knots of interpretation
  actor knot, 165–6
  ascertainment knot, 159–62, 258, 327
  functional reconstruction and, 76–8
  goal knot, 147–50
  intertemporal knot, 172–82, 211–13
  participation knot, 167–9, 331–2
  perception and, 210–11
  qualitative agreement knot, 166–7, 259, 329
  quantitative agreement knot, 166
  source knot and, 167–9, 331–2
  subject knot, 159–62
Konstantin Markin case, 292–4
Koroma (Judge), 246–51
Koselleck, Reinhard, 3–5
Koskenniemi, Martti, 4n.8, 67–71, 74n.444, 147–50
Kratochwil, Friedrich, 124–5
Kress case, 301–5

language
  philosophy of, 156, 255
  treaty interpretation and, 8–13
Lasswell, Harold, 135–7
Lauterpacht, Elihu, xiii–xviii, 27, 101
law-making treaties
  ECtHR jurisprudence and, 306–9
  interpretation and, 15–16
  structure of, 33–4
law-making treaties (*traité loi*), 120–1
Lawrence, T. J., 95–7, 143–4
League of Nations
  ICJ justificatory patterns and, 257–8, 269–71
  International Status of South West Africa and, 216–17
  South West Africa cases (Ethiopia, Liberia and Namibia) and, 220, 231–4, 236–9, 255
Lebedev case, 284–5
Legality of the Threat or Use of Nuclear Weapons case, 224–5, 258–62, 267–9
Legality of the Use of Force case, 262–3
  ICJ jurisprudence and, 223–4
legal personality doctrine, ICJ jurisprudence and, 231–4
legal theory, functional reconstruction in, 71–6
legitimacy, in treaty interpretation, xi–xiii
Lessig, Lawrence, 56–8
lex posterior maxim, norm conflict and, 194–5
lex specialis, express regulation in treaties and, 184–9
Leyla Şhahın case, 295–6
liberty and security, right to, ECtHR jurisprudence concerning, 284–5
libre évolution scientifique, Saleilles' concept of, 62–4
Linderfalk, U., 156–7
linguistics
  interpretation and, 8–13, 88–90
  ordinary and special meaning and, 153–7
  semantic change and, 18–21
  semiotic triangle and, 11–13

literal interpretation, 86–8
  flexibility and, 91–7
  Vattel's maxim and, 88–90
living instrument doctrine
  devolution of rights and, 309–14
  ECtHR jurisprudence and, 26n.137, 301–5, 337–8, 354–6
loci, maxims of interpretation and, 116–18
locus standi, in South West Africa cases, 236–9
Loizidou case, 296–7, 301–9, 328–34
L v. Lithuania case, 286–9

MacCormick, Neil, 73–4
Mamatkulov case, 298–9
Mangouras case, 284–5
Marckx case, 292–4, 305
margin of appreciation, ECtHR jurisprudence and, 306–9
marriage, rights concerning, ECtHR jurisprudence and, 291–2, 321–2
material breach, termination or suspension of treaties and, 197–8
material impossibility, termination or suspension of treaties and, 197–8
material principles
  good faith in interpretation and, 150–3
  in ICJ rulings, 263–7
  perception and, 210–11
  properties of, 122
Matthews case, 295–6
maxims of interpretation, 116–18, 173
McDougal, Myres, 105–6, 131–2, 134–8, 162–7
McNair, Arnold, 93–4, 257–8
MC v. Bulgaria, 281–3
McVeigh case, 284–5, 309–14
meaning of treaties
  defined, 11–13, 347–50
  flexible interpretative approaches and role of, 94–5
  harmonisation of, 140–1n.329
  in *Kasikili Sedudu* case, 226–7
  mechanical approaches to treaty interpretation and, 85–91
  natural and ordinary meaning, 52–4
  ordinary and special meaning, 153–7

means of interpretation, 22–7
  core principles for, 114–25
  Grotius' interpretive methods and, 86–8
  historical evolution of, 83–108
  techniques, 114–25
mechanical approaches to treaty interpretation, 85–91, 359–61
  hierarchies of interpretation and, 129–34
  intertemporality and, 176–8
  precedence and, 267–9
media technology, devolution of interpretation and, 309–14, 321–2
method and methodology of interpretation
  defined, 3–5, 347–50
  Suárez's interpretive methods and, 85–6
méthode evolutive, interpretation of French *Code Civil* and, 60–5
méthode scientifique, evolutive interpretation of French *Code Civil* and, 60–5
Miller, James C., 135–7
misconduct of interpreter, good faith in interpretation and, 150–3
modification
  interpretation and, 15–16
  through practice, ILC draft on intertemporality and, 41–7
most-favoured-nations principle, International Court of Justice jurisprudence and, 217–18
Mouvement Raëlien Suisse case, 290
Mowbray, A. R., 26n.137
multilateral treaties, evolutive interpretation and, 32–4
multilingual treaties, flexibility in interpretation of, 94–5

Namibia. See also South West Africa cases (Ethiopia, Liberia and Namibia)
  ECtHR jurisprudence concerning, 301–5, 354–6
  ICJ jurisprudence concerning, 220, 231–4, 236–9, 257–8, 354–6

national courts, interpretation and, 101–2
Nationality Decrees Issued in Tunisia and Morocco case, 231–4, 267–9
national law
  ECtHR jurisprudence and, 316–18, 320–1
  legality of VCLT cores and, 109–14
nature of the treaty
  inferences from, 119–20
  supplementary means and, 174
Navigational and Related Rights case, 228–30, 243–6, 258–62, 264n.319, 267–9, 269–71, 354–6
ne bis in idem prohibition, ECtHR jurisprudence and, 295–6
necessary implications, interpretive results as, 22–7
Netherlands, resistance to intertemporal doctrine in, 39–41
Neuberger (Lord), 65–6
New Haven School of interpretation, 105–6, 134–8
new rights, creation of, 306–9
Nolte, Georg, 28–31
non-derogable norms. *See jus cogens* principle
normative argument
  functional reconstruction and, 73–6
  originalism and, 56–8
  peremptory norms of international law and, 199–201
norm conflict, treaty interpretation and, 194–5
nuclear weapons, ICJ jurisprudence concerning, 224–5, 258–62

object and purpose
  circularity in treaty interpretation and, 67–71
  consensus and, 334–6
  ECtHR jurisprudence and, 326–7, 354–6
  hierarchies of interpretation and, 131–2
  in ICJ justificatory patterns, 251–63

inferences from nature of the treaty and, 119–20
  in *Navigational and Related Rights* case and, 243–6
  subject knot and, 158–62
objective approach to interpretation, 102–4
objective inquiry, evolutive interpretation and, 62–4
obligations
  Grotius on role of, 86–8
  rules of interpretation and role of, 88–90
  structural features of treaties and, 121–2
Öcalan v. Turkey case, 280n.427, 329–31
openness core, rules of interpretation and, 134–8
opinio juris sive necessitatis principle
  customary international law and, 109–14
  ECtHR jurisprudence and, 328–9
Oppenheim, Lassa, 95–7, 361–3
ordinary and special meaning
  ECtHR jurisprudence and, 324–6
  ICJ justificatory patterns and, 251–63
  International Court of Justice jurisprudence and, 222–3
  in *Navigational and Related Rights* case and, 243–6
  rules of interpretation and, 153–7
originalism
  evolutive interpretation and, 31–54
  ICJ trend toward, 246–51
Ovid, xiii–xviii

pace of judicial interpretation, 211–13
  ECtHR jurisprudence and, 338–43
  ICJ rules of interpretation and, 208–9, 269–71
Pacific Settlement of International Disputes of 1928, 222–3
pacta sunt servanda principle
  good faith in interpretation and, 150–3

pacta sunt servanda principle (cont.)
  internal law and treaty interpretation and, 193
  material breach/material impossibility and, 197–8
  modification of intertemporal doctrine and, 46–7
parental rights, ECtHR jurisprudence and, 292–4, 316–19
Parra-Arranguren (Judge), 258–62
participation knot, 167–9, 331–2
path dependency, functions of treaty rules and, 145–6
Pauwelyn, J., 16n.71
peaceful co-existence, ICJ jurisprudence and, 235–6
perception
  in ECtHR jurisprudence, 338–43
  in ICJ jurisprudence, 210–11, 269–71
Perelman, Chaim, 124–5
Petroleum Development Ltd v. *Sheikh of Abu Dhabi* case, 267–9
Phillimore, Robert, 51–2, 84n.4
Philosophical Investigations (Wittgenstein), 67–71
Pichkur, 292–4, 331–2
political methods, ICJ jurisprudence and, 263–7
Port Royal Topics, 124–5
power 208–9
  of ECtHR jurisprudence, 338–43
  in ICJ jurisprudence, 208–9, 269–71
practice
  circularity in treaty interpretation concerning, 67–71
  defined, 347–50
  functional reconstruction and, 73–6
Preah Vihear case, 219–20, 242–3, 258–62, 267–9
precedent
  in ECtHR jurisprudence, 337–8
  in ICJ jurisprudence, 267–9
Preparatory Committee for the Codification Conference (League of Nations), 97–8

presumption
  flexible interpretative approaches and role of, 94–5
  in ICJ jurisprudence, 263–7
  inferences from nature of the treaty and, 119–20
  rules of interpretation and, 30–1, 118–19
  as supplementary means, 174
pretium, interpretation and principle of, 8–9
Pretty case, ECtHR jurisprudence in, 280–1
principles in international law, 32–4, 122–3
  intertemporality and, 178–81
private life, right to, ECtHR jurisprudence and, 286–9
property rights, ECtHR jurisprudence and, 294–5
proportionality
  balanced interpretation and, 16–17
  ECtHR intertemporality and, 278–301
  freedom of expression and, 290
public law in treaties, 120–1
Pufendorf, Samuel, 84n.4, 88
Pulp Mills on the River Uruguay case, 229–30, 263–7
purposive interpretation
  codification and, 102–4
  competing principles and, 32–4

qualitative agreement knot, 166–7, 258–62, 328–9
quantitative agreement knot, 166

Ranjeva (Judge), 258–62
Rantsev case, 283, 324–6, 331–2
ratio decidendi, of precedent, 22–7
ratio legis, analogies and, 22–7
reality, text and, 14–15
reasonably assumed intentions concept, ICJ jurisprudence and, 243–6
rebalancing, in ECtHR jurisprudence, 286–9
Rechtsfortbildung, 23, 26–7

reciprocal obligations
  ICJ jurisprudence and, 222–3
  VCLT rules of interpretation and, 33–4
reconstruction. *See* functional reconstruction in treaty interpretation
Rees case, 286–9, 291–2, 338–43
referent, defined, 11–13
referential evolution, 20–1
  ICJ justificatory discourse on, 262
  ILC draft article on intertemporal law and, 39
  International Court of Justice jurisprudence and, 217–18
relevant rules
  in ECtHR jurisprudence, 283–4n.440, 331–2
  ICJ justificatory interpretations and, 262
religion, freedom of, ECtHR jurisprudence concerning, 289
Reparations for Injuries Suffered in the Service of the United Nations case, 231–4
reservations concerning treaties, 189–92, 367–8
restrictive interpretions, in ICJ jurisprudence, 263–7
results of interpretation, 22–7
retroactive evolutive interpretation, ECtHR jurisprudence and, 305
right to life, ECtHR intertemporality concerning, 280–1
Roman law
  maxims of interpretation and, 116–18
  rules of interpretation and, 111–12
Rosa, Hartmut, 211–13
rule core of VCLT, legality of, 109–14
rule of interpretation. *See also* cardinal cores of VCLT; maxims
  amendments to treaties and, 193–4
  application and obedience to, 69–70n.414
  canons of treaty construction, 84n.4
  circularity in interpretation of, 67–71
  codification and, 97–106
  contextual analysis and, 157–8

ECtHR jurisprudence and, 323–34
functional reconstruction and, 71–6
function as cardinal core, 140–6
goal knot of interpretation, 147–50
hierarchies in, 129–34
historical overiew of pre-VCLT methods, 83–108, 350–4
ICJ jurisprudence and, 214–16, 251–63
international law rules relevant to, 167–9
invalidity, termination and suspension rules, 195–201
legality of, 109–14
mechanical approaches to, 85–91
openness core in, 134–8
ordinary and special meaning and, 153–7
perception and, 210–11
power and, 208–9
reservations on interpretations, 189–92
travaux préparatoires and, 170–1
in VCLT, 28–31, 350–4
rule of lawyer's considerations, functional reconstruction and, 73–6
rule on intertemporal law, 178–81
rulers of law considerations, functional reconstruction and, 73–6
Rutherforth, Thomas, 49–51, 84n.4, 90–1, 361

Saleilles, Raymond, 62–4
same sex marriage
  ECtHR jurisprudence and, 291–4, 316–18
  internal practices of states and, 316–18
Schalk and Kopf case, 286–9, 291–4, 338–43
schools of interpretation
  codification and, 102–4
  supplementary means and, 173–4
  VCLT rules and, 34–5
Schröder, J., 4n.9
Schwarzenberger, G., 16n.70

Schwizgebel case, 292–4
scientific method
  ECtHR jurisprudence and, 321–2
  functional reconstruction in, 72–3
  rules of interpretation and, 123–4
Scoppola No. 3 case, 295–6, 309–14
Second Restatement (American Law Institute), 102–4, 129–34, 365–6
Selmouni case, 281–3
semantic change, evolutive interpretation and, 18–21
semiotic triangle
  application of, 14–15
  defined, 11–13
sermo humilis, Auerbach's concept of, xiii–xviii
Seventh International Conference of American States, 109–14
severity requirements, prohibition against torture and, 281–3
sex-change operations, ECtHR jurisprudence concerning, 286–9
shared expectations, codification of interpretation and, 105–6
Sheffield and Horsham case, 286–9, 291–2, 321–2, 338–43
Shi (Judge), 246–51, 258–62
sign, defined, 11–13
Sigurjónsson case, 290–1
Simma, Bruno, 34–5
Sitaropoulos case, 295–6
Skinner, Quentin, 3–5
Skotnikov (Judge), 253–6, 258–67
slavery, ECtHR jurisprudence concerning, 283
Smend, Rudolf, 162–7
social factors in interpretation
  ECtHR jurisprudence and, 321–2, 336–7
  functional reconstruction in, 72–3
  ICJ jurisprudence and, 263–7
  temporal aspects of treaties and, 211–13, 246–51
Société Colas Est case, 286–9, 338–43
Soering case, 280–1, 329–31

soft-law instruments, ECtHR jurisprudence and, 332–3
Sørensen, Max, 28–31, 273–8, 301–5, 334–6
source knot, 167–9
  in ECtHR jurisprudence, 331–2
source thesis, rules of interpretation and, 71–2n.422
South West Africa cases (Ethiopia, Liberia and Namibia), 354–6
  ECtHR jurisprudence concerning, 301–5
  ICJ jurisprudence and, 220, 231–4, 236–9, 255, 263–9
sovereignty
  evolutive interpretations of, 250n.236
  flexible interpretative approaches and, 91–7
  ICJ jurisprudence and, 219–20, 264n.319
  intertemporal law and, 30–5
  treaty interpretation and, 3–5
specification, interpretation and, 22–7
Spender (Judge), 235–9, 243–51, 258–67
state practice
  authentic interpretation and, 132–4
  continuation of treaties in succession of states, 183n.487
  ECtHR jurisprudence and Member States practices, 286–9, 315–16, 328–9
  evolutive interpretation and, 188–9
  flexible interpretive methods and role of, 91–7
  freedom of states in treaty interpretation, 143–4
  ICJ justificatory patterns concerning, 258–62
  internal practice, 316–18
  International Court of Justice jurisprudence and, 223–4
  legality of VCLT and, 109–14
  presumptions in, 118–19
  reservations on interpretation and, 189–92
  of respondent states, 320–1

subsequent agreement and practice and, 165–6
static interpretation, 22–7
　classification of terms and, 255–63
　comparative law and solutions to, 54–66
　ECtHR jurisprudence and, 298–301, 323–34, 338–43, 354–6
　express regulation in treaties and, 184–9
　ICJ jurisprudence and, 236–9, 246–51, 269–71, 354–6
　ILC draft article on intertemporal law and, 39–41
　living instrument doctrine and, 301–5
　maxims for, 116–18
　ordinary and special meaning and, 153–7
　voting rights and, 295–6
STEC case, 328–9
stocktaking
　ECtHR intertemporal interpretations and, 278–301, 338–43, 354–6
　ICJ jurisprudence and, 229–30, 354–6
　profile of international courts and, 205–8
Stoll case, 290, 309–14, 321–2
Strauss, David, 56–8
structural features of treaties
　evolutive interpretation and, 32–4
　inferences from, 121–2
　supplementary means and, 174
Stummer case, 283
Suárez, Francisco, 85–6
subjective interpretation, 102–4
subject knot, rules of interpretation and, 159–62
subsequent agreement and practice
　ECtHR jurisprudence and, 280n.425, 280n.426, 283–4n.440, 285–6n.448, 328–9
　in ICJ justificatory patterns, 251–63, 269–71
　intertemporal doctrine and, 41–7, 52–4

in *Navigational and Related Rights* case and, 243–6
rules of interpretation and, 162–7
suicide, right to, ECtHR jurisprudence and, 286–9
Summers, Robert, 72–3
supplementary means
　hierarchies of interpretation and, 129–34
　intertemporal knot and, 172–81
Supreme Court (Canada), 26
suspension of treaties
　inferences from nature of the treaty and, 119–20
　rules on, 195–201
　severance of diplomatic/consular relations and, 198–9
Sutherland v. the United Kingdom, 292–4
synonymous terms, ICJ jurisprudence concerning, 255–63
synthesis, rules of interpretation and, 138–9
Syria, resistance to intertemporal doctrine in, 39–41
system-oriented perspective, functional reconstruction and, 73–6

table of cases, 20–6
Tanaka (Judge), 243–6, 263–7
techniques of interpretation, 115–16. *See also* mechanical approaches to treaty interpretation
　actor dimension in, 208–9
　in ECtHR jurisprudence, 323–34
　ICJ justificatory patterns and, 251–63
　as means in VCLT, 124–5
　weighing and balancing and, 126–8
technological acceleration, temporal aspects of treaties and, 211–13
teleological approach
　competing principles and, 32–4
　ICJ justificatory patterns and, 258
temporal aspects of treaties
　applicability of treaty and, 192
　ordinary and special meaning and, 153–7

temporal aspects of treaties (cont.)
  pace of judicial interpretation and, 211–13
  techniques of interpretation and, 124–5
termination of treaties, 195–201
  ICJ jurisprudence and, 231–4
  severance of diplomatic/consular relations and, 198–9
territorial issues, evolutive interpretation of, 48
terrorism, devolution of rights and, 309–14
textualist approach to interpretation, 102–4
  openness core and, 134–8
  ordinary and special meaning and, 153–7
Tomuschat, Christian, 30–1, 162–7
topoi
  maxims of interpretation and, 116–18
  means of interpretation and, 124–5
Torres Bernárdez (Judge ad hoc), 263–7
torture, prohibition of, ECtHR jurisprudence and, 281–3
trade unions, ECtHR jurisprudence concerning, 290–1
trafficking jurisprudence, ECtHR interpretations and, 283, 336–7
traité contrat. See contract treaties
traité loi. See law-making treaties (*traité loi*)
transgender rights, ECtHR jurisprudence and, 286–9, 291–2, 324–6
translation, originalism and non-originalism and, 56–8
travaux préparatoires, 102–4
  contractual right of denunciation and withdrawal and, 196–7
  ECtHR jurisprudence and, 333–4
  functions of rules of interpretation and, 140–6
  history of treaty interpretation and, 91–7, 350–4
  ICJ judicial interpretations and, 262–3

rules of interpretation and, 170–1
state practice and, 223–4
static interpretations and, 159–62
Treaty of Granada, 48
Treaty of Limits, ICJ jurisprudence and, 228–9
Treaty of Peace and Friendship, 217–18
Treaty of Separation, 253–5
Treaty on the Functioning of the European Union (TFEU), application of, 14–15
Tulkens, Françoise, 273–8
Tunisia, ICJ jurisprudence concerning, 231–4, 267–9
Turkey, *Aegean Sea Continental Shelf* case and, 222–3
T v. the United Kingdom case, 281–3
Tyrer case, 281–3, 301–5, 337–8, 354–6

unaffected parties, ECtHR jurisprudence including, 297
UN Charter
  circularity in interpretation of, 67–71
  ICJ jurisprudence and, 246–51, 258, 263–7
  treaty interpretation and, 194–5
UNCITRAL Rules on Transparency in Treaty-based Investor-State Arbitration, 188–9
United Kingdom, evolutive interpretation discourse in, 65–6
United Nations, ICJ jurisprudence and, 228
United States
  codification of treaty interpretation in, 101–2
  originalism debate in, 31–54
  resistance to intertemporal doctrine in, 39–41
Universal Declaration of Human Rights, 332–3
unmarried parents, ECtHR jurisprudence concerning, 292–4
use of force, ICJ jurisprudence on, 223–4
uti possidetis principle, border treaty cases and, 240–1n.184

validation of treaties. *See also* invalidity of treaties
  ICJ jurisprudence and, 231–4
  internal law and, 193
  techniques of interpretation and, 115–16
Vallianatos case, 292–4, 316–18
van der Mussele case, 301–5
Van Wyk (Judge), 243–6
Vattel, Emer de, 49–51, 53–4, 84n.4
  on art of interpretation, 138–9
  balancing and weighing in treaty rules and, 126–8
  codification of rules of interpretation and, 98–100
  hierarchies of interpretation and, 129–34
  interpretive methods of, 347–50, 88–90
Vattel's maxim of interpretation, 88–90
Verfassungswandel, discourse concerning, 65–6
victims, ECtHR jurisprudence and, 297
Viehweg, Theodor, 124–5
Vienna Conference, ILC rules of treaty interpretation and, 37–47
Vienna Convention on Diplomatic Relations, 193–4
Vienna Convention on the Law of Treaties (VCLT)
  amendments to treaties and, 193–4
  argumentative process in, 129–34
  cardinal cores of, 350–4
  circularity in rules of, 67–71, 347–50
  circumstances at conclusion of, 171–2
  complementary approaches to rules of, 30–5
  contractual right of denunciation and withdrawal, 196–7
  ECtHR interpretations and rules of, 273–8, 323–36
  evolutive interpretation in context of, 183–202
  express regulation in, 184–9
  functional reconstruction of rules in, 71–6
  function in practice of, 76–8
  historical evolution of interpretation prior to, 83–5, 107–8, 350–4
  ICJ justificatory patterns in conformance with, 251–63
  ILC modification of, 41–7
  International Court of Justice and, 214–16
  international law rules relevant to, 167–9
  international legal method in, 18–21
  interpretive method and methodology, xi–xiii, 28–35, 73–7
  intertemporal openness and, 357–8
  invalidity, termination and suspension rules in, 195–201
  legal v. non-legal issues in, 135n.302
  méthode scientifique and *méthode evolutive* interpretations of *Code Civil* and, 62–4
  norm conflict and, 194–5
  presumptions in, 118–19
  profile of international courts and, 205–8
  relevant rules defined in, 262
  reservations on interpretation in, 189–92
  rigidity and flexibility questions concerning, 75
  rule of interpretation in, 28–31
  structure of treaties and, 121–2
  techniques as means of, 124–5
Vilho Eskelinen and others, 285–6, 305
Vogenauer, Stefan, 62–4
von Jhering, Rudolf, 60–2
voting rights, ECtHR jurisprudence on, 295–6
VO v. France, 280–1

Waldock, Humphrey (Sir), 37, 109–14, 347–50
  balancing and weighing in draft of, 126–8
  draft article on intertemporal law and, 37–41
  intertemporal doctrine and, 152–3
  on maxims of interpretation, 116–18

Waldock, Humphrey (Sir) (cont.)
  modification of intertemporal
    doctrine and, 41–7
  object and purpose concept and,
    158–62
  on synthesis in rules of
    interpretation, 138–9
  on techniques of interpretation,
    115–16, 124–5
  techniques of interpretation and,
    147–50
Wall Opinion, 228, 258–62
Weeramantry (Judge), 263–7
weighing, 126–8. *See also* balancing
Westlake, John, 92
Whittington, Keith, 56

Wildhaber, Luzius, 277n.412, 309–14
withdrawal from treaties
  contractual right of denunciation
    and withdrawal, 196–7
  inferences from nature of the treaty
    and, 119–20
Wittgenstein, Ludwig, 67–71,
  69–70n.414, 76–8

X and others case, 309–14, 316–18,
  320–1
X v. Austria case, 292–4
X, Y and Z case, 286–9, 337–8

Zaunegger case, 292–4
Zolotukhin case, 295–6

CAMBRIDGE STUDIES IN INTERNATIONAL
AND COMPARATIVE LAW

Static and Evolutive Treaty Interpretation: A Functional Reconstruction
Christian Djeffal

Civil Liability in Europe for Terrorism-Related Risk
Lucas Bergkamp, Michael Faure, Monika Hinteregger and Niels Philipsen

Proportionality and Deference in Investor-State Arbitration: Balancing Investment Protection and Regulatory Autonomy
Caroline Henckels

International Law and Governance of Natural Resources in Conflict and Post-Conflict Situations
Daniëlla Dam-de Jong

Proof of Causation in Tort Law
Sandy Steel

Taking Economic, Social and Cultural Rights Seriously in International Criminal Law
Evelyne Schmid

Climate Change Litigation: Regulatory Pathways to Cleaner Energy?
Jacqueline Peel and Hari Osofsky

Mestizo International Law: A global intellectual history 1842–1933
Arnulf Becker Lorca

Sugar and the Making of International Trade Law
Michael Fakhri

Strategically Created Treaty Conflicts and the Politics of International Law
Surabhi Ranganathan

Investment Treaty Arbitration as Public International Law: Procedural Aspects and Implications
Eric De Brabandere

The New Entrants Problem in International Fisheries Law
Andrew Serdy

Substantive Protection under Investment Treaties: A Legal and Economic Analysis
Jonathan Bonnitcha

Popular Governance of Post-Conflict Reconstruction: The Role of International Law
Matthew Saul

Evolution of International Environmental Regimes: The Case of Climate Change
Simone Schiele

Judges, Law and War: The Judicial Development of International Humanitarian Law
Shane Darcy

Religious Offence and Human Rights: The Implications of Defamation of Religions
Lorenz Langer

Forum Shopping in International Adjudication: The Role of Preliminary Objections
Luiz Eduardo Ribeiro Salles

International Law and the Arctic
Michael Byers

Cooperation in the Law of Transboundary Water Resources
Christina Leb

Underwater Cultural Heritage and International Law
Sarah Dromgoole

State Responsibility: The General Part
James Crawford

The Origins of International Investment Law
Kate Miles

The Crime of Aggression under the Rome Statute of the International Criminal Court
Carrie McDougall

Crimes against Peace and International Law
Kirsten Sellars

The Non-Legal in International Law
Fleur Johns

Armed Conflict and Displacement: The Protection of Refugees and Displaced Persons under International Humanitarian Law
Mélanie Jacques

Foreign Investment and the Environment in International Law
Jorge Viñuales

The Human Rights Treaty Obligations of Peacekeepers
Kjetil Larsen

Cyberwarfare and the Laws of War
Heather Harrison Dinniss

The Right to Reparation in International Law for Victims of Armed Conflict
Christine Evans

Global Public Interest in International Investment Law
Andreas Kulick

State Immunity in International Law
Xiaodong Yang

Reparations and Victim Support in the International Criminal Court
Conor McCarthy

Reducing Genocide to Law: Definition, Meaning, and the Ultimate Crime
Payam Akhavan

Decolonizing International Law: Development, Economic Growth and the Politics of Universality
Sundhya Pahuja

Complicity and the Law of State Responsibility
Helmut Philipp Aust

State Control over Private Military and Security Companies in Armed Conflict
Hannah Tonkin

'Fair and Equitable Treatment' in International Investment Law
Roland Kläger

The UN and Human Rights: Who Guards the Guardians?
Guglielmo Verdirame

Sovereign Defaults before International Courts and Tribunals
Michael Waibel

Making the Law of the Sea: A Study in the Development of International Law
James Harrison

Science and the Precautionary Principle in International Courts and Tribunals: Expert Evidence, Burden of Proof and Finality
Caroline E. Foster

Transition from Illegal Regimes in International Law
Yaël Ronen

Access to Asylum: International Refugee Law and the Globalisation of Migration Control
Thomas Gammeltoft-Hansen

Trading Fish, Saving Fish: The Interaction between Regimes in International Law
Margaret Young

The Individual in the International Legal System: Continuity and Change in International Law
Kate Parlett

The Participation of States in International Organisations: The Role of Human Rights and Democracy
Alison Duxbury

'Armed Attack' and Article 51 of the UN Charter: Evolutions in Customary Law and Practice
Tom Ruys

Science and Risk Regulation in International Law
Jacqueline Peel

Theatre of the Rule of Law: Transnational Legal Intervention in Theory and Practice
Stephen Humphreys

The Public International Law Theory of Hans Kelsen: Believing in Universal Law
Jochen von Bernstorff

Vicarious Liability in Tort: A Comparative Perspective
Paula Giliker

Legal Personality in International Law
Roland Portmann

Legitimacy and Legality in International Law: An Interactional Account
Jutta Brunnée and Stephen J. Toope

The Concept of Non-International Armed Conflict in International Humanitarian Law
Anthony Cullen

The Challenge of Child Labour in International Law
Franziska Humbert

Shipping Interdiction and the Law of the Sea
Douglas Guilfoyle

International Courts and Environmental Protection
Tim Stephens

Legal Principles in WTO Disputes
Andrew D. Mitchell

War Crimes in Internal Armed Conflicts
Eve La Haye

Humanitarian Occupation
Gregory H. Fox

The International Law of Environmental Impact Assessment: Process, Substance and Integration
Neil Craik

The Law and Practice of International Territorial Administration: Versailles to Iraq and Beyond
Carsten Stahn

Cultural Products and the World Trade Organization
Tania Voon

United Nations Sanctions and the Rule of Law
Jeremy Farrall

National Law in WTO Law: Effectiveness and Good Governance in the World Trading System
Sharif Bhuiyan

The Threat of Force in International Law
Nikolas Stürchler

Indigenous Rights and United Nations Standards
Alexandra Xanthaki

International Refugee Law and Socio-Economic Rights
Michelle Foster

The Protection of Cultural Property in Armed Conflict
Roger O'Keefe

Interpretation and Revision of International Boundary Decisions
Kaiyan Homi Kaikobad

Multinationals and Corporate Social Responsibility: Limitations and Opportunities in International Law
Jennifer A. Zerk

Judiciaries within Europe: A Comparative Review
John Bell

Law in Times of Crisis: Emergency Powers in Theory and Practice
Oren Gross and Fionnuala Ní Aoláin

Vessel-Source Marine Pollution: The Law and Politics of International Regulation
Alan Tan

Enforcing Obligations Erga Omnes in International Law
Christian J. Tams

Non-Governmental Organisations in International Law
Anna-Karin Lindblom

Democracy, Minorities and International Law
Steven Wheatley

Prosecuting International Crimes: Selectivity and the International Law Regime
Robert Cryer

*Compensation for Personal Injury in English, German and Italian Law:
 A Comparative Outline*
Basil Markesinis, Michael Coester, Guido Alpa, Augustus Ullstein

Dispute Settlement in the UN Convention on the Law of the Sea
Natalie Klein

The International Protection of Internally Displaced Persons
Catherine Phuong

Imperialism, Sovereignty and the Making of International Law
Antony Anghie

Necessity, Proportionality and the Use of Force by States
Judith Gardam

*International Legal Argument in the Permanent Court of International Justice:
 The Rise of the International Judiciary*
Ole Spiermann

Great Powers and Outlaw States: Unequal Sovereigns in the International Legal Order
Gerry Simpson

Local Remedies in International Law
C. F. Amerasinghe

*Reading Humanitarian Intervention: Human Rights and the Use of Force in
 International Law*
Anne Orford

*Conflict of Norms in Public International Law: How WTO Law Relates to Other
 Rules of International Law*
Joost Pauwelyn

Transboundary Damage in International Law
Hanqin Xue

European Criminal Procedures
Edited by Mireille Delmas-Marty and John Spencer

The Accountability of Armed Opposition Groups in International Law
Liesbeth Zegveld

Sharing Transboundary Resources: International Law and Optimal Resource Use
Eyal Benvenisti

International Human Rights and Humanitarian Law
René Provost

Remedies Against International Organisations
Karel Wellens

Diversity and Self-Determination in International Law
Karen Knop

The Law of Internal Armed Conflict
Lindsay Moir

International Commercial Arbitration and African States: Practice, Participation and Institutional Development
Amazu A. Asouzu

The Enforceability of Promises in European Contract Law
James Gordley

International Law in Antiquity
David J. Bederman

Money Laundering: A New International Law Enforcement Model
Guy Stessens

Good Faith in European Contract Law
Reinhard Zimmermann and Simon Whittaker

On Civil Procedure
J. A. Jolowicz

Trusts: A Comparative Study
Maurizio Lupoi

The Right to Property in Commonwealth Constitutions
Tom Allen

International Organizations Before National Courts
August Reinisch

The Changing International Law of High Seas Fisheries
Francisco Orrego Vicuña

Trade and the Environment: A Comparative Study of EC and US Law
Damien Geradin

Unjust Enrichment: A Study of Private Law and Public Values
Hanoch Dagan

Religious Liberty and International Law in Europe
Malcolm D. Evans

Ethics and Authority in International Law
Alfred P. Rubin

Sovereignty Over Natural Resources: Balancing Rights and Duties
Nico Schrijver

The Polar Regions and the Development of International Law
Donald R. Rothwell

Fragmentation and the International Relations of Micro-States: Self-determination and Statehood
Jorri Duursma

Principles of the Institutional Law of International Organizations
C. F. Amerasinghe